PHYSICS HANDBOOK and STUDY GUIDE™

PHYSICS MADE EASY

A comprehensive summary of Grade 11 and 12 Physics

Simple, logical summaries with example exam questions and worked through solutions

COVERS THE FUNDAMENTALS OF GRADE 11 and 12 PHYSICS AND COMPLEMENTS THE MATERIAL IN ANY CLASS TEXT

GRADES 11 & 12

KEVIN SMITH

WRITTEN ESPECIALLY FOR THE IEB CURRICULUM

TABLE OF CONTENTS

CHAPTER 1 – PHYSICS DATA SHEET

CHAPTER 2 – PHYSICS DEFINITIONS

CHAPTER 3 – EQUATIONS AND GRAPHS OF MOTION

CHAPTER 4 – FORCES AND NEWTONS LAWS

CHAPTER 5 – VECTORS

CHAPTER 6 – MOMENTUM AND ENERGY

CHAPTER 7 – ELECTRIC CIRCUITS

CHAPTER 8 – ELECTROSTATICS

CHAPTER 9 – ELECTROMAGNETISM

CHAPTER 10 – PHOTONS AND ELECTRONS

1. EXAMINATION DATA SHEET FOR THE PHYSICAL SCIENCES (PHYSICS)

TABLE 1 PHYSICAL CONSTANTS

NAME	SYMBOL	VALUE
Acceleration due to gravity	g	$9{,}8\ \text{m}\cdot\text{s}^{-2}$
Speed of light in a vacuum	c	$3{,}0\times10^{8}\ \text{m}\cdot\text{s}^{-1}$
Universal gravitational constant	G	$6{,}7\times10^{-11}\ \text{N}\cdot\text{m}^{2}\cdot\text{kg}^{-2}$
Coulomb's constant	k	$9\times10^{9}\ \text{N}\cdot\text{m}^{2}\cdot\text{C}^{-2}$
Magnitude of charge on electron	e	$1{,}6\times10^{-19}\ \text{C}$
Mass of an electron	m_e	$9{,}1\times10^{-31}\ \text{kg}$
Planck's constant	h	$6{,}6\times10^{-34}\ \text{J}\cdot\text{s}$
1 electron volt	eV	$1{,}6\times10^{-19}\ \text{J}$

TABLE 2 PHYSICS FORMULAE

MOTION

$v = u + at$ **or** $v_f = v_i + a\Delta t$	$s = \left(\frac{v+u}{2}\right)t$ **or** $\Delta x = \left(\frac{v_f + v_i}{2}\right)\Delta t$
$v^2 = u^2 + 2as$ **or** $v_f^{\,2} = v_i^{\,2} + 2a\Delta x$	$s = ut + \frac{1}{2}at^2$ **or** $\Delta x = v_i\Delta t + \frac{1}{2}a\Delta t^2$

FORCE AND MOMENTUM

$F_{net} = ma$	$F_{net} = \frac{\Delta p}{\Delta t}$ **or** $F_{net}\Delta t = m\Delta v$	$J = \Delta p = mv - mu$ **or** $J = \Delta p = mv_f - mv_i$
$p = mv$	$F_g = mg$	$F_{fs}^{max} = \mu_s F_N$ $F_{fk} = \mu_k F_N$

WORK, ENERGY AND POWER

$W = Fs$ **or** $W = F\Delta x$ **or** $W = F\Delta x\cos\theta$	$P = \frac{W}{t}$	$P = Fv$

$E_p = mgh$	$E_k = \frac{1}{2}mv^2$	$W_{net} = \Delta E_k$	$\text{efficiency} = \frac{\text{power}_{out}}{\text{power}_{in}}\times100$

GRAVITATIONAL AND ELECTRIC FIELDS

$F = G\dfrac{m_1 m_2}{r^2}$	$g = \dfrac{F}{m}$	$g = G\dfrac{M}{r^2}$
$F = k\dfrac{q_1 q_2}{r^2}$	$E = \dfrac{F}{q}$	$E = \dfrac{kQ}{r^2}$

ELECTRIC CIRCUITS

$I = \dfrac{q}{t}$	$V = \dfrac{W}{q}$
$R = \dfrac{V}{I}$	$emf = I(R_{ext} + r)$ **or** $emf = V_{load} + V_{internal\ resistance}$
$R_s = R_1 + R_2 + \ldots\ldots$	$\dfrac{1}{R_P} = \dfrac{1}{R_1} + \dfrac{1}{R_2} + \ldots\ldots$
$P = \dfrac{W}{t}$ **or** $W = Pt$	
$W = VIt$ **or** $W = I^2Rt$ **or** $W = \dfrac{V^2}{R}t$	
$P = VI$ **or** $P = I^2R$ **or** $P = \dfrac{V^2}{R}$	

ELECTRODYNAMICS

$\Phi = BA\cos\theta$	$emf = -\dfrac{N\Delta\Phi}{\Delta t}$	$F = IB\ \sin\theta$
$V_p I_p = V_s I_s$	$\dfrac{N_s}{N_p} = \dfrac{V_s}{V_p}$	

PHOTONS AND ELECTRON

$c = f\lambda$	$E = hf$ **or** $E = \dfrac{hc}{\lambda}$	
$E = W_o + E_{k(\max)}$	$W_o = hf_o$	$E_{k(max)} = \dfrac{1}{2}mv_{max}^2$

2. PHYSICS DEFINITIONS

VECTORS

Term	Definition
Vector quantity	A physical quantity that has both magnitude and direction.
Scalar quantity	A physical quantity that has magnitude only.
Resultant vector	A single vector which has the same effect as the original vectors acting together.

DISPLACEMENT, VELOCITY AND ACCELERATION

Term	Definition
Distance	The length of path travelled. (Scalar)
Displacement	A change in position. (Vector)
Speed	The rate of change of distance. (Scalar)
Velocity	The rate of change of position or the rate of displacement or the rate of change of displacement. (Vector)
Acceleration	The rate of change of velocity. (Vector)

NEWTON'S LAWS

Term	Definition
Weight (F_g)	The gravitational force the Earth exerts on any object on or near its surface.
Normal force (F_N)	The perpendicular force exerted by a surface on an object in contact with it.
Frictional force (F_f)	The force that opposes the motion of an object and acts parallel to the surface with which the object is in contact.
Newton's first law	An object continues in a state of rest or uniform (moving with constant) velocity unless it is acted upon by a net or resultant force.
Inertia	The property of an object that causes it to resist a change in its state of rest or uniform motion.
Newton's Second Law	When a net force, F_{net}, is applied to an object of mass, m, it accelerates in the direction of the net force. The acceleration, *a*, is directly proportional to the net force and inversely proportional to the mass.
Newton's Second Law (In terms of Momentum)	The net force acting on an object is equal to the rate of change of momentum.
Newtons Third Law	When object A exerts a force on object B, object B simultaneously exerts an oppositely directed force of equal magnitude on object A.

MOMENTUM

Term	Definition
Linear momentum	The product of the mass and velocity of the object.
Law of conservation of linear momentum	The total linear momentum of an isolated system remains constant (is conserved).
Elastic collision	A collision in which both momentum and kinetic energy are conserved.
Inelastic collision	A collision in which only momentum is conserved.
Impulse (J)	The product of the net force and the contact time.

WORK, ENERGY AND POWER

Term	Definition
Work	The product of the displacement and the component of the force parallel to the displacement.
Gravitational potential energy	The energy an object possesses due to its position relative to a reference point.
Kinetic energy	The energy an object has as a result of the object's motion.
Mechanical energy	The sum of gravitational potential and kinetic energy at a point.
Law of conservation of energy	The total energy in a system cannot be created nor destroyed; only transformed from one form to another.
Principle of conservation of mechanical energy	In the absence of air resistance or any external forces, the mechanical energy of an object is constant.
Work-energy theorem	The work done by a net force on an object is equal to the change in the kinetic energy of the object.
Power	The rate at which work is done or the rate at which energy is transferred.
Watt	The power when one joule of work is done in one second.
Efficiency	The ratio of output power to input power.

GRAVITATIONAL AND ELECTRIC FEILDS

Term	Definition
Newton's Law of Universal Gravitation	Every particle with mass in the universe attracts every other particle with a force which is directly proportional to the product of their masses and inversely proportional to the square of the distance between their centres.
Gravitational field	The force acting per unit mass. It is described as a region in space where a mass will experience a force.
Coulomb's law	Two point charges in free space or air exert forces on each other. The force is directly proportional to the product of the charges and inversely proportional to the square of the distance between the charges.
Magnitude of an electric field at a point	The force per unit positive charge.

ELECTRIC CIRCUITS

Term	Definition
Potential difference	The work done per unit positive charge
Current	The rate of flow of charge
Ohm's Law	Current through a conductor is directly proportional to the potential difference across the conductor at constant temperature.
Resistance	Material's opposition to the flow of electric current.
EMF	The total energy supplied per coulomb of charge by the cell.

ELECTROMAGNETIC INDUCTION

Term	Definition
Magnetic flux Density	A representation of the magnitude and direction of the magnetic field.
Magnetic flux linkage	The product of the number of turns on the coil and the flux through the coil.
Faraday's law of electromagnetic induction	The emf induced is directly proportional to the rate of change of magnetic flux.
Lenz's Law	The induced current flows in a direction so as to set up a magnetic field to oppose the change in magnetic flux.

ALTERNATING CURRENT

Term	Definition
Diode	A component that only allows current to flow in one direction.

PHOTONS AND ELECTRONS

Term	Definition
Threshold (cut-off) frequency (f_o)	The minimum frequency of incident radiation at which electrons will be emitted from a particular metal.
Work function (W_o)	The minimum amount of energy needed to emit an electron from the surface of a metal.

TOC
1 Data Sheet
2 Definitions
3
3 solutions
4
4 solutions
5
5 solutions
6
6 solutions
7
7 solutions
8
8 solutions
9
9 solutions
10
10 solutions

3. EQUATIONS AND GRAPHS OF MOTIONS

EQUATIONS:

Symbols		Meaning
v	v_f	Final Velocity
u	v_i	Initial Velocity
s	Δx	Displacement
t	Δt	Change in time
a	a	Acceleration

If an object is in free fall the only force acting on the object is weight. The objects acceleration will be due only to gravitational acceleration and the symbol for acceleration is sometimes changed to *g* in the formulas.

Equation		When to use
$v = u + at$	$v_f = v_i + a\Delta t$	Displacement is not given
$s = ut + \frac{1}{2}at^2$	$\Delta x = v_i\Delta t + \frac{1}{2}a\Delta t^2$	Final velocity is not given
$v^2 = u^2 + 2as$	$v_f^2 = v_i^2 + 2a\Delta x$	Time is not given
$s = \left(\frac{v+u}{2}\right)t$	$\Delta x = \left(\frac{v_f + v_i}{2}\right)\Delta t$	Acceleration is not given

- Try to **draw a diagram** of the situation.
- **Choose a direction as positive** and use that convention throughout each question. Make sure you indicate the chosen direction as positive.
- If **up is positive, gravitational acceleration is always negative**.
- If **down is positive, gravitational acceleration is always positive**.
- **From rest** means $v_i = 0$ $(u = 0)$
- At **maximum height velocity is 0**. However, **gravitational acceleration** is still **9,8 m.s^{-2} downwards**. Gravitational force acts on an object at any point in its motion, even when at rest.
- If an object is **slowing down, acceleration** is in the **opposite direction to motion**.
- If **velocity is constant**, **acceleration is 0**. Use the equation $\Delta x = v\,t$ for constant velocity.
- To **convert** ***km.h^{-1}*** **to** ***m.s^{-1}*** **divide by 3,6**.
- **Velocity, displacement and acceleration** are **vector quantities**. You must give direction in words in your final answer for vector quantities. Never leave the sign ('+' or '–') in your final answer.
- **Speed, distance and height are scalars**. **Do not give direction for scalars**.
- If the question asks for **magnitude**, **do not give direction**.
- If **up is taken as positive** and an **object ends below its starting point,** the **displacement** of the object is **negative**.

GRAPHS OF MOTION:

- **Area** under a **acceleration**-time **graph is velocity**.
- **Area** under a **velocity-time graph is displacement**.
- **Gradient** of a **displacement**-time **graph is velocity**.
- **Gradient** of a velocity-time **graph is acceleration**.

Area Gradient

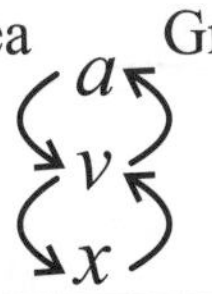

Stationary object

Acceleration-time

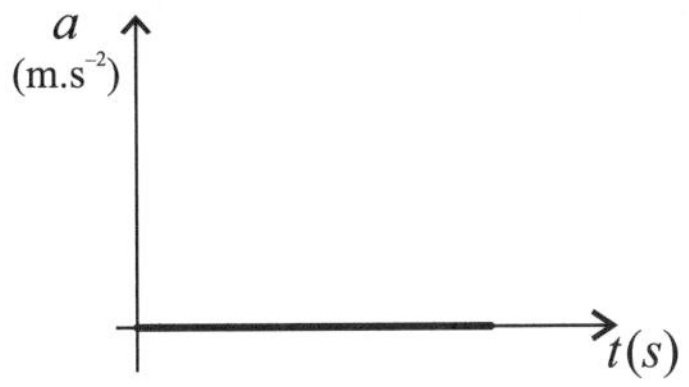

Acceleration is zero

Velocity-time

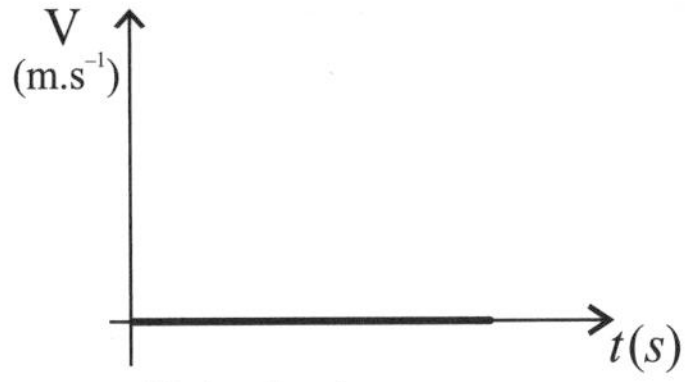

Velocity is constant
(gradient and velocity is zero)

Displacement-time

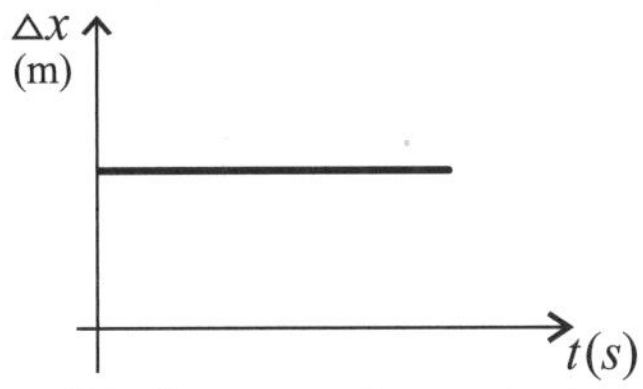

Displacement is constant
(gradient is zero)

Object moving at a constant velocity

Acceleration-time

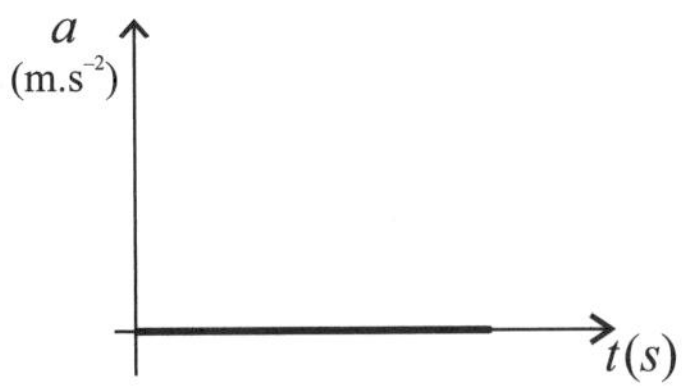

Acceleration is zero

Velocity-time

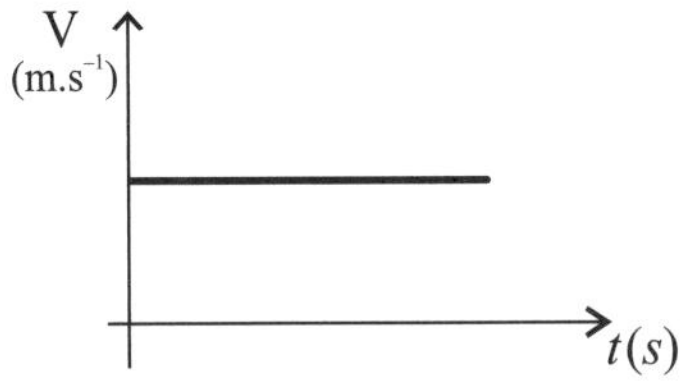

Velocity is constant
(gradient is zero)
(velocity is constant)

Displacement-time

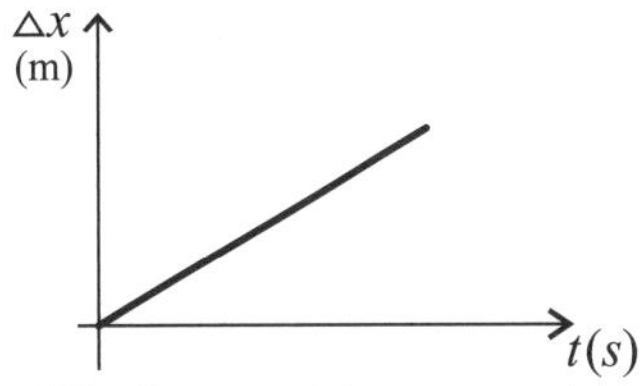

Displacement increases at a constant rate
(gradient is constant)

Object moving with an increasing velocity

Acceleration-time

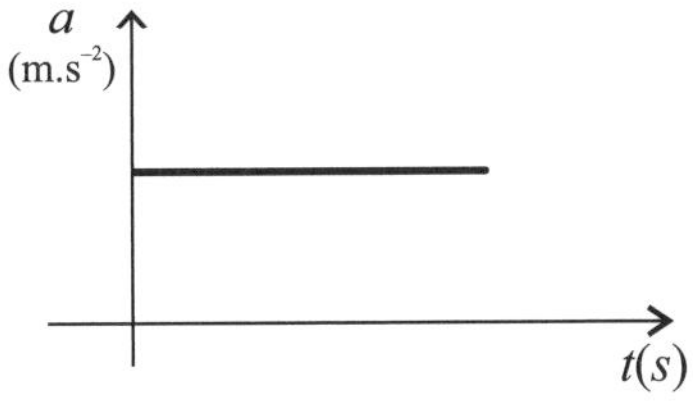

Acceleration is constant

Velocity-time

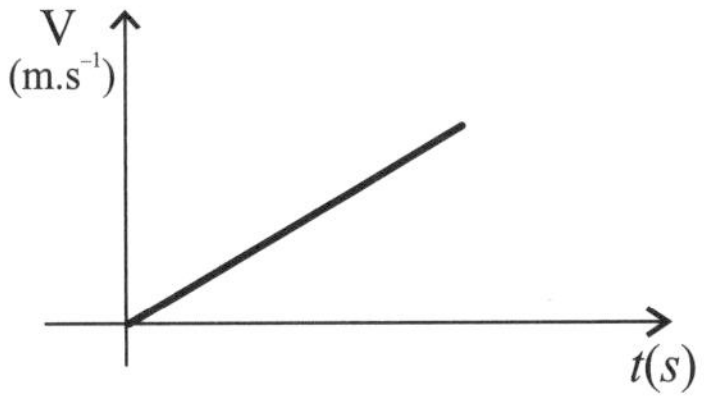

Velocity increases at a constant rate
(gradient is constant)

Displacement-time

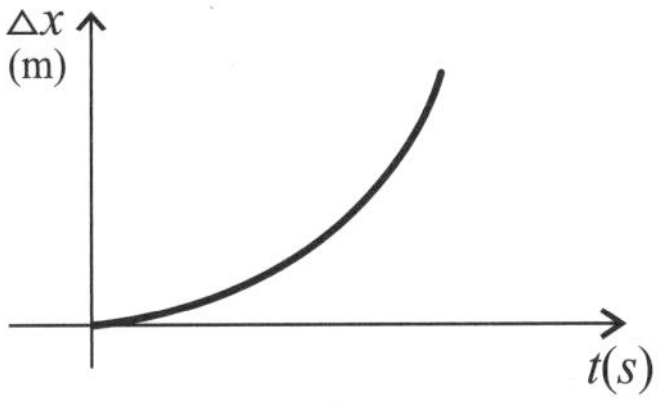

Displacement increases at an increasing rate
(gradient is increasing)
(graph is getting steeper)

Object moving with a decreasing velocity

Acceleration-time

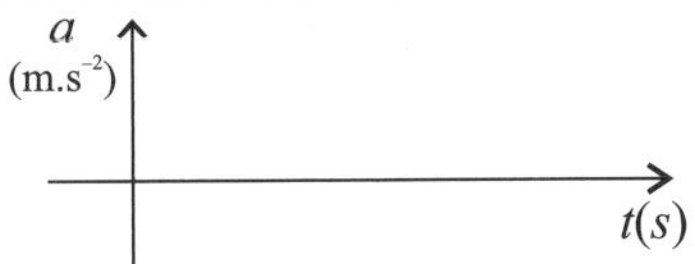

Acceleration is constant and negative

Velocity-time

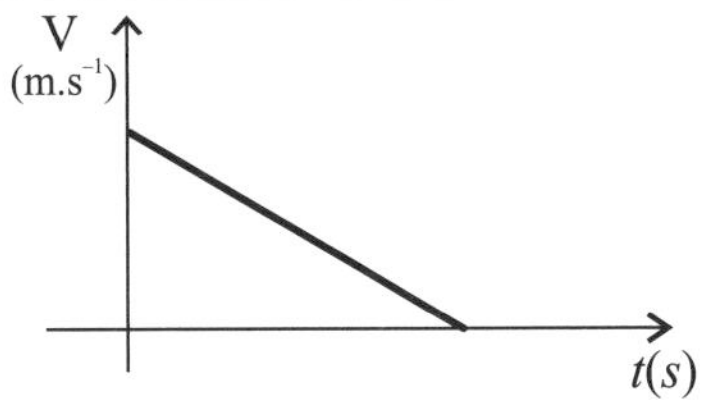

Velocity Decreasing at a constant rate
(constant negative gradient)

Displacement-time

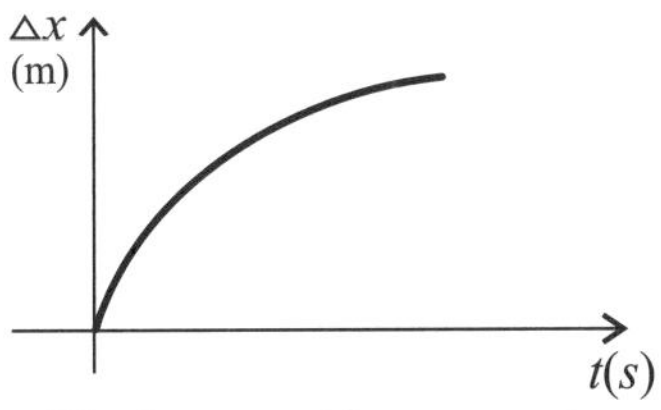

Displacement increases at a decreasing rate
(gradient is decreasing)
(graph is getting flatter)

SHAPE OF DISPLACEMENT-TIME GRAPHS:

Speed Increasing Displacement increasing	**Speed Decreasing Displacement increasing**	**Constant Speed Displacement Increasing**
V ↑ △x ↑ 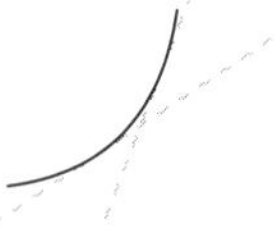	V ↓ △x ↑ 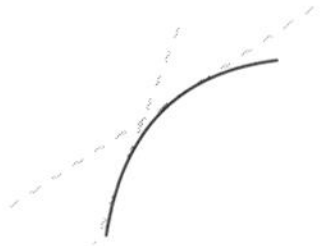	V=k △x ↑ 
Speed Increasing Displacement Decreasing	**Speed Decreasing Displacement Decreasing**	**Constant Speed Displacement Decreasing**
V ↑ △x ↓ 	V ↓ △x ↓ 	V=k △x ↓ 
Zero velocity (displacement is constant)		
V=0 △x=k		

The points below apply to a velocity time graph:

- If the graph is **above the time axis, displacement** is **increasing**.
- If the graph is **below the time axis, displacement** is **decreasing**.
- If the graph moves **away from the time axis, velocity** is **increasing** (object is speeding up).
- If the graph moves **towards the time axis, velocity** is **decreasing** (object is slowing down).

Away from the time axis: speed increases (V↑) **Toward the time axis: speed decreases**(V↓)

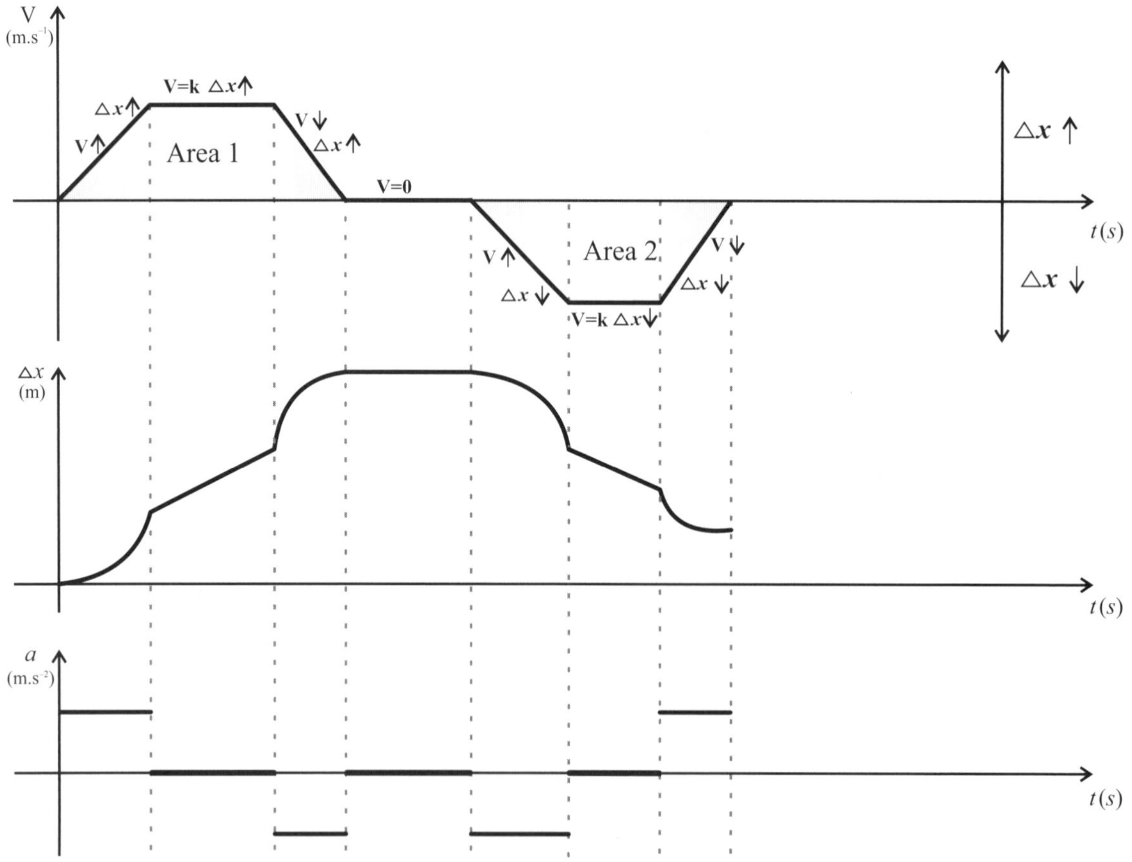

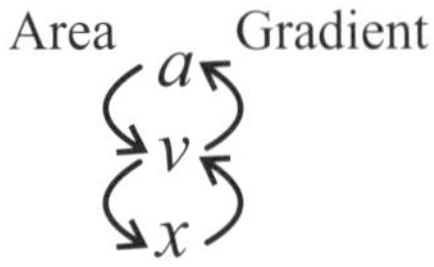

Note: The above displacement-time graph shows the shape that would be obtained from the velocity-time graph shown. whether or not the displacement time graph will go below the time axis depends on the area underneath the velocity time graph.

If **Area 1 > Area 2** then the displacement time graph will **end above the time axis.**
If **Area 1 < Area 2** then the displacement time graph will **end below the time axis.**
If **Area 1 = Area 2** then the displacement time graph will **end on the time axis.**

GRAPHS OF BOUNCING BALLS

Taking down as positive	Taking up as positive
Ball is dropped (initial velocity is 0)	**Ball is dropped (initial velocity is zero)**

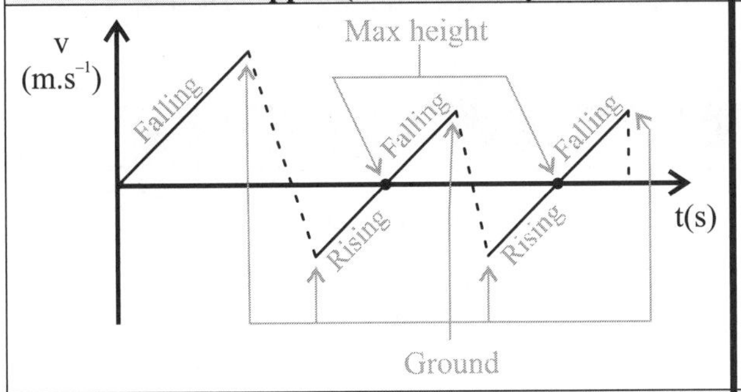

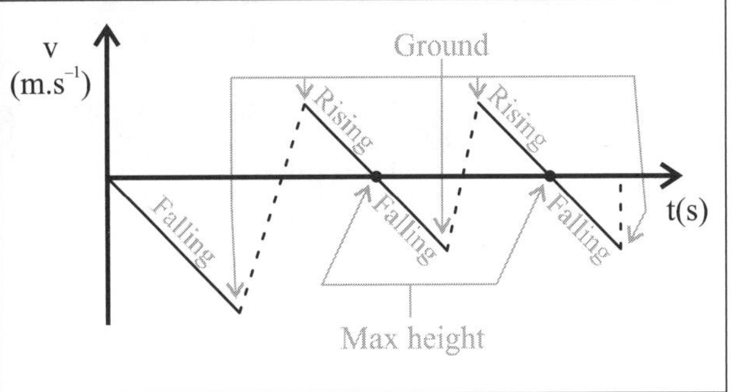

Position time graph starting point as zero displacement	Position time graph starting point as zero displacement

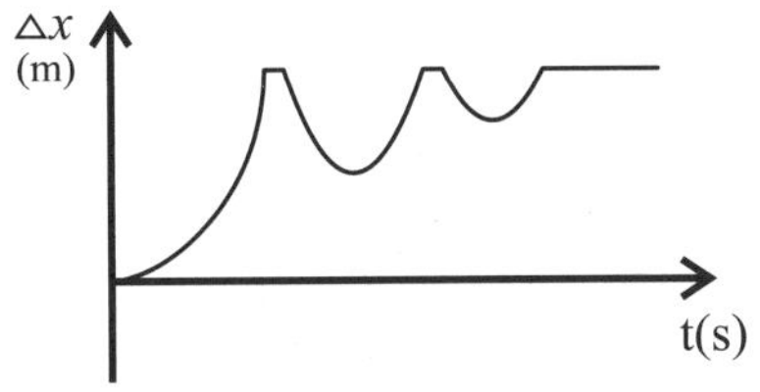

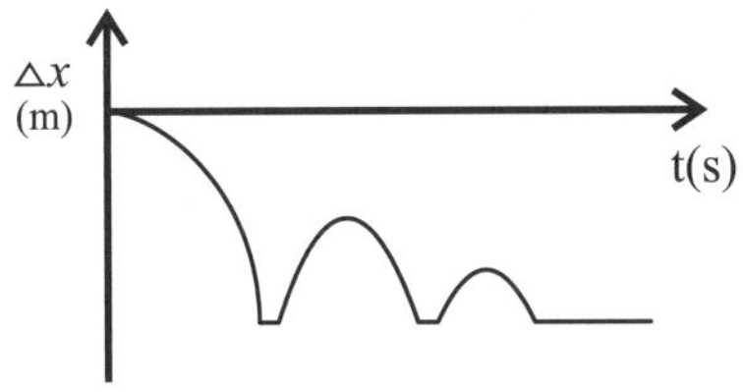

Position time graph ground as zero displacement	Position time graph ground as zero displacement

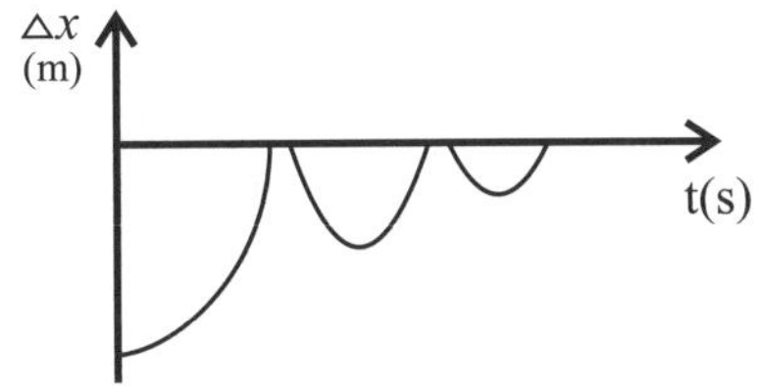

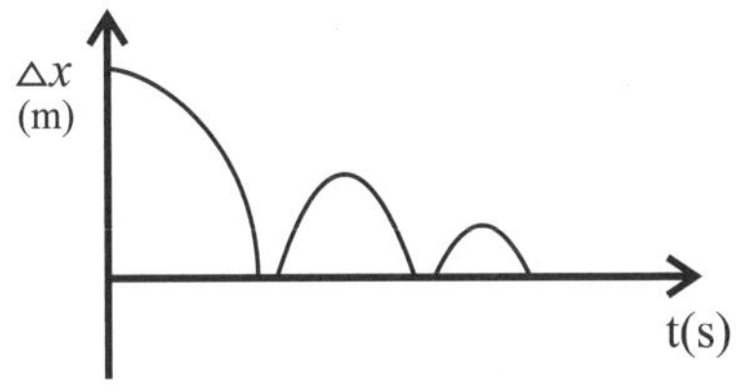

The dotted line in the velocity time graph represents the time the ball is on the ground.
If the ball is thrown up or down first the initial velocity will not start at 0.
The shapes of the displacement time graphs will not change if the ball has an initial velocity.
If there is no friction, the gradient of a velocity time graph will be equal to –9,8 m.s^{-2} (if up is positive) or 9,8 m.s^{-2} (if down is positive).

Taking down as positive	Taking up as positive
Ball is thrown down	**Ball is thrown down**

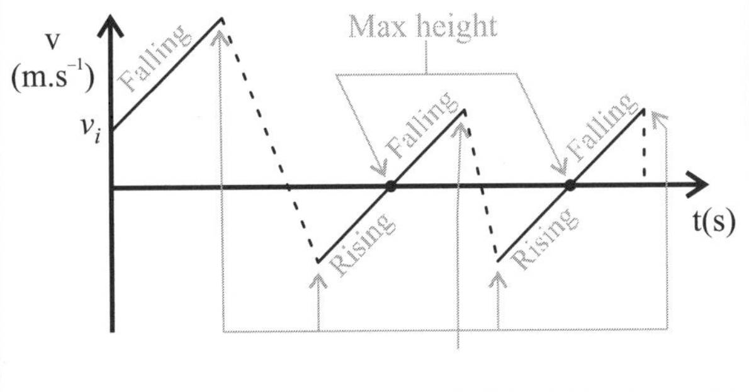

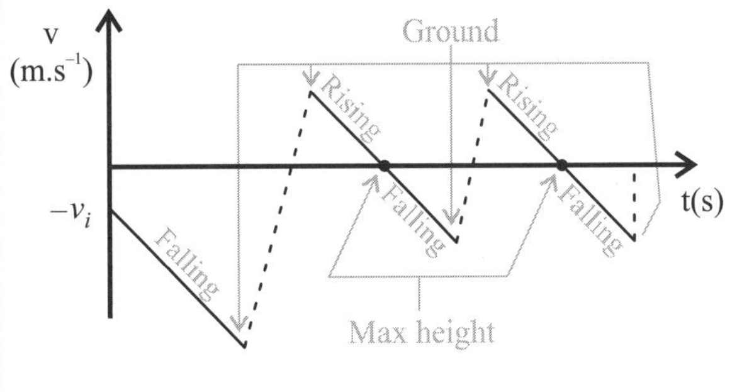

Ball is thrown up	Ball is thrown up

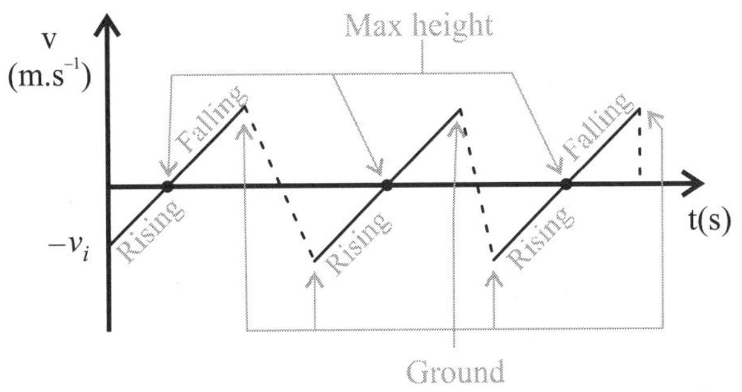

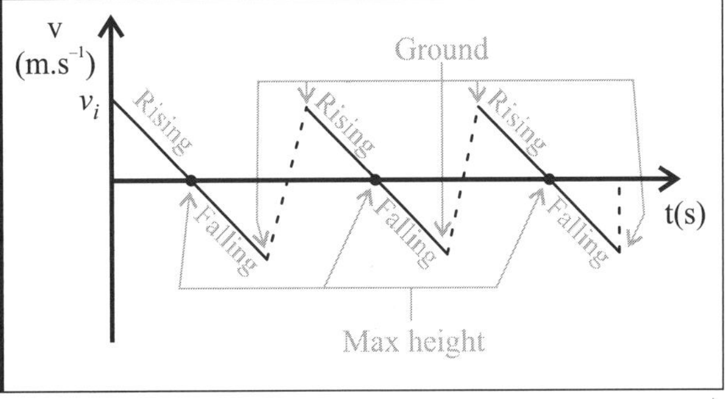

Question 1 (Solutions on page 58)

1.1 A ball is thrown vertically upwards and returns to the thrower's hand. Ignore air resistance. Which one of the following best describes the direction of the ball's acceleration during its flight?

	Travelling up	Maximum Height	Travelling down
A	Downward	Downward	Downward
B	Upward	Zero	Downward
C	Downward	Zero	Downward
D	Upward	Downward	Upward

(2)

1.2 Car P and Q are travelling towards each other. Initially, Car P is travelling at a speed of 10 m.s^{-1} and accelerating with a magnitude of 2 m.s^{-2} causing it to increase its speed. Initially, Car Q is travelling with a speed of 20 m.s^{-1} and accelerating with a magnitude of 1 m.s^{-2}, also causing it to increase its speed.
After 5 seconds the cars pass each other.

Which of the graphs below could be a velocity time graph to represent the situation above?

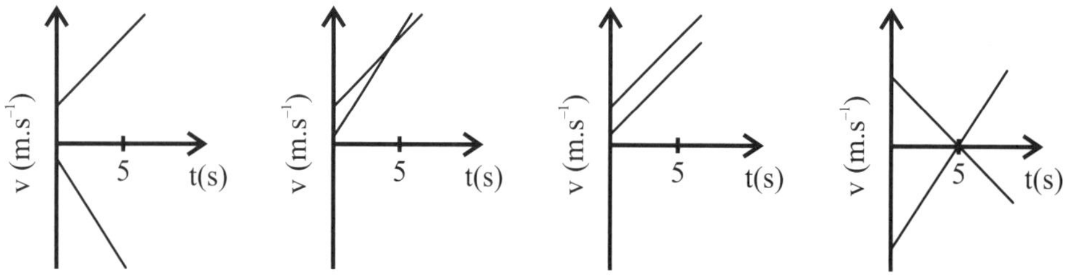

A B C D

(2)

1.3 Tommy is working on a building site and throws a hammer to his friend above him. Unfortunately, his friend does not catch the hammer and it falls to the soft ground below and embeds itself in the ground. Which one of the acceleration time graphs below best represents the motion of the hammer from the time it leaves Tommy's hand to when it embeds in the ground?

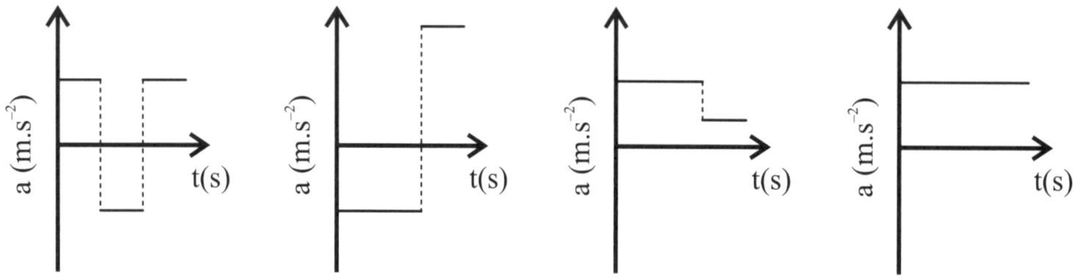

A B C D (2)

1.4 A ball is dropped from rest. After time t the ball has travelled a distance of x. After time $5t$ the ball has travelled a distance of:

A $5x$
B x
C $10x$
D $25x$

(2)

1.5 The velocity vs time graph below shows the motion of two different objects sliding in a straight line across a horizontal surface.

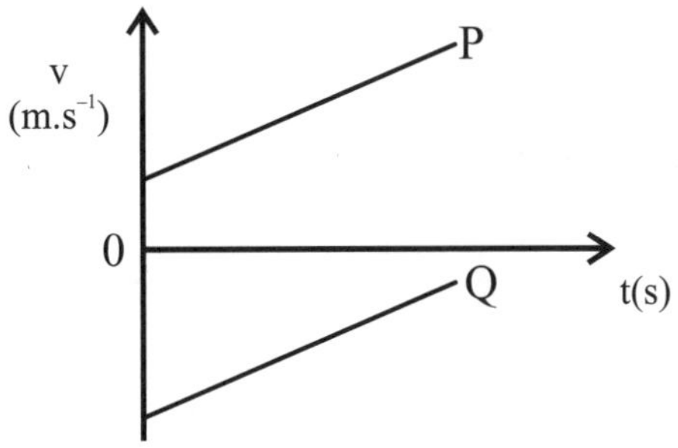

If East is positive which of the statements below is true?

A The resultant forces acting on P and Q are opposite in direction.

B There is no resultant force acting on P or Q.

C The resultant force on P is East whilst the resultant force on Q is West.

D The resultant force on P and Q are both East. (2)

1.6 A Stone of mass 100g is projected vertically upwards with an initial velocity u. The stone reaches a maximum height s. What initial velocity would the stone have to be projected with to reach a maximum height of $2s$?

A $2u$

B $u\sqrt{2}$

C $4u$

D $8u$ (2)

1.7 The velocity time graph below shows two objects, P and Q, which initially start from rest.

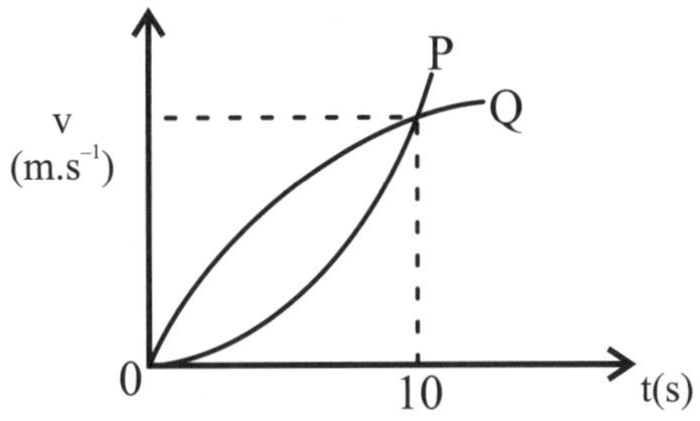

At 10 seconds:

A The velocity of Q is greater than that of P.

B The velocity of P is greater than that of Q.

C Q has travelled a greater distance than P.

D The displacement of P and Q are equal. (2)

1.8 A car accelerates uniformly from rest. After travelling a distance, d, in a straight line in t seconds, it has a velocity v. At what time and distance during its motion did it reach a velocity of $0{,}5v$?

	Time	Distance
A	$0{,}25t$	$0{,}25d$
B	$0{,}5\ t$	$0{,}5d$
C	$0{,}25t$	$0{,}5d$
D	$0{,}5\ t$	$0{,}25d$

1.9 Three identical balls (A, B and C) are thrown from the same height above the ground.
Ball A is thrown up with an initial speed of 20 $m.s^{-1}$.
Ball B is thrown down with an initial speed of 20 $m.s^{-1}$.
Ball C is dropped from rest.

Which one of the following statements concerning the magnitude of the final velocity of the balls is true if air resistance is ignored?

A All three balls will hit the ground with the same velocity.
B Ball B hits the ground with greatest velocity and C with the lowest.
C Ball A and B will hit the ground with same velocity.
D Ball C will hit the ground with a greater velocity than ball A. (2)

1.10 A ball is thrown vertically upwards. The ball is in contact with a hand for 0,5 s while it is thrown. Ignore air resistance. Which of the following is the most likely velocity versus time graph for the motion of the ball?

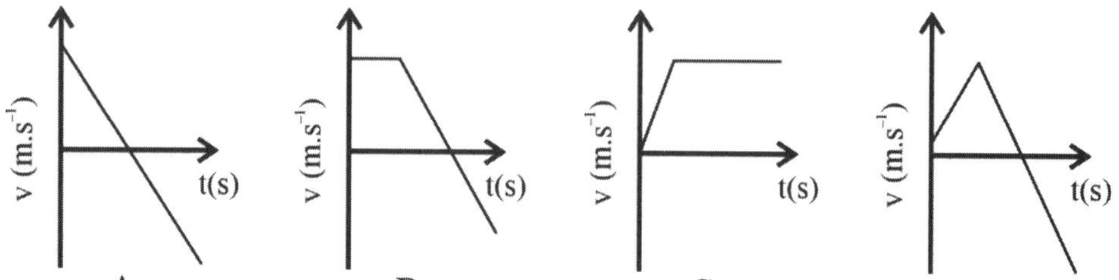

A B C D (2)

1.11 Which of the following descriptions correctly describes the motion of an object travelling with uniform acceleration along a straight line?

The object…..

A moves with an increasing velocity.
B moves with the same distance in equal time intervals.
C has the same increase or decrease in speed in equal time intervals.
D has the same increase in distance in equal time intervals. (2)

1.12 At the highest point of a ball's trajectory, which of the following are correct regarding the magnitudes and directions of the velocity, force and acceleration acting on the ball?

	Velocity	Force	Acceleration
A	Zero	Downwards	Downwards
B	Upwards	Zero	Zero
C	Zero	Zero	Zero
D	Zero	Downwards	Zero

1.13 An object is thrown vertically upwards leaving the thrower's hand at time t = 0. Which graph shows how speed v varies with t as the object rises and falls?

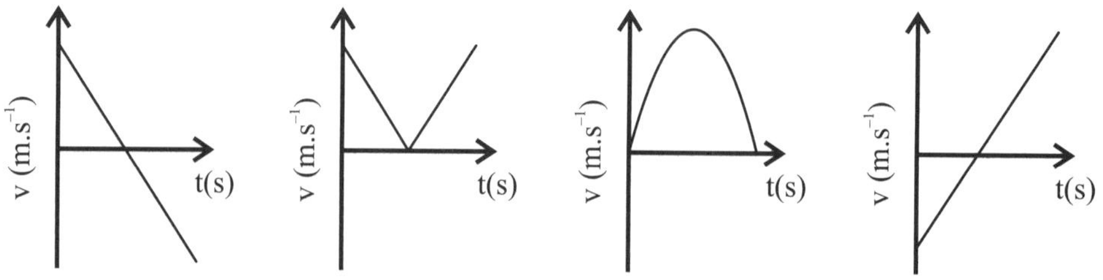

A B C D (2)

1.14 The graph below indicates how the velocity of an object which initially starts moving due East, changes with time.

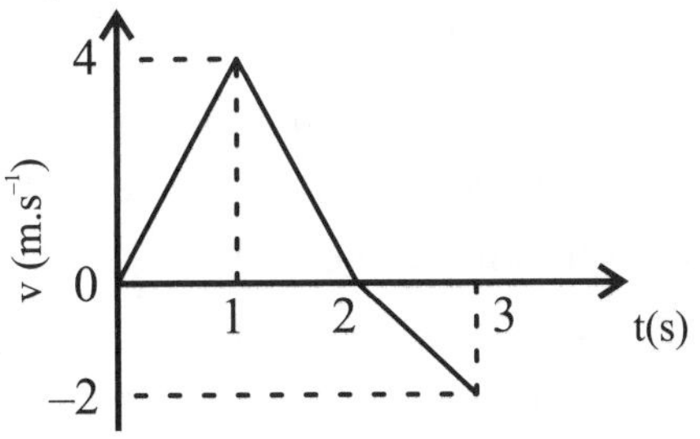

After 3 seconds the object is:

A 3 m West of its starting point.

B 3 m East of the its starting point.

C back at its starting point.

D slowing down and moving West. (2)

1.15 Tom is training for a cycling race around a 400 m circular track. He completes a warmup lap travelling at an average speed of 2,5 m.s^{-1}. He then completes his next lap at an average speed of v. His average speed for both laps was 4 m.s^{-1}. What was Tom's average speed for his second lap?

A 6,25 m.s^{-1}

B 10 m.s^{-1}

C 5,5 m.s^{-1}

D 7,5 m.s^{-1} (2)

1.16 Which of the displacement time graphs below could represent an object in free fall on Earth?

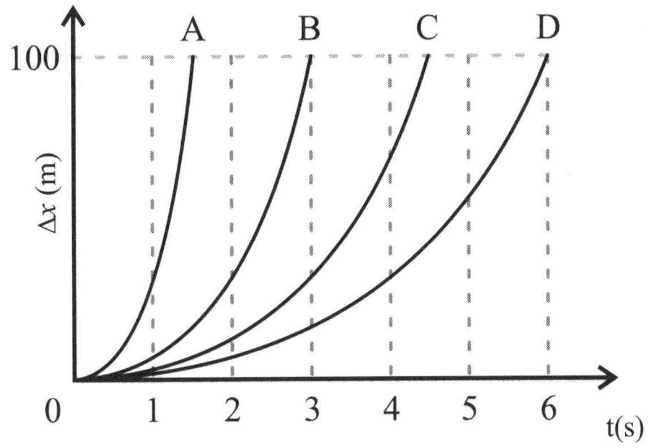

(2)

1.17 Refer to the following displacement vs. time graph for the motion of an object travelling in a straight line on a horizontal surface. North is the positive direction.

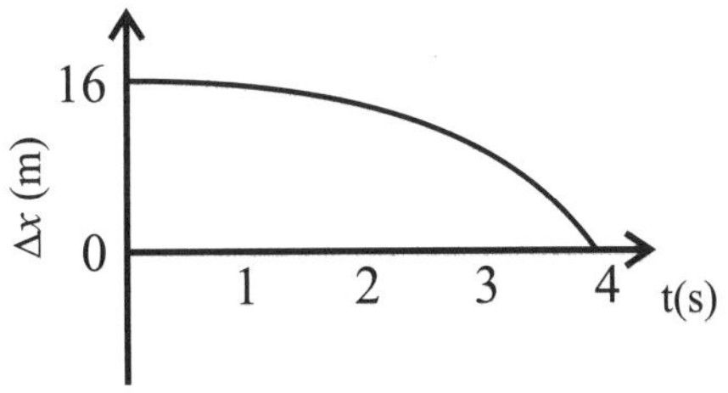

A The magnitude of the average velocity of the object is 4 m.s^{-1}.

B The object is travelling South and its speed is increasing.

C The object is travelling North and its speed is decreasing.

D The object is travelling North at a constant speed. (2)

TOC
1 Data Sheet
2 Definitions
3
3 solutions
4
4 solutions
5
5 solutions
6
6 solutions
7
7 solutions
8
8 solutions
9
9 solutions
10
10 solutions

1.18 A ball of mass m is thrown vertically upwards and reaches a height h above the ground. Another identical ball of mass $2m$ is also thrown vertically upwards and reaches the same height h. Ignore all effects of friction.

A The lighter ball will take a shorter time to reach a height of h.
B Both balls have the same kinetic energy when they are thrown.
C Both balls have the same initial velocity.
D Both balls have the same momentum as they are thrown. (2)

1.19 An object falls freely from rest. After falling a distance d its velocity is v. What is its velocity after it has fallen a distance of $3d$?

A $3v$
B $6v$
C $9v$
D $v\sqrt{3}$ (2)

1.20 A package is dropped from two different heights. In the first instance the package is dropped from a height of H and it takes t seconds for the package to reach the ground. In the second instance the package is dropped from a height of $4H$.

The time for the package, dropped from the height of $4H$, to reach the ground compared to the time t of the package dropped from H is:

A t
B $2t$
C $4t$
D $16t$ (2)

1.21 A ball reaches the bottom of a smooth slope travelling at a constant velocity. The ball rolls up the slope, stops briefly at some point on its way up and rolls back to the bottom of the slope.

Which one of the following velocity-time graphs best shows the motion of the ball from the time it starts rolling up the slope to the time it reaches the bottom of the slope?

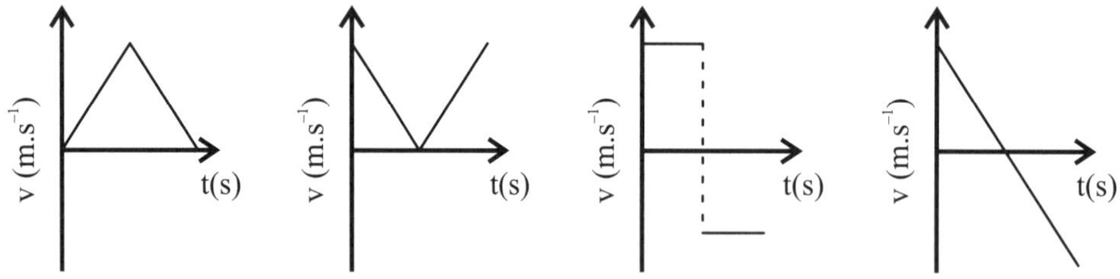

A B C D (2)

1.22 The velocity time graph below is of an object that has been projected vertically upwards from the edge of a cliff. The displacement of the object is:

A $(y-2x)[Q+0,5(R-Q)]$
B $(0,5R)(y-x)$
C $(0,5y)(P-R)$
D $0,5R(y-x)$

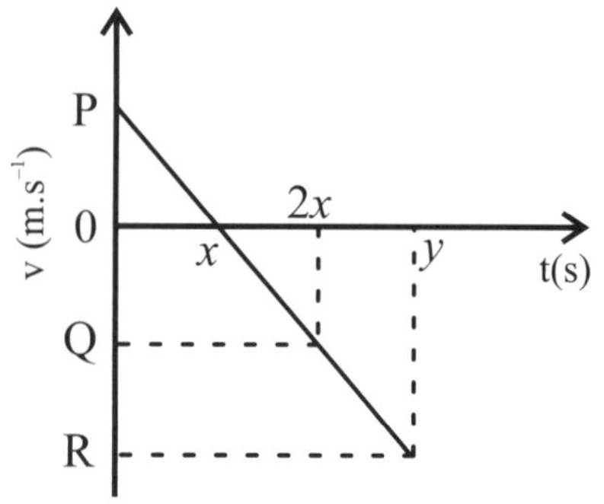

(2)

1.23 An object undergoes a constant negative acceleration. Which one of the velocity time graphs would be a possible description of the object's motion?

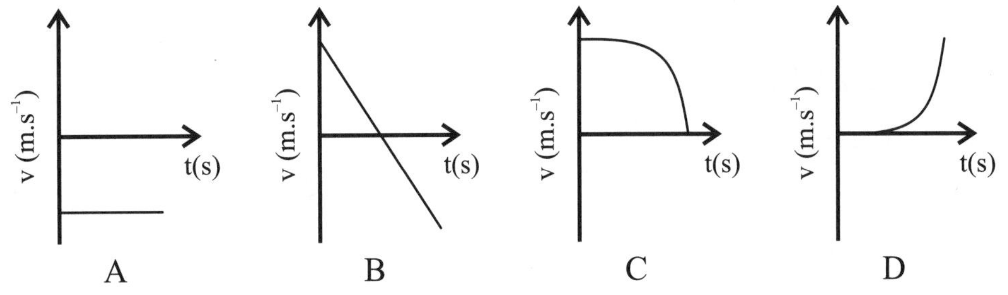

(2)

1.24 A brick is dropped from a height of x. After time t, the brick's velocity is v. At the same instant the brick is a dropped a half brick is also dropped. After time $3t$ the velocity of the half brick will be:

A $3v$ B $2v$ C v D $9v$

(2)

1.25 An object accelerates uniformly from rest in a straight line. After travelling a distance of x the velocity of the object is v. After travelling a distance of $4x$ the objects velocity is:

A v B $2v$ C $16v$ D $4v$

(2)

1.26 An object accelerates uniformly from rest in a straight line. After travelling a distance of x the velocity of the object is v. What distance has the object travelled when its velocity is $3v$?

A x B $3x$ C $9x$ D $x\sqrt{3}$

(2)

1.27 An object accelerates uniformly from rest. After travelling distance $2x$ its velocity is $2v$. what will the objects velocity be after travelling a distance of $8x$?

A $6v$ B $4v$ C $8v$ D $v\sqrt{6}$

(2)

1.28 A ball rolls down a slope from P to Q. While rolling down the slope it experiences a constant frictional force of 2 N. On reaching point Q, a level surface at the bottom of the slope, the ball continues to roll to point R experiencing a constant frictional force of 1 N. R to S is covered in a sheet of black ice and is essentially frictionless. Which one of the following velocity time graphs is a representation of the object's velocity from P to S?

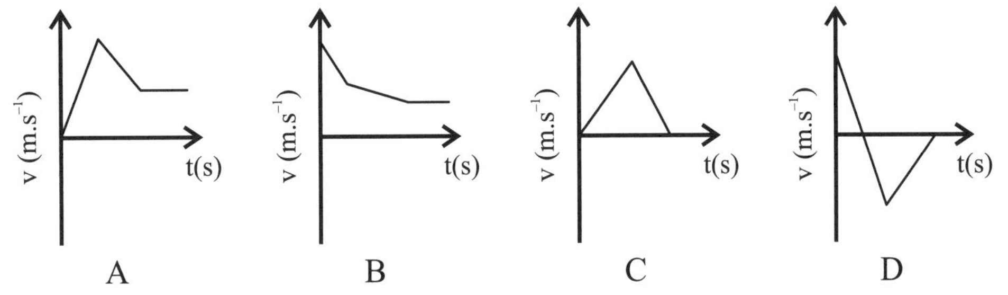

(2)

TOC
1 Data Sheet
2 Definitions
3
3 solutions
4
4 solutions
5
5 solutions
6
6 solutions
7
7 solutions
8
8 solutions
9
9 solutions
10
10 solutions

1.29 The graph shows the position (x) of two soccer players, K and L, moving along the same horizontal straight line.

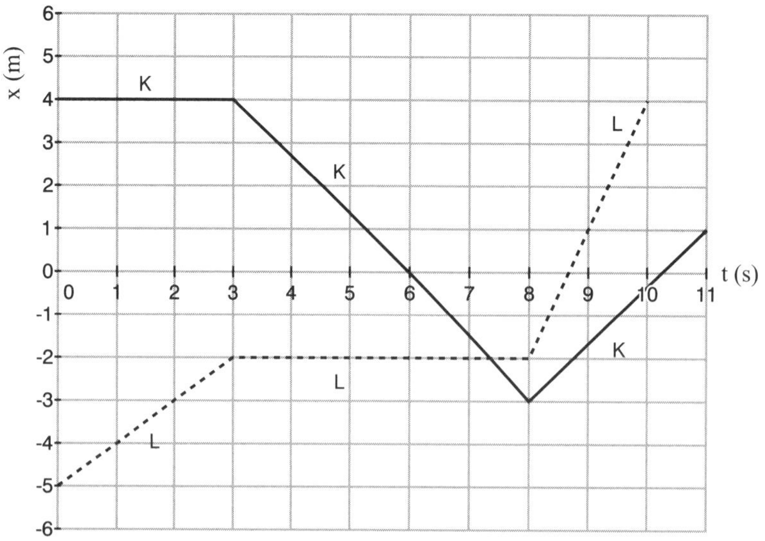

At t = 3 s, what is the distance between K and L?

A –2 m B 2 m C 4 m D 6 m

(The above question is from the 2014 IEB Exemplar Examination) (2)

1.30 The motion of a car moving along a straight road is shown in the speed-time graph below.

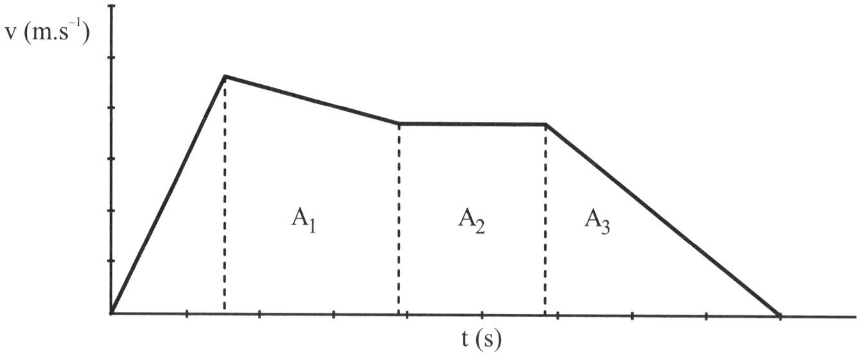

Which area represents the total distance moved by the car during the time its speed is decreasing?

A A_1 B A_3 C $A_1 + A_3$ D $A_1 + A_2 + A_3$

(The above question is from the 2014 IEB Exemplar Examination) (2)

1.31 An athlete runs around the athletics track at a constant speed in an anticlockwise direction. The athletics track is shown in the diagram below.

Which one of the following statements is true as the athlete runs past point X to Z via Y? The instantaneous velocity of the athlete is …

A constant between X and Y only.

B constant between Y and Z only.

C constant at all points between X and Z.

D never constant anywhere between X and Z.

(The above question is from the 2014 IEB Final Examination) (2)

1.32 You have two identical marbles. You drop the first marble and throw the second marble down from the same height. Air resistance is negligible. While the marbles are in the air, which statement is NOT correct?

A The second marble will spend less time in the air.

B The first marble will have a smaller velocity when it reaches the ground.

C The second marble will experience a larger force.

D Both marbles will have the same acceleration.

(The above question is from the 2015 IEB Final Examination) (2)

1.33 A sketch of the velocity-time graph for a moving object is shown below.

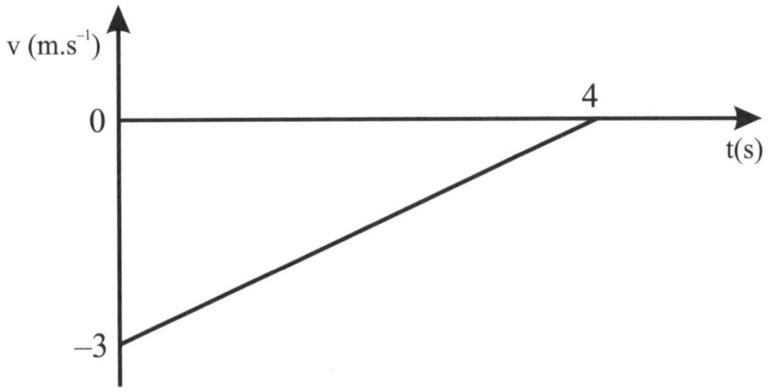

Which answer best describes the magnitude of the object's velocity and the sign of the acceleration?

	v (m.s^{-1})	a (m.s^{-2})
A	Decreasing	+
B	Decreasing	–
C	Increasing	+
D	Increasing	–

(The above question is from the 2015 IEB Final Examination) (2)

1.34 A car is travelling west at 12 m.s^{-1} when the driver notices a stop sign. The driver applies brakes, and the car stops at the stop sign. Which is the best description of the velocity and acceleration of the car while it is slowing down?

	Velocity (m.s^{-1})	Acceleration (m.s^{-2})
A	East	East
B	West	East
C	East	West
D	West	West

(The above question is from the 2016 IEB Final Examination) (2)

1.35 A small aeroplane starting from rest can achieve a high enough speed to take off from a runway that is 400 m long. Another, heavily loaded aeroplane, also starting from rest, has the same acceleration but needs to achieve twice the speed to take off. What is the minimum length of runway that will be needed for the heavy plane to take off?

A 400 m

B 800 m

C 1 200 m

D 1 600 m.

(The above question is from the 2016 IEB Final Examination) (2)

1.36 Velocity vs time graphs are shown for three racing cars, a red car, a green car and a blue car. At t = 5 s, which car has travelled the furthest?

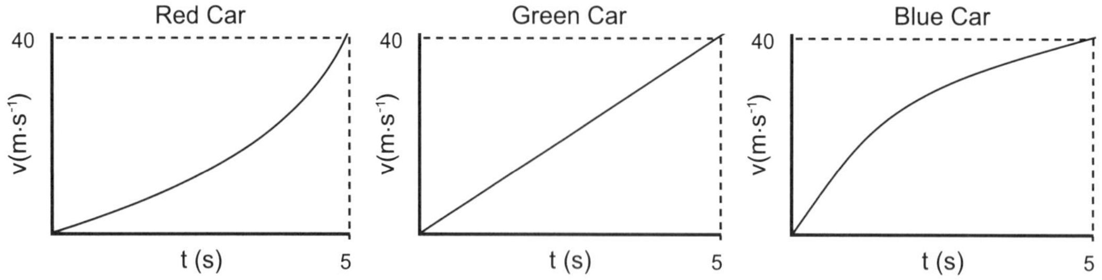

A The red car

B The green car

C The blue car

D all cars travelled the same distance

(The above question is from the 2016 IEB Supplementary Examination) (2)

1.37 You throw a small ball vertically upwards and measure that it takes time ***t*** to come back to you. You then throw the same ball upwards so that it takes time ***2t*** to come back to you. Which statement is true about the motion of the ball for the second throw?

A The ball's initial speed for the second throw was twice the initial speed for the first throw

B The ball travelled twice as high in the second throw than the original throw

C The ball had double the acceleration on the way up for the second throw

D The ball stopped at the highest point and had zero acceleration at that point

(The above question is from the 2016 IEB Supplementary Examination)

1.38 The velocity vs time graph for the motion of a car on a straight road is shown in the diagram. Assume that the car starts at the origin $x = 0$ at time $t = 0$.

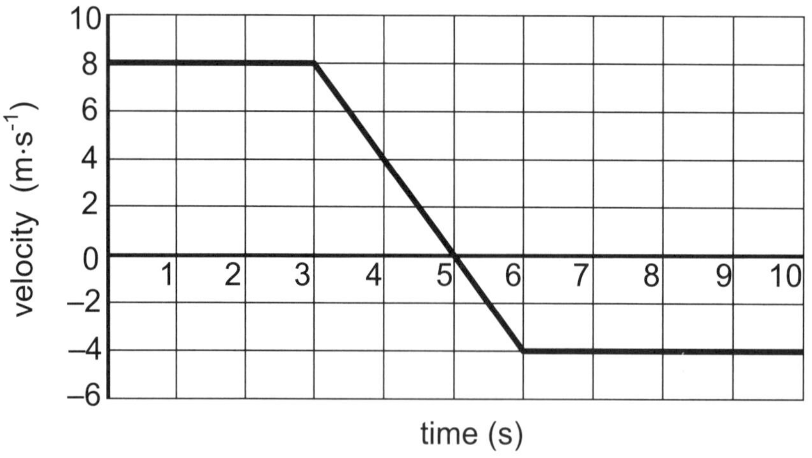

At which time is the car the greatest distance from the origin?

A 10 s

B 6 s

C 5 s

D 3 s

(The above question is from the 2017 IEB Final Examination) (2)

1.39 An object moves along a horizontal line with **increasing speed**. Which one of the following choices could be the best description of the velocity and the acceleration for the object to achieve this motion?

	Velocity ($m.s^{-1}$)	Acceleration ($m.s^{-2}$)
A	Positive	Zero
B	Positive	Negative
C	Negative	Positive
D	Negative	Negative

(The above question is from the 2017 IEB Final Examination) (2)

1.40 The velocity vs time graph for a moving object is sketched below. Upwards is taken as positive.

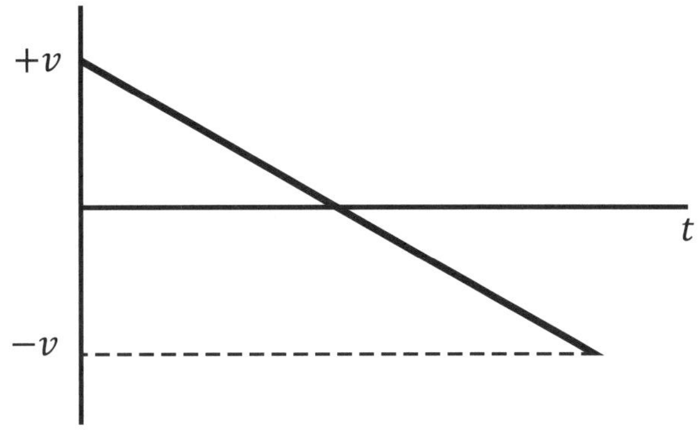

The motion of the object can be described as:

A the object is travelling downwards throughout its motion

B the object is travelling with a constant velocity throughout its motion

C the object's speed is decreasing throughout its motion

D the object is travelling with a constant acceleration throughout its motion

(The above question is from the 2017 IEB Supplementary Examination) (2)

1.41 A ball is dropped vertically from rest above a hard, horizontal surface. The motion for the bouncing ball is represented on the velocity vs time graph shown below. Air resistance is negligible.

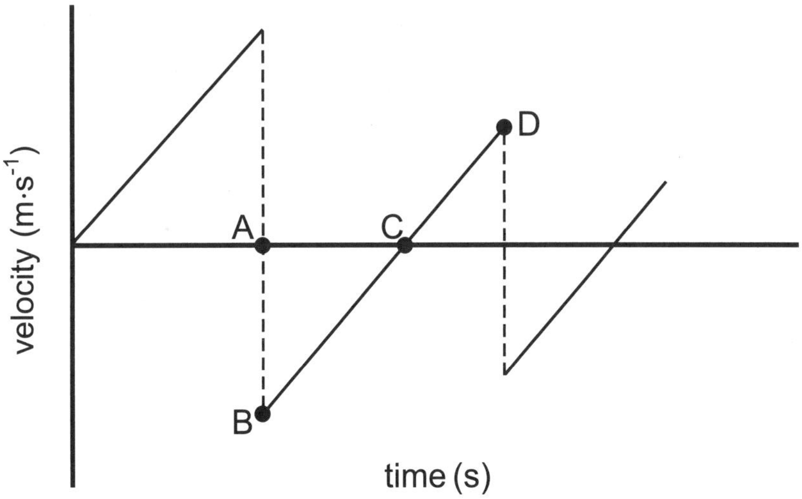

At which point labelled on the graph does the ball reach its maximum height after the first bounce?

(The above question is from the 2018 IEB Final Examination) (2)

TOC 1 Data Sheet 2 Definitions 3 3 solutions 4 4 solutions 5 5 solutions 6 6 solutions 7 7 solutions 8 8 solutions 9 9 solutions 10 10 solutions

1.42 A bike starts at the origin and its velocity along a straight line is represented on the velocity vs time graph shown. During which intervals is the bike moving **towards** the origin?

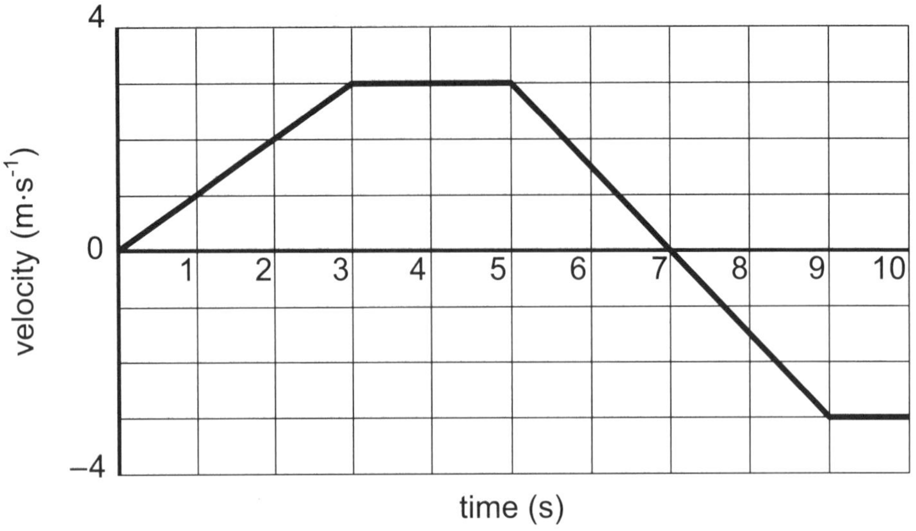

A For times between 0 s and 3 s.

B For times between 0 s and 7 s.

C For times between 5 s and 7 s.

D For times greater than 7 s.

(The above question is from the 2018 IEB Supplementary Examination) (2)

1.43 A model car completes one lap around a circular track of 400 m at an average speed of 5 $m.s^{-1}$ and then a second lap at an average speed of v. The average speed for the completion of both laps was 8 $m.s^{-1}$. What was the average speed of the second lap?

A 11,0 $m.s^{-1}$

B 12,5 $m.s^{-1}$

C 15,0 $m.s^{-1}$

D 20,0 $m.s^{-1}$

(The above question is from the 2018 IEB Supplementary Examination) (2)

1.44 An object initially at rest travels a distance d in a time t at a constant acceleration. What is the time taken for the object to travel 16 d from rest at the same acceleration?

A 2 t

B 4 t

C 8 t

D 16 t

(The above question is from the 2019 IEB Final Examination) (2)

1.45 The graph shows how the velocity of an object changes with time.

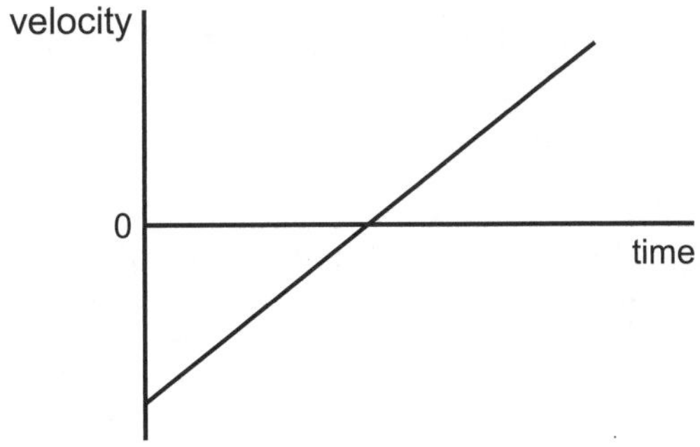

Which one of the following graphs correctly shows how the acceleration of the object changes with time?

A
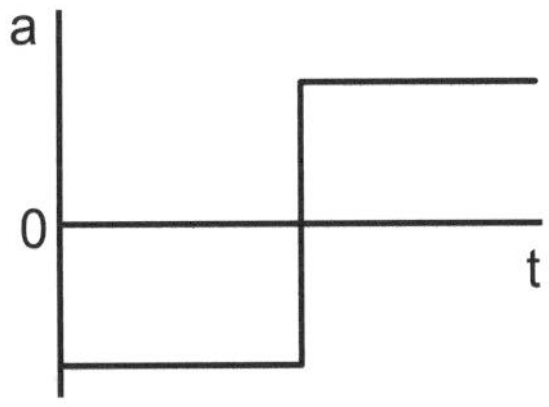

B
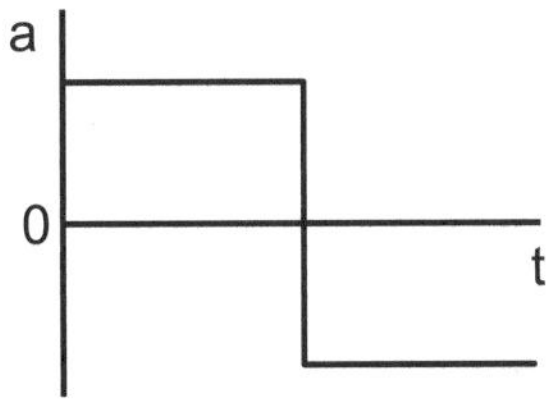

C
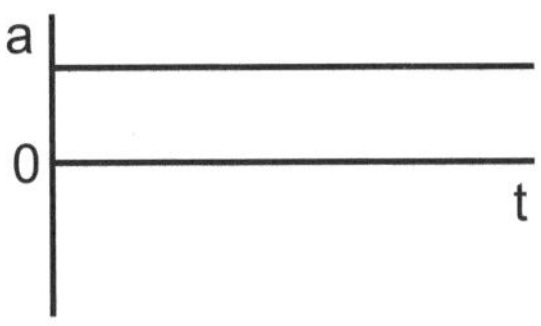

D
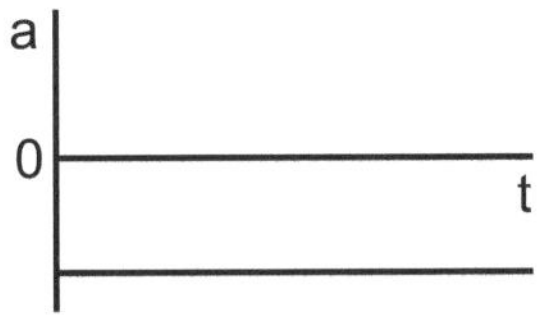

(The above question is from the 2019 IEB Final Examination) (2)

1.46 A ball is dropped from a certain height above the ground and bounces a few times after it hits the ground. The velocity-time graph below describes the motion of the ball from the time it is dropped. Ignore the effects of air friction.

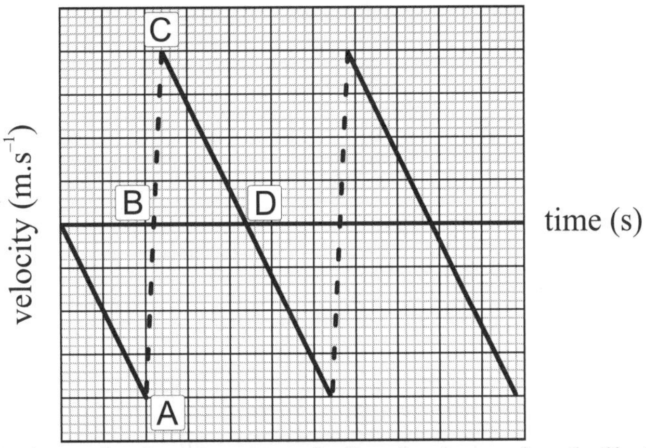

In relation to the velocity-time graph for the bouncing ball shown above, which statement below is correct?

A Down is taken as the positive direction and the ball is at the highest position of its first bounce at C.

B Down is taken as the negative direction and the ball is at the highest position of its first bounce at D.

C Down is taken as the negative direction and the ball is at the highest position of its first bounce at C.

D Down is taken as the positive direction and the ball is at the highest position of its first bounce at D.

(The above question is from the 2019 IEB Supplementary Examination) (2)

[48]

TOC 1 Data Sheet 2 Definitions 3 3 solutions 4 4 solutions 5 5 solutions 6 6 solutions 7 7 solutions 8 8 solutions 9 9 solutions 10 10 solutions

Question 2 (Solutions on page 58)

A child throws a coin vertically upwards from the top of a high building with an initial velocity of $20 m.s^{-1}$. The coin strikes the ground at $58 m.s^{-1}$. Air resistance is negligible and take upward as the positive direction.

2.1 Describe the acceleration of the coin as it leaves the child's hand.
Use the words constant upwards, constant downwards or non-constant (2)

2.2 Calculate the time it takes for the coin to reach the ground (4)

2.3 Determine the height of the building (4)

2.4 Calculate the distance travelled during the last second of the coins motion. (5)

[15]

Question 3 (Solutions on page 59)

Ball, B, is thrown vertically upward from a height, h, with a speed of $4,9 m.s^{-1}$. At the same instant, a second identical ball, A, is dropped from the same height as ball B as shown in the diagram below.

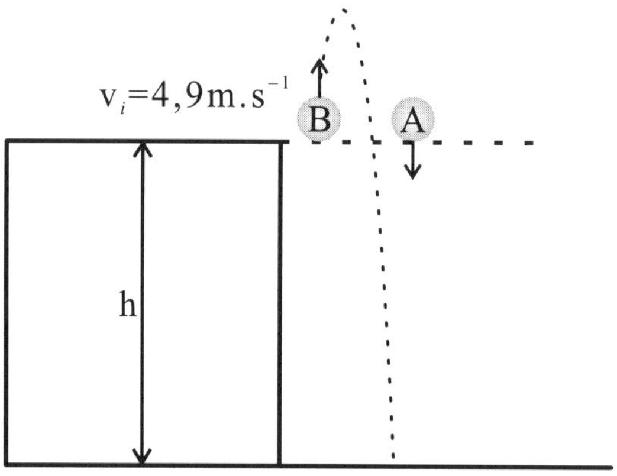

3.1 Define acceleration. (1)

3.2 Calculate the time it takes for ball B to reach its maximum height. (3)

3.3 Determine distance between the balls when B is at its maximum height. (7)

3.4 Sketch a velocity-time graph for the motion of ball **B** from the time it is projected until it hits the ground.
Clearly show the following points on your graph:
- The initial velocity
- The time it takes to reach its maximum height
- The time it takes to return to its starting point (4)

[15]

Question 4 (Solutions on page 59 and 60)

A tennis ball with a mass of 60 grams is dropped from a height of 19,6m above the ground. It rebounds from the ground and rises to a maximum height of 7,35m. The effects of air resistance are negligible.

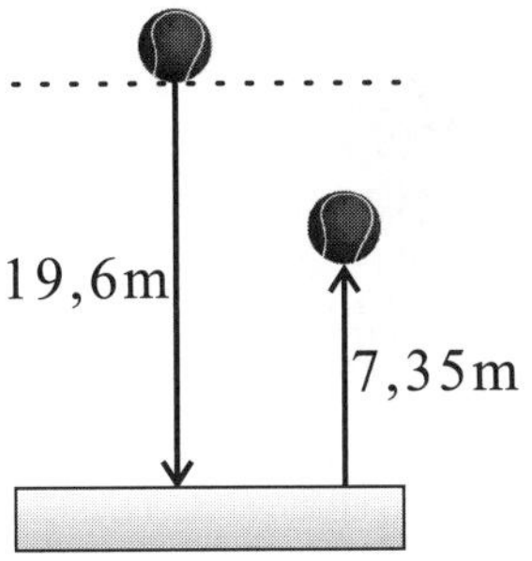

4.1 Determine the time taken for the ball to reach the ground after it was dropped. (3)

4.2 Determine the magnitude of the velocity that the ball strikes the ground. (3)

4.3 At what speed does the ball rebound from the ground? (4)

4.4 How long does the ball take to reach it maximum height after the rebound? (3)

4.5 Draw a sketch graph of displacement versus time, from the time the ball is dropped until it reaches its maximum height. Use the ground as the reference point and label all relevant points. (5)

4.6 Determine the force that the ground applies on the ball to rebound it to a height of 7,35m if it is in contact with the ground for 0,5 seconds. (5)

[23]

Question 5 (Solutions on page 60)

Zipho stands at the bottom of a 40 metre high building. He throws ball A vertically up with a velocity of $18 m.s^{-1}$. One second later Nthombi throws ball B vertically down with a velocity of $6 m.s^{-1}$. At what height above the ground will ball A and B pass each other?

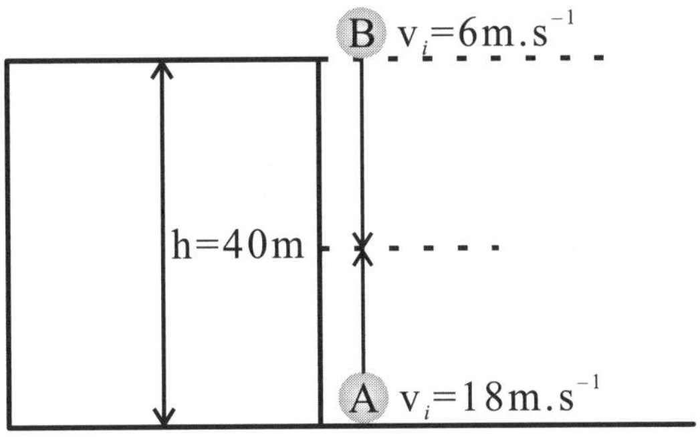

[8]

Question 6 (Solutions on page 60 and 61)

A hot air balloon is ascending at a constant velocity. At a height of 92,5 metres a sandbag is accidently dislodged. From this height, it would take the sandbag 5 seconds to reach the ground. The effects of air resistance are negligible.

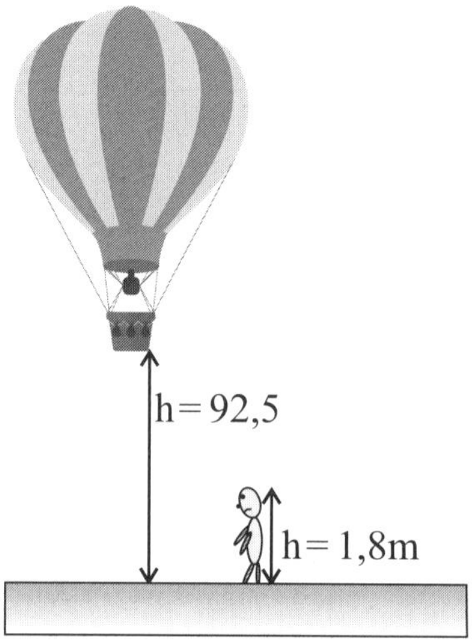

6.1 Calculate the velocity of the balloon when the sandbag is dislodged. (3)

6.2 Using the balloon as the reference point, draw a sketch graph of displacement versus time. Take up as positive. (4)

6.3 A man is walking at $2m.s^{-1}$ on the ground below. At the instant the sandbag is dislodged, he is 3 metres from the base of the balloon. If he is 1,8 metres tall, is the man safe? (5)

[12]

Question 7 (Solutions on page 61)

James is attempting to determine the height of a flagpole. A science student suggests that he should throw a golf ball so that it reaches its maximum height at the top of the flagpole. James throws the golf ball up from height of 1,2m and catches it at the same height. If the golf ball is the air for a total time of 1,6 seconds, determine the height of the flagpole.

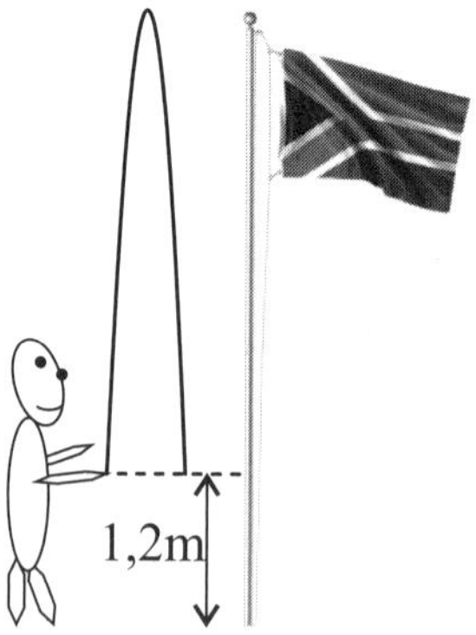

[8]

Question 8 (Solutions on page 61 and 62)

A super hero and villain are fighting on the roof of a 50m high building. The villain manages to gain the upper hand on the superhero. He holds him over the edge of the building and throws him vertically upwards with a speed of $10 m.s^{-1}$. Luckily for the superhero, a shade awning is open at a height of 4 meters above the ground. The super hero lands on the awning and is safely brought to rest in a time of 1,2 seconds. Ignore the effects of air resistance.

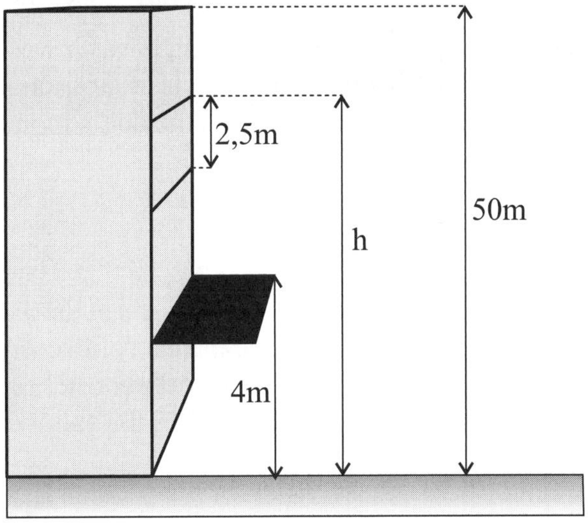

8.1 Determine the time taken for the superhero to reach his maximum height. (4)

8.2 What is the superhero's maximum height above the ground? (4)

8.3 Using the ground as the reference point, draw a sketch graph of displacement versus time for the superhero from the moment he leaves the villain's hands up to the point he lands on the awning. It is not necessary to include time values in your diagram. However, include 3 values of displacement. (5)

8.4 On his way down, the superhero passes a window of length 2,5 meters as shown on the diagram above. If the superhero takes 0,2s to pass the window, determine the value of h, the height of the window above the ground, as shown on the diagram. (8)

8.5 If the superhero has a mass of 120kg, calculate the change in his momentum when the awning brings him to rest. (5)

8.6 Hence, determine the force the awning exerts on the superhero to bring him to rest. (4)

[30]

TOC
1 Data Sheet
2 Definitions
3
3 solutions
4
4 solutions
5
5 solutions
6
6 solutions
7
7 solutions
8
8 solutions
9
9 solutions
10
10 solutions

Question 9 (Solutions on page 62)

A man and woman are playing with their dog in a park. They are 50m apart and the dog is at a point between them. The dog accelerates uniformly from rest towards the woman and reaches a maximum speed of 5 $m.s^{-1}$ in a time of 10 seconds. 10 seconds after the dog starts running the woman throws a ball vertically upwards with a speed of 14,7 $m.s^{-1}$.

9.1 Determine the time taken for ball to reach its maximum height. (3)

9.2 If the dog arrives at the ball just in time to catch it, how far was the dog from the man when it started running? Ignore the effects of air friction and assume the ball was thrown up from the same height as the dog's mouth. (7)

[10]

Question 10 (Solutions on page 63)

A car, travelling at a constant velocity, passes a stationary police car. 2 seconds later, the officer accelerates at 0,8 $m.s^{-2}$ and begins to chase the car for exceeding the speed limit. At this point, the officer is 60m behind the car. When the officer catches up to the car the driver denies that he was speeding. Ignore the length of cars for the following questions.

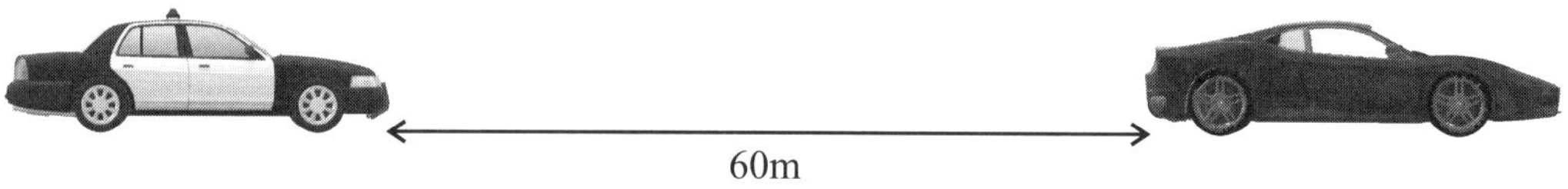

10.1 The speed limit on the road is 60km/h. Was the driver speeding? (3)

10.2 How long did it take the traffic officer to catch the car? (6)

10.3 What was the magnitude of the traffic officer's velocity when he caught the car? (3)

[12]

Question 11 (Solutions on page 63)

A rocket is launched vertically upwards with a uniform acceleration. At some point the rocket runs out of fuel and later returns to earth. A sketch graph of velocity against time (not drawn to scale) of the rockets motion is shown below. Using only the graph and NOT equations of motion answer the questions on the next page.

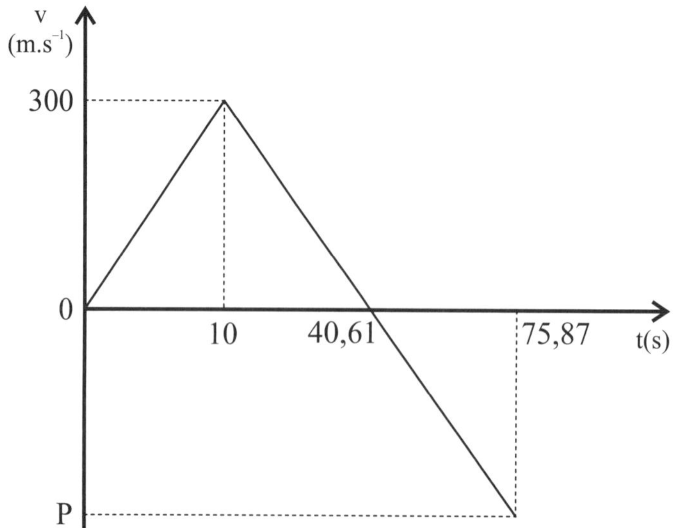

11.1 How long did it take for the rocket run out of fuel? (1)

11.2 Determine the rockets acceleration before it ran out of fuel. (3)

11.3 What was the rockets maximum height above the ground? (1)

11.4 Without any calculations, state the value of the gradient of the graph after 10 seconds. Give a reason for your answer. (3)

11.5 Determine the value of P, the velocity the rocket hit the ground with. (4)

11.6 Draw a sketch graph of displacement against time for the rockets entire motion if it ran out of fuel at a height of 1 500 metres. (5)

[17]

Question 12 (Solutions on page 64)

A hot air balloon is rising at constant velocity when a tourist leans over the edge and accidently drop his camera. When the camera lands on the ground it bounces once and then comes to rest. The graph below shows the entire motion of the camera from the instant it is released until it comes to rest on the ground. Air friction has been ignored.

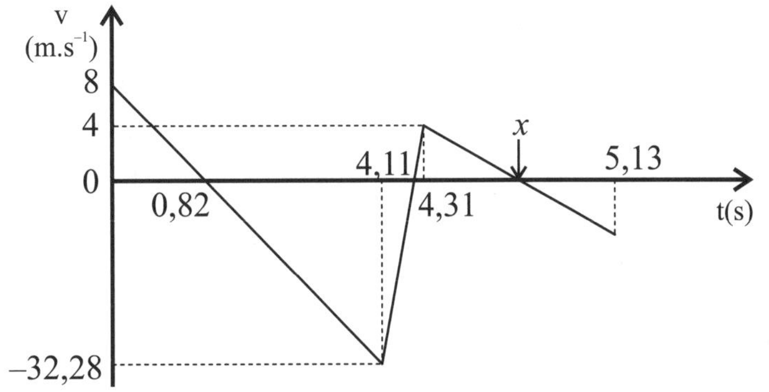

12.1 What velocity was the balloon ascending at? (1)

12.2 How high was the balloon when the camera was dropped? (4)

12.3 How long was the camera in contact with the ground during the bounce? (2)

12.4 Determine the value of x. (3)

12.5 What is the magnitude of the maximum height the camera reaches after it has bounced? (3)

12.6 At time x, what is the distance between the camera and the hot air balloon? (6)

[19]

TOC
1 Data Sheet
2 Definitions
3
3 solutions
4
4 solutions
5
5 solutions
6
6 solutions
7
7 solutions
8
8 solutions
9
9 solutions
10
10 solutions

Question 13 (Solutions on page 64 and 65)

A Grade 12 science class setup an experiment to determine gravitational acceleration. The class finds a tall building and drops a tennis ball from different heights. They use a light gate to determine the velocity of the ball as it hits the ground. The results of their experiment are tabulated below.

Drop Height Δx **(m)**	**Final velocity** v_f **(m.s^{-1})**	**Final velocity squared** v_f **(m^2.s^{-2})**
5	9,9	
10	14,0	
15	16,2	
20	19,1	
25	21,9	
30	23,5	
35	25,5	

13.1 Define acceleration. (2)

13.2 Fill in the last column of the above table correct to the nearest whole number. (3)

13.3 Use the graph paper on the next page to plot a graph of final velocity squared against drop height. (6)

13.4 Explain why final velocity squared should be plotted as opposed to final velocity? (2)

13.5 Determine the gradient of the graph you plotted. Clearly mark the points you use to calculate the gradient. (3)

13.6 Use your answer to determine the acceleration of the tennis ball. (4)

13.7 Why is the value you calculated for acceleration less than 9,8m.s^{-2}. (2)

[22]

Question 13.3
Graph paper

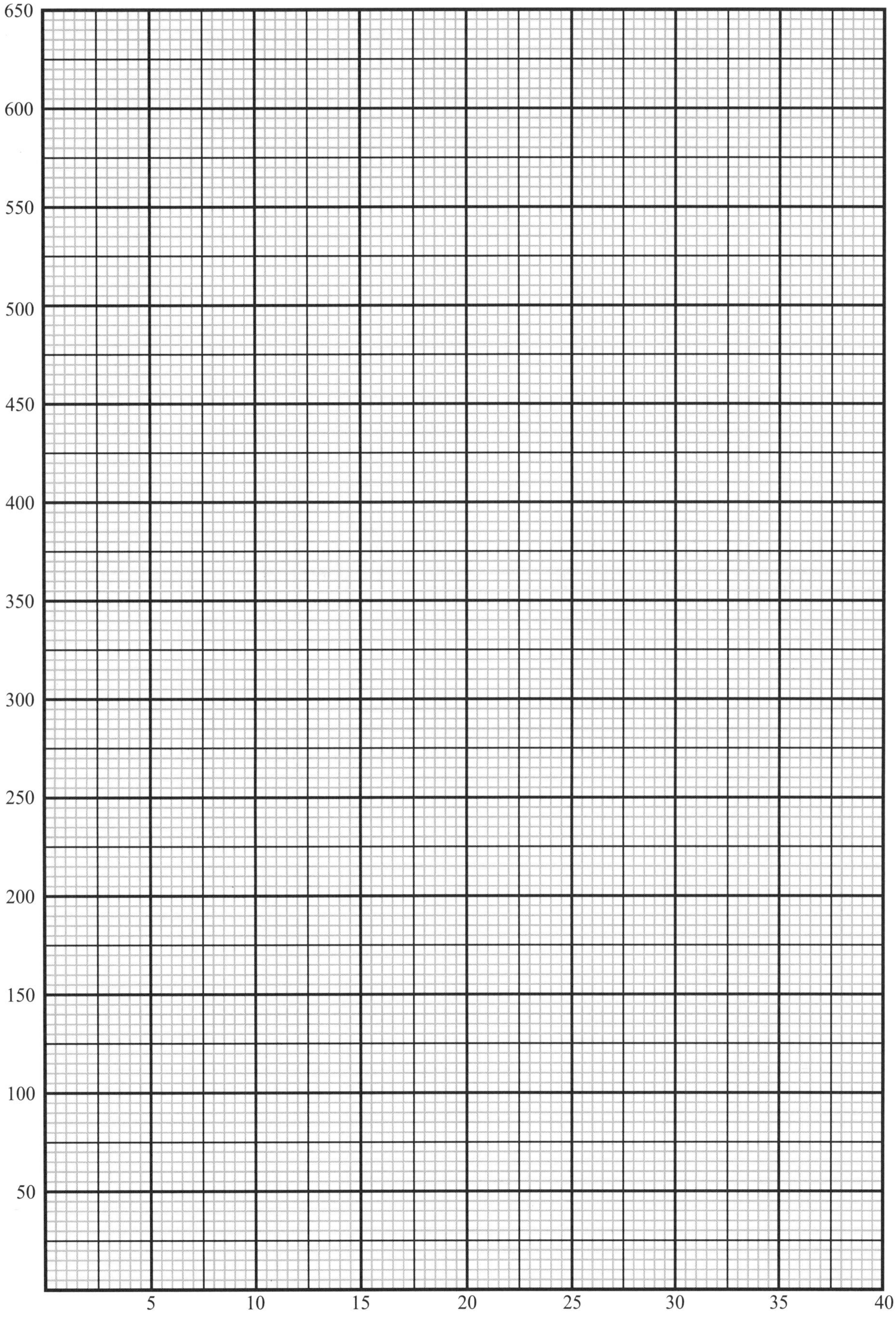

Question 14 (Solutions on page 66)

In an investigation, a small light ball was projected horizontally off a table 1,5m above the ground. A high-speed camera recorded the balls journey for 0,4 seconds, taking a picture of the ball every 0,1 seconds. The trail of the pictures are shown on the graph below.

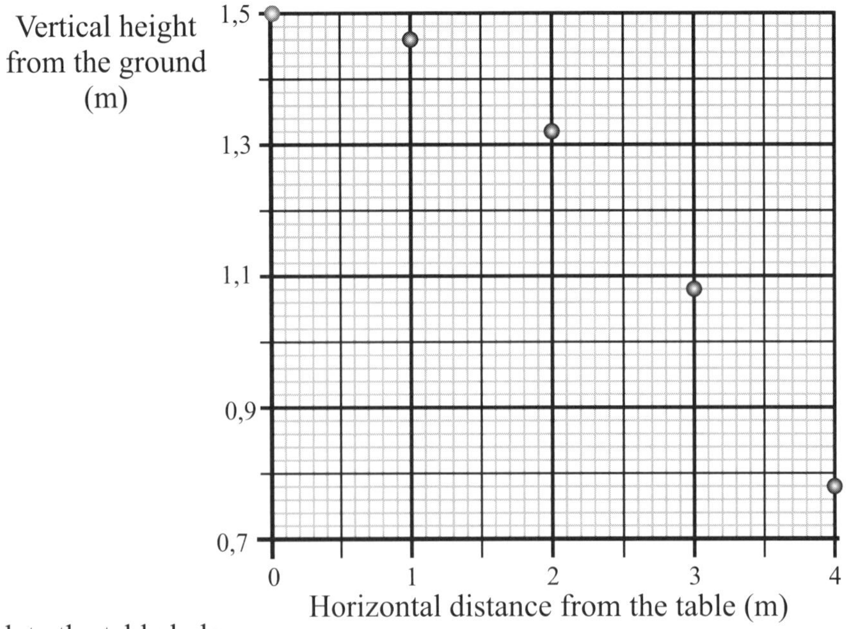

14.1 Complete the table below: (4)

Time (s)	Vertical Distance Travelled (m)	Horizontal Distance Travelled (m)	Time squared (s^2)
0,0	0	0	0
0,1			
0,2			
0,3			
0,4			

14.2 What can be deduced about the horizontal velocity of the ball from the table? Hence, determine the speed at which the ball was projected off the table. (4)

14.3 Plot a graph of vertical distance travelled against time squared on the graph paper below: (6)

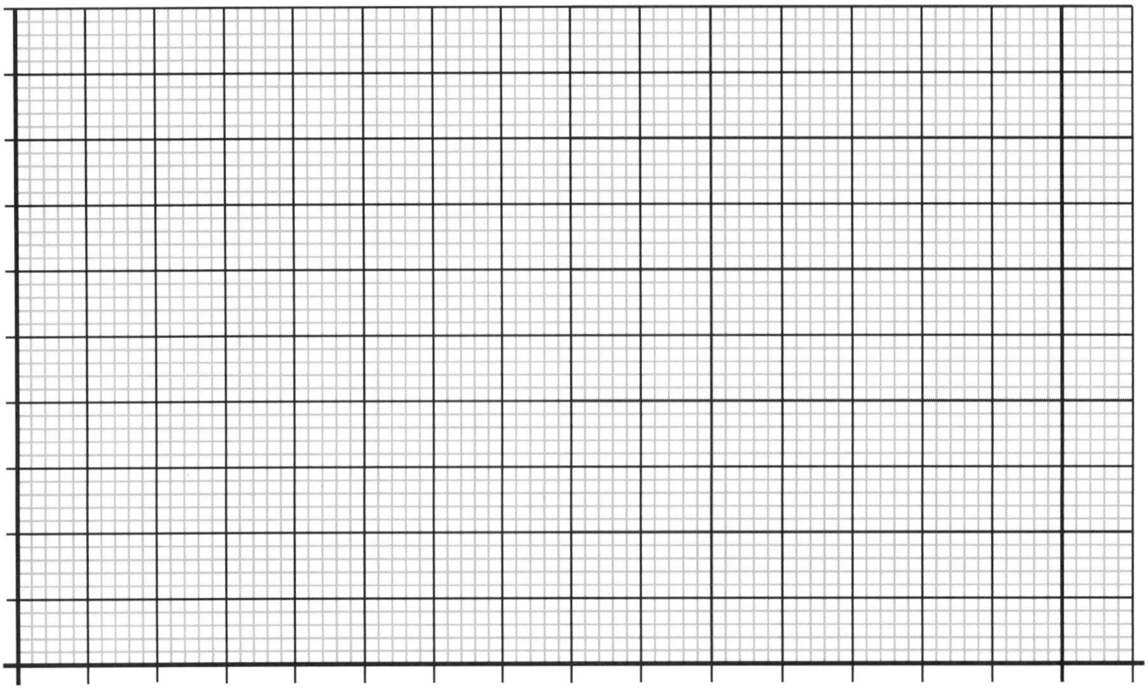

14.4 State the relationship shown on your graph? (2)

14.5 Write an equation of motion that represents your graph in the form $y = mx + c$ (1)

14.6 Use your equation and the graph to determine the acceleration of the ball. Clearly label the points on your graph which you used. (5)

14.7 Was air friction negligible in this question? Substantiate your answer. (2)

[28]

Question 15 (Solutions on page 67)

A naughty school boy throws a stone vertically downwards from a 1st floor balcony. The velocity versus time graph below represents the motion of the stone.

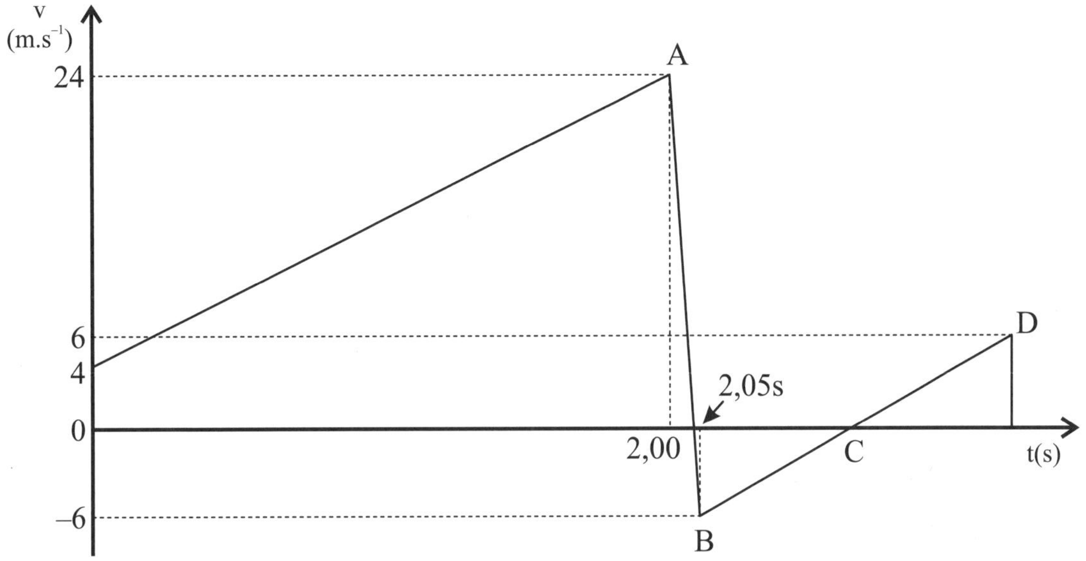

15.1 At what speed was the stone thrown? (1)

15.2 At which point did the stone hit the ground for the first time? (A, B, C or D) (2)

15.3 Where on the graph did the stone reach its maximum height after bouncing? (A. B. C or D) (2)

15.4 Where is the stone between A and B. (2)

15.5 Use the graph and not equations of motion to determine the height of the balcony above the ground. (4)

15.6 If the stone has a mass of 100g, what force does the ground exert on the stone between A and B? (5)

15.7 Sketch a displacement versus time graph to represent the change in position of the stone for the same period given in the velocity versus time graph. No values need to be shown, but the positions A, B, C and D must be clearly shown. Take the ground as your frame of reference. (6)

15.8 Sketch an acceleration versus time graph for same period given in the velocity versus time graph. Positions A and B must be clearly shown. (4)

[26]

Question 16 (Solutions on page 67)

A coin is dropped from the top of a tall building. Two seconds later another heavier coin is dropped. Ignoring air friction, answer the following questions.

16.1 How will the impact speed when the heavier coin hits the ground compare to that of the lighter coin? Write only **greater than**, **less than** or **the same**. (2)

16.2 How long after the lighter coin hits the ground will the heavier coin land? (2)

16.3 After the lighter coin has fallen for *t* seconds, what is the distance between the coins in terms of *t*. (8)

16.4 At the instant the heavier coin is released, the lighter coin is travelling at 19,6 $m.s^{-1}$. When the lighter coin impacts the ground, it is travelling at 98 $m.s^{-1}$. What is the velocity of the heavier coin at the instant the lighter coin impacts the ground? (3)

[15]

Question 17 (Solutions on page 68)

A ball is projected vertically downwards from an unknown height with an initial velocity v. After the ball has fallen 6m its velocity is 2v. After falling a further unknown distance the ball is travelling at $24m.s^{-1}$.

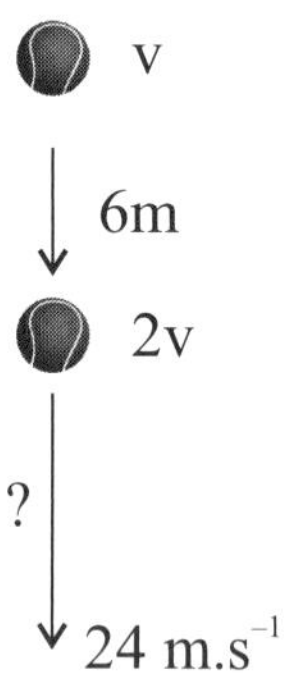

17.1 Determine the unknown distance. (6)

17.2 The ball strikes the ground 2 seconds after it was thrown. At what height above the ground was the ball initially thrown from? (3)

17.3 At what velocity does the ball strike ground? (2)

17.4 The ball rebounds from the ground at speed of $4m.s^{-1}$. Draw a velocity-time graph for the motion of the ball until it reaches its highest point above the ground on the rebound. Include all relevant values given that it takes the ball 0,82s to reach the floor after its bounce. (5)

17.5 Determine the maximum height reached by the ball after its bounce. (3)

17.6 Sketch a displacement-time graph for the balls entire journey if it only bounces once. Take down as positive and the release point as your frame of reference. The contact time with the floor may be ignored. (6)

[25]

Question 18 (Solutions on page 69)

In the distant future an astronaut's navigation system fails and his spaceship crash lands on a planet with no atmosphere (no air). The astronaut is not sure which planet he has landed on but has a table of the gravitational acceleration on different planets in his solar system.

At his disposal is an electronic ball which tracks its velocity and plots a graph on the ships computer screen. The astronaut stands on the edge of a deep crater and throws the ball vertically upwards over the edge of the crater. The velocity-time graph displayed on the ships screen is shown below:

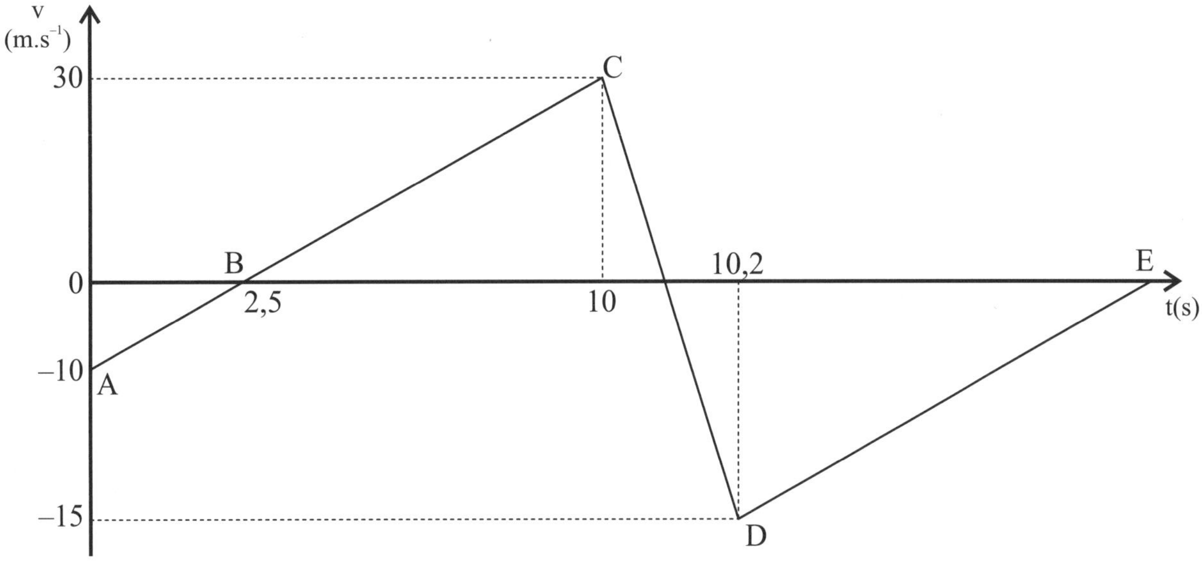

18.1 For the section on the graph labelled A to B describe the balls velocity and acceleration. (4)

18.2 Using the astronaut's table below, determine what planet he is on:

Acromia: 3,2 $m.s^{-2}$	**Fenope**: 4,2 $m.s^{-2}$	**Eskion**: 5,0 $m.s^{-2}$
Iotis: 9,2 $m.s^{-2}$	**Spides 18**: 4,0 $m.s^{-2}$	**Soylia**: 9,8 $m.s^{-2}$

(4)

18.3 How deep was the crater? (4)

18.4 Draw a sketch displacement-time graph for the balls entire motion up to E. Take the ball's release point as your zero reference. Label A to E on your time axis. The only displacement value necessary is the value you calculated in question 18.3. (5)

18.5 If the ball has a mass of 4kg, determine the rate of change of momentum of the ball, while it is in contact with the ground at the bottom of the crater. (5)

18.6 Hence, determine the force which the ground exerts on the ball. (3)

[25]

TOC | 1 Data Sheet | 2 Definitions | 3 | 3 solutions | 4 | 4 solutions | 5 | 5 solutions | 6 | 6 solutions | 7 | 7 solutions | 8 | 8 solutions | 9 | 9 solutions | 10 | 10 solutions

Question 19 (Solutions on page 69)

Six children are playing hide and seek. The children hiding stand 2 metres from a tree and run in different directions. The seeker waits at the tree for brief period and then runs to look for the children hiding. The displacement-time graph for the children is shown below.

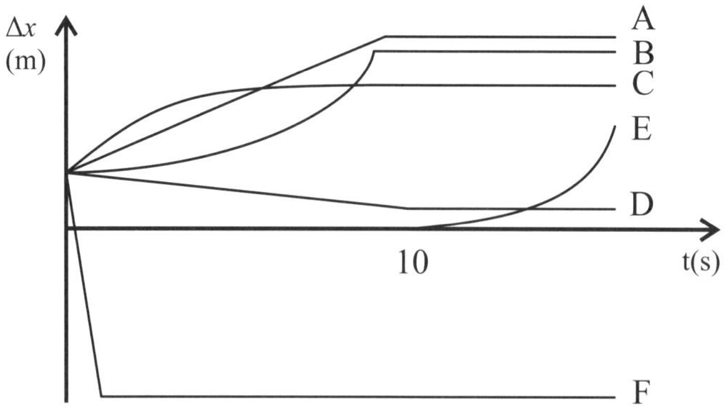

19.1 Which child labelled on the graph is the seeker? (2)

19.2 How long did the seeker wait to start looking for the other children? (2)

19.3 How can it be seen on the graph that the children have reached their hiding spots? (2)

19.4 Which of the children initially ran towards the tree? (2)

19.5 Which child or children ran past the tree to hide from their starting point? (2)

19.6 Which children ran to their hiding place at a constant velocity? (3)

19.7 Which of the children are slowing down as they run? (2)

19.8 Which child had the highest average speed in getting to their hiding place? Give a reason for your answer. (3)

[18]

Question 20 (Solutions on page 70)

Two cars, A and B are driving at a constant velocity of 30 $m.s^{-1}$. The cars are separated by a distance of 45 meters. The driver of car A sees a cow in the road ahead and brakes hard, coming to rest in 5 seconds. The driver of car B has a reaction time of 0,8 seconds from the time he sees the brake lights of car A.

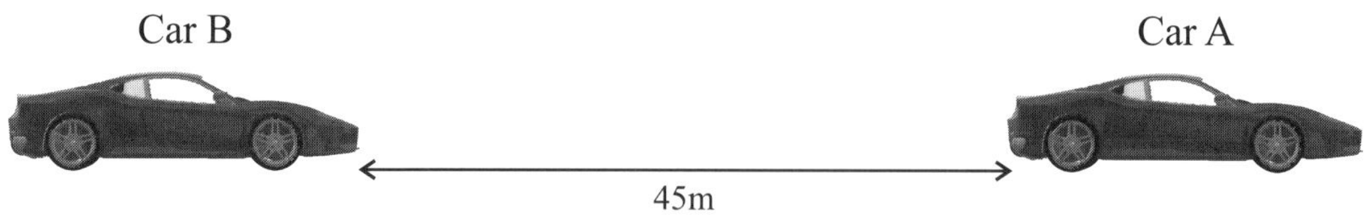

20.1 Calculate the magnitude of car A's average acceleration while braking. (3)

20.2 The brakes of car B can decelerate the car at a maximum of 8 $m.s^{-2}$. Will car B be able to stop before hitting car A? (9)

20.3 What is the minimum following distance car B should keep to avoid an accident? (3)

[15]

Question 21 (2014 IEB Final Examination) (Solutions on page 70 and 71)

21.1 A coconut of mass 5,4 kg falls from a tree and breaks the glass roof of a greenhouse directly below it. The unbroken coconut continues to fall freely until it hits the ground. The velocity-time graph below represents the motion of the coconut from when it left the tree until it hit the ground. Air resistance is negligible.

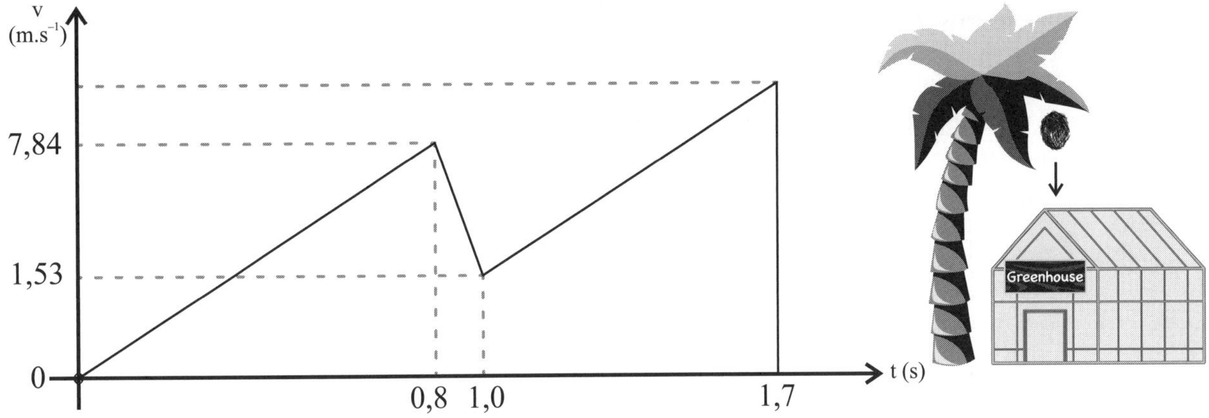

21.1.1 Calculate the distance fallen by the coconut from when it left the tree until it hit the glass roof at time t = 0,8 s. (3)

21.1.2 Calculate the speed of the coconut at time t = 1,7s as it hits the ground. (4)

21.1.3 Calculate the net force acting on the coconut while it was in contact with the glass roof. (5)

21.1.4 How does the magnitude of the force exerted by the coconut on the glass roof compare with the magnitude of the force exerted by the glass roof on the coconut? Name the law which you used to determine your answer. (2)

21.1.5 Draw an acceleration-time sketch graph to represent the motion of the coconut over the time period t = 0s to t = 1,7s. It is not necessary to show any numerical values. (3)

21.1.6 Consider the following information regarding two coconuts X and Y which fall from different heights:

- The mass of coconut X is greater than the mass of coconut Y.
- As they reach the roof of the greenhouse the momentum of coconut X is equal to the momentum of coconut Y.

a) At the roof, is the kinetic energy of coconut X greater than, less than or equal to the kinetic energy of coconut Y? (1)

b) Fully explain your answer to Question 20.1.6 (a) making reference to relevant formulae. (4)

21.2 An object which is dropped on a unknown planet 'P' falls a distance of 11,2 m in its 4th second of motion. There is no air resistance on planet 'P'. Calculate the magnitude of the acceleration due to gravity on planet 'P'.

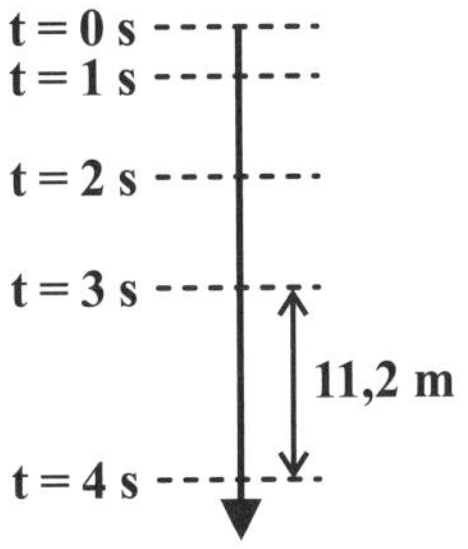

(5)

[27]

TOC
1 Data Sheet
2 Definitions
3
3 solutions
4
4 solutions
5
5 solutions
6
6 solutions
7
7 solutions
8
8 solutions
9
9 solutions
10
10 solutions

Question 22 (2014 IEB Exemplar Examination) (Solutions on page 72)

A gymnast is training by jumping on a trampoline.

22.1 Define acceleration. (2)

22.2 State the acceleration of the gymnast while she is in the air. (2)

22.3 While the gymnast is in contact with the trampoline mat, her acceleration is different to your answer in Question 22.2 Explain. (2)

Unfortunately, the gymnast is still learning. She manages to bounce up, but she misses the trampoline on the way down. She leaves the trampoline mat with a velocity of 7,84 $m.s^{-1}$ up. The velocity-time graph for her vertical motion from the moment she leaves the mat to the moment she lands on the ground is given below. Up is the positive direction.

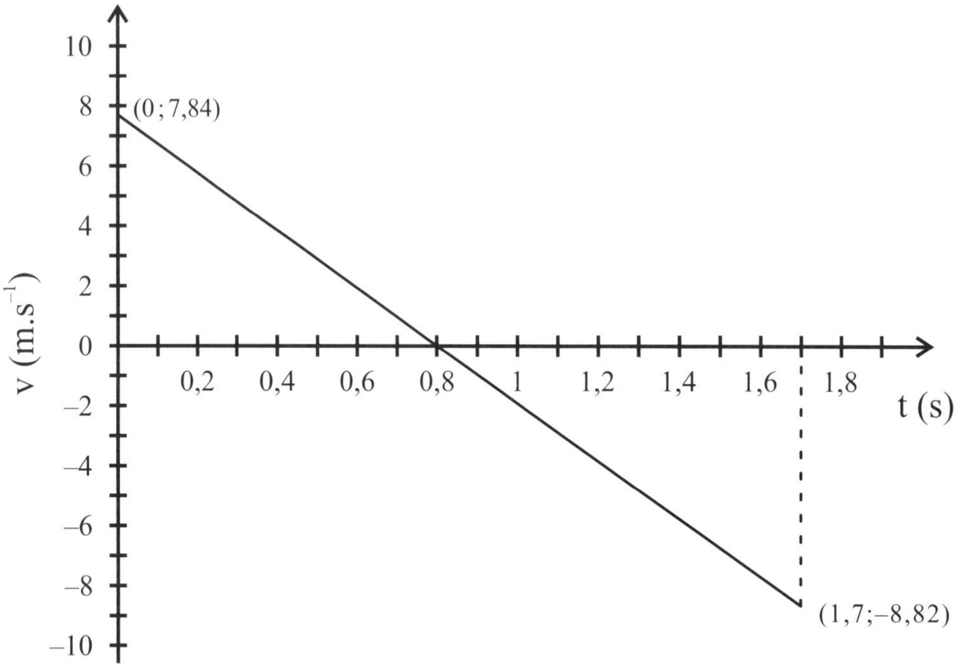

22.4 Use the graph to determine the height of the trampoline above the ground. (5)

22.5 Draw a sketch graph of the gymnast's displacement against time. Take displacement to be zero on the mat of the trampoline (frame of reference). Label A as the point she leaves the trampoline, B as the highest point and C as the point where she reaches the ground. No values are necessary on either of the axes. You also do not need to give the graph a heading. (3)

[14]

Question 23 (2015 IEB Final Examination) (Solutions on page 72 and 73)

23.1 A model car starts from rest and initially travels east. A velocity vs time graph of the motion is shown below.

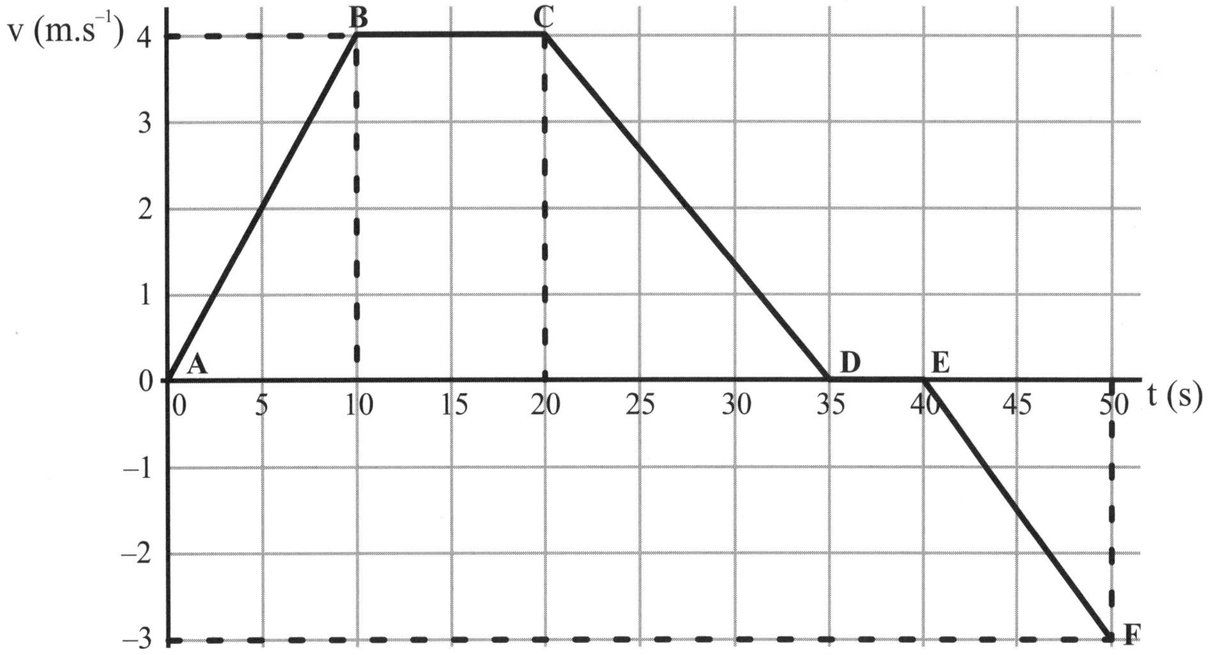

23.1.1 Use the graph to determine the acceleration of the car between 20 s and 35 s of the motion. (4)

23.1.2 During which time interval/s is the speed of the car increasing? (2)

23.1.3 Define *displacement.* (2)

23.1.4 Use the graph to determine the displacement of the car after 50 s. (4)

23.1.5 Calculating the distance travelled by this car from the graph would give you a value greater than the calculated displacement. Is the distance travelled for any object always greater than its displacement? Explain your answer. (2)

23.1.6 Sketch a position vs time graph for the car from 0 s to 50 s on the axes provided on the next page. Values are not required but you must use the labels A – F. (5)

Axes for Question 23.1.6

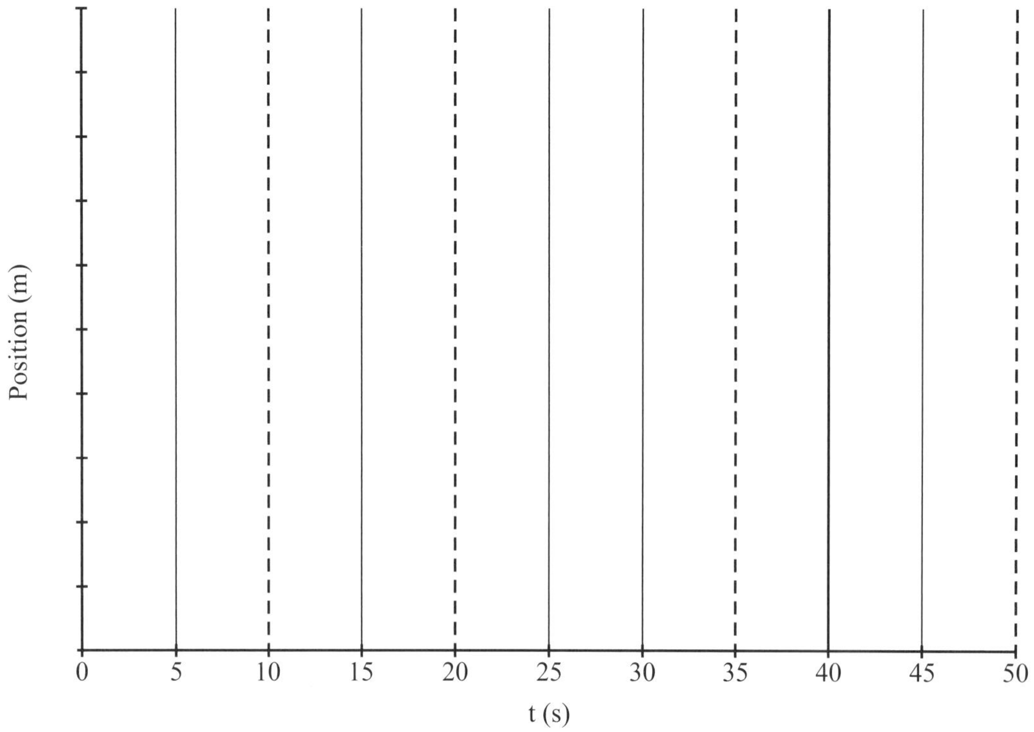

23.2 Motorists on the N3 highway in KwaZulu-Natal are often fined because their average speed exceeds the speed limit.

A camera at position X takes a photo of a Toyota and records the time. At position Y, a distance of 12 km further along the road, a second camera takes a photo and again records the time.

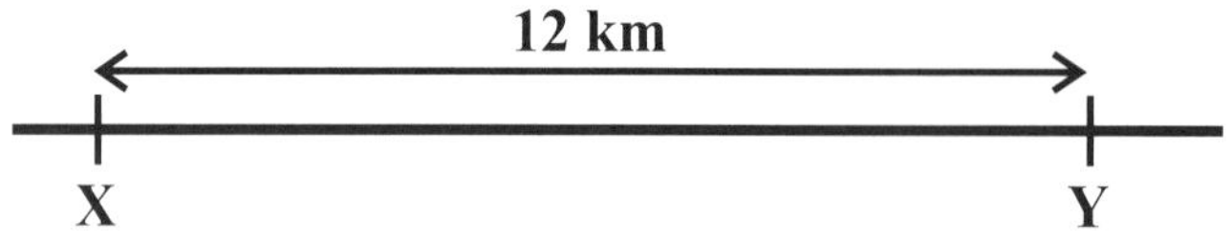

23.2.1 The Toyota takes 7,6 minutes to travel the 12 km between X and Y. Calculate the average speed of the car in $m.s^{-1}$. (4)

The speed limit in the area is 100 km/h.

23.2.2 Convert 100 km/h to $m.s^{-1}$. (2)

23.2.3 Should the driver of the Toyota car be fined for exceeding the speed limit? (1)

A BMW car travelling on the same road is stuck behind a slow truck for 6 km and only manages a speed of 60 km/h. The driver passes the truck and knowing that the average speed limit is 100 km/h, he travels at 140 km/h for the next 6 km.

23.2.4 Calculate the average speed of the BMW. For this question use km and hours (5)

[31]

TOC | 1 Data Sheet | 2 Definitions | 3 | 3 solutions | 4 | 4 solutions | 5 | 5 solutions | 6 | 6 solutions | 7 | 7 solutions | 8 | 8 solutions | 9 | 9 solutions | 10 | 10 solutions

Question 24 (2015 IEB Supplementary Examination) (Solutions on page 73 and 74)

On January 21, 2013, the Hennessey Venom GT set a new Guinness World Record by accelerating from 0 to 83,3 $m.s^{-1}$ in a time of 13,63 s.

24.1 Convert 83,8 $m.s^{-1}$ to $km.h^{-1}$. (2)

24.2 Calculate the distance covered (in metres) during this period of rapid acceleration. (4)

24.3 The stopping distance is the sum of the reaction distance and the braking distance. The reaction distance is how far the car travels before the driver reacts and applies brakes. The table below shows typical stopping distances given in the Highway Code (rules of the road).

Speed ($m.s^{-1}$)	Reaction distance (m)	Braking distance (m)	Stopping Distance (m)
10	7	7	14
20	14	28	42
30	21	63	84
40	28	112	140

24.3.1 State the relationship between **reaction** distance and speed. (2)

24.3.2 The equation $v_f^2 = v_i^2 + 2a\Delta x$ (or $v^2 = u^2 + 2as$) can be used to derive the mathematical relationship between the **braking** distance and the initial speed of a car which brakes uniformly to rest. Use the equation to prove that braking distance is directly proportional to initial speed squared. (2)

24.3.3 Use the data in the table to prove that these results obey the relationship given in Question 23.3.2. (4)

24.3.4 The stopping distances given in the table are just a general guide.

a) Give one factor (other than speed) which would affect the reaction distance. (1)

b) Give one factor (other than speed) which would affect the braking distance. (1)

24.4 The Bugatti Veyron is known for its ultra-fast deceleration. James is test driving the Bugatti Veyron. Whilst travelling at its top speed of 113 $m.s^{-1}$ James sees a fallen tree in the road 600 m ahead. He takes 0,7 s to react before slamming on brakes and decelerating at 12,1 $m.s^{-2}$. By means of suitable calculations determine whether or not James hits the tree. (6)

[22]

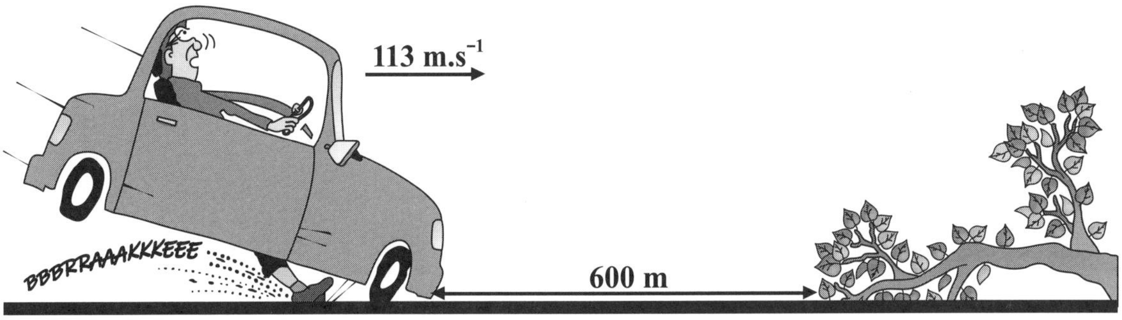

TOC 1 Data Sheet 2 Definitions 3 3 solutions 4 4 solutions 5 5 solutions 6 6 solutions 7 7 solutions 8 8 solutions 9 9 solutions 10 10 solutions

Question 25 (2016 IEB Final Examination) (Solutions on page 74 and 75)

An experimental rocket, designed to land upright, was tested recently. During lift-off, the following velocity-time graph was recorded.

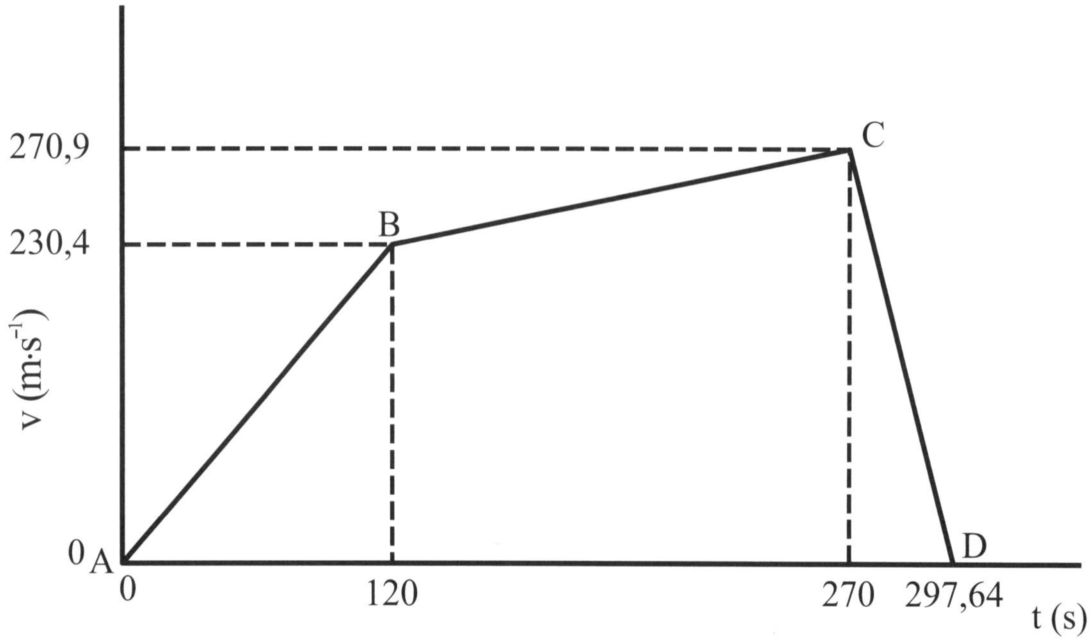

25.1 Define *acceleration*. (2)

25.2 Calculate the acceleration of the rocket during the first stage (from A to B). (4)

The rocket then fired a second stage (from B to C) before turning off at 270 s.

25.3 Describe the rocket's **velocity** and **acceleration** from C to D. Directions must be included. (4)

25.4 At what time did the rocket reach its maximum height of 55 165,34 m? (2)

The rocket then fell freely from rest from the height of 55 165,34 m. At a height of 6 000 m, the rocket engines fire and provide a constant acceleration until the rocket reaches the ground at a speed of 1 m·s^{-1}.

25.5 Define *speed.* (2)

25.6 Calculate the magnitude of the rocket's velocity at a height of 6 000 m. (3)

25.7 Calculate the magnitude of the rocket's acceleration during the last 6 000 m. (3)

The rocket has a mass of 5 800 kg.

25.8 Draw a labelled free-body diagram of the rocket during the last 6 000 m. The relative sizes of the forces must be clear. (2)

25.9 Calculate the thrust exerted on the rocket during the last 6 000 m. (5)

[27]

Question 26 (2016 IEB Final Examination) (Solutions on page 75)

26.1 Five children (A, B, C, D and E) are playing in the street outside their homes. The street runs in an east–west direction. The positions of the children are plotted on the position vs time graph below. Define east as positive.

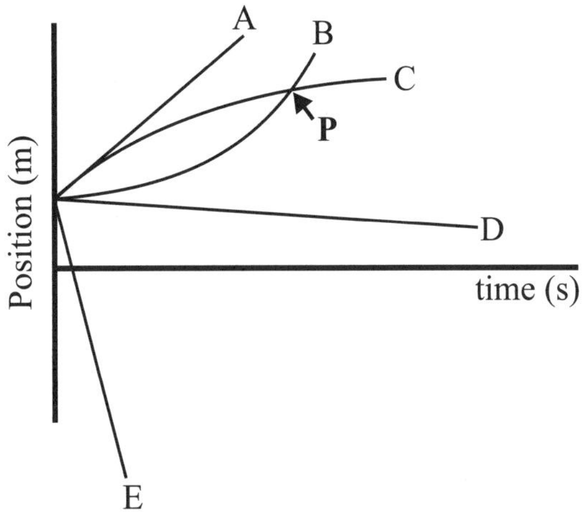

Use the graph to answer the questions that follow. Use only the correct letter(s) in your answer.

26.1.1 Which of the children are running West? (2)

26.1.2 Which of the children are running at a constant velocity? (3)

26.1.3 Which of the children are slowing down? (1)

26.1.4 Which of the children has the highest average speed? (1)

26.1.5 Describe what happened at point labelled P on the graph. (2)

26.2 A puppy is running at a constant speed of 2 $m.s^{-1}$ towards a mud puddle that is a distance of 6 m away.

26.2.1 Define *distance.* (2)

26.2.2 How long does the puppy take to get to the mud puddle? (3)

Lauren is 10 m behind the puppy and is running at a constant speed of 4 $m.s^{-1}$ chasing the puppy.

26.2.3 How far does Lauren run in the time it takes the puppy to get to the mud puddle? (2)

26.2.4 How far is Lauren from the mud puddle when the puppy reaches the mud puddle? (2)

Lauren doesn't want the puppy to get dirty. Her initial speed is 4 $m.s^{-1}$ and she accelerates uniformly to ensure she catches the puppy at the instant just before it reaches the mud puddle.

26.2.5 Calculate the magnitude of Lauren's acceleration. (3)

[21]

Question 27 (2016 IEB Supplementary Examination) (Solutions on page 75 and 76)

27.1 Two athletes, Grant and Sue, challenge each other to a race over 100 m. The velocity - time graphs for both Sue and Grant running the race are shown.

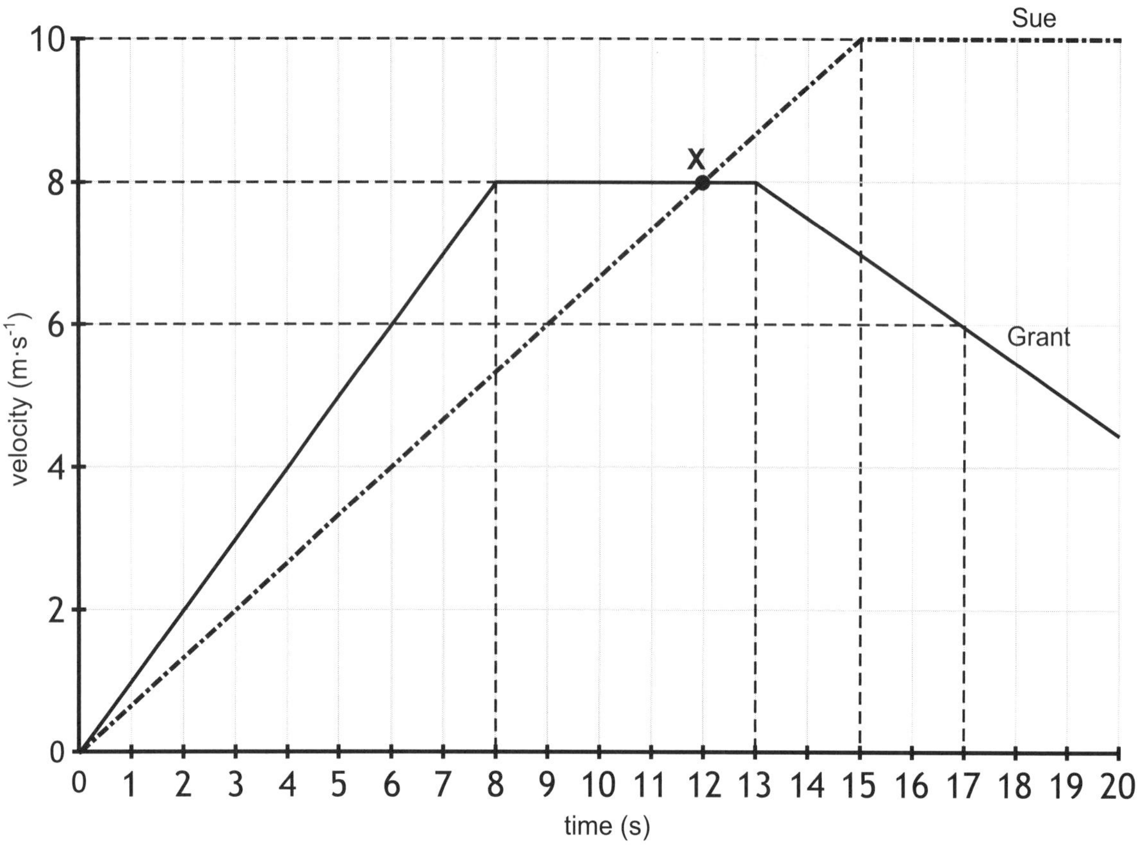

27.1.1 Define *acceleration*. (2)

27.1.2 Determine the magnitude of Grant's acceleration during the first 8 s of the race. (3)

27.1.3 Describe Grant's motion between 8 s and 13 s. (2)

27.1.4 Determine how far Grant ran in 17 s. (4)

27.1.5 The two graphs intersect at point X. What can you conclude about the athletes at that point? (2)

27.1.6 Determine how long Sue takes to complete the 100 m race. (4)

27.2 The springbok is the national animal of South Africa. It gets its name as the springbok has the ability to jump very high.

When a springbok is startled, it crouches down and then pushes on the ground accelerating vertically up at 35 $m.s^{-2}$ for a distance of 0,70 m while it straightens its legs. When the legs are fully straightened, the springbok leaves the ground and rises into the air.

27.2.1 Identify the action-reaction pair of forces involved in the process of the springbok jumping. (2)

27.2.2 Explain why the springbok accelerates upwards even though the forces in Question 26.2.1 are equal. Use one of Newton's laws to help you in your explanation. (4)

Treat the springbok as single particle for the following questions.

27.2.3 At what speed does the springbok leave the ground? (3)

27.2.4 How high above the ground does the springbok jump? (3)

[29]

Question 28 (2017 IEB Final Examination) (Solutions on page 76 and 77)

28.1 A child is holding a red ball and a blue ball over the edge of a roof. The child throws the red ball vertically up in the air and, at the same moment drops the blue ball over the edge. On the same set of axes, sketch the **velocity vs time** graph for both balls. Label the two lines red and blue. Choose **up** as the **positive** direction for your graph. (3)

28.2 A cat is 6 m from a mouse and walking slowly.

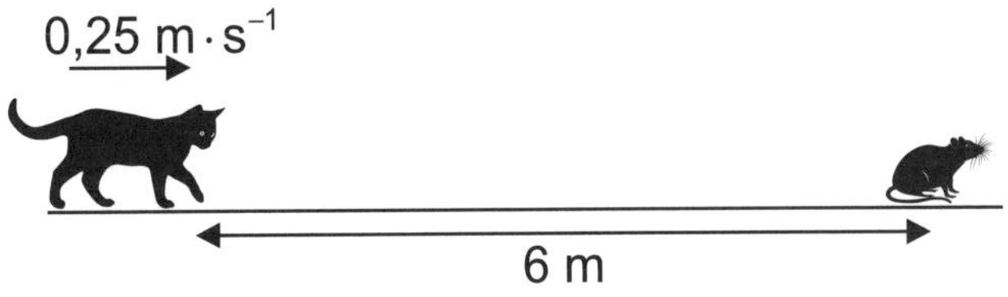

The cat hunts the mouse for 10 s in two stages. For the first 8 s the cat stalks the mouse slowly at a constant 0,25 $m.s^{-1}$ and for the last 2 s runs at a constant faster speed and catches the mouse. The mouse did not see the cat coming and sat still.

28.2.1 Calculate how far the cat is from the mouse after 8 s. (3)

28.2.2 Draw a position vs time graph for the cat for 0–10 s. Relevant values of position and time must be shown on the axes. Consider the mouse's position as position zero. (3)

28.2.3 Calculate how fast the cat ran for the last 2 s of the hunt. (2)

TOC 1 Data Sheet 2 Definitions 3 3 solutions 4 4 solutions 5 5 solutions 6 6 solutions 7 7 solutions 8 8 solutions 9 9 solutions 10 10 solutions

28.3 A model rocket is fired vertically upwards from rest at ground level. The rocket accelerates upwards at 20 $m.s^{-2}$ for 15 s and then runs out of fuel. Air resistance is negligible.

28.3.1 Calculate the rocket's maximum height above the ground. (6)

28.3.2 Calculate the time the rocket is in the air from launch to crashing on the ground. (5)

28.3.3 At which position will the rocket experience a maximum velocity? (2)

[24]

Question 29 (2017 IEB Final Examination) (Solutions on page 77 and 78)

A cyclist is riding north at 2 $m.s^{-1}$ along a straight road. A velocity vs time graph of the motion of the cyclist for 10 s is shown below.

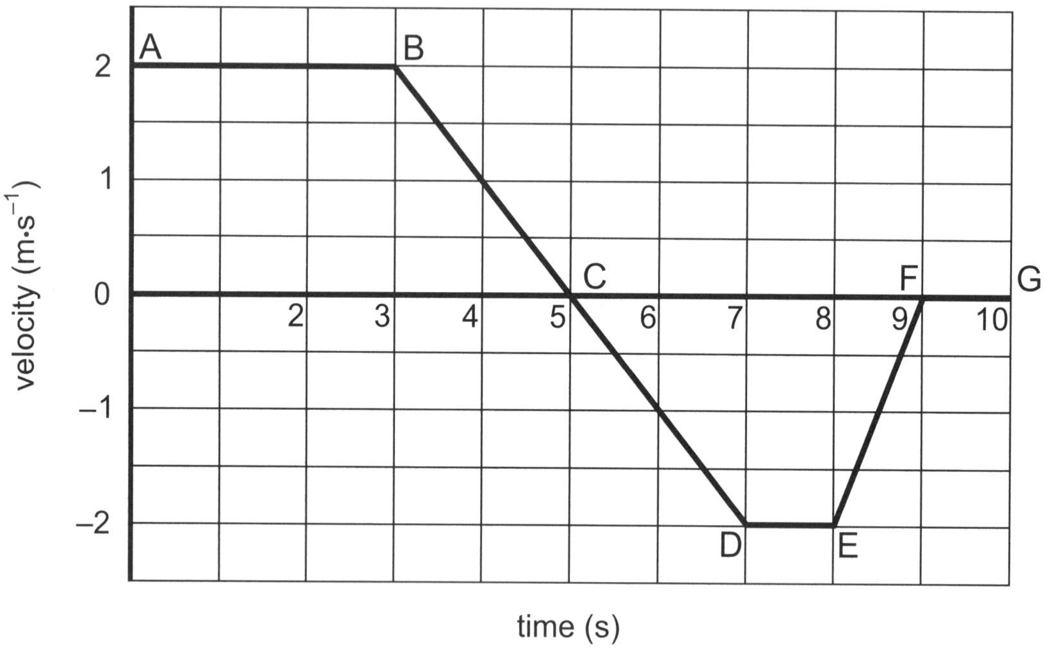

29.1 Define *velocity.* (2)

29.2 During which time interval(s) is the cyclist's velocity constant? (3)

29.3 During which time interval(s) is the cyclist slowing down? (2)

29.4 During which time interval(s) is the cyclist travelling south? (2)

29.5 Define *acceleration.* (2)

29.6 Calculate the acceleration of the cyclist between 3 s and 7 s. (4)

29.7 Sketch a position vs time graph for the cyclist on the axes provided on the next page. Values are not required but you must use the labels A–G. The cyclist's position is zero at t = 0 s. (6)

[21]

Axes for Question 29.7

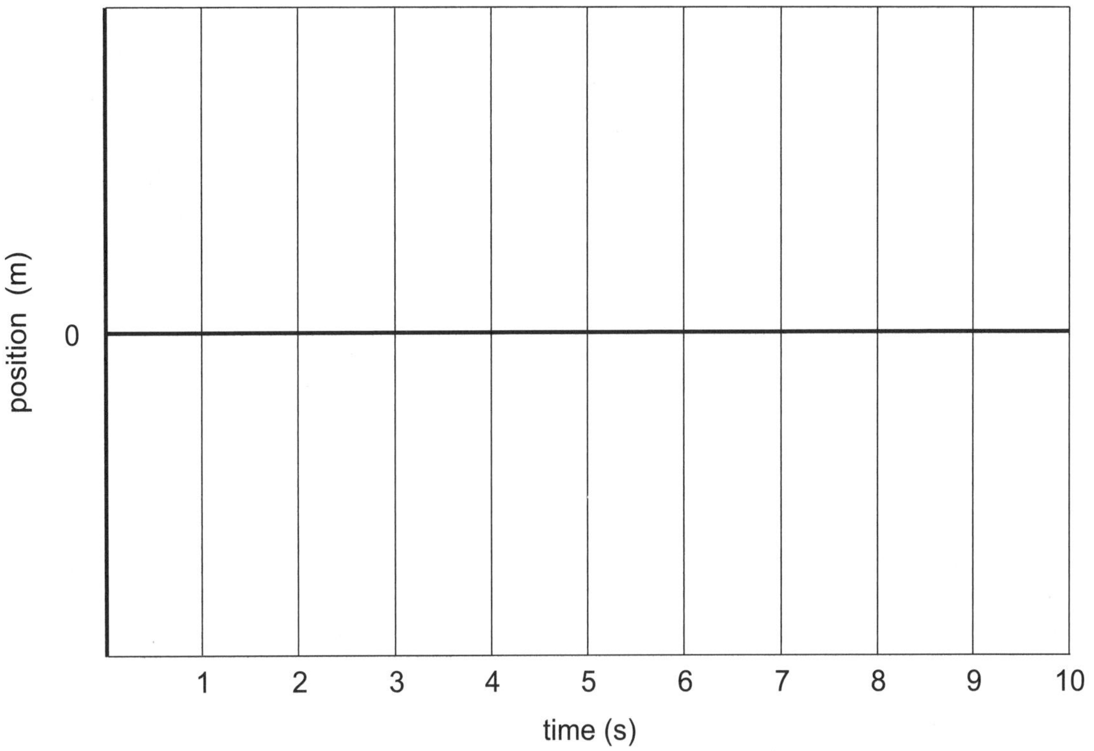

Question 30 (2017 IEB Supplementary Examination) (Solutions on page 78)

A slide in a playground has a structure as shown in the diagram below.

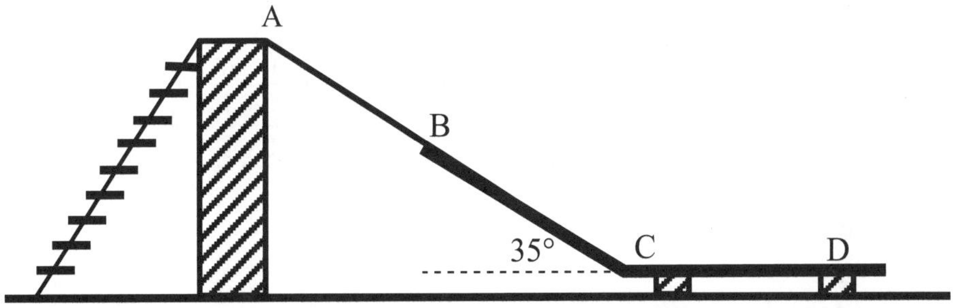

Children climb up the stairs and slide down starting at point A. The surface AB is smooth, while the surface BD has been covered so that there is friction present along BD.
A boy of mass 30 kg slides down the slide. The magnitude of the boy's velocity is represented on the velocity-time graph shown.

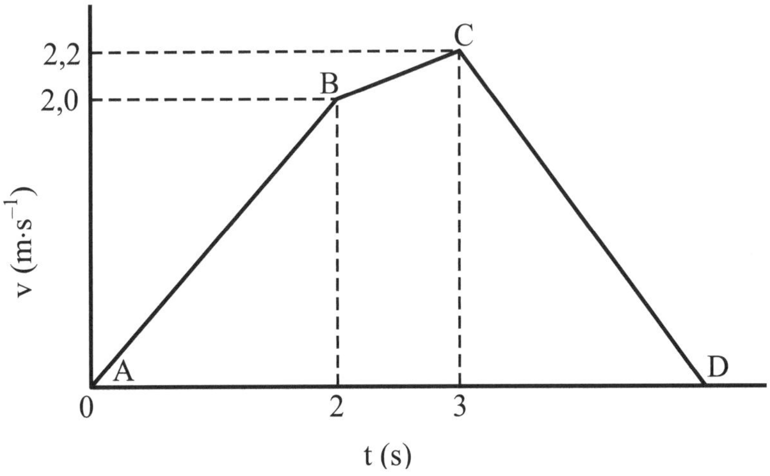

30.1 Define *velocity*. (2)

TOC
1 Data Sheet
2 Definitions
3
3 solutions
4
4 solutions
5
5 solutions
6
6 solutions
7
7 solutions
8
8 solutions
9
9 solutions
10
10 solutions

30.2 Define *acceleration*. (2)

30.3 Calculate the magnitude of the boy's acceleration while sliding on slope BC. (3)

30.4 Draw a labelled, free-body diagram of the boy while sliding on BC. (3)

30.5 Calculate the magnitude of the frictional force acting on the boy while sliding on slope BC. (5)

30.6 Calculate the length of the slide ABC. (4)

The boy slows down on the flat surface CD at 1,1 $m.s^{-2}$

30.7 Calculate the time taken from C for the boy to stop. (3)

30.8 What is the minimum length of CD required to ensure the boy comes to rest and does not slide over the edge at D? (3)

[25]

Question 31 (2017 IEB Supplementary Examination) (Solutions on page 79)

A group of students decided to measure the acceleration due to gravity. They carried out an experiment by dropping a small steel ball (mass 10 g) from different heights and measured the time taken (t) for the ball to fall through the particular height (h).

The results are recorded in the table below:

***h* (m)**	***t* (s)**	**t^2 (s^2)**
0,4	0,27	0,07
0,7	0,40	0,16
1,2	0,47	0,22
1,7	0,60	0,36
2,1	0,64	0,41
2,5	0,72	0,52

The students decided to plot *h* vs t^2.

31.1 Why is it necessary to plot *h* vs t^2 rather than *h* vs *t*? (2)

31.2 Use the data in the table to plot a graph of *h* (*y*-axis) vs t^2 (*x*-axis) on the graph paper on the next page. (6)

31.3 Calculate the gradient of the graph. Indicate the values you used for this calculation on your graph. (4)

31.4 Write an equation of motion that describes the relationship between *h* and t^2. (2)

31.5 Use your answer from Question 31.4 and your knowledge that the equation $y = mx + c$ describes a straight line to determine the acceleration due to gravity. (2)

31.6 The students repeated the experiment with a ball of twice the mass. Describe the graph of *h* vs t^2 for the heavier mass in comparison with the graph plotted for the 10 g ball. Briefly explain your answer. (2)

[19]

Graph paper for 31.2

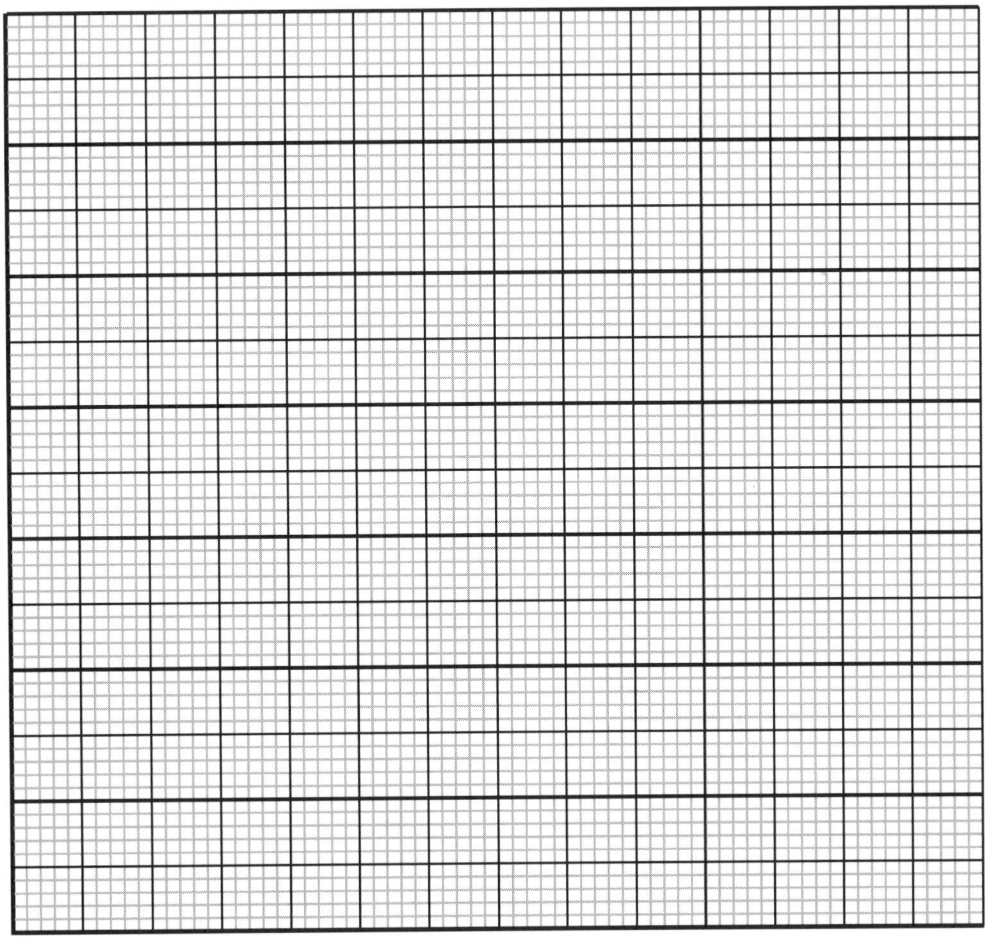

Question 32 (2018 IEB Final Examination) (Solutions on page 79 and 80)

32.1 A toy car is pushed in a northerly direction along the ground for several seconds and then released. The car continues to move until friction brings it to rest. The velocity-time graph shown below represents the motion of the toy car.

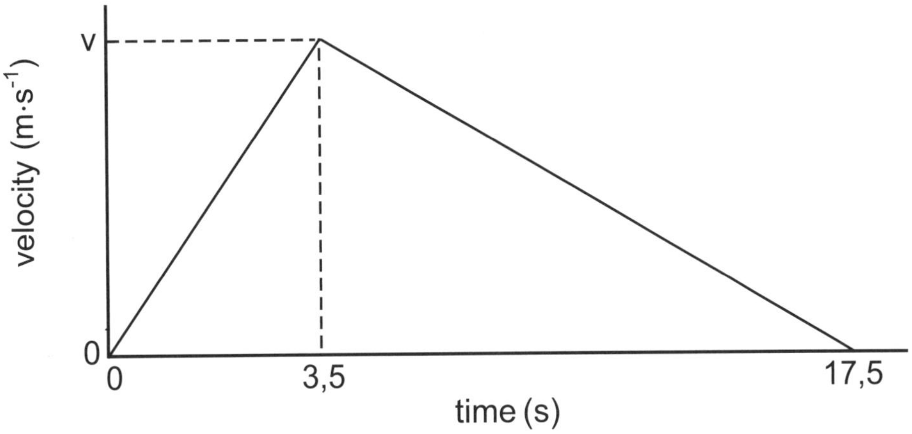

The total distance travelled by the toy car in 17,5 s is 29,8 m.

32.1.1 Define *velocity*. (2)

32.1.2 Calculate the magnitude of the maximum velocity of the car. (4)

The car has a mass of 20 kg. The only forces acting on the car during the last 14 s are weight and friction.

32.1.3 Calculate the frictional force on the car during the last 14 s. (6)

TOC
1 Data Sheet
2 Definitions
3
3 solutions
4
4 solutions
5
5 solutions
6
6 solutions
7
7 solutions
8
8 solutions
9
9 solutions
10
10 solutions

32.2 In 1997, a high-speed car broke the world land-speed record. The car accelerated uniformly in two stages as shown by the information provided in the table. The car started from rest.

	Time (s)	Speed at end of stage ($m.s^{-1}$)
Stage 1	0,0 – 4,0	44
Stage 2	4,0 – 12,0	280

32.2.1 Calculate the average acceleration during stage 1. (3)

32.2.2 Calculate the total distance travelled by the car in 12 s. (6)

[21]

Question 33 (2018 IEB Final Examination) (Solutions on page 80)

33.1 The velocity vs time graph shows the motion of two different objects sliding in a straight line across a horizontal surface.

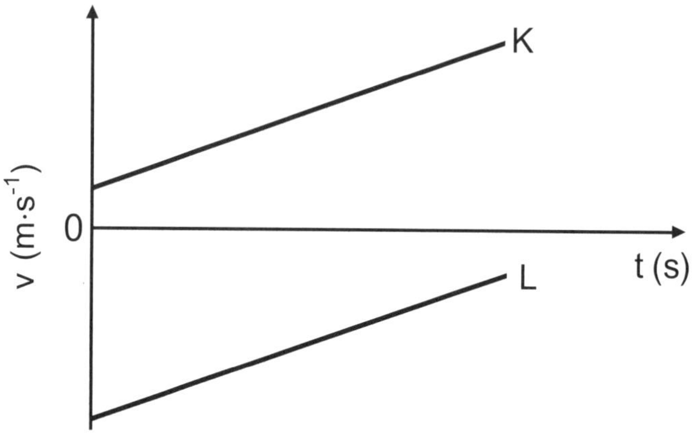

33.1.1 Could friction be the cause of the change in the velocity for object K? Explain your answer. (3)

33.1.2 Could friction be the cause of the change in velocity for object L? Answer yes or no. (1)

33.2 A hail stone of mass 0,7 kg falls from rest from the top of a storm cloud. The average acceleration of the hail stone while falling through air is 0,21 $m.s^{-2}$. The hail stone reaches the ground with a speed of 34 $m.s^{-1}$.

33.2.1 Define *acceleration.* (2)

33.2.2 Calculate the distance the hail stone travelled from the top of the storm cloud to the ground. (4)

33.2.3 Falling objects normally have an acceleration of 9,8 $m.s^{-2}$. Explain why the acceleration of the hail stone is much less. (2)

On reaching the ground, the hail stone pierces 12 cm into the ground before coming to rest.

33.2.4 Calculate the acceleration of the hail stone while piercing the ground. (4)

33.2.5 Hence, calculate the magnitude of the force the ground exerts on the hail stone. (5)

[21]

Question 34 (2018 IEB Supplementary Examination) (Solutions on page 81)

A ball on a distant planet is dropped from a certain height. The velocity-time graph represents the motion of the ball as it bounces vertically on a solid floor. The time of the bounce is negligible. The planet has no atmosphere so there is zero air resistance.

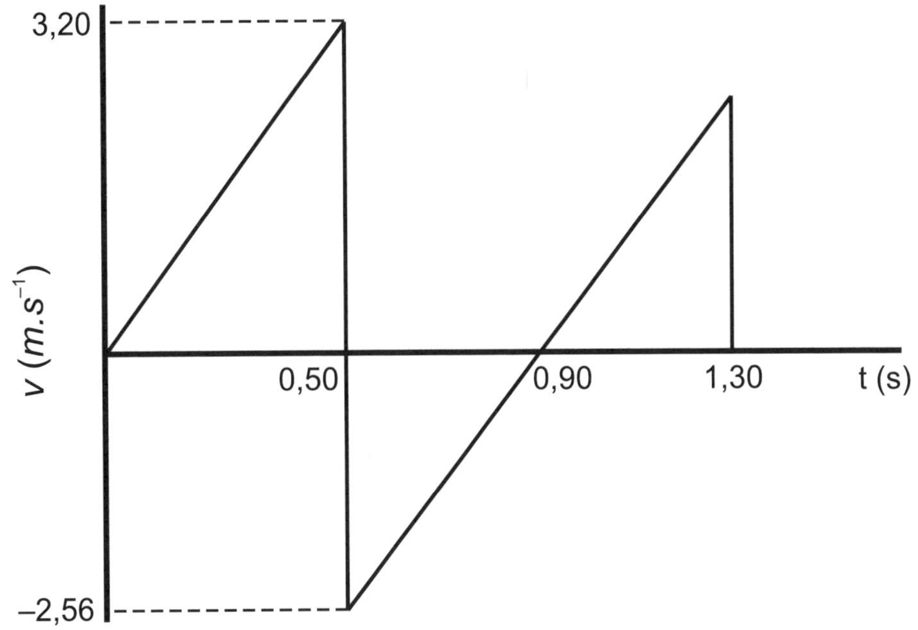

34.1 Define *acceleration*. (2)

34.2 Calculate the magnitude of the acceleration of the ball on this planet. (3)

34.3 Calculate the height from which the ball was dropped. (3)

34.4 Draw a labelled free-body diagram showing the forces acting on the ball at 0,7 s. Ignore air resistance. (2)

34.5 Is the collision with the floor elastic or inelastic? Briefly explain your answer. (2)

34.6 State the magnitude of the velocity with which the ball hits the ground at 1,30 s. (2)

34.7 On the set of axes below, sketch the corresponding position-time graph for the motion of the ball from 0 s to 1,3 s. Use the ground as position zero. (3)

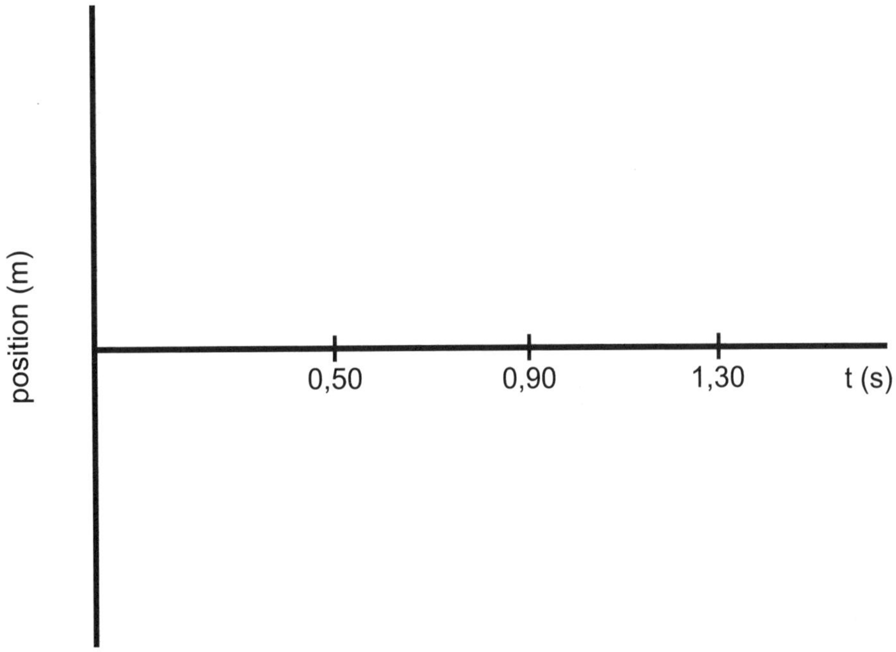

TOC
1 Data Sheet
2 Definitions
3
3 solutions
4
4 solutions
5
5 solutions
6
6 solutions
7
7 solutions
8
8 solutions
9
9 solutions
10
10 solutions

The Earth has a mass M and a radius R. The distant planet has the same mass as Earth but has a different radius.

34.8 Use the answer from Question 34.2 to calculate the radius of the planet in terms of R. (4)

[21]

Question 35 (2018 IEB Supplementary Examination) (Solutions on page 81 and 82)

A hot air balloon is rising vertically upwards at a constant velocity. A cell phone is accidentally dropped from the balloon when the balloon is at a height of 104,40 m as shown in the diagram. The cell phone strikes the ground 6 s after it is dropped. Ignore air resistance.

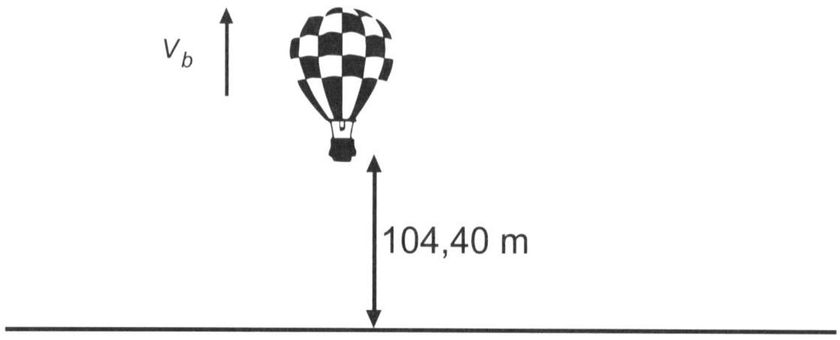

35.1 Calculate the speed v_b with which the balloon is rising when the cell phone is dropped. (4)

35.2 State the velocity of the cell phone at the instant it is dropped. (2)

35.3 Calculate the maximum height that the cell phone reaches above the ground. (5)

35.4 Calculate the height of the balloon when the cell phone strikes the ground. (4)

[15]

Question 36 (2019 IEB Supplementary Examination) (Solutions on page 82, 83 and 84)

36.1 A boy standing on a very high bridge, projects **ball A** vertically upwards at a velocity of 15 $m.s^{-1}$. The velocity-time graph for the motion of **ball A** is shown below. (Ignore air resistance for **ball A**).

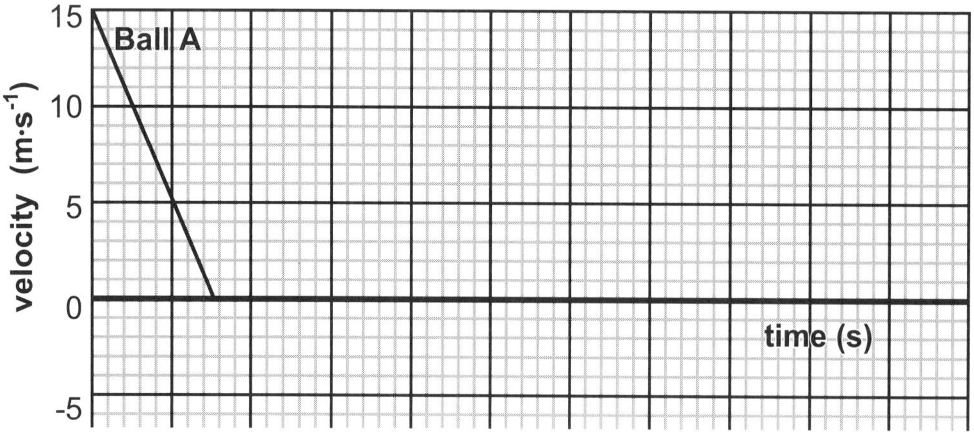

36.1.1 Define *acceleration.* (2)

36.1.2 Determine the magnitude and direction of the acceleration of ball A. (2)

36.1.3 Show that the time taken for ball A to reach a maximum height above the bridge is 1,53s. (2)

36.1.4 Calculate the maximum height reached by the ball above the bridge. (3)

Ball A continues in its motion and hits the ground 5s **after it was originally projected**.

36.1.5 The speed of ball A when it hits the ground is 34 $m.s^{-1}$. Calculate the height of the bridge. (4)

36.1.6 Complete the velocity-time graph for ball A on the graph below, ensuring that you fill in the correct scale on the time axis. (3)

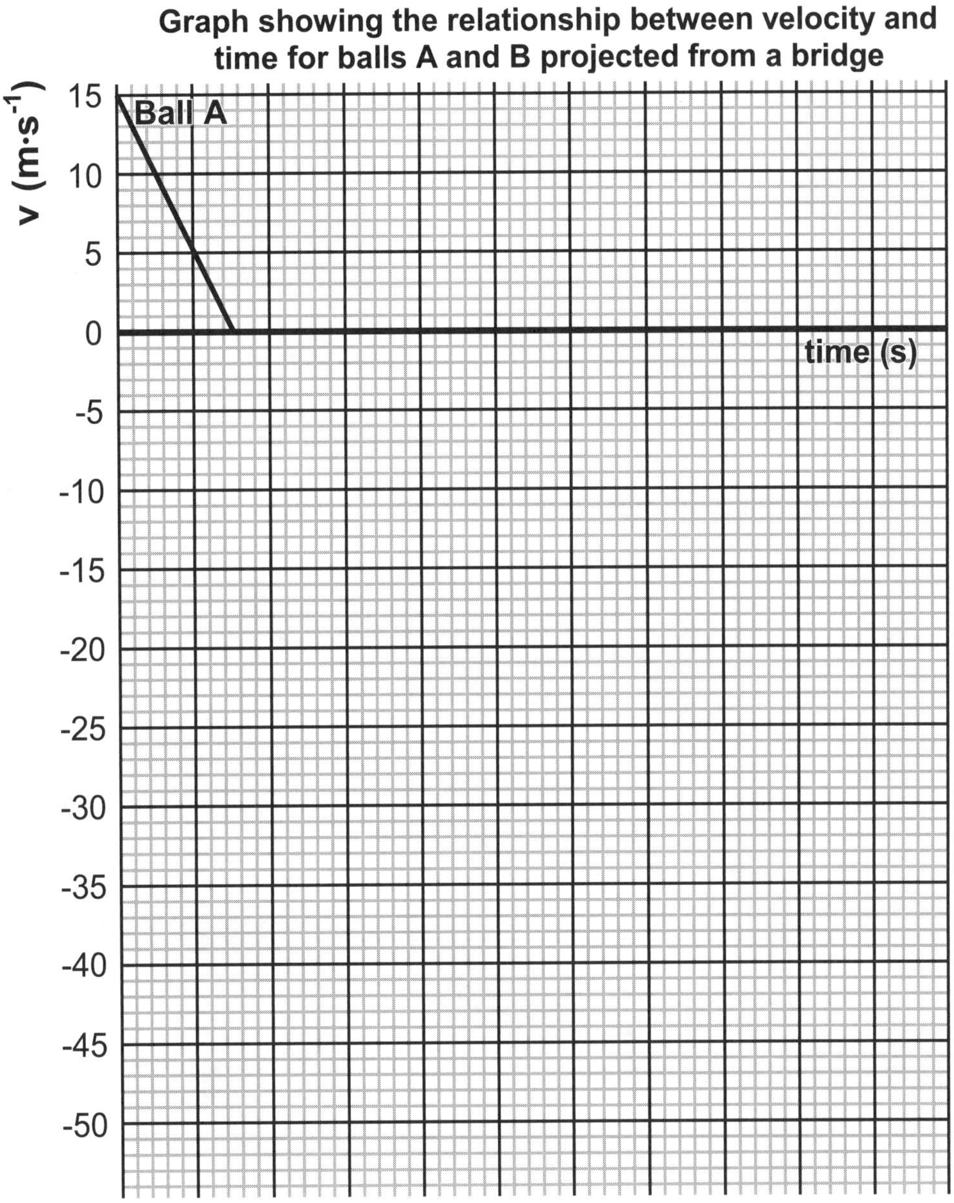

Ball B is dropped from the bridge at exactly the same time as **ball A** is projected upwards. **Ball B** is attached to a small parachute containing a measuring device which records the velocity of ball B every second. The results are recorded in the table below:

Time (s)	Magnitude of velocity B ($m.s^{-1}$)
0	0
1	3,1
2	5,9
3	9,2
4	11,9
5	15

36.1.7 On the same set of axes as the graph drawn in Question 35.1.6 on the previous page, draw the velocity-time graph for ball **B**. (3)

36.1.8 From the graph drawn in Question 36.1.7, determine the time at which the balls have the same velocity. (1)

36.1.9 Comment on the relative positions of ball A and ball B at the time mentioned in Question 36.1.8 above. Just answer:
Ball A is above ball B
OR
Ball B is above ball A
OR
Ball A and ball B are at the same height above the ground. (1)

36.1.10 Justify your choice in Question 31.1.9, WITHOUT PERFORMING A CALCULATION. (2)

36.1.11 Calculate the time at which the balls have the same displacement above the ground. (5)

36.1.12 Draw position-time sketch graphs for the entire motion of balls A and B on the graph paper provided below. No scale is required on the *y*-axis, but show the times on the *x*-axis. (5)

Graph showing the relationship between position and time for balls A and B

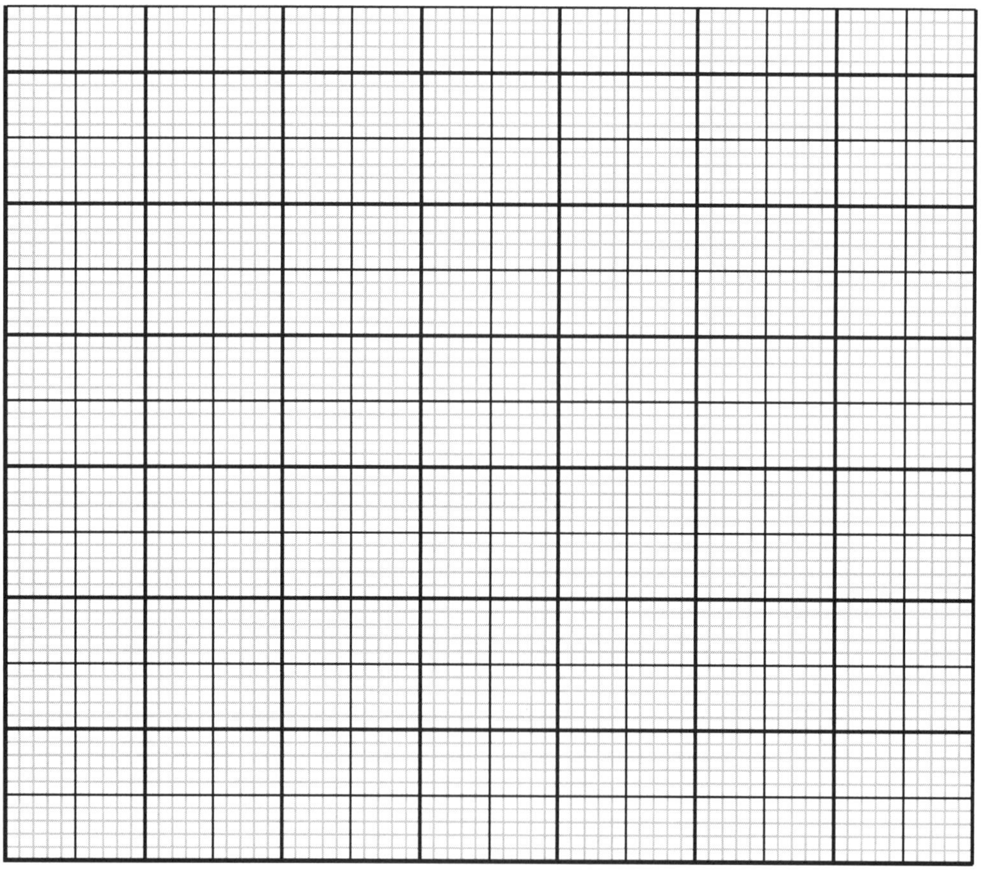

36.2 An athlete runs in an anticlockwise direction around an 800 m long track shown below. The athlete starts from point A, running east.

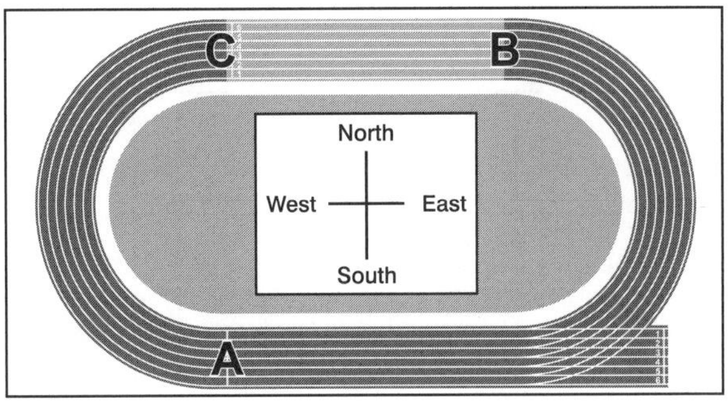

36.2.1 Define *speed*. (2)

36.2.2 It takes the athlete 1 minute and 45 seconds to run halfway around the track to point B. Calculate the average speed of the athlete. (3)

36.2.3 Suppose the athlete continues running at a constant speed, what is the athlete's **instantaneous velocity** at point C? (2)

[40]

Question 37 (2019 IEB Final Examination) (Solutions on page 84 and 85)

37.1 Tsholofelo runs **North** along a straight track. A velocity vs time graph of his motion is shown below.

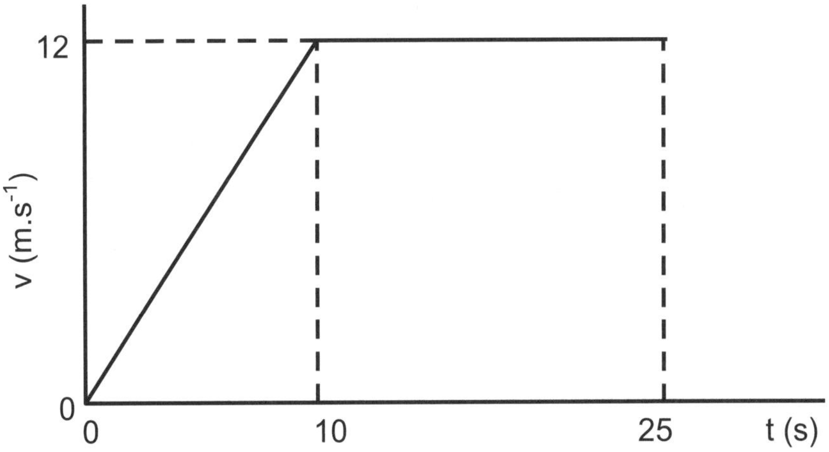

37.1.1 Define *velocity*. (2)

37.1.2 Determine Tsholofelo's instantaneous velocity at 25 s. (2)

37.1.3 Calculate the magnitude of Tsholofelo's average velocity for 25 s. (6)

37.1.4 Define *acceleration*. (2)

37.1.5 Calculate the magnitude of Tsholofelo's acceleration for the first 10 s of his run. (3)

37.2 Helen and Matthew are riding their scooters. Matthew is at rest when Helen passes him moving at a constant speed of 0,37 $m.s^{-1}$ going in a straight line. After 1,8 s Matthew decides to chase Helen and try and catch her. Matthew accelerates at 0,91 $m.s^{-2}$. How much time does Helen have from the moment she passed Matthew until Matthew is side by side with her? (7)

[22]

TOC
1 Data Sheet
2 Definitions
3
3 solutions
4
4 solutions
5
5 solutions
6
6 solutions
7
7 solutions
8
8 solutions
9
9 solutions
10
10 solutions

Question 38 (2019 IEB Final Examination) (Solutions on page 85)

38.1 The position vs time graph for objects A and B moving in a straight line in the same direction is shown below.

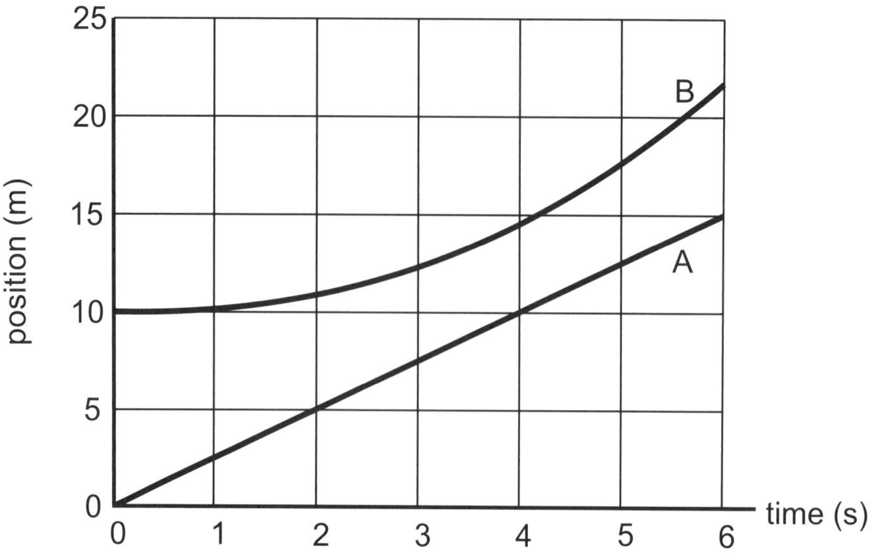

38.1.1 At the instant, t = 1 s, is the speed of object A greater than or less than the speed of object B? Use the graph to explain your answer. (3)

38.1.2 Do object A and object B ever reach the same speed? If so, at approximately what time are the speeds the same? (2)

38.1.3 Which object has the greater displacement over the 6 s? (2)

38.2 A helicopter is flying vertically upwards at a constant speed of 2 $m.s^{-1}$ when a stuntman steps out of an open door. The stuntman lands on a trampoline 4,32 s later.

38.2.1 Calculate the height of the helicopter above the trampoline as the stuntman jumped. (4)

38.2.2 Calculate the velocity of the stuntman when he reaches the trampoline. (5)

As the stuntman lands on the trampoline, the trampoline sags 1,5 m before launching the stuntman back into the air.

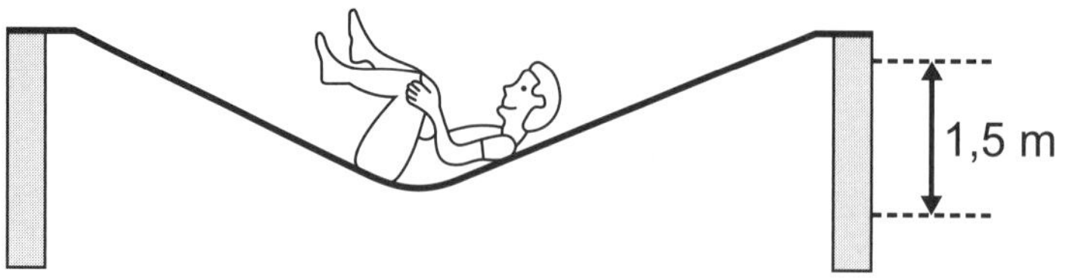

38.2.3 Draw a labelled free-body diagram of the stuntman when the sag is greatest. The relative sizes of the forces must be clear. (3)

38.2.4 At the very bottom, where the sag is greatest, is the stuntman's acceleration upward, downward or zero? Explain your answer. (2)

[21]

3. EQUATIONS AND GRAPHS OF MOTION (SOLUTIONS)

Question 1

1.1	A	(2)	1.24	A	(2)
1.2	A	(2)	1.25	B	(2)
1.3	B	(2)	1.26	C	(2)
1.4	D	(2)	1.27	B	(2)
1.5	D	(2)	1.28	A	(2)
1.6	B	(2)	1.29	D	(2)
1.7	C	(2)	1.30	C	(2)
1.8	D	(2)	1.31	B	(2)
1.9	C	(2)	1.32	C	(2)
1.10	D	(2)	1.33	A	(2)
1.11	C	(2)	1.34	B	(2)
1.12	A	(2)	1.35	D	(2)
1.13	B	(2)	1.36	C	(2)
1.14	B	(2)	1.37	A	(2)
1.15	B	(2)	1.38	C	(2)
1.16	C	(2)	1.39	D	(2)
1.17	B	(2)	1.40	D	(2)
1.18	C	(2)	1.41	C	(2)
1.19	D	(2)	1.42	D	(2)
1.20	B	(2)	1.43	D	(2)
1.21	D	(2)	1.44	B	(2)
1.22	A	(2)	1.45	C	(2)
1.23	B	(2)	1.46	B	(2)

[92]

Question 2

2.1 Constant **Downwards**. (acceleration due to gravity is always in the downwards direction.) (2)

2.2

$v_f = v_i + a\Delta t$

$-58 = 20 + (-9,8)\Delta t$

$\therefore \Delta t = 7,96\,\text{s}$ (4)

2.3

$v_f^2 = v_i^2 + 2a\Delta x$

$(-58)^2 = (20)^2 + 2(-9,8)\Delta x$

$\therefore \Delta x = -151,22\,\text{m}$

$= 151,22\,\text{m}$ downwards

$\therefore$ The height of the building is 151,22 m (4)

2.4 First calculate the distance covered in 6,96s:

$\Delta x = v_i\Delta t + \frac{1}{2}a\Delta t^2$

$= 20(6,96) + \frac{1}{2}(-9,8)(6,96)^2$

$= -98,16$

$= 98,16\,\text{m}$ downwards

Therefore, distance travelled in last second = 151,22 – 98,16 =53,06 m (5)

[15]

Question 3

3.1 The rate of change of velocity. (1)

3.2 $v_f = v_i + a\Delta t$

$0 = 4{,}9 + (-9{,}8)\Delta t$

$\therefore \Delta t = 0{,}5\,\text{s}$ (3)

3.3 Ball A:

$\Delta x = v_i\Delta t + \frac{1}{2}a\Delta t^2$

$= (0)(0{,}5) + \frac{1}{2}(-9{,}8)(0{,}5)^2$

$= -1{,}225$

Ball B:

$\Delta x = v_i\Delta t + \frac{1}{2}a\Delta t^2$

$= (4{,}9)(0{,}5) + \frac{1}{2}(-9{,}8)(0{,}5)^2$

$= 1{,}225\,\text{m}$

$\therefore$ Distance apart $= 1{,}225 + 1{,}225$

$= 2{,}45\,\text{m} \rightarrow 2{,}46\,\text{m}$ is correct if answers above were rounded off (7)

3.4

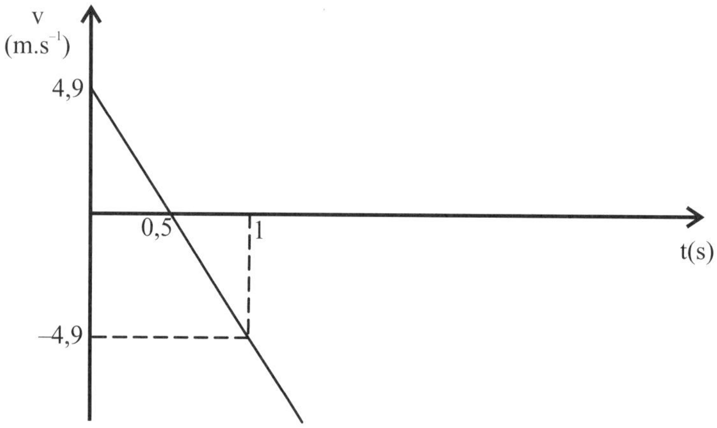

(4)

[15]

Question 4

4.1 $\Delta x = v_i\Delta t + \frac{1}{2}a\Delta t^2$

$19{,}6 = 0 + \frac{1}{2}(9{,}8)\Delta t^2 \rightarrow$ down has been taken as positive

$\therefore \Delta t = 2\,\text{s}$ (3)

4.2 $v_f = v_i + a\Delta t$

$= 0 + (9{,}8)(2)$

$= 19{,}6\,\text{m.s}^{-1} \rightarrow$ do not give direction as the question asked for magnitude (3)

4.3 $v_f^2 = v_i^2 + 2a\Delta x$

$0^2 = v_i^2 + 2(9{,}8)(\mathbf{-7{,}35}) \rightarrow$ displacement is negative as down was taken as positive

$\therefore v_i = 12\,\text{m.s}^{-1} \rightarrow$ do not give direction as the question asked for **speed** (4)

4.4 $v_f = v_i + a\Delta t$

$0 = -12 + (9{,}8)\Delta t \rightarrow v_i$ is negative because down was taken as positve

$\therefore \Delta t = 1{,}22\,\text{s}$ (3)

[15]

4.5

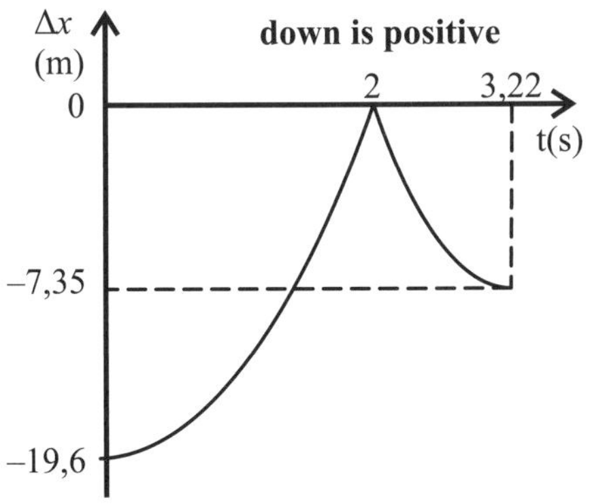

or

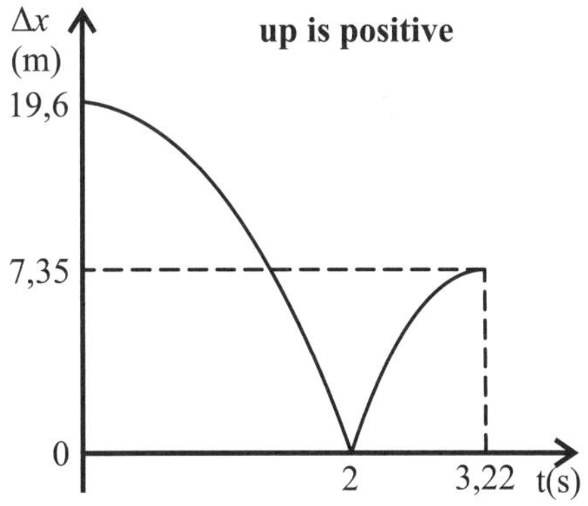

(5)

4.6 Taking up as positive:

$$F_{net} = \frac{\Delta p}{\Delta t}$$

$$F_{ground} - F_{gravity} = \frac{m(v_f - v_i)}{\Delta t}$$

$$F_{ground} - (0,06)(9,8) = \frac{0,06[12-(-19,6)]}{0,5}$$

$$\therefore F_{ground} = 4,38\,\text{N upwards}$$

Taking down as positive:

$$F_{net} = \frac{\Delta p}{\Delta t}$$

$$F_{gravity} - F_{ground} = \frac{m(v_f - v_i)}{\Delta t}$$

$$(0,06)(9,8) - F_{ground} = \frac{0,06[-12-19,6]}{0,5}$$

$$\therefore F_{ground} = 4,38\,\text{N upwards}$$

(5)

Question 5

$\Delta x_A + \Delta x_B = 40 \rightarrow$ taking up as positive for A and down as positive for B

$$\underbrace{18t + \frac{1}{2}(-9,8)t^2}_{\Delta x_A} + \underbrace{6(t-1) + \frac{1}{2}(9,8)(t-1)^2}_{\Delta x_B} = 40$$

$$\therefore 18t - 4,9t^2 + 6t - 6 + 4,9\left(t^2 - 2t + 1\right) = 40$$

$$\therefore 18t - 4,9t^2 + 6t - 6 + 4,9t^2 - 9,8t + 4,9 = 40$$

$$\therefore t = 2,89\,\text{s}$$

$$\therefore \text{Height above the ground} = 18(2,89) + \frac{1}{2}(-9,8)(2,89)^2$$

$$= 11,09\,\text{m} \rightarrow \text{if time is not rounded off the answer is } 11,05\,\text{m}$$

[8]

Question 6

6.1 $$\Delta x = v_i \Delta t + \frac{1}{2} a \Delta t^2$$

$$-92,5 = v_i(5) + \frac{1}{2}(-9,8)(5)^2 \rightarrow \text{displacement is negative as up was taken as positive}$$

$$\therefore v_i = 6\,\text{m.s}^{-1}\ \text{upwards}$$

(3)

6.2

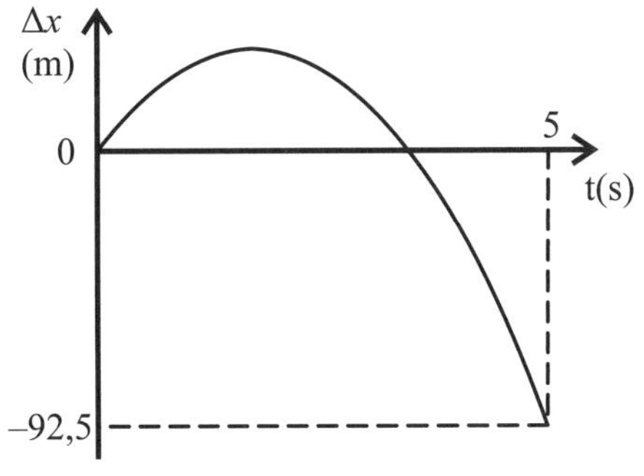

(4)

6.3 $\Delta x = v_i \Delta t + \frac{1}{2} a \Delta t^2$

$-90,7 = 6t + \frac{1}{2}(-9,8)t^2$ → displacement is negative as up was taken as positive

$\therefore t = 4,96\text{s}$ or $t = -3,73$ → N/A as time cannot be negative

$\Delta x_{man} = vt$ → constant velocity

$= 2(4,96)$

$= 9,92\text{m}$

∴ The man is safe as he is 6,92m past the sandbag when it is at the height of his head. (5)

[12]

Question 7

$v_f = v_i + a\Delta t$

$0 = v_i + (-9,8)(0,8)$ → at max height the ball is in the air for half the total time

$\therefore v_i = 7,84\,\text{m.s}^{-1}$ upwards

$\Delta x = v_i \Delta t + \frac{1}{2} a \Delta t^2$

$= (7,84)(0,8) + \frac{1}{2}(-9,8)(0,8)^2$

$= 3,14$

$\therefore$ Height $= 3,14 + 1,2$

$= 4,34\,\text{m}$

[8]

Question 8

8.1 $v_f = v_i + a\Delta t$

$0 = 10 + (-9,8)\Delta t$

$\therefore \Delta t = 1,02\,\text{s}$ (4)

8.2 $\Delta x = v_i \Delta t + \frac{1}{2} a \Delta t^2$

$= 10(1,02) + \frac{1}{2}(-9,8)(1,02)^2$

$= 5,1\,\text{m}$

$\therefore$ Max height $= 55,1\,\text{m}$ → the height of the building has to be added in (4)

8.3

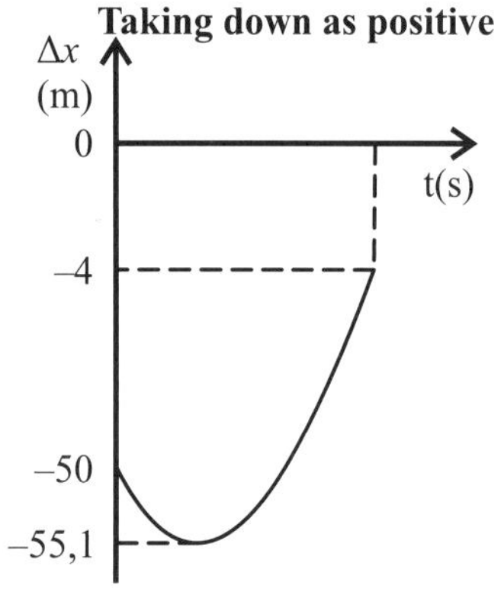

or

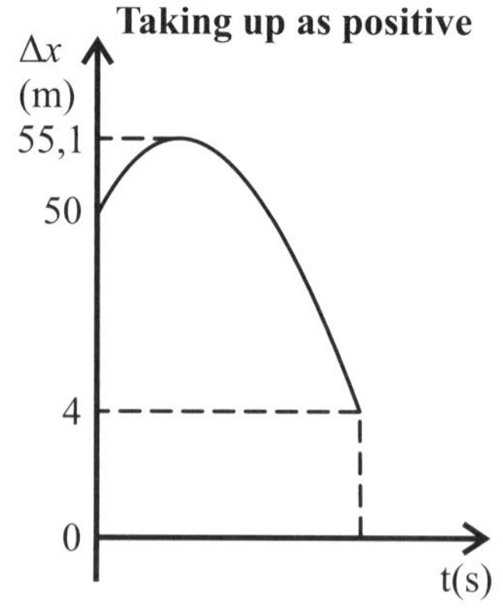

(5)

8.4 $\Delta x = v_i\Delta t + \frac{1}{2}a\Delta t^2$

$2,5 = v_i(0,2) + \frac{1}{2}(9,8)(0,2)^2$ → taking down as positive

$\therefore v_i = 11,52\,\text{m.s}^{-1}$ → this is the velocity at the top of the window

$v_f^2 = v_i^2 + 2a\Delta x$

$(11,52)^2 = (-10)^2 + 2(9,8)\Delta x$

$\therefore \Delta x = 1,67\,\text{m}$ → this is the distance from the top of the building to the top of the window

$\therefore \text{h} = 50 - 1,67$

$= 48,33\,\text{m}$ (8)

8.5 $v_f^2 = v_i^2 + 2a\Delta x$

$= (-10)^2 + 2(9,8)(46)$ → down has been taken as positive

$\therefore v_f = 31,65\,\text{m.s}^{-1}$

$\Delta \text{p} = m(v_f - v_i)$

$= 120(0 - 31,65)$ → v_i is the velocity the superhero lands on the canvas with

$= -3798$

$= 3798\,\text{kg.m.s}^{-1}$ upwards (5)

8.6 $\text{F}_{net} = \frac{\Delta \text{p}}{\Delta t}$

$\text{F}_{awning} - \text{F}_g = \frac{\Delta \text{p}}{\Delta t}$

$\text{F}_{awning} - 120(9,8) = \frac{3798}{1,2}$

$\therefore \text{F}_{awning} = 4341\,\text{N}$ upwards (4)

[30]

Question 9

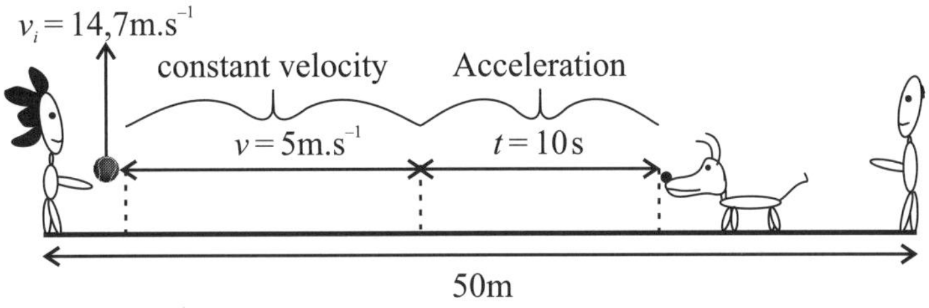

9.1 $v_f = v_i + a\Delta t$

$0 = 14,7 + (-9,8)\Delta t$

$\therefore \Delta t = 1,5\,\text{s}$ (3)

9.2 While accelerating:

$v_f = v_i + a\Delta t$

$5 = 0 + a(10)$

$\therefore a = 0,5\,\text{m.s}^{-1}$

$\Delta x = v_i\Delta t + \frac{1}{2}a\Delta t^2$

$= 0 + \frac{1}{2}(0,5)(10)^2$

$= 25\,\text{m}$ → while accelerating the dog covers a distance of 25m

As there is no air resistance, time up = time down:

$t = 3\,\text{s}$

$\Delta x = v\Delta t$ → constant velocity

$= 5(3)$

$= 15\,\text{m}$

$\therefore \Delta x_{\text{total}} = 40\,\text{m}$

$\therefore$ The dog is 10 m from the man. (7)

TOC
1 Data Sheet
2 Definitions
3
3 solutions
4
4 solutions
5
5 solutions
6
6 solutions
7
7 solutions
8
8 solutions
9
9 solutions
10
10 solutions

TOC | 1 Data Sheet | 2 Definitions | 3 | 3 solutions | 4 | 4 solutions | 5 | 5 solutions | 6 | 6 solutions | 7 | 7 solutions | 8 | 8 solutions | 9 | 9 solutions | 10 | 10 solutions

Question 10

10.1 speed limit $= 16,67\ \text{m.s}^{-1} \rightarrow \div$ by 3,6 to convert km.h^{-1} to m.s^{-1}

$\Delta x = v\Delta t$

$60 = v(2) \rightarrow$ in 2s the car covered a distance of 60m

$\therefore v_{car} = 30\,\text{m.s}^{-1}$

$\therefore$ The car was speeding. (3)

10.2 At the moment the officer catches the car his displacement is 60m more than the car's:

$\Delta x_{police} = \Delta x_{car} + 60$

police

car

$v_i\Delta t + \frac{1}{2}a\Delta t^2 = v\Delta t + 60$

$0 + \frac{1}{2}(0,8)\Delta t^2 = (30)\Delta t + 60$

$0,4t^2 - 30t - 60 = 0$

$t = 76,95\,\text{s}$ or $t = -1,95\,\text{s} \rightarrow$ N/A (6)

10.3 $v_f = v_i + a\Delta t$

$= 0 + (0,8)(76,95)$

$= 61,56\,\text{m.s}^{-1} \rightarrow$ do not give direction as the question asked for magnitude (3)

[12]

Question 11

11.1 10 seconds. (1)

11.2 $a = \frac{300 - 0}{10 - 0} \rightarrow$ gradient

$= 30\,\text{m.s}^{-2}$ upwards (6)

11.3 $\Delta x = \frac{1}{2}(\text{base})(\perp \text{height}) \rightarrow$ displacement is area under the graph

$= \frac{1}{2}(40,61)(300)$

$= 6\,091,5\,\text{m}$ (3)

11.4 $-9,8\ \text{m.s}^{-2}$. The rocket is in freefall and its acceleration is therefore due to gravitational force. (1)

11.5 $-9,8 = \frac{P - 300}{75,87 - 10} \rightarrow$ gradient is $-9,8\,\text{m.s}^{-2}$

$P = -345,53$

$= 345,53\,\text{m.s}^{-1}$ downwards (4)

11.6

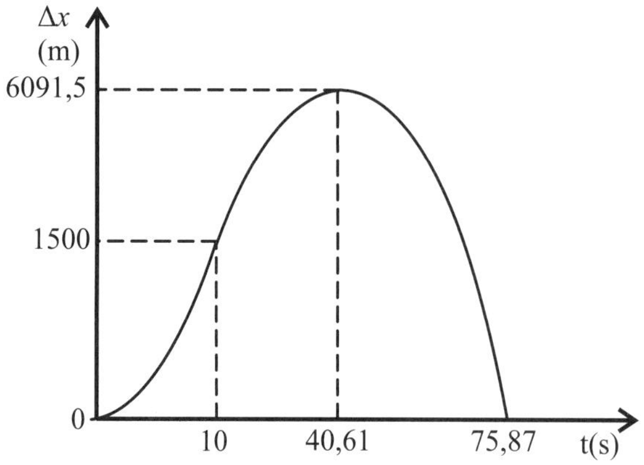

(5)

[17]

Question 12

12.1 $8\,\text{m.s}^{-1}$ upwards (1)

12.2 $\Delta x = \frac{1}{2}(0,82)(8) + \frac{1}{2}(4,11 - 0,82)(-32,28)$

$= -49,82$

$\therefore$ The balloon is 49,82 m above the ground. (4)

12.3 0,2 seconds (2)

12.4 $v_f = v_i + a\Delta t$

$0 = 4 + (-9,8)\Delta t$

$\Delta t = 0,41\,\text{s}$

$\therefore x = 4,72\,\text{s}$ (3)

12.5 $\Delta x = \frac{1}{2}(4,72 - 4,31)(4)$

$= 0,82\,\text{m}$ (3)

12.6 Height of balloon above the ground after 4,72 seconds:

$\Delta x = 8(4,72) + 49,82$

$= 87,58\,\text{m}$

$\therefore$ distance apart $= 87,58 - 0,82$

$= 86,76\,\text{m}$ (6)

[19]

Question 13

13.1 The rate of change of velocity. (1)

13.2

Drop Height Δx (m)	Final velocity v_f (m.s^{-1})	Final velocity squared v_f^2 ($\text{m}^2.\text{s}^{-2}$)
5	9,9	98
10	14,0	196
15	16,2	262
20	19,1	365
25	21,9	480
30	23,5	552
35	25,5	650

(3)

13.3 Graph of (final velocity)^2 against drop height

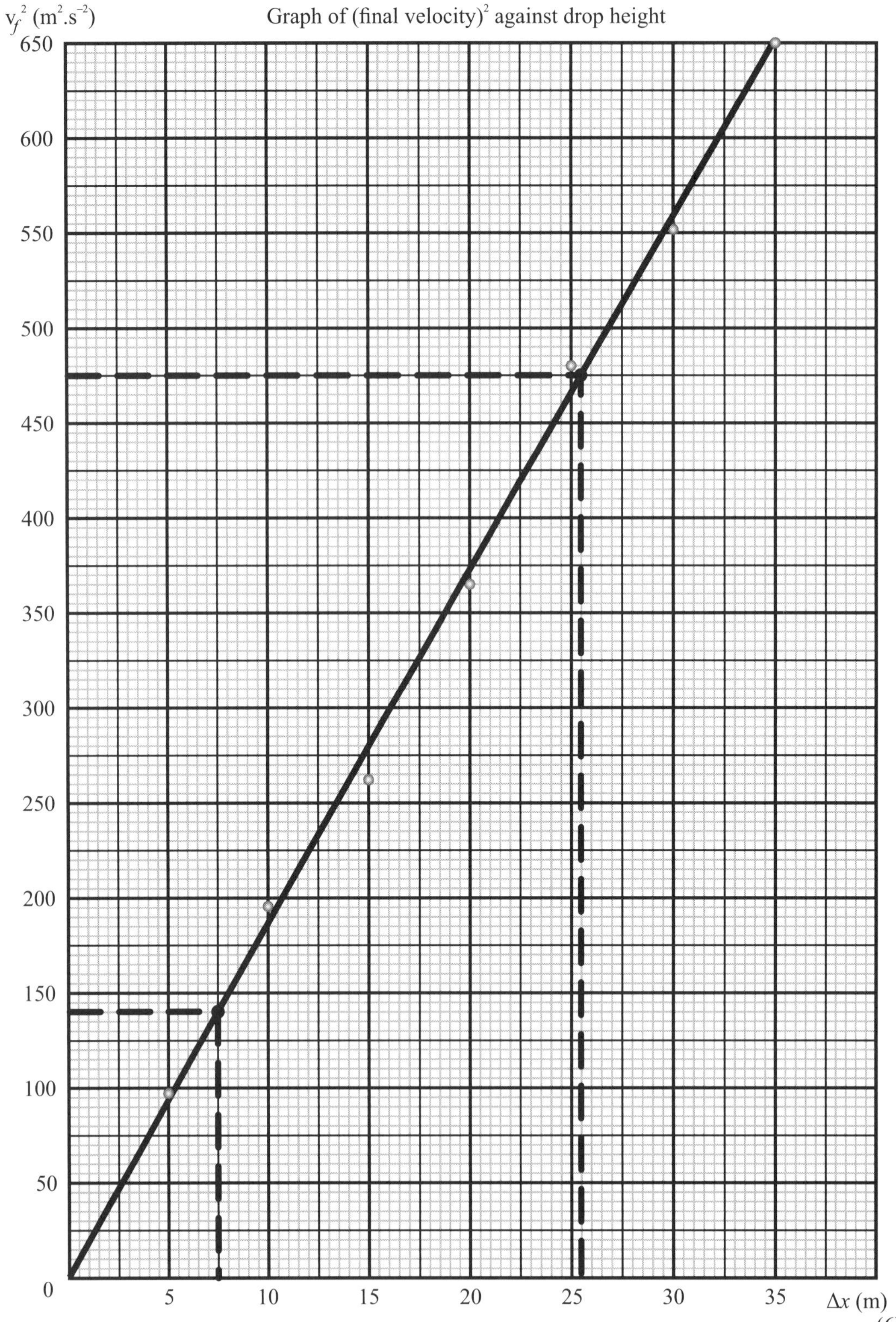

(6)

13.4 Displacement is directly proportional to (velocity)^2 not velocity. (2)

13.5 $\text{gradient} = \dfrac{475-140}{25,5-7,5} = 18,61\,\text{m.s}^{-2}$ → points must be on the line and not from the table (3)

13.6 $v_f^2 = 2a\Delta x + v_i^2 \rightarrow y = mx + c \rightarrow m = 2a$

$\therefore 18,61 = 2a$

$\therefore a = 9,31\,\text{m.s}^{-2}$ (4)

13.7 There is air friction which reduces the net force acting on the tennis ball, reducing acceleration. (2)

[22]

Question 14

14.1

Time (s)	Vertical Distance Travelled (m)	Horizontal Distance Travelled (m)	Time squared (s^2)
0,0	0	0	0
0,1	0,04	1	0,01
0,2	0,18	2	0,04
0,3	0,42	3	0,09
0,4	0,72	4	0,16

(4)

14.2 It is constant. (The displacement is increasing by the same amount each time interval)

$v = \frac{\Delta x}{t} \rightarrow$ constant velocity

$= \frac{4}{0,4} \rightarrow$ any corresponding values from the table could have been used

$= 10 \text{ m.s}^{-1}$ (4)

14.3

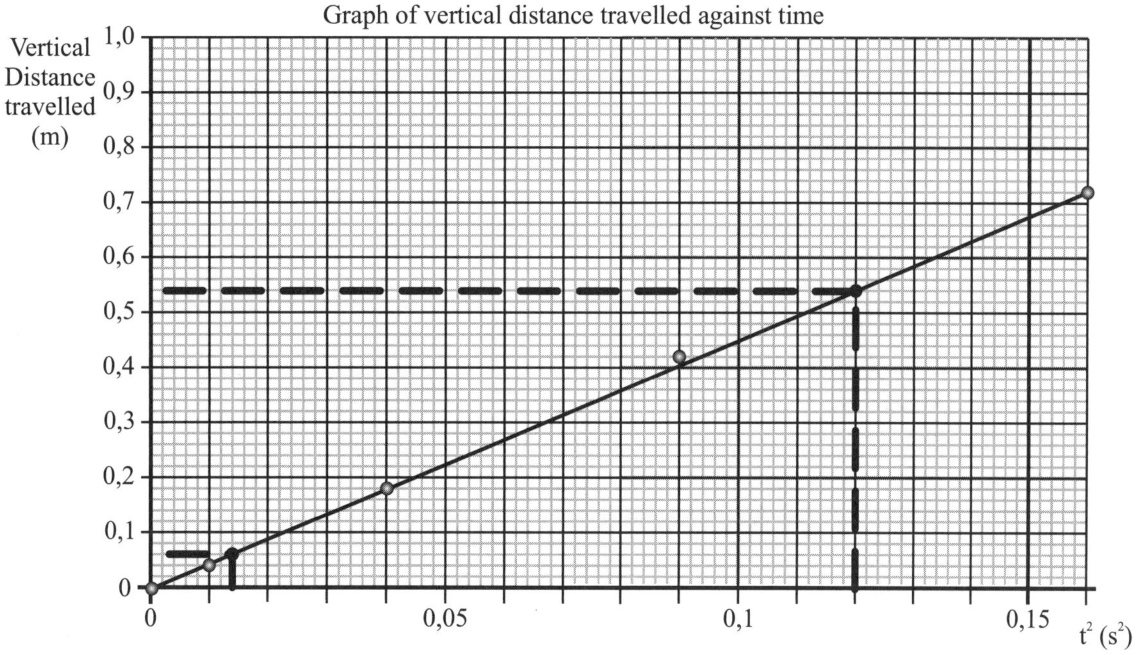

(6)

14.4 Vertical distance travelled is directly proportional to time squared. (2)

14.5 $\Delta x = \frac{1}{2}a\Delta t^2 + v_i\Delta t \rightarrow y = mx + c$ (1)

14.6 $\text{Gradient} = \frac{0,54 - 0,06}{0,12 - 0,014}$

$= 4,53 \text{ m.s}^{-2}$

$\text{Gradient} = \frac{1}{2}a \rightarrow$ this can be seen from the equation in the form $y = mx + c$

$\therefore \frac{1}{2}a = 4,53$

$\therefore a = 9,06 \text{ m.s}^{-2}$ (5)

14.7 No, if air friction were negligible the acceleration would have been $9,8 \text{ m.s}^{-2}$ (2)

[28]

TOC | 1 Data Sheet | 2 Definitions | 3 | 3 solutions | 4 | 4 solutions | 5 | 5 solutions | 6 | 6 solutions | 7 | 7 solutions | 8 | 8 solutions | 9 | 9 solutions | 10 | 10 solutions

Question 15

15.1 $4\,\text{m.s}^{-1} \rightarrow$ don't give direction for speed (1)

15.2 A (2)

15.3 C (2)

15.4 In contact with the ground. (2)

15.5 $\Delta x = 2(4) + \frac{1}{2}(2)(20)$

$= 28\,\text{m}$ above the ground (4)

15.6

Method 1:

$$a = \frac{-6-24}{2,05-2} \rightarrow \text{gradient between A and B}$$

$$= -600$$

$$= 600\,\text{m.s}^{-2} \text{ upwards}$$

Taking up as positive :

$$F_{net} = ma$$

$$F_{ground} - F_{gravity} = 0,1(600)$$

$$F_{ground} - (0,1)(9,8) = 60$$

$$F_{ground} = 60,98\,\text{N upwards}$$

Method 2:

$$F_{net} = \frac{\Delta p}{\Delta t}$$

$$F_{gravity} - F_{ground} = \frac{m(v_f - v_i)}{\Delta t}$$

$$(0,1)(9,8) - F_{ground} = \frac{0,1[-6-24]}{0,05}$$

$$\therefore F_{ground} = 60,98\,\text{N upwards}$$

(5)

15.7

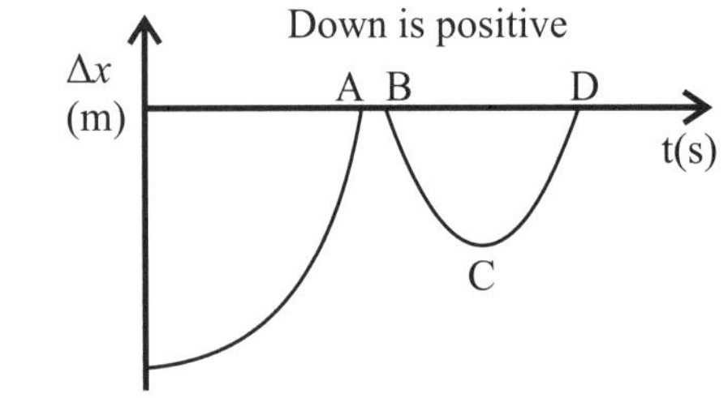

(6)

15.8

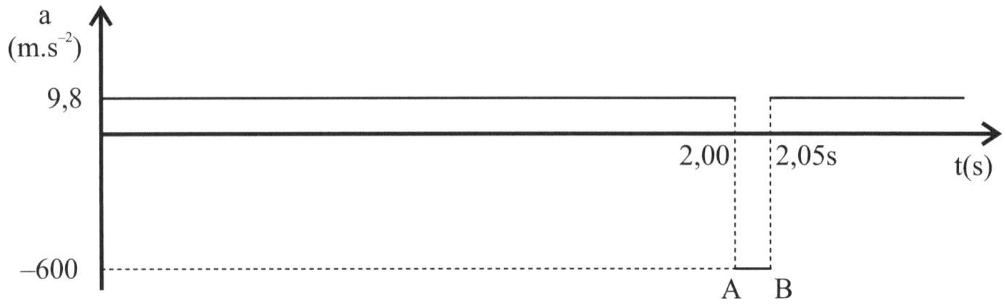

(4)

[19]

Question 16

16.1 The same. $\rightarrow$ acceleration is constant and the same for both coins (2)

16.2 2 seconds. $\rightarrow$ coins are dropped 2s apart and take the same amount of time to reach the floor (2)

16.3

$$\Delta x_{lighter} = v_i \Delta t + \frac{1}{2} a \Delta t^2$$

$$= 0 + \frac{1}{2}(9,8)t^2$$

$$= 4,9t^2$$

$$\Delta x_{heavier} = v_i \Delta t + \frac{1}{2} a (\Delta t - 2)^2$$

$$= 0 + \frac{1}{2}(9,8)(t^2 - 4t + 4)$$

$$= 4,9t^2 - 19,6t + 19,6$$

Distance between coins $= \Delta x_{lighter} - \Delta x_{heavier}$

$$= 4,9t^2 - (4,9t^2 - 19,6t + 19,6)$$

$$= 19,6t - 19,6 \quad t \geq 2$$

(8)

16.4 $78,4\,\text{m.s}^{-1}$. $\rightarrow$ The heavier coin will always be $19,6\,\text{m.s}^{-1}$ slower than the lighter coin (3)

[15]

TOC 1 Data Sheet 2 Definitions 3 3 solutions 4 4 solutions 5 5 solutions 6 6 solutions 7 7 solutions 8 8 solutions 9 9 solutions 10 10 solutions

Question 17

17.1 $v_f^2 = v_i^2 + 2a\Delta x$

$(2v)^2 = v^2 + 2(9,8)(6)$

$4v^2 = v^2 + 117,6$

$3v^2 = 117,6$

$\therefore v = 6,26\,\text{m.s}^{-1}$

$v_f^2 = v_i^2 + 2a\Delta x$

$24^2 = (2\times 6,26)^2 + 2(9,8)\Delta x$

$\therefore \Delta x = 21,39\,\text{m}$ (6)

17.2 $\Delta x = v_i\Delta t + \frac{1}{2}a\Delta t^2$

$= 6,26(2) + \frac{1}{2}(9,8)(2)^2$

$= 32,12\,\text{m}$ (3)

17.3 $v_f = v_i + a\Delta t$

$= 6,26 + 9,8(2)$

$= 25,86\,\text{m.s}^{-1}$ downwards (2)

17.4

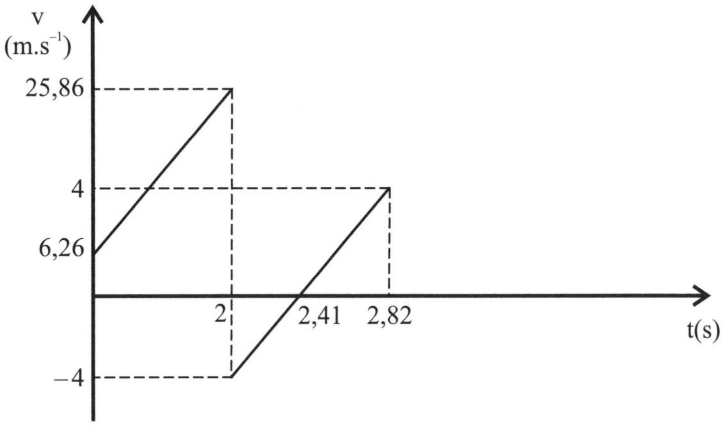

(5)

17.5 $v_f^2 = v_i^2 + 2a\Delta x$

$0 = (-4)^2 + 2(9,8)\Delta x$

$\therefore \Delta x = -0,82$

$= 0,82\,\text{m}$ above the ground (3)

17.6

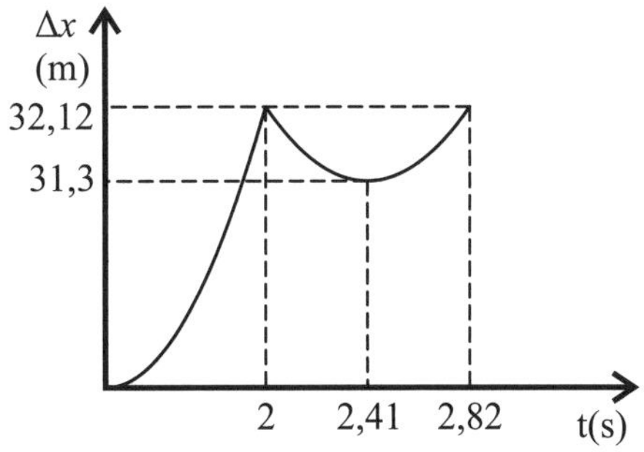

(6)

[25]

Question 18

18.1 Velocity is decreasing at a constant rate in the upwards direction.
Acceleration is constant in the downwards direction, (4)

18.2 $a = \frac{30-(-10)}{10-0}$ → acceleration is the gradient of a velocity-time graph

$= 4\,\text{m.s}^{-2}$

∴ He is on planet Spides 18 (4)

18.3 $\Delta x = \frac{1}{2}(2{,}5)(-10) + \frac{1}{2}(10-2{,}5)(30) \rightarrow \text{Area}_{AB} + \text{Area}_{BC}$

$= 100\,\text{m}$ (4)

18.4

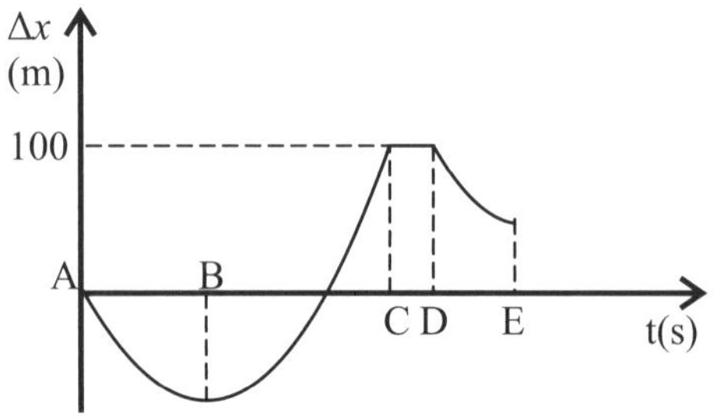

(5)

18.5 $a = \frac{-15-30}{10{,}2-10}$

$= -225$

$= 225\,\text{m.s}^{-2}$

$F_{net} = ma$

$= 4(225)$

$= 900\,\text{N upwards}$ (5)

18.6 $F_{net} = F_{ground} - F_{gravity}$

$900 = F_{ground} - 4(4)$

$F_{ground} = 916\,\text{N upwards}$ (3)

[25]

Question 19

19.1 E → The child is stationary for 10 seconds (2)

19.2 10 seconds. (2)

19.3 When the graph becomes horizontal the children have stopped moving and have reached their hiding place. (2)

19.4 D and F (2)

19.5 F (2)

19.6 A, D and F. (3)

19.7 C (2)

19.8 F. Child F covered the largest distance in the shortest amount of time. (3)

[18]

Question 20

20.1 $v_f = v_i + a\Delta t$

$0 = 30 + a(5)$

$\therefore a = -6\,\text{m.s}^{-2}$

$= 6\,\text{m.s}^{-2}$ (3)

20.2 **First calculate the distance car A travels while coming to rest:**

$\Delta x = v_i\Delta t + \frac{1}{2}a\Delta t^2$

$= 30(5) + \frac{1}{2}(-6)(5)^2$

$= 75\,\text{m}$

$\therefore$ Total stopping distance B has to avoid hitting A $= 75 + 45$

$= 120\,\text{m}$

Calculate the distance car B travels during the 0,8 seconds reaction time:

$\Delta x = v\Delta t \rightarrow$ constant velocity

$= 30(0,8)$

$= 24\,\text{m}$

Calculate the distance car B travels while coming to rest:

$v_f^2 = v_i^2 + 2a\Delta x$

$(0)^2 = (30)^2 + 2(-8)\Delta x$

$\therefore \Delta x = 56,25\,\text{m}$

$\therefore$ Total stopping distance $= 56,25 + 24$

$= 80,25\,\text{m}$

As 80,25 m is less than 120 m, car B does manage to stop in time. (9)

20.3 Minimum distance $= 80,25 - 75 \rightarrow$ distance B needs to stop $-$ distance travelled by A

$= 5,25\,\text{m}$ (3)

[15]

Question 21 (2014 IEB Final Examination)

21.1.1 **Method 1: Area under the graph**

$\Delta x = \frac{1}{2}(0,8)(7,84)$

$= 3,14\,\text{m}$

Method 2: Using equations of motion

$\Delta x = v_i\Delta t + \frac{1}{2}a\Delta t^2$

$= 0 + \frac{1}{2}(9,8)(0,8)^2$

$= 3,14\,\text{m}$ (3)

There are many equations of motion which could have been used to solve this problem but not all have been shown. The law of conservation of mechanical energy could also have been used.

21.1.2 **Method 1:**

$v_f = v_i + a\Delta t$

$= 1,53 + (9,8)(0,7)$

$= 8,39\,\text{m.s}^{-1}$

Method 2:

$\Delta x = v_i\Delta t + \frac{1}{2}a\Delta t^2$

$= (1,53)(0,7) + \frac{1}{2}(9,8)(0,7)^2$

$= 3,472\,\text{m}$

$v_f^2 = v_i^2 + 2a\Delta x$

$= (1,53)^2 + 2(9,8)(3,472)$

$= 70,3921$

$\therefore v_f = 8,39\,\text{m.s}^{-1}$ (4)

21.1.3 **Method 1: Using Impulse**

$$F_{net} = \frac{m(v_f - v_i)}{\Delta t}$$
$$= \frac{5,4(1,53-7,84)}{0,2}$$
$$= -170,37$$
$$= 170,37\text{ N up}$$

Method 2: Using Newton's 2nd law

$$v_f = v_i + a\Delta t$$
$$1,53 = 7,84 + a(0,2)$$
$$\therefore a = -31,55$$
$$= 31,55\text{ m.s}^{-2}\text{ up}$$
$$F_{net} = ma$$
$$= 5,4(-34,55)$$
$$= -170,37$$
$$= 170,37\text{ N up}$$

Method 3: Using Work-energy theorem

$$\Delta x = \frac{(v_f + v_i)}{2}\Delta t$$
$$= \frac{(7,84+1,53)}{2}(0,2)$$
$$= 0,937\text{ m}$$
$$\Delta Ek = \frac{1}{2}m(v_f^2 - v_i^2)$$
$$= \frac{1}{2}(5,4)(1,53^2 - 7,84^2)$$
$$= -159,637\text{ J}$$
$$F_{net}\Delta x = \Delta Ek$$
$$F_{net}(0,937) = -159,637$$
$$\therefore F_{net} = -170,37$$
$$\therefore F_{net} = 170,37\text{ N up}$$

(5)

21.1.4 According to Newton's 3rd law they are equal. (2)

21.1.5

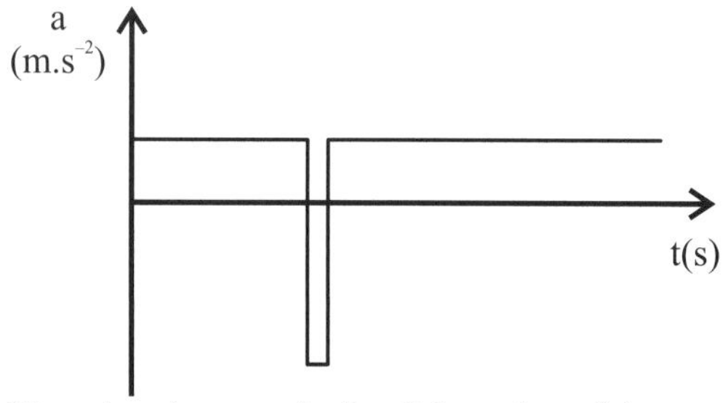

Note that the magnitude of the value of the negative acceleration must be greater than the positive value. (3)

21.1.6

a) Less than (1)

b) $E_k = \frac{1}{2}mv^2$

$= \frac{1}{2}mv \times v$

$= \frac{1}{2}pv$

As momentum is the same for both, but the velocity of X is smaller, the kinetic energy of X must also be smaller. (4)

21.2 After 4 seconds: $\Delta x_4 = v_i\Delta t + \frac{1}{2}a\Delta t^2$

$$\Delta x_4 = 0 + \frac{1}{2}a(4)^2$$
$$= 8a$$

After 3 seconds: $\Delta x_3 = v_i\Delta t + \frac{1}{2}a\Delta t^2$

$$\Delta x_3 = 0 + \frac{1}{2}a(3)^2$$
$$= \frac{9}{2}a$$

$$\Delta x_4 - \Delta x_3 = 11,2$$
$$8a - \frac{9}{2}a = 11,2$$
$$3,5a = 11,2$$
$$a = 3,2\text{ m.s}^{-2}$$

[27]

Question 22 (2014 IEB Exemplar Examination)

22.1 The rate of change of velocity. (2)

22.2 9,8 m.s^{-2} downwards (2)

22.3 There are forces other than gravity acting on the gymnast while in contact with the trampoline. Therefore, acceleration is not 9,8 m.s^{-2}. (2)

22.4 displacement = area under the velocity time graph

$$= \frac{1}{2}(0,8)(7,84) - \frac{1}{2}(1,7-0,8)(8,82)$$

$$= -0,83$$

$\therefore$ height of trampoline = 0,83 m (5)

22.5

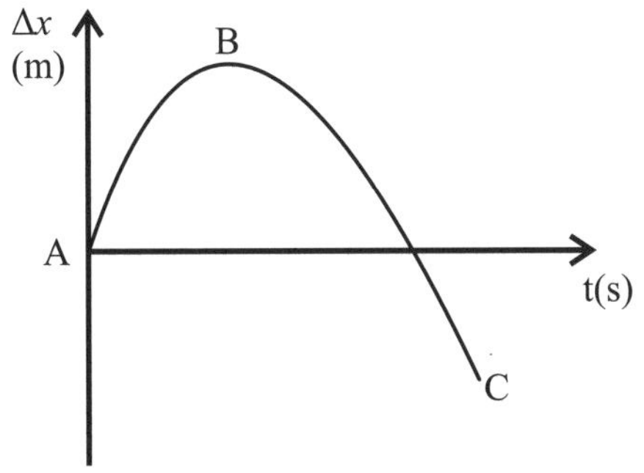

(3)

[14]

Question 23 (2015 IEB Final Examination)

23.1.1 $a =$ gradient of a velocity time graph $= \dfrac{4-0}{20-35}$

$$= -0,27$$

$$= 0,27 \text{ m.s}^{-2} \text{ West}$$ (4)

23.1.2 0 - 10 s (A - B) and 40 - 50 s (E - F) (2)

23.1.3 Displacement is a change in position. (2)

23.1.4 displacement = area under the velocity time graph

$$= \frac{1}{2}(10)(4) + (10)(4) + \frac{1}{2}(15)(4) - \frac{1}{2}(10)(3)$$

= 75 m East (4)

23.1.5 No, it will not always be true. Displacement and distance can be equal only if the object travels in a straight line in one direction. (2)

23.1.6

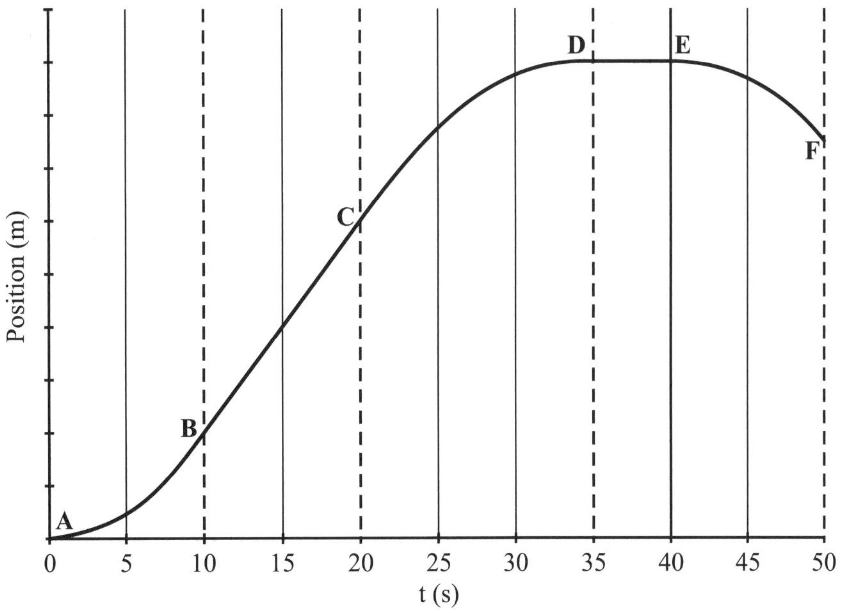

(5)

23.2.1 $\text{average speed} = \frac{\text{total distance}}{\text{total time}} = \frac{12\,000}{7,6 \times 60} = 26,32 \text{ m.s}^{-1}$ (4)

23.2.2 $100 \text{ km.h}^{-1} \div 3,6 = 27,78 \text{ m.s}^{-1}$ (2)

23.2.3 No (1)

23.2.4 $\text{Time for } 1^{st}\ 6\text{km} = \frac{6}{60} = 0,1 \text{ hours}$

$\text{Time for } 2^{nd}\ 6\text{km} = \frac{6}{140} = 0,04 \text{ hours}$

$$\text{average speed} = \frac{\text{total distance}}{\text{total time}}$$

$$= \frac{12}{0,1 + 0,04}$$

$= 85,71 \text{ km.h}^{-1} \rightarrow$ without rounding the answer would be 84 km.h^{-1} (5)

[31]

Question 24 (2015 IEB Supplementary Examination)

24.1 $83,8 \times 3,6 = 301,68 \text{ km.h}^{-1}$ (2)

24.2 **Method 1:**

$$\Delta x = \frac{(v_f + v_i)}{2}\Delta t$$

$$= \frac{(83,3+0)(13,63)}{2}$$

$$= 567,69 \text{ m}$$

Method 2:

$v_f = v_i + a\Delta t$

$83,3 = 0 + a(13,63)$

$\therefore a = 6,11 \text{m.s}^{-2}$

$v_f^2 = v_i^2 + 2a\Delta x$

$(83,3)^2 = 0^2 + 2(6,11)\Delta x$

$\therefore \Delta x = 567,83 \text{ m}$

or

$$\Delta x = v_i\Delta t + \frac{1}{2}a\Delta t^2$$

$$= 0 + \frac{1}{2}(6,11)(13,63)^2$$

$$= 567,55 \text{ m}$$ (4)

The different answers in each method is due to rounding. All will be marked correct.

24.3.1 Reaction distance is directly proportional to speed. (2)

24.3.2 $v_f^2 = v_i^2 + 2a\Delta x$

$0^2 = v_i^2 + 2a\Delta x$

$$\Delta x = -\frac{v_i^2}{2a}$$

As acceleration is constant: $\Delta x \propto v_i^2$ (2)

24.3.3

Braking distance (Δx)	Initial speed squared (v_i^2)	$\frac{\Delta x}{v_i^2}$
7	100	**0,07**
28	400	**0,07**
63	900	**0,07**
112	1 600	**0,07**

As $\frac{\Delta x}{v_i^2}$ is constant the braking distance is directly proportional to inital speed squared. (4)

24.3.4 a) Mental state of driver, tiredness, alcohol consumption, etc… (any one answer) (1)

b) Road surface (oil/ice/wet), state of tyres (worn/good tread), state of brakes, etc… (1)

24.4

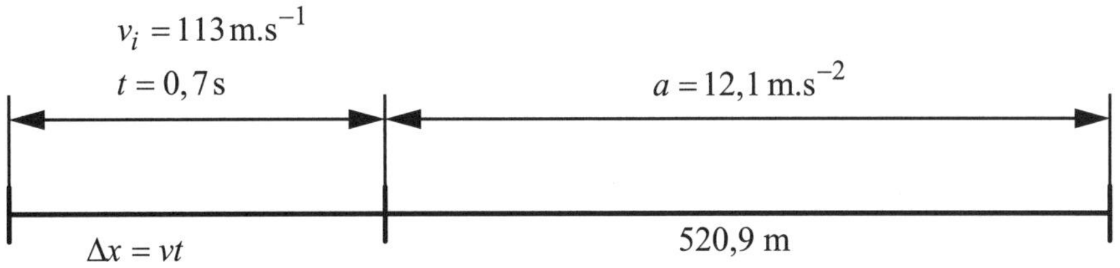

$\Delta x = vt$

$= (113)(0,7)$

$= 79,1\,\text{m}$

Distance covered before brakes are applied:

$v_i = 113\,\text{m.s}^{-1}$

$t = 0,7\,\text{s}$

$\Delta x = vt \rightarrow$ constant

$= (113)(0,7)$

$= 79,1\,\text{m}$

Method 1 :

Distance required to stop once the brakes applied:

$v_f^2 = v_i^2 + 2a\Delta x$

$0 = 113^2 + 2(-12,1)\Delta x$

$\Delta x = 527,64\ \text{m}$

Distance available to stop $= 600 - 79,1$

$= 520,9\,\text{m}$

$\therefore$ He does not stop in time.

Method 2 :

Acceleration required to stop in 520,9 m

$v_f^2 = v_i^2 + 2a\Delta x$

$0 = 113^2 + 2(a)(520,9)$

$a = -12,26$

$\therefore$ He does not stop in time as the car's deceleration is to small. (6)

[22]

Question 25 (2016 IEB Final Examination)

25.1 The rate of change of velocity. (2)

25.2 **Method 1: Using the gradient of the graph**

$a =$ gradient of a velocity time graph $= \dfrac{230,4 - 0}{120 - 0}$

$= 1,92\ \text{m.s}^{-2}$ up

Method 2: Using equations of motion

$v_f = v_i + a\Delta t$

$230,4 = 0 + a(120)$

$\therefore a = 1,92\ \text{m.s}^{-2}$ up (4)

25.3 Velocity: Velocity is upwards and decreasing in magnitude (slowing down)
Acceleration: Acceleration is downwards and constant in magnitude. (4)

25.4 297,64 s (2)

25.5 The rate of change of distance. (2)

25.6 $v_f^2 = v_i^2 + 2a\Delta x$

$v_f^2 = 0 + 2(9,8)(55165,34 - 6000)$

$v_f = 981,65 \text{ m.s}^{-1}$ (3)

25.7 $v_f^2 = v_i^2 + 2a\Delta x$

$1 = 981,65^2 + 2a(6000)$

$a = -80,30$

$= 80,30 \text{ m.s}^{-2}$ (3)

25.8

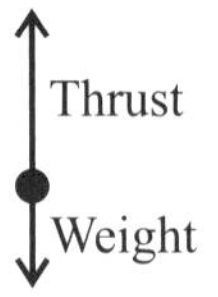

(2)

25.9 $F_{net} = ma$

$\text{Thrust} - F_g = ma$

$\text{Thrust} - (5800)(9,8) = (5800)(80,3)$

$\text{Thrust} = 522\,580,0 \text{ N upwards}$ (5)

Question 26 (2016 IEB Final Examination)

26.1.1 D and E (2)

26.1.2 A, D and E (3)

26.1.3 C (1)

26.1.4 E (1)

26.1.5 Child B and C are in the same position (2)

26.2.1 The length of path travelled (2)

26.2.2 $\Delta x = vt \rightarrow$ constant velocity

$6 = 2t$

$t = 3\text{s}$ (3)

26.2.3 $\Delta x = vt \rightarrow$ constant velocity

$= 4(3)$

$= 12\text{m}$ (2)

26.2.4 $16 - 12 = 4$ m away (2)

26.2.5 $\Delta x = v_i\Delta t + \frac{1}{2}a\Delta t^2$

$16 = 4(3) + \frac{1}{2}a(3)^2$

$a = 0,89 \text{ m.s}^{-2}$ (3)

[21]

Question 27 (From the 2016 IEB NSC Supplementary Examination)

27.1.1 The rate of change of velocity (2)

27.1.2 $a =$ gradient of a velocity time graph $= \frac{8-0}{8-0}$

$= 1 \text{ m.s}^{-2}$ (3)

27.1.3 Grant is running at a constant velocity (2)

27.1.4 distance = area under a velocity time graph

$$= \frac{1}{2}(8)(8) + (13-8)(8) + \frac{1}{2}(17-13)(2) + (17-13)(6)$$

$$= 100\,\text{m}$$ (2)

27.1.5 They have the same velocity. (2)

27.1.6 distance = area under a velocity time graph

$$100 = \frac{1}{2}(15)(10) + (t-15)(10)$$

$$t = 17{,}5\,\text{s}$$ (4)

27.2.1 Springbok exerts a force on the ground, ground exerts a force on the springbok (2)

27.2.2

- The action-reaction pairs act on different objects
- force of ground on springbok is greater than weight of the springbok
- resultant force on springbok is up
- by Newton's second law, resultant force produces an acceleration upwards. (4)

27.2.3 $v_f^2 = v_i^2 + 2a\Delta x$

$v_f^2 = 0 + 2(35)(0,7)$

$v_f^2 = 49$

$v_f = 7\ \text{m.s}^{-1}$ (3)

27.2.4 $v_f^2 = v_i^2 + 2a\Delta x$

$0 = 49 + 2(-9,8)\Delta x$

$\Delta x = 2,5\ \text{m}$ (3)

[29]

Question 28 (2017 IEB Final Examination)

28.1

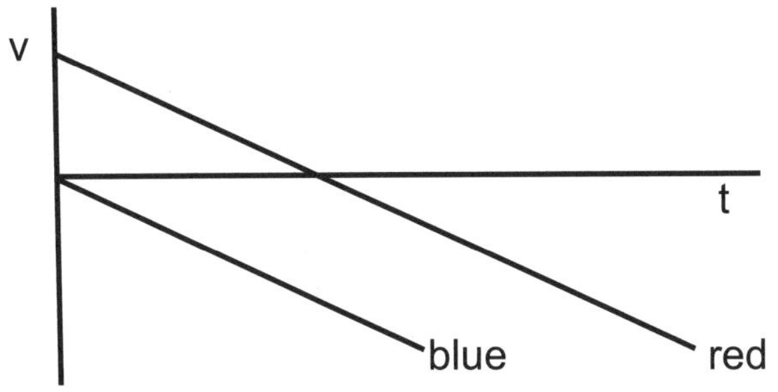

(3)

28.2.1 $\Delta x = vt \rightarrow$ constant velocity

$= 0,25(8)$

$= 2\ \text{m}$

$\therefore$ the cat is $6 - 2 = 4$ m from the mouse (3)

28.2.2

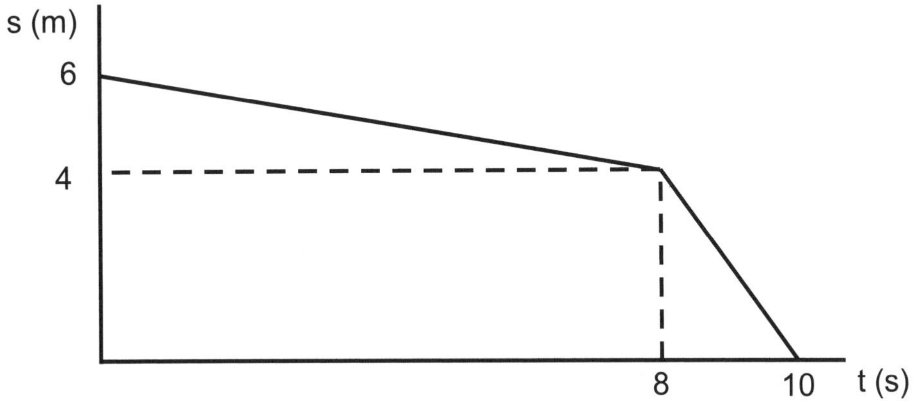

(3)

TOC
1 Data Sheet
2 Definitions
3
3 solutions
4
4 solutions
5
5 solutions
6
6 solutions
7
7 solutions
8
8 solutions
9
9 solutions
10
10 solutions

28.2.3 $\Delta x = vt \rightarrow$ constant velocity

$4 = v(2)$

$v = 2 \text{ m.s}^{-1}$ (2)

28.3.1 While acceleration is 20 m.s^{-2}:

$$\Delta x = v_i \Delta t + \frac{1}{2} a \Delta t^2$$
$$= 0 + \frac{1}{2}(20)(15)^2$$
$$= 2\,250 \text{ m}$$

at the point where the fuel runs out:

$$v_f = v_i + a\Delta t$$
$$= 0 + (20)(15)$$
$$= 300 \text{ m.s}^{-1}$$
$$v_f^2 = v_i^2 + 2a\Delta x$$

$0 = 300^2 + 2(-9,8)\Delta x \rightarrow$ once the rocket runs out of fuel $a = 9,8 \text{ m.s}^{-2}$

$\Delta x = 4\,591,84 \text{ m}$

max height $= 2\,250 + 4\,591,84$

$= 6\,841,84 \text{ m}$ (6)

28.3.2 Time to max height after rocket runs out of fuel:

$$v_f = v_i + a\Delta t$$
$$0 = 300 + (-9,8)t$$
$$t = 30,61 \text{ s}$$

Time to reach the ground from max height:

$$-6\,841,84 = 0 + \frac{1}{2}(-9,8)\Delta t^2$$
$$\Delta t = 37,37 \text{ s}$$
$$\therefore t_{tot} = 15 + 30,61 + 37,37$$
$$= 82,98 \text{ s}$$ (5)

28.3.3 At the instant it hits the ground.

[24]

Question 29 (2017 IEB Final Examination)

29.1 The rate of change of position or the rate of displacement or the rate of change of displacement. (2)

29.2 AB (0 – 3 s); DE (7 – 8 s); FG (9 – 10 s) (3)

29.3 BC (3 – 5 s); EF (8 – 9 s) (2)

29.4 CF (5 – 9 s) (2)

29.5 The rate of change of velocity (2)

29.6 **Method 1:**

$a =$ gradient of a velocity time graph

$$= \frac{-2-2}{7-3}$$
$$= -1$$
$$= 1 \text{ m.s}^{-2} \text{ South}$$

Method 2:

$$v_f = v_i + a\Delta t$$
$$-2 = 2 + a(4)$$
$$a = -1$$
$$= 1 \text{ m.s}^{-2} \text{ South}$$

(4)

29.7

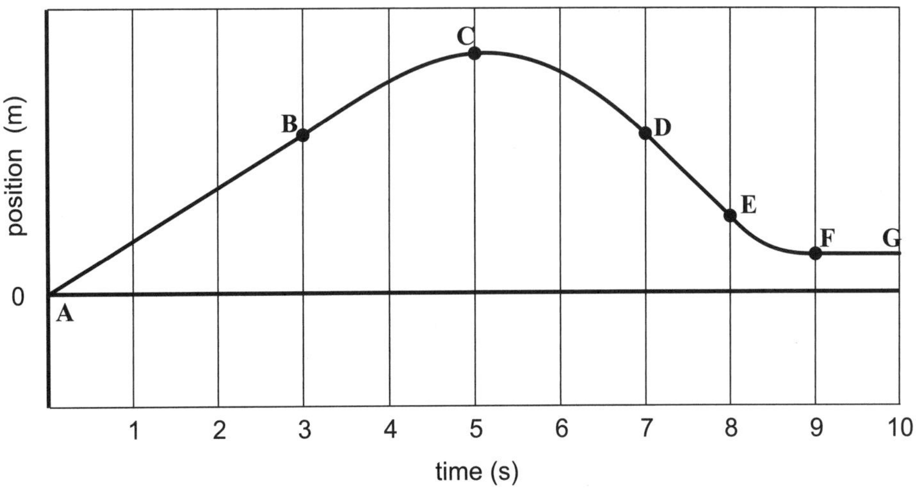

(6)

[21]

Question 30 (2017 IEB Supplementary Examination)

30.1 The rate of change of position or the rate of displacement or the rate of change of displacement. (2)

30.2 The rate of change of velocity. (2)

30.3 **Method 1:**

$a =$ gradient of a velocity time graph

$= \dfrac{2,2-2,0}{3-2}$

$= 0,2 \text{ m.s}^{-2}$

Method 2:

$v_f = v_i + a\Delta t$

$2,2 = 2,0 + a(1)$

$a = 0,2 \text{ m.s}^{-2}$

(4)

30.4

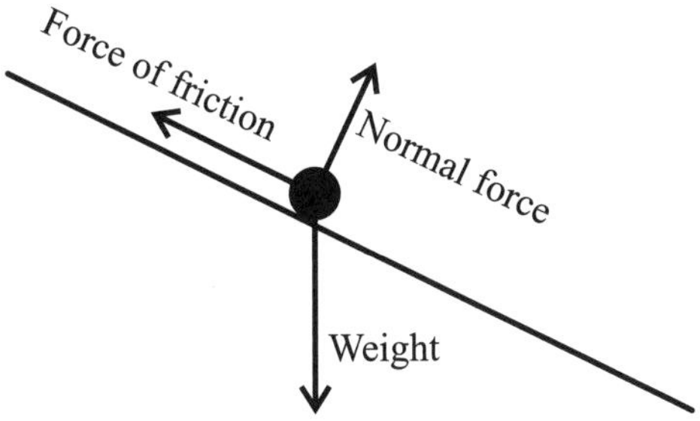

(3)

30.5 $\text{F}_{net} = ma$

$\text{F}_{g//} - \text{F}_f = ma$

$mg\sin 35 \; - \text{F}_f = 30(0,2)$

$(30)(9,8)\sin 35 \; - \text{F}_f = 30(0,2)$

$\text{F}_f = 162,63 \text{ N}$

(5)

30.6 distance = area under a velocity time graph

$= \frac{1}{2}(2)(2) + \frac{1}{2}(1)(0,2) + (1)(2)$

$= 4,1 \text{ m}$

(4)

30.7 $v_f = v_i + a\Delta t$

$0 = 2,2 + (-1,1)t$

$t = 2 \text{ s}$

30.8 **Method 1:**

distance = area under a velocity time graph

$= \frac{1}{2}(2)(2,2)$

$= 2,2 \text{ m}$

Method 2:

$v_f^2 = v_i^2 + 2a\Delta x$

$0 = 2,2^2 + 2(-1,1)\Delta x$

$\Delta x = 2,2 \text{ m}$

(4)

Question 31 (2017 IEB Supplementary Examination)

31.1 To carry out analysis, a straight line is needed to determine gradient/show relationship. The graph of h vs t yields a curved line while h vs t^2 is linear. (3)

31.2 **Graph of height vs time squared**

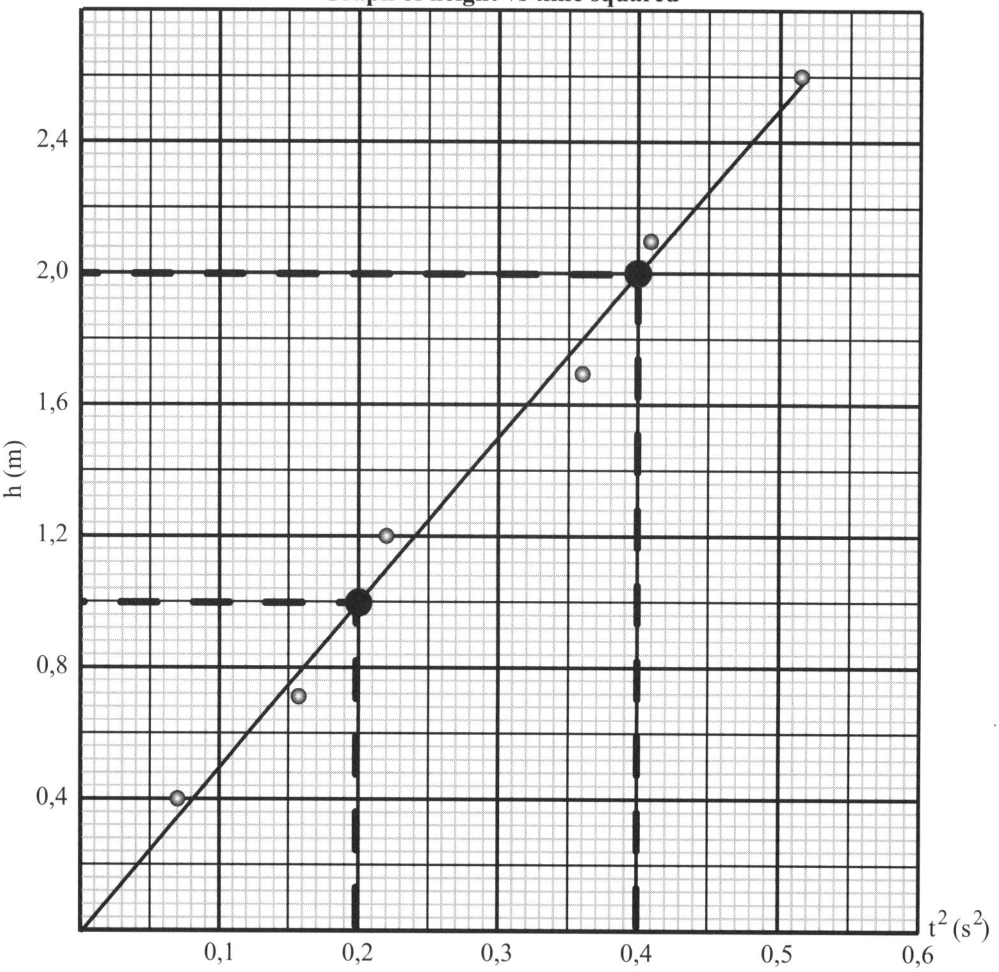

(6)

31.3 $$\text{Gradient} = \frac{2,0-1,0}{0,4-0,2}$$
$$=5$$ (4)

31.4 $$h = \frac{1}{2}a\Delta t^2 + v_i\Delta t$$ (2)

31.5 $$\text{Gradient} = \frac{1}{2}a$$
$$5 = \frac{1}{2}a$$
$$a = 10\ \text{m.s}^{-2}$$ (2)

31.6 The graph would not change as acceleration due to gravity is independent of the mass of the falling object. (2)

[19]

Question 32 (2018 IEB Final Examination)

32.1.1 The rate of change of position or the rate of displacement or the rate of change of displacement. (2)

32.1.2 Method 1:
distance = area under a velocity time graph
$$29,8 = \frac{1}{2}(3,5)v + \frac{1}{2}(14)v$$
$$v = 3,41\ \text{m.s}^{-1}$$

Method 2:
distance = area under a velocity time graph
$$29,8 = \frac{1}{2}(17,5)v$$
$$v = 3,41\ \text{m.s}^{-1}$$ (4)

32.1.3 **Method 1:**

$a =$ gradient of a velocity time graph

$= \frac{0-3,41}{17,5-3,5}$

$= -0,24 \text{ m.s}^{-2}$

$F_f = ma$

$= 20(-0,24)$

$= -4,87$

$= 4,87 \text{ N South}$

Method 2:

$F_f = \frac{m\Delta v}{\Delta t}$

$= \frac{20(0-3,41)}{14}$

$= -4,87$

$= 4,87 \text{ N South}$

(6)

32.2.1 **Stage 1:**

$v_f = v_i + a\Delta t$

$44 = 0 + a(4)$

$a = 11 \text{ m.s}^{-2}$

(3)

32.2.2 **Stage 1:**

$v_f^2 = v_i^2 + 2a\Delta x$

$44^2 = 0^2 + 2(11)\Delta x$

$\Delta x = 88 \text{ m}$

Stage 2:

$v_f = v_i + a\Delta t$

$280 = 44 + a(8)$

$a = 29,5 \text{ m.s}^{-2}$

$v_f^2 = v_i^2 + 2a\Delta x$

$280^2 = 44^2 + 2(29,5)\Delta x$

$\Delta x = 1296 \text{ m}$

Total distance $= 88 + 1296$

$= 1384 \text{ m}$

(6)

[21]

Question 33 (From the 2018 IEB NSC Final Examination)

33.1.1 No, velocity is increasing, and friction opposes motion. This would cause the speed of K to decrease, not increase. (3)

33.1.2 Yes. (1)

33.2.1 The rate of change of velocity. (2)

33.2.2 $v_f^2 = v_i^2 + 2a\Delta x$

$34^2 = 0^2 + 2(0,21)\Delta x$

$\Delta x = 2752,37 \text{ m}$

(4)

33.2.3 There are forces other than weight acting on the hailstone. (2)

33.2.4 $v_f^2 = v_i^2 + 2a\Delta x$

$0^2 = 34^2 + 2a(0,12)$

$a = 4816,67 \text{ m.s}^{-2}$ upwards

(4)

33.2.5 $F_{net} = ma$

$F_{ground} - F_g = ma$

$F_{ground} - mg = ma$

$F_{ground} - 0,7(9,8) = 0,7(4816,67)$

$F_{ground} = 3378,53 \text{ N}$

(5)

[21]

Question 34 (2018 IEB Supplementary Examination)

34.1 The rate of change of velocity. (2)

34.2 **Method 1:**

$a =$ gradient of a velocity time graph

$$= \frac{3,2-0}{0,5-0}$$

$$= 6,40 \text{ m.s}^{-2}$$

Method 2:

$$v_f = v_i + a\Delta t$$

$$3,2 = 0 + a(0.5)$$

$$a = 6,40 \text{ m.s}^{-2}$$

(3)

34.3 distance = area under a velocity time graph

$$= \frac{1}{2}(0,5)(3,2)$$

$$= 0,8 \text{ m}$$

(3)

34.4

(2)

34.5 Inelastic as it doesn't bounce back to the same height. (2)

34.6 $2,56 \text{ m.s}^{-1}$. (2)

34.7

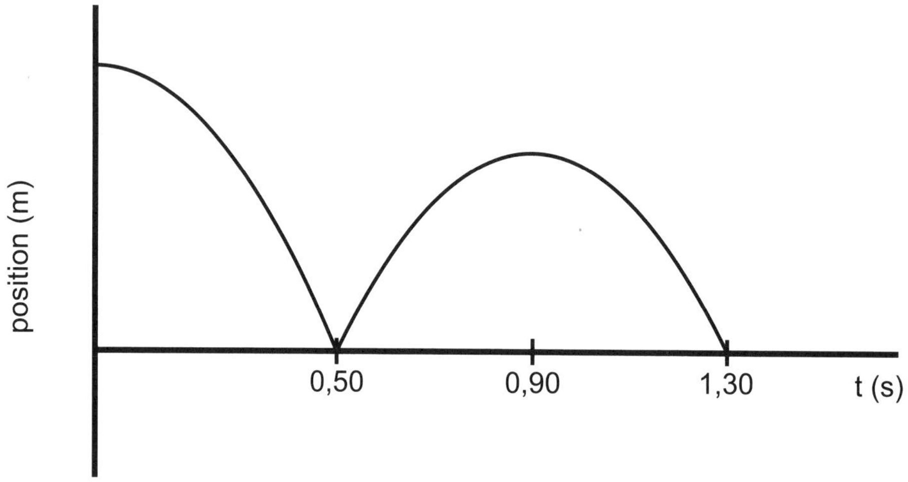

(3)

34.8

$$g_{earth} = \frac{GM}{r_{earth}^2} \qquad g_{planet} = \frac{GM}{r_{planet}^2}$$

$$\frac{g_{planet}}{g_{earth}} = \frac{GM}{r_{planet}^2} \div \frac{GM}{r_{earth}^2}$$

$$\frac{g_{planet}}{g_{earth}} = \frac{GM}{r_{planet}^2} \times \frac{r_{earth}^2}{GM}$$

$$\frac{6,4}{9,8} = \frac{r_{earth}^2}{r_{planet}^2}$$

$$r_{planet}^2 = \frac{9,8}{6,4} r_{earth}^2$$

$$r_{planet} = 1,24 r_{earth}$$

(4)

[21]

Question 35 (2018 IEB Supplementary Examination)

35.1

$$\Delta x = v_i \Delta t + \frac{1}{2} a \Delta t^2$$

$$-104,4 = v_b(6) + \frac{1}{2}(-9,8)(6)^2$$

$$v_b = 12 \text{ m.s}^{-1}$$

(4)

35.2 12 $m.s^{-1}$ upwards. (2)

35.3 $v_f^2 = v_i^2 + 2a\Delta x$

$0^2 = 12^2 + 2(-9,8)\Delta x$

$\Delta x = 7,35$ m

Max height $= 104,4 + 7,35$

$= 111,75$ m (5)

35.4 $\Delta x = v\Delta t \rightarrow$ constant velocity

$= (12)(6)$

$= 72$ m

Max height $= 104,4 + 72$

$= 176,40$ m (4)

[21]

Question 36 (2019 IEB Supplementary Examination)

36.1.1 The rate of change of velocity. (2)

36.1.2 9,8 $m.s^{-2}$ downwards (2)

36.1.3 $v_f = v_i + a\Delta t$

$0 = 15 + (-9,8)\Delta t$

$\Delta t = 1,53$ s (2)

36.1.4 **Method 1:**

$\Delta x = v_i\Delta t + \frac{1}{2}a\Delta t^2$

$= 15(1,53) + \frac{1}{2}(-9,8)(1,53)^2$

$= 11,48$ m

Method 2:

distance $=$ area under a velocity time graph

$= \frac{1}{2}(1,53)(15)$

$= 11,48$ m (3)

36.1.5 $v_f^2 = v_i^2 + 2a\Delta x$

$(-34)^2 = 15^2 + 2(-9,8)\Delta x$

$\Delta x = -47,5$

$= 47,5$ m (4)

36.1.6 & 36.1.7

Graph showing the relationship between velocity and time for balls A and B projected from a bridge

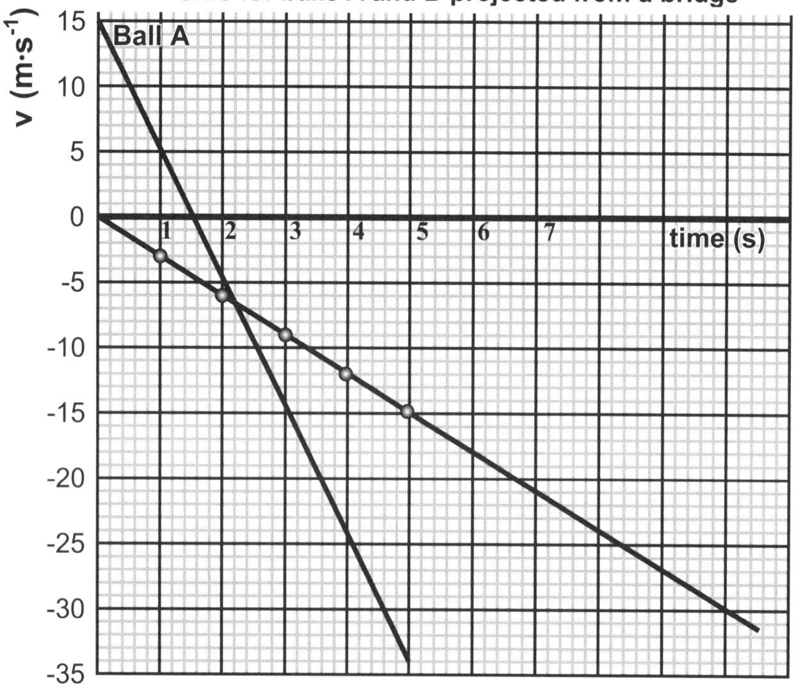

(6)

36.1.8 2,2 s (1)

36.1.9 A is above B. (1)

36.1.10 displacement is given by area under the graph.
Area UNDER AXIS for B > area Under X-axis for A (2)

36.1.11 **Ball A:**

$$\Delta x = v_i \Delta t + \frac{1}{2} a \Delta t^2$$

$$\Delta x = -15\Delta t + \frac{1}{2}(9,8)\Delta t^2 \rightarrow \boxed{1}$$

Substitute $\boxed{2}$ into $\boxed{1}$:

$$1,5\Delta t^2 = -15\Delta t + 4,9\Delta t^2$$

$$3,4\Delta t^2 - 15\Delta t = 0$$

$$\Delta t(3,4\Delta t - 15) = 0$$

$$\Delta t = 4,41 \text{ s}$$

Ball B:

$$\Delta x = v_i \Delta t + \frac{1}{2} a \Delta t^2$$

$$\Delta x = 0 + \frac{1}{2}(3)\Delta t^2$$

$$\Delta x = 1,5\Delta t^2 \rightarrow \boxed{2}$$

(5)

36.1.12 **Graph showing the relationship between position and time for balls A and B**

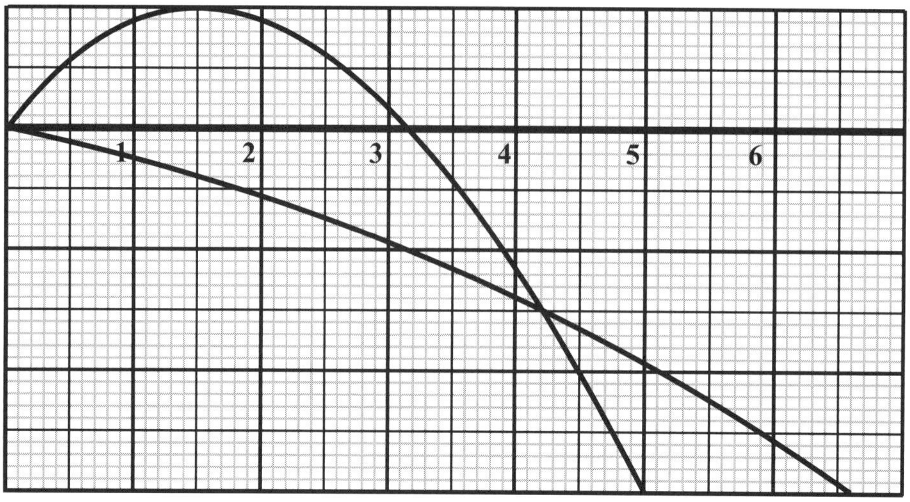

(5)

36.2.1 The rate of change of distance. (2)

36.2.2
$$\text{speed} = \frac{\text{distance}}{\text{time}}$$
$$= \frac{400}{105}$$
$$= 3{,}8\,\text{m.s}^{-1}$$
(3)

36.2.3 $3{,}8\,\text{m.s}^{-1}$ West (2)

[40]

Question 37 (2019 IEB Final Examination)

37.1.1 The rate of change of position or the rate of displacement or the rate of change of displacement. (2)

37.1.2 $12\,\text{m.s}^{-1}$ North (2)

37.1.3 displacement = area under a velocity time graph
$$= \frac{1}{2}(10)(12) + (25-10)(12)$$
$$= 240\,\text{m}$$
$$\text{average velocity} = \frac{\text{total displacement}}{\text{total time}}$$
$$= \frac{240}{25}$$
$$= 9{,}6\,\text{m.s}^{-1}$$
(6)

37.1.4 The rate of change of velocity. (2)

37.1.5 $a =$ gradient of a velocity time graph
$$= \frac{12-0}{10-0}$$
$$= 1{,}2\ \text{m.s}^{-2}$$
(3)

37.2 **Method 1:** Taking the displacement from the moment Helen passes Matthew. In this case Matthew catches Helen when their displacements are equal, and Matthew's time is 1,8 s less than Helen's.

$$\Delta x_H = v\Delta t \rightarrow \text{constant velocity}$$
$$= 0{,}37\Delta t$$

$$\Delta x_M = v_i\Delta t + \frac{1}{2}a\Delta t^2$$
$$= 0 + \frac{1}{2}(0{,}91)(\Delta t - 1{,}8)^2$$
$$= 0{,}455(\Delta t - 1{,}8)^2$$

$$\Delta x_M = \Delta x_H$$
$$0{,}455(\Delta t - 1{,}8)^2 = 0{,}37\Delta t$$
$$0{,}455\Delta t^2 - 2\Delta t + 0{,}455(3{,}24) = 0$$
$$\Delta t = 3{,}48\ \text{s}$$

37.2 **Method 2:** Taking the displacement from the moment Matthew begins to chase Helen. In this case, the time taken for them to meet is the same, but Matthew must travel the additional distance that Helen moved before Matthew started to accelerate.

Distance Helen travels before Matthew begins to chase Helen:

$$\Delta x_H = v\Delta t \rightarrow \text{constant velocity}$$
$$= 0{,}37(1{,}8)$$
$$= 0{,}666 \text{ m}$$

$$\Delta x_H = v\Delta t \rightarrow \text{constant velocity} \qquad \Delta x_M = v_i\Delta t + \frac{1}{2}a\Delta t^2$$
$$= 0{,}37\Delta t \qquad = 0 + \frac{1}{2}(0{,}91)\Delta t^2$$
$$= 0{,}455\Delta t^2$$

When Matthew catches Helen $\Delta x_M = \Delta x_H + 0{,}666$

$$0{,}455\Delta t^2 = 0{,}37\Delta t + 0{,}666$$
$$0{,}455\Delta t^2 - 0{,}37\Delta t - 0{,}666 = 0$$

$\Delta t = 1{,}68\text{ s} \rightarrow$ time taken for Matthew to catch Helen from when he starts moving

$\therefore$ Time form when Helen passes Matthew $= 1{,}68 + 1{,}8$
$= 3{,}48 \text{ s}$ (7)

[22]

Question 38 (2019 IEB Final Examination)

38.1.1 A is greater than B, speed = gradient of position-time graph and gradient A > gradient B. (2)

38.1.2 Yes, at 4 s. (any answer between 3 and 5 seconds is acceptable) (2)

38.1.3 Object A (2)

38.2.1 $\Delta x = v_i\Delta t + \frac{1}{2}a\Delta t^2$

$$= 2(4{,}32) + \frac{1}{2}(-9{,}8)(4{,}32)^2$$
$$= -82{,}81$$

$\therefore$ The helicopter is 82,81 m above the trampoline. (4)

38.2.2 **Method 1:**

$$v_f = v_i + a\Delta t$$
$$= 2 + (-9{,}8)(4{,}32)$$
$$= -40{,}34$$
$$= 40{,}34 \text{ m.s}^{-1} \text{ downwards}$$

Method 2:

$$v_f^2 = v_i^2 + 2a\Delta x$$
$$= 2^2 + 2(-9{,}8)(-82{,}81)$$
$$= 1627{,}08$$
$$v_f = 40{,}34 \text{ m.s}^{-1}$$ (4)

38.2.3

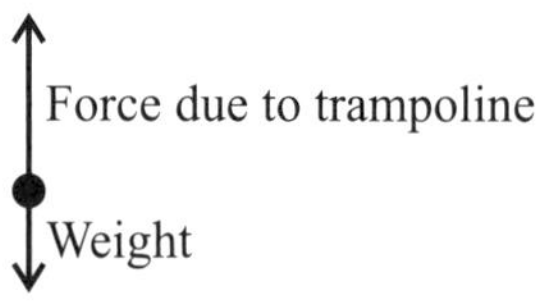

Arrow of trampoline must be longer than weight (3)

38.2.4 Upwards. The man is launched back into the air and therefore must experience a net force up. (2)

[21]

4. FORCES AND NEWTON'S LAWS

TYPES OF FORCES:

There are two types of forces that can be exerted on an object:

1. **Contact Forces:**
   These are **forces exerted between objects** which are **in contact** with each other. Examples of these forces are:
   - Applied forces on an object
   - Tension
   - Friction
   - Normal force

2. **Non-contact Forces:**
   These are **forces exerted between objects over a distance without any physical contact**.
   Examples of these forces:
   - Gravitational force
   - Electrostatic force (forces between charged particles)
   - Magnetic force

THE NORMAL FORCE

The **normal force** is the **perpendicular force exerted by a surface on an object** in contact with it.

Illustrative Example 1:
An object of mass 10kg rests on a flat horizontal surface with no applied forces acting on it.

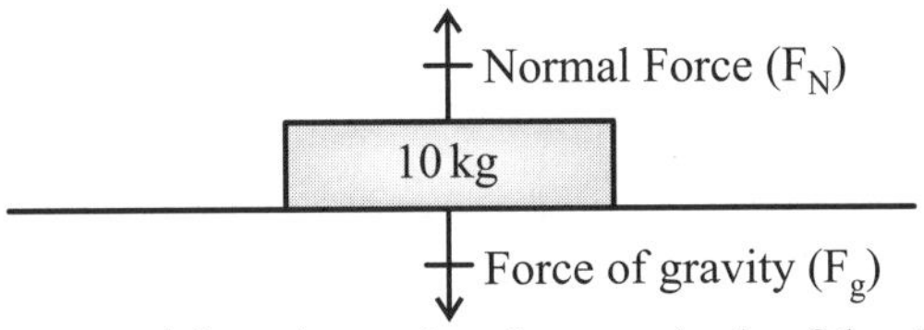

In this case the magnitude of the normal force is equal to the magnitude of the objects weight (force of gravity)

$$F_N = F_g$$

$$\begin{aligned} F_N &= F_g \\ &= ma \\ &= 10(9,8) \\ &= 98\text{ N} \end{aligned}$$

Illustrative Example 2:
An object of mass 10kg rests on a flat horizontal surface with a horizontal force applied.

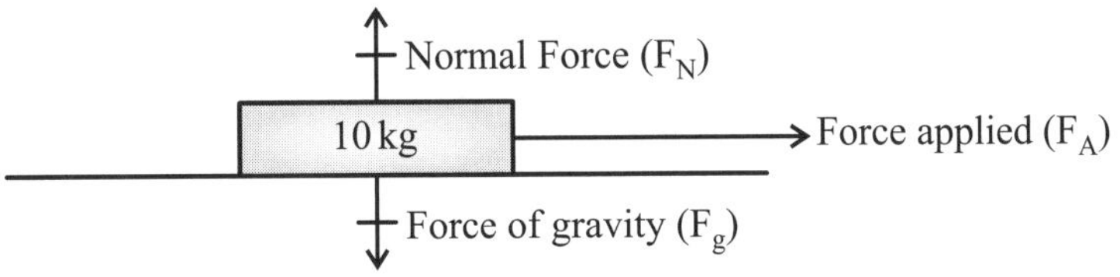

The horizontal force has no effect on the normal force.
The magnitude of the normal force is equal to the magnitude of objects weight (force of gravity)

$$F_N = F_g$$

$$\begin{aligned} F_N &= F_g \\ &= ma \\ &= 10(9,8) \\ &= 98\text{ N} \end{aligned}$$

Illustrative Example 3:

An object of mass 10kg is on a flat horizontal surface and is pulled by a force of 100N at an angle of 30°.

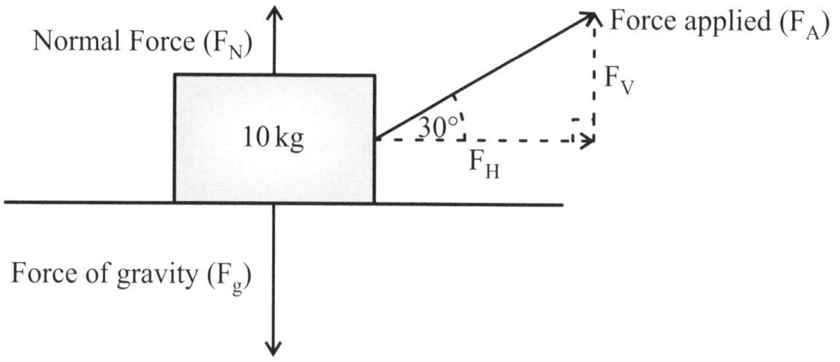

When a mass is **pulled at an angle** the force has a **horizontal (F_H)** and **vertical component (F_V)**.
The **vertical component** reduces the force pushing into the ground and therefore **reduces the normal force**.

$$F_N = F_g - F_v$$

$$\begin{aligned} F_N &= F_g - F_v \\ &= ma - F_A \sin\theta \\ &= 10(9,8) - 100\sin 30^\circ \\ &= 48 \text{ N} \end{aligned}$$

Illustrative Example 4:

An object of mass 10kg rests on a flat horizontal surface and is pushed by a force of 100N at an angle of 30°.

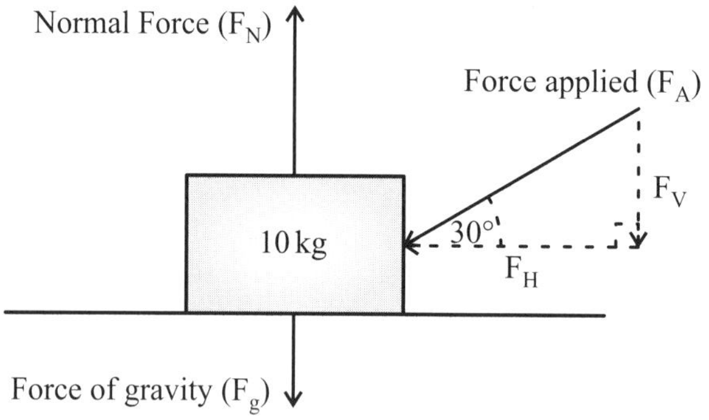

When a mass is **pushed at an angle** the force has a **horizontal (F_H)** and **vertical component (F_V)**.
The **vertical component** increases the force pushing into the ground and therefo**increases the normal force**.

$$F_N = F_g + F_v$$

$$\begin{aligned} F_N &= F_g + F_v \\ &= ma + F_A \sin\theta \\ &= 10(9,8) + 100\sin 30^\circ \\ &= 148 \text{ N} \end{aligned}$$

INCLINED PLANES

When an object rests on an inclined plane, the force of gravity acts straight down. The force of gravity is broken into two components.

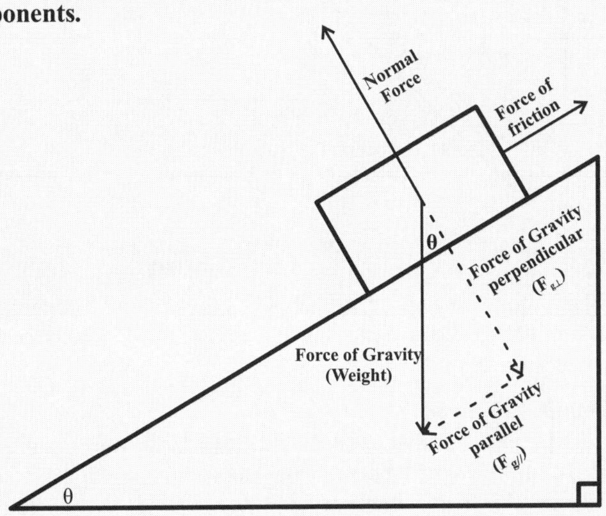

1. **A parallel component:**
   The parallel component acts parallel to the slope and pulls the object down the incline.

$$F_{//} = F_g \sin\theta$$

2. **A perpendicular component:**
   The perpendicular component acts perpendicular to the slope and pushes the object into the incline. This component is used in the calculation of the normal force.

$$F_{\perp} = F_g \cos\theta$$

> **If there are no applied or tension forces acting on the box at an angle, the perpendicular component of gravity is equal to the normal force.**
>
> **The frictional force always acts to oppose motion. If the mass slides down the slope, friction acts up the incline. If the mass moves up the incline, friction acts down the slope.**
>
> **The parallel component of gravity always acts down the incline.**

FRICTION

Friction is the force that opposes the motion of an object and acts parallel to the surface with which the object is in contact.
Frictional forces occur when an object is in contact with a surface. The **frictional force** an object experiences, is **due to the material that the object and surface are made of**. The rougher the object and surface are, the greater the force of friction between them. **Frictional forces** always **oppose motion.**

The coefficient of friction (μ_s and μ_k) is a description of the frictional force that an object will experience on a surface.
The **greater the coefficient of friction the greater the force of friction**.

There are two types of frictional forces:

1. **Static friction:**
   Static friction is the frictional force on a **stationary object** that opposes motion of the object.
   As the **parallel component of the applied force increases**, the **magnitude of the force of static friction will also increase**, until the maximum force of friction (F_{fs}^{max}) is reached.

   At this point the object will **just start to move.**

$$F_{fs}^{max} = \mu_s F_N$$

$F_{fs}^{max} \rightarrow$ maximum force of static friction (measured in Newtons)

$\mu_s \rightarrow$ coefficient of static friction (does not have units)

$F_N \rightarrow$ Normal force (measured in Newtons)

TOC 1 Data Sheet 2 Definitions 3 3 solutions 4 4 solutions 5 5 solutions 6 6 solutions 7 7 solutions 8 8 solutions 9 9 solutions 10 10 solutions

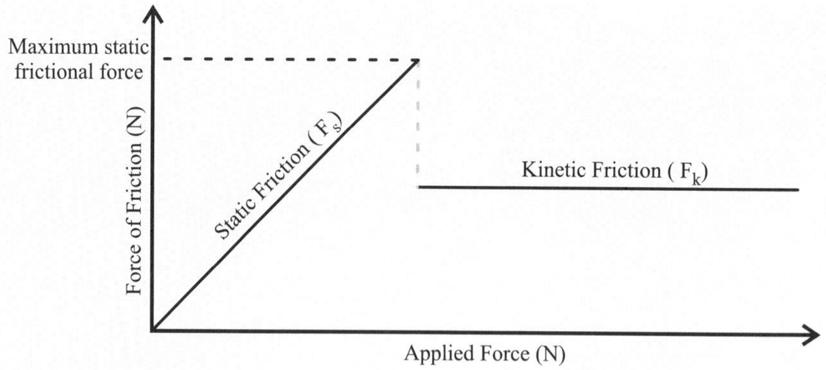

The above graph illustrates how the force of friction changes as the applied force increases up to the maximum frictional force. Once maximum frictional force is reached the object will start to move and the force of friction will decrease to kinetic friction (see below).

2. **Kinetic Friction (Dynamic Friction):**
   Kinetic friction is the frictional force that opposes the motion of a **moving object**.
   The force is constant and acts while the object is in motion.
   Kinetic friction is always smaller than static friction.

$$\mathbf{F}_{fk} = \mu_k \mathbf{F}_N$$

F_{fk} → Kinetic friction (measured in Newtons)

μ_k → coefficient of kinetic friction (does not have units)

F_N → Normal force (measured in Newtons)

If an object is pulled at an angle the normal force decreases and the force of friction decreases. If an object is pushed at an angle the normal force increases and the force of friction increases. Therefore, it is easier to pull an object at an angle than it is to push it at an angle.

Illustrative Example 1:

A crate of mass 50 kg is at rest on a flat horizontal surface. The coefficient of static friction between the crate and the surface is 0,3.

a) Determine the magnitude of the maximum force of static friction between the crate and the surface.

b) A force of 20 N to the right is applied to the crate. What is the force of friction while this force is applied?

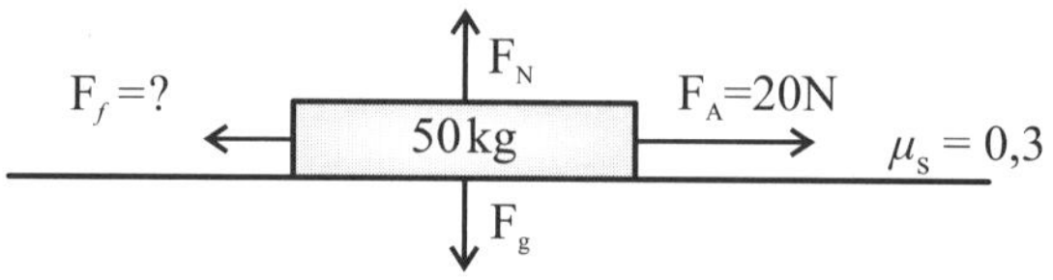

a) $F_{f\,max} = \mu_s F_N$

$= 0,3(9,8)(50)$

$= 147\ N$

b) 20N to the left. As the applied force is less than the maximum force of static friction, friction will apply the same force in the opposite direction to stop the crate from moving.
Friction cannot be greater than the applied force.

Illustrative Example 2:

A crate of mass 50 kg accelerates along a flat horizontal surface. The coefficient of kinetic friction between the crate and the surface is 0,1. While accelerating, a force of 100 N acts on the crate at an angle of 30° to the horizontal. Determine the magnitude of the force of friction acting on the crate while it is accelerating.

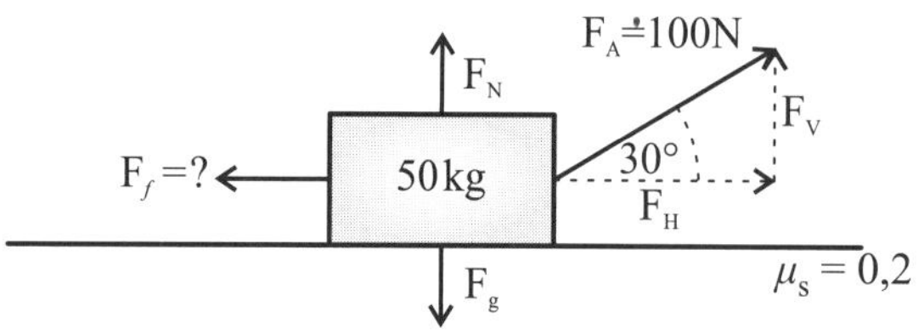

$F_V = 100 \sin 30$

$F_N = F_g - F_V$

$= 50(9,8) - 100 \sin 30$

$= 440\ N$

$F_f = \mu_k F_N$

$= 0,1(440)$

$= 44\ N$

Illustrative Example 3:

A crate of mass 10 kg slides down a slope inclined at 60° to the horizontal. The coefficient of kinetic friction between the crate and the surface of the slope is 0,4. Determine the magnitude of the frictional force acting on the crate as it slides down the slope.

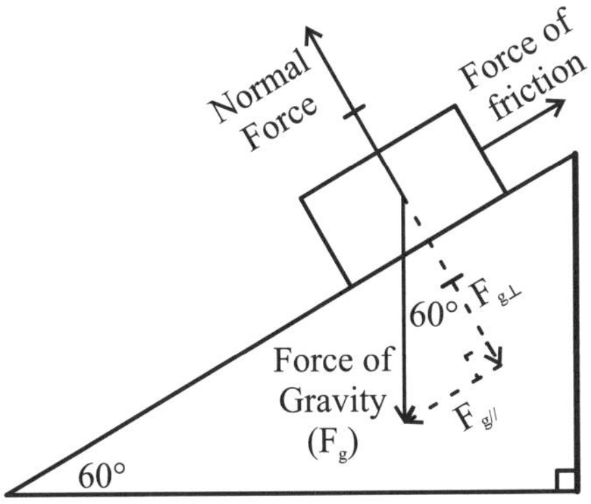

$$F_N = F_{g\perp}$$
$$= 10(9,8)\cos 60$$
$$= 49\text{ N}$$
$$F_f = \mu_k F_N$$
$$= 0,4(49)$$
$$= 19,6\text{ N}$$

NEWTON'S FIRST LAW OF MOTION (THE PROPERTY OF INERTIA):

Inertia is the **property** of an object **that causes it to resist a change in its state of rest or uniform motion.**

Newton's first law states:
An object continues in a state of rest or uniform (moving with constant) velocity unless it is acted upon by a net or resultant force.

Newton's first law **applies** to all cases where the **net or resultant force is zero.**
An objects **inertia** is dependent on its **mass.**

If an object is at rest or moving at a constant velocity the resultant force on the object is zero.
Inertia is a property of an object due to its mass. It is not a force.

Illustrative Examples:

1. When travelling in a car without a seatbelt, if the car suddenly stops, the passenger continues moving.
2. A magician quickly pulls a tablecloth off a table leaving the cutlery in place.
3. A ball is held above a small bucket inside a high-speed train. When it is released it lands in the bucket directly below it. This is because the ball continues to move at the same velocity and lands directly beneath it when dropped. The ball does not move backwards.
4. When standing on a bus, a passenger falls backwards when the bus accelerates.
This is because the body wishes to remain stationary and resists the change in its motion due to inertia.

NEWTON'S SECOND LAW OF MOTION:

When a **net force**, F_{net}, is **applied to an object** of mass, m, **it accelerates in the direction of the net force.** The **acceleration**, *a*, is **directly proportional** to the **net force** and **inversely proportional to the mass.**

$$\mathbf{F_{net} = ma}$$

Illustrative Example 1:

A force of 100 N East is applied to an object of mass 10kg. There is a frictional force of 25N that acts between the surface and the object. Determine the acceleration of the object.

Taking East as positive:

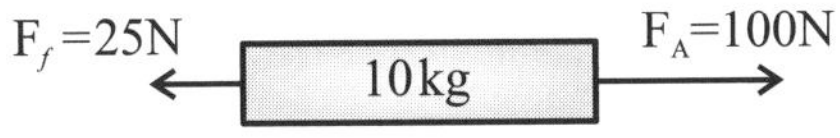

$$F_{net} = ma$$
$$F_A - F_f = ma$$
$$100 - 25 = 10a$$
$$75 = 10a$$
$$a = 7,5\text{ m.s}^{-2}\text{ East}$$

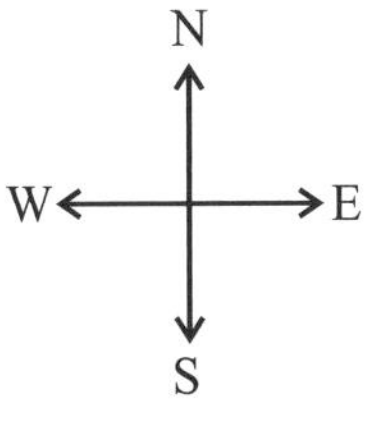

Illustrative Example 2:

A force of 100 N pulls an object of mass 10 kg to the right at an angle of 60° above the horizontal as shown in the diagram below. The coefficient of kinetic friction between the box and the surface is 0,1. Determine the acceleration of the object.

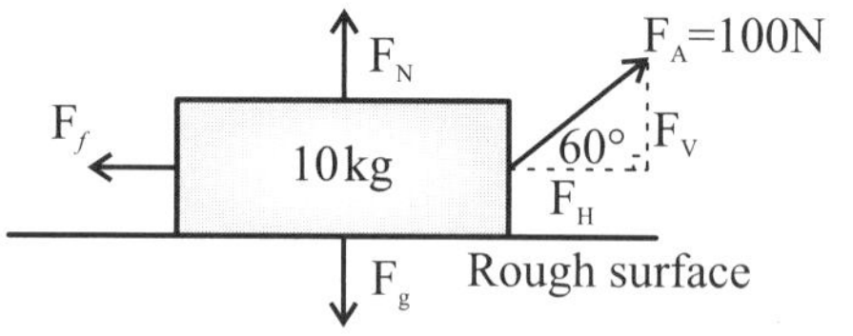

$$F_H = F_A \cos\theta$$
$$= 100\cos 60$$
$$= 50\,N$$

$$F_N = F_g - F_v$$
$$= 10(9,8) - 100\sin 60$$
$$= 11,40\,N$$

$$F_f = \mu_k F_N$$
$$= 0,1(11,40)$$
$$= 1,14\,N$$

$$F_{net} = ma$$
$$F_H - F_f = ma$$
$$50 - 1,14 = 10a$$
$$48,86 = 10a$$
$$a = 4,89\,m.s^{-2} \text{ right}$$

Illustrative Example 3:

A force of 100 N is pushes an object of mass 10kg to the right at an angle of 60° to the horizontal as shown in the diagram below. The coefficient of kinetic friction between the box and the surface is 0,1. Determine the acceleration of the object.

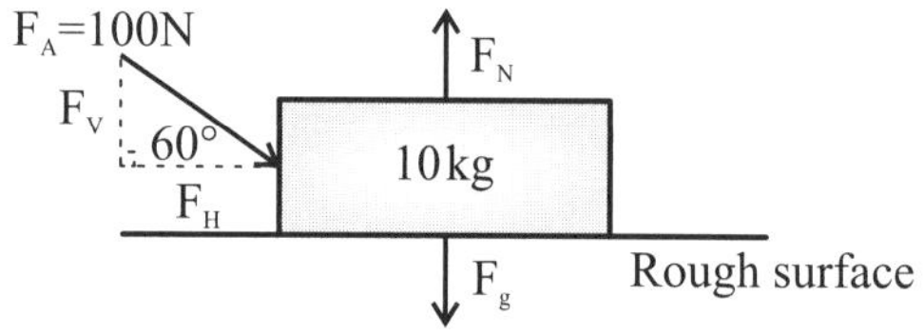

$$F_H = F_A \cos\theta$$
$$= 100\cos 60$$
$$= 50\,N$$

$$F_N = F_g + F_v$$
$$= 10(9,8) + 100\sin 60$$
$$= 184,60\,N$$

$$F_f = \mu_k F_N$$
$$= 0,1(184,60)$$
$$= 18,46\,N$$

$$F_{net} = ma$$
$$F_H - F_f = ma$$
$$50 - 18,46 = 10a$$
$$31,54 = 10a$$
$$a = 3,15\,m.s^{-2} \text{ right}$$

Illustrative Example 4:

An object is pulled up an incline angled at 30° to the horizontal. An applied force of 600 N acts at an angle of 20° to the incline and causes the object to accelerate up the incline at 4,62 m.s^{-2}. Determine the coefficient of kinetic friction as the object accelerates up the slope.

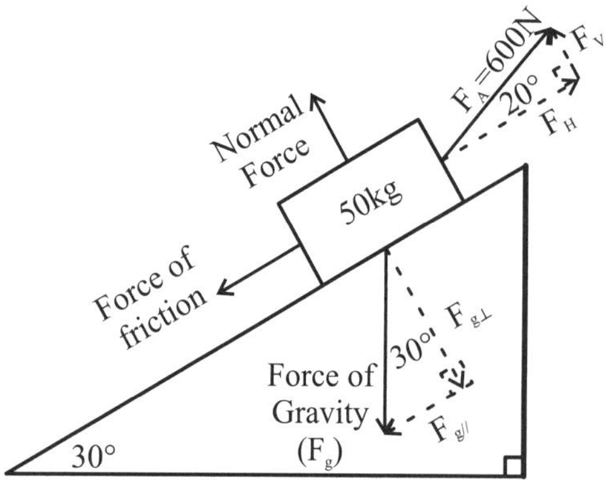

$$F_H = F_A \cos 20$$
$$= 600\cos 20$$

$$F_{g//} = F_g \sin 30$$
$$= 50(9,8)(\sin 30)$$
$$= 245\,N$$

$$F_{net} = ma$$
$$F_H - F_{//} - F_f = ma$$
$$600\cos 20 - 245 - F_f = 50(4,62)$$
$$F_f = 87,82\,N$$
$$F_N = F_\perp - F_V$$
$$= 490\cos 30 - 600\sin 20$$
$$F_f = \mu F_N$$
$$87,82 = \mu(490\cos 30 - 600\sin 20)$$
$$\mu = 0,4$$

Illustrative Example 5:

A cars engine applies force of 5 200 N to keep the car moving up an incline at a constant speed. The car has a mass of 1200 kg and the frictional forces acting on the car while moving up the incline are 1800 N.

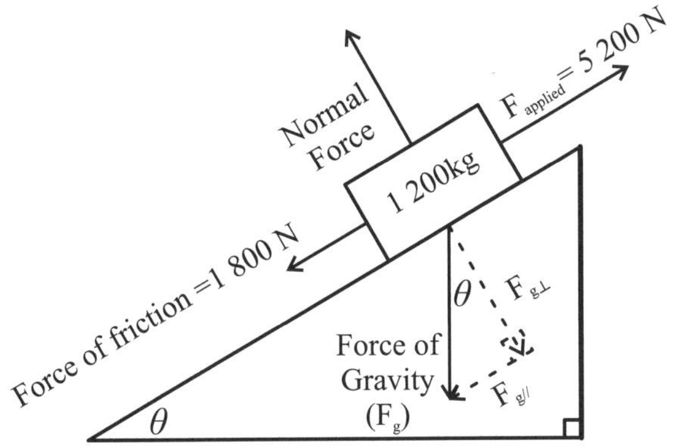

a) Draw a free body diagram showing all of the forces acting on the car.
b) Calculate the magnitude of the cars weight acting down the slope.
c) Calculate the angle of the incline.
d) Calculate the coefficient of kinetic friction between the car and the slope.

a)

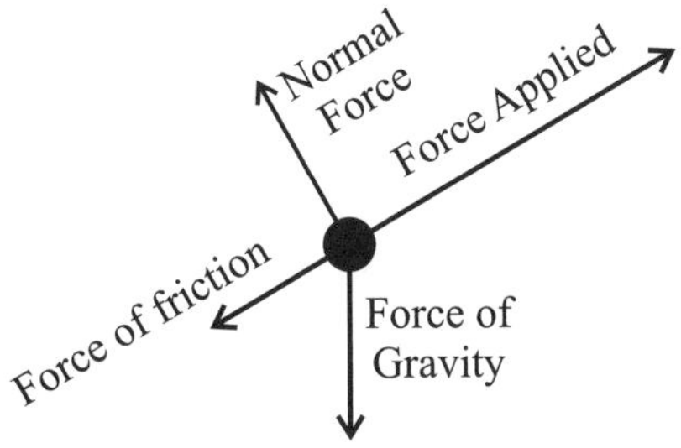

> **When drawing a free body diagram of an object on a slope, do not include the perpendicular and parallel component of gravity. These are vectors which sum to the weight of the object. If these were included, you would be placing weight on the diagram twice.**
>
> **Alternatively, you can include the components of gravity on the diagram. However, you would then not include force of gravity acting straight down.**

b) $F_{net} = ma \rightarrow$ the car is travelling at a constant velocity, this means that acelleration is 0

$$F_A - F_f - F_{//} = 0$$
$$5\,200 - 1800 = F_{//}$$
$$F_{//} = 3\,400 \text{ N}$$

c) $F_{//} = F_g \sin\theta$

$$F_{//} = mg\sin\theta$$
$$3\,400 = 1200(9{,}8)\sin\theta$$
$$\sin\theta = \frac{3\,400}{1200(9{,}8)}$$
$$\theta = 16{,}81$$

d) $F_f = \mu F_N$

$F_f = \mu(mg\cos\theta) \rightarrow$ the normal force is equal in magnitude to the perpindicular component of weight

$$3\,400 = \mu$$
$$\mu = \frac{3\,400}{(1200)(9{,}8)(\cos 16{,}81)}$$
$$= 0{,}30$$

TOC 1 Data Sheet 2 Definitions 3 3 solutions 4 4 solutions 5 5 solutions 6 6 solutions 7 7 solutions 8 8 solutions 9 9 solutions 10 10 solutions

CONNECTED OBJECTS

When dealing with **connected objects**, **each object** in the system has the **same acceleration**.
There are two methods which can be used to solve problems with connected objects.

Method 1:
Treat each object individually and draw a free body diagram of each object in the system.
Use simultaneous equations to first determine the acceleration of the system and the force (tension) connecting the objects.

Method 2:
Treat the system as one object (ignoring the tension force) connecting the objects to determine the acceleration.
The force connecting the objects can be ignored as it does not affect the acceleration.
After determining the acceleration, use one of the objects to determine the force (tension) connecting the objects.
Method 2 can only be used if all objects are accelerating in the same direction.

> **Take note of the important points below:**
> - **The magnitude of the force exerted on different objects by a single rope, bar or string is the same on all objects.**
> - **An applied force only acts on one object. It does not transfer to a connected or touching object.**
> - **It is normally easiest to take the direction of acceleration as positive.**

Illustrative Example 1:

A horizontal force of 100N is applied to a 15kg block which is connected to a 10kg block by a light inextensible string. The force of friction on the 15kg block is 10N whilst the force of friction acting on the 10kg block is 7N. Determine the magnitude of the acceleration of the system as well as the tension in the connecting string.

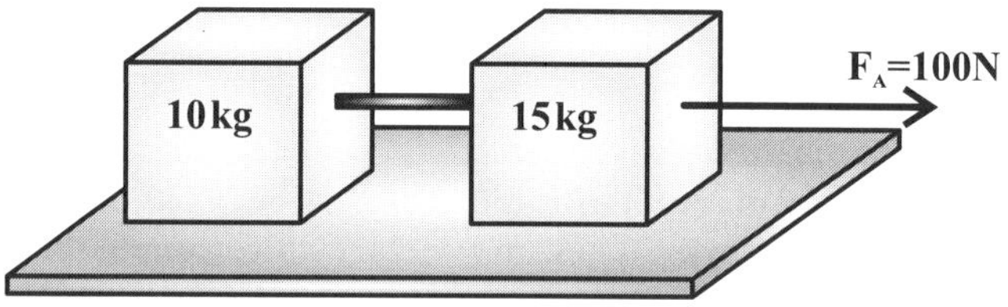

Method 1:

10kg:

$F_{net} = ma$

$T - 7 = 10a \rightarrow \boxed{1}$

Substitute $\boxed{2}$ into $\boxed{1}$:

$90 - 15a - 7 = 10a$

$a = 3{,}32\,m.s^{-2} \rightarrow \boxed{3}$

Substitute $\boxed{3}$ into $\boxed{1}$:

$T - 7 = 10(3{,}32)$

$T = 40{,}2\,N$

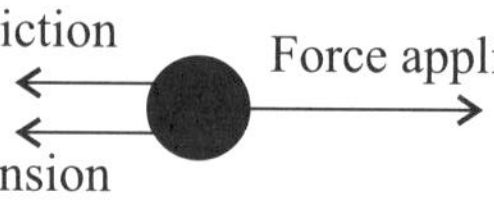

15kg:

$F_{net} = ma$

$F_A - F_f - T = ma$

$100 - 10 - T = 15a$

$T = 90 - 15a \rightarrow \boxed{2}$

Method 2:

10kg:

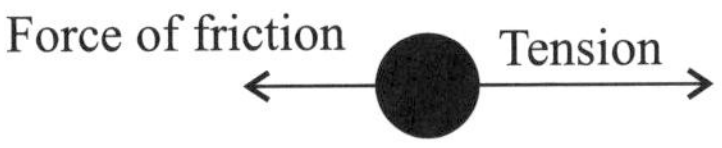

15kg:

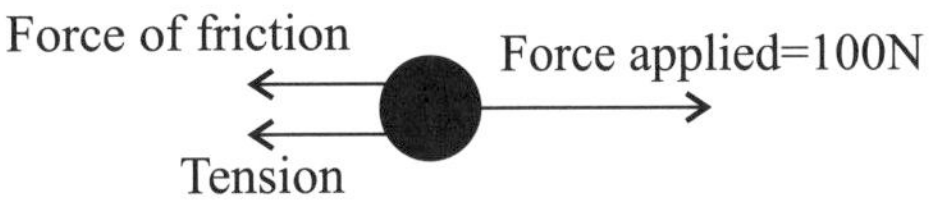

$F_{net} = ma$

$F_A - F_{f15kg} - F_{f10kg} = ma$

$100 - 10 - 7 = (15 + 10)a$

$83 = 25a$

$a = 3{,}32\,m.s^{-1}$

Now use either the 15kg or 10kg block to calculate the tension:

Using the 10kg mass:	**OR**	Using the 15kg mass:
$T - 7 = ma$		$F_A - F_f - T = ma$
$T = 10(3{,}32) + 7$		$100 - 10 - T = 15(3{,}32)$
$= 40{,}2\ N$		$T = 40{,}2\ N$

<u>Illustrative Example 2</u>:

A 15kg block is connected to a 10kg block by a light inextensible string running over a frictionless pulley as shown in the diagram below. The force of friction between the table and the 10kg block is 7N. Determine the magnitude of the acceleration of the system as well as the tension in the connecting string.

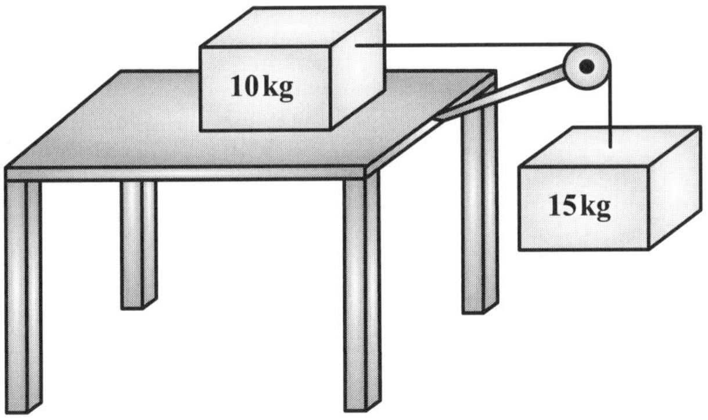

10kg: (take right as positive)

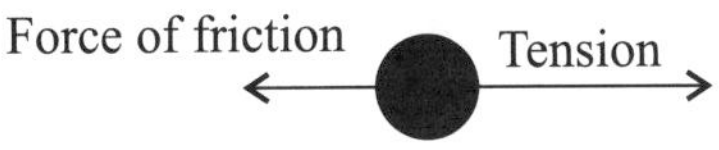

15kg: (take down as positive)

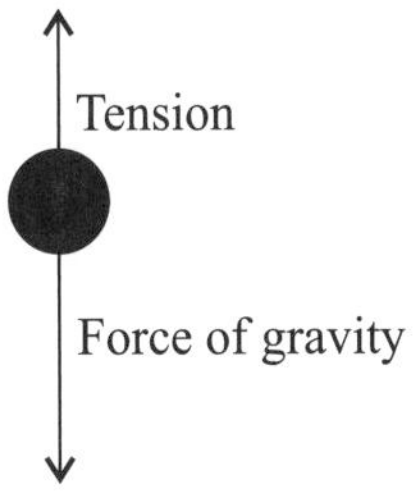

10kg:

$F_{net} = ma$

$T - F_f = ma$

$T - 7 = 10a$

$T = 10a + 7 \rightarrow \boxed{1}$

15kg:

$F_{net} = ma$

$F_g - T = ma$

$15(9{,}8) - T = 15a$

$147 - T = 15a \rightarrow \boxed{2}$

Substitute $\boxed{1}$ into $\boxed{2}$:

$147 - (10a + 7) = 15a$

$140 - 10a = 15a$

$a = 5{,}6\,m.s^{-2} \rightarrow \boxed{3}$

Substitute $\boxed{3}$ into $\boxed{2}$:

$147 - T = 15(5{,}6)$

$T = 63\,N$

Method 2 cannot be used in this example as the direction of the acceleration of each block is different. Therefore, the objects cannot be treated as a single system.

TOC 1 Data Sheet 2 Definitions 3 3 solutions 4 4 solutions 5 5 solutions 6 6 solutions 7 7 solutions 8 8 solutions 9 9 solutions 10 10 solutions

Illustrative Example 3:

A 10kg block rests against 15kg block on a rough surface. A 100N horizontal force is applied to the 10kg block. The 10kg block experiences a frictional force of 7N while the 15kg block experiences a frictional force of 10N. Determine the magnitude of the acceleration of the system and the force the 10kg block exerts on the 15kg block.

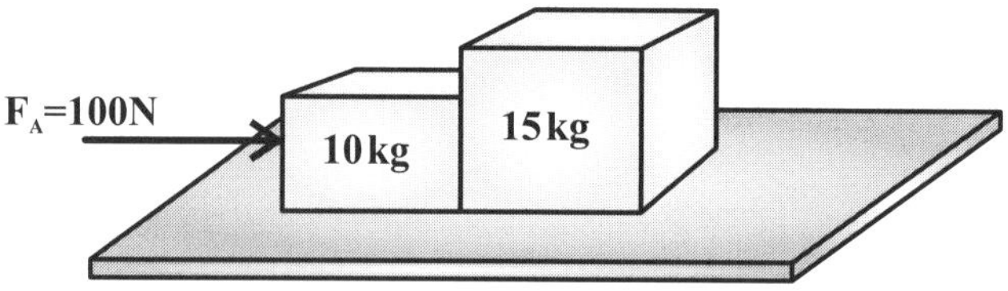

From Newton's 3rd Law (see page 98), the force the 10kg block exerts on the 15kg block is equal in magnitude to the force of the 15kg block on the 10kg block.

Method 1:

10kg:

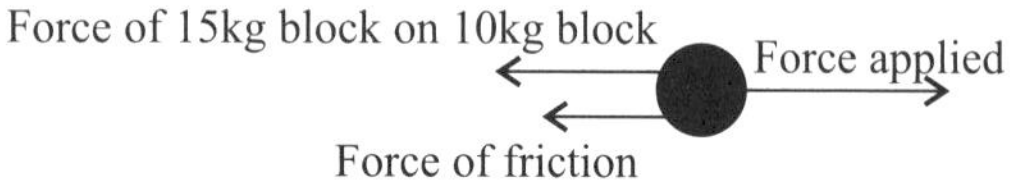

15kg:

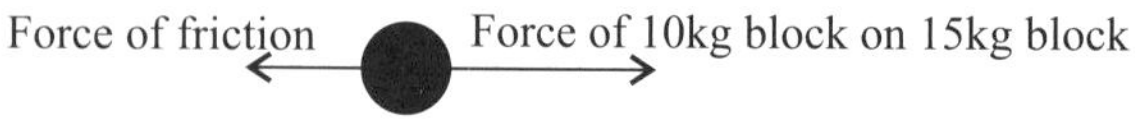

Let the magnitude of the force of the 15kg block on the 10kg block be x.

10kg:

$F_{net} = ma$

$F_A - F_f - x = ma$

$100 - 7 - x = 10a$

$x = 93 - 10a \rightarrow \boxed{1}$

15kg:

$F_{net} = ma$

$x - F_f = ma$

$x - 10 = 15a \rightarrow \boxed{2}$

Substitute $\boxed{1}$ into $\boxed{2}$:

$93 - 10a - 10 = 15a$

$83 = 25a$

$a = 3{,}32\,\text{m.s}^{-2} \rightarrow \boxed{3}$

Substitute $\boxed{3}$ into $\boxed{2}$:

$x - 10 = 15(3{,}32)$

$x = 59{,}8\,\text{N}$ to the right

Method 2:

10kg:

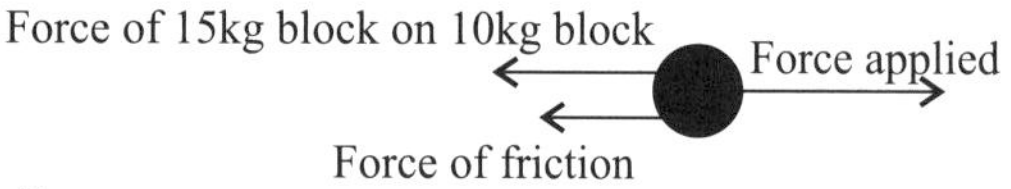

15kg:

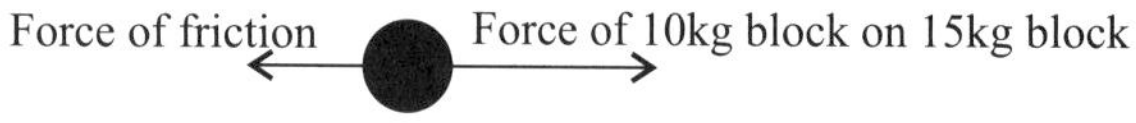

$F_{net} = ma$

$F_A - F_{f10kg} - F_{f15kg} = ma$

$100 - 7 - 10 = (10 + 15)a$

$83 = 25a$

$a = 3{,}32\,\text{m.s}^{-2}$

Let the magnitude of the force of the 15kg block on the 10kg block be x.
Using the 10kg mass:

$F_A - F_{f10kg} - x = ma$

$100 - 7 - x = 10(3{,}32)$

$x = 59{,}8$ N to the right

LIFT PROBLEMS:

When dealing with **elevator problems** it is easiest to **choose the direction of acceleration as positive.**

If a lift **accelerates upwards** the **tension** in the cable is **greater** than the force of **gravity**.

If a lift **accelerates downwards** the force of **gravity** is **greater than** the **tension** in the cable.

If a lift is **stationary or moves at a constant the velocity** the **tension** in the cable **equals** the force of **gravity**

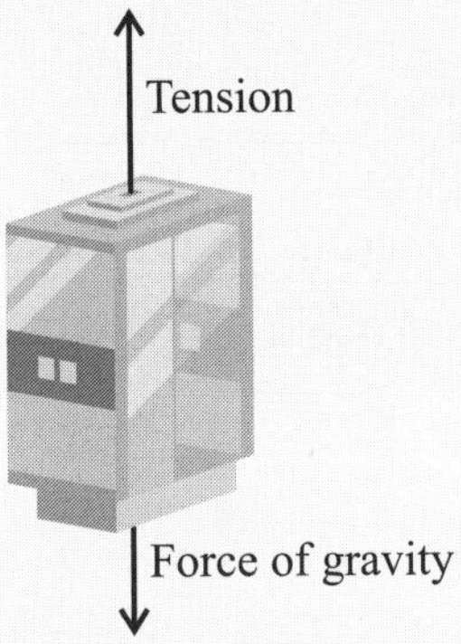

Acceleration upwards
Tension > Gravity
$T - F_g = ma$

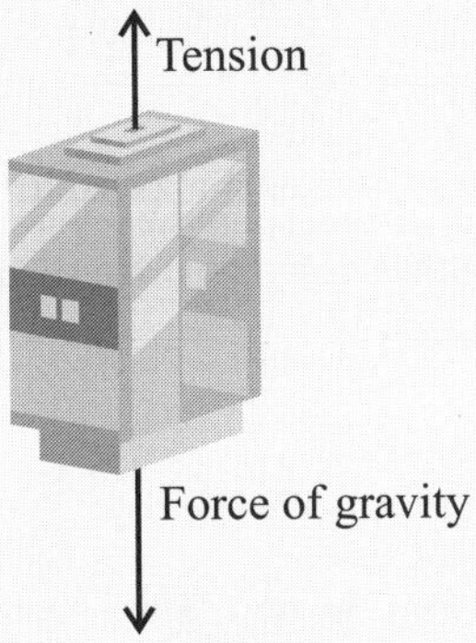

Acceleration downwards
Gravity > Tension
$F_g - T = ma$

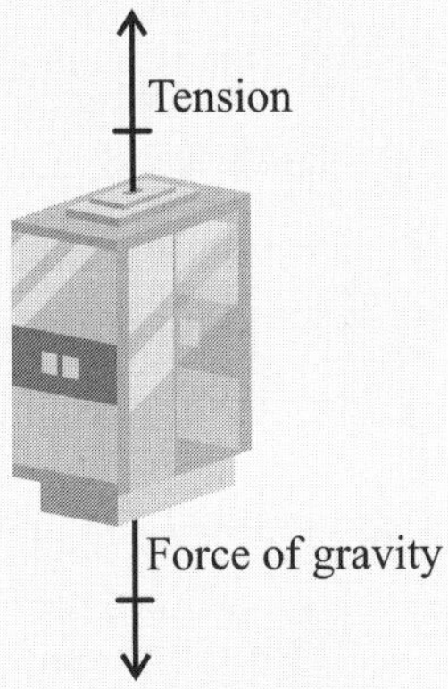

Constant velocity / Stationary
Tension = Gravity
$F_g = T$

OBJECTS IN A LIFT:

If an object is on a scale in a lift the **scale reads the normal force.**

If a lift **accelerates upwards** the **normal force** is **greater than** the force of **gravity**.

If a lift **accelerates downwards** the **normal force** is **less than** the force of **gravity**.

If a lift is **stationary or moves at a constant the velocity** the **normal force equals** the force of **gravity**.

If the **cable snaps** the object and the scale are in freefall and the **scale reads zero.**

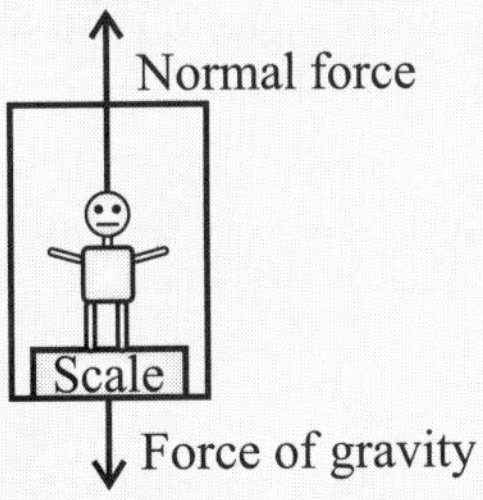

Acceleration upwards
Normal force > Gravity
Scale reads greater than actual weight
$F_N - F_g = ma$

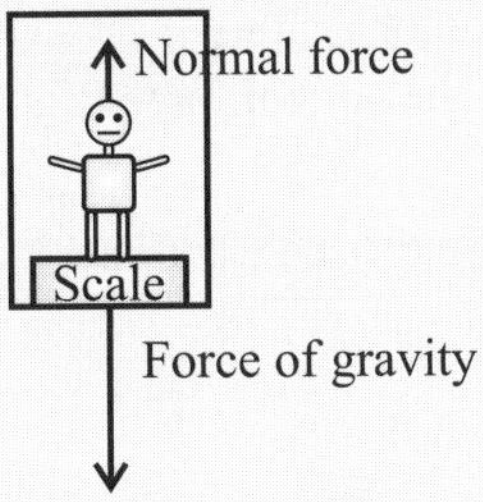

Acceleration downwards
Normal force < Gravity
Scale reads less than actual weight
$F_g - F_N = ma$

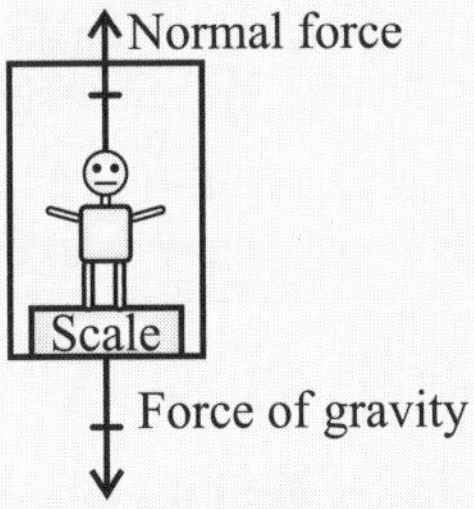

Constant velocity / Stationary
Normal force = Gravity
Scale reads actual weight
$F_N = F_g$

> **The direction of motion is not always the same as the direction of acceleration.**
> **If a lift is slowing down the direction of acceleration is opposite to the direction of motion.**

Illustrative Example 1:

A person of mass 60 kg stands on a bathroom scale in a lift. What will be the reading, in Newton, on the scale if the lift accelerates upwards at 2 m.s^{-2}?

$F_{net} = ma$

$F_N - F_g = ma$ → The normal force is greater than gravity as acceleration is upwards

$F_N - 60(9{,}8) = 60(2)$

$F_N = 708$ N

∴ The scale will read 708 N

> **When standing on a scale, the scale reading is equal to the normal force.**

TOC | 1 Data Sheet | 2 Definitions | 3 | 3 solutions | 4 | 4 solutions | 5 | 5 solutions | 6 | 6 solutions | 7 | 7 solutions | 8 | 8 solutions | 9 | 9 solutions | 10 | 10 solutions

Illustrative Example 2:

A man with a weight of 750N places a bathroom scale on the floor of a stationary lift and stands on the scale. Explain how the reading on the scale will compare to the man's weight if:

a) The lift is travelling upwards at a constant velocity.

b) The lift is stationary.

c) The lift is accelerating upwards.

d) The lift is accelerating downwards.

e) The lift is moving upwards and slows down as it approaches the floor it is to stop at.

f) The lift is moving downwards and slows down as it approaches the floor it is to stop at.

g) The cable of the lift breaks and the lift goes into freefall.

Solutions:

a) The scale will read 750N.
At a constant velocity, the resultant force is zero. The normal force is equal to the force of gravity.

b) The scale will read 750N.
When the lift is stationary the resultant force is zero. The normal force is equal to the force of gravity.

c) The scale will read a value greater than 750N.
When the lift accelerates up, the normal force is greater than the force of gravity.

d) The scale will read a value less than 750N.
When the lift accelerates downwards, the normal force is less than the force of gravity.

e) The scale will read a value less than 750N.
If the lift is moving up, but its velocity is decreasing, the direction of acceleration is downwards.
When the lift accelerates downwards, the normal force is less than the force of gravity.

f) The scale will read a value greater than 750N.
If the lift is moving downwards, but its velocity is decreasing, the direction of acceleration is upwards.
When the lift accelerates upwards, the normal force is greater than the force of gravity.

g) The scale will read 0 N.
In freefall there is no force acting on the scale and therefore no normal force.

Illustrative Example 3:

A lift of mass 500 kg is certified to carry a maximum mass of 800 kg. The lift is designed so that magnitude of its acceleration does not exceed 1,5 m.s^{-2}.

a) What is the greatest tension in the cable at an acceleration of 1,5 m.s^{-2}?

b) The maximum force the lifts cable can withstand is 15 990 N. What is the maximum acceleration the lift can maintain without breaking the cable?

a) Greatest tension is when acceleration is upwards.

$$F_{net} = ma$$

$$T - F_g = ma$$

$$T - 1300(9,8) = 1300(1,5)$$

$$T = 14690\text{ N}$$

b)

$$F_{net} = ma$$

$$T - F_g = ma$$

$$15990 - 1300(9,8) = 1300a$$

$$a_{max} = 2,5\text{ m.s}^{-2}$$

NEWTONS THIRD LAW OF MOTION:

When **object A exerts a force on object B**, **object B** simultaneously **exerts** an **oppositely directed** force of **equal magnitude on object A.** These are known as **action reaction force pairs**.

In the above diagram the **boy exerts a force on the wall** and the **wall exerts the same force back on the boy** but **in the opposite direction**. As **these forces act on different objects**, they **cannot cancel** each other out and the boy would accelerate backwards due to the force the wall exerts on him.

Examine the diagram below:

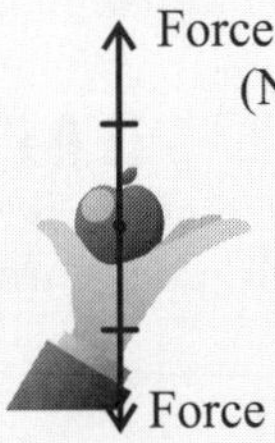

In the above diagram, there are four forces acting.

1. Force of earth on the apple (the apples weight).
2. Force of apple on the hand.
3. Force of hand on apple (normal force).
4. Force of apple on earth.

There are two action reaction force pairs:

1. Force of earth on the apple and force of apple on earth.
2. Force of apple on the hand and force of hand on apple.

The **weight of an object** is the **force that the earth exerts on an object**. The **reaction force of an objects weight** is always the **force of the object on the earth.**

The force of the hand on the apple and the force of the earth on apple are not action reaction pairs.

Action reaction force pairs act on different objects and never cancel with each other. Newton's laws always apply. In any situation, the force one object exerts on the other are always equal in magnitude and opposite in direction.

Illustrative Example 1:

Using two of Newton's laws explain how a rocket moves in the vacuum of space.

Solution:
When fuel is burnt in the engine, gases are forced out of the rocket engine. This means the rocket exerts a force on the gases and according to Newton's 3rd law the gases exert a force equal in magnitude but opposite in direction on the rocket. This causes the rocket to experience a resultant force and according to Newton's 2nd law the rocket will accelerate in the direction of the resultant force.

Illustrative Example 2:

A girl of mass m stands behind a boy of mass $2m$ on a frictionless surface. The girl pushes the boy to the right with a force of F and he accelerates to the right with acceleration a. Using Newton's laws describe what would happen to the girl. Make specific reference to the acceleration that the girl would experience.

Solution:
When the girl pushes on the boy the boy experiences a force F to the right. According to Newton's 3rd law the girl will experience a force of magnitude F to the left. According to Newton's 2nd law the girl will accelerate to the left.

From Newton's 2nd law: $a = \frac{F_{net}}{m}$

This means that acceleration is inversely proportional to mass. (as long as force is constant). The force acting on the boy and the girl are the same, but the girl has half the mass of the boy. Therefore, the girl will accelerate to the left with an acceleration of $2a$.

NEWTON'S UNIVERSAL LAW OF GRAVITATION

Every particle with mass in the universe attracts every other particle with a force which is directly proportional to the product of their masses and inversely proportional to the square of the distance between their centres.

$$\mathbf{F = \frac{G\,m_1 m_2}{r^2}}$$

$F \rightarrow$ Force of attraction between two objects (measured in Newtons)

$G \rightarrow$ Universal gravitational constant $\left(6{,}7\times10^{-11}\ \text{N.m}^2.\text{kg}^{-2}\right)$

$m_1 \rightarrow$ Mass of object 1 (measured in kilograms)

$m_2 \rightarrow$ Mass of object 2 (measured in kilograms)

$r \rightarrow$ distance between the **centres** of the two objects (measured in metres)

DETERMINING GRAVITATIONAL ACCELERATION ON A PLANET

The **gravitational acceleration** on a planet is **independent of the mass of an object** on the planet. It is only **dependant** on the **mass of the planet** and the **distance from the centre of the planet**.

$$\mathbf{g = \frac{G\,M_p}{r^2}}$$

$g \rightarrow$ gravitational acceleration (measured in m.s^{-2})

$G \rightarrow$ Universal gravitational constant $\left(6{,}7\times10^{-11}\ \text{N.m}^2.\text{kg}^{-2}\right)$

$M_p \rightarrow$ Mass of the planet (measured in kilograms)

$r \rightarrow$ distance from the centre of the planet (measured in metres)

Proof:

From Newton's 2nd law $F_g = m_{object}\,g$:

$$F_g = \frac{G\,M_{planet}\,m_{object}}{r^2}$$

$$m_{object}\,g = \frac{G\,M_{planet}\,m_{object}}{r^2} \rightarrow \div \text{ both sides by } m_{object}$$

$$g = \frac{G\,M_{planet}}{r^2}$$

> **Do not confuse Fg with *g*. Fg is the gravitational force experienced between two objects due to their mass and is measured in Newtons.**
>
> ***g* is gravitational acceleration which is specific to a planet and is measured in m.s^{-2}.**

MASS VS WEIGHT

Mass	Weight (Force of gravity)
The **amount of substance** that an object is made from.	The **force** of attraction between a planet and an object.
Constant anywhere in the universe.	**Differs** depending on the mass of the planet and the distance from the planets centre.
Measured in **kilograms** (kg).	Measured in **Newtons** (N).
Scalar quantity.	**Vector quantity**.

Illustrative Example 1:

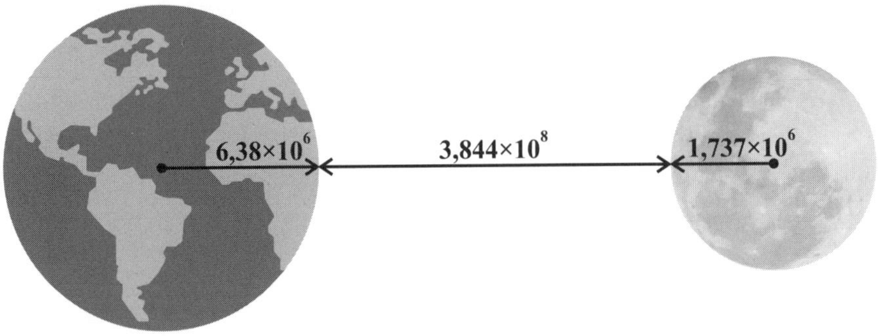

The Earth has a radius $6,38\times10^{6}$ m and is $3,844\times10^{8}$ m from the moon which has radius of $1,737\times10^{6}$ m. If the mass of the Earth is $5,97\times10^{24}$ kg and the mass of the Moon is $7,35\times10^{22}$ kg. Determine the gravitational force experienced between the planets.

$$F = \frac{G m_1 m_2}{r^2}$$

$$= \frac{\left(6,7\times10^{-11}\right)\left(5,97\times10^{24}\right)\left(7,35\times10^{22}\right)}{\left(6,38\times10^{6}+3,844\times10^{8}+1,737\times10^{6}\right)^2}$$

$$= 1,91\times10^{20}\text{ N}$$

Illustrative Example 2:

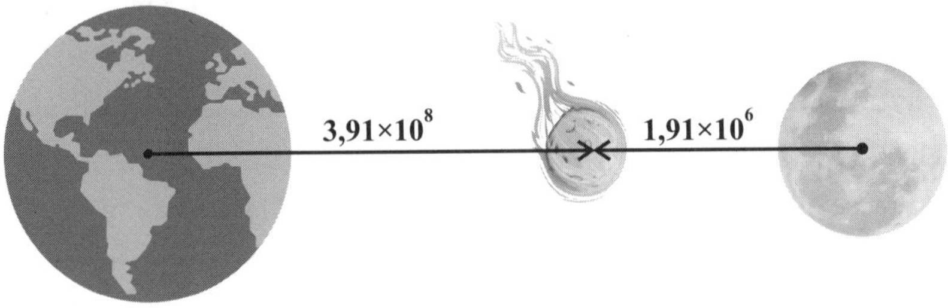

An asteroid with a mass of 200 tons passes between the earth and the moon. At the point where all three are in a straight line the centre of the asteroid is $3,91\times10^{8}$ m from the centre of the Earth and $1,91\times10^{6}$ m from the centre of the Moon. Determine the resultant force acting on the asteroid. You may use masses given in the example above for the Earth and the Moon.

Force of Earth on asteroid

$$F_{EA} = \frac{G m_1 m_2}{r^2}$$

$$= \frac{\left(6,7\times10^{-11}\right)\left(5,97\times10^{24}\right)\left(200\times10^{3}\right)}{\left(3,91\times10^{8}\right)^2}$$

$$= 523,27\text{ N towards the Earth}$$

Force of Moon on asteroid

$$F_{MA} = \frac{G m_1 m_2}{r^2}$$

$$= \frac{\left(6,7\times10^{-11}\right)\left(7,35\times10^{22}\right)\left(200\times10^{3}\right)}{\left(1,91\times10^{6}\right)^2}$$

$$= 269976,15\text{ towards the Moon}$$

$$F_{net} = 269976,15 - 523,27$$

$$= 269452,88\text{ N towards the Moon}$$

When dealing with small objects such as people and satellites, the distance from their centre to the surface of the object is small and may be ignored.

When dealing with large objects such as planets and asteroids, you must take the distance from the centre of the planet or object to its surface into account.

DEALING WITH RATIOS

When dealing with ratios you are considering the factor that each mass or distance has changed by.

Illustrative Example 1:

Two objects of mass M and m have centres which are separated by a distance of r. At this distance they exert a force of F on each other. If the distance between them is doubled what force will they exert on each other?

$$F_{new} = F\left[\frac{(1)(1)}{(2)^2}\right] \rightarrow \text{from } \frac{Gm_1m_2}{r^2} \rightarrow \text{the radius increased by a factor of 2}$$

$$= \frac{F}{4}$$

Illustrative Example 2:

Object A of mass M and object B of Mass 3M have centres separated by a distance of x. At this distance they exert a force of F on each other. If the distance between the objects is halved and the mass of A is doubled what is the new force experienced between the objects?

$$F_{new} = F\left[\frac{(2)(1)}{\left(\frac{1}{2}\right)^2}\right] \rightarrow \text{from } \frac{Gm_1m_2}{r^2}$$

$$= 8F$$

The numbers used in the formula are not the distances between the object's centres or the actual mass of the objects. It is the factor that the distance between the objects or the mass of the objects changes by.

Illustrative Example 3:

Two objects exert a force of F on each other. The distance is changed by a factor of x so that the new force between the objects is now $4F$. Determine the value of x.

$$4F = F\left[\frac{(1)(1)}{(x)^2}\right]$$

$$4 = \frac{1}{x^2}$$

$$x^2 = \frac{1}{4}$$

$$x = \frac{1}{2}$$

Illustrative Example 4:

On Earth a satellite has weight W. What will it's weight be when it orbits the Earth at distance of twice the radius of the Earth?

$$W_{new} = W\left[\frac{(1)(1)}{(3)^2}\right] \rightarrow \text{the distance has increased by a factor of 3}$$

$$= \frac{W}{9}$$

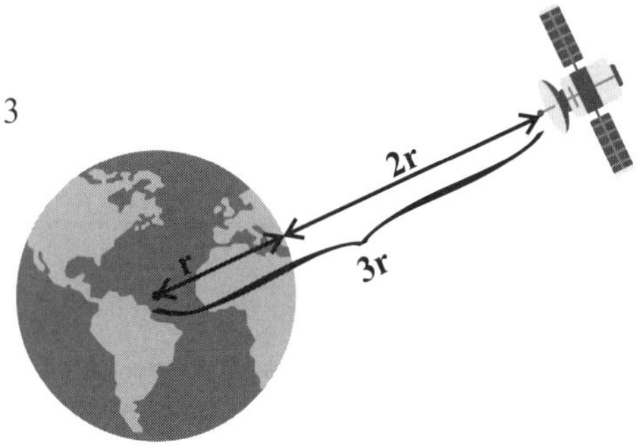

Question 1 (Solutions on page 128)

1.1 If an object is travelling at a constant velocity it can be concluded that

A there are no external forces acting on the object
B there is a constant force applied to the object
C the net force on the object is zero
D there is a constant net force which acts on the object (2)

1.2 An object is travelling due east when it is suddenly acted upon by a resultant force acting due south.

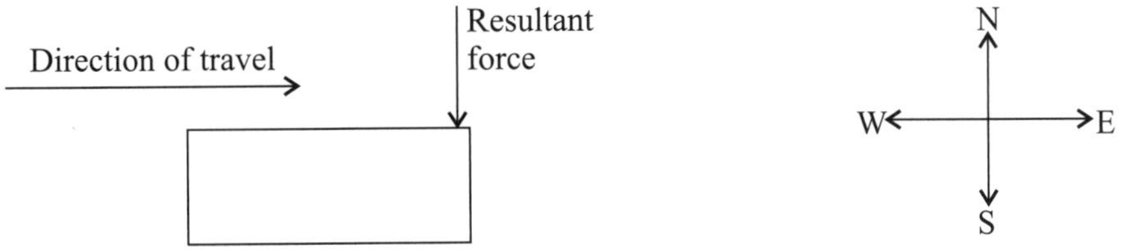

The object will accelerate:

A south east
B south west
C south
D 20° south of east (2)

1.3 The mass of an object on Earth is 500 kg. What would the mass be of the same object on a planet with double the mass and half the radius of the Earth?

A 4900N
B 39200N
C 500kg
D 4000kg (2)

1.4 Which one of the following graphs best represents the relationship between mass (m) and acceleration (a) for a constant force?

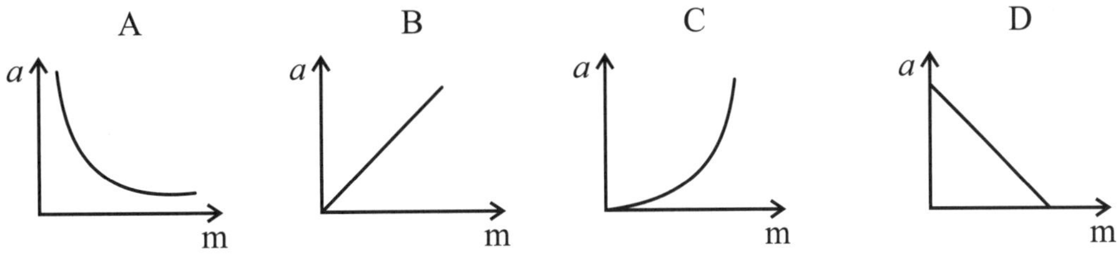

(2)

1.5 A rocket on earth has a mass of 1000kg. It is designed to orbit at a height twice the radius of the earth. During take-off the rocket burns 200kg of fuel. What will the weight of the rocket be in orbit?

A 2450N
B 1960N
C 871,11N
D 1088,89N (2)

1.6 A ball is suspended from the ceiling of a car as shown in the diagram below. If the car rapidly accelerates to the right, select the picture which will correspond to the movement of the ball as well as the law responsible.

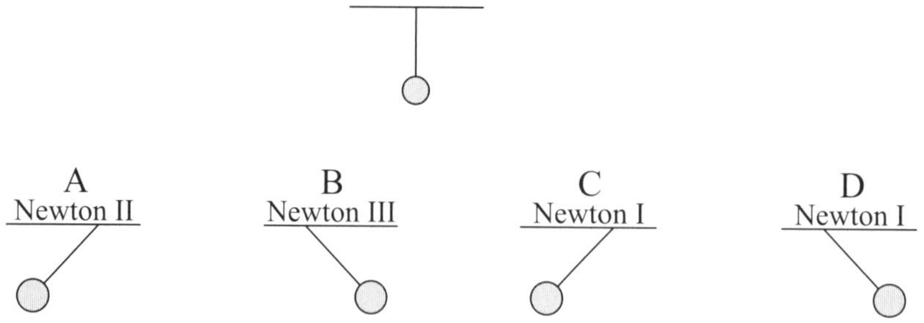

(2)

1.7 The displacement versus time graphs for 3 different objects are shown below. Which of the objects has a net force acting on it?

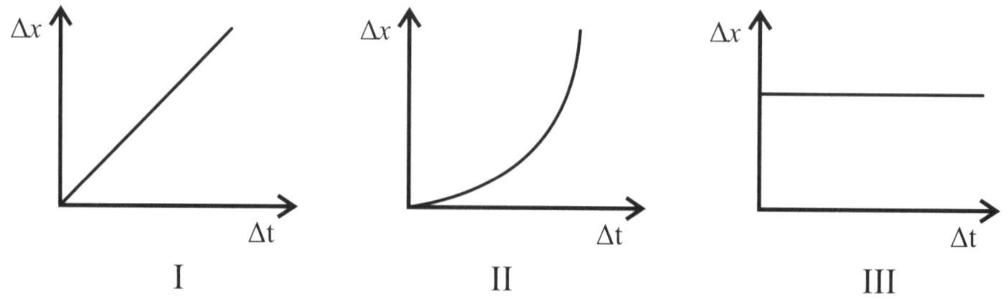

A I and II
B I only
C II only
D III only

(2)

1.8 The radius of the earth is given as x. which of the graphs below represent an astronaut of 100kg as the astronaut moves away from the surface of the earth?

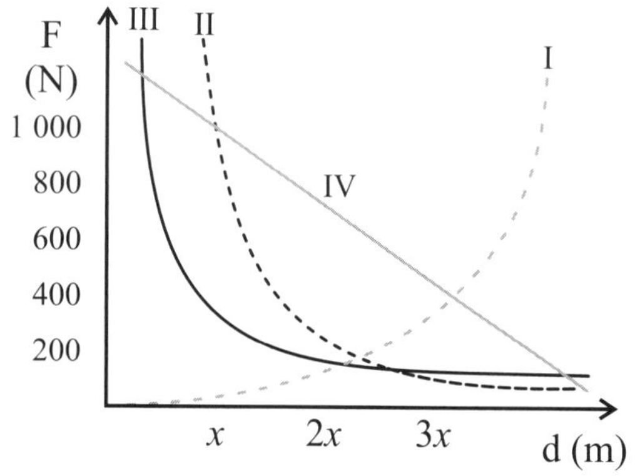

A I
B II
C III
D IV

(2)

1.9 A satellite experiences a gravitational force of magnitude F on the surface of the Earth. The radius of the Earth is R. The satellite now circles the Earth at an unknown height above the surface of the Earth and experiences a gravitational force of magnitude $\frac{F}{16}$. The unknown height is:

A R
B 2R
C 3R
D 4R

(2)

1.10 Two forces of 5N and 20N act on an object simultaneously. Which of the forces below could be the resultant force acting on the object due to these forces?

A 20 N
B 5 N
C 30 N
D 10 N

(2)

1.11 An astronaut has mass *m* and weight *W* on earth. What is the astronaut's mass and weight on a planet which has twice the mass and twice the radius of earth?

	Mass	Weight
A	m	W
B	m	$\frac{W}{2}$
C	$2m$	2W
D	$\frac{m}{2}$	$\frac{W}{2}$

(2)

1.12 It is known that the earth rotates at approximately 1 600 km.h^{-1} at the equator. A movement known as Flat Earther's believe that the earth is flat and does not rotate. A statement used by a Flat Earther to justify their belief is:
"If the earth is rotating at thousands of kilometres per hour, why can people not feel the movement?"
Which of Newton's Laws could be used to explain to a Flat Earther as to the reason people don't feel the earth's movement?

A Newton I
B Newton II
C Newton III
D None, the earth is flat

(2)

1.13 Pulley system A on the left shows a block with a weight of 100 N connected by a light inextensible string running over a frictionless pulley to a block of weight 200 N.
Pulley system B on the right is identical except that the block is replaced with a force of 200 N downwards.
Initially the systems are at rest. The moment the 200 N block is released, the 200 N force is applied to system B. In both cases the 100 N blocks accelerate upward and hits the pulley. Which 100 N block hits the pulley first?

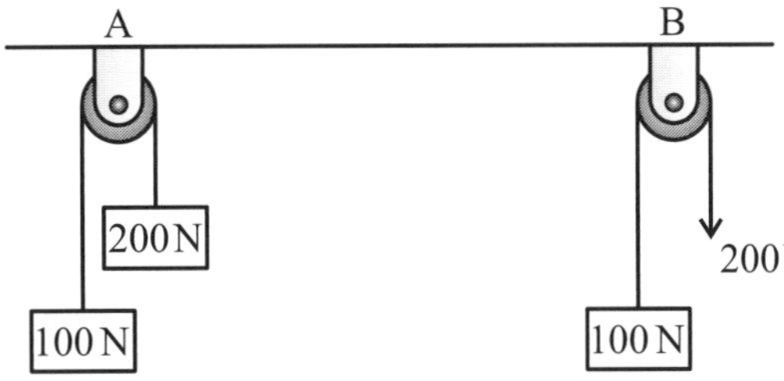

A System A
B System B
C They hit at the same time
D It is not possible to tell from the given information

(2)

1.14 Two objects of Mass M and m respectively are placed with their centres a distance, r, apart. Under these conditions they exert a force F on each other. The mass of each object and the distance between the centres of the objects, is doubled. The new force experienced between the objects, in terms of F, is:

A $\frac{F}{2}$
B F
C 4F
D 8F (2)

1.15 A force of 100 N is applied to a 8 kg trolley at 30° to the horizontal as shown in the diagram below.

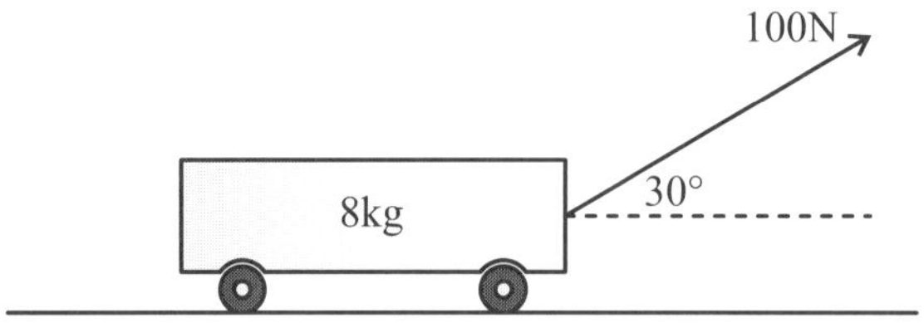

Which of the following statements are true?

A The trolley will accelerate to the right
B The trolley will lift off the floor
C The trolley won't move
D The normal force acting on the trolley is 28,4N (2)

1.16 Two masses of 10 kg and 5 kg respectively are connected by an elastic band on a frictionless surface. The masses are pulled apart so that the elastic band is stretched as far as it can.

The masses are then released simultaneously. Which statement describes their subsequent motion immediately after their release?

A The 10kg mass will remain stationary and the 5kg block will accelerate left
B The 10kg mass and 5kg mass will accelerate towards each other with the same acceleration
C The 10kg mass and 5kg mass will accelerate towards each other but the 10kg mass will have a greater acceleration
D The 10kg mass and 5kg mass will accelerate towards each other but the 5kg mass will have a greater acceleration (2)

1.17 A ball rests in a person's hand. According to Newton's 3rd law what is the reaction force to the weight of the ball?

A The force of the hand on the ball
B The normal force
C The force of the Earth on the ball
D The force of the ball on the earth (2)

1.18 The diagram below is free body diagram of a passenger at the instant after they are involved in a car accident. If the person is not wearing a seat belt, which of the forces (if any) are incorrect?

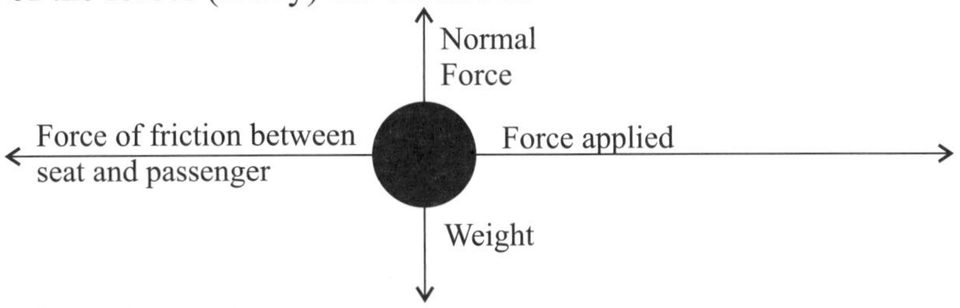

A Force Applied
B Force of Friction between seat and passenger
C Normal force and weight
D None of the above forces are correct (2)

1.19 Four planets are Shown below. Which planets would have the same gravitational acceleration on the surface of the planets?

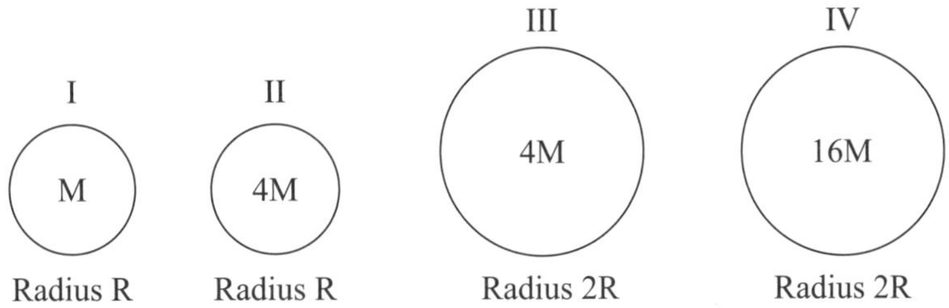

A I and II as well as III and IV
B I and III as well as II and IV
C II, III and IV
D I, III and IV (2)

1.20 Tom attempts to move a box of mass 100kg by applying a force of 95N. The coefficient of friction between the box and surface it is resting on is 0,1. Which of the following are true?

A The force of friction acting on the box is 98N
B The force of friction acting on the box is 95N
C The box will accelerate
D The box doesn't move because it applies a force back on Tom of 95N according to Newton's 3rd Law (2)

1.21 A box rests on a rough inclined plane which makes an angle of θ with the horizontal. The angle is increased to $1{,}5\theta$ and the box remains at rest. Which one of the following is the best description of how the force of gravity, normal force and force of friction changes as the angle is increased?

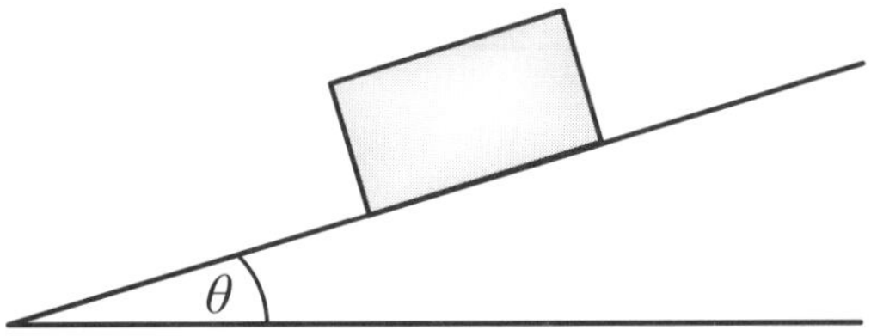

	Force of Gravity	Normal Force	Force of Friction
A	Increases	Decreases	Decreases
B	Stays the same	Decreases	Increases
C	Increases	Increases	Increases
D	Stays the same	Increases	Decreases

(2)

[42]

TOC 1 Data Sheet 2 Definitions 3 3 solutions 4 4 solutions 5 5 solutions 6 6 solutions 7 7 solutions 8 8 solutions 9 9 solutions 10 10 solutions

Question 2 (Solutions on page 128 and 129)

A box of mass 14kg is connected by a rigid, massless bar to an 8kg box. The system is pulled up a slope inclined at 50° by a force of 460N. The coefficient of kinetic friction between the surface and the boxes is 0,55 whilst the static coefficient of friction is 0,8.

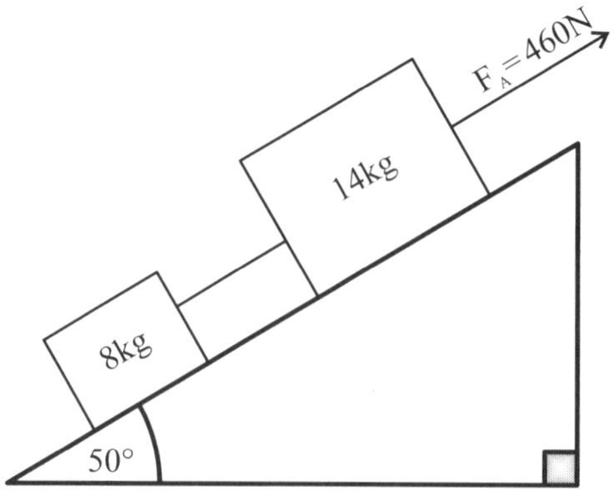

2.1 Draw free body diagram showing all the forces acting on the blocks. (7)

2.2 Calculate the force of friction acting on each block. (4)

2.3 Determine the acceleration of the system. (5)

2.4 Hence, calculate the tension in the bar connecting the blocks. (3)

[19]

Question 3 (Solutions on page 129)

A boat accelerates at 0,5 $m.s^{-2}$ to tow a water-skier across a lake. The tow rope makes an angle of 30° with the horizontal. The coefficient of friction between the water and the skier is 0,15. The mass of the water skier (with all kit) is 100kg.

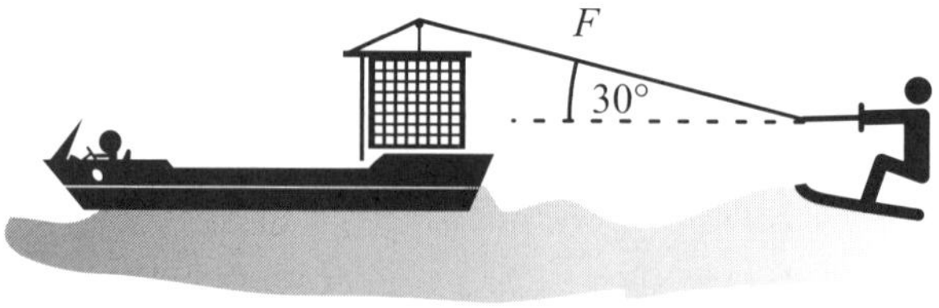

3.1 Define acceleration (2)

3.2 Would decreasing the angle of the tow rope to 15° have any effect on the force of friction? Explain your answer using relative physic principles. Include any relevant formulae in your explanation. (5)

3.3 Determine the magnitude of F, the force in the tow rope. (6)

[10]

Question 4 (Solutions on page 129 and 130)

Crate Q of mass 6 kg is attached to crate P of mass 8 kg by a light inextensible string which passes over a frictionless pulley as shown in the diagram below. Crate P is at rest on slope XY. When Q is released it falls to the ground and P moves up the slope accelerating at 0,43 $m.s^{-2}$.

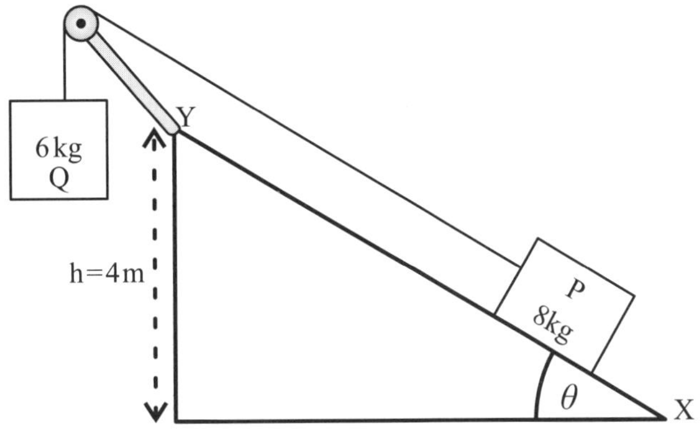

4.1 Draw a labelled free body diagram to show all the forces acting on P and Q as P moves up the slope. (6)

4.2 Calculate the magnitude of the tension in the string. (3)

4.3 If the frictional force acting on P as it moves up the slope is 13,58N, determine the angle of the slope and the coefficient of kinetic friction. (7)

4.4 Determine the speed at which Q strikes the ground. (3)

4.5 The pully is adjusted so that that P is pulled at an angle of 15°. Determine the magnitude of the new force of friction acting on P. In this scenario the acceleration changes to 0,5 $m.s^{-2}$. You may assume that the angle of the slope is 30°. (4)

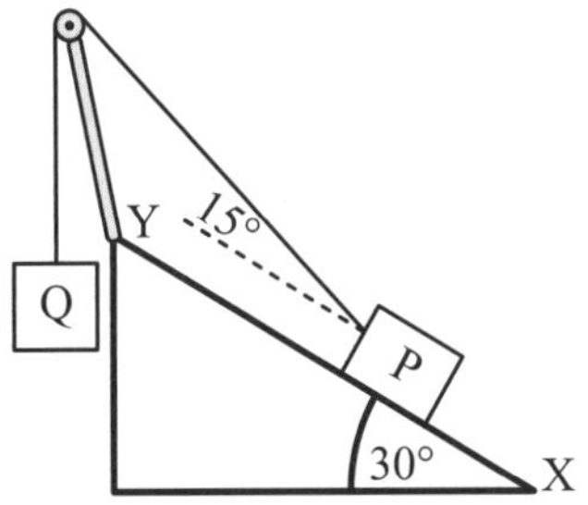

4.6 Explain why the force of friction calculated in 4.5 is less than that given in 4.3. (3)

[26]

Question 5 (Solutions on page 130)

A horizontal force of 40N is applied to a 5kg block placed on a frictionless surface as shown. A second 2kg block is placed on the rough upper surface of the 5kg block. The two blocks are joined by a massless inextensible string running over a frictionless pulley. The force of friction between the blocks is 2N while they are moving. The tension in the string which joins the blocks is T.

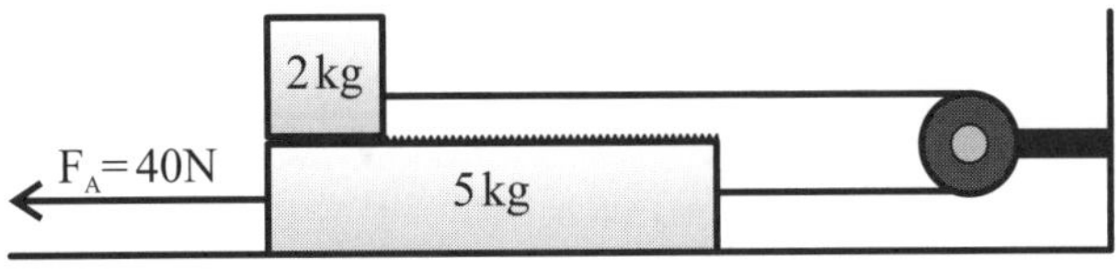

5.1 Draw two separate labelled force diagrams showing all the horizontal forces acting on the blocks while they are moving. (5)

5.2 Write an expression to show the net force acting on the 5kg block. (3)

5.3 Write an expression to show the net force acting on the 2kg block. (3)

5.4 Use your equations above to determine the magnitude of the acceleration of the 2kg block. (4)

[15]

TOC 1 Data Sheet 2 Definitions 3 3 solutions 4 4 solutions 5 5 solutions 6 6 solutions 7 7 solutions 8 8 solutions 9 9 solutions 10 10 solutions

Question 6 (Solutions on page 131)

An 18,4kg block resting on a level frictionless surface is attached to a hanging block m by a light, inextensible string over a frictionless pulley. The block is initially at rest 1,5m above the ground.

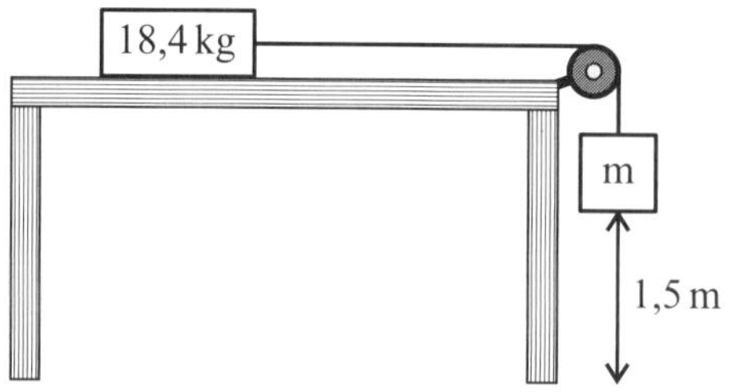

When the hanging block is released, it takes 2 seconds to reach the floor.

6.1 State Newton's second law of motion. (2)

6.2 Calculate the magnitude of the acceleration of block m (4)

6.3 Determine the value of m, the mass of the hanging block. (5)

[11]

Question 7 (Solutions on page 131)

A coal mine uses a motor to pull carts of coal up a slope out of the mine. The motor is connected to the cart over a frictionless pully and the slope in inclined at 52°. The system is illustrated in the diagram below. A fully loaded cart has a mass of 4,5 tons. The coefficient of kinetic friction between the cart and slope is 0,35. (1 ton = 1 000 kg)

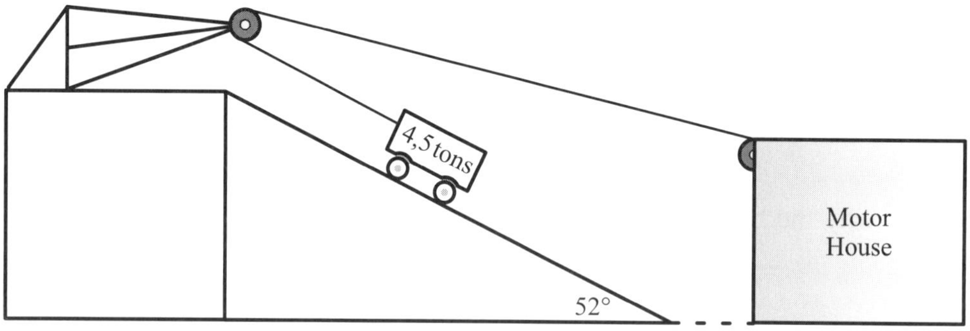

7.1 Draw a labelled free body diagram of all the forces acting on the cart while the cart is accelerating up the slope. (4)

7.2 State Newton's second law of motion. (2)

7.3 If the cart accelerates at $0{,}25\,m.s^{-2}$, calculate the magnitude of the resultant force on the cart. (3)

7.4 Calculate the magnitude of the maximum force of kinetic friction on the cart. (4)

7.5 What force does the motor need to exert to pull the cart out of the mine. (5)

7.6 As the front wheels of the cart reach the level surface of the slope, the rope snaps. Explain using physics principles, how it is possible that the cart still makes it to the top of the slope. (3)

[21]

Question 8 (Solutions on page 132)

Two blocks have masses of 8 kg and 24 kg and are joined together by a light inextensible rope. A force, F, is applied to the 24 kg block at an angle of 20° to the horizontal as shown. The coefficient of static friction between the surface on which the blocks rest and the blocks is 0,6. The blocks do not move when the force is applied and both blocks are made from the same material.

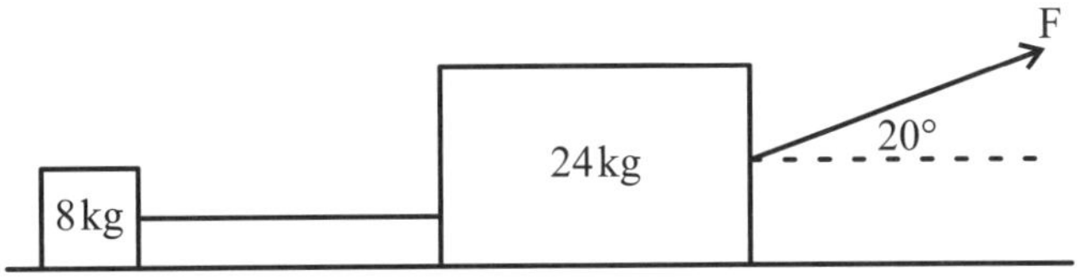

8.1 State Newtons first law. (2)

8.2 Calculate the maximum frictional force that could act on the 8 kg block. (3)

8.3 State the magnitude of the tension in the rope joining the blocks when the blocks are about to start sliding. Give a reason for your answer. (2)

8.4 Draw a labelled free body diagram showing all the forces acting on the 24 kg block. (5)

8.5 Determine the magnitude of Force F, when the blocks are just about to start to move. (6)

[18]

Question 9 (Solutions on page 132 and 133)

A deep space NASA probe arrives at planet Nibiru in a galaxy far away from earth. When the probe lands it discovers that Nibiru has a gravitational acceleration of 14m.s^{-2}.

9.1 In words, state Newton's Universal Law of Gravitation. (3)

9.2 The probe experiences a gravitational force of 280×10^3 N on the surface of Nibiru. Calculate the mass of the space probe. (2)

9.3 If Nibiru has a mass of 1×10^{21} tons, determine the radius of Nibiru. Give your answer to the nearest kilometre. (4)

On its journey to planet Nibiru the space probe stopped between two asteroids whose centres were 1000km apart. The asteroids had the same radii, but one was double the mass of the other. At a certain distance *x*, from the centre of the lighter asteroid, the probe experienced zero force.

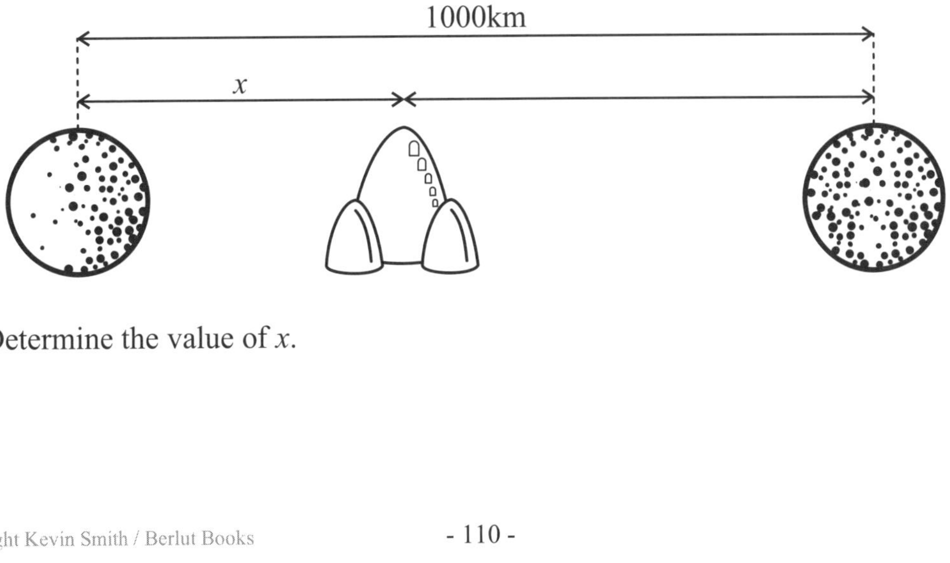

9.4 Determine the value of *x*. (6)

[15]

Question 10 (Solutions on page 133)

A block of mass M is attached to a block of mass 5,6 kg via a light inextensible string which is passed over a frictionless pulley as shown in the diagram below. The block of mass 5,6 kg is at rest on a horizontal surface with a coefficient of kinetic friction of 0,65 and a coefficient of static friction of 0,8. If the hanging mass M was any heavier the system would not remain in equilibrium.

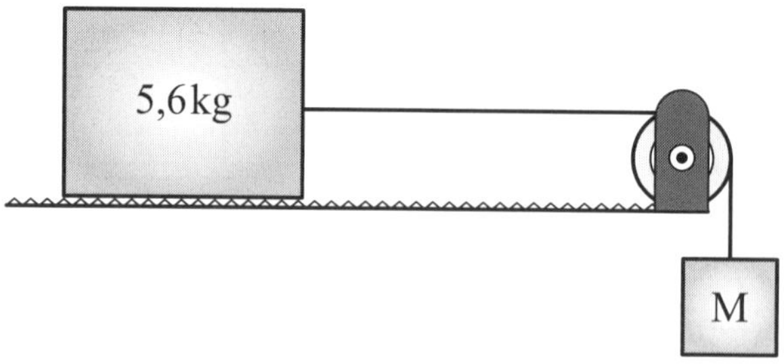

10.1 State Newton's second law of motion. (2)

10.2 Draw a labelled free-body diagram of all the horizontal forces acting on the 5,6 kg block. (2)

10.3 Calculate the magnitude of the tension in the string while the system is in equilibrium. (3)

10.4 The mass is increased so that the system starts to accelerate at $0{,}25 m.s^{-2}$. Determine the mass of the block which causes this acceleration. (5)

[12]

Question 11 (Solutions on page 134)

A lawnmower of mass 20 kg is pushed at an angle of 30° to the horizontal. A force of 200 N is required to get the lawnmower to move.

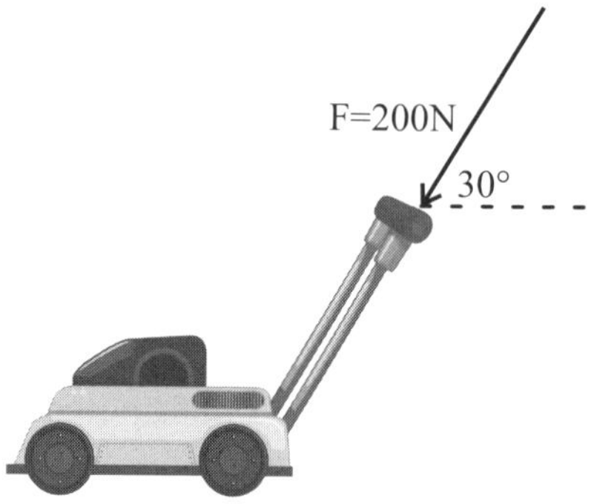

11.1 Draw a fully labelled free-body diagram of all the forces acting on the lawnmower. (4)

11.2 Calculate the coefficient of maximum static friction correct to 3 decimal places. (6)

11.3 Once the lawnmower is moving at a constant velocity, the coefficient of kinetic friction reduces to 0,50. Calculate the new force (acting at the same angle) which must be applied to keep the lawnmower moving at a constant velocity. (6)

[16]

Question 12 (Solutions on page 134)

An applied force of 80N pulls a cart of mass 10 kg up a slope with an incline of 35° at constant velocity of 3 m.s^{-1}. While moving up the slope, the cord pulling the cart suddenly breaks. The cart continues to move and then comes to rest at a point on the slope. At the instant the cart comes to rest a man grabs the broken rope and prevents it from sliding down the hill by applying a force of 16N. Assume the man applies the minimum force needed to keep the cart at rest.

12.1 Determine the coefficient of kinetic friction between the cart and the incline. (6)

12.2 Determine the coefficient of static friction between the cart and the incline. (6)

[12]

Question 13 (Solutions on page 135 and 136)

To investigate the frictional forces between different surfaces, some learners set up a basket on a mat. They performed multiple experiments and increased the mass of the basket each time by adding mass pieces in the basket and then determined the force needed to just get the basket to move (to just overcome friction).

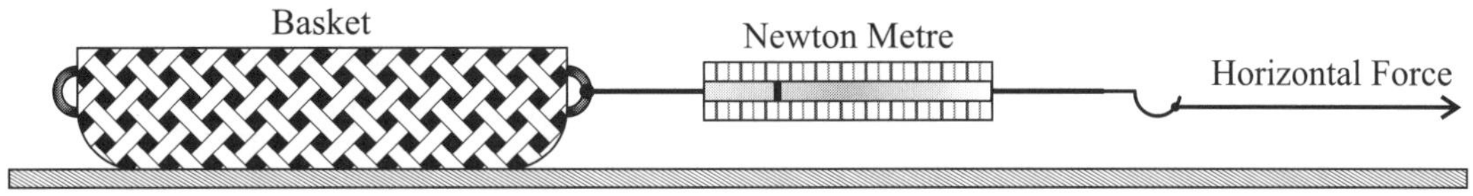

The table below shows their results:

Mass of the basket and mass piece (kg)	Force on the meter (N)
1,0	3,7
1,5	5,9
2,0	7,8
3,0	12,2
5,0	20,0
6,0	23,7

13.1 Define frictional force. (2)

13.2 On the graph paper provided on the next page, plot a graph of the force on the meter vs the total mass of the block and the mass pieces. (6)

13.3 Determine the gradient of the graph clearly showing the units of the gradient. (Show clearly on the graph the values used) (4)

13.4 What relationship is shown by this graph? (2)

13.5 Use the equation for static friction to write down an equation that links the mass of the object with the frictional force. (2)

13.6 Use your answers for 13.3, 13.5. and your knowledge of the straight-line equation $y = mx + c$ to determine the coefficient of static friction for the block on the mat. (4)

[20]

TOC
1 Data Sheet
2 Definitions
3
3 solutions
4
4 solutions
5
5 solutions
6
6 solutions
7
7 solutions
8
8 solutions
9
9 solutions
10
10 solutions

TOC
1 Data Sheet
2 Definitions
3
3 solutions
4
4 solutions
5
5 solutions
6
6 solutions
7
7 solutions
8
8 solutions
9
9 solutions
10
10 solutions

Question 13.2

Graph paper

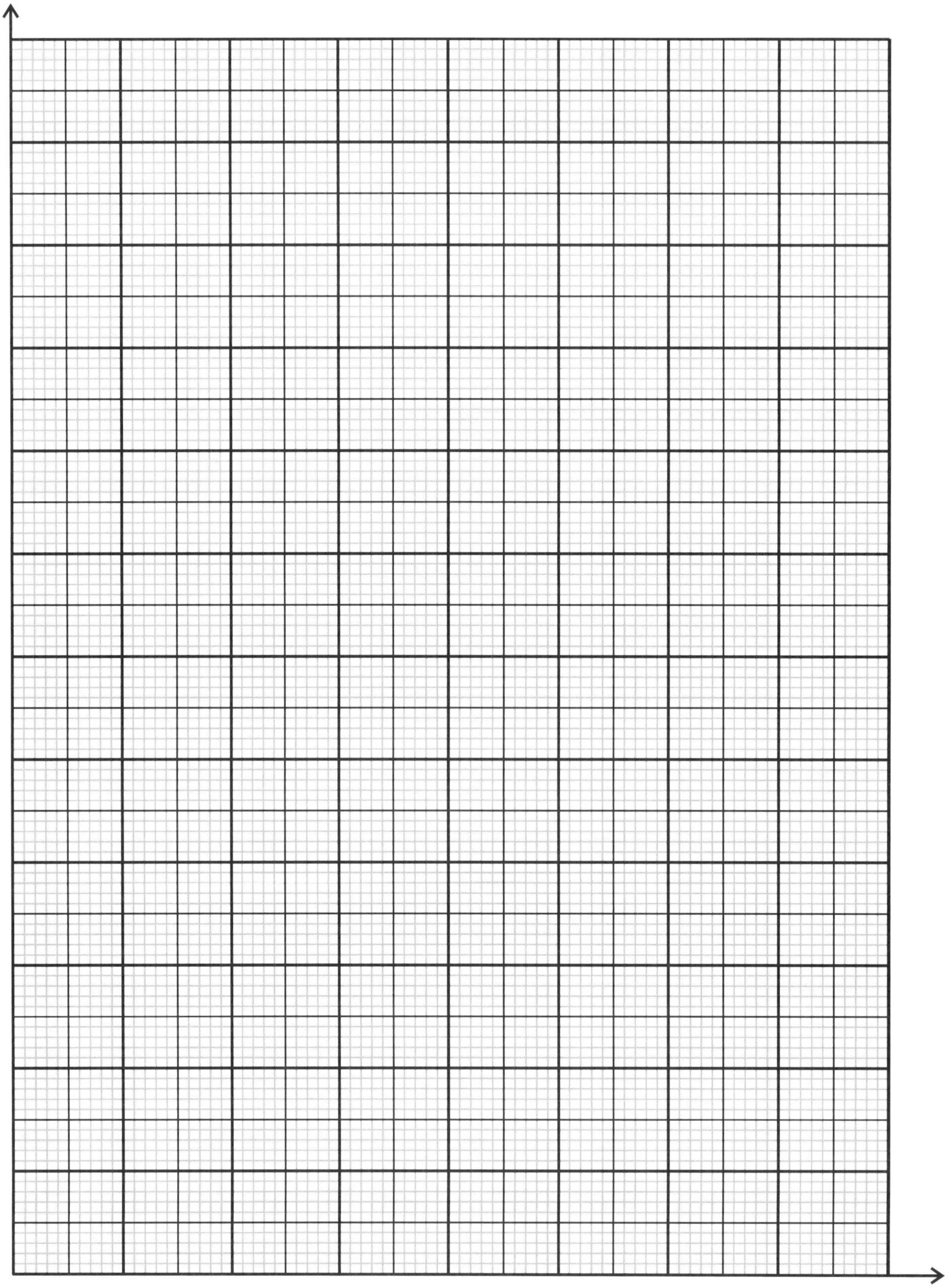

Question 14 (Solutions on page 136)

On the 26th of November 2018 NASA landed "InSight" on the surface of Mars. Insight entered the atmosphere of Mars with a mass of 608 kg at height of 128km above the planet's surface. Several minutes later InSight touched down on the surface of Mars. At this point its mass had reduced to 358 kg.

14.1 State Newton's law of Universal Gravitation. (3)

14.2 Calculate the magnitude of the gravitational force exerted on insight when it was at a height of 128 km above the surface of the planet.

Given: Mass of Mars = $6{,}4\times10^{23}$ kg. Radius of Mars = 3 397 km. (4)

14.3 Tom states that when InSight lands on the surface of Mars, its weight will be larger than when it entered the atmosphere. This is due to the distance between the planet's centre and InSight decreasing.

Gina states that Tom is incorrect, and InSight's weight will decrease. Who is correct? Performa a calculation to explain your answer. (5)

14.4 Calculate the acceleration due to gravity on Mars. (4)

[16]

Question 15 (Solutions on page 136 and 137)

Two blocks made of the same materials are shown below. An 80N force is applied at an angle of 20° to the 2,5kg block as shown in the diagram. The 2,5kg block is connected to the 5kg block by a light inextensible rod. The applied force causes both blocks to accelerate across a rough floor which has kinetic coefficient of friction of 0,25.

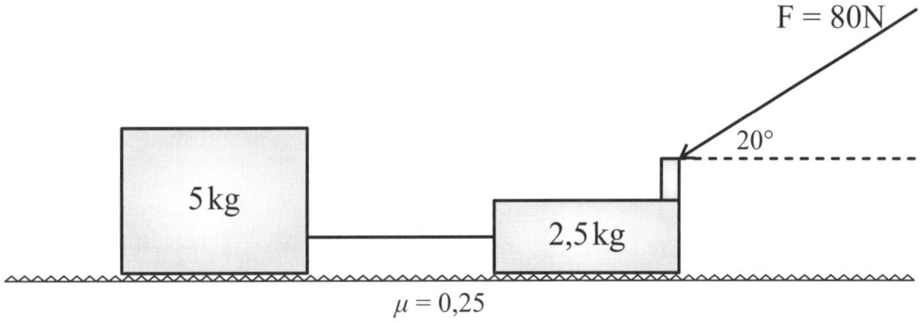

15.1 State Newton's second law of motion. (2)

15.2 Calculate the magnitude of the frictional force acting on the 5kg block. (3)

15.3 Draw a fully labelled free body diagram of the forces acting on the 2,5kg block (5)

15.4 Determine the tension in the bar connecting the blocks (8)

[18]

Question 16 (Solutions on page 137)

A man standing on a scale in an elevator has mass of 80kg. When the lift accelerates upwards the scale reads 944N. The elevator has a mass of 1000kg. What is the magnitude of the force in the cable which causes the lift to accelerate?

[8]

Question 17 (Solutions on page 138)

A man stands on a scale in a lift graduated in Newtons. The lift is on the 50th floor of a 100-floor building. The scale reading against time graph below shows the reading on the scale, **starting at the instant the lift begins to move** until it reaches the selected floor.

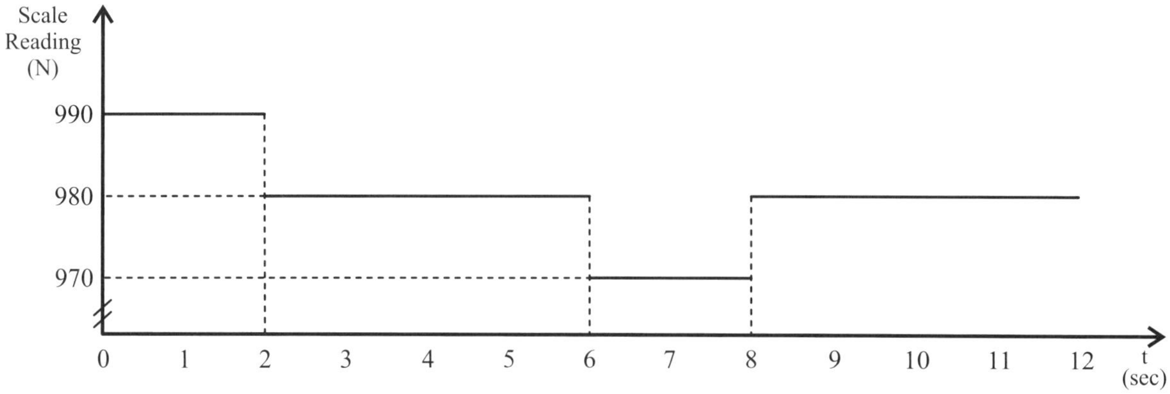

17.1 What direction does the lift initially move in? (2)

17.2 What is the man's mass? (3)

17.3 In what direction is the lift moving between 6 and 8 seconds? Explain your answer. (3)

17.4 When the lift accelerates, what is the magnitude of its acceleration? (3)

17.5 What is the velocity of the lift at 10 seconds? (1)

17.6 If the cable suddenly snaps at 1 second, what direction will the lift be moving immediately after the cable snaps? Give a reason for your answer, making reference to one of Newton's Laws. (3)

17.7 What will the scale read at the instant the cable snaps? (1)

[16]

Question 18 (Solutions on page 138)

Tom is standing on a scale in an elevator that has a constant acceleration upward. The scale reads 960 N. When Tom picks up a 20 kg box, the scale reads 1200 N. Determine Tom's weight.

[8]

Question 19 (Solutions on page 138 and 139)

A rope is attached to a box of mass 60 kg. The magnitude of the force in the rope is F and it makes angle of θ with the horizontal. The coefficient of static friction between the box and the floor is 0,3. With force F applied, the magnitude of the maximum static frictional force between the floor and the box is 140 N. The applied force does not cause the box to lift off the ground.

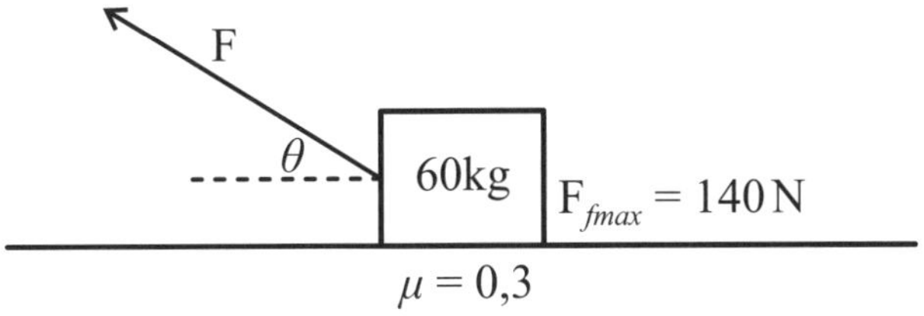

19.1 Draw a free-body diagram showing all the forces acting on the box. (4)

19.2 Define frictional force. (2)

19.3 Calculate the magnitude of the normal force that the floor exerts on the box when static friction is at a maximum. (3)

19.4 Determine the magnitude of force F and the angle θ that the rope makes with the horizontal. (8)

[17]

Question 20 (2014 Exemplar IEB Examination) (Solutions on page 139 and 140)

20.1 Some boxes are loaded into a trailer to take to a new house. A car of mass 1 600 kg pulls the loaded trailer of mass 700 kg as shown in the diagram. There is a frictional force of 4 800 N acting on the trailer and a frictional Force of 10 900 N acting on the car. The car's engine provides a driving force of 21 220 N.

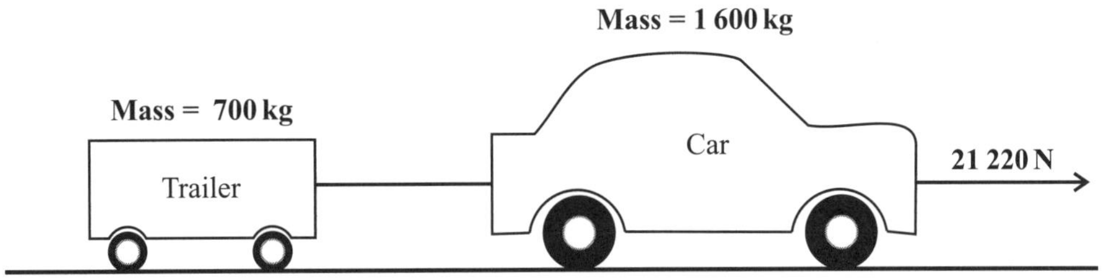

20.1.1 State Newton's second law of motion. (4)

20.1.2 Draw a labelled force diagram to represent the horizontal forces acting on

a) The car. (3)

b) The trailer. (2)

20.1.3 Calculate the magnitude of

a) the acceleration of the system, and (3)

b) the tension in the tow bar. (2)

20.2 While moving house, a safe of mass 180 kg needs to be moved. It is too heavy to lift, so the movers tie a rope around the safe and pull it **horizontally** to the right. The coefficient of static friction between the safe and the ground is 0,5. The movers are not able to move the safe.

20.2.1 Draw a labelled free body diagram to represent all of the forces acting on the safe. (4)

20.2.2 Calculate the magnitude of the maximum frictional force. (4)

The movers decide to pull on the rope so that the applied force makes an angle of 40° to the horizontal.

20.2.3 Why does pulling on the rope at an angle to the horizontal make it easier to move the safe? (2)

20.2.4 Calculate the magnitude of the force in the rope when it is at an angle of 40° to the horizontal, that will just cause the safe to start sliding. (4)

[28]

Question 21 (2014 IEB Final Examination) (Solutions on page 140)

Tom, Thuli and Tessa conduct an investigation using a box on an inclined plane. Their aim is to determine how the mass of an object placed on an inclined plane affects the maximum angle (θ) to which the plane can be tilted before the object just starts to slide down the plane.

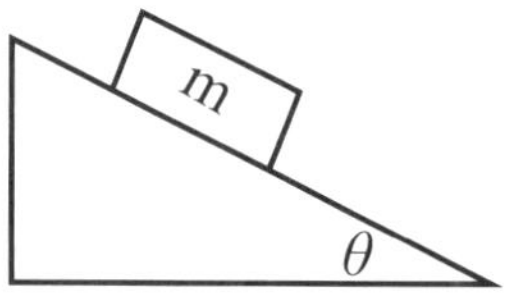

They place an empty box on a flat horizontal track and gradually tilt the track until the box just starts to slide. They record the angle of the incline (θ) at which this happens.
They then add a 1 kg mass piece to the empty box and repeat the experiment.
They continue to increase the mass of the box by 1 kg at a time and record the angle θ each time the box starts to slide.

21.1 Name the dependent variable in this experiment. (2)

21.2 Why was it necessary to use the same track and the same box for each experiment? (2)

21.3 Draw a labelled free body diagram to represent the forces acting on the box at rest on the inclined plane. Show relevant angles and name the forces. (4)

Before conducting their investigation, the learners make the following hypotheses:

Tom: "The greater the mass of the box the smaller the angle (θ) of the incline at which the box will start to slide."

Thuli: "The greater the mass of the box the greater the angle (θ) of the incline at which the box will start to slide."

Tessa: "The mass of the box will not affect the angle (θ) of the incline at which the box will just start to slide."

21.4 Use your knowledge and understanding of the forces acting on the box to predict which learner's hypothesis is correct. Justify your choice by referring to relevant physics principles and formulae. (5)

[13]

Question 22 (2018 IEB Supplementary Examination) (Solutions on page 140 and 141)

Two scale pans each of mass 0,1 kg are attached to a light inextensible cable which passes over a smooth pulley. A mass of 0,5 kg is placed on one pan and a mass of 0,3 kg is placed on the other pan as shown in the diagram. The system is released from rest.

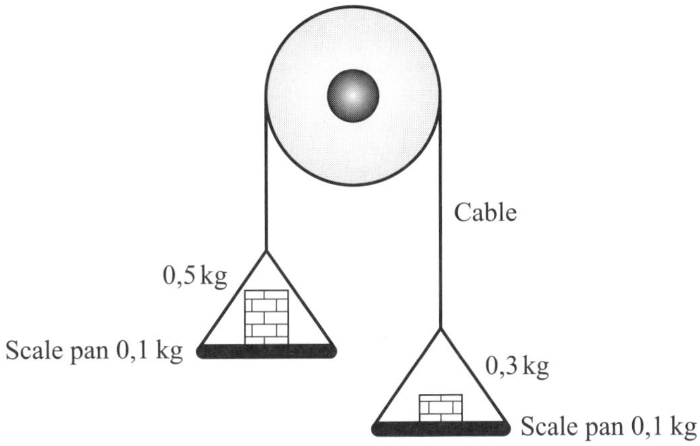

22.1 State Newton's second law of motion. (2)

22.2 Consider each side separately and use Newton's second law to write an equation for each side. (3)

22.3 Hence, calculate the magnitude of the acceleration of the system and the magnitude of the tension in the cable. (2)

22.4 Draw a free-body diagram for the 0,5 kg mass piece while the system is accelerating. The relative sizes of the forces must be clear. (3)

22.5 Calculate the force that the scale pan exerts on the 0,5 kg mass. (3)

22.6 State Newton's third law of motion. (2)

22.7 Describe the force that is the Newton third law pair to the force that the scale pan exerts on the 0,5 kg mass. (2)

[17]

Question 23 (2017 IEB Final Examination) (Solutions on page 141 and 142)

23.1 An experiment was conducted to investigate the relationship between the force exerted on an object and the object's acceleration. An electric fan is mounted on a zero-friction cart to accelerate the cart along a **smooth** track. The speed of the fan and hence the force exerted on the cart is adjusted and the acceleration of the cart determined.

23.1.1 Name and state the Newton's Law that is under investigation. (3)

23.1.2 State the dependent variable in the investigation. (2)

The experimental results are recorded in the table.

Force (mN) due to fan	Acceleration ($m.s^{-1}$)
25	0,09
80	0,30
135	0,52
190	0,68
245	0,92
300	1,05

23.1.3 Using the graph paper on the next page, plot a graph of acceleration (on the y-axis) against force due to the fan (on the x-axis). (6)

23.1.4 Calculate the gradient of the graph. Include the appropriate unit in your answer. (4)

23.1.5 Use your answer for Question 22.1.4 to determine the mass of the cart. (3)

The experiment is conducted again, but on a track with friction. The cart experiences a frictional forcc of 50 mN.

23.1.6 On the same set of axes used for Question .1.3, sketch a line that you would expect to obtain for the experiment conducted with friction. Label your predicted line P. (2)

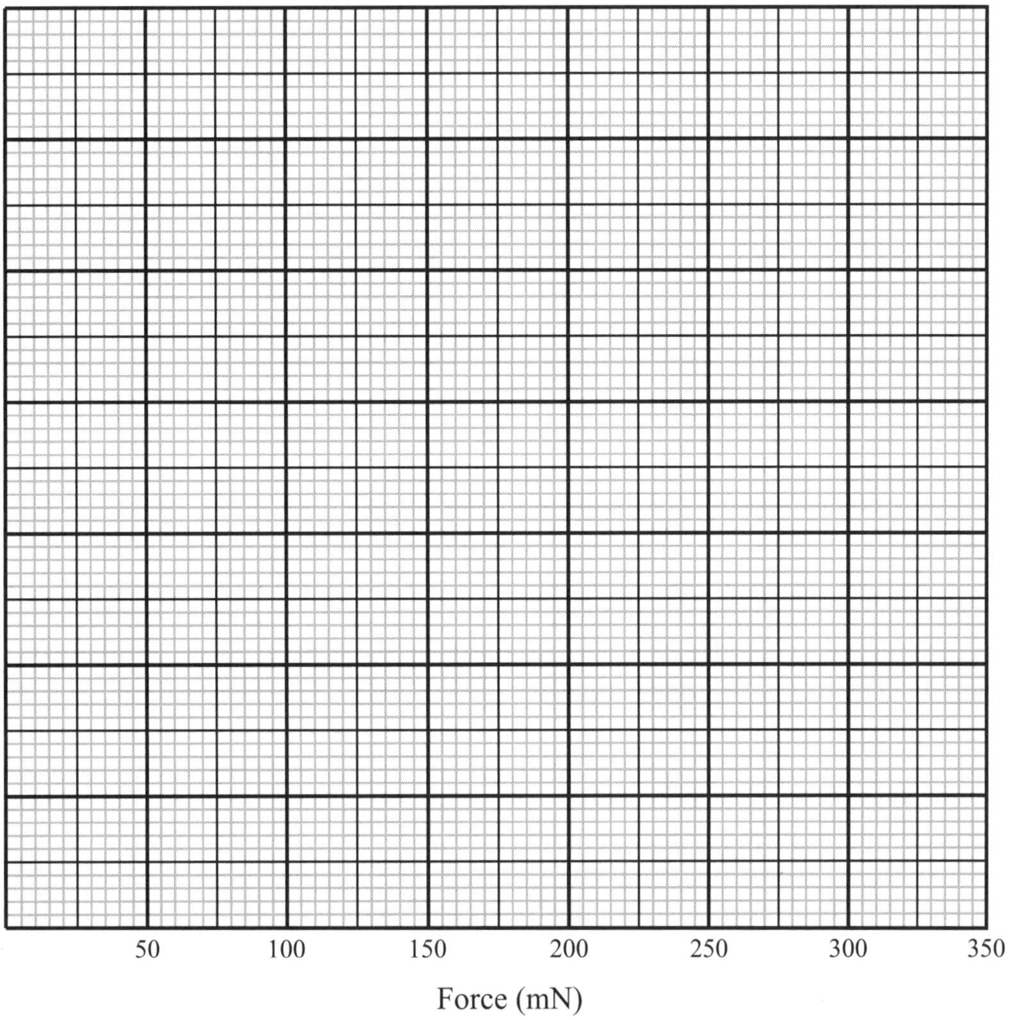

23.2 A box of mass 150 kg is prevented from sliding down the slope by a force, F, of 100 N acting at 40° to the rough inclined plane as shown. The plane is inclined at 35° to the horizontal and the coefficient of static friction between the box and the surface is 0,7.

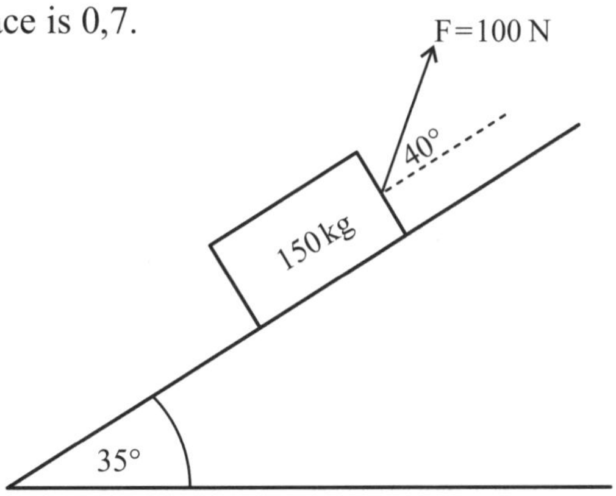

23.2.1 Draw a labelled free-body diagram showing all the forces acting on the box. (4)

23.2.2 Calculate the component of the weight parallel to the inclined plane. (3)

23.2.3 Calculate the magnitude of the frictional force that is acting on the box. (4)

The size of force F is slowly reduced from 100 N until the box is about to slide.

23.2.4 Calculate the minimum value of the force F for the box to remain at rest. (4)

[35]

Question 24 (2018 IEB Final Examination) (Solutions on page 143)

An athlete trains by pushing a heavy box A of mass 23 kg, which is in contact with an even heavier box B of mass 31 kg, across the rough surface of a field as shown in the diagram below. The athlete exerts a force F = 134 N at an angle of 36° to the horizontal on box A and each box experiences a frictional force of 45 N. The boxes accelerate horizontally.

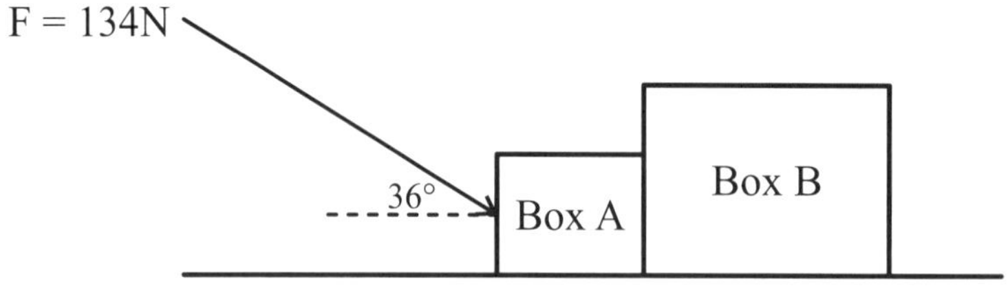

24.1 Draw a labelled free-body diagram for box A. (5)

24.2 Draw a labelled free-body diagram for box B. (4)

24.3 State Newton's second law. (2)

24.4 Use Newton's second law to write the equation $F_{net} = ma$ in terms of all the horizontal forces acting on **box A**. (4)

24.5 State Newton's third law. (2)

24.6 Calculate the force that box B exerts on box A. (3)

24.7 Define frictional force due to a surface. (2)

Box A and box B are made of identical material, yet each box experiences the same frictional force.

24.8 Use a suitable equation to help you explain why box A experiences the same magnitude frictional force even though box A has a smaller mass than box B. (3)

[25]

Question 25 (2015 IEB Supplementary Examination) (Solutions on page 144 and 145)

25.1 Two identical blocks, A and B, joined by a light inextensible string are pulled by a constant force, F, across a frictionless horizontal surface as shown in the diagram below.

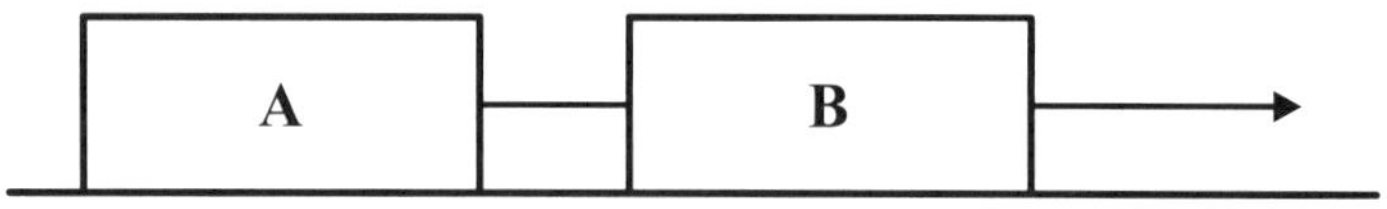

After they have been pulled for a certain time, t, the string between the blocks snaps. Force F continues to act on block B.
Draw a velocity-time sketch graph on the axes provided on the next page to represent the motion of blocks A and B before and after the string snaps.
Clearly label the following lines on your graph;

- **A and B** together before time t
- **A** after time t
- **B** after time t (3)

25.1 Axes for question 25.1

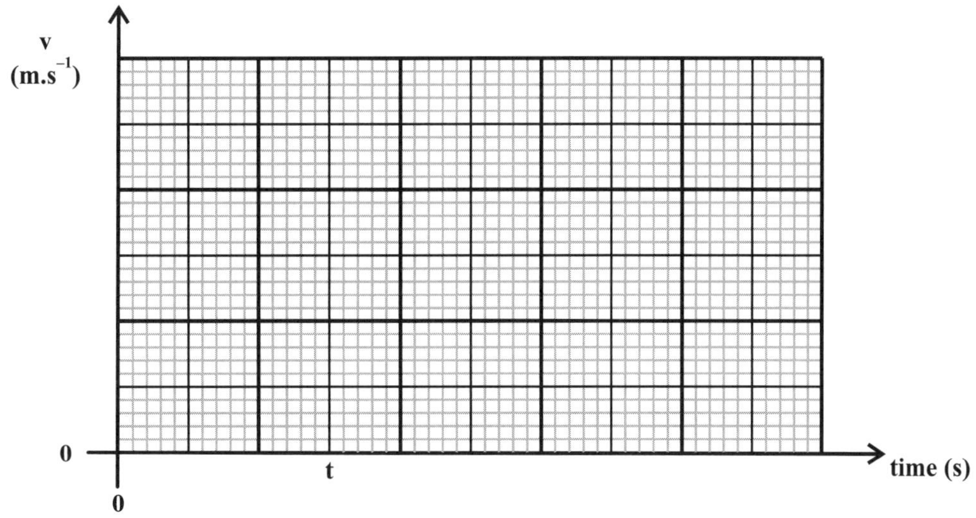

25.2 The same two identical blocks, A and B, joined by a light inextensible string are now pulled by a constant force, F, across a **rough** horizontal surface at **constant speed**.

After they have been pulled for a certain time, t, the string between the blocks snaps. Force F continues to act on block B.

Draw a velocity-time sketch graph on the axes provided on the axes below to represent the motion of blocks A and B before and after the string snaps.

Clearly label the following lines on your graph;

- **A and B** together before time t
- **A** after time t
- **B** after time t (3)

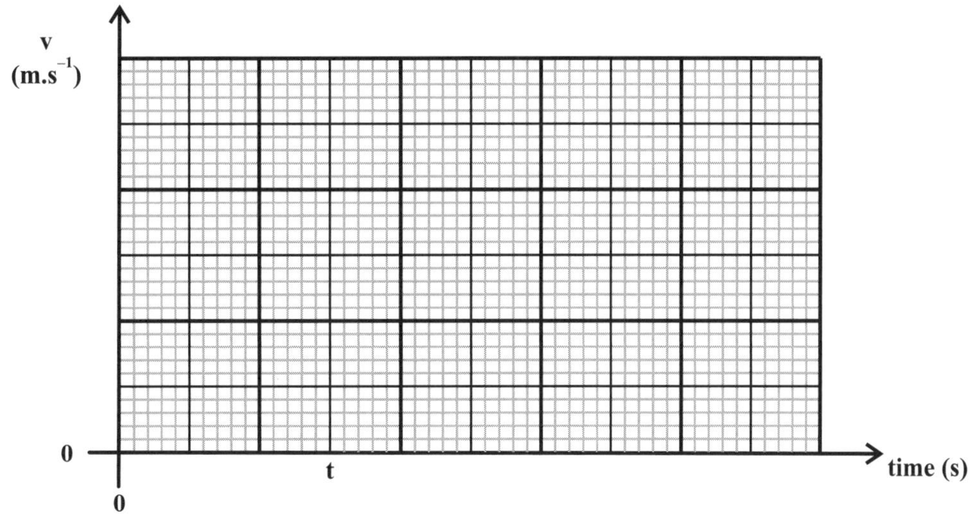

TOC
1 Data Sheet
2 Definitions
3
3 solutions
4
4 solutions
5
5 solutions
6
6 solutions
7
7 solutions
8
8 solutions
9
9 solutions
10
10 solutions

25.3 Two different blocks A and B of masses 16 kg and 24 kg respectively are pulled across a smooth (frictionless) surface by means of a light inextensible rope, Y, inclined at 64° to the horizontal.

The rope, Y, exerts a constant force of 120 N on block B. The blocks are joined by a light inextensible bar, X.

The masses of rope Y and bar X are negligible compared with those of blocks A and B.

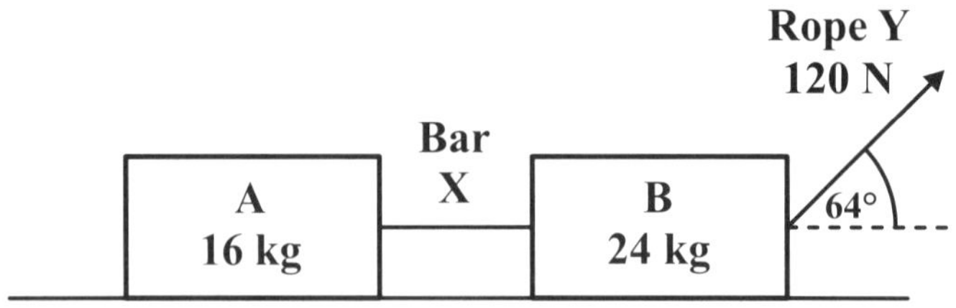

25.3.1 State *Newton's second law.* (3)

25.3.2 Calculate the magnitude of the acceleration of both blocks A and B. (4)

25.3.3 Draw a labelled free-body diagram to represent the forces acting on block A only. The labels must have the names of the forces, not just symbols. (4)

25.3.4 Calculate the magnitude of the tension in the bar, X, between blocks A and B. (4)

25.3.5 Calculate the work done by rope Y on the system as it pulls the blocks for a distance of 5 m. (4)

25.4 A block of mass 15 kg is at rest on a rough horizontal surface. The block is pulled by means of a light inextensible rope which exerts a force at an angle of 55° to the horizontal. The maximum force which the rope can exert before the block starts to move is 80 N. Calculate the co-efficient of static friction between the block and the surface.

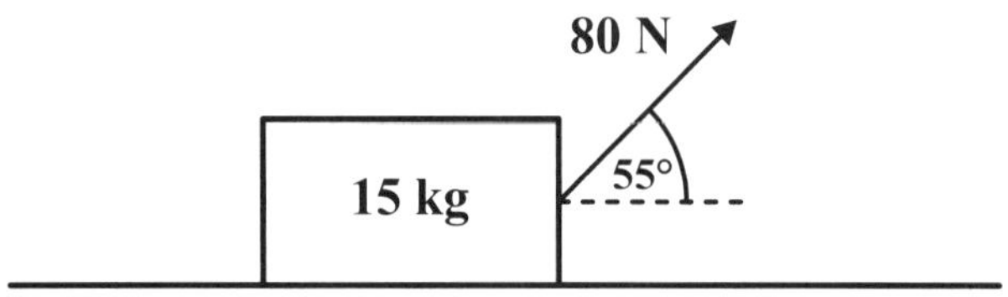

(6)

[31]

Question 26 (2016 IEB Supplementary Examination) (Solutions on page 145)

Two blocks are made of the same material. The blocks have masses of 12 kg and 36 kg and are joined together by a light inextensible rope. A force, F, is applied to the 36 kg block at an angle of 20° to the horizontal as shown. The coefficient of static friction between the surface on which the blocks rest and the blocks is 0,7. The blocks do not slide.

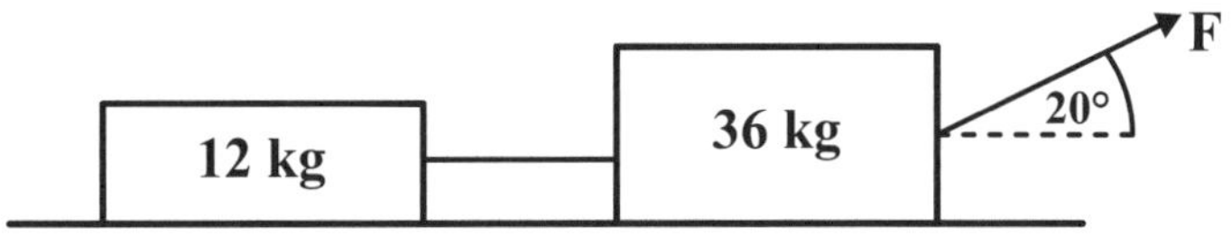

26.1 Calculate the maximum frictional force that could act on the 12 kg block. (3)

26.2 State *Newton's first law.* (2)

26.3 State the magnitude of the tension in the rope joining the blocks when the blocks are about to start sliding. Give a reason for your answer. (2)

26.4 Draw a labelled free-body diagram showing all the forces acting on the 36 kg block. (5)

26.5 Write an expression for the normal force, acting on the 36 kg block. (2)

26.6 Hence, calculate the magnitude of force F when the blocks are just about to start sliding. (4)

[18]

Question 27 (2016 IEB Final Examination) (Solutions on page 146)

Block A has a weight of 44 N and Block B has a weight of 22 N. Block A is placed on a rough table that has a coefficient of static friction of 0,2. Block A and Block B are connected via a light, inextensible rope over a frictionless pulley and Block C is placed on top of Block A as shown in the diagram below.

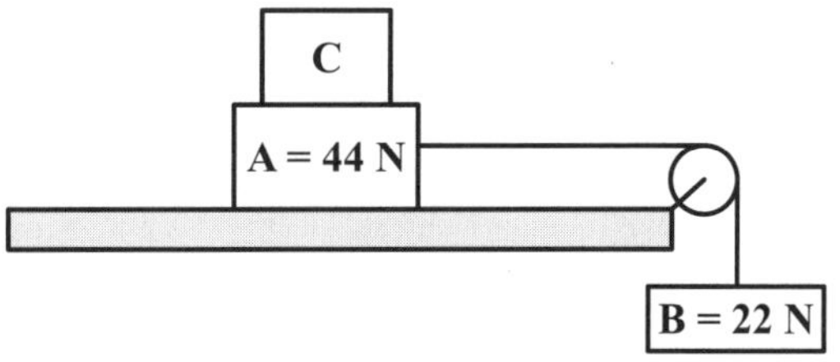

The system, as shown in the diagram, is only just at rest and on the limit of sliding.

27.1 Determine the tension in the rope joining Block A and Block B while the system is at rest. (2)

27.2 Define *frictional force due to a surface.* (2)

27.3 State the magnitude of the frictional force required for Block A to be at rest. (2)

27.4 Calculate the minimum weight of Block C to stop Block A from sliding. (5)

Block C is removed and the system starts accelerating.

27.5 State *Newton's second law.* (2)

27.6 Draw a labelled, free-body diagram for Block B while it is accelerating. (2)

The magnitude of the acceleration of the system is 2,3 $m.s^{-2}$.

27.7 Calculate the tension in the rope joining the blocks. (4)

27.8 Calculate the frictional force acting on Block A while it is accelerating. (3)

27.9 State two reasons why the frictional force between Block A and the surface is smaller than the value stated in question 27.3. Briefly explain your answer. (4)

[26]

Question 28 (2017 IEB Supplementary Examination) (Solutions on page 146 and 147)

Two identical blocks A and B are connected by a light, inextensible string that passes over a frictionless pulley as shown in the diagram. Each block has a mass of 2 kg. Initially block B is resting on the ground while block A is 4 m above the ground.

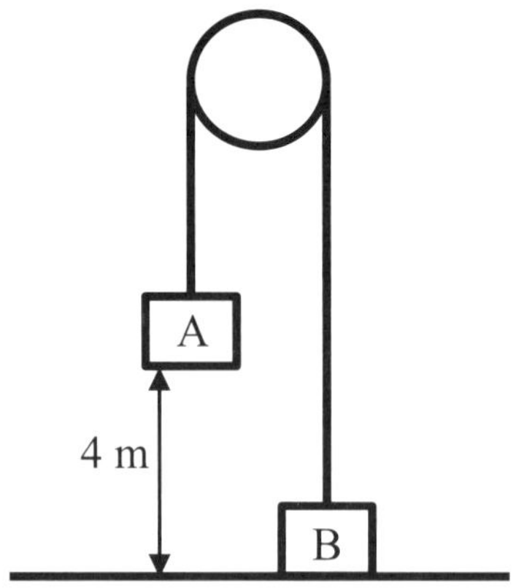

A block of mass 1 kg is placed on block A. The system accelerates as a result.

28.1 Draw a labelled free-body diagram of the forces acting on block B after it has left the ground and while it is accelerating upwards. The relative sizes of the forces must be clear. (3)

28.2 State *Newton's second law of motion*. (2)

28.3 Calculate the magnitude of the acceleration of the system. (5)

28.4 Calculate the tension in the string joining block A and block B while the blocks are accelerating. (2)

Block A hits the floor with a speed of 3,96 $m.s^{-1}$ and comes to rest almost immediately.

28.5 Determine the resultant force acting on block B just after block A has reached the floor. (2)

28.6 Define *mechanical energy*. (2)

28.7 Explain why the conservation of mechanical energy may be used to calculate the maximum height reached by block B. (2)

28.8 Use the principle of conservation of mechanical energy to calculate the maximum height from the ground reached by block B. (4)

[22]

Question 29 (2019 IEB Supplementary Examination) (Solutions on page 147)

29.1 A child of mass 40 kg is holding a dog stationary when the dog pulls forward on an inextensible leash. The dog exerts a force of 200 N, so that the leash makes an angle of 30° to the horizontal as shown below.

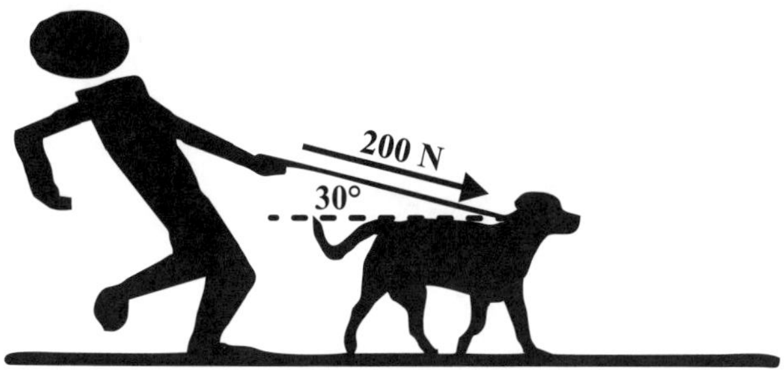

29.1.1 Calculate the horizontal and vertical components of the 200 N force applied by the dog. (4)

29.1.2 Calculate the magnitude of the normal force experienced by the child. (3)

29.1.3 Given that the coefficient of static friction between the child's foot and the ground is 0,4, calculate the maximum force of static friction experienced between the child's foot and the ground. (3)

29.1.4 Decide whether the child's foot will slip or not when the dog exerts the 200 N force at this angle and justify your answer. (2)

29.2 A child on a skateboard is pulled by a rope and experiences a horizontal force T to the right as shown in the sketch below. The mass of the child and the skateboard together is 55 kg. A total force of 80 N, due to friction, opposes the motion. The child and skateboard accelerate at 2 $m.s^{-2}$ to the right.

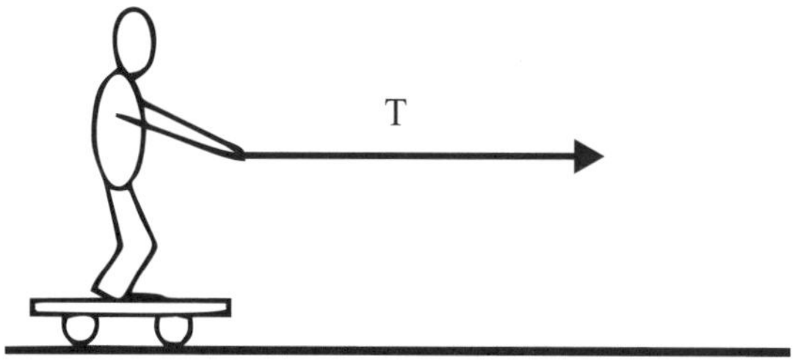

29.2.1 Calculate the magnitude of the force T. (4)

29.2.2 The force T is increased and the acceleration is measured, for each value of T. All other forces remain constant. Draw a sketch graph for the system showing the relationship between acceleration and T. No values need to be given on the axes. (3)

29.2.3 Sometime later, the force T is removed and the child and skateboard continues to move to the right for a short distance. The skateboard then hits a stone in the path and stops. State and explain what happens to the child. (3)

29.2.4 Name the Law of Physics which you applied in Question 29.2.3. (1)

[23]

TOC | 1 Data Sheet | 2 Definitions | 3 | 3 solutions | 4 | 4 solutions | 5 | 5 solutions | 6 | 6 solutions | 7 | 7 solutions | 8 | 8 solutions | 9 | 9 solutions | 10 | 10 solutions

Question 30 (2019 IEB Final Examination) (Solutions on page 148)

30.1 A child of mass 48 kg is on a water slide. The child slides down a steep slope and then travels up a gentle slope inclined at an angle θ to the horizontal. The coefficient of kinetic friction is 0,12.

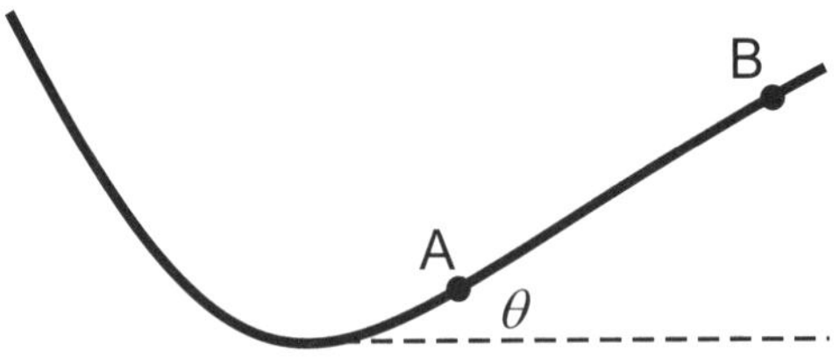

The child passes point A with a speed of 15 $m.s^{-1}$. The child just reaches point B.

30.1.1 Draw a labelled free-body diagram showing all the forces acting on the child while sliding **from A to B**. (3)

The component of the child's weight down the slope is 52,52 N.

30.1.2 Calculate the value of θ. (3)

30.1.3 Calculate the frictional force acting on the child. (4)

30.1.4 State *Newton's second law of motion*. (2)

30.1.5 Calculate the acceleration of the child (4)

On reaching point B, the child immediately slides back down the slope towards point A.

30.1.6 Explain if the magnitude of the acceleration of the child from A to B is the same as, greater than or less than the magnitude of the child's acceleration from B to A. (3)

30.2 A rocket in deep space is moving sideways, with its rockets off, from A to B as shown in the diagram.

On reaching point B, the rocket fires its engines for 2 s while the rocket travels to some point C. At point C, the engines are turned off.

On the diagram above, draw in

30.2.1 point C and the path the rocket follows from B to C. (2)

30.2.2 the path the rocket follows from C onwards. (2)

[23]

4. FORCES AND NEWTON'S LAWS (SOLUTIONS)

Question 1

1.1	C	(2)	1.12	A	(2)
1.2	C	(2)	1.13	B	(2)
1.3	C	(2)	1.14	B	(2)
1.4	A	(2)	1.15	D	(2)
1.5	C	(2)	1.16	D	(2)
1.6	C	(2)	1.17	D	(2)
1.7	C	(2)	1.18	A	(2)
1.8	B	(2)	1.19	B	(2)
1.9	C	(2)	1.20	B	(2)
1.10	A	(2)	1.21	B	(2)
1.11	B	(2)			

[42]

Question 2

2.1 8kg mass:

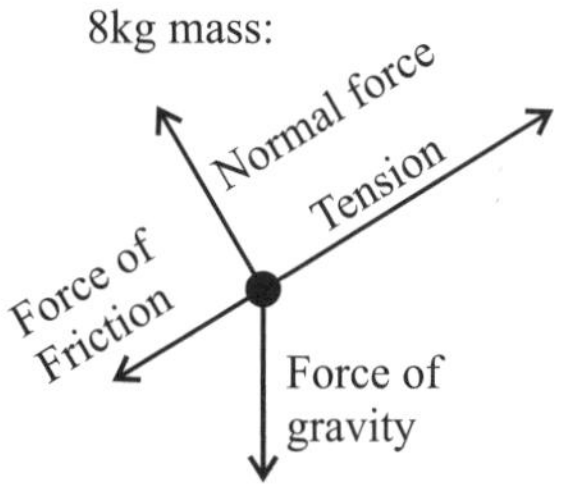

14kg mass:

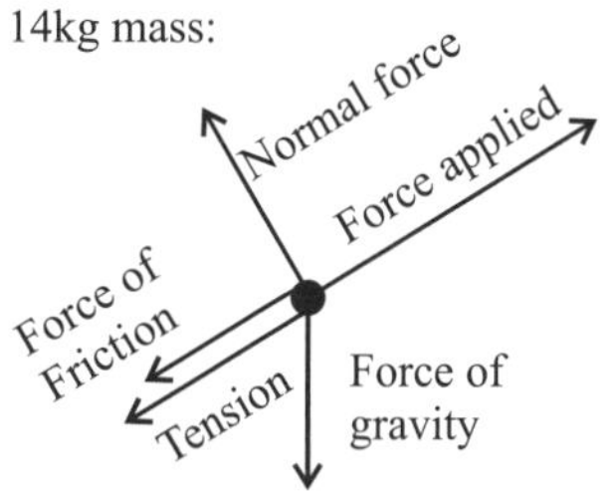

(7)

2.2 8kg:

$F_f = \mu F_N$

$= 0,55\left(9,8 \times 8\cos 50\right)$

$= 27,72\,\text{N}$

14kg:

$F_f = \mu F_N$

$= 0,55\left(9,8 \times 14\cos 50\right)$

$= 48,5\,\text{N}$

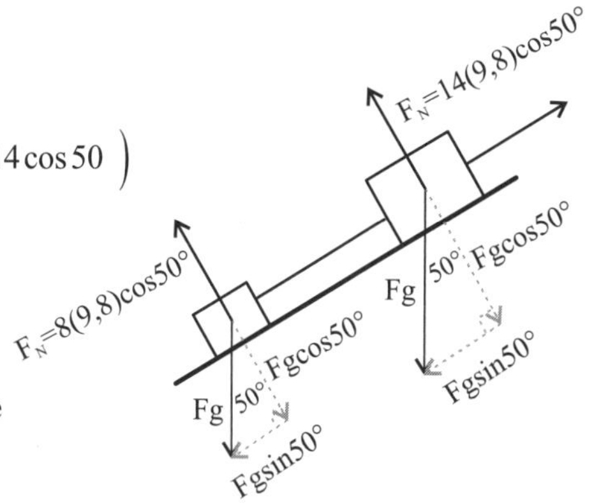

(4)

2.3 **Method 1: Working with the system as a whole**

$F_{net} = ma$

$F_A - F_{f14} - F_{g//14} - F_{f8} - F_{g//8} = ma$

$460 - 48,5 - 14(9,8)\sin 50 - 27,71 - 8(9,8)\sin 50 = 22a$

$a = 9,94\,\text{m.s}^{-2}$

Method 2: Working with each block individually:

14kg:

$F_{\text{net}} = ma$

$F_A - F_g \sin\theta - F_f - T = ma$

$460 - 14(9,8)\sin 50 - 48,5 - T = 14a$

$T = 411,5 - 137,2\sin 50 - 14a \rightarrow$ sub into T for the 8kg block

8kg:

$F_{\text{net}} = ma$

$T - F_g \sin\theta - F_f = ma$

$T - 8(9,8)\sin 50 - 27,72 = 8a$

$411,5 - 137,2\sin 50 - 14a - 78,4\sin 50 - 27,72 = 8a$

$a = 9,94\,\text{m.s}^{-2}$ up the slope

(5)

TOC | 1 Data Sheet | 2 Definitions | 3 | 3 solutions | 4 | 4 solutions | 5 | 5 solutions | 6 | 6 solutions | 7 | 7 solutions | 8 | 8 solutions | 9 | 9 solutions | 10 | 10 solutions

TOC
1 Data Sheet
2 Definitions
3
3 solutions
4
4 solutions
5
5 solutions
6
6 solutions
7
7 solutions
8
8 solutions
9
9 solutions
10
10 solutions

2.4 Using the 14kg block:

$$T = F_A - F_g \sin\theta - F_f - ma$$
$$= 460 - 14(9,8)\sin 50 - 48,5 - 14(9,94)$$
$$= 167,24\,\text{N}$$

[19]

Question 3

3.1 The rate of change of velocity. (2)

3.2 The force of friction would increase.
The force in the tow rope has a vertical component upwards which decreases the normal force.
$F_f = \mu F_N$
By decreasing the angle, the vertical component will decrease, and the normal force will increase. The frictional force is directly proportional to the normal force. Therefore, the force of friction will increase. (5)

3.3

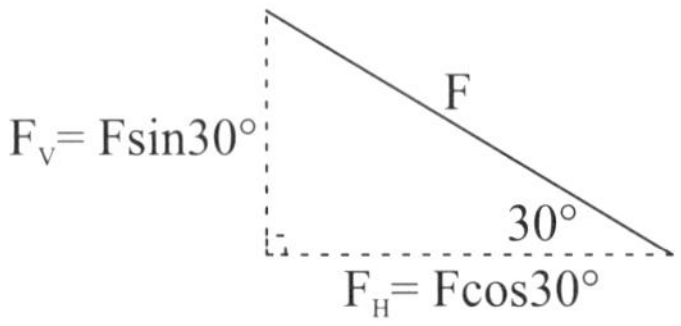

$$F_N = F_g - F_V$$
$$= mg - F\sin 30$$
$$= 100(9,8) - 0,5F$$
$$= 980 - 0,5F$$
$$F_f = \mu F_N$$
$$= 0,15(980 - 0,5F)$$
$$= 147 - 0,075F$$
$$F_{net} = ma$$
$$F\cos 30 - F_f = ma$$
$$F\cos 30 - (147 - 0,075F) = 100(0,5)$$
$$\frac{\sqrt{3}}{2}F + 0,075F = 197$$
$$F\left(\frac{\sqrt{3}}{2} + 0,075\right) = 197$$
$$F = 209,35\,\text{N}$$

(6)

[13]

Question 4

4.1 Q:

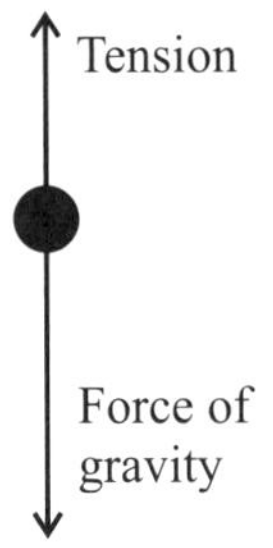

P:

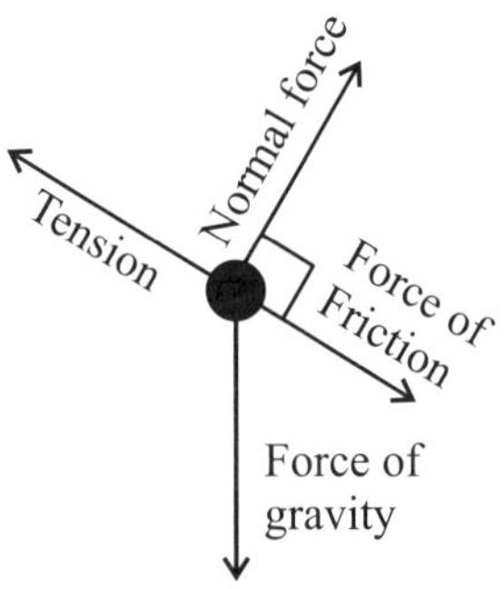

(6)

4.2 Using crate Q:

$$F_{net} = ma$$
$$F_g - T = ma$$
$$9,8(6) - T = 6(0,43)$$
$$T = 56,22\text{N}$$

(3)

4.3 Using crate P:

$F_{net} = ma$

$T - F_{g//} - F_f = ma$

$T - mg\sin\theta - F_f = ma$

$56,22 - 8(9,8)\sin\theta - 13,58 = 8(0,43)$

$\sin\theta = 0,5$

$\theta = 30$

$F_f = \mu F_N$

$13,58 = \mu\left[8(9,8)\cos 30\right]$

$\mu = 0,2$ (7)

4.4 $v_f^2 = v_i^2 + 2a\Delta x$

$= 0 + 2(0,43)(4)$

$= 3,44$

$\therefore v_f = 1,85\,\text{m.s}^{-1}$ (3)

4.5 **Method 1:**

$F_{net} = ma \rightarrow$ Using crate Q

$F_g - T = ma$

$9,8(6) - T = 6(0,5)$

$T = 55,8\,\text{N}$

$F_{net} = ma$

$T_H - F_{g//} - F_f = ma$

$T\cos 15 - mg\sin 30 - F_f = ma$

$55,8\cos 15 - F_f - 8(9,8)\sin 30 = 8(0,5)$

$F_f = 10,7\,\text{N}$

Method 2:

$F_{net} = ma \rightarrow$ Using crate Q

$F_g - T = ma$

$9,8(6) - T = 6(0,5)$

$T = 55,8\,\text{N}$

$F_f = \mu F_N$

$= 0,2\left[F_{g\perp} - T_V\right]$

$= 0,2\left[8(9,8)\cos 30 - 55,8\sin 15\right]$

$= 10,7\,\text{N}$ (4)

4.6 Frictional force is directionally proportional to the normal force.
As the force applied is at an angle the vertical component will decrease the normal force which decreases the force of friction. (3)

[26]

Question 5

5.1 

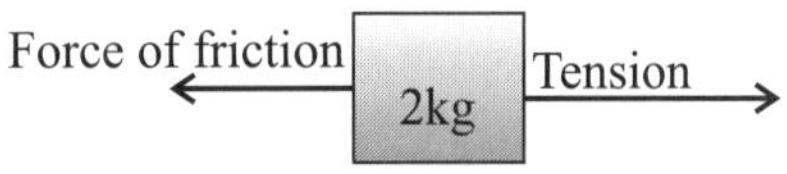

(5)

5.2 $\text{F}_{net\,5kg} = ma$

$\text{F}_\text{A} - \text{F}_f - \text{T} = 5a$

$40 - 2 - \text{T} = 5a$

$38 - \text{T} = 5a$ (3)

5.3 $\text{F}_{net\,2kg} = ma$

$\text{T} - \text{F}_f = 2a$

$\text{T} - 2 = 2a$ (3)

5.4 $\text{T} - 2 = 2a$

$\text{T} = 2a + 2 \rightarrow$ substitute into the equation for the 5kg block

$38 - (2a + 2) = 5a$

$36 = 7a$

$a = 5,14\,\text{m.s}^{-2}$ (4)

[15]

TOC 1 Data Sheet 2 Definitions 3 3 solutions 4 4 solutions 5 5 solutions 6 6 solutions 7 7 solutions 8 8 solutions 9 9 solutions 10 10 solutions

Question 6

6.1 When a net force, Fnet, is applied to an object of mass, m, it accelerates in the direction of the net force. The acceleration, *a*, is directly proportional to the net force and inversely proportional to the mass. (2)

6.2 $\Delta x = v_i \Delta t + \frac{1}{2} a \Delta t^2$

$1{,}5 = 0 + \frac{1}{2}(a)(2)^2$

$a = 0{,}75\,\text{m.s}^{-2}$ (4)

6.3 **18,4 kg block:**

$F_{net} = ma$

$T = 18{,}4(0{,}75)$

$= 13{,}8\,\text{N}$

Block m:

$F_{net} = ma$

$F_g - T = ma$

$9{,}8m - 13{,}8 = m(0{,}75)$

$9{,}05m = 13{,}8$

$m = 1{,}52\,\text{kg}$

[11]

Question 7

7.1

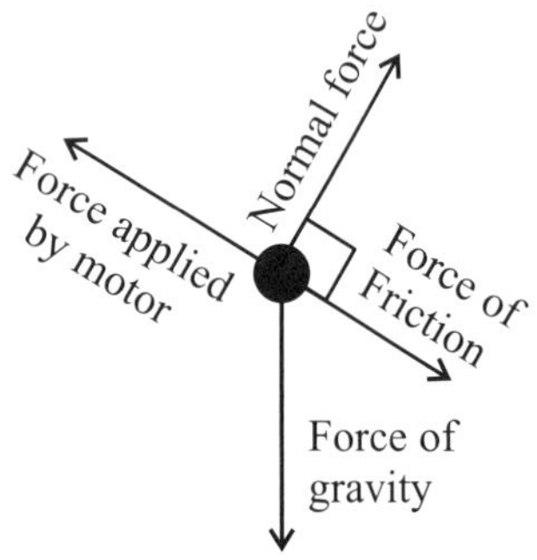

(4)

7.2 When a net force, Fnet, is applied to an object of mass, m, it accelerates in the direction of the net force. The acceleration, *a*, is directly proportional to the net force and inversely proportional to the mass. (2)

7.3 $F_{net} = ma$

$= 4500(0{,}25)$

$= 1125\,\text{N}$ (3)

7.4 $F_f = \mu F_N$

$= 0{,}35(4500)(9{,}8)(\cos 52)$

$= 9502{,}73\,\text{N}$ (4)

7.5 $F_{net} = F_{motor} - F_f - F_{//}$

$1125 = F_{motor} - 9502{,}73 - 4500(9{,}8)(\sin 52)$

$F_{motor} = 45379\,\text{N}$ up the slope (5)

7.6 When the rope snapped, the cart has inertia and will continue moving. It is possible that the cart will reach the top before the force of friction and/or force of gravity brings it to rest. (3)

[21]

Question 8

8.1 An object continues in a state of rest or uniform (moving with constant) velocity unless it is acted upon by a net or resultant force. (2)

8.2 $F_f = \mu F_N$

$= 0,6(9,8 \times 8)$

$= 47,04\,\text{N}$ (3)

8.3 $T = 47,04\,\text{N}$. The minimum force required to make the block move is equal to the maximum frictional force on the $8\,\text{kg}$ block. (2)

8.4

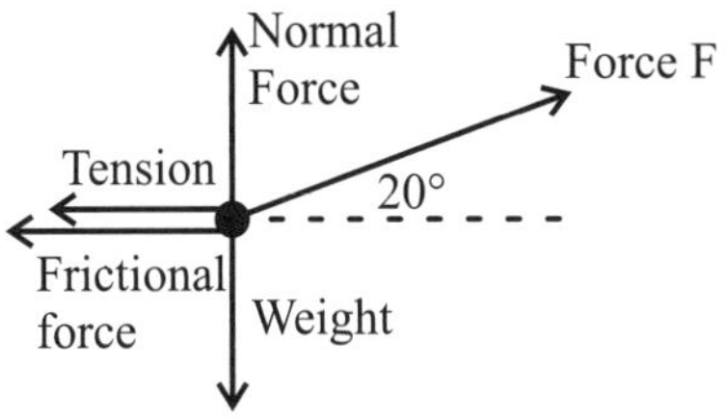

(5)

8.5 $F_{f24kg} = \mu\left(F_g - F_v\right)$

$= 0,6\left[24(9,8) - F\sin 20\right]$

$= 141,12 - F\left(0,6\sin 20\right)$

When the blocks are just about to move:

$F_H = T + F_f$

$F\cos 20 = 47,04 + 141,12 - F\left(0,6\sin 20\right)$

$F\left(\cos 20 + 0,6\sin 20\right) = 188,16$

$F = 164,35\,\text{N}$ (6)

[18]

Question 9

9.1 Every particle with mass in the universe attracts every other particle with a force which is directly proportional to the product of their masses and inversely proportional to the square of the distance between their centres. (3)

9.2 $F = mg$

$280 \times 10^3 = m(14)$

$m = 20\,000\,\text{kg}$ (2)

9.3 $g = \dfrac{Gm_p}{r^2}$

$r^2 = \dfrac{\left(6,7 \times 10^{-11}\right)\left(1 \times 10^{21} \times 1000\right)}{14}$

$r = 2\,187\,627,55\,\text{m}$

$= 2188\,\text{km}$ (4)

TOC 1 Data Sheet 2 Definitions 3 3 solutions 4 4 solutions 5 5 solutions 6 6 solutions 7 7 solutions 8 8 solutions 9 9 solutions 10 10 solutions

9.4 Note that the probe would have to be closer to the lighter asteroid.

Lighter asteroid:

$$F_1 = \frac{Gm_1m_2}{r^2}$$

$$F_1 = \frac{Gm_am_p}{x^2}$$

Heavier asteroid:

$$F_2 = \frac{Gm_1m_2}{r^2}$$

$$F_2 = \frac{G(2m_a)m_p}{\left(1000\times10^3 - x\right)^2}$$

$$F_1 = F_2$$

$$\frac{Gm_am_p}{x^2} = \frac{G(2m_a)m_p}{\left(1000\times10^3 - x\right)^2}$$

$$\frac{1}{x^2} = \frac{2}{1\times10^{12} - 2\,000\,000x + x^2}$$

$$1\times10^{12} - 2\,000\,000x + x^2 = 2x^2$$

$$x^2 + 2\,000\,000x - 1\times10^{12} = 0$$

$x = 4\,14\,213{,}27\,\text{m} \rightarrow x$ has to be positive (6)

[15]

Question 10

10.1 When a net force, Fnet, is applied to an object of mass, m, it accelerates in the direction of the net force. The acceleration, *a*, is directly proportional to the net force and inversely proportional to the mass. (2)

10.2

(2)

10.3

$$F_{net} = 0$$
$$T = F_f$$
$$= \mu_s F_N$$
$$= 0{,}8(9{,}8)(5{,}6)$$
$$= 43{,}9\,\text{N}$$

(3)

10.4

5,6 kg:

$$F_{net} = ma$$
$$T - F_f = ma$$
$$T - \mu_k mg = ma$$
$$T - (0{,}65)(5{,}6)(9{,}8) = (5{,}6)(0{,}25)$$
$$T = 37{,}07\,\text{N}$$

M:

$$F_{net} = ma$$
$$F_g - T = ma$$
$$M(9{,}8) - 37{,}07 = M(0{,}25)$$
$$9{,}8M - 0{,}25M = 37{,}07$$
$$9{,}55M = 37{,}07$$
$$M = 3{,}88\,\text{kg}$$

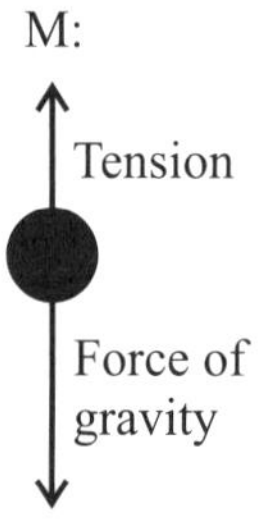

(5)

[12]

Question 11

11.1

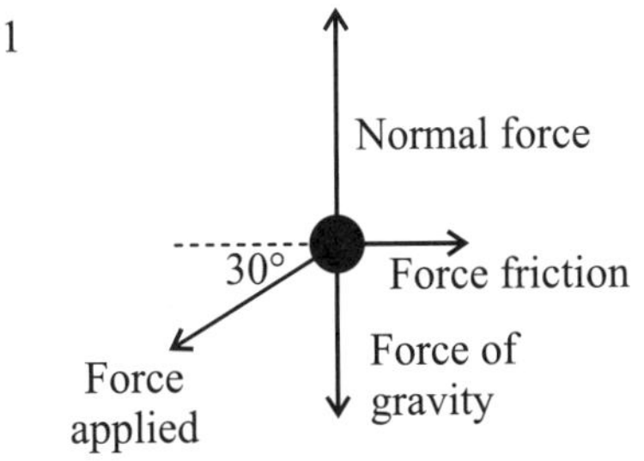

(4)

11.2

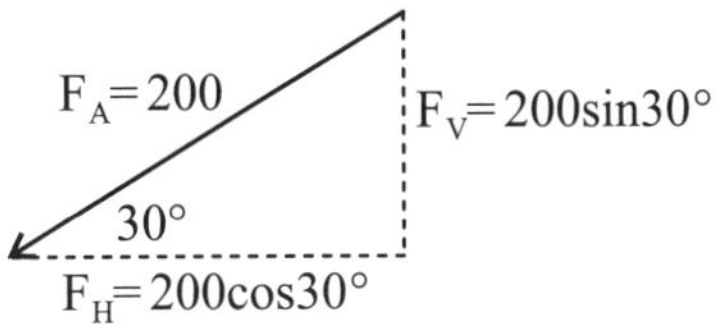

$$F_H = F_f$$
$$200\cos 30^\circ = \mu F_N$$
$$200\cos 30^\circ = \mu\left(F_g + F_V\right)$$
$$200\cos 30^\circ = \mu\left[(20)(9,8) + 200\sin 30^\circ\right]$$
$$\mu = \frac{200\cos 30^\circ}{(20)(9,8) + 200\sin 30^\circ}$$
$$= 0,585$$

(6)

11.3

$$F_H = F_f$$
$$F_A \cos 30^\circ = \mu F_N$$
$$F_A \cos 30^\circ = 0,5\left(F_g + F_V\right)$$
$$F_A \cos 30^\circ = 0,5\left[(20)(9,8) + F_A \sin 30^\circ\right]$$
$$F_A \cos 30^\circ = 98 + 0,25 F_A$$
$$F_A \cos 30^\circ - 0,25 F_A = 98$$
$$F_A\left(\cos 30^\circ - 0,25\right) = 98$$
$$F_A = \frac{98}{\cos 30^\circ - 0,25}$$
$$= 159,08\,N$$

(6)

[16]

Question 12

12.1

$$F_f + F_{g//} = F_A$$
$$\mu_k F_N + mg\sin 35^\circ = F_A$$
$$\mu_k mg\cos 35^\circ + mg\sin 35^\circ = F_A$$
$$\mu_k (10)(9,8)\cos 35^\circ + (10)(9,8)\sin 35^\circ = 80$$
$$\mu_k = 0,3$$

(6)

12.2

$$F_f + F_A = F_{g//}$$
$$\mu_s F_N + F_A = mg\sin 35^\circ$$
$$\mu_s mg\cos 35^\circ + F_A = mg\sin 35^\circ$$
$$\mu_s (10)(9,8)\cos 35^\circ + 16 = (10)(9,8)\sin 35^\circ$$
$$\mu_s = 0,5$$

(6)

[12]

Question 13

13.1 The force that opposes the motion of an object and acts parallel to the surface with which the object is in contact. (2)

13.2 Graph of Force against Mass

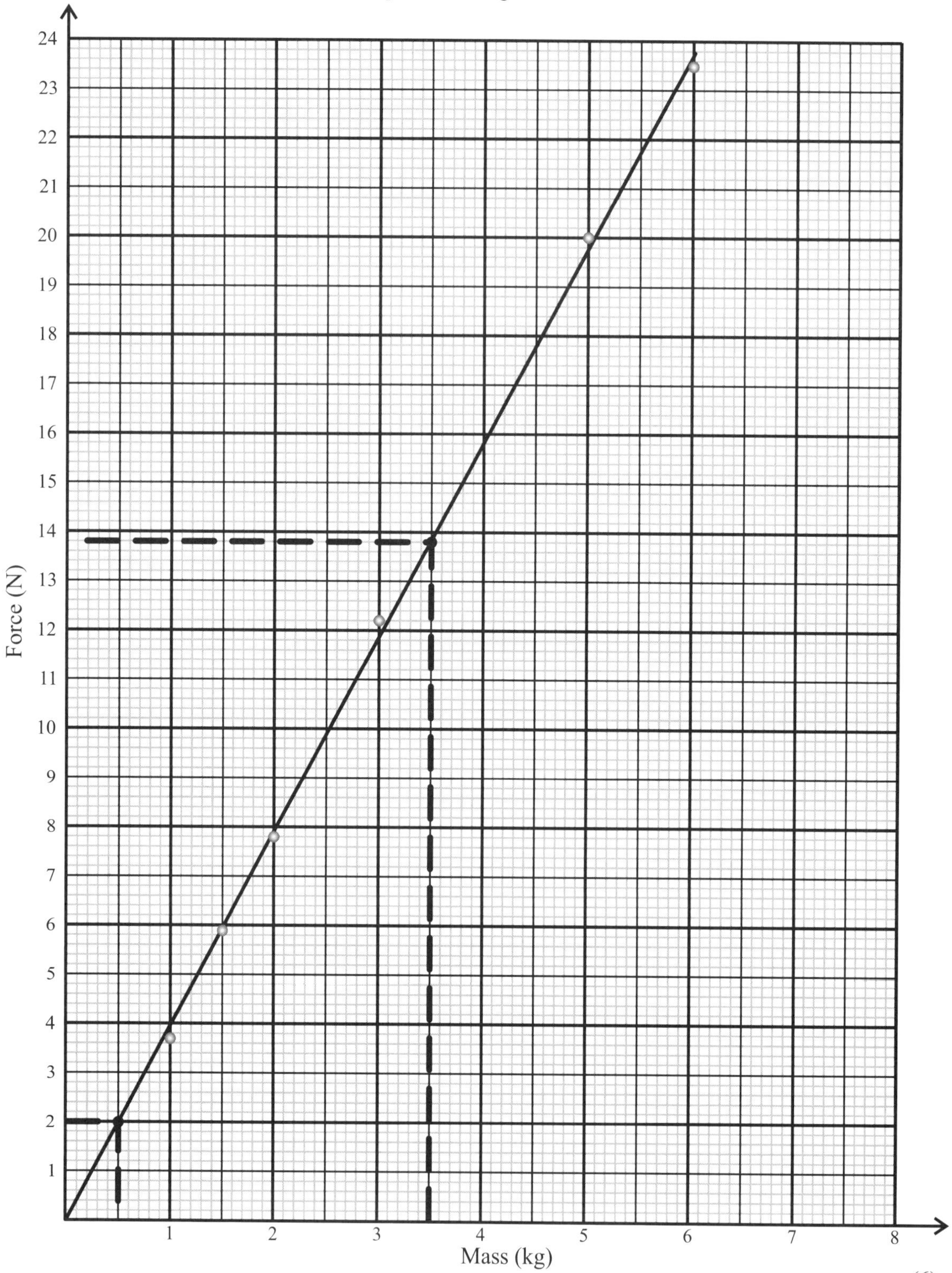

(6)

13.3 $m = \dfrac{13,8-2}{3,5-0,5}$

$= 3,93$ (4)

13.4 The force required to pull the block is directly proportional to the mass of the block. (2)

13.5 $F_f = \mu F_N$

$= \mu mg$ (2)

13.6 $y = m\,x + c \rightarrow m$ in this equation is the gradient

$F_f = \mu g\, m + 0 \rightarrow$ it can be seen from the equation that the gradient $= \mu g$

$\mu g = 3{,}93$

$\mu(9{,}8) = 3{,}93$

$\mu = 0{,}4$ (4)

[20]

Question 14

14.1 Every particle with mass in the universe attracts every other particle with a force which is directly proportional to the product of their masses and inversely proportional to the square of the distance between their centres. (3)

14.2

$$F_g = \frac{GM_pM_{in}}{r^2}$$

$$= \frac{\left(6{,}7\times10^{-11}\right)\left(6{,}4\times10^{23}\right)(608)}{\left(3525\times10^{3}\right)^2}$$

$$= 2{,}61\times10^{16}\ \text{N}$$

(4)

14.3

$$F_{g\ \text{on the surface}} = \frac{GM_pM_{in}}{r^2}$$

$$= \frac{\left(6{,}7\times10^{-11}\right)\left(6{,}4\times10^{23}\right)(358)}{\left(3397\times10^{3}\right)^2}$$

$$= 1330{,}29\ \text{N}$$

Gina is correct. Although distance decreased, the decrease is relatively small compared to the overall radius of Mars. This means the large decrease in mass takes preference and the weight will decrease. (5)

14.4

$$g = \frac{GM_p}{r^2}$$

$$= \frac{\left(6{,}7\times10^{-11}\right)\left(6{,}4\times10^{23}\right)}{\left(3397\times10^{3}\right)^2}$$

$$= 3{,}72\ \text{m.s}^{-2}$$

(4)

[16]

Question 15

15.1 When a net force, Fnet, is applied to an object of mass, m, it accelerates in the direction of the net force. The acceleration, *a*, is directly proportional to the net force and inversely proportional to the mass. (2)

15.2

$$F_f = \mu F_N$$

$$= 0{,}25(5)(9{,}8)$$

$$= 12{,}25\ \text{N}$$

(3)

TOC
1 Data Sheet
2 Definitions
3
3 solutions
4
4 solutions
5
5 solutions
6
6 solutions
7
7 solutions
8
8 solutions
9
9 solutions
10
10 solutions

15.3 2,5kg block:

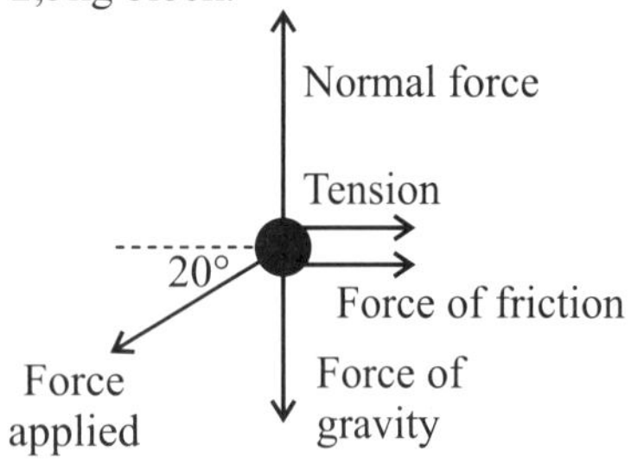

(5)

15.4 **Method 1: Working with the system as a whole**

$F_{net} = ma$

$F_H - F_{f\,2,5kg} - F_{f\,5kg} = ma$

$80\cos 20^\circ - \mu F_{N2,5kg} - \mu F_{N2,5kg} = 7,5a$

$80\cos 20^\circ - 0,25\left[2,5(9,8) + 80\sin 20^\circ\right] - 0,25\left[5(9,8)\right] = 7,5a$

$49,96 = 7,5a$

$a = 6,66\ \text{m.s}^{-2}$

$5kg$ block:

$F_{net} = ma$

$T - F_f = ma$

$T - 12,25 = 5(6,66)$

$T = 45,55\ \text{N}$

Method 2: Working with each block individually:

2,5kg block:

$F_{net} = ma$

$F_H - T - F_f = ma$

$80\cos 20^\circ - T - \mu F_N = 2,5a$

$80\cos 20^\circ - T - 0,25\left[2,5(9,8) + 80\sin 20^\circ\right] = 2,5a$

$80\cos 20^\circ - T - 6,125 - 20\sin 20 = 2,5a$

$80\cos 20^\circ - (5a + 12,25) - 6,125 - 20\sin 20 = 2,5a$

$a = 6,66\ \text{m.s}^{-2}$

$T = 5(6,66) + 12,25$

$= 45,55\ \text{N}$

5kg block:

$F_{net} = ma$

$T - F_f = ma$

$T - 12,25 = 5a$

$T = 5a + 12,25$

(8)

[18]

Question 16

First determine the acceleration of the man (this is the same as the acceleration of the elevator)

$F_N - F_g = ma$

$944 - 80(9,8) = 80a$

$a = 2\,\text{m.s}^{-2}$ upwards

Man:

$T - F_g = ma$

$T - 1080(9,8) = 1080(2)$

$T = 12\,744\text{N}$

Elevator:

[8]

Question 17

17.1 Upwards (2)

17.2 $m = \dfrac{980}{9{,}8}$

$= 100\,\text{kg}$ (3)

17.3 Upwards, the lift is slowing down (accelerating downwards) between 6 and 8 seconds. (3)

17.4 $F_N - F_g = ma$ **or** $F_g - F_N = ma$

$990 - 980 = 100a$ **or** $980 - 970 = 100a$

$a = 0{,}1\,\text{m.s}^{-2}$ **or** $a = 0{,}1\,\text{m.s}^{-2}$ (3)

17.5 $0\ \text{m.s}^{-2}$ (1)

17.6 Upwards. According to Newton's first law, An object continues in a state of rest or uniform (moving with constant) velocity unless it is acted upon by a net or resultant force. The lift is moving upwards when the cable snaps and will continue to move upwards. (3)

17.7 0 N (1)

[16]

Question 18

First determine the acceleration of the elevator using the weight of the box:

Box weight = 1200 – 960

= 240N

$F_N - F_g = ma$

$240 - 20(9{,}8) = 20a$

$a = 2{,}2\,\text{m.s}^{-2}$

Now determine Tom's weight:

$F_N - F_g = ma$

$960 - m(9{,}8) = m(2{,}2)$

$960 = 12m$

$m = 80\,\text{kg}$

$\text{Weight} = 80(9{,}8) = 784\,\text{N}$ **[8]**

Question 19

19.1

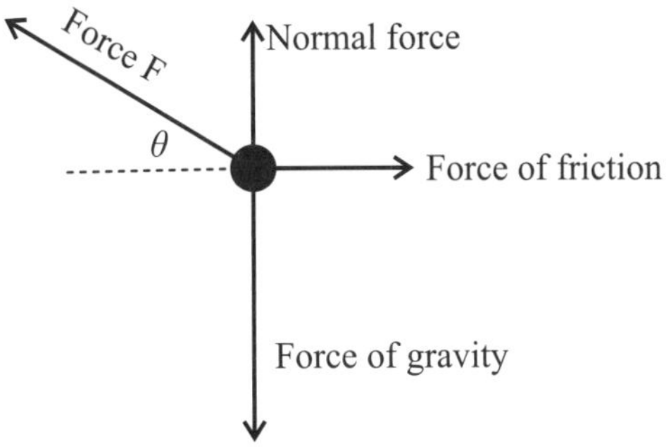

Note:
The normal force must be shorter than force of gravity.

(4)

19.2 The force that opposes the motion of an object and acts parallel to the surface with which the object is in contact. (2)

19.3 $F_f = \mu F_N$

$140 = 0{,}3F_N$

$F_N = 466{,}67\,\text{N}$ (3)

19.4 $F_H = F_f = 140\,N$

$F_N = F_g - F_v$

$466,67 = 60(9,8) - F_v$

$F_v = 121,33\,N$

$F^2 = 140^2 + 121,33^2$

$= 34320,9689$

$F = 185,26\,N$

$\tan\theta = \dfrac{121,33}{140}$

$\theta = 40,91^\circ$ (8)

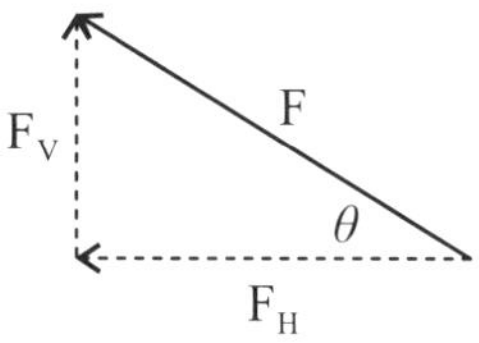

[17]

Question 20 (2014 Exemplar IEB Examination)

20.1.1 When a net force, Fnet, is applied to an object of mass, m, it accelerates in the direction of the net force. The acceleration, *a*, is directly proportional to the net force and inversely proportional to the mass. (4)

20.1.2

a) Note that the Driving force arrow must be longer than the combined arrows of Tension and force of friction

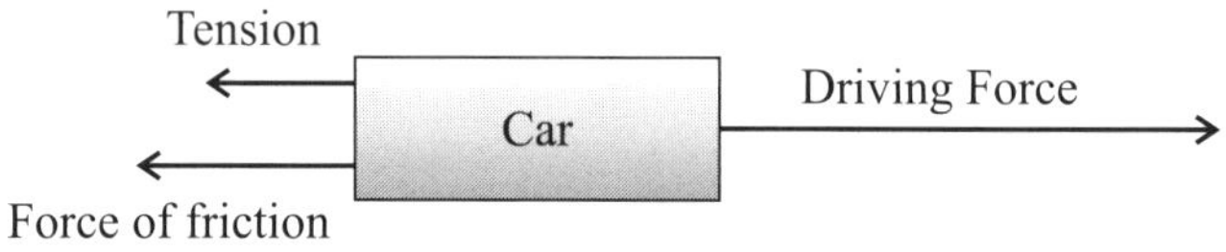

(3)

b) Note that the Tension arrow must be longer than the Force of friction arrow.

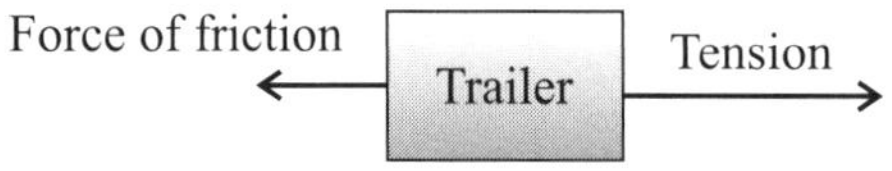

20.1.3 (5)

a) $F_{net} = ma$

$F_D - F_{f\,car} - F_{f\,trailer} = ma$

$21220 - 10900 - 4800 = (1600 + 700)a$

$a = 2,4\ m.s^{-2}$ (3)

b) Using the trailer:

$F_{net} = ma$

$T - F_{f\,trailer} = ma$

$T - 4800 = 700(2,4)$

$T = 6480\ N$ (2)

20.2.1

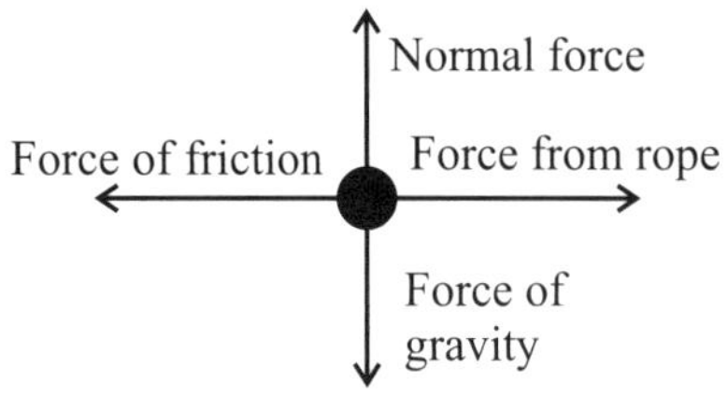

(4)

20.2.2 $F_{f\,max} = \mu F_N$

$= \mu mg$

$= (0,5)(180)(9,8)$

$= 882\ N$ (4)

20.2.3 The force of friction is directly proportional to the normal force. By pulling at an angle the normal force is reduced. Therefore, the force of friction is reduced. (2)

20.2.4 $F_{f\,max} = \mu F_N$

$= \mu\left(mg - F\sin 40\right)$

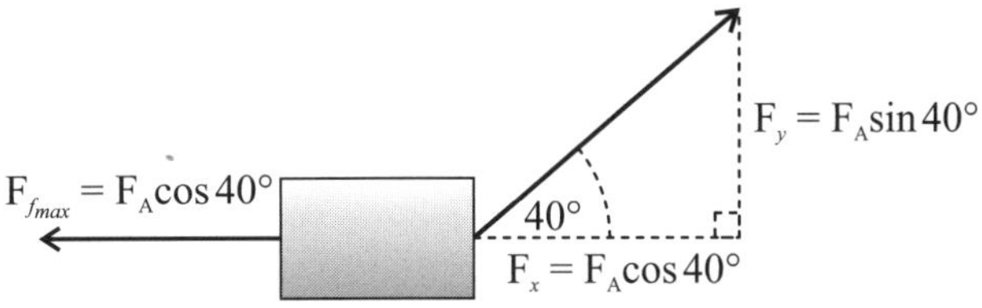

$F_{f\,max} = F\cos 40$

$\mu\left(mg - F\sin 40\right) = F\cos 40$

$0,5\left[(180)(9,8) - F\sin 40\right] = F\cos 40$

$882 - 0,5F\sin 40 = F\cos 40$

$882 = F\left(\cos 40 + 0,5\sin 40\right)$

$F = 811,08\,N$ (4)

[28]

Question 21 (2014 IEB Final Examination)

21.1 The angle (θ) of the incline. (2)

21.2 The surfaces need to be the same so that they have the same coefficient of friction. (2)

21.3

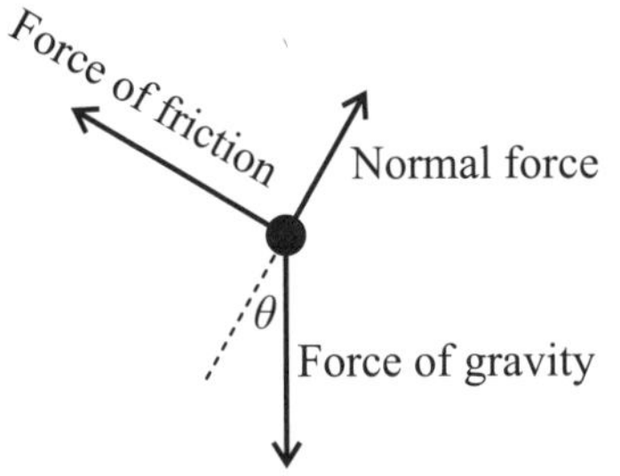

(4)

21.4 Tessa is correct. The box will be on the point of sliding when the component of the gravitational force down the slope (Fsin θ) is equal (OR greater than) in magnitude to the maximum static frictional force up the slope ($\mu F_g\cos\theta$).

$\mu F_g\cos\theta = F_g\sin\theta$

$\mu = \dfrac{F_g\sin\theta}{F_g\cos\theta}$

$= \tan\theta$

This means that the angle at which the box begins to slide is independent of mass and only depends on the coefficient of friction. (5)

[13]

Question 22 (2018 IEB Supplementary Examination)

22.1 When a net force, Fnet, is applied to an object of mass, m, it accelerates in the direction of the net force. The acceleration, a, is directly proportional to the net force and inversely proportional to the mass. (2)

22.2 Left side:

$F_{net} = ma$

$F_g - T = ma$

$(0,6)(9,8) - T = 0,6a$

$5,88 - T = 0,6a$

Right Side:

$F_{net} = ma$

$T - F_g = ma$

$T - (0,4)(9,8) = 0,4a$

$T - 3,92 = 0,4a$ (3)

22.3 From the right side:

$T = 0,4a + 3,92$

Substitute into the left side equation:

$5,88 - T = 0,6a$

$5,88 - 0,4a - 3,92 = 0,6a$

$a = 1,96\,m.s^{-2}$

$T = 0,4(1,96) + 3,92$

$= 4,70\,N$ (2)

22.4

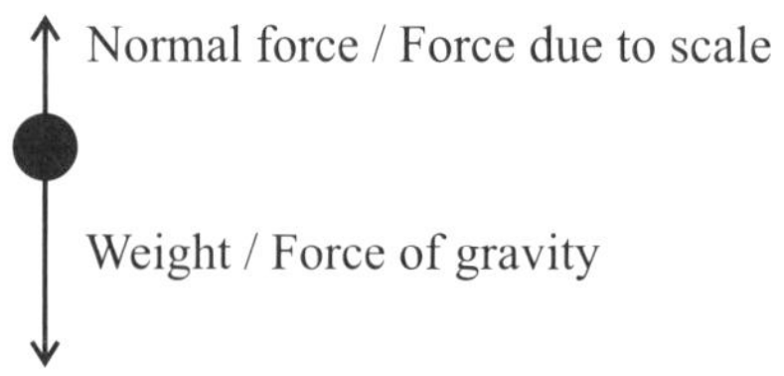

(3)

22.5 $F_{net} = ma$

$F_g - F_N = ma$

$(0{,}5)(9{,}8) - F_N = 0{,}5(1{,}96)$

$F_N = 3{,}92 \text{ N}$ (3)

22.6 When object A exerts a force on object B, object B simultaneously exerts an oppositely directed force of equal magnitude on object A. (2)

22.7 The force of the 0,5kg mass on the scale pan. (2)

[17]

Question 23 (2017 IEB Final Examination)

23.1.1 Newtons II law.
When a net force, Fnet, is applied to an object of mass, m, it accelerates in the direction of the net force. The acceleration, *a*, is directly proportional to the net force and inversely proportional to the mass. (3)

23.1.2 Acceleration (2)

23.1.3 (6)

Graph of acceleration vs force

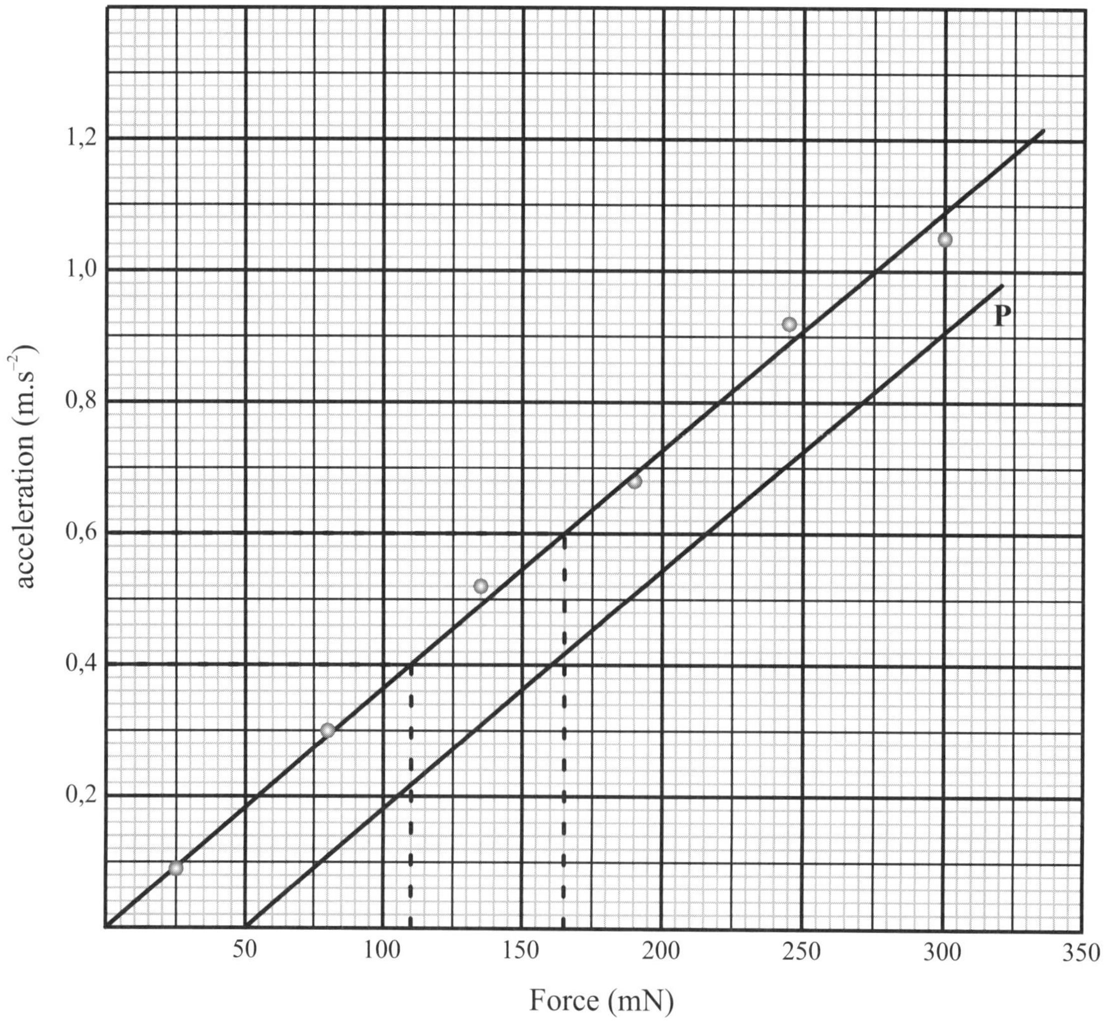

23.1.4 Gradient $= \frac{\Delta a}{\Delta F}$

$$= \frac{0,6-0,4}{165\times10^{-3}-110\times10^{-3}}$$

$$= 3,63\,\text{kg}^{-1}$$

Units calculation:

$$\text{units} = \frac{Acceleration}{Force} \rightarrow \frac{y}{x}$$

$$= \frac{\text{m.s}^{-2}}{\text{N}} \rightarrow \text{Newton} \Rightarrow m\times a \Rightarrow \text{kg.m.s}^{-2}$$

$$= \frac{\text{m.s}^{-2}}{\text{kg.m.s}^{-2}}$$

$$= \text{kg}^{-1}$$ (4)

23.1.5 $\frac{1}{m} = 3,63$

$$m = \frac{1}{3,63}$$

$$= 0,275\,\text{kg}$$ (3)

23.1.6 Shown on the graph. Line P must be parallel to the original line (have the same gradient). (2)

23.2.1

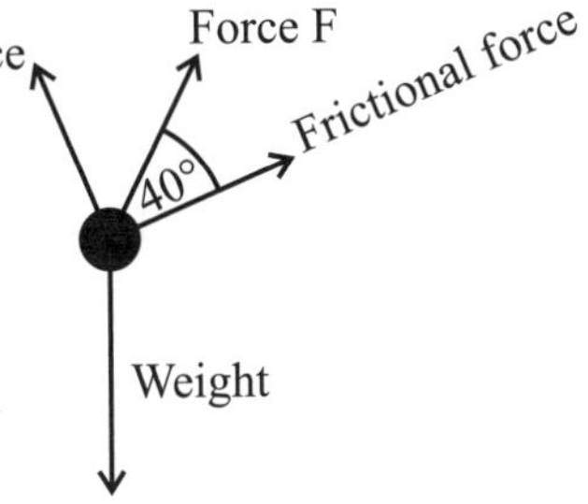

(4)

23.2.2 $W_{//} = F_g \sin\theta$

$$= 150(9,8)\sin 35$$

$$= 843,16\text{ N}$$ (3)

23.2.3 $F_f + F\cos 40 = W_{//}$

$$F_f + 100\cos 40 = 843,16$$

$$F_f = 766,56\text{ N}$$ (4)

23.2.4 $F_{f\,max} = \mu F_N$

$$= \mu\left(W_\perp - F\sin 40\right)$$

$$= 0,7\left[(150)(9,8)\cos 35 - F\sin 40\right]$$

$$= 842,91 - 0,7F\sin 40$$

$$F_{f\,max} + F\cos 40 = W_{//}$$

$$842,91 - 0,7F\sin 40 + F\cos 40 = 843,16$$

$$-0,7F\sin 40 + F\cos 40 = 0,25$$

$$F\left(-0,7\sin 40 + \cos 40\right) = 0,25$$

$$F = \frac{0,25}{-0,7\sin 40 + \cos 40}$$

$$= 0,79\text{ N}$$ (4)

[35]

TOC
1 Data Sheet
2 Definitions
3
3 solutions
4
4 solutions
5
5 solutions
6
6 solutions
7
7 solutions
8
8 solutions
9
9 solutions
10
10 solutions

Question 24 (2018 IEB Final Examination)

24.1 **Box A:**

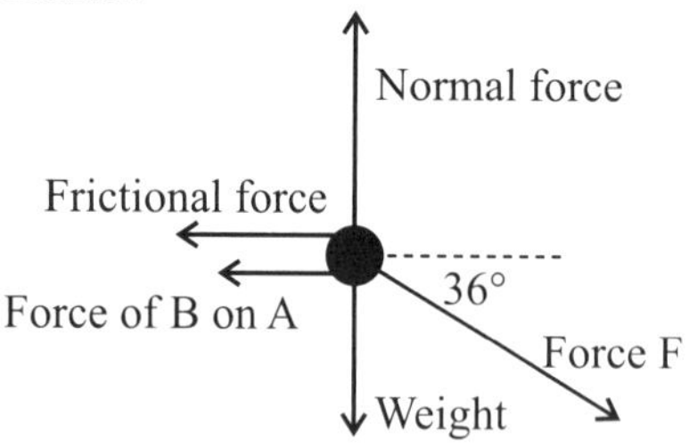

24.2 **Box B:**

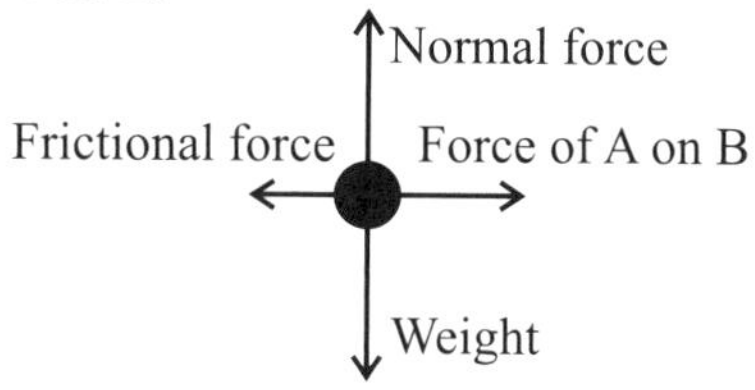

(5)

24.3 Newtons II law.
When a net force, Fnet, is applied to an object of mass, m, it accelerates in the direction of the net force. The acceleration, *a*, is directly proportional to the net force and inversely proportional to the m (4)

24.4 $F_{net} = ma$

$134\cos 36 \ -(45 + F_{B \text{ on } A}) = 23a$ (4)

24.5 When object A exerts a force on object B, object B simultaneously exerts an oppositely directed force of equal magnitude on object A. (2)

24.6 **Method 1: Working with the system as a whole**

$F_{net} = ma$

$F_H - F_{fA} - F_{fB} = ma$

$134\cos 36 \ -45 - 45 = (23+31)a$

$a = 0{,}34\,\text{m.s}^{-2}$

Magnitude of $F_{A \text{ on } B} = F_{B \text{ on } A} = x$

Box B:

$F_{net} = ma$

$x - F_f = ma$

$x - 45 = 31(0{,}34)$

$x = 55{,}54$ N to the left (3)

Method 2: Working with each block
Let the magnitude of force of B on A and A on B = x

Box A:

$F_{net} = ma$

$134\cos 36 \ -45 - x = 23a$

$134\cos 36 \ -45 - (31a + 45) = 23a$

$a = 0{,}34$

$x = 31(0{,}34) + 45$

$= 55{,}54$ N to the left

Box B:

$F_{net} = ma$

$x - 45 = 31a$

$x = 31a + 45$

24.7 The force that opposes the motion of an object (2)

24.8 $F_f = \mu F_N$

$F_N = F_g + F_V$ where F_V is the vertical component of F

Although, box B has a greater mass than A, they both have the same normal force due to the vertical component of force F. (3)

[25]

Question 25 (2015 IEB Supplementary Examination)

25.1

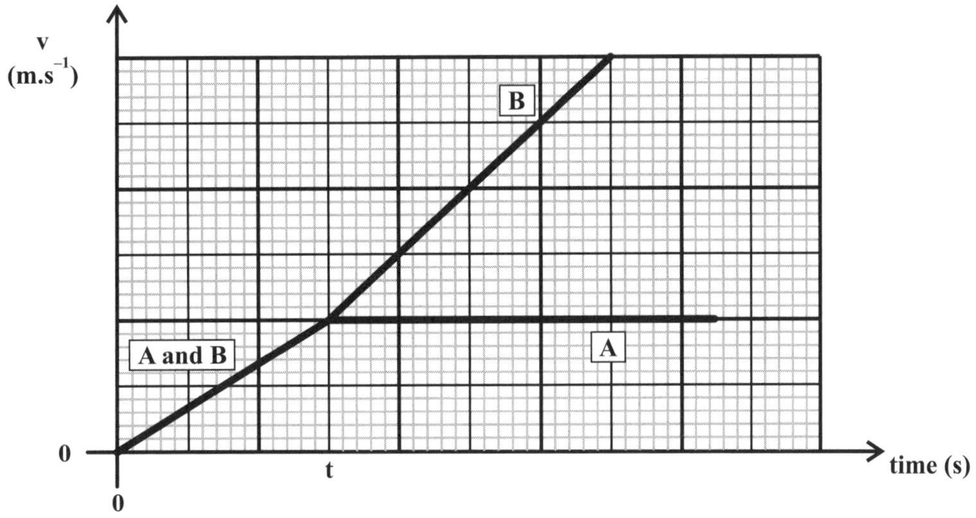

(3)

25.2

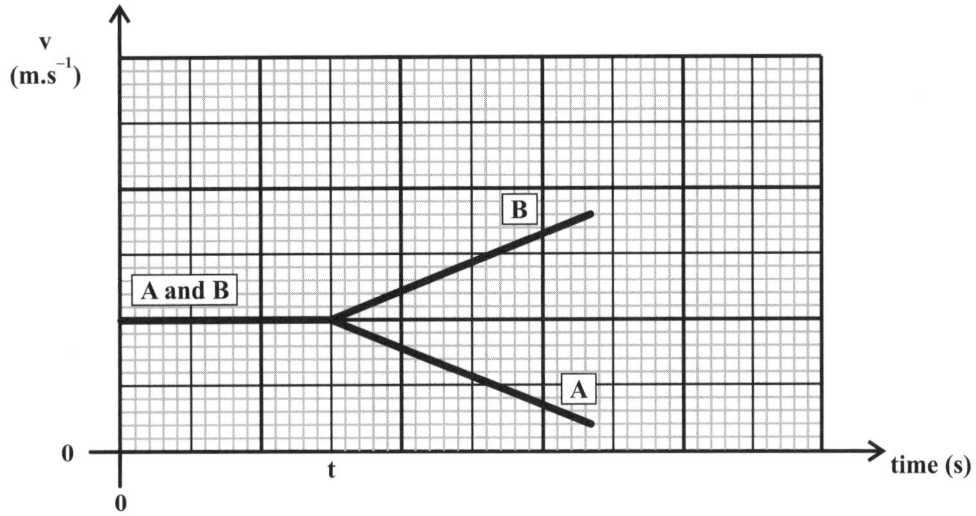

(3)

25.3.1 When a net force (Fnet) is applied to an object (of mass) it accelerates in the direction of the net force. The acceleration (a) is directly proportional to the net force and inversely proportional to the mass.

OR

The net force acting on a body is equal to (or directly proportional to) its rate of change of momentum. (3)

25.3.2 $F_{net} = ma$

$120\cos 64 \ = (16+24)a$

$52,6 = 40a$

$a = 1,32 \text{ m.s}^{-1}$ (4)

25.3.3

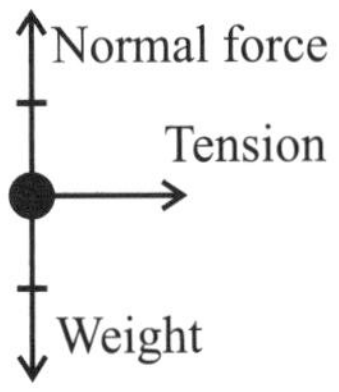

(3)

25.3.4 **Method 1: using block A**

$F_{net} = ma$

$T = (16)(1,32)$

$= 21,12 \text{ N}$

Method 1: using block B

$F_{net} = ma$

$F_A - T = ma$

$120\cos 64 \ - T = (24)(1,32)$

$T = 20,92 \text{ N}$ (4)

The difference in the answers above is due to the rounding in acceleration

TOC 1 Data Sheet 2 Definitions 3 3 solutions 4 4 solutions 5 5 solutions 6 6 solutions 7 7 solutions 8 8 solutions 9 9 solutions 10 10 solutions

TOC 1 Data Sheet 2 Definitions 3 3 solutions 4 4 solutions 5 5 solutions 6 6 solutions 7 7 solutions 8 8 solutions 9 9 solutions 10 10 solutions

25.3.5 $W = F_H \Delta x$

$= 20\cos 64\ (5)$

$= 263{,}02\ J$ (4)

25.4 $F_x = 80\cos 55$

$= 45{,}866\ N$ right

$F_y = 80\sin 55$

$= 65{,}532\ N$ upwards

$F_g = 15(9{,}8)$

$= 147\ N$ downwards

$F_N = 147 - 65{,}532$

$= 81{,}468\ N$ upwards

$F_f = \mu_s F_N$

$45{,}866 = \mu_s (81{,}468)$

$\mu_s = 0{,}56$ (6)

[31]

Question 26 (2016 IEB Supplementary Examination)

26.1 $F_{f\,max} = \mu_s F_N$

$= \mu_s mg$

$= 0{,}7(12)(9{,}8)$

$= 82{,}32\ N$ (3)

26.2 An object continues in a state of rest or uniform velocity unless it is acted upon by a net or resultant force. (2)

26.3 Using the 12kg mass:

$T = F_{f\,max}$

$= 82{,}32\ N$ (2)

26.4

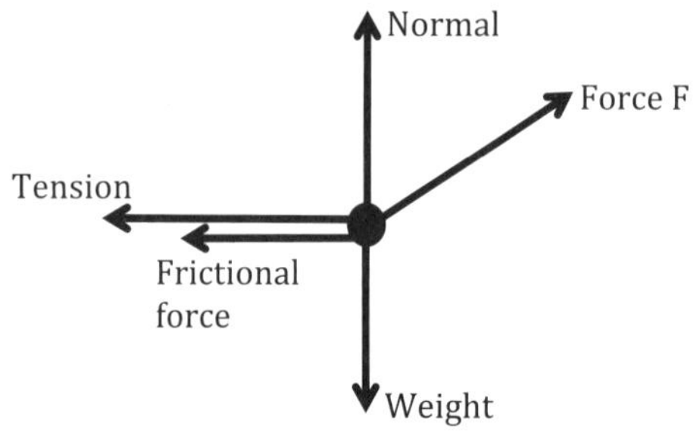

(5)

26.5 $F_N = mg - F\sin 20$ (2)

26.6 When the blocks are about to slide:

$F_H = T + \mu_s F_N$

$F\cos 20 = T + \mu_s F_N$

$F\cos 20 = T + \mu_s (mg - F\sin 20)$

$F\cos 20 = 82{,}32 + 0{,}7[(36)(9{,}8) - F\sin 20]$

$F\cos 20 + 0{,}7F\sin 20 = 82{,}32 + 0{,}7(36)(9{,}8)$

$F(\cos 20 + 0{,}7\sin 20) = 82{,}32 + 0{,}7(36)(9{,}8)$

$F = 279{,}26\ N$ (4)

[18]

Question 27 (2016 IEB Final Examination)

27.1 22 N (2)

27.2 The force that opposes the motion of the object and acts parallel to the surface with which the object is in contact. (2)

27.3 22 N (2)

27.4 $F_f = \mu_s F_N$

$22 = (0,2)F_N$

$F_N = 110 \text{ N}$

$W_A + W_C = 110$

$44 + W_C = 110$

$W_C = 66 \text{ N}$ (5)

27.5 When a net force (Fnet) is applied to an object (of mass) it accelerates in the direction of the net force. The acceleration (a) is directly proportional to the net force and inversely proportional to the mass.

OR

The net force acting on a body is equal to (or directly proportional to) its rate of change of momentum. (2)

27.6

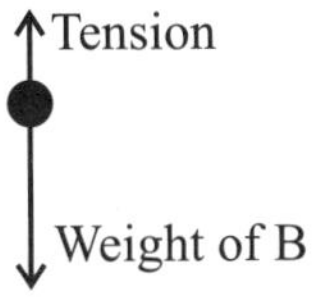

(2)

27.7 Using block B:

$F_{net} = ma$

$F_g - T = ma$

$22 - T = \frac{22}{9,8}(2,3) \rightarrow \text{mass of block B} = \frac{22}{9,8}$

$T = 16,84 \text{ N}$ (4)

27.8 Using block A:

$F_{net} = ma$

$T - F_f = ma$

$16,84 - F_f = \frac{44}{9,8}(2,3) \rightarrow \text{mass of block A} = \frac{44}{9,8}$

$F_f = 6,51 \text{ N}$ (3)

27.9
1) The norml force is less as block C has been removed. Force of friction is directly proportional to the normal force. As the normal force decreases so does friction.
2) The objects are now moving. Kinetic friction is less than static friction. Therefore, the force of friction would be less. (4)

Question 28 (2017 IEB Supplementary Examination)

28.1

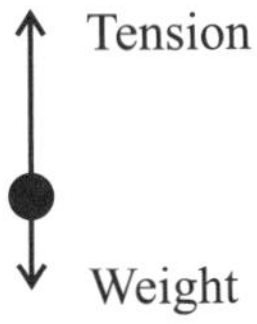

(2)

28.2 When a net force (Fnet) is applied to an object (of mass) it accelerates in the direction of the net force. The acceleration (a) is directly proportional to the net force and inversely proportional to the mass.

OR

The net force acting on a body is equal to (or directly proportional to) its rate of change of momentum. (2)

28.3 Block A:

$F_{net} = ma$

$F_g - T = ma$

$mg - T = ma$

$3(9,8) - 2a - 19,6 = 3a$

$a = 1,96 \text{ m.s}^{-2}$

Block B:

$T - mg = ma$

$T - 2(9,8) = 2a$

$T = 2a + 19,6$

(5)

28.4 $T = 2a + 19,6$

$= 2(1,96) + 19,6$

$= 23,52 \text{ N}$

(2)

28.5 $F_g = mg \rightarrow$ once block B hits the floor Block A is in freefall

$= 2(9,8)$

$= 19,6 \text{ N}$

(2)

28.6 Sum of gravitational potential energy and kinetic energy at a point. (2)

28.7 No external forces or friction are acting on block B once A has hit the floor. (2)

28.8 $E_{k \text{ of B}}$ when A hits the ground = $E_{p \text{ of B}}$ at the top

$\frac{1}{2}(2)(3,96)^2 = 2(9,8)(h)$

$h = 0,80 \text{m}$

$\therefore$ Height above the ground $= 4+,08 = 4,8 \text{m}$

(4)

[22]

Question 29 (2019 IEB Supplementary Examination)

29.1.1 $F_H = 200 \cos 30$

$= 173,21$ N right

$F_V = 200 \sin 30$

$= 100$ N down

(4)

29.1.2 $F_N = F_g + F_V$

$= 40(9,8) + 100$

$= 492 \text{ N}$

(3)

29.1.3 $F_{f \max} = \mu_s F_N$

$= 0,4(492)$

$= 196,8 \text{ N}$

(3)

29.1.4 Her foot will not slip as the horizontal componenet the dog is pulling with is less than the maximum force of static friction. (2)

29.2.1 $F_{net} = ma$

$T - 80 = 55(2)$

$T = 190 \text{ N}$

(4)

29.2.2 Graph of Acceleration vs Tension

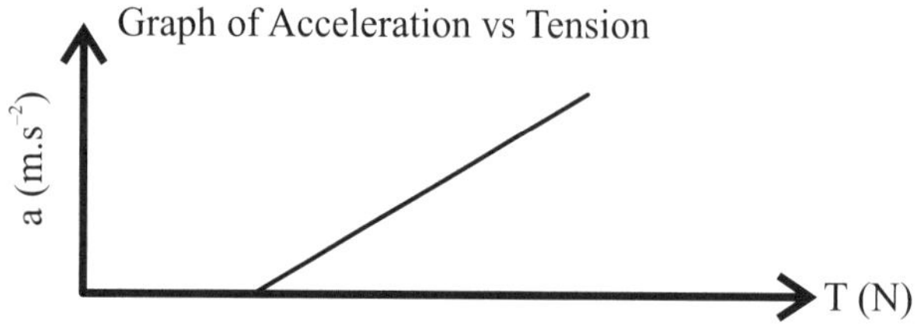

(3)

29.2.3 The child continues to move forward when the T is removed and also continues to move forward when the board strikes the stone as the child does not experience a net force. (3)

29.2.3 Newton's first law (1)

[23]

Question 30 (2019 IEB Final Examination)

30.1.1

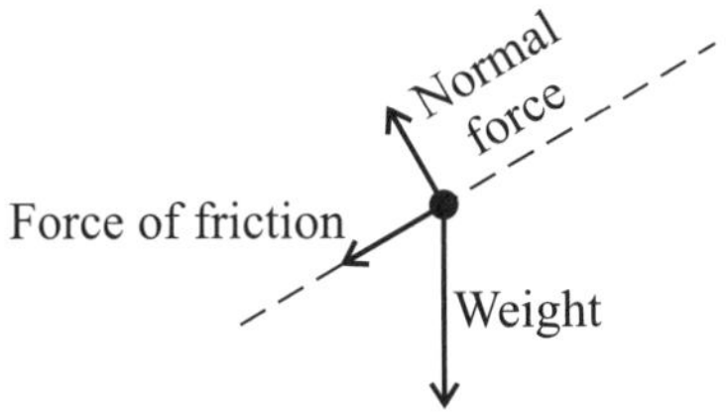

(3)

30.1.2 $F_{g//} = mg\sin\theta$

$52,52 = 48(9,8)\sin\theta$

$\sin\theta = \dfrac{52,52}{470,4}$

$\theta = 6,41$ (3)

30.1.3 $F_N = mg\cos\theta$

$F_f = \mu_k F_N$

$= \mu_k mg\cos\theta$

$= 0,12(48)(9,8)\cos(6,41)$

$= 56,10$ N (4)

30.1.4 When a net force (Fnet) is applied to an object (of mass) it accelerates in the direction of the net force. The acceleration (a) is directly proportional to the net force and inversely proportional to the mass.

OR

The net force acting on a body is equal to (or directly proportional to) its rate of change of momentum. (2)

30.1.5 $F_{net} = ma$

$F_{g//} + F_f = ma$

$52,52 + 56,10 = 48a$

$a = 2,26$ m.s^{-2} down the slope (4)

30.1.6 Greater from A to B Friction and component of weight in the same direction So resultant force is more.

OR

Less from B to A As friction acting up slope, opposite to component of weight So resultant force is less (3)

30.2.1 BC must follow the path of a parabola (2)

30.2.2 From C onwards must be straight tangential (in the same direction) as before C (2)

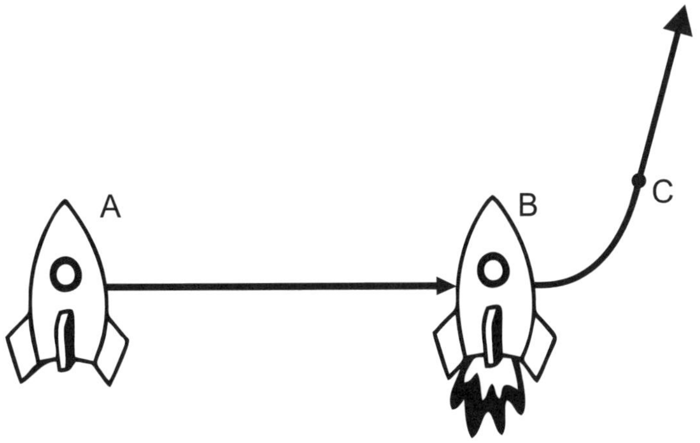

[23]

5. VECTORS

RESULTANT OF VECTORS ACTING FROM THE SAME POINT

There are 3 methods that can be used to determine the resultant of two vectors acting at a point.

1. **Resolving the vectors into their components**
2. **Parallelogram method**
3. **Head to tail method**

Illustrative Example 1:

Two forces act at point A as shown in the diagram below. Determine the resultant of the forces.

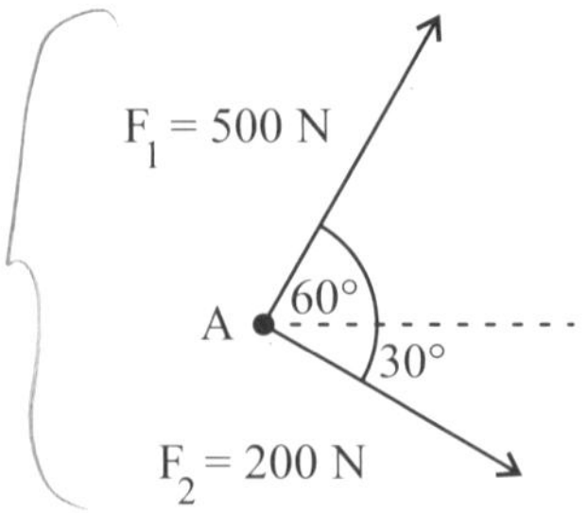

Method 1: Resolving the vectors into their components

Step 1: Choose a direction as positive for the horizontal and vertical components

Choose right and up as positive.

Step 2: Resolve each vector into their horizontal and vertical components

F_1	F_2
$F_{1H} = 500\cos 60^\circ$ $= 250\,N$ $F_{1V} = 500\sin 60^\circ$ $= 433,01\,N$ 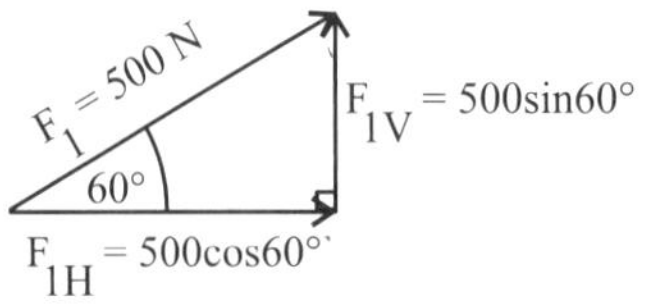 	$F_{2H} = 200\cos 30^\circ$ $= 173,21\,N$ $F_{2V} = -200\sin 30^\circ$ $= -100\,N$ 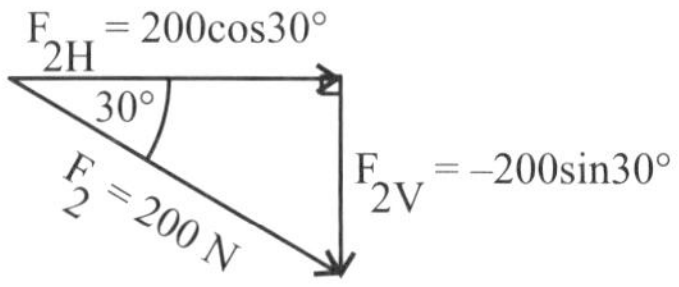 Note that the vertical component of F_2 negative as it is in the downwards direction.

Step 3: Construct a new triangle by adding the horizontal and vertical components of each force together.

Sum of horizontal components	Sum of vertical components
$F_{1H} + F_{2H} = 250 + 173,21$ $= 423,21\,N$ right	$F_{1V} + F_{2V} = 433,01 - 100$ $= 333,01\,N$ upwards

The hypotenuse of the vector sum of the horizontal and vertical components will be the resultant of the vectors.

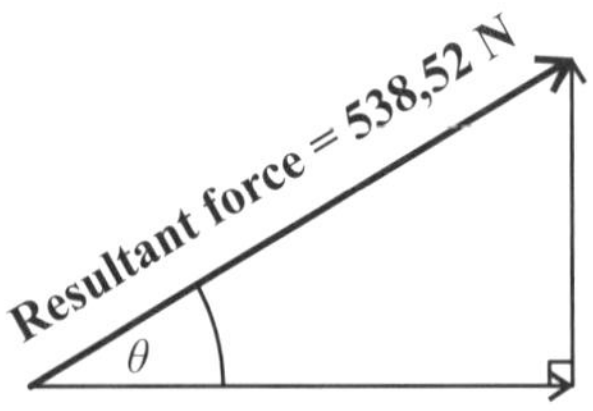

Resultant/net Force:

$$F_{net}^2 = 423,21^2 + 333,01^2$$
$$= 290\,002,36$$
$$F_{net} = 538,52\,N$$

Now calculate the direction of the resultant (vectors must have direction unless the question says magnitude)

$$\tan\theta = \frac{333,01}{423,21}$$

$$\theta = 38,2^\circ$$

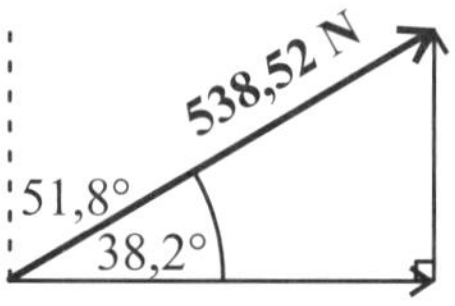

$\therefore F_{net} = 538,52$ N on a bearing of $51,8^\circ \rightarrow$ bearing is measured clockwise from North

This could also be written as: $F_{net} = 538,52$ N at an angle of $38,2^\circ$ North of East

Method 2: Parallelogram method

In this method you **construct a parallelogram** using both vectors.
The **resultant is the diagonal from the starting point to the opposite end of the parallelogram**. (where all the heads of the arrows meet)
This method is shown in the diagram below

This angle is calculated using co-interior angles

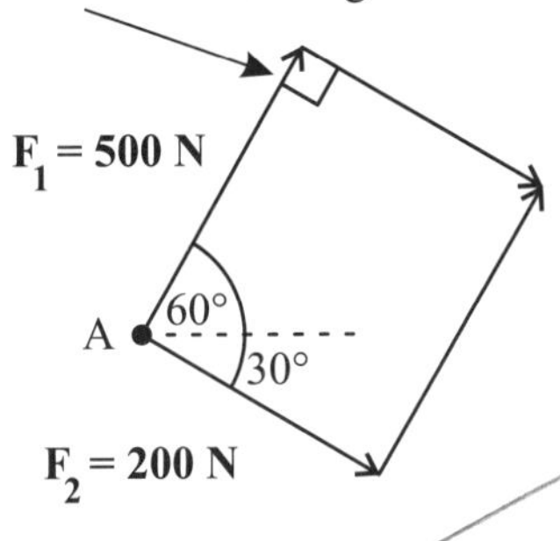

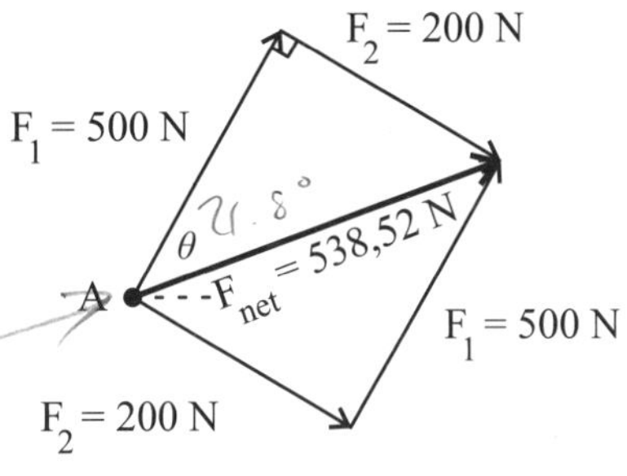

$F_{net}{}^2 = 500^2 + 200^2$

$= 29\,000$

$F_{net} = 538,52\ N$

$\tan\theta = \dfrac{200}{500}$

$\theta = 21,8^\circ$

$\therefore F_{net} = 538,52$ N on a bearing of $51,8^\circ$ → bearing is measured clockwise from North

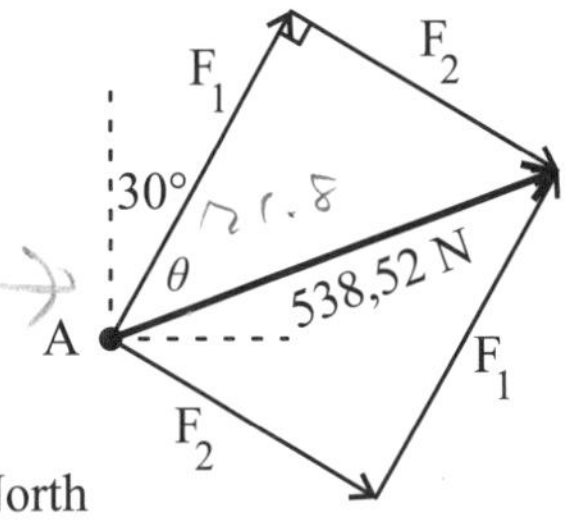

This could also be written as: $F_{net} = 538,52$ N at an angle of $38,2^\circ$ North of East

> **When giving the direction on a bearing the 30° angle from North to F_1 has to be added to the calculated angle.**
> **The resultant force is drawn to the point where two arrow heads meet.**
> **Bearing is always measured clockwise from North to the vector.**

Method 3: Head to tail method

This method is almost the same as the parallelogram method.
Instead of drawing a parallelogram, draw the **tail of force F_2 at the head of F_1.**
The resultant is the vector drawn from the starting point to the head of F_2.

Using this method, you only draw the top triangle of the parallelogram.
You could also draw the tail of F_1 at the head of F_2. This would result in the bottom triangle of the parallelogram.

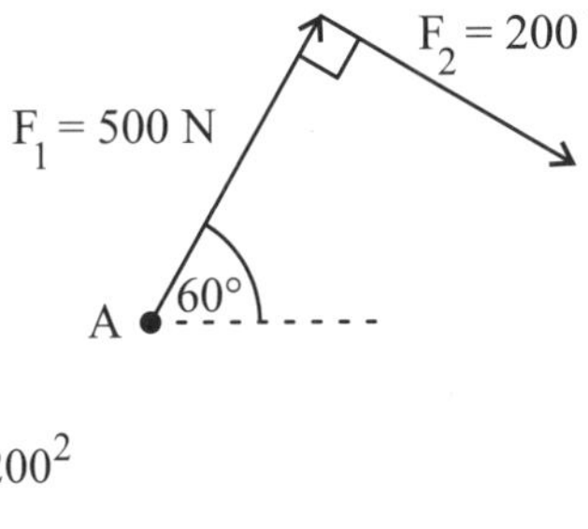

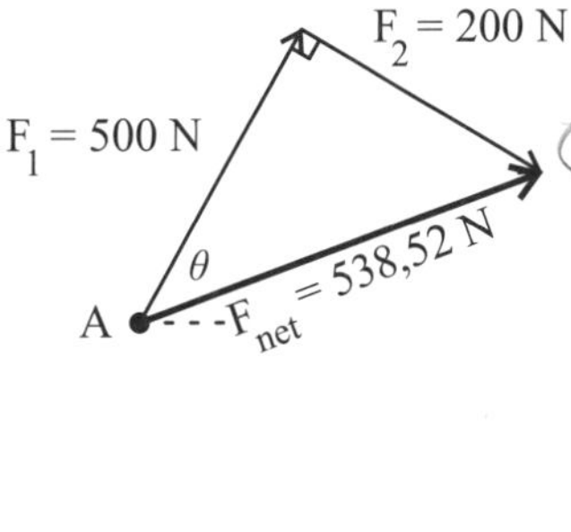

$F_{net}{}^2 = 500^2 + 200^2$

$= 29\,000$

$F_{net} = 538,52\ N$

$\tan\theta = \dfrac{200}{500}$

$\theta = 21,8^\circ$

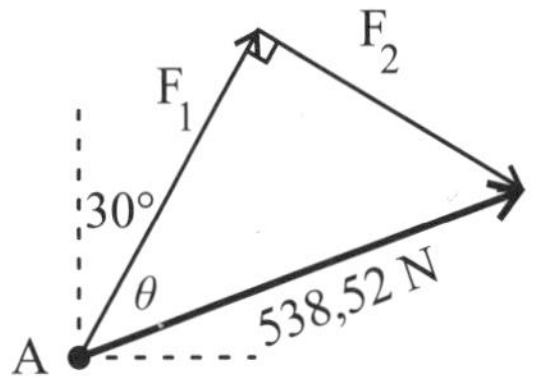

$\therefore F_{net} = 538,52$ N on a bearing of $51,8^\circ$ → bearing is measured clockwise from North

This could also be written as: $F_{net} = 538,52$ N at an angle of $38,2^\circ$ North of East

WORKING WITH MORE THAN 2 VECTORS FROM THE SAME POINT

When determining the resultant of more **than two vectors method 1** on the previous page should be used.

Illustrative Example 2:

Four forces act at point A as shown in the diagram below. Determine the resultant of the forces.

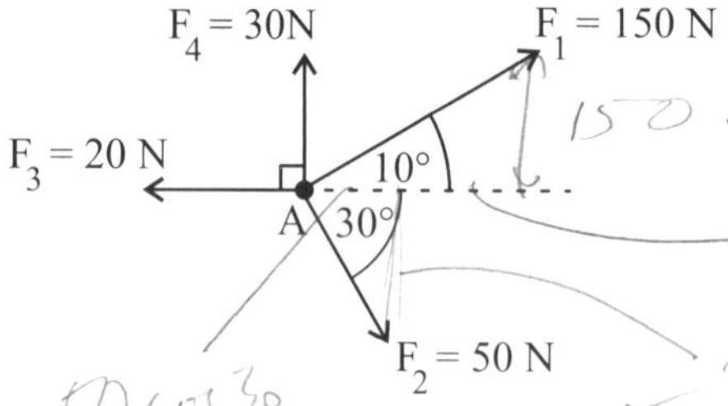

Taking right and up as positive

F_1	F_2	F_3	F_4
$F_{1H} = 150\cos 10^\circ$ $= 147,72\text{ N}$ $F_{1V} = 150\sin 10^\circ$ $= 26,05\text{ N}$	$F_{2H} = 50\cos 30^\circ$ $= 43,30\text{ N}$ $F_{2V} = -50\sin 30^\circ$ $= -25\text{ N}$	$F_{3H} = -20\text{ N}$ $F_{3V} = 0\text{ N}$	$F_{4H} = 0\text{ N}$ $F_{4V} = 30\text{ N}$

Sum of horizontal components	Sum of vertical components
$F_{1H} + F_{2H} + F_{3H} = 147,72 + 43,3 - 20$ $= 171,02\text{ N right}$	$F_{1V} + F_{2V} + F_{4V} = 26,05 - 25 + 30$ $= 31,05\text{ N upwards}$

Resultant/net Force:

$$F_{net}^2 = 171,02^2 + 31,05^2$$
$$= 30211,9429$$
$$F_{net} = 173,82\text{ N}$$

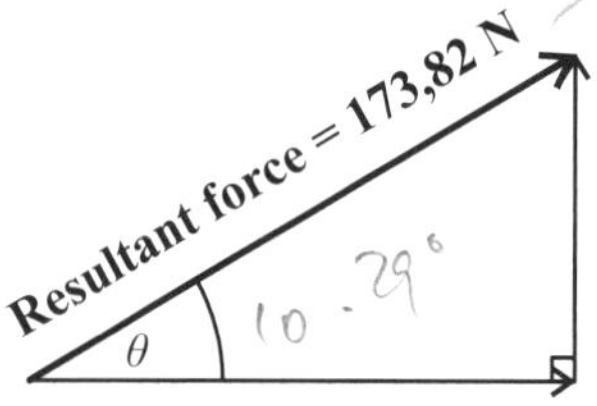

Now calculate the direction of the resultant force (vectors must have direction unless the question says magnitude)

$$\tan\theta = \frac{31,05}{171,02}$$

$$\theta = 10,29^\circ$$

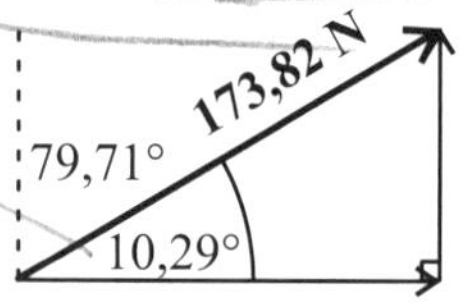

$\therefore F_{net} = 173,82\text{ N}$ on a bearing of $79,71^\circ$ → bearing is measured clockwise from North

This could also be written as: $F_{net} = 173,82\text{ N}$ at an angle of $10,29^\circ$ North of East

> **The maximum resultant force occurs when two or more vectors act in the same direction (at 0° to each other).**
> **The minimum resultant force occurs when the vectors act in the opposite direction (at 180° to each other).**

Illustrative Example 3:

Two forces, A and B act on object O. Force A has a magnitude of 600 N and acts at on a bearing of 70°. Force B has a magnitude of 1000 N and acts on a bearing of 120°.

a) Draw a free body diagram showing all forces acting on object O.
b) Using components, determine the resultant force on object O.
c) What additional force is required so that the resultant force on object O is 1 429,85 N on a bearing of 90°?

a)

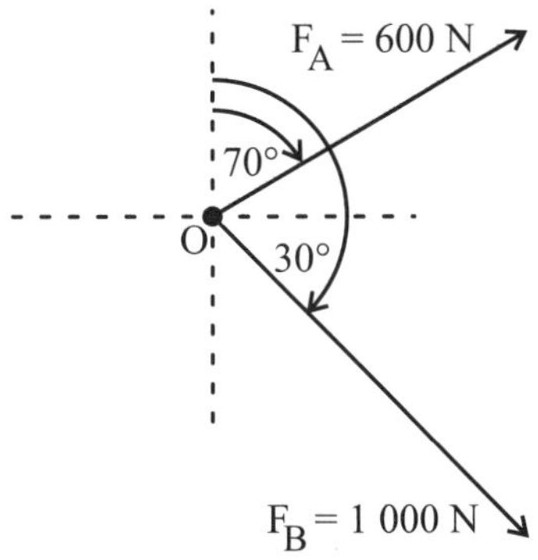

b)

Step 1: Choose a direction as positive for the horizontal and vertical components

Choose right and down as positive.

Step 2: Resolve each vector into their horizontal and vertical components

F_A	F_B
$F_{AH} = 600\cos 20^{\circ} = 563,82\text{ N}$ $F_{AV} = -600\sin 20^{\circ} = -205,21\text{ N}$ 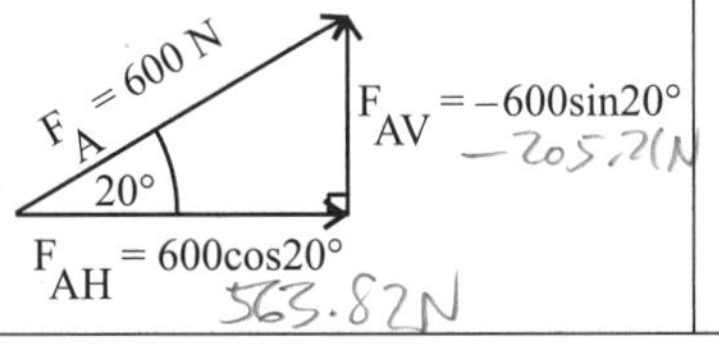	$F_{BH} = 1000\cos 30^{\circ} = 866,03\text{ N}$ $F_{BV} = 1000\sin 30^{\circ} = 500\text{ N}$ 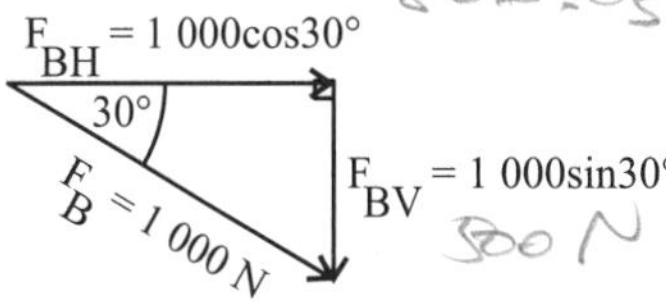

Step 3: Construct a new triangle by adding the horizontal and vertical components of each force together.

Sum of horizontal components	Sum of vertical components
$F_{AH} + F_{BH} = 563,82 + 866,03 = 1429,85\text{ N right}$	$F_{AV} + F_{BV} = -205,21 + 500 = 294,79\text{ N downwards}$

The hypotenuse of the vector sum of the horizontal and vertical components will be the resultant of the vectors.

Sum of horizontal forces = 1429,85 N

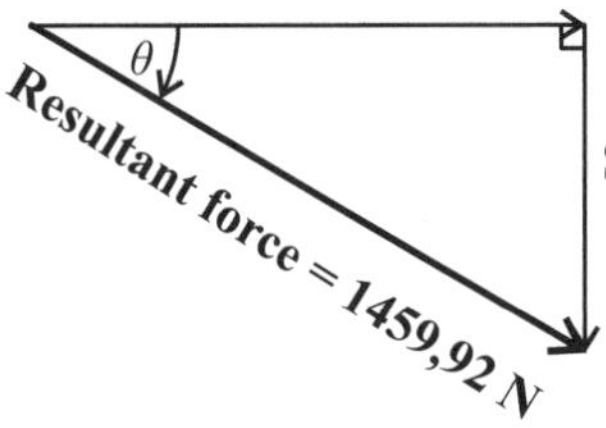

Resultant/net Force:

$$F_{net}^2 = 1429,85^2 + 294,79^2 = 2131372,167\text{ N}$$

$$F_{net} = 1459,92\text{ N}$$

Now calculate the direction of the resultant (vectors must have direction unless the question says magnitude)

$$\tan\theta = \frac{294,79}{1429,85}$$

$$\theta = 11,65^{\circ}$$

$\therefore F_{net} = 1459,92$ N on a bearing of $101,65^{\circ}$ → bearing is measured clockwise from North

This could also be written as: $F_{net} = 1459,92$ N $11,65^{\circ}$ South of East

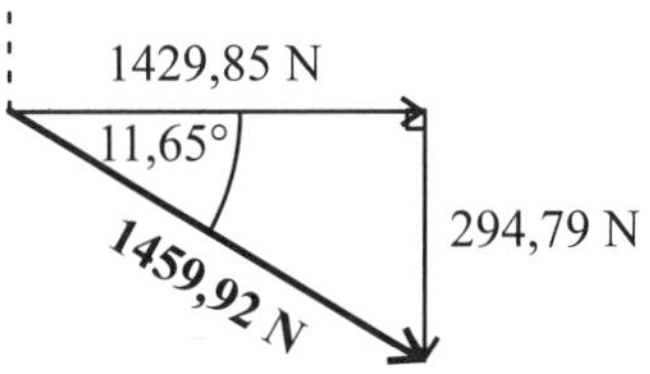

c) 294,79 N upwards (North).

FORCES IN EQUILIBRIUM

When forces are in **equilibrium** the **resultant force is zero**.
The **sum of the horizontal forces** will be **zero**.
The **sum of the vertical forces** will be **zero**.

Illustrative Example 1:

A hanging lamp of mass 10 kg is suspended by two strings as shown in the diagram below. Determine the magnitude of force F_1 and F_2.

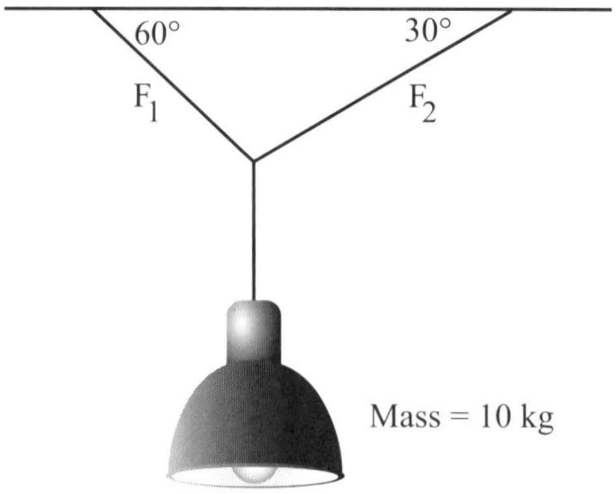

Method 1: Using components

Draw a free body diagram showing all the forces acting on the lamp and calculate the horizontal and vertical components of each force.

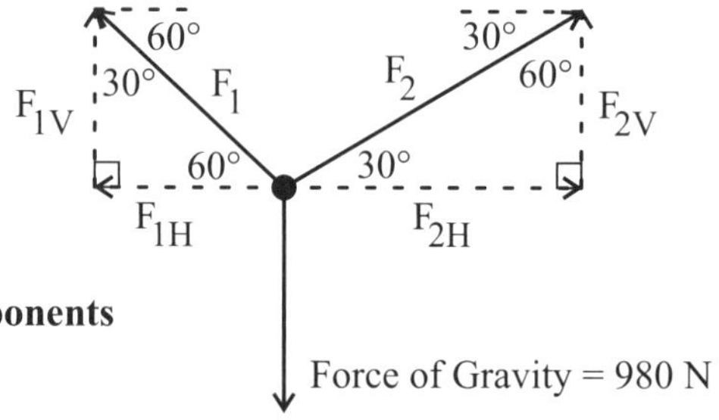

$F_{1V} = F_1 \sin 60^\circ$

$F_{1H} = F_1 \cos 60^\circ$

$F_{2V} = F_2 \sin 30^\circ$

$F_{2H} = F_2 \cos 30^\circ$

As the lamp is hanging (not moving) it is in equilibrium.
This means that the sum of the vertical and horizontal components both sum to zero.

$F_{1V} + F_{2V} = F_g \rightarrow$ force up = force down

$F_1 \sin 60^\circ + F_2 \sin 30^\circ = 10(9,8) \rightarrow \boxed{1}$

$F_{1H} = F_{2H}$

$F_1 \cos 60^\circ = F_2 \cos 30^\circ$

$F_1 = \dfrac{F_2 \cos 30^\circ}{\cos 60^\circ} \rightarrow \boxed{2}$

Substitute $\boxed{2}$ into $\boxed{1}$

$\dfrac{F_2 \cos 30^\circ}{\cos 60^\circ} \times \sin 60^\circ + F_2 \sin 30^\circ = 980$

$F_2\left(\dfrac{\cos 30^\circ \sin 60^\circ}{\cos 60^\circ} + \sin 30^\circ\right) = 980$

$F_2 = 980 \div \left(\dfrac{\cos 30^\circ \sin 60^\circ}{\cos 60^\circ} + \sin 30^\circ\right)$

$= 490 \text{ N} \rightarrow \boxed{3}$

Substitute $\boxed{3}$ into $\boxed{2}$

$F_1 = \dfrac{490 \cos 30^\circ}{\cos 60^\circ}$

$= 848,70 \text{ N}$

<u>Method 2</u>: Draw a closed vector diagram using the head to tail method

When objects are in **equilibrium the resultant force is zero.**
When the **resultant force is zero**, the **forces acting head to tail form a closed vector diagram with no arrow heads meeting.**

Step 1:
Draw a free body diagram and mark all alternate angles.

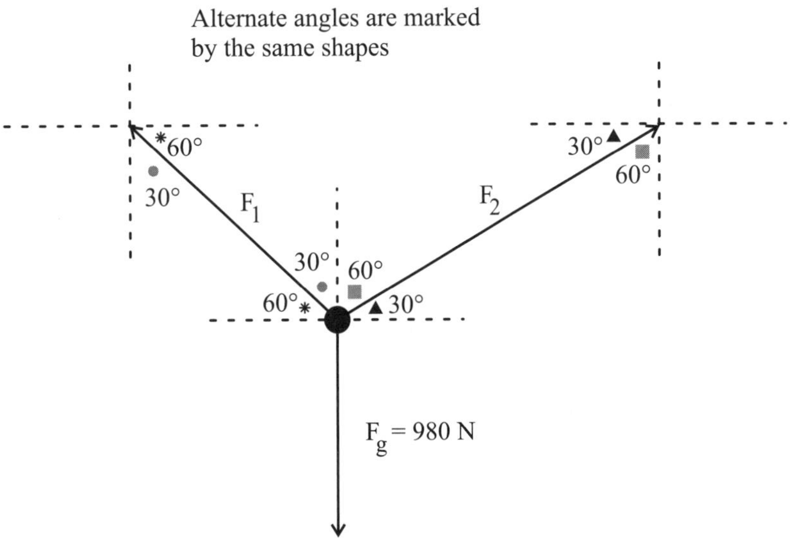

Step 2:
Draw a free body diagram and mark all alternate angles.
The angles at the head and tail of each vector must match the original free body diagram.

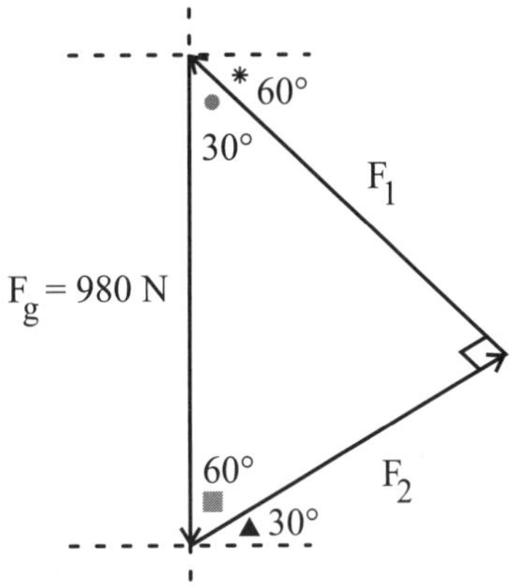

$$\sin 60^\circ = \frac{F_1}{980}$$

$$F_1 = 980 \sin 60^\circ$$
$$= 848,70\ \text{N}$$

$$\cos 60^\circ = \frac{F_2}{980}$$

$$F_2 = 980 \cos 60^\circ$$
$$= 490\ \text{N}$$

> **If a closed vector diagram does not form a 90° triangle you have to either use a scale diagram or the sine and cosine rule to solve unknowns using method 2.**

TOC | 1 Data Sheet | 2 Definitions | 3 | 3 solutions | 4 | 4 solutions | 5 | 5 solutions | 6 | 6 solutions | 7 | 7 solutions | 8 | 8 solutions | 9 | 9 solutions | 10 | 10 solutions

<u>Illustrative Example 2</u>:

An ornament is suspended in the air by two cables attached to the ceiling and wall of a room as shown below. The tension in the cables are T_1 and T_2.

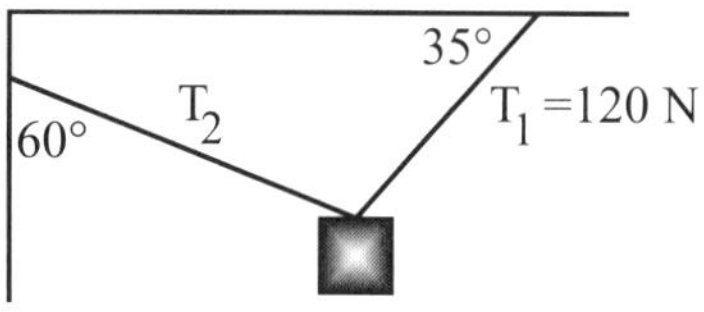

If $T_1 = 120$ N, calculate the value of:

a) T_2, the tension in the other cable.
b) The mass of the ornament.

<u>Method 1</u>: Using components

a)
Draw a free body diagram showing all the forces acting on the ornament and calculate the horizontal and vertical components of each force.

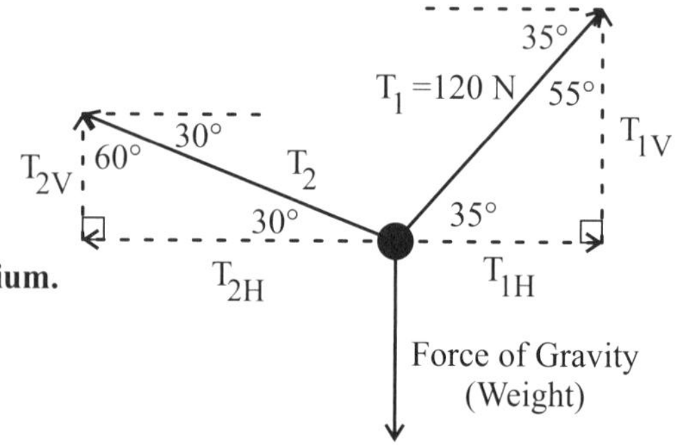

$T_{1V} = 120\sin 35^\circ$ $\qquad$ $T_{2V} = T_2 \sin 30^\circ$

$T_{1H} = 120\cos 35^\circ$ $\qquad$ $T_{2H} = T_2 \cos 30^\circ$

As the ornament is hanging (not moving) it is in equilibrium.
The sum of the horizontal components sum to zero.
Therefore, T_{2H} must be equal to T_{1H}

$$T_{2H} = T_{1H}$$

$$T_2 \cos 30^\circ = 120\cos 35^\circ$$

$$T_2 = \frac{120\cos 35^\circ}{\cos 30^\circ} = 113{,}51\,\text{N}$$

b) **The sum of the vertical forces equal zero:**

$$F_g = T_{1V} + T_{2V}$$

$$mg = T_{1V} + T_{2V}$$

$$m(9{,}8) = 120\sin 35^\circ + 113{,}51\sin 30^\circ$$

$$m = 12{,}81\,\text{kg}$$

<u>Method 2</u>: Draw a closed vector diagram using the head to tail method

Step 1:
Draw a free body diagram and mark all alternate angles.

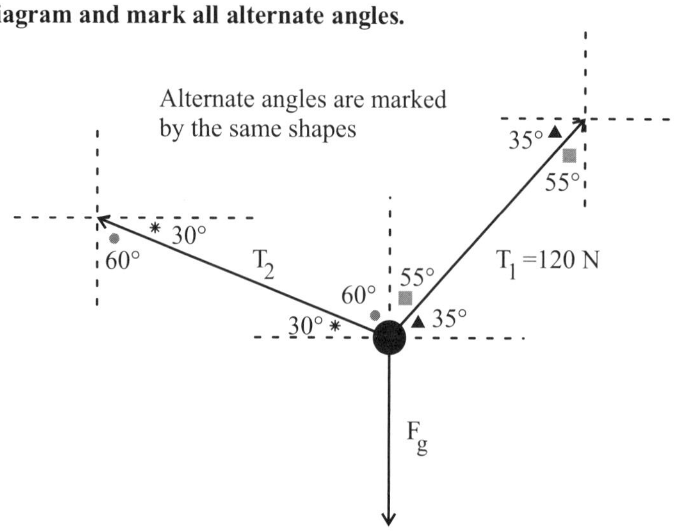

Step 2:

Draw a free body diagram and mark all alternate angles.

The angles at the head and tail of each vector must match the original free body diagram.

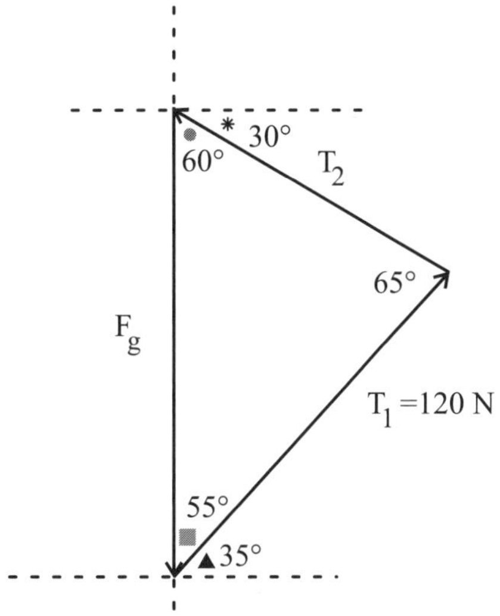

As the angles do not form right a angled triangle, the sign rule must be used to determine the tension, T₂, and mass of the ornament.

a) $\dfrac{T_2}{\sin 55^\circ} = \dfrac{T_1}{\sin 60^\circ}$

$\dfrac{T_2}{\sin 55^\circ} = \dfrac{120}{\sin 60^\circ}$

$T_2 = 113{,}51\,\text{N}$

b) $\dfrac{F_g}{\sin 65^\circ} = \dfrac{T_1}{\sin 60^\circ}$

$\dfrac{mg}{\sin 65^\circ} = \dfrac{120}{\sin 60^\circ}$

$m(9{,}8) = \dfrac{120 \sin 65^\circ}{\sin 60^\circ}$

$m = 12{,}81\,\text{kg}$

When using method 2, if a closed vector diagram does not form a 90° triangle you have to either use a scale diagram or the sine and cosine rule to solve unknown sides and angles.

For these triangles method 1 is recommended.

The Sine Rule is:

$$\frac{a}{\sin \hat{A}} = \frac{b}{\sin \hat{B}} = \frac{c}{\sin \hat{C}}$$

The Cosine Rule is:

$$a^2 = b^2 + c^2 - 2ab\cos \hat{A}$$

DISPLACEMENT VECTORS

Displacement vectors usually **occur in sequence**.
The **head to tail method** is used to calculate the **resultant of displacement vectors**.
The **resultant** is always from **the origin to the head of the last vector**.

Illustrative Example:

A cyclist travels 1 km North, 3 km West and 5 km South. Use a diagram to determine the resultant displacement of the cyclist.

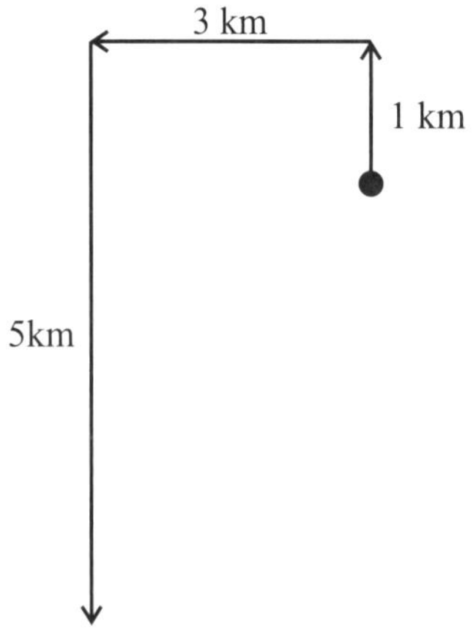

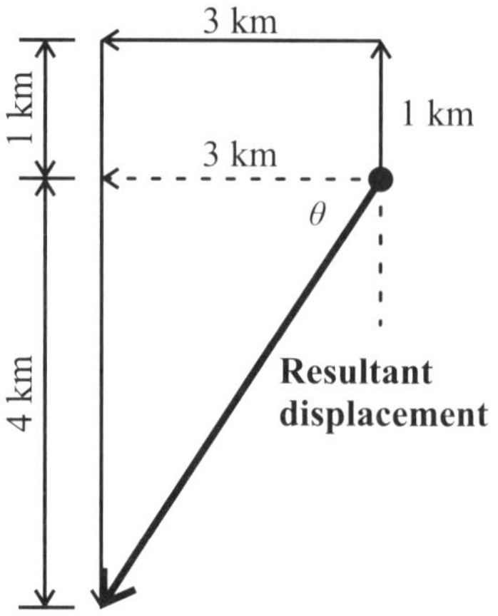

$\Delta x_{res}{}^2 = 3^2 + 4^2 \rightarrow$ Pythag

$= 25$

$\Delta x_{res} = 5$ km

$\tan\theta = \dfrac{4}{3}$

$\theta = 53{,}13^\circ$

$\therefore \Delta x_{res} = 5$ km $53{,}13^\circ$ South of West

Alternatively

$\therefore \Delta x_{res} = 5$ km on a bearing of $216{,}87^\circ$ $\left(180^\circ + 36{,}87^\circ\right)$

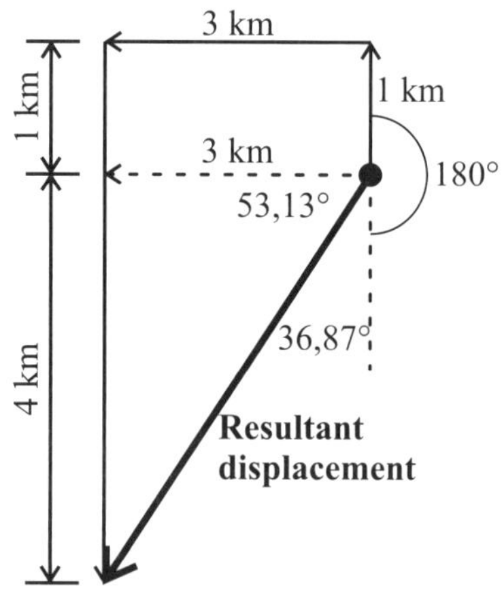

VELOCITY VECTORS

Velocity vectors are added together using the **head to tail method to obtain a resultant** velocity.
When measuring **velocity**, it **must be relative to a reference point**. For instance, when standing stationary on the Earth's surface you are moving at the same velocity that the Earth is rotating. However relative to the Earth you are stationary.

When labelling velocity vectors:
The **resultant is relative to the ground**.
The **velocity of the medium** (wind, water, etc…) is **relative to the ground**.
The **velocity of the object** (airspeed, velocity in still water, etc…) is **relative to the medium** the object is in.

Only add vectors of the same type. Never add velocity vectors with displacement vectors.

Illustrative example 1:

A man swims North across a river at a speed of 2 m.s^{-1}. The river flows East with a velocity of 1,5 m.s^{-1}.

a) Draw a vector diagram and use it to determine the resultant velocity of the man.
b) If it takes the man 10 minutes to cross the river, determine the width of the river.

a)

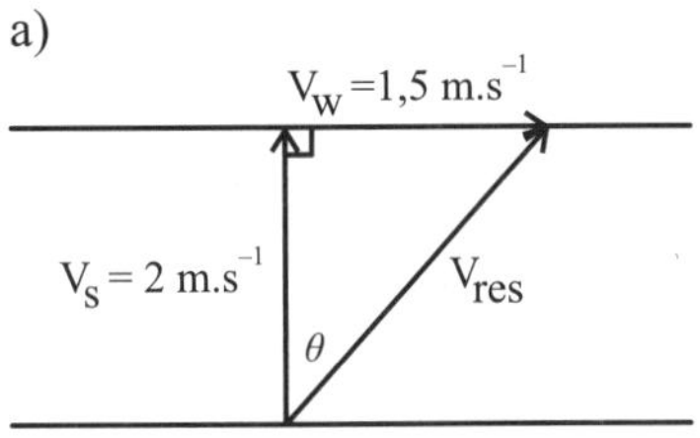

Key: V_S = velocity of swimmer relative to the water

V_W = velocity of the water (river) relative to the ground

V_{res} = velocity of the swimmer relative to the ground (resultant velocity)

$$v_{res}{}^2 = 2^2 + 1,5^2$$
$$= 6,25$$
$$v_{res} = 2,5 \text{ m.s}^{-1}$$
$$\tan\theta = \frac{1,5}{2}$$
$$\theta = 36,87^\circ$$
$$\therefore v_{res} = 2,5 \text{ m.s}^{-1} \text{ on a bearing of } 36,87^\circ$$

b) $\Delta x = vt$
$= 2(10 \times 60) \rightarrow$ convert minutes to seconds
$= 1200\,\text{m}$

As all components occur simultaneously, the time taken for each component is the same.

TOC
1 Data Sheet
2 Definitions
3
3 solutions
4
4 solutions
5
5 solutions
6
6 solutions
7
7 solutions
8
8 solutions
9
9 solutions
10
10 solutions

Illustrative example 2:

A man wants to swim directly North across a river which is flowing East with a velocity of 1,5 m.s^{-1}. The man can swim at 2 m.s^{-1}.

a) Draw vector diagram and use it to determine the resultant velocity of the man.
b) At what angle must the man swim in order move directly across the river?
c) If the river is 1200 m wide, how long will it take him to cross the river?

a)

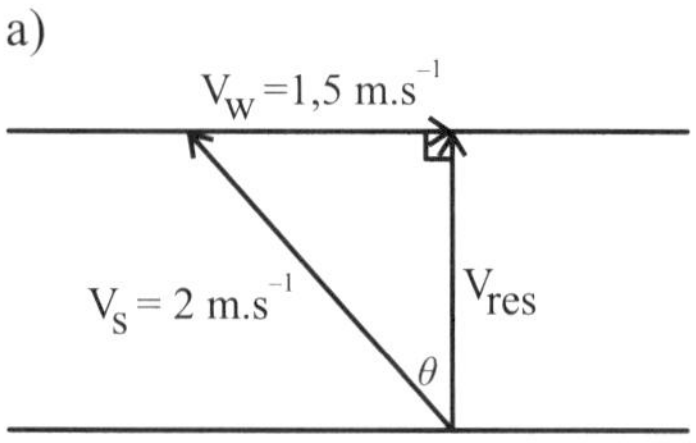

Key: V_S = velocity of swimmer relative to the water

V_W = velocity of the water (river) relative to the ground

V_{res} = velocity of the swimmer relative to the ground (resultant velocity)

$$v_{res}^{\ 2} = 2^2 - 1,5^2$$
$$= 1,75$$
$$v_{res} = 1,32 \text{ m.s}^{-1} \text{ North}$$

b) $\sin\theta = \dfrac{1,5}{2}$

$\theta = 48,6^\circ$

$\therefore$ He must swim at an angle of $48,6^\circ$ W of N $\rightarrow$ this could be written as on a bearing of $311,4^\circ$

c) $\Delta x = vt$
$1200 = 1,32t$
$t = 909,09\,\text{s}$

Illustrative example 3:

A pilot wishes to fly from town A to town B. Town B is 1000 km due North of town A. The pilot flies on a bearing of 330° to reach town B. A wind blows at a constant speed of 90 km.h^{-1} on bearing of 60°.

a) Use a vector diagram to determine the speed at which the pilot must fly in order to reach town B.
b) Determine how long it takes the pilot to reach town B.

a)

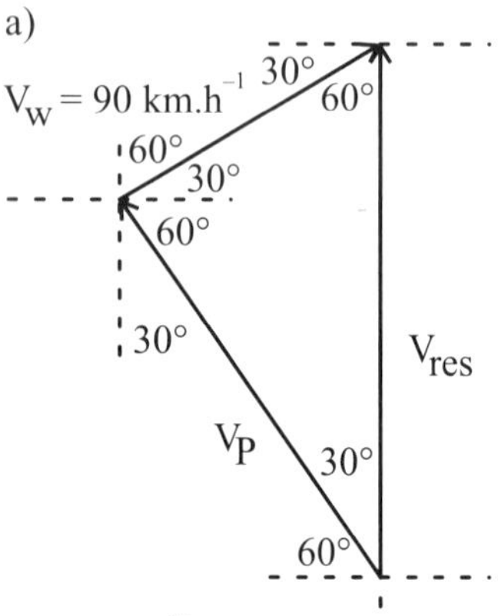

Key: V_P = velocity of plane relative to the wind

V_W = velocity of the wind relative to the ground

V_{res} = velocity of the plane relative to the ground (resultant velocity)

$$\tan 60^\circ = \frac{v_P}{90}$$
$$v_P = 155,88 \text{ km.h}^{-1}$$

b) $\sin 30^\circ = \dfrac{90}{v_{res}}$

$v_{res} = 180\,\text{km.h}^{-1}$

$\Delta x = vt$

$1000 = 180t$

$t = 5,56\,\text{hours}$

Question 1 (Solutions on page 171)

1.1 An aircraft is flying East in a wind that blows from the North. The pilot draws the following vector diagram to determine the aircraft's correct heading.

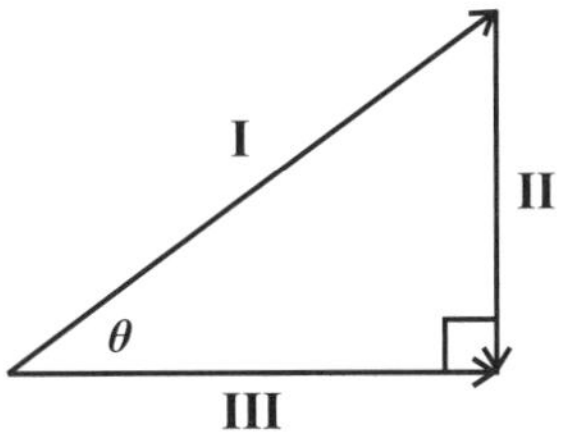

What is the correct label for the vector marked **I** in the diagram?

A Velocity of plane relative to the ground.
B Velocity of wind relative to the ground.
C Velocity of plane relative to wind.
D Velocity of wind relative to the plane. (2)

1.2 The diagram below shows a neon sign of weight 500 N suspended from point P by a rigid strut PR fixed to the wall at R and a light chain PQ attached to the wall at Q.

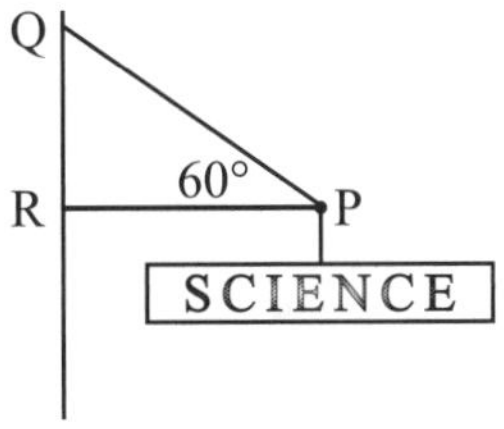

A The vertical component of the tension in chain QP is equal to 500 N.
B The tension in chain QP is equal to 500 N.
C The vector sum of the three forces acting at point P is 500 N.
D The vertical component of the tension in chain QP is equal to 250 N. (2)

1.3 Refer to the diagram in question 1.2.

A The strut exerts a force of approximately 289 N to the left.
B The resultant of the forces acting on the sign is 500 N upwards.
C The strut exerts a force of approximately 289 N to the right.
D The resultant of the forces acting on the sign is 500 N downwards. (2)

1.4 The back of a heavy square picture with dimensions of 100 cm x 100 cm is shown below. A string 120 cm long is used to hang the picture. Which arrangement below would result in the smallest tension in the string?

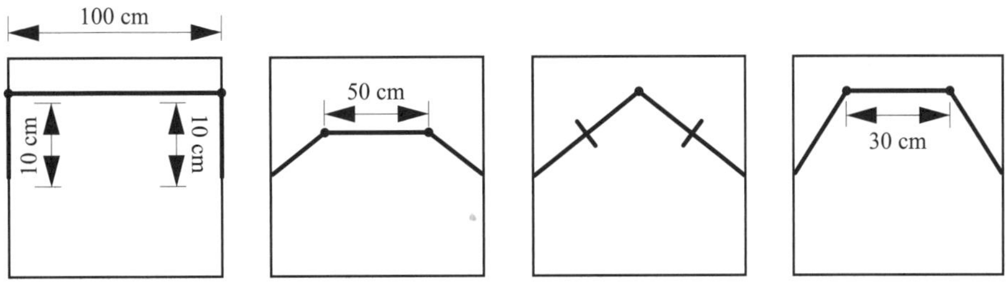

A B C D (2)

TOC
1 Data Sheet
2 Definitions
3
3 solutions
4
4 solutions
5
5 solutions
6
6 solutions
7
7 solutions
8
8 solutions
9
9 solutions
10
10 solutions

1.5 A pot plant of weight W, is suspended from two light strings T and F. The angle between the strings is θ. F acts horizontally. Which of the following force diagram are correct?

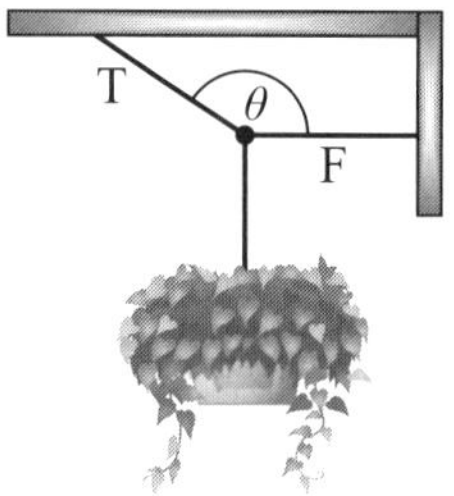

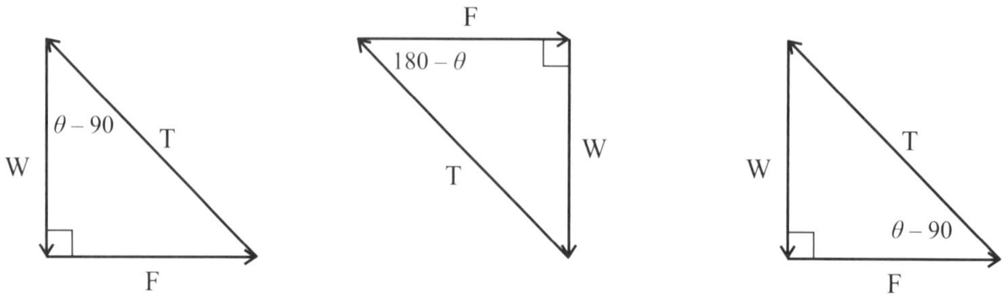

I **II** **III**

A I B II C I and III D I and II (2)

1.6 A sign of mass m is held stationary by three light ropes as shown alongside. Ropes 1, 2 and 3 experience tension of magnitudes T_1, T_2 and T_3 respectively. The diagram is not drawn to scale.

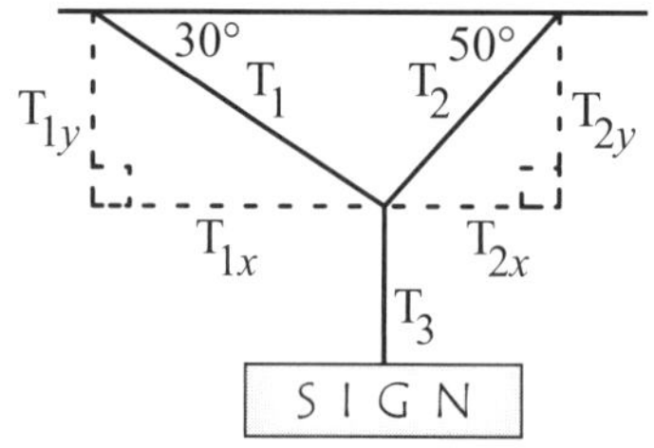

Which one of the following mathematical expressions is **incorrect**?

A $T_{1x} = T_{2x}$

B $T_{1y} + T_{2y} = T_3$

C $T_1 > T_2$

D $T_{1y} + T_{2y} = mg$

(2)

1.7 A box is suspended from a string as shown below. The string makes an angle of 55° with the ceiling. Force F, with a magnitude of 56 N, pulls East and holds the box stationary. What is the mass of the box?

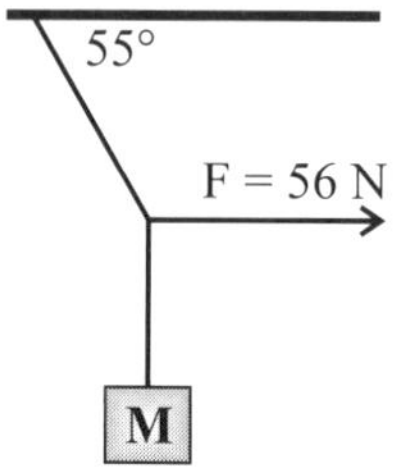

A 79,98 kg
B 8,16 kg
C 39,2 kg
D 4 kg

(2)

1.8 An object of weight W hangs from two strings, x and y, attached to the ceiling. String y makes an angle of θ to the vertical as shown in the diagram below.

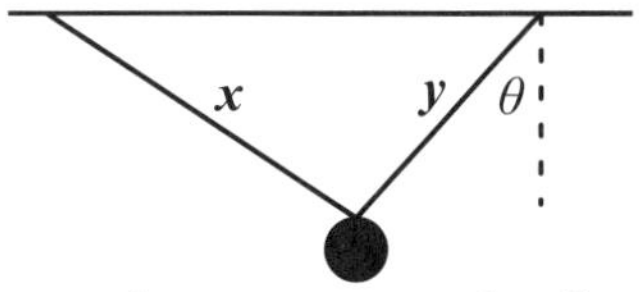

Which vector diagram correctly represents the forces acting on the hanging object?

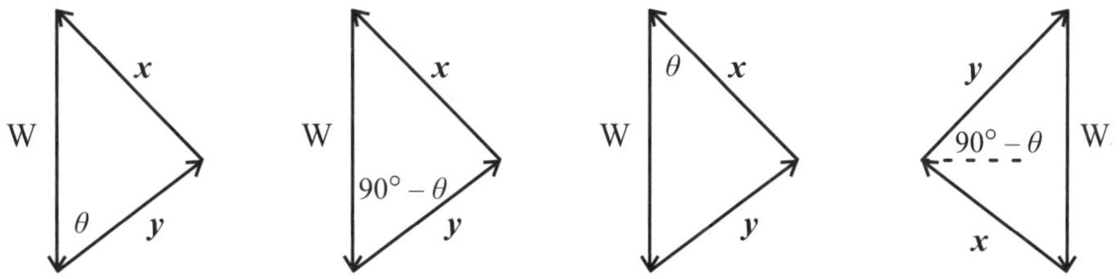

I **II** **III** **IV**

A I only
B I and IV only
C III only
D I and II only (2)

1.9 Two forces, F_1 of magnitude 100 N and F_2 of magnitude 150 N act on a box from the same point as shown below. The angle (α and θ) between the box and each force can vary between 0° and 90°.

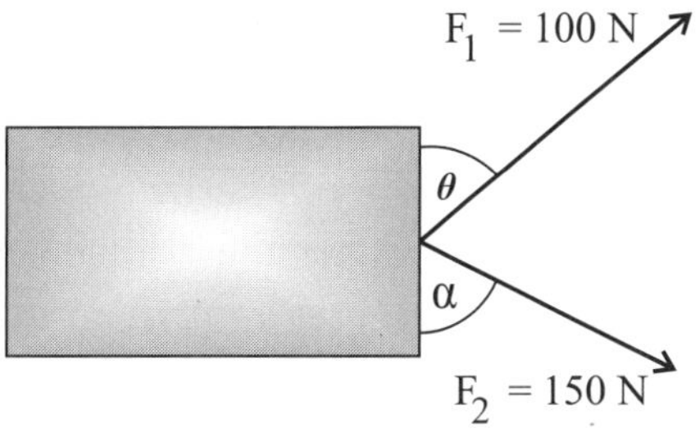

Which of the following forces could be the magnitude of the resultant of the two forces?

A 260 N
B 50 N
C 360 N
D 40 N (2)

1.10 The magnitude of the resultant force in the vector diagram below is:

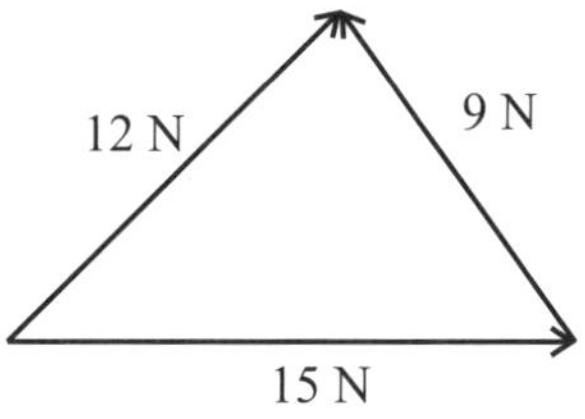

A 0 N
B 9 N
C 12 N
D 15 N (2)

TOC 1 Data Sheet 2 Definitions 3 3 solutions 4 4 solutions 5 5 solutions 6 6 solutions 7 7 solutions 8 8 solutions 9 9 solutions 10 10 solutions

1.11 The vector diagram shows two forces in the same plane acting on an object P.

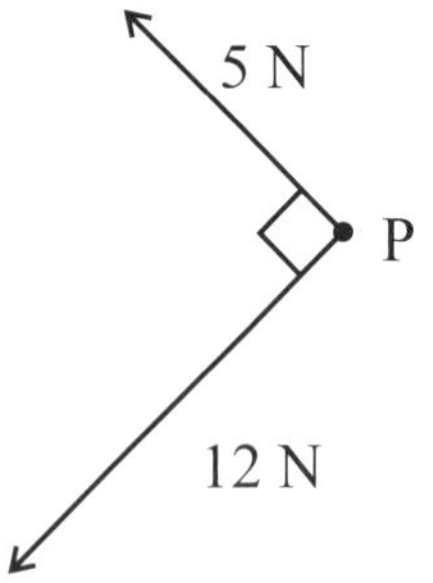

A 13 N force, in the same plane as the other forces, is applied on object P. Which of the following represents the direction at which the 13 N force must be applied to ensure object P is in equilibrium?

(2)

1.12 Two vectors X and Y are shown in the following diagrams.
For which diagram will the magnitude of the resultant of X + Y be a minimum?

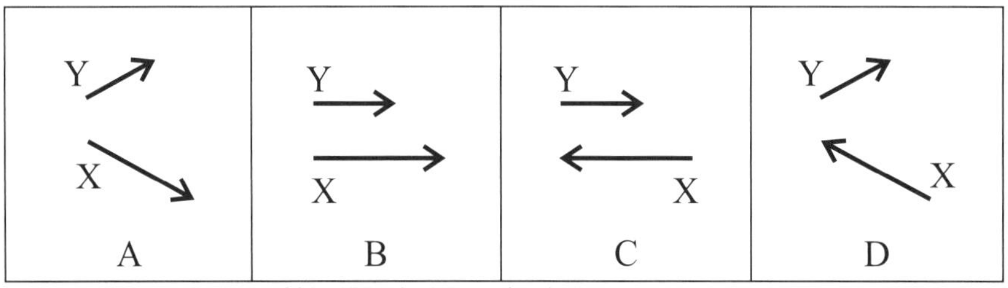

(The above question is from the 2015 IEB Final Examination) (2)

1.13 An orange ball is travelling along a smooth surface with an initial velocity u, when it is struck by another ball. After the collision, the orange ball is travelling with a speed v, which is greater in magnitude than u, in the direction shown below.

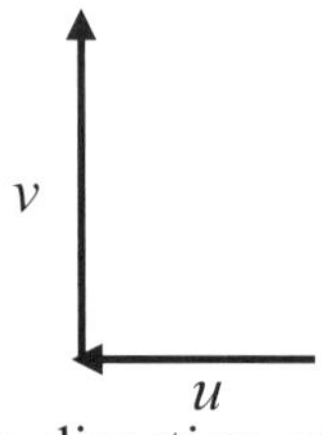

Which vector best indicates the direction of the acceleration of the orange ball during this collision?

(The above question is from the 2017 IEB Supplementary Examination) (2)

[26]

Question 2 (Solutions on page 171)

A heavy beam of mass M is lifted by means of rope S over a pulley to reach the first floor of a construction site. The construction workers take a lunch break and secure the beam using a second rope T, which pulls the beam horizontally to the left causing the beam to hang in equilibrium.

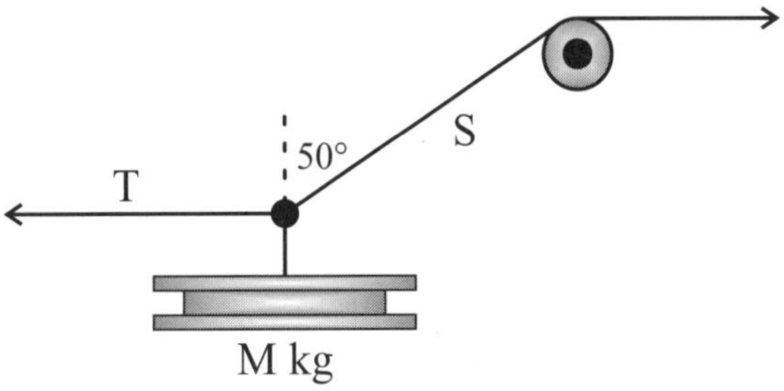

The tension in the rope T is 13 000N.

2.1 Draw a closed vector diagram showing all the forces acting at point O. (4)

2.2 Use your diagram to determine the mass of the crate and the tension in the rope S. (6)

2.3 The tension in rope T is now increased (to raise the beam) and the beam is pulled further to the left. Will the tension in rope S increase, decrease or remain the same? Explain your answer fully referring to a suitable formula. (5)

[15]

Question 3 (Solutions on page 171)

A man can push with a force of 600 N. He is unable to move a heavy crate by pushing it. Instead he ties an inextensible cable of negligible mass to a pole and attaches the other end to the crate. He then stands in the middle of the cable and pushes forward as hard as he can. As the cable makes an angle of 10° the crate just starts to move. This is shown in the diagram below.

Top view

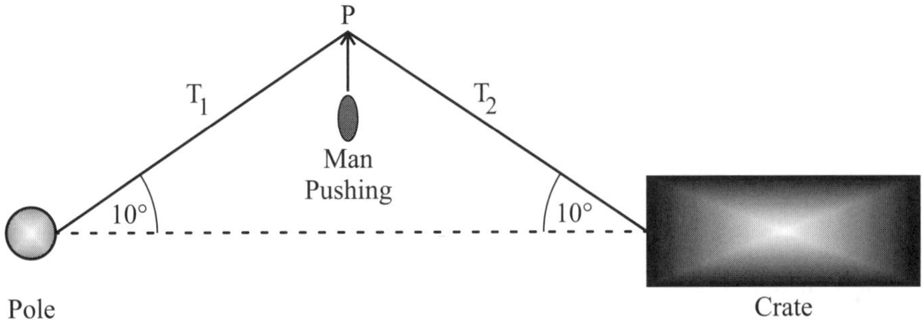

3.1 Draw a labelled free body diagram of the which represents the forces acting at point P. (3)

As the crate is about to move the acceleration of the crate is zero and the system is in equilibrium

3.2 What is the sum of the horizontal components in each section of the cable T_1 and T_2? (1)

3.3 Calculate the magnitude of the tension in the cable when the crate is about to move. (4)

3.4 By using this technique how many times greater is the force the man can exert? (2)

[8]

TOC | 1 Data Sheet | 2 Definitions | 3 | 3 solutions | 4 | 4 solutions | 5 | 5 solutions | 6 | 6 solutions | 7 | 7 solutions | 8 | 8 solutions | 9 | 9 solutions | 10 | 10 solutions

Question 4 (Solutions on page 172)

A gymnast suspends himself from two ropes as shown below. For simplicity, the gymnast is depicted as a block. The tension in rope 1 is 450 N.

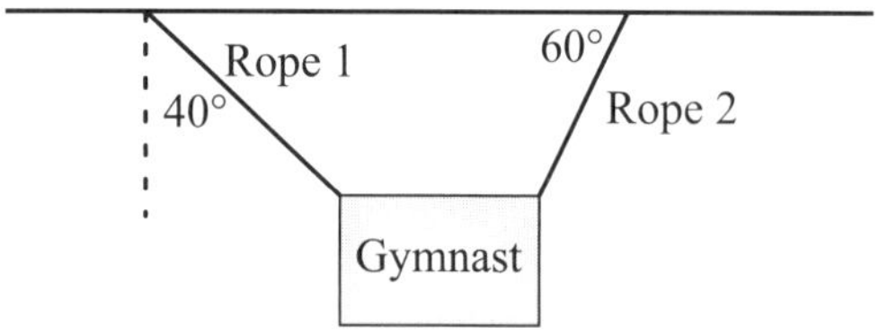

4.1 Define a vector. (2)

4.2 Determine the magnitude of the horizontal component of rope 1. (2)

4.3 Determine the magnitude of the tension rope 2. (3)

4.4 Determine the mass of the gymnast (5)

[12]

Question 5 (Solutions on page 172)

In an experiment to determine the unknown mass of an object, two 500 g masses and an object of unknown mass, M, are suspended from three strings, as shown in the diagram (not drawn to scale) below. The strings are light and inextensible and run over frictionless pulleys. When the three forces acting on knot O are in equilibrium, the angles between the two strings and the vertical are 45° as shown on the diagram below.

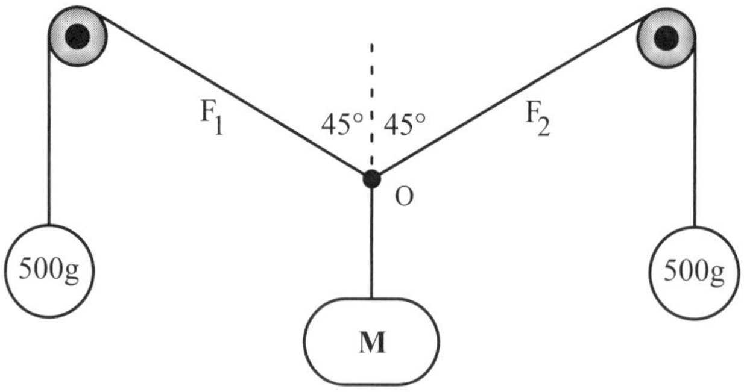

5.1 Draw a free body diagram of the forces acting on the knot at O. (3)

5.2 Draw a closed vector diagram of the forces which can be used to determine the mass of the object. (4)

5.3 Determine the mass of M. (3)

[10]

Question 6 (Solutions on page 173)

A small aeroplane takes off from a local airport travelling at 300 $km.h^{-1}$. The pilot heads on a bearing of 295°. At the same time there is a wind blowing at 45 $km.h^{-1}$ on a bearing of 25°. It takes the pilot 45 minutes to reach his destination.

6.1 Draw a fully labelled vector diagram to illustrate the above situation. (5)

6.2 Calculate the resultant velocity of the plane. (4)

6.3 Calculate the displacement of the plane. (3)

[12]

Question 7 (Solutions on page 173)

A large Christmas decoration of mass 100 kg is suspended from the ceiling of a shopping centre by two light inextensible strings as shown in the diagram below.

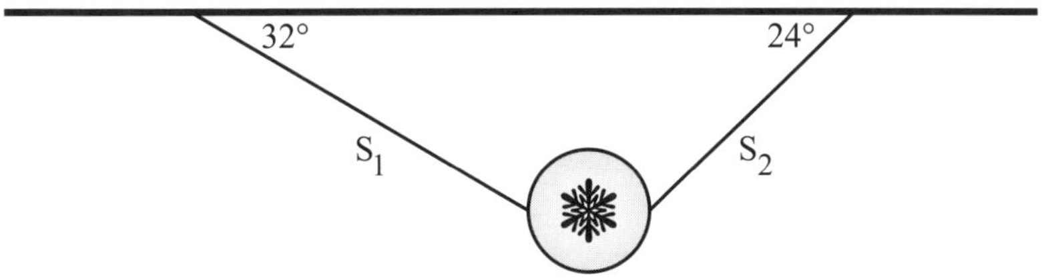

7.1 Draw a labelled free body diagram showing the forces acting on the decoration as it hangs suspended by the strings. (3)

7.2 Write down an equation representing the horizontal components of the forces acting in the strings. (3)

7.3 Write down an equation representing the vertical components acting in the strings. (3)

7.4 Use your answers from 7.2 and 7.3 to determine the magnitude of the forces acting in each string. (4)

[13]

Question 8 (Solutions on page 174)

The sign in the diagram below has a mass of 4 kg. It is held stationary by a horizontal steel strut and a light chain that forms an angle 35° with the wall.

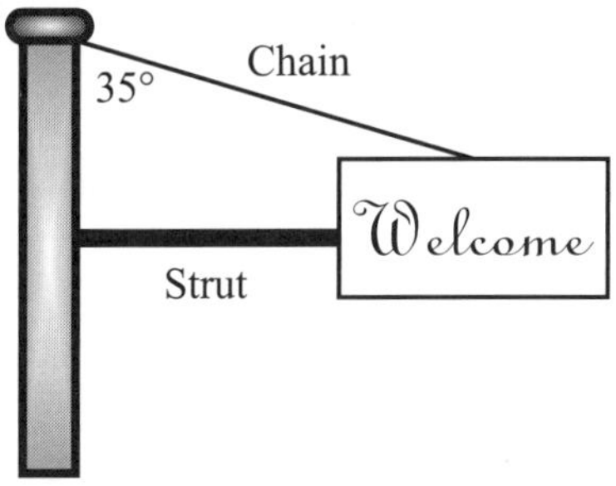

8.1 Sketch a fully labelled free body diagram of the forces acting on the sign. (3)

8.2 Define weight. (2)

8.3 Determine the tension in the chain. (3)

8.4 The steel strut will bend if the it experiences a force greater than 120 N. Calculate the maximum weight of the sign before the strut bends. (4)

[12]

TOC | 1 Data Sheet | 2 Definitions | 3 | 3 solutions | 4 | 4 solutions | 5 | 5 solutions | 6 | 6 solutions | 7 | 7 solutions | 8 | 8 solutions | 9 | 9 solutions | 10 | 10 solutions

TOC 1 Data Sheet 2 Definitions 3 3 solutions 4 4 solutions 5 5 solutions 6 6 solutions 7 7 solutions 8 8 solutions 9 9 solutions 10 10 solutions

Question 9 (Solutions on page 174)

Demi is studying hard for her physical science exam. She has a lamp hanging in the centre of the room and would like some more light over her table. She pulls the lamp sideways and attaches it to a weight on her shelf so that light hang directly over her desk. She attaches the weight to the lamp via a light inextensible string at a knot at point P as shown in the diagram below. This causes the lamp to form a 30° angle with the ceiling.

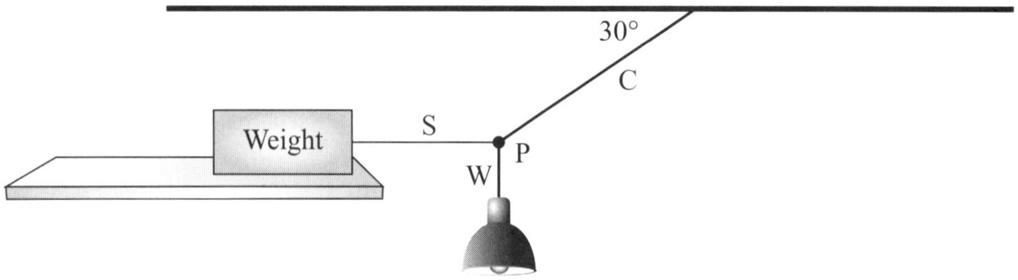

9.1 Draw a closed vector triangle for the forces acting on the knot at point P. (4)

9.2 The coefficient of static friction between the weight and the shelf is 0,8. If the weight has a mass of 2 kg, calculate the maximum force of static friction. (3)

9.3 Determine the maximum mass the lamp can be before the weight begins to slide. (4)

9.4 When the lamp is at the maximum weight, what is the tension in cable C? (3)

[14]

Question 10 (Solutions on page 175)

A 120 kg block, is at rest on a horizontal rough surface. Block M is just held in equilibrium by the 120 kg block and a massless rope which is connected to the ceiling. The rope connecting the 120 kg block makes an angle of 40° with the vertical and the rope connected to the ceiling makes an angle of 60° with the ceiling. The static frictional force the 120 kg block experiences is 400 N. The above situation is shown in the diagram below.

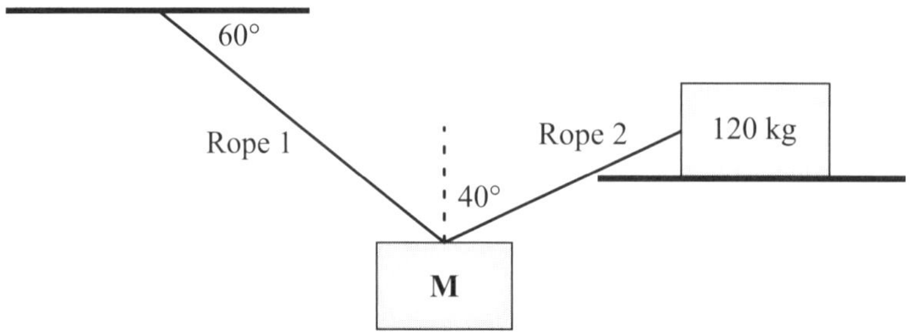

10.1 Explain what it means that the system is in equilibrium. (2)

10.2 Draw a fully labelled free body diagram of the forces acting on the 120 kg block (4)

10.3 Calculate the coefficient of static friction between the surface and the 120 kg block. (6)

10.4 If the 120kg block was replaced with a 200 kg block, what would happen to the force of friction the block experiences in comparison to the 120 kg block?
Write only increase, decrease or remains the same. (1)

10.5 Explain your answer to 10.4. (4)

10.6 Determine the mass of block M. (6)

[23]

Question 11 (2014 IEB Final Examination) (Solutions on page 175)

Lucy's doll is suspended by means of two light inextensible strings from the ceiling in the corner of her room as shown. String A makes an angle of 40° with the ceiling and string B makes an angle of 90° with the wall. The tension in string A is 12,2 N.

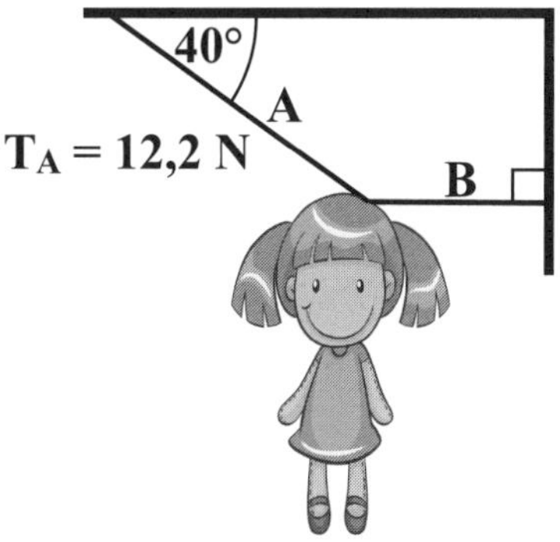

11.1 Calculate the magnitude of the vertical component of the tension in string A. (2)

11.2 Calculate the mass of Lucy's doll. (4)

11.3 Calculate the magnitude of the tension in string B. (2)

[8]

Question 12 (2015 IEB Supplementary Examination) (Solutions on page 176)

Thandi drives a motorboat in still water across a dam directly from point A to a jetty at point C, as shown in the diagram below. Susie walks 240 m at an average speed of 1,5 $m.s^{-1}$ across a bridge from point A to point B and then jogs for 100 m from B to meet Thandi at the jetty at point C. It takes Susie a total time of 3 minutes to get from point A to the jetty at point C.

Diagram is not to scale

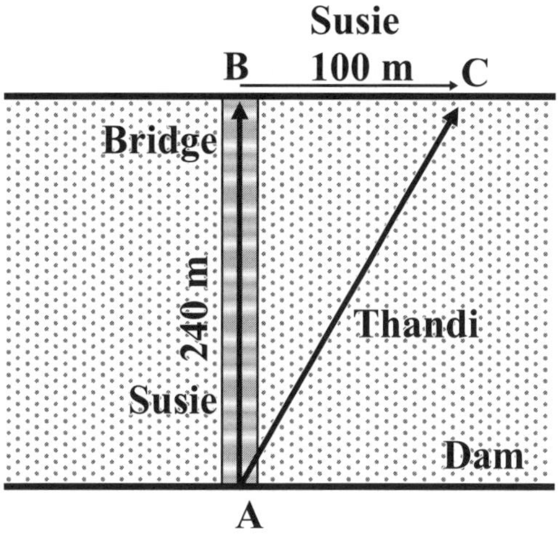

12.1 Define distance and hence state who travels the greater distance in going from A to C. (Thandi, Susie or neither) (2)

12.2 Define displacement and hence state whose displacement from A is greatest upon arriving at C. (Thandi, Susie or neither) (2)

12.3 Calculate Susie's average speed between B and C. (Give your answer in $m.s^{-1}$.) (6)

12.4 Calculate Susie's average speed from A to C. (Give your answer in $m.s^{-1}$.) (3)

12.5 Calculate the magnitude and direction of Susie's average velocity from A to C. (Give your answer in $m.s^{-1}$.) (5)

[18]

TOC 1 Data Sheet 2 Definitions 3 3 solutions 4 4 solutions 5 5 solutions 6 6 solutions 7 7 solutions 8 8 solutions 9 9 solutions 10 10 solutions

Question 13 (2016 IEB Supplementary Examination) (Solutions on page 176 and 177)

13.1 Simon is hanging at rest from a hoop, which is attached to the ceiling by two ropes. The ropes make angles to the horizontal ceiling of 50° and 60° as shown in the diagram. The tension in the rope P is 500 N.

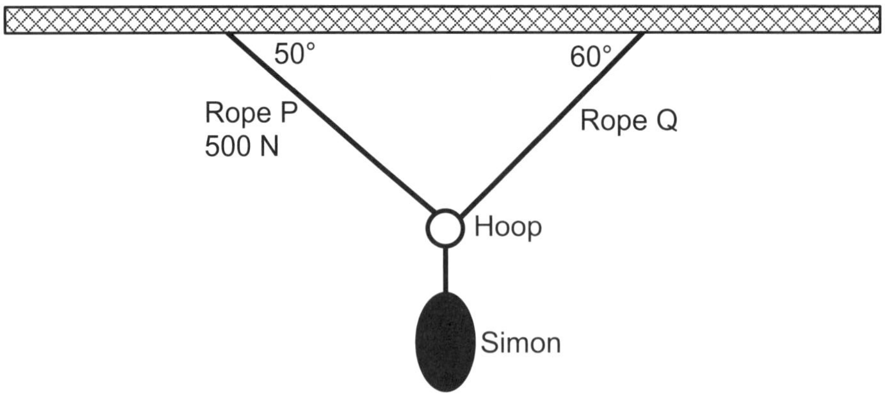

13.1.1 Define a *vector.* (2)

13.1.2 Determine the magnitude of the horizontal component of the tension in rope P. (2)

13.1.3 Calculate the magnitude of the tension in the rope Q. (3)

13.1.4 Determine Simon's mass. (5)

13.2 A sportsman is busy training and is sprinting a marked out pattern on a field. The diagram below shows the path taken by the sportsman. He started the stopwatch at point W. The positions of all the points and the reading on the stopwatch are given in the table after the diagram.

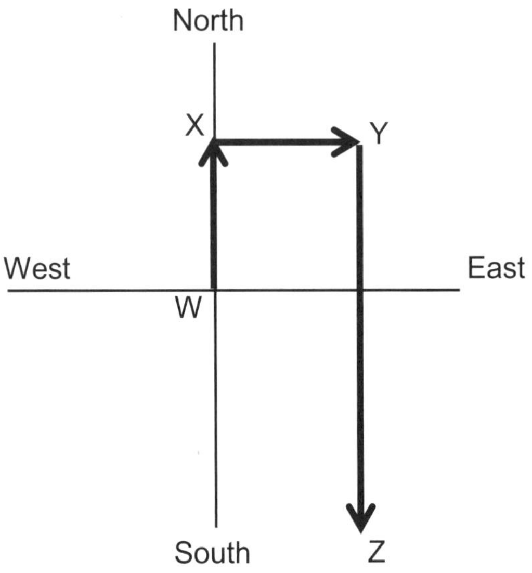

	Stopwatch Reading (s)	Position from W
W	0	0
X	5	40 m North
Y	10	40 m East, 40 m North
Z	25	40 m East, 80 m South

13.2.1 Define *distance.* (2)

13.2.2 Determine the sportsman's distance for the 25 s illustrated. (2)

13.2.3 Determine the sportsman's displacement for the 25 s illustrated. (5)

13.2.4 Determine the average speed for the sportsman for the 25 s illustrated. (3)

[24]

Question 14 (2014 IEB Exemplar Examination) (Solutions on page 177)

A cruise ship is being towed out of the harbour by two tugboats. One tugboat pulls with a force of 3 200 N on a bearing of 205°, while the other tugboat pulls with a force of 2 600 N directly south.

14.1 Draw a labelled free body diagram to represent only the forces applied by the tugboats to the cruise ship. (2)

14.2 Calculate the westerly component of the 3 200 N force. (3)

14.3 The cruise ship needs to go directly south to exit the harbour, but it is going off course. A third tugboat is requested to help. State the magnitude and direction of the minimum force which the third tugboat needs to apply to the cruise ship, to steer it safely out of the harbour. (2)

[7]

5. VECTORS (SOLUTIONS)

Question 1

1.1	C	(2)	1.8	B	(2)
1.2	A	(2)	1.9	B	(2)
1.3	C	(2)	1.10	C	(2)
1.4	A	(2)	1.11	B	(2)
1.5	D	(2)	1.12	C	(2)
1.6	C	(2)	1.13	C	(2)
1.7	B	(2)			

[26]

Question 2

2.1

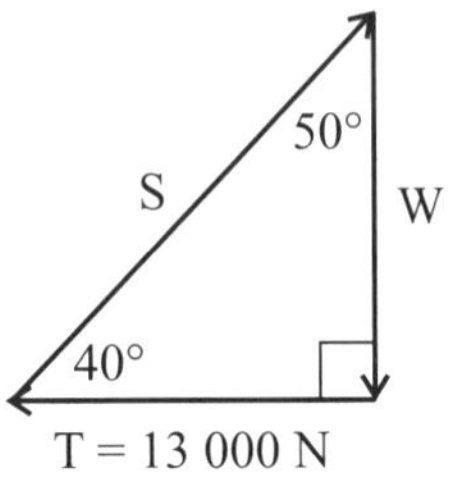

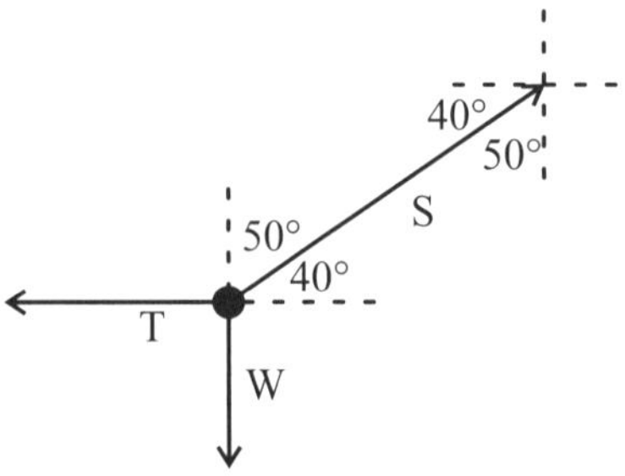

(4)

2.2 $\tan 40^\circ = \dfrac{W}{13000}$ $\qquad\cos 40^\circ = \dfrac{13000}{S}$

$W = 13000 \tan 40^\circ$ $\qquad S = \dfrac{13000}{\cos 40^\circ}$

$mg = 13000 \tan 40^\circ$ $\qquad = 16970,29\,\text{N}$

$m = 1113,09\,\text{kg}$

(6)

2.3 Increase.
As the system is in equilibrium:
$S_{vertical} = W$
$S\sin\theta = W$
As tension increases the angle (40°) will decrease and the value of $\sin\theta$ will also decrease.
For the vertical component to remain equal to W the tension in S must increase. (5)

[15]

Question 3

3.1

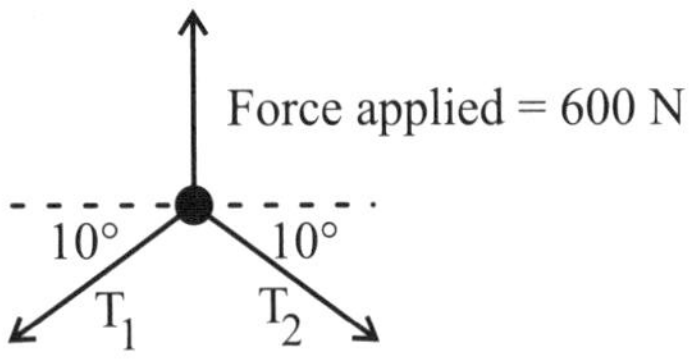

(3)

3.2 As the system is in equilibrium the sum of the horizontal components is zero. (1)

3.3 $T_1 = T_2 = x$

$2x\sin 10^\circ = 600$

$x = 1727,63\,\text{N}$

(4)

3.4 Force magnification $= \dfrac{1727,63}{600}$

= 2,88 times greater

(2)

[8]

Question 4

4.1 A physical quantity that has both magnitude and direction. (2)

4.2 $R_{1H} = 450 \sin 40°$

$= 289,25 \text{ N}$ (2)

4.3 As the system is in equilibrium: $R_{1H} = R_{2H}$

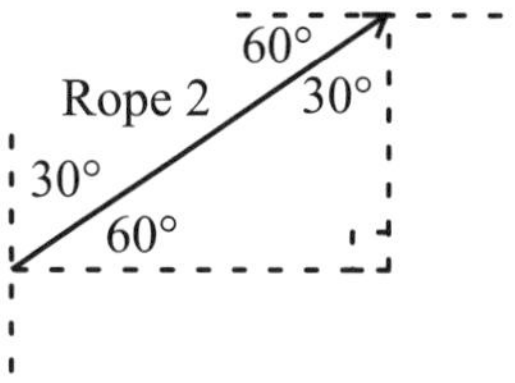

$R_{2H} = 289,25 \text{ N}$

$\cos 60° = \dfrac{R_{2H}}{R_2}$

$R_2 = \dfrac{289,25}{\cos 60°}$

$= 578,5 \text{ N}$ (4)

4.4 As the system is in equilibrium: $W = R_{1V} + R_{2V}$

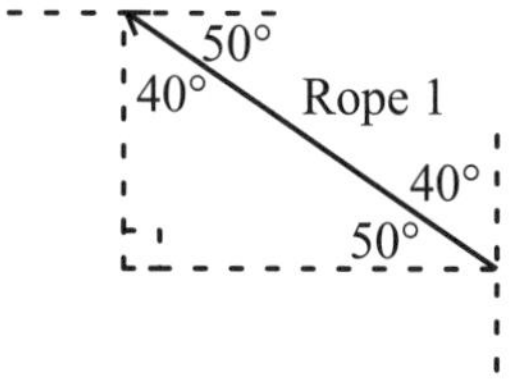

$W = 450 \cos 40° + 578,5 \sin 60°$

$= 845,72 \text{ N}$

$W = mg$

$845,72 = m(9,8)$

$m = 86,30 \text{ kg}$ (5)

[4]

Question 5

5.1

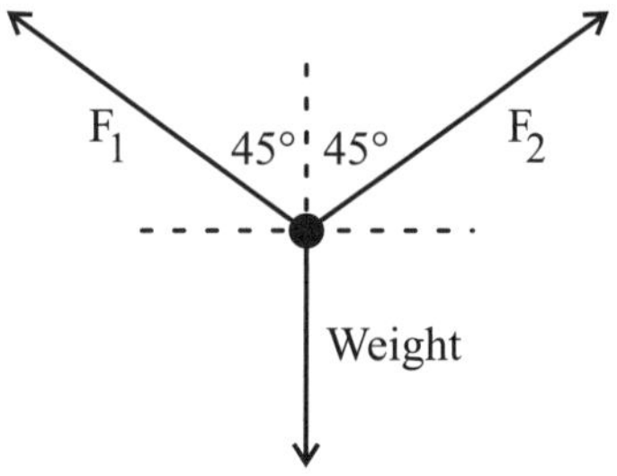

(3)

5.2 As the object is hanging, F_1 and F_2 are equal to the weight of the hanging masses:

$F_1 = F_2 = 0,5(9,8)$

$= 4,9 \text{ N}$

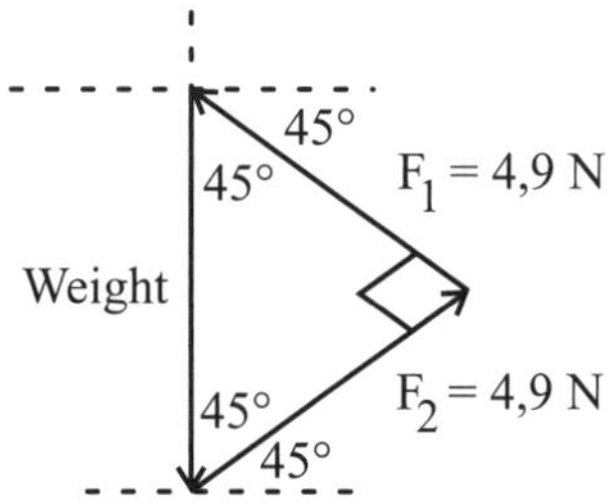

(4)

5.3

$\sin 45° = \dfrac{4,9}{W}$

$W = 6,93 \text{ N}$

$mg = 6,93$

$m = 0,71 \text{ kg}$ (3)

[10]

Question 6

6.1

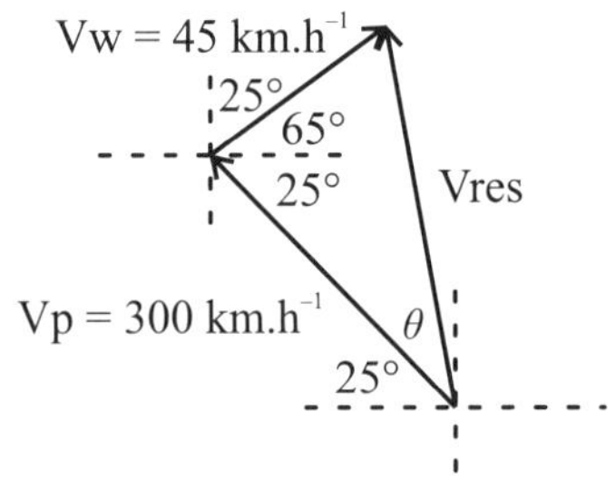

Key: Vp = velocity of plane relative to wind
Vw = velocity of wind relative to ground
Vres = resultant velocity

(5)

6.2 $v_{res}^2 = 300^2 + 45^2$

$= 92\,025$

$v_{res} = 303,36\,\text{km.h}^{-1}$

$\tan\theta = \frac{45}{300}$

$\theta = 8,53^\circ$

$\therefore v_{res} = 303,36\,\text{km.h}^{-1}$ on a bearing of $303,53^\circ$ (4)

6.3 $\Delta x = vt$

$= 303,36(0,75)$

$= 227,52\,\text{km}$ (3)

[12]

Question 7

7.1

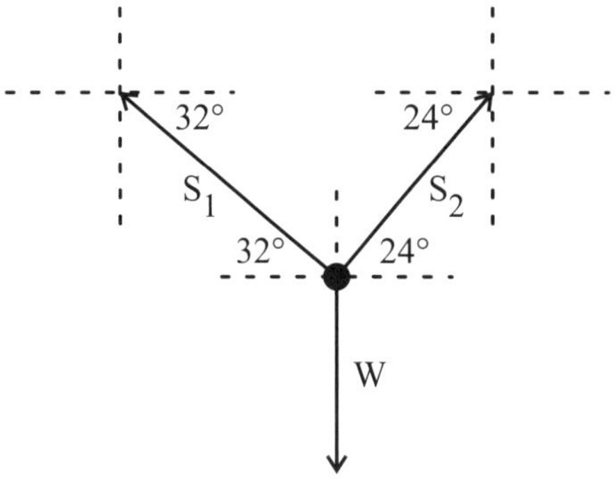

(3)

7.2 $S_{1H} = S_{2H}$

$S_1 \cos 32^\circ = S_2 \cos 24^\circ$ (3)

7.3 $S_{1V} + S_{2V} = W$

$S_1 \sin 32^\circ + S_2 \sin 24^\circ = 980 \rightarrow W = mg = 100(9,8)$ (3)

7.4 $S_1 = \frac{S_2 \cos 24^\circ}{\cos 32}$

$\frac{S_2 \cos 24^\circ \sin 32^\circ}{\cos 32} + S_2 \sin 24^\circ = 980$

$S_2 = \frac{980}{\frac{\cos 24^\circ \sin 32^\circ}{\cos 32} + \sin 24^\circ}$

$= 1002,47\,\text{N}$

$S_1 = \frac{1002,47 \cos 24^\circ}{\cos 32}$

$= 1079,89\,\text{N} \rightarrow$ without rounding the answer would be $1079,90\,\text{N}$ (4)

[16]

Question 8

8.1

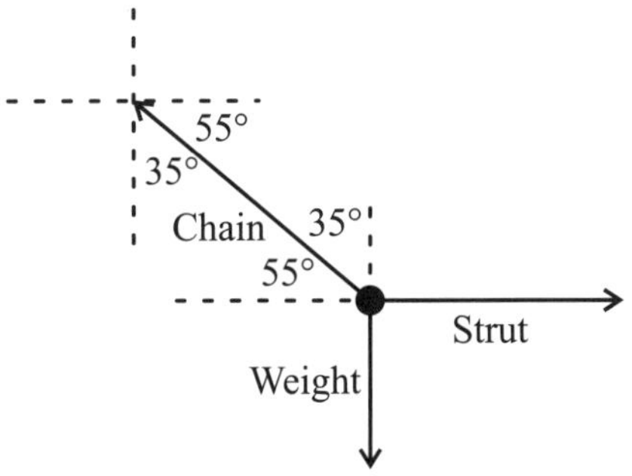

(3)

8.2 The gravitational force the Earth exerts on any object on or near its surface. (2)

8.3 As the system is in equilibrium: $C_v = W$

$C_v = W$

$C\sin 55^\circ = mg$

$C = \dfrac{4(9{,}8)}{\sin 55^\circ}$

$= 47{,}85\ \text{N}$ (3)

8.4 $\tan 55^\circ = \dfrac{W}{120}$

$mg = 120\tan 55^\circ$

$m = \dfrac{120\tan 55^\circ}{9{,}8}$

$= 17{,}49\ \text{kg}$

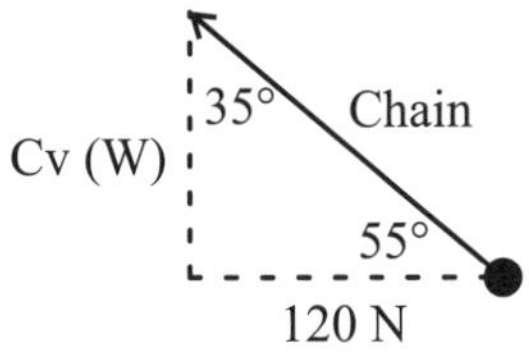

(4)

[12]

Question 9

9.1

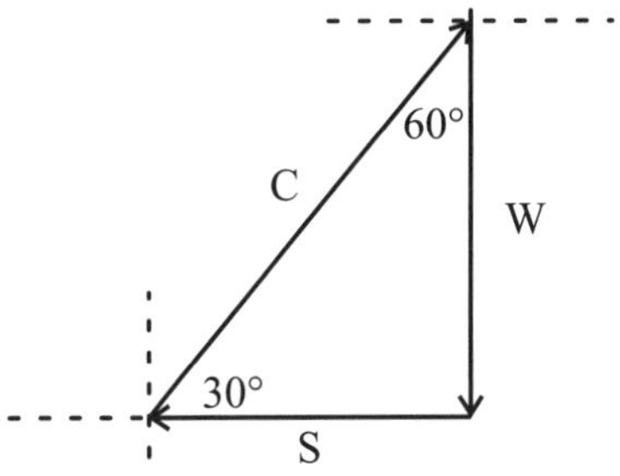

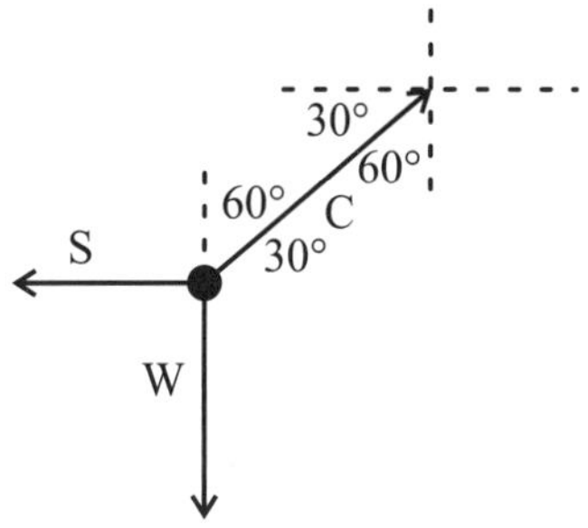

(4)

9.2 $F_{f\,max} = \mu F_N$

$= 0{,}8(2)(9{,}8)$

$= 15{,}68\ \text{N}$ (3)

9.3 $\tan 30^\circ = \dfrac{W}{15{,}68}$

$W_{max} = 15{,}68\tan 30^\circ$

$= 9{,}05\ \text{N}$

$W_{max} = m_{max}g$

$m_{max} = \dfrac{9{,}05}{9{,}8}$

$= 0{,}92\ \text{kg}$

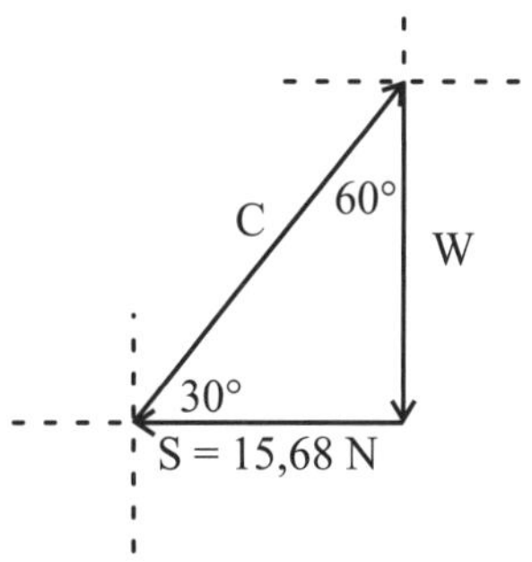

(4)

9.4 $\cos 30^\circ = \dfrac{15{,}68}{C}$

$C = 18{,}11\ \text{N}$ (1)

[14]

Question 10

10.1 The sum of the vertical and horizontal components is equal to zero. (2)

10.2

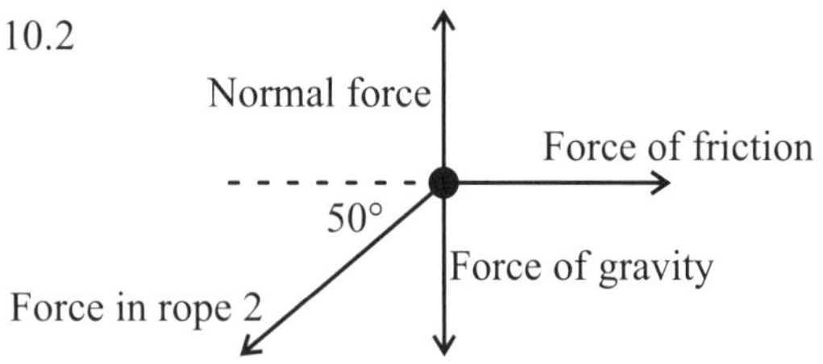

(4)

10.3 $R_{2H} = F_f = 400\,N$

$R_{2V} = R_{2H} \tan 50^\circ$

$= 400 \tan 50^\circ$

$= 476,70\,N$

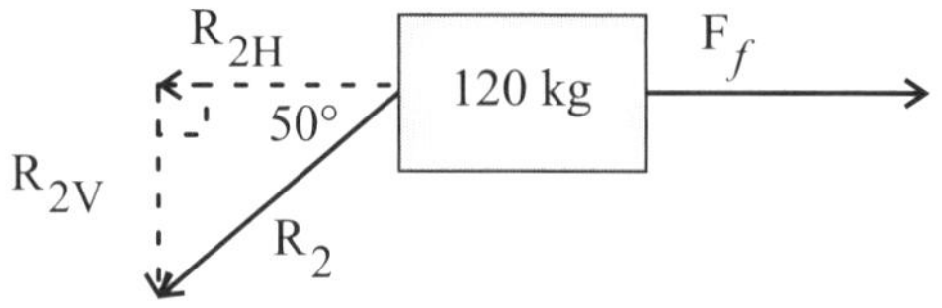

$F_f = \mu F_N$

$F_f = \mu\left(F_g + R_{2V}\right)$

$$\mu = \frac{400}{120(9,8)+476,70}$$

$= 0,24$ (6)

10.4 Remain the same. (1)

10.5 Although the **maximum** static frictional force increases the force of friction will not change as only 400 N is required to maintain the equilibrium of the system. (4)

10.6 $F_g = R_{1V} + R_{2V}$

$R_{2H} = R_{1H} = 400\,N$

$$\tan 60^\circ = \frac{R_{1V}}{R_{1H}}$$

$R_{1V} = 400 \tan 60^\circ$

$= 692,82\,N$

$mg = 692,82 + 476,70$

$m(9,8) = 1169,52$

$m = 119,34\,kg$ (6)

[23]

Question 11 (2014 IEB Final Examination)

11.1 $T_{Av} = 12,2 \sin 40^\circ$

$= 7,84\,N$ (2)

11.2 $F_g = T_{Av}$

$= 7,84\,N$

$F_g = mg$

$7,84 = m(9,8)$

$m = 0,8\,kg$ (3)

11.3 $T_B = T_{AH}$

$= 12,2 \cos 40^\circ$

$= 9,35\,N$ (4)

[8]

Question 12 (2015 IEB Supplementary Examination)

12.1 The length of path travelled. Susie travels the greater distance. (2)

12.2 A change in position. Neither, they have the same displacement. (2)

12.3 $\text{time}_{AB} = \dfrac{\text{distance}_{AB}}{\text{speed}_{AB}}$

$= \dfrac{240}{1,5}$

$= 160\,\text{s}$

Average $\text{Speed}_{BC} = \dfrac{\text{distance}_{BC}}{\text{time}_{BC}}$

$= \dfrac{100}{20} \rightarrow \text{time} = 180 - 160 = 20\,\text{s}$

$= 5\,\text{m.s}^{-1}$ (6)

12.4 Average $\text{Speed}_{AC} = \dfrac{\text{distance}_{AC}}{\text{time}_{AC}}$

$= \dfrac{240 + 100}{180}$

$= 1,89\,\text{m.s}^{-1}$ (3)

12.5 $AC^2 = 240^2 + 100^2$

$AC = 260\,\text{m}$

Average velocity $= \dfrac{\text{displacement}}{\text{time}}$

$= \dfrac{260}{180}$

$= 1,44\,\text{m.s}^{-1}$

$\tan\theta = \dfrac{100}{240}$

$\theta = 22,62^\circ$

$\therefore$ Average velocity $= 1,44\,\text{m.s}^{-1}$ on a bearing of $22,62^\circ$ (5)

[18]

Question 13 (2016 IEB Supplementary Examination)

13.1.1 A physical quantity that has both magnitude and direction. (2)

13.1.2 $P_H = 500\cos 50^\circ$

$= 321,39\,\text{N}$ (2)

13.1.3 $P_H = Q_H$

$321,39 = Q\cos 60^\circ$

$Q = 642,79\ \text{N}$ (3)

13.1.4 $P_V + Q_V = W$

$500\sin 50^\circ + 642,79\sin 60^\circ = mg$

$939,69 = m(9,8)$

$m = 95,89\ \text{kg}$ (5)

13.2.1 The length of path travelled. (2)

13.2.2 $\text{distance} = 40 + 40 + 40 + 80$

$= 200\,\text{m}$ (2)

13.2.3 $\text{displacement} = \sqrt{40^2 + 80^2}$

$= 89,44\,\text{m}$

$\tan\theta = \dfrac{80}{40}$

$\theta = 63,43^\circ$

$\therefore$ displacement $= 89,44\,\text{m}$ on a bearing of $153{,}43^\circ \rightarrow$ this is the same as $63,43^\circ$ S of E (5)

13.2.4 $\text{Average Speed} = \dfrac{\text{distance}}{\text{time}}$

$= \dfrac{200}{25}$

$= 8\,\text{m.s}^{-1}$

[24]

Question 14 (2014 IEB Exemplar Examination)

14.1

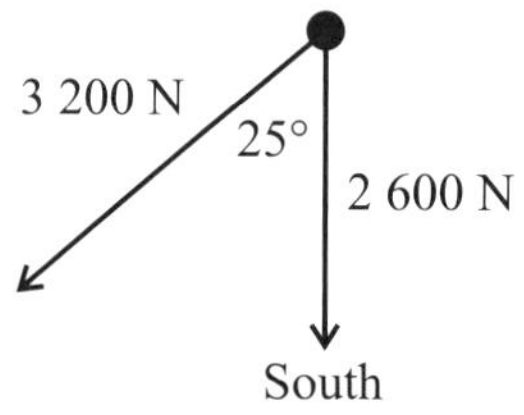

(2)

14.2 $\text{Westerly component} = 3\,200 \sin 25^\circ$

$= 1352,38$ N West (3)

14.3 1352,38 N East (2)

[7]

6. MOMENTUM AND ENERGY

MOMENTUM:

Momentum is the **product** of an object's **mass** and **velocity**.
Momentum is a method of quantifying the motion of a moving object.

> **Momentum**:
> $$p = mv$$
> Where:
>
> $p \rightarrow$ momentum $\left(\text{kg.m.s}^{-1}\right)$
>
> $m \rightarrow$ mass (kg)
>
> $v \rightarrow$ velocity $\left(\text{m.s}^{-1}\right)$

> **Momentum is a vector. This means it has magnitude and direction.**
> **The direction of momentum is in the same direction as the objects velocity.**
> **If mass is constant, momentum is directly proportional to velocity.**

Illustrative Example:

A truck of mass 4 580 kg is travelling South at 30 m.s^{-1}. Calculate the momentum of the truck.

$$\begin{aligned} p &= mv \\ &= (4580)(30) \\ &= 137\,400\,\text{kg.m.s}^{-1} \text{ South} \end{aligned}$$

CHANGE IN MOMENTUM

When a **moving object collides with another object**, the velocity of the objects will change.
This causes a change in the momentum of both objects.

> **Change in Momentum**:
> $$\begin{aligned} \Delta p &= p_f - p_i \\ &= m\Delta v \\ &= m\left(v_f - v_i\right) \end{aligned}$$

Illustrative Example 1:

A ball of mass 2kg travelling East hits a wall with a velocity of 5m.s^{-1} and rebounds at the same speed. Determine the change in momentum of the ball.

Taking East as positive:

$$\begin{aligned} \Delta p &= m\left(v_f - v_i\right) \\ &= 2\left[(-5)-(+5)\right] \\ &= -20 \\ &= 20\,\text{kg.m.s}^{-1} \text{ West} \end{aligned}$$

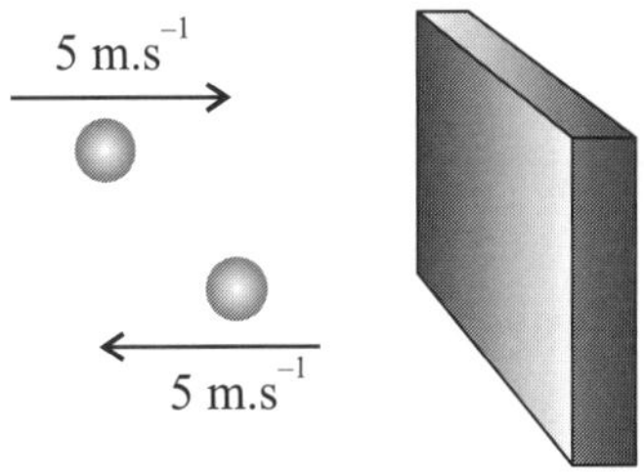

> **Direction is important when dealing with momentum. When an object rebounds the change in momentum is never zero.**

TOC 1 Data Sheet 2 Definitions 3 3 solutions 4 4 solutions 5 5 solutions 6 6 solutions 7 7 solutions 8 8 solutions 9 9 solutions 10 10 solutions

Illustrative Example 2:

A ball of putty with mass 2kg travelling East hits a wall with a velocity of 5m.s^{-1} and sticks to the wall. Determine the change in momentum of the ball.

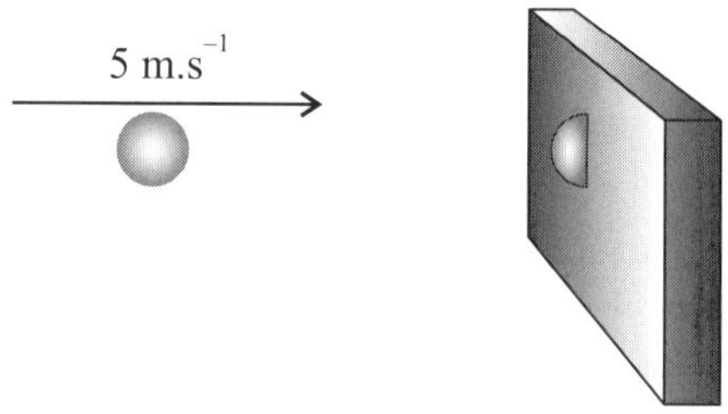

$$\Delta p = m\left(v_f - v_i\right)$$
$$= 2\left(0-5\right)$$
$$= -10$$
$$= 10\,\text{kg.m.s}^{-1}\text{ West}$$

In a collision, the change in momentum of an object that rebounds is always greater than an object which remains stationary after the collision.

IMPULSE (J)

Impulse is the product of the net force and contact time.

Impulse (J):

$$\mathbf{F}_{net}\Delta t = \Delta p$$

The formula can also be written as:

$$\mathbf{F}_{net}\Delta t = \mathbf{J}$$

Where:

F_{net} → net force (N)

Δt → collision time (s)

Δp / J → change in momentum / Impulse $\left(\text{kg.m.s}^{-1}\right)$

It can be seen from the equation above that **an objects impulse is the same as its change in momentum (Δp)**. They **symbol** used for **impulse** (or change in momentum) is **J**.

Impulse is **directly proportional** to the magnitude of the **net force** applied to an object and the **contact time** of the force.

Impulse is a vector. It has the same direction as the net (resultant) force acting on an object.

Illustrative Example 1:

A cricket ball of mass 163g is travelling at 44m.s^{-1} West when it is struck by a cricket bat. The ball leaves the cricket bat at 38m.s^{-1} travelling directly back to the bowler. If the ball is in contact with the bat for 0,02 seconds, what force does the bat exert on the ball?

$$F_{net}\Delta t = \Delta p$$

$$F_{net} = \frac{m\left(v_f - v_i\right)}{\Delta t}$$

$$F_{net} = \frac{\left(163\times10^{-3}\right)\left[-38-\left(44\right)\right]}{\left(0{,}02\right)}$$

$$= -668{,}3\text{ N}$$

$$= 668{,}3\text{ N East}$$

Illustrative Example 2:

A golfer strikes a golf ball with force F. Using physics principles explain why two identical balls, hit with the same force, could leave the club head with different velocities.

From the formula $F_{net}\Delta t = \Delta p$, it can be seen that if the force is constant, $\Delta p \ \alpha \ \Delta t$ (impulse is directly proportional to change in time). The longer the club is contact with the ball, the greater the change in momentum. As both balls have the same mass and initial velocity of 0, a larger change in momentum will result in a larger velocity leaving the club.

In a collision where force is constant, increasing the contact time increases the change in momentum of the object.

Illustrative Example 3:

The graph below shows the force exerted on a stationary hockey ball.

a) Calculate the impulse experienced by the hockey ball.

b) Determine the mass of the hockey ball if it leaves the hockey stick with a speed of 162,5 m.s^{-1}.

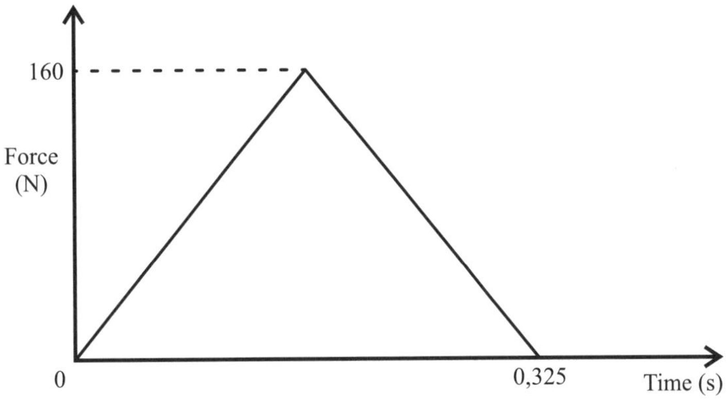

a) **The area under a force time graph represents the impulse (change in momentum) experienced by the ball.**

$$F_{net}\Delta t = \text{Area under the graph}$$
$$= \frac{1}{2}(\text{base})(\perp \text{height})$$
$$= \frac{1}{2}(0{,}325)(160)$$
$$= 26 \text{ kg.m.s}^{-1}$$

b) $\Delta p = m(v_f - v_i)$

$26 = m(162{,}5 - 0)$

$m = 0{,}16 \text{ kg}$

> **When calculating the <u>area under a graph</u>, the units of the answer represent the quantity on the *y*-axis multiplied by the quantity on the *x*-axis.**
>
> **When calculating the <u>gradient of a graph</u>, the units of the answer represent the quantity on the *y*-axis divided by the quantity on the *x*-axis.**

RATE OF CHANGE OF MOMENTUM (F_{NET})

The **rate of change of momentum** is the **net (resultant) force** acting on an object.

Rate of change of momentum:

$$F_{net} = \frac{\Delta p}{\Delta t}$$

From the formula above, it can be seen that if the change in momentum is constant, the **force** experienced by an object is **inversely proportional to the contact time** of the collision $F_{net} \propto \frac{1}{t}$.

Illustrative Example:

Two identical cars with the same mass crash into a steel barrier with the same velocity and are brought to rest. One of the cars is designed with a crumple zone while the other is not. Explain the benefits of a crumple zone in a collision making reference to the above case.

As both cars have the same mass, initial velocity and final velocity, the change in momentum is the same for both cars. However, the car with the crumple zone will take longer to come to rest. As the net force acting on the car is inversely proportional to time $\left(F_{net} \propto \frac{1}{t}\right)$, the car with the crumple zone will experience less force in coming to rest than the car without the crumple zone. This reduces the injuries the passengers experience.

> **Do not confuse rate of change of momentum with impulse or change in momentum. Rate of change of momentum is the net force an object experiences in a collision.**

TOC | 1 Data Sheet | 2 Definitions | 3 | 3 solutions | 4 | 4 solutions | 5 | 5 solutions | 6 | 6 solutions | 7 | 7 solutions | 8 | 8 solutions | 9 | 9 solutions | 10 | 10 solutions

CONSERVATION OF LINEAR MOMENTUM

The total linear momentum of an isolated system remains constant.
An **isolated system** is a system with **no external forces** (such as friction and applied forces).

When dealing with conservation of linear momentum there are 4 general types of collisions/events:

1. **Collisions where objects move separately after the collision.**
2. **Collisions where objects stick together after the collision.**
3. **Collisions where objects are dropped vertically onto a moving object.**
4. **Explosions.**

Note that the total linear momentum before a collision/event, is equal to the total linear momentum after a collision/event.

$$p_{bef} = p_{aft}$$

1. Collisions where objects move separately after the collision

$$p_{bef} = p_{aft}$$

$$m_1 v_{1_i} + m_2 v_{2_i} = m_1 v_{1f} + m_2 v_{2f}$$

Illustrative Example 1:

Object A of mass 60kg is travelling at 4m.s^{-1} East, when it collides head on with object B of mass 20kg travelling at 2m.s^{-1} West. After the collision, Object A moves East at 1,5m.s^{-1}.

Before collision **After collision**

a) Determine the velocity of Object B immediately after the collision.

b) Which object, if any, experienced the greater change in momentum?

a) $p_{bef} = p_{aft}$

$m_1 v_{1_i} + m_2 v_{2_i} = m_1 v_{1f} + m_2 v_{2f}$

$60(4) + 20(-2) = 60(1,5) + (20) v_{2_f}$

$v_{2_f} = 5,5\,\text{m.s}^{-1}$ East

b) Both objects experienced the same change in momentum.

> **According to Newton III, when two objects collide, the force exerted on both objects will be equal in magnitude. The time of contact will also be the same.**
> **From the formula $F_{net}\Delta t = \Delta p$ it can be seen that if the net force and contact time is the same for two objects, the change in momentum will be the same for both objects.**

Illustrative Example 2:

Object A of mass 10kg is travelling right at 2m.s^{-1}. It collides head on with object B of mass 5kg travelling to the left at 1m.s^{-1}. After the collision, Object A moves off to the right at 0,5m.s^{-1}. Determine the velocity of object B after the collision.

Before collision **After collision**

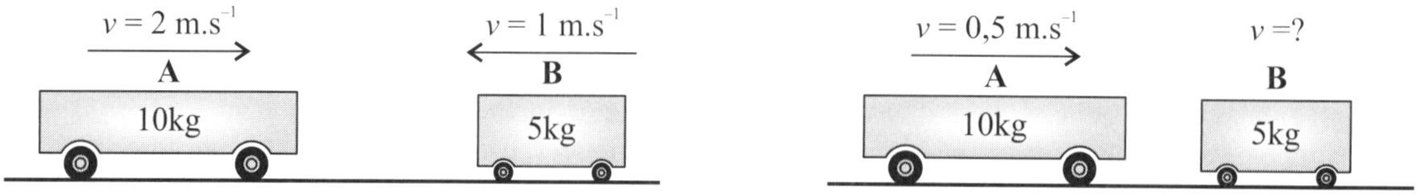

$p_{bef} = p_{aft}$

$m_1 v_{1_i} + m_2 v_{2_i} = m_1 v_{1f} + m_2 v_{2f}$

$10(2) + 5(-1) = 10(0,5) + (5) v_{2_f}$

$v_{2_f} = 2\,\text{m.s}^{-1}$ right

2. Collisions where objects stick together after the collision

$$p_{bef} = p_{aft}$$
$$m_1 v_{1_i} + m_2 v_{2_i} = (m_1 + m_2) v_f$$

Illustrative Example 1:

Object A of mass 3kg is travelling right at 5m.s^{-1}. It collides with object B of mass 7kg which is stationary. After the collision, the objects stick together. Determine the velocity of the objects after the collision.

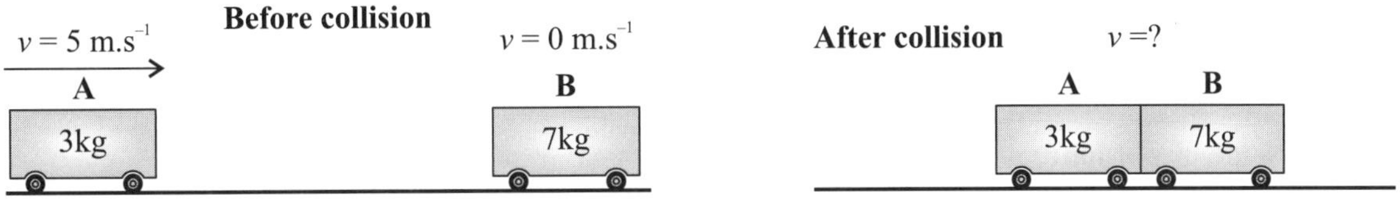

$p_{bef} = p_{aft}$

$m_1 v_{1_i} + m_2 v_{2_i} = (m_1 + m_2) v_f$

$3(5) + (7)0 = (3+7) v_f$

$v_f = 1{,}5\,\text{m.s}^{-1}$ right

Illustrative Example 2:

Object A of mass 3kg is travelling right at 5m.s^{-1}. It collides with object B of mass 7kg travelling left at 1m.s^{-1}. After the collision, the objects stick together. Determine the velocity of the objects after the collision.

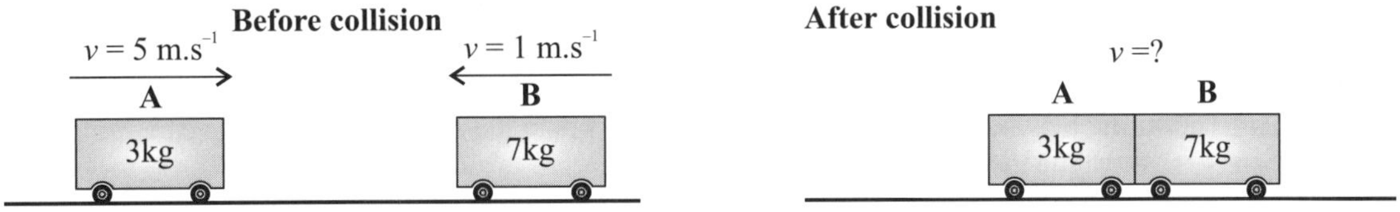

$p_{bef} = p_{aft}$

$m_1 v_{1_i} + m_2 v_{2_i} = (m_1 + m_2) v_f$

$3(5) + (7)(-1) = (3+7) v_f$

$v_f = 0{,}8\,\text{m.s}^{-1}$ right

3. Collisions where objects are dropped vertically onto a moving object

$$p_{bef} = p_{aft}$$
$$m_1 v_{1_i} + m_2 (0) = (m_1 + m_2) v_f$$
The object moving vertically has a horizontal velocity of zero

Illustrative Example:

Object A of mass 10kg is moving right at 5m.s^{-1}. Object B of mass 20kg is dropped vertically onto object A. Determine the velocity of Object A and B together after the collision.

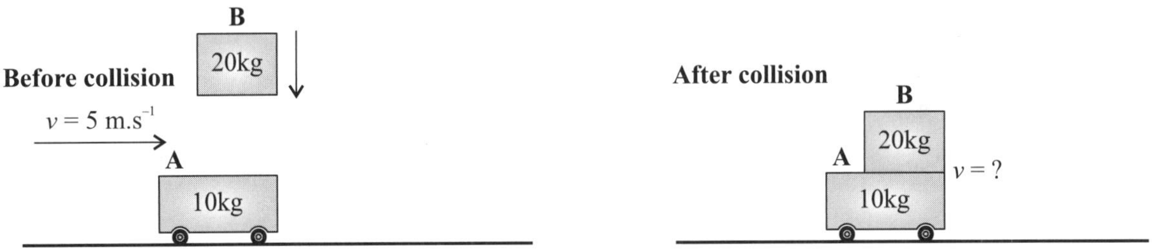

$p_{bef} = p_{aft}$

$m_1 v_{1_i} + m_2 v_{2_i} = (m_1 + m_2) v_f$

$10(5) + (20)0 = (10+20) v_f$

$v_f = 1{,}67\,\text{m.s}^{-1}$ right

4. Explosions

Explosions occur when a stationary or moving object breaks apart into two or more objects. As with all collisions, the objects all experience the same force.

$$p_{bef} = p_{aft}$$
$$(m_1 + m_2)v_i = m_1 v_{1_f} + m_2 v_{2_f}$$

Illustrative Example 1:

A stationary object of mas 20kg explodes into two pieces. One piece with a mass of 12kg moves to the left with a velocity of 1m.s^{-1}. Determine the velocity of the other piece.

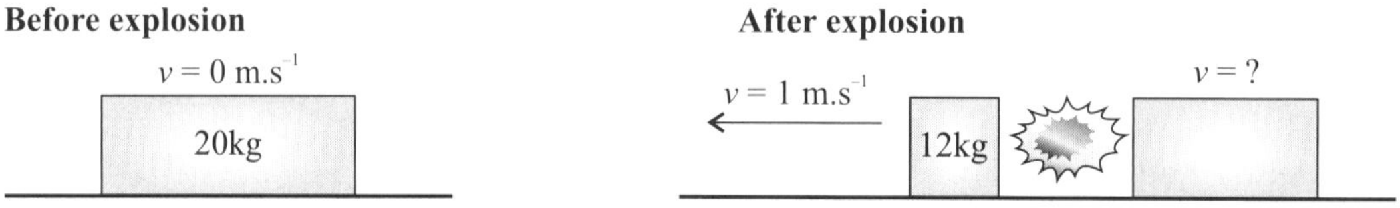

$p_{bef} = p_{aft}$

$(m_1 + m_2)v_i = m_1 v_{1_f} + m_2 v_{2_f}$

$(20)(0) = (12)(-1) + (8)v_{2_f}$ → taking right as positive, $m_2 = 20 - 12 = 8\,kg$

$v_{2_f} = 1{,}5\,m.s^{-1}$ right

Illustrative Example 2:

Two carts, A and B are travelling to the right at 3m.s^{-1} with a compressed spring between them. Cart A has a mass of 5kg. The spring between them releases and cart B moves to the right at 7m.s^{-1} while cart A moves to the left at 4m.s^{-1}. Determine the mass of cart B.

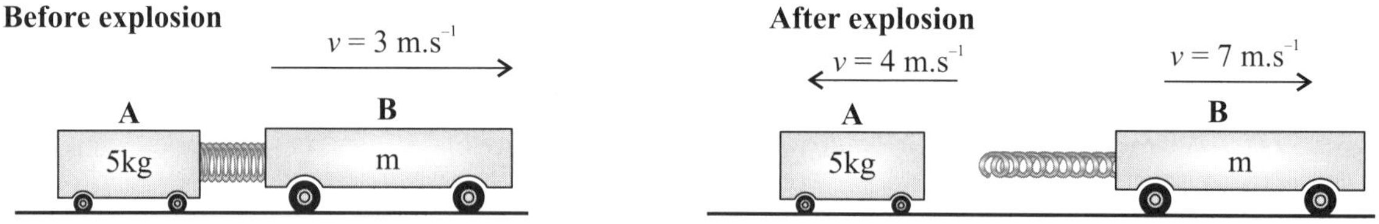

$p_{bef} = p_{aft}$

$(m_1 + m_2)v_i = m_1 v_{1_f} + m_2 v_{2_f}$

$(5 + m)(3) = (5)(-4) + 7m$ → taking right as positive

$15 + 3m = -20 + 7m$

$-4m = -35$

$m = 8{,}75\,kg$

Illustrative Example 2:

A fully loaded handgun of mass 850g fires a bullet that has a mass of 7,5g. The bullet exits the barrel of the gun at 380 m.s^{-1} travelling to the right. Determine the recoil velocity of the gun.

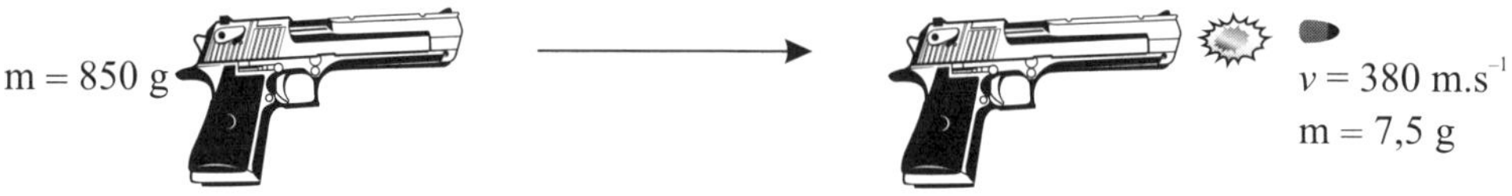

$p_{bef} = p_{aft}$

$mv_i = m_1 v_{1_f} + m_2 v_{2_f}$

$(850\times10^{-3})(0) = (842{,}5\times10^{-3})v_{1_f} + (7{,}5\times10^{-3})(380)$ → the guns mass is 7,5g less after the bullet is fired

$v_{1_f} = -3{,}38$

$= 3{,}38\,m.s^{-1}$ left

ELASTIC AND INELASTIC COLLISIONS

An **elastic collision** is a collision in which **both momentum and kinetic energy are conserved.**

An **inelastic collision** is a collision in which **only momentum is conserved.** (kinetic energy is not conserved)

Kinetic energy is the energy of an object as a result of its motion. It is calculated using the formula below.

Kinetic Energy:

$$E_k = \frac{1}{2}mv^2$$

Where:

$E_k \rightarrow$ kinetic energy (J)

$m \rightarrow$ mass (kg)

$v \rightarrow$ velocity $(m.s^{-1})$

Illustrative Example 1:

Object A of mass 2kg is travelling right at $12 m.s^{-1}$, when it collides head on with a stationary object B of mass 6kg. After the collision, Object A moves left at $6 m.s^{-1}$.

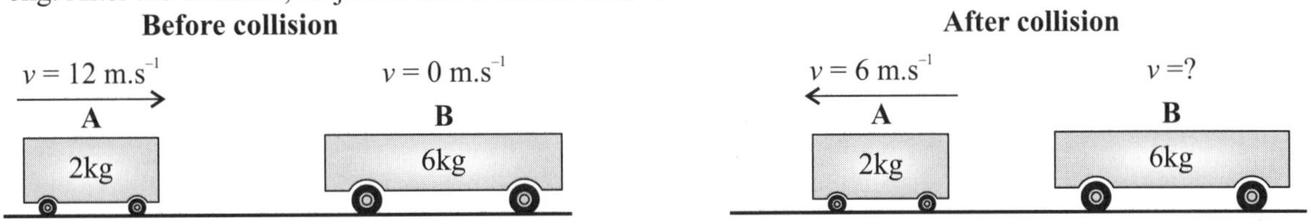

a) Determine the velocity of Object B immediately after the collision.

b) Showing all calculations, determine whether the collision was elastic or inelastic.

a) $p_{bef} = p_{aft}$

$m_1 v_{1_i} + m_2 v_{2_i} = m_1 v_{1_f} + m_2 v_{2_f}$

$2(12) + 6(0) = 2(-6) + (6) v_{2_f}$

$v_{2_f} = 6 m.s^{-1}$ right

b) $E_{k_{bef}} = \frac{1}{2} m_1 v_{1_i}^2 + \frac{1}{2} m_2 v_{2_i}^2$

$= \frac{1}{2}(2)(12)^2 + \frac{1}{2}(6)(0)^2$

$= 144 J$

$E_{k_{aft}} = \frac{1}{2} m_1 v_{1_f}^2 + \frac{1}{2} m_2 v_{2_f}^2$

$= \frac{1}{2}(2)(-6)^2 + \frac{1}{2}(6)(6)^2$

$= 144 J$

$\therefore$ The collision is elastic as $E_{k_{bef}} = E_{k_{aft}}$.

Energy is a scalar, not a vector. Energy does not have a direction.

TOC | 1 Data Sheet | 2 Definitions | 3 | 3 solutions | 4 | 4 solutions | 5 | 5 solutions | 6 | 6 solutions | 7 | 7 solutions | 8 | 8 solutions | 9 | 9 solutions | 10 | 10 solutions

Illustrative Example 2:

A 10kg ball traveling at 2m.s^{-1} to the right collides elastically with a 2kg ball traveling at 4m.s^{-1} in the opposite direction. After the collision the 10kg ball moves with a velocity x and the 2kg mass moves off with a velocity y. Determine the final velocities of both objects.

$p_{bef} = p_{aft}$

$m_1 v_{1_i} + m_2 v_{2_i} = m_1 v_{1f} + m_2 v_{2_f}$

$10(2) + 2(-4) = 10x + 2y$

$12 = 10x + 2y$

$y = 6 - 5x \rightarrow \boxed{1}$

$E_{k_{bef}} = E_{k_{aft}} \rightarrow$ collision is elastic

$\frac{1}{2} m_1 v_{1_i}{}^2 + \frac{1}{2} m_2 v_{2_i}{}^2 = \frac{1}{2} m_1 v_{1_f}{}^2 + \frac{1}{2} m_2 v_{2_f}{}^2$

$\frac{1}{2}(10)(2)^2 + \frac{1}{2}(2)(-4)^2 = \frac{1}{2}(10)(x)^2 + \frac{1}{2}(2)(y)^2$

$36 = 5x^2 + y^2 \rightarrow \boxed{2}$

Substitute $\boxed{1}$ into $\boxed{2}$

$36 = 5x^2 + (6 - 5x)^2$

$36 = 5x^2 + 36 - 60x + 25x^2$

$0 = 30x^2 - 60x$

$0 = 30x(x - 2)$

$x = 0$ or $x \neq 2 \rightarrow \boxed{3}$

Substitute $\boxed{3}$ into $\boxed{1}$

$y = 6 - 5(0)$

$= 6$

$\therefore x = 0\,\text{m.s}^{-1}$ and $y = 6\,\text{m.s}^{-1}$ right

> **In the above example $x \neq 2$ as this would result in a negative value of y. This would mean that after the collision, the 10kg mass would continue moving right and the 2kg mass would continue moving left, which is not possible.**

SUMMARY OF CONSERVATION OF MOMENTUM FORMULAS

1. **Collisions where objects move separately after the collision**

$$m_1 v_{1_i} + m_2 v_{2_i} = m_1 v_{1f} + m_2 v_{2_f}$$

2. **Collisions where objects stick together after the collision**

$$m_1 v_{1_i} + m_2 v_{2_i} = (m_1 + m_2) v_f$$

3. **Collisions where objects are dropped vertically onto a moving object**

$$m_1 v_{1_i} + m_2 (0) = (m_1 + m_2) v_f$$

4. **Explosions**

$$(m_1 + m_2) v_i = m_1 v_{1_f} + m_2 v_{2_f}$$

GRAVITATIONAL POTENTIAL ENERGY AND KINETIC ENERGY

Energy is the **ability to do work.**
It is measured in **joules (J).**
Energy cannot be created or destroyed only transferred from one form to another.
This means that the **total energy** in a system **is always conserved.**

Gravitational potential energy is the energy an object possesses due to its position relative to a reference point. It is calculated using the formula below:

Gravitational Potential Energy:

$$\mathbf{E}_p = \boldsymbol{mgh}$$

Where:

$E_p \rightarrow$ gravitational potential energy (J)

$m \rightarrow$ mass (kg)

$g \rightarrow$ gravitational acceleration $\left(\text{m.s}^{-2}\right)$

$h \rightarrow$ height (m)

Kinetic Energy is the energy an object has as a result of the object's motion.

Kinetic Energy:

$$\mathbf{E}_k = \frac{1}{2}\boldsymbol{mv}^2$$

Where:

$E_k \rightarrow$ kinetic energy (J)

$m \rightarrow$ mass (kg)

$v \rightarrow$ velocity $\left(\text{m.s}^{-1}\right)$

MECHANICAL ENERGY

Mechanical energy is the **sum of gravitational potential and kinetic energy** of an object **at a point.**

Mechanical Energy:

$$\mathbf{E_M} = \mathbf{E}_p + \mathbf{E}_k$$

$$\mathbf{E_M} = \boldsymbol{mgh} + \frac{1}{2}\boldsymbol{mv}^2$$

PRINCIPLE OF CONSERVATION OF MECHANICAL ENERGY

In the absence of air resistance or any external forces, the mechanical energy of an object is constant.
This means that the **sum of potential and kinetic energy** remains **constant** if there are **no external forces or friction** present.

Conservation of Mechanical Energy:

$$\mathbf{E}_{\mathbf{M}_{before}} = \mathbf{E}_{\mathbf{M}_{after}}$$

$$\left(\mathbf{E}_p + \mathbf{E}_k\right)_{before} = \left(\mathbf{E}_p + \mathbf{E}_k\right)_{after}$$

$$\left(\boldsymbol{mgh} + \frac{1}{2}\boldsymbol{mv}^2\right)_{before} = \left(\boldsymbol{mgh} + \frac{1}{2}\boldsymbol{mv}^2\right)_{after}$$

As total energy in a system is conserved, if friction is present the formula can be adjusted as shown below:

Conservation of Total Energy:

$$\mathbf{E}_{\mathbf{M}_{before}} = \mathbf{E}_{\mathbf{M}_{after}} + \mathbf{W}_f$$

$W_f \rightarrow$ work done against / by friciton

TOC | 1 Data Sheet | 2 Definitions | 3 | 3 solutions | 4 | 4 solutions | 5 | 5 solutions | 6 | 6 solutions | 7 | 7 solutions | 8 | 8 solutions | 9 | 9 solutions | 10 | 10 solutions

TOC | 1 Data Sheet | 2 Definitions | 3 | 3 solutions | 4 | 4 solutions | 5 | 5 solutions | 6 | 6 solutions | 7 | 7 solutions | 8 | 8 solutions | 9 | 9 solutions | 10 | 10 solutions

Illustrative Example 1:

A 5kg ball is dropped from point A, which is 10m above the ground. Point B is 8m above the ground. At point C the ball is travelling at a velocity of 8,85m.s^{-1}. The ball hits the ground at D.
Ignoring air resistance, determine the:

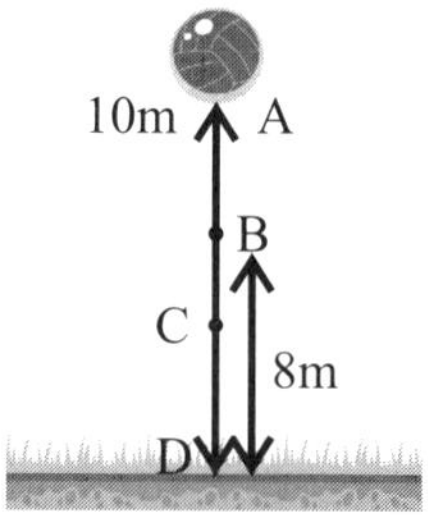

a) mechanical energy of the ball at point A.
b) speed of the ball at point B.
c) height above the ground at point C.
d) speed the ball strikes the ground with at point D

a) $$E_{M_A} = E_p + E_k$$
$$= mgh + \frac{1}{2}mv^2$$
$$= 5(9,8)(10) + 0$$
$$= 490\,\text{J}$$

b) $$E_{M_A} = E_{M_B}$$
$$490 = mgh + \frac{1}{2}mv^2$$
$$490 = 5(9,8)(8) + \frac{1}{2}(5)v^2$$
$$v^2 = 39,2$$
$$v = 6,26\,\text{m.s}^{-1}$$

c) $$E_{M_A} = E_{M_C}$$
$$490 = mgh + \frac{1}{2}mv^2$$
$$490 = 5(9,8)h + \frac{1}{2}(5)(8,85)^2$$
$$h = 6\,\text{m}$$

d) $$E_{M_A} = E_{M_D}$$
$$490 = mgh + \frac{1}{2}mv^2$$
$$490 = 5(9,8)(0) + \frac{1}{2}(5)v^2$$
$$v^2 = 196$$
$$v = 14\,\text{m.s}^{-1}$$

Illustrative Example 2:

A soccer ball rolling on a frictionless surface reaches an incline travelling at 3 m.s^{-1} at A. Assuming the incline is frictionless, determine the maximum height the soccer ball will reach at B.

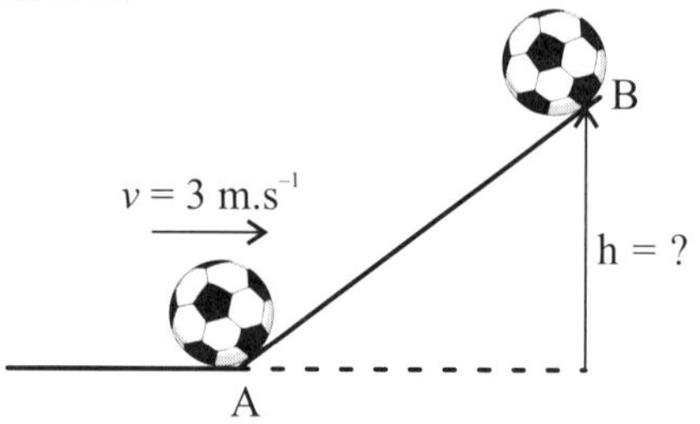

$$E_{M_A} = E_{M_B}$$
$$(E_p + E_k)_A = (E_p + E_k)_B$$
$$mgh + \frac{1}{2}mv^2 = mgh + \frac{1}{2}mv^2 \rightarrow \text{divide both sides by } m$$
$$(9,8)(0) + \frac{1}{2}(3)^2 = (9,8)h + \frac{1}{2}(0)^2$$
$$0 + \frac{1}{2}(3)^2 = (9,8)h + 0$$
$$h = 0,46\,\text{m}$$

Illustrative Example 3:

A soccer ball of mass 450g rolling on a frictionless surface reaches an incline travelling at 3 m.s^{-1} at A. The work done against friction while rolling up the incline is 0,25 J. Determine the maximum height the soccer ball will reach at B.

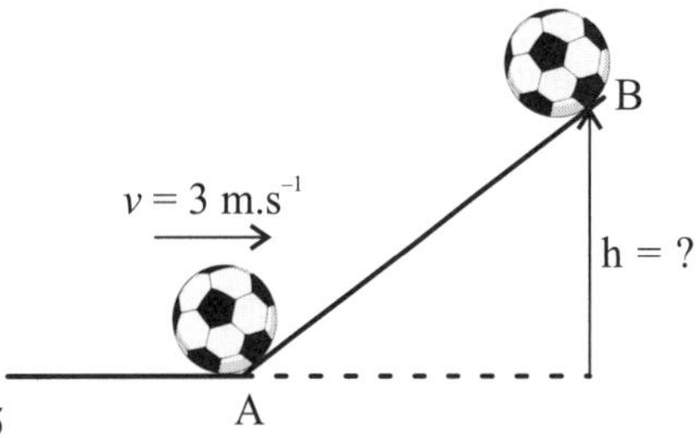

$$E_{M_A} = E_{M_B} + W_f$$

$$(E_p + E_k)_A = (E_p + E_k)_B + W_f$$

$$mgh + \frac{1}{2}mv^2 = mgh + \frac{1}{2}mv^2 + W_f$$

$$(0,45)(9,8)(0) + \frac{1}{2}(0,45)(3)^2 = (0,45)(9,8)h + \frac{1}{2}(0,45)(0)^2 + 0,25$$

$$0 + \frac{1}{2}(0,45)(3)^2 = (0,45)(9,8)h + 0 + 0,25$$

$$h = 0,4\,\text{m}$$

Illustrative Example 4:

A 145g baseball rolls from point A, 15m above the ground with a velocity of 2m.s^{-1}. The balls rolls down a rough incline to B. The ball continues rolling to C reaching C at 8,13m.s^{-1}.
The work done against friction from A to B is 2,605 J and there is no friction from B to C.
Determine the height of C above the ground.

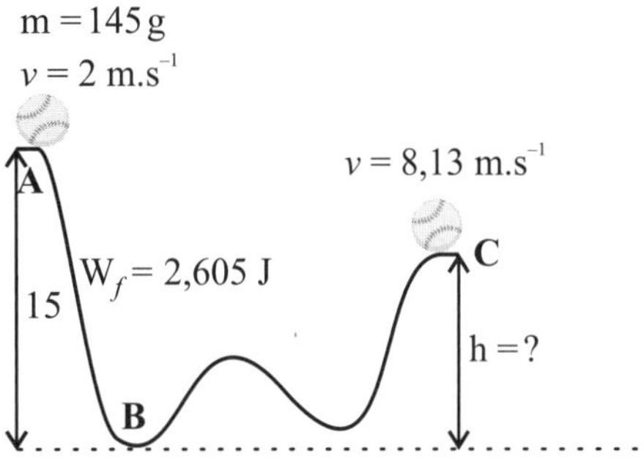

$$E_{M_A} = E_{M_C} + W_f$$

$$(E_p + E_k)_A = (E_p + E_k)_B + W_f$$

$$mgh + \frac{1}{2}mv^2 = mgh + \frac{1}{2}mv^2 + W_f$$

$$(0,145)(9,8)(15) + \frac{1}{2}(0,145)(2)^2 = (0,145)(9,8)h + \frac{1}{2}(0,145)(8,13)^2 + 2,605$$

$$h = 10\,\text{m}$$

Illustrative Example 5:

A pendulum is released from rest. It swings from A through B and C to D. The velocity of the pendulum at C, the lowest point in its swing is 7,67 m.s^{-1}. At point B the pendulum is 2m above C.

a) Determine the length of the pendulum's string.
b) Determine the velocity of the pendulum at B

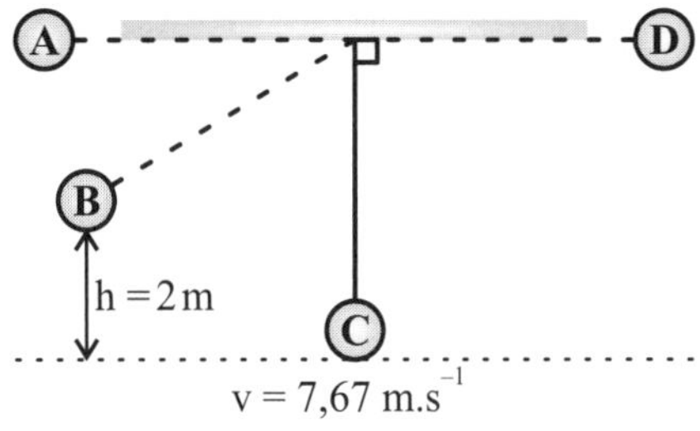

a) $E_{M_A} = E_{M_C}$

$$(E_p + E_k)_A = (E_p + E_k)_C$$

$$mgh + \frac{1}{2}mv^2 = mgh + \frac{1}{2}mv^2 \rightarrow \text{divide both sides by } m$$

$$(9,8)h + 0 = 0 + \frac{1}{2}(7,67)^2$$

$$h = 3\,\text{m}$$

$\therefore$ The string is 3 m long

b) $E_{M_A} = E_{M_B}$

$$(E_p + E_k)_A = (E_p + E_k)_B$$

$$mgh + \frac{1}{2}mv^2 = mgh + \frac{1}{2}mv^2 \rightarrow \text{divide both sides by } m$$

$$(9,8)(3) + 0 = 9,8(2) + \frac{1}{2}v^2$$

$$v = 4,43\,\text{m.s}^{-1}$$

TOC 1 Data Sheet 2 Definitions 3 3 solutions 4 4 solutions 5 5 solutions 6 6 solutions 7 7 solutions 8 8 solutions 9 9 solutions 10 10 solutions

CONSERVATION OF ENERGY AND COLLISIONS

Illustrative Example 1:

An arrow of mass 25g is fired horizontally into an apple of mass 150g. The arrow lodges in the apple and the arrow-apple combination rises to a vertical height of 0,8m above the ground. You may assume that there are no frictional forces present.

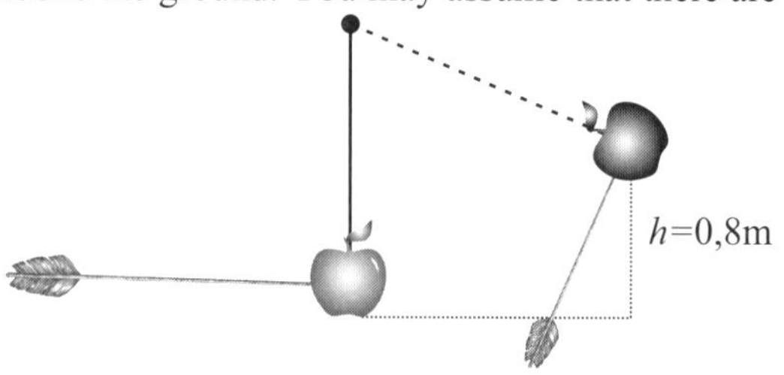

a) Determine the magnitude of the velocity of the apple-arrow combination immediately after the arrow gets imbedded in the apple.

b) Determine the speed at which the arrow strikes the apple.

a) $E_{M_{\text{bottom}}} = E_{M\ \text{top}}$

$E_p + E_k = E_p + E_k$

$$0+\frac{1}{2}\left(150\times10^{-3}+25\times10^{-3}\right)v^2=\left(150\times10^{-3}+25\times10^{-3}\right)(9,8)(0,8)+0$$

$v^2 = 15,68$

$v = 3,96\,\text{m.s}^{-1}$

b) **The initial velocity that the arrow-apple combination starts with, is the final velocity for the collision between the arrow and the apple when using the principle of conservation of linear momentum.**

$p_{bef} = p_{aft}$

$m_1v_{1_i} + m_2v_{2_i} = (m_1+m_2)v_f$

$$\left(25\times10^{-3}\right)v_{1_i}+\left(150\times10^{-3}\right)0=\left(25\times10^{-3}+150\times10^{-3}\right)(3,96)$$

$v_{1_i} = 27,72\,\text{m.s}^{-1}$

Illustrative Example 2:

A box of mass 10kg is suspended on a light inextensible string 2m above the ground. At the bottom of its arc it collides with a stationary box of mass 8kg. The 8kg mass moves off with a velocity of 0,5m.s^{-1}. Determine the maximum height that the 10kg box will reach above the ground after striking the 8 kg box.

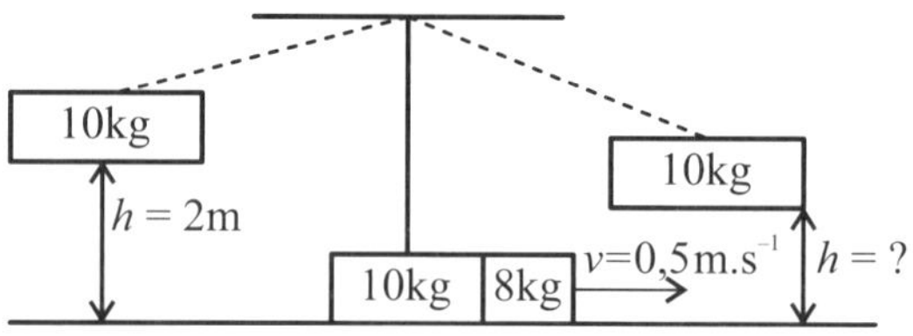

Step 1:
Using conservation of mechanical energy, find the speed of the 10kg block as it strikes the 8kg block.

$E_{M_{\text{top}}} = E_{M_{\text{bottom}}}$

$(E_p + E_k)_{\text{top}} = (E_p + E_k)_{\text{bottom}}$

$mgh + \frac{1}{2}mv^2 = mgh + \frac{1}{2}mv^2$

$(10)(9,8)(2) + 0 = 0 + \frac{1}{2}(10)v^2$

$v = 6,26\,\text{m.s}^{-1}$

Step 2: Use conservation of linear momentum to find the speed of the 10kg block after the collision.

$p_{bef} = p_{aft}$

$m_1v_{1_i} + m_2v_{2_i} = m_1v_{1_f} + m_2v_{2_f}$

$10(6,26) + 8(0) = 10v_{1_f} + (8)(0,5)$

$v_{2_f} = 5,86\,\text{m.s}^{-1}$

Step 3: Use conservation of mechanical energy to determine the height the 10kg box will reach.

$E_{M_{\text{bottom}}} = E_{M_{\text{top}}}$

$(E_p + E_k)_{\text{bottom}} = (E_p + E_k)_{\text{top}}$

$mgh + \frac{1}{2}mv^2 = mgh + \frac{1}{2}mv^2$

$0 + \frac{1}{2}(10)(5,86)^2 = (10)(9,8)h + 0$

$h = 1,75\,\text{m}$

WORK

Work done by a force is the **product of the displacement** and the component of the **force parallel to the displacement**.

> **Work:**
> $$W = F\Delta x$$
> Where:
> $W \rightarrow$ work (J)
> $F \rightarrow$ Force applied (N)
> $\Delta x \rightarrow$ displacement (m)

For **work to be done by a force**, the **force** must be **parallel to the direction of motion**.

> **Work is a scalar, not a vector. It does not have a direction.**

POSITIVE AND NEGATIVE WORK

If a **force acts in the same direction as the motion** of an object, the **work done by the force is positive**.
Only components of the force parallel to the direction of motion do work.

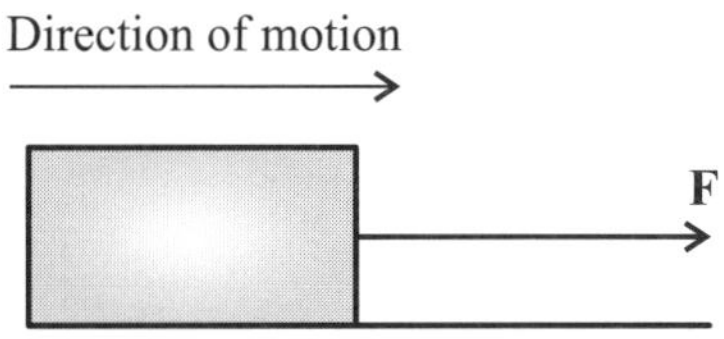

Force is in the same direction as motion
Work done by the force is positive

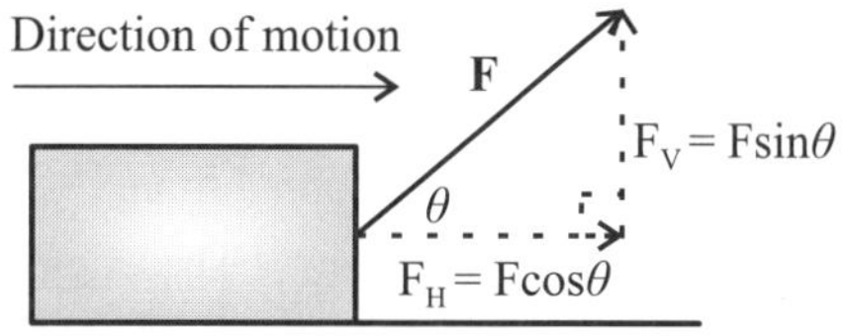

Only the horizontal component (F_H) of the force does work
Horizontal force is in the same direction as motion
Work done by the horizontal force is positive

If a force acts perpendicular to the direction of motion, no work is done by the force.
In the diagram below a man is standing on a moving sidewalk holding a briefcase.
He is applying a **force vertically** upwards, but his **motion is horizontal** to the right.
This means that **no work is done** by the force that the man is applying to the briefcase.

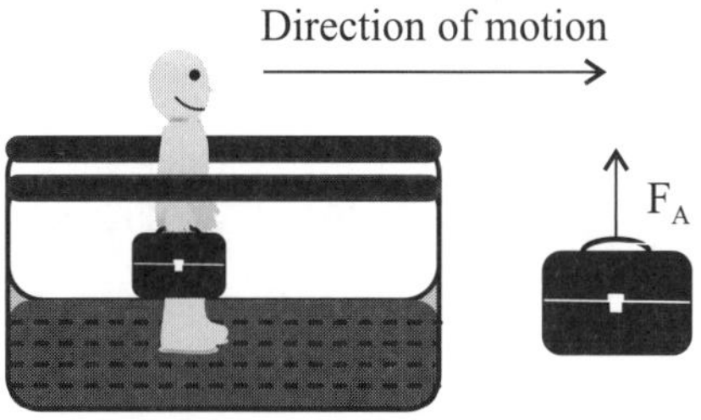

> **If work is positive, it means that energy is being added to a system**

If a **force acts in the opposite direction of the motion** of an object, the **work done by the force is negative**.
If **work is negative**, it **decreases the energy** of the object it acts on.

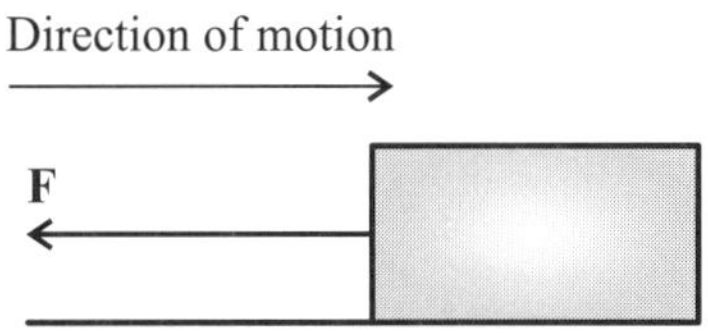

Force is in the opposite direction of motion
Work done by the force is negative

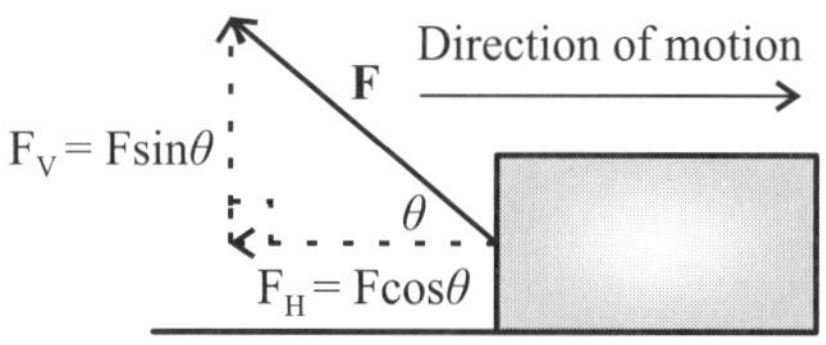

Only the horizontal component (F_H) of the force does work
Horizontal force is in the opposite direction of motion
Work done by the horizontal force is negative

> **If work is negative, it means that energy is being removed from a system**

ALTERNATIVE WORK FORMULA ON THE DATA SHEET

Work:
$$\mathbf{W = F\Delta x\cos\theta}$$

Where:

$W \rightarrow$ work (J)

$F \rightarrow$ Force applied (N)

$\Delta x \rightarrow$ displacement (m)

$\theta \rightarrow$ angle between the force vector and the displacement vector

When using the above formula, **the angle (θ) is the angle between the applied force and the direction of the displacement** of the object. If an object is on an **inclined plane**, the **angle** in the above formula **is not** the **angle of the inclined plane**.

When using this formula, if the force is in the opposite direction to motion the angle is 180°. This accounts for the fact that the work would be negative. You do not make the force or work negative when using this formula.

Illustrative Example:

A box is pulled across a floor by a force of 300N as shown in the diagram below. The force of friction between the box and floor is 120N and the box is pulled a distance of 10m, Determine:

a) The work done by the applied force.

b) The work done by the frictional force.

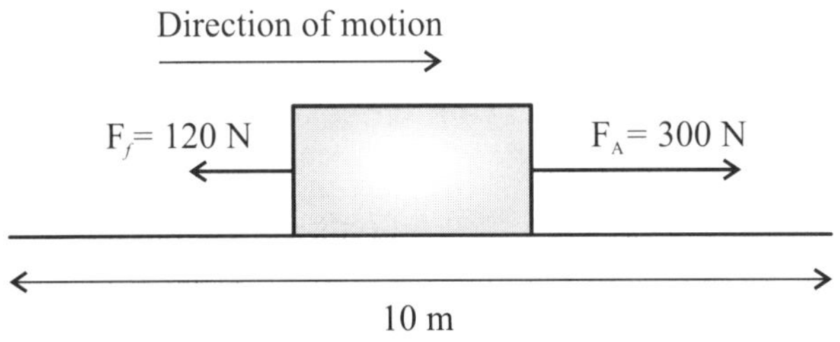

Using the formula: $W = F\Delta x$	Using the formula: $W = F\Delta x\cos\theta$
a) $W_A = F\Delta x$ $= 300(10)$ $= 3000\,J$	a) $W_A = F\Delta x\cos\theta$ $= 300(10)\cos 0^\circ$ $= 3000\,J$
b) $W_f = F\Delta x$ $= (-120)(10)$ $= -1200\,J$ $= 1200\,J$	b) $W_f = F\Delta x\cos\theta$ $= (120)(10)\cos 180^\circ$ $= (120)(10)(-1)$ $= -1200\,J$ $= 1200\,J$

Work is a scalar not a vector.
If work is positive it means energy is added to the system.
If work is negative it means that energy is removed from the system.

NET WORK ON AN OBJECT

When multiple forces act on an object, each force does work on the object to change its energy.
The **net work** done on an object is the **sum of the work done by each force** acting on the object **parallel to the objects motion**.

Illustrative Example 1:

A box is pulled horizontally across a floor. The work done by the applied force is 65J and the work done against friction is 25J. Calculate the net work done on the box.

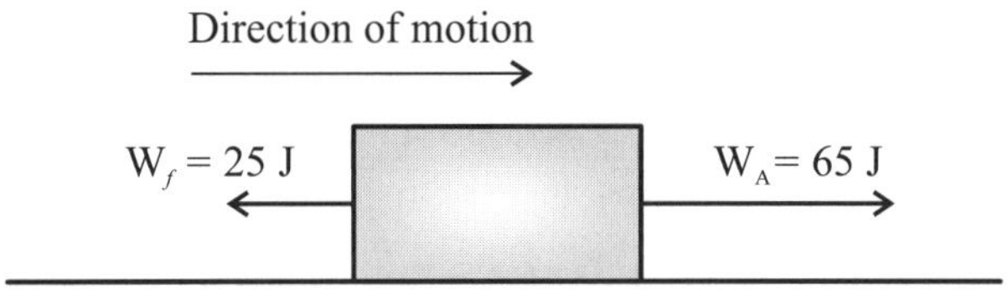

$$\begin{aligned} W_{net} &= W_A - W_f \\ &= 65 - 25 \\ &= 40\,\text{J} \end{aligned}$$

> **The gravitational and normal force do not do work on the box.**
> **This is because they are perpendicular to the direction of the displacement.**
> **For work to be done, there must be a component of force in the same (or opposite) direction of the displacement of the object.**

Illustrative Example 2:

A box is pulled horizontally across a floor by an applied force 100N at an angle of 60° to the horizontal. The force of friction acting on the box is 20N as it moves a distance of 5m across the floor.

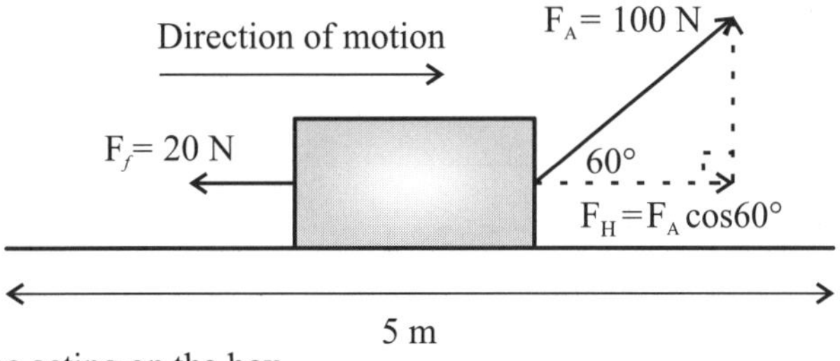

a) Calculate the net force acting on the box.
b) Calculate the net work done on the box.

a) $$\begin{aligned} F_{net} &= F_H - F_f \\ &= 100\cos 60^\circ - 20 \\ &= 30\,\text{N right} \end{aligned}$$ → force is a vector and has to have a direction

> **Only include forces (or components of forces) that act in the same (or opposite) direction of motion. You don't include the gravitational force, normal force or vertical components as these are perpendicular to the direction of motion and do no work on the box.**

b) $$\begin{aligned} W_{net} &= F_{net}\Delta x \\ &= 30(5) \\ &= 150\,\text{J} \end{aligned}$$

NON-CONSERVATIVE FORCES

The work done by a non-conservative force is dependent on the path taken.
In general, all forces you deal with in school, other than gravitational force, are non-conservative forces. These include forces such as applied forces, frictional forces, and forces of tension.

> **Non-conservative forces do not conserve mechanical energy.**

CONSERVATIVE FORCES AND THE WORK DONE BY GRAVITY

If the **total work done in moving** an object **from point A to B is independent of the path taken**, then the force is **conservative**.
The only **conservative force** we will deal with in this section is the **force of gravity**.
If an object **moves vertically** (up or down), **work is done by gravitational force**.

Gravitational force is a **conservative force**. This means that the **work done by gravity** (or against gravity) **to reach a point above the ground is independent of the path taken** to reach the point. In other words, in the diagram below, the work done by gravity on the ball moving from A to B is the same in all 3 scenarios. **The work done by gravity is only dependent on the height that the ball moves through**.

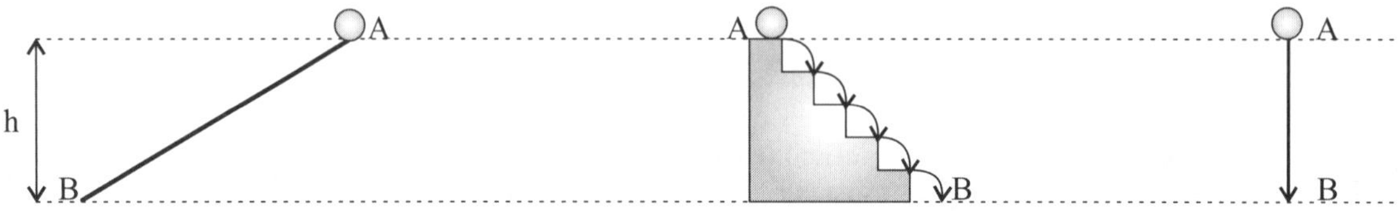

> **Conservative forces conserve mechanical energy.**

<u>Illustrative Example</u>:

A box slides down a frictionless slope Δx metres long from point A to B. Show that the work done by gravity moving the box from point A to B is the same as the work done by gravity in moving the Box from A to C.

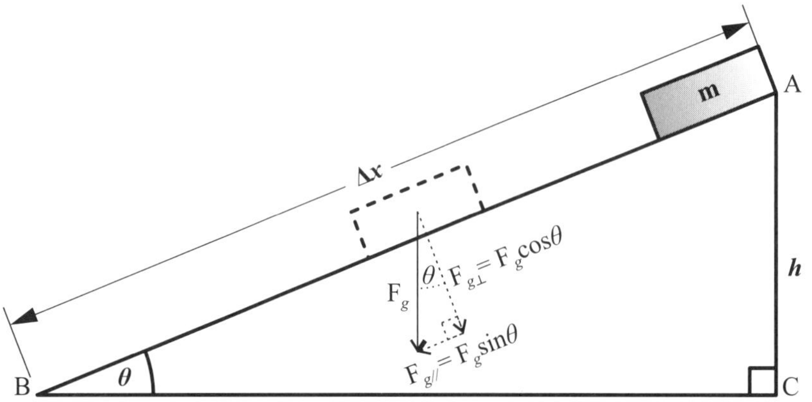

$$\sin\theta = \frac{h}{\Delta x}$$
$$\therefore h = \sin\theta\Delta x$$

Work done by Gravity from A to B	Work done by Gravity from A to C
$W_g = F\Delta x$	$W_g = F\Delta x$
$= F_{g//}\Delta x$	$= F_g h$
$= F_g \sin\theta\Delta x$	$= mgh \rightarrow$ note that this is the change in potential energy
$= mg\sin\theta\Delta x$	$= mg\sin\theta\Delta x \rightarrow h = \sin\theta\Delta x$

> **The work done by gravity can always be expressed as the change in potential energy.**
> $W_g = mgh$

WORK ENERGY THEOREM

The work done by a net force on an object is equal to the change in kinetic energy of the object.

Work Energy Theorem:

$$W_{net} = \Delta E_k$$

$$F_{net}\Delta x = \frac{1}{2}m\left(v_f^2 - v_i^2\right)$$

Illustrative Example 1:

A 10kg box is pulled up a slope by a force of 800N. The slope is inclined at 30° to the horizontal and the force of friction between the box and the slope is 25N. If the box started from rest determine the magnitude of the velocity of the box at the top of the slope.

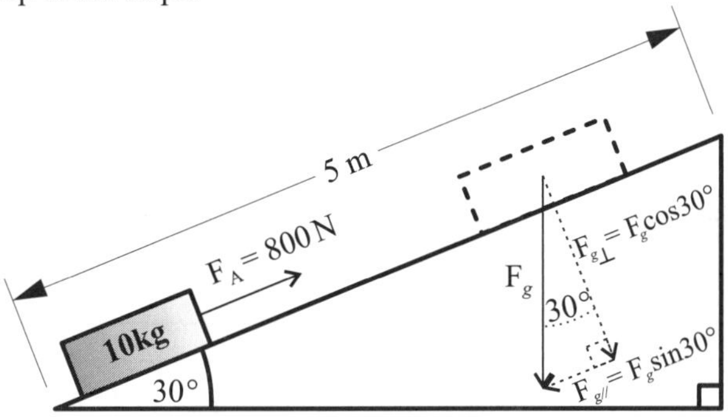

$$W_{net} = \Delta E_k$$

$$W_A - W_f - W_g = \frac{1}{2}m\left(v_f^2 - v_i^2\right)$$

$$F_A\Delta x - F_f\Delta x - mg\sin\theta\,\Delta x = \frac{1}{2}m\left(v_f^2 - v_i^2\right)$$

$$800(5) - 25(5) - 10(9,8)\sin 30^\circ(5) = \frac{1}{2}(10)\left(v_f^2 - 0\right)$$

$$v_f^2 = 726$$

$$v_f = 26,94\,\text{m.s}^{-1}$$

Illustrative Example 2:

A 10kg box is travelling on a frictionless surface at 2,5m.s^{-1}. The box encounters a rough slope and rises to a height *h* before coming to rest. Given that the work done against friction on the slope is 1,25 J, calculate the vertical height that the box reaches on the slope.

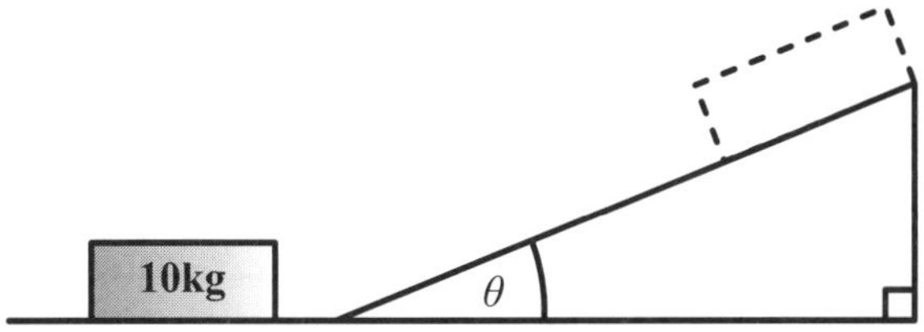

$$W_{net} = \Delta E_k$$

$$-W_f - W_g = \frac{1}{2}m\left(v_f^2 - v_i^2\right)$$

$$-W_f - mgh = \frac{1}{2}m\left(v_f^2 - v_i^2\right) \rightarrow W_g \text{ can be expressed as } mgh$$

$$-1,25 - 10(9,8)h = \frac{1}{2}(10)\left(0 - 2,5^2\right)$$

$$h = 0,31\text{m}$$

POWER

Power is the rate at which work is done or the rate at which energy is transferred.

Power:

$$\mathbf{P = \frac{W}{\Delta t}}$$

Where:

$P \rightarrow \text{Power}\ (W)$

$W \rightarrow \text{work}\ (J)$

$\Delta t \rightarrow \text{time}\ (s)$

If an object is travelling at **constant velocity** the **average power** required to keep it at a constant velocity is:

Average Power at a Constant Velocity:

$$\mathbf{P = F\,v}$$

Where:

$P \rightarrow \text{power}\ (W)$

$F \rightarrow \text{force}\ (N)$

$v \rightarrow \text{velocity}\ (m.s^{-1})$

Power is a scalar quantity.

PERCENTAGE EFFICIENCY

When a motor does work, all the input power is not always transferred to the output. To determine how efficient a motor is the formula below is used.

$$\mathbf{\%\,Efficiency = \frac{Power\ Output}{Power\ Input} \times 100\%}$$

Illustrative Example 1:

It takes a motor 2 minutes to lift a carton of mass 2000kg through a height of 10 metres from rest. At a height of 10 metres the carton is travelling at 1,5 $m.s^{-1}$. Determine:

a) The work done by the motor in lifting the carton 10 metres.
b) The output power of the motor.
c) The percentage efficiency of the motor if it is rated 220V and 10A.

a)
$$W_{net} = \Delta E_k$$
$$W_M - W_g = \frac{1}{2}m\left(v_f^{\,2} - v_i^{\,2}\right)$$
$$W_M - mgh = \frac{1}{2}m\left(v_f^{\,2} - v_i^{\,2}\right) \rightarrow W_g \text{ can be expressed as } mgh$$
$$W_M - 2000(9,8)(10) = \frac{1}{2}(2000)\left(1,5^2 - 0^2\right)$$
$$W_M = 198250\text{J}$$

b)
$$\text{Power output} = \frac{W}{t} = \frac{198250}{2 \times 60} = 1652,08\text{ W}$$

c)
$$\%\,\text{Efficiency} = \frac{\text{Power Output}}{\text{Power Input}} \times 100\%$$
$$= \frac{1652,08}{220 \times 10} \times 100\% \rightarrow \text{Power input} = VI = 220(10)$$
$$= 75,09\%$$

Illustrative Example 2:

A motorcycle travels up a rough inclined slope at a constant velocity of 72 $km.h^{-1}$. At this speed, the output power of the engine is 125 kW.

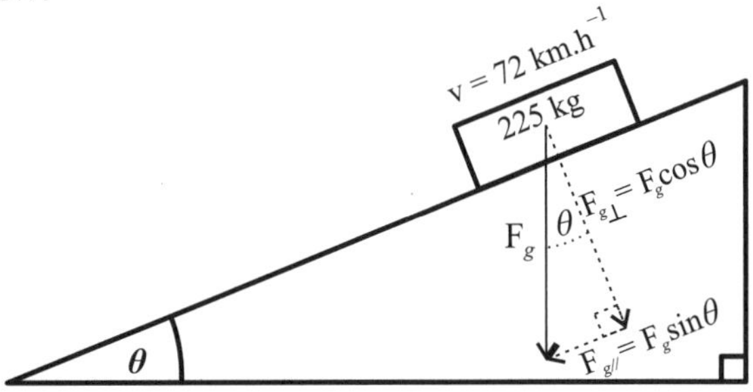

a) Determine the motorcycle's velocity in metres per second ($m.s^{-1}$).
b) Determine the force applied by the motor.
c) The motorcycle has a mass of 225 kg and the length of the slope is 20m. If the force of friction on the hill is 5 150 N, determine the angle of the incline.

a) $v = 72 \div 3,6$

$= 20\,m.s^{-1}$

b) $P = F v$

$125 \times 10^3 = F(20)$

$F = 6250\,N$

c) As the car is travelling at a constant velocity the net force acting on the car is zero.

$F_{net} = 0$

$F_A - F_{g//} - F_f = 0$

$F_A - mg\sin\theta - F_f = 0$

$6250 - 225(9,8)\sin\theta - 5150 = 0$

$\sin\theta = 0,50$

$\theta = 30^\circ$

Illustrative Example 3:

A motor rated as 750W is 80% efficient. It takes 30 seconds to lift an object of mass *m* through a height of 3 meters. The object starts at rest and is travelling at a velocity of 0,2$m.s^{-1}$ at the instant it reaches 3m off the ground. Determine the mass of the object.

$$\%\,\text{Efficiency} = \frac{\text{Power Output}}{\text{Power Input}} \times 100\%$$

$$80 = \frac{\text{Power Output}}{750} \times 100$$

$$\text{Power Output} = 600\,W$$

$$W_m = Pt$$

$$= 600(30)$$

$$= 18000\,J$$

$$W_{net} = \Delta E_k$$

$$W_m - W_g = \frac{1}{2}m\left(v_f^2 - v_i^2\right)$$

$$W_m - mgh = \frac{1}{2}m\left(v_f^2 - v_i^2\right) \rightarrow W_g \text{ can be expressed as } mgh$$

$$18000 - m(9,8)(3) = \frac{1}{2}m\left(0,2^2 - 0^2\right)$$

$$18000 = 29,42m$$

$$m = 611,83\,kg$$

TOC | 1 Data Sheet | 2 Definitions | 3 | 3 solutions | 4 | 4 solutions | 5 | 5 solutions | 6 | 6 solutions | 7 | 7 solutions | 8 | 8 solutions | 9 | 9 solutions | 10 | 10 solutions

TOC | 1 Data Sheet | 2 Definitions | 3 | 3 solutions | 4 | 4 solutions | 5 | 5 solutions | 6 | 6 solutions | 7 | 7 solutions | 8 | 8 solutions | 9 | 9 solutions | 10 | 10 solutions

Question 1 (Solutions on page 227)

1.1 Which of the following quantities would be equal to the work done in moving an object along a frictionless surface?

A change in momentum
B change in velocity
C change in kinetic energy
D change in potential energy (2)

1.2 A ball, with mass 160g, is bowled towards a batsman at 42 m.s^{-1}. The batsman hits the ball back at 45 m.s^{-1}. The magnitude of the ball's impulse will be…

A 480 kg.m.s^{-1}
B 0,48 kg.m.s^{-1}
C 13,92 kg.m.s^{-1}
D 13 920 kg.m.s^{-1} (2)

1.3 Two trolleys approach each other from opposite directions with speed *v*. The mass of trolley A is double the mass of trolley B.

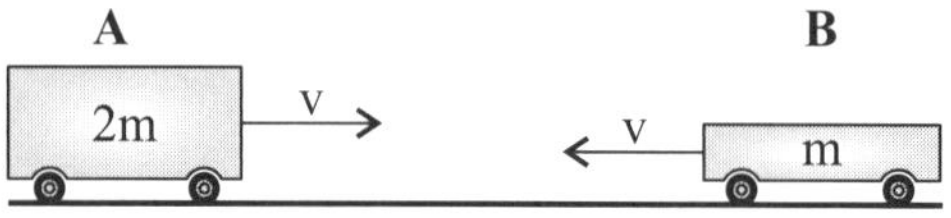

The trolleys collide head on with each other. After the collision, trolley A moves off to the left with speed $\frac{v}{2}$ and trolley B moves off to the right.

The magnitudes of the change in momentum of A and the resultant force A experiences is Δp and F respectively.
Which one of the following is correct?

	Magnitude of Impulse on B	Magnitude of rate of change of momentum experienced by B	Speed of B after the collision
A	$\frac{\Delta p}{2}$	F	$2v$
B	Δp	$\frac{F}{2}$	$\frac{v}{2}$
C	Δp	F	$2v$
D	$2\Delta p$	$2F$	v

(2)

1.4 Two objects of different masses undergo an elastic collision in the absence of any external force.
Which option gives the effect on the total kinetic energy of the masses and the magnitudes of the forces exerted on the masses during the collision?

	Total Kinetic Energy	Magnitude of Forces
A	constant	equal on both objects
B	constant	greater on the smaller object
C	decreases	equal on both objects
D	decreases	greater on the smaller object

(2)

1.5 Choose the correct row.

	Velocity	Momentum	Mass
A	vector	vector	vector
B	vector	vector	scalar
C	vector	scalar	vector
D	scalar	vector	scalar

(2)

1.6 A worker pushes a trolley loaded with a box up a ramp of length 1,8 m and on to a loading dock. The loading dock is 0,7 m above the ground. The trolley box combination weighs 1200N.

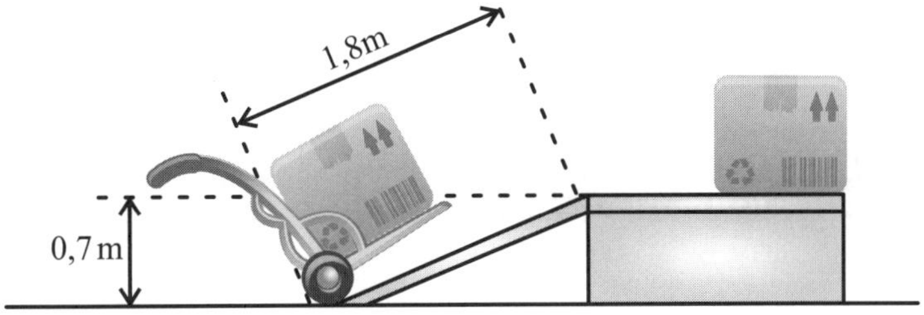

What is the work done against gravity on the trolley box combination?

A 2 160 J
B 1 200 J
C 8 232 J
D 840 J

(2)

1.7 A child shoots a pellet gun at an apple. His first shot penetrates and becomes embedded in the apple. His second shot misses the apple and hits the steel base the apple is sitting on. The second bullet rebounds back at 180°.

Choose the correct statement regarding the impulse of the second bullet.

The impulse of the second bullet…

A is smaller than the impulse of the first bullet
B is greater than the impulse of the first bullet
C and the first bullet is equal to zero
D is the same as the impulse of the first bullet

(2)

1.8 A pendulum swings from position A to D passing through B and C. The speed of the ball at C is V_C. What is the relationship between the speed of the ball at positions B and C?

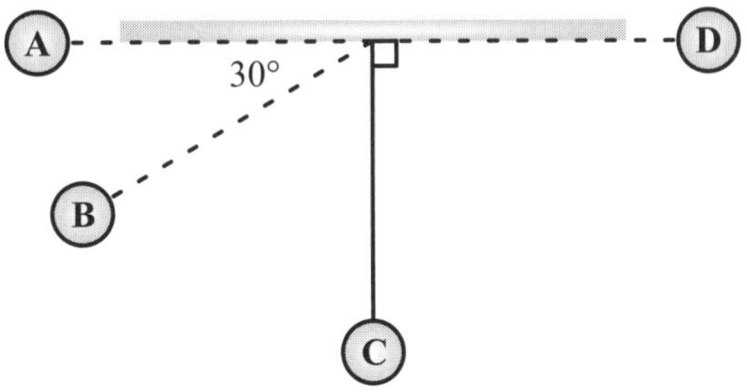

A $V_B = V_C$

B $V_B = 2V_C$

C $V_B = \frac{V_C}{2}$

D $V_B = \frac{V_C}{\sqrt{2}}$

(2)

TOC 1 Data Sheet 2 Definitions 3 3 solutions 4 4 solutions 5 5 solutions 6 6 solutions 7 7 solutions 8 8 solutions 9 9 solutions 10 10 solutions

1.9 Which one of the following statements is correct? The rate of change of momentum is equivalent to…

A net force
B impulse
C net work
D change in momentum (2)

1.10 Two trolleys, X and Y, of masses m and 4m respectively, move to the right across a horizontal frictionless surface with speed V and total energy E. They are joined by means of a compressed spring. When the spring is released, the trolleys move apart.

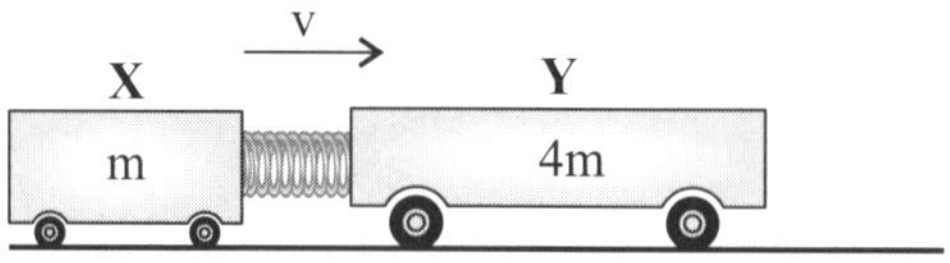

The magnitude of the change in momentum of trolley X is p.

	Magnitude of change in momentum of Y	Total energy after the spring is released
A	$4p$	E
B	$2p$	$0{,}5E$
C	p	E
D	$0{,}5p$	$4E$

(2)

1.11 Which one of the following is also a unit of momentum?

A N.s
B N.m
C J.s
D $J.s^{-1}$ (2)

1.12 A ball of mass m is thrown vertically upwards and reaches a height h above the ground. At the same time, another ball of mass $2m$ is thrown vertically upwards and reaches a height h. Ignoring the effects of friction which statement below is true?

A the ball of mass $2m$ will reach a height of h first
B both balls have the same kinetic energy at the instant they are thrown
C both balls have the same momentum at the instant they are thrown
D both balls both have the same initial velocity (2)

1.13 A ball of mass m hits a wall at a speed of v and rebounds in a straight line in the opposite direction with the same speed. What is the magnitude of the change in momentum of the ball?

A 0
B $-2mv$
C $2mv$
D mv (2)

1.14 The kinetic energy of object A is E. An object B has double the mass and moves with half the velocity of A. What would the kinetic energy be of object B?

A $2E$
B $4E$
C E
D $0{,}5E$ (2)

1.15 Consider the following diagram with a cart passing point A at a constant velocity. It rolls down the frictionless slope, past B and then up to C, D and E.

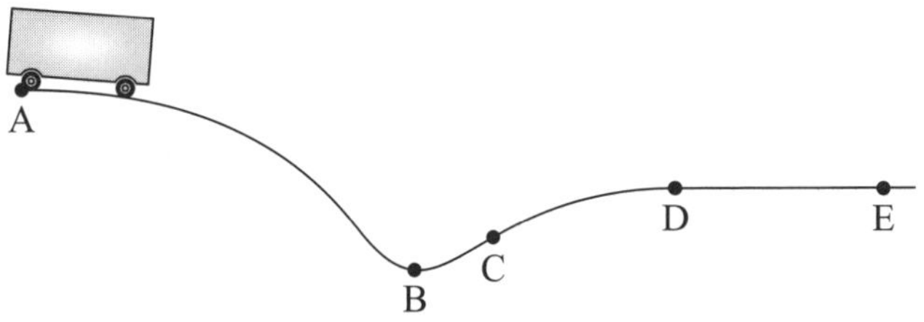

	Kinetic energy at point C is less than the kinetic energy at...	Potential energy at point C is greater than the potential energy at...
A	A and B	D and E
B	B	B
C	A	A and B
D	A and B	B

(2)

1.16 Using the diagram in question 1.15 choose the graph which best represents the mechanical energy of the cart as it moves from position A to E.

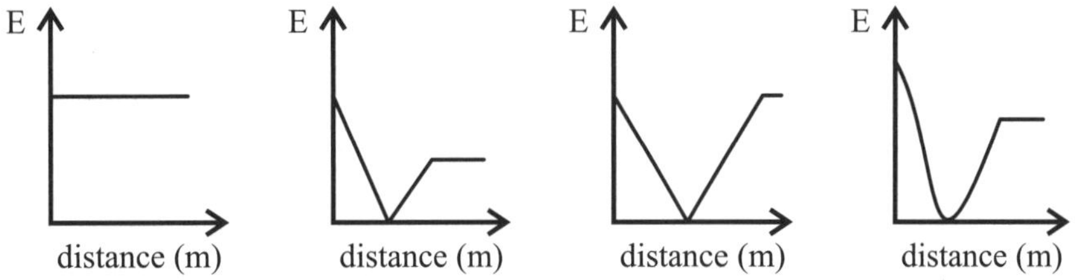

A B C D

(2)

1.17 The graph shows the resultant force variation which acts on an object over a time interval of 6 seconds.

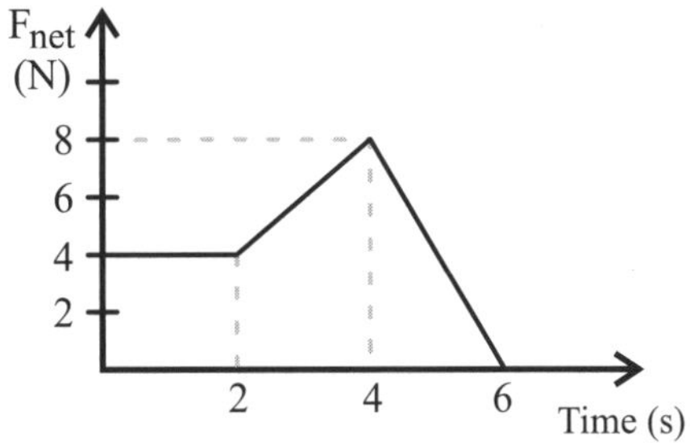

The change in momentum of the object over the interval is...

A 48 kg.m.s^{-1}

B 24 kg.m.s^{-1}

C 28 kg.m.s^{-1}

D 36 kg.m.s^{-1}

(2)

TOC
1 Data Sheet
2 Definitions
3
3 solutions
4
4 solutions
5
5 solutions
6
6 solutions
7
7 solutions
8
8 solutions
9
9 solutions
10
10 solutions

1.18 Two trolleys of mass M and m are joined by a compressed spring. When the spring is released the stationary trolleys separate. Mass M attains velocity V and mass m attains velocity v. If $M > m$.

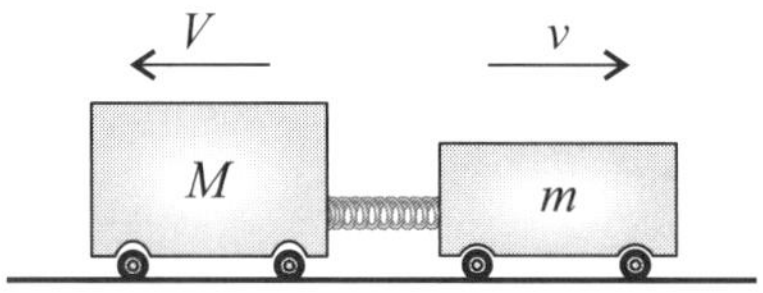

Which of the relationships below is true for the trolleys after they have separated?

A $V = v$

B $MV + mv = 0$

C $MV = mv$

D $\frac{1}{2}MV^2 = \frac{1}{2}mv^2$ (2)

1.19 Two people, of unequal mass, run towards each other and collide head on. Ignoring all forces of friction, which of the following statements is true?

A During the collision, the magnitude of the force that they exert on each other will be zero.

B During the collision, the person with the greater mass will exert the greater force.

C During the collision, the person with the smaller mass will exert the greater force.

D During the collision, the magnitude of the forces they exert on one another will be equal. (2)

1.20 When the sluice gates of a large dam open, water flows over the edge at a rate of $5{,}5 \times 10^8$ kg per minute. If the height of the dam is 100m the power delivered by the water falling is…

A $5{,}39 \times 10^{11}$ W

B $8{,}99 \times 10^9$ W

C $1{,}5 \times 10^8$ W

D $8{,}98 \times 10^9$ W (2)

1.21 A block of mass 50 kg moves at a constant velocity on a horizontal frictionless surface. It encounters a surface with a coefficient of kinetic friction of 0,5 and travels 20 m before coming to rest. What is the work done by the frictional force?

A 4 900 J

B 3 200 J

C 1 800 J

D 980 J (2)

1.22 An object of mass m travelling at speed v hits a wall in a direction perpendicular to the wall. The collision is elastic.

What is the magnitude of the change in momentum and the kinetic energy of the object?

	Magnitude of change in momentum	**Change in kinetic energy**
A	0	$2mv^2$
B	$2mv$	0
C	0	mv^2
D	mv	0

(2)

1.23 Two objects of different masses are travelling toward each other at different speeds and collide head on. Which of the statements below best describes the magnitudes of the forces experienced by the objects during the collision?

A The heavier object experiences a larger force.
B The lighter object experiences a larger force.
C It depends on the ratios of the masses and velocities of the objects.
D They experience equal forces. (2)

1.24 A stuntman jumps off a 5-storey building onto a large airbag and escapes injury. How does the airbag help the stuntman to avoid injury?

A It reduces the change in momentum of the stuntman.

B It increases the change in momentum of the stuntman.

C It decreases the net force on the stuntman by decreasing the time it takes to bring the stuntman to rest.

D It decreases the net force on the stuntman by increasing the time it takes to bring the stuntman to rest. (2)

1.25 In an inelastic collision and the absence of any external forces…

i Linear momentum is conserved
ii Kinetic energy is conserved
iii Total linear momentum and total energy is conserved

Which of the following are true:

A i and iii C iii only

B i and ii D i only (2)

1.26 A small car engine develops 90 000 W of power to keep the car at a constant velocity of 30 $m.s^{-1}$. What is the magnitude of the frictional force acting on the car?

A 3 000 N C 300 000 N

B 30 000 N D 300 N (2)

1.27 A ball is thrown vertically upwards. Neglecting air resistance, which one of the following statements is incorrect?

A The potential energy of the ball is largest at the maximum height.

B By the principle of conservation of linear momentum, the momentum of the ball is constant throughout its motion.

C The kinetic energy of the ball decreases as the ball moves up.

D By the principle of conservation of mechanical energy, the total mechanical energy of the ball is constant throughout its motion. (2)

1.28 Use the information in the table below relating to object A and B.

	Object A	**Object B**
Velocity	v	$2v$
Mass	M	$2M$
Kinetic energy	E	?

A $4E$ C $2E$

B E D $8E$

1.29 Tom and Lerato are ice skating towards each other on a frictionless surface. Tom has a mass of 50kg and is moving to the left at a velocity of $2m.s^{-1}$. Lerato has a mass of 30kg and is moving to the right at a velocity of $3m.s^{-1}$.

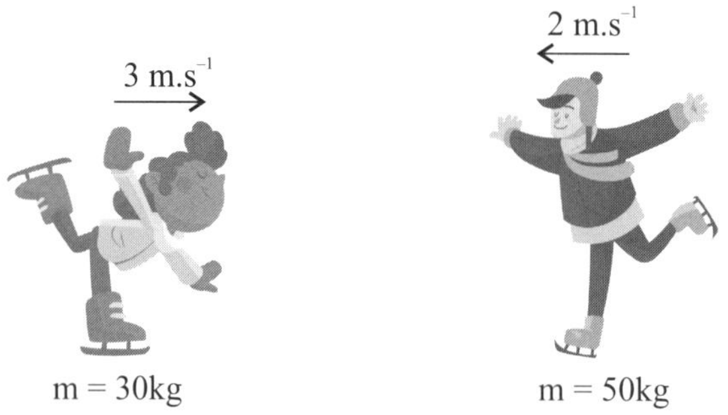

They collide and after the collision Lerato moves to the left at $1m.s^{-1}$. Who experienced the greater magnitude of acceleration during the collision?

A Lerato, as her mass is smaller than Jerry's.

B By Newton's III law the magnitude of the forces acting on both people are the same and therefore the magnitude of the acceleration is the same for both people.

C Jerry, as his mass is larger than Lerato's.

D It cannot be calculated without knowing if the collision was elastic or inelastic. (2)

1.30 A ball rolls down a frictionless slope and attains a velocity of v at the bottom of the slope. In order to double the speed of the ball at the bottom of the slope you would…

A Increase the height of the slope by a factor of 2.

B Increase the height of the slope by a factor of 4.

C Increase the steepness of the slope so that it's gradient increased by a factor of 2.

D Increase the height of the slope by a factor of $\sqrt{2}$. (2)

1.31 A projectile is launched vertically upwards and reaches a maximum height of 20 metres above the ground. A second projectile, with half the mass of the first, is launched vertically upwards with double the velocity. Ignoring friction, the second projectile will reach a height of…

A 20 metres

C 40 metres

B 80 metres

D 10 meters (2)

1.32 Two identical trolleys of mass m move towards each other at speed v and collide head on in an isolated system.

Which of the following statements are true?

A The collision is elastic as it is an isolated system.

B The trolleys rebound off each other and move in opposite directions with speed v.

C The trolleys stick together after impact.

D By the principle of conservation of linear momentum, the total momentum before and after the collision is $2mv$. (2)

1.33 A fully loaded fighter jet has a mass $10m$ and is travelling at an unknown velocity. The fighter jet fires a missile of mass $2m$ with velocity $2v$. After the missile is fired the fighter jet is moving at velocity v in the same direction as the missile.

The magnitude of the jets momentum before the missile fired is...

A $4mv$ C $10mv$

B $14mv$ D $12mv$ (2)

1.34 A stationary gun fires a bullet of mass m. The bullet is emitted with momentum p and kinetic energy E. The mass of the recoiling gun is 60 times greater than the mass of the bullet.

What are the magnitudes of the momentum and kinetic energy of the recoiling gun?

	Momentum	Kinetic Energy
A	p	$\frac{E}{3\,600}$
B	p	$\frac{E}{60}$
C	$\frac{p}{60}$	E
D	$\frac{p}{60}$	$\frac{E}{60}$

1.35 Cart A, of mass m, is travelling at velocity $2v$ East and is behind cart B, of mass $5m$, travelling at velocity v East. The carts collide and stick together on impact. What is the velocity of the carts after the collision?

A $7v$ East

B $\frac{7}{6}v$ West

C $7v$ West

D $\frac{7}{6}v$ East

[72]

TOC | 1 Data Sheet | 2 Definitions | 3 | 3 solutions | 4 | 4 solutions | 5 | 5 solutions | 6 | 6 solutions | 7 | 7 solutions | 8 | 8 solutions | 9 | 9 solutions | 10 | 10 solutions

Question 2 (Solutions on page 227)

In a crash test, it is discovered that a car can withstand a frontal force of 350 kN before the integrity of the driver cabin is compromised. A car loaded with crash test dummies has a mass of 2 500 kg. The car is crashed into a solid steel barrier at a speed of 80 km.h^{-1}, coming to rest in 0,18 seconds. Will the driver cabin be compromised in the collision?

[5]

Question 3 (Solutions on page 227 and 228)

A stationary trolley of mass 18 kg, is left unattended at the top of a slope of vertical height h. The trolley rolls 12 m down the slope to reach a speed of 2 m.s^{-1} at the bottom of the slope. The total frictional force acting on the trolley as it rolls down the slope is 33 N.

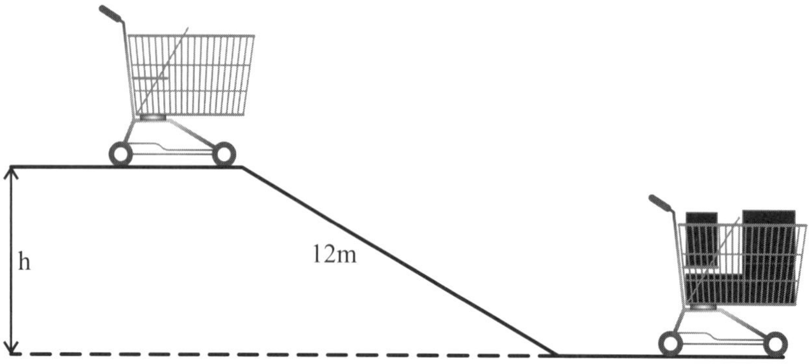

3.1 Calculate the work done by the frictional force as the trolley rolls down the slope. (3)

3.2 Hence, determine the vertical height, h, of the slope. (5)

As the trolley reaches the bottom of the slope it collides with an identical stationary trolley filled with boxes with a total mass of *m*. Immediately after the collision the trolley filled with boxes moves with a velocity of 3 m.s^{-1} to the right and the empty trolley moved to the left with a velocity of 1,7 m.s^{-1}.

3.3 Calculate the distance taken for the trolley filled with boxes to come to rest after the collision if the magnitude of its acceleration is 0,8 m.s^{-2}. (3)

3.4 State the law of conservation of linear momentum. (2)

3.5 Calculate the mass of the boxes in the trolley. (5)

3.6 Define impulse (2)

3.7 The collision between the trolleys lasted 0,2 s. Calculate the magnitude of the net force exerted by the loaded trolley on the empty trolley. (3)

[23]

Question 4 (Solutions on page 228)

A bullet with a mass of 40 g is shot horizontally at 720 m.s^{-1} into a stationary wooden block with a mass of 0,8 kg. The bullet becomes embedded in the block causing it to slide 0,3 m along a rough horizontal surface before coming to rest.

4.1 State the Law of conservation of linear momentum. (2)

4.2 Calculate the speed of the bullet and block immediately after the collision. (4)

4.3 Showing all relevant calculations, State whether the collision was elastic or inelastic. (4)

4.4 State the work energy theorem. (2)

4.5 Use the work-energy theorem to calculate the magnitude of the frictional force which brings the bullet and block combination to rest. (5)

[17]

Question 5 (Solutions on page 229)

A stationary rifle with a mass of 1,5 kg fires a 6 g bullet horizontally to the right into a stationary block of wood which has a mass of 150 g. The bullet embeds in the block of wood causing it to slide along the surface it is resting on. The block experiences a frictional force of 5 N while sliding. The block and bullet come to rest after covering a distance of 11,5 m.

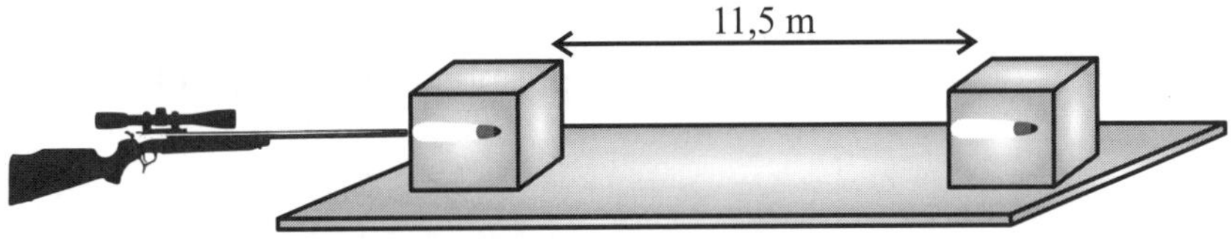

5.1 State the work energy theorem. (2)

5.2 Show that the initial velocity of the bullet block system was 27,15 ms^{-1}. (4)

5.3 State the law of conservation of linear momentum. (2)

5.4 Determine the recoil velocity of the gun when it is fired. (7)

[15]

Question 6 (Solutions on page 229 and 230)

A trolley loaded with sandbags moves from rest down a frictionless inclined plane. When it reaches the bottom of the incline at point B, it continues toward C at a constant speed of 2 m.s^{-1} to the left. The sandbags and trolley have a combined mass of 4 kg. A bullet of mass 0,15 kg is fired as shown and gets embedded in the sandbag. Immediately after the collision the trolley-sandbags-bullet combination travels backwards towards B, at 5,3 m.s^{-1}.

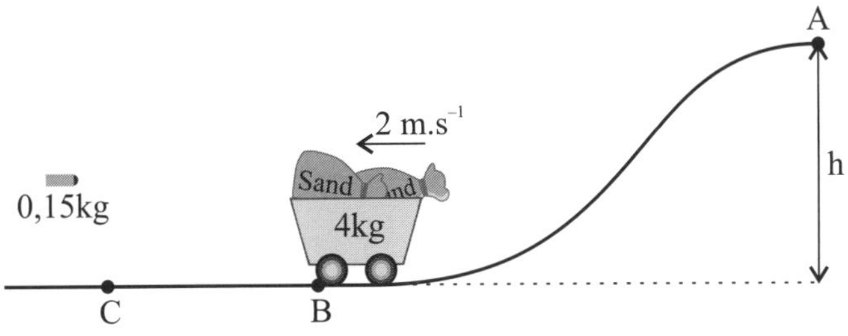

6.1 State the law of conservation of linear momentum. (2)

6.2 Determine the velocity of the bullet just before it hits the sandbags. (5)

6.3 Determine the vertical height of the incline, h, if the trolley-sandbags-bullet combination reaches the top of the incline at point A with a velocity of 2,5 m.s^{-1}. You may ignore all frictional forces. (7)

[14]

Question 7 (Solutions on page 230)

A ski resort has a 50 metre training slope for children which is inclined at an angle of 20° to the horizontal. A motor at the top is used to pull skiers up the slope.

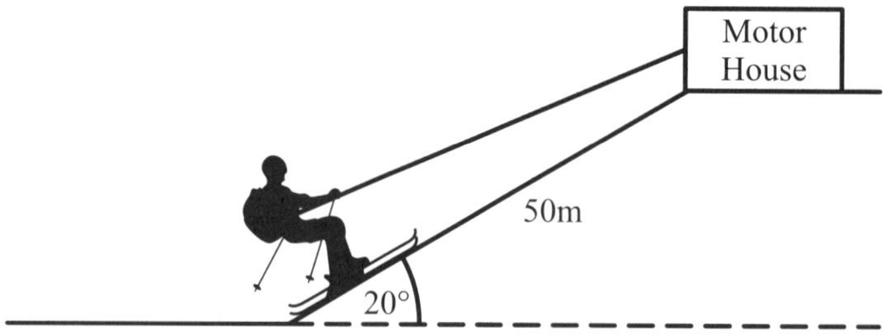

A child with a mas of 25 kg is pulled up the slope at constant velocity. The child experiences a frictional force of 15 N while being pulled up the slope.

7.1 Calculate the work done by the motor to overcome friction. (3)

7.2 What is the increase in the child's potential energy when moving from the bottom to the top of the slope? (5)

7.3 Determine the power output of the motor if it takes 22 seconds to pull the skier up the slope. (4)

7.4 If the motor is 75% efficient what is the input power to the motor. (2)

[14]

Question 8 (Solutions on page 230)

Jolene has a mass of 55kg and is running at 1 $m.s^{-1}$ East towards a stationary skateboard which has a mass of 4,5kg. Thabo has a mass of 75kg and is running at 1,5 $m.s^{-1}$ West towards the same skateboard. Both people jump onto the skateboard and land at the same time. Determine the velocity of the skateboard after Jolene and Thabo have jumped on.

[5]

Question 9 (Solutions on page 231)

Block A with a mass of 3 kg is released from height h and collides with block B with a mass of 6kg at the bottom of its swing. Immediately after the collision block A moves at 0,5 $m.s^{-1}$ to the left and block B moves at 2,25 $m.s^{-1}$ to the right.

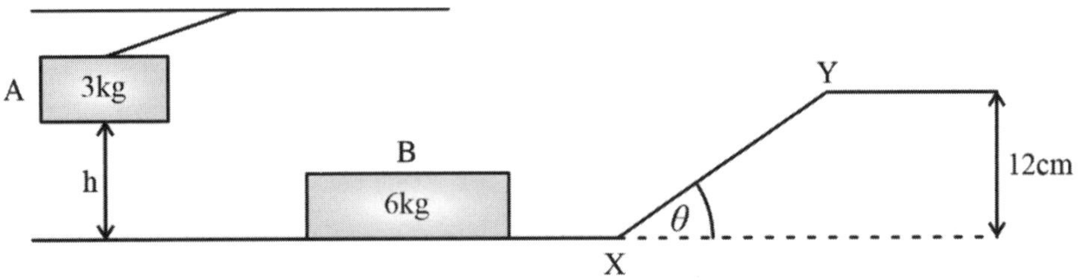

9.1 State the law of conservation of linear momentum. (2)

9.2 Calculate the speed of block A before the collision at the bottom of its swing. (4)

9.3 Determine the height, h, that block A was released from. (4)

9.4 If the collision lasts for 0,01s, calculate the magnitude of the force exerted by the 3 kg block on the 6 kg block during the collision. (3)

After the collision, block B moves up a rough incline XY. A constant frictional force of 20,5 N acts on the block and causes it to come to rest at point Y.

9.5 Define the work energy theorem. (2)

9.6 Determine the angle of the incline. (8)

[23]

Question 10 (Solutions on page 231 and 232)

A bullet of mass 2,5 g is travelling east at velocity of 450 $m.s^{-1}$, collides with a wooden block of mass 1,5 kg, initially at rest. The bullet passes through the block and emerges with a velocity of 105 $m.s^{-1}$. The block slides 20 cm along the surface from its initial position before coming to rest again.

10.1 State the law of conservation of linear momentum. (2)

10.2 Determine the velocity of the block immediately after the bullet has exited the block. Assume that the block's mass remains constant. Give your answer correct to 3 decimal places. (5)

10.3 Was the collision elastic or inelastic? (5)

10.4 Determine the magnitude of the average frictional force acting on the block as its slides across the horizontal surface. (5)

[12]

Question 11 (Solutions on page 232)

A monkey named Bob swings on a vine to pick up his friend Sam who is sitting on the floor eating bananas. After colliding, Bob and Sam swing to a maximum height of 5 metres and land on a ledge. Bob has a mass of 25kg and Sam has a mass of 30kg.
Ignore all frictional forces.

11.1 Determine the velocity that Bob and Sam leave the ground with after colliding. (5)

11.2 Determine the height that Bob started his swing from. (8)

11.3 Was the collision between Bob and Sam elastic or inelastic? Use calculations to verify your answer. (4)

[17]

Question 12 (Solutions on page 233)

At a golf tournament, Judd positions himself to take a shot. Using his golf club, he applies a force of 3 800 N on the golf ball of mass 46 grams and it accelerates away from him. A constant frictional force of 0,4 N acts on the ball while it is in contact with the club.

12.1 If the ball is in contact with the club for 0,8 milliseconds, calculate the speed with which the ball leaves the golf club. (5)

Unfortunately, Judd's ball hits a stationary tree branch which has a mass of 600g. At the instant the ball strikes the branch it is travelling at 22 $m.s^{-1}$, causing the branch to snap. The ball rebounds off the branch at 6 $m.s^{-1}$.

12.2 State the Law of Conservation of Momentum. (2)

12.3 Calculate the magnitude of the velocity of the branch after the impact. (5)

12.4 Determine whether the collision between the ball and the branch is an elastic or inelastic collision. (5)

[17]

Question 13 (Solutions on page 233 and 234)

Thabo, standing on the ground, throws a ball, of mass 500 g, vertically upwards to Celeste, who is on a balcony directly above him 5m from the ground. The ball leaves Thabo's hand at a speed of 10 m·s^{-1} from point Q, which is at a height of 1,5m above the ground. At a height of 3,5 m above the ground, the ball passes through the branches of a tree, but continues vertically upwards. Ignore the effects of air resistance.

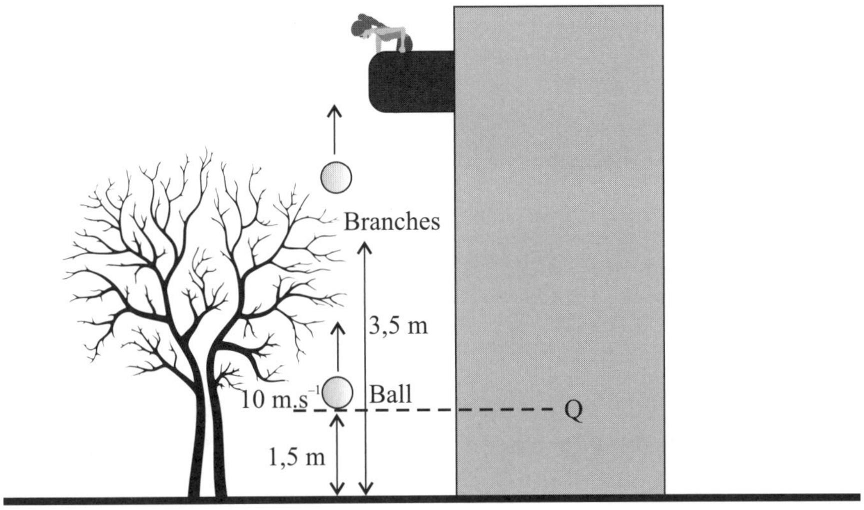

13.1 Calculate the maximum height above point Q that the package could have reached, if the branches had not been in the way. (3)

13.2 State, in words, the Law of Conservation of Mechanical Energy. (2)

13.3 Using energy principles, calculate the speed of the package just as it reaches the branches. (5)

The ball, on the way upwards, leaves the branches at a velocity of 5 m·s^{-1} at a height of 3,60 m above the ground.

13.4 Calculate the work done by the ball in passing through the branches. (4)

13.5 Calculate whether it would be possible for Celeste to catch the ball. (4)

[20]

Question 14 (Solutions on page 235)

The sketches A, B and C, show the positions of a pendulum at different times. Assume the height above the ground of the pendulum is the same at position A and C. Ignore friction.

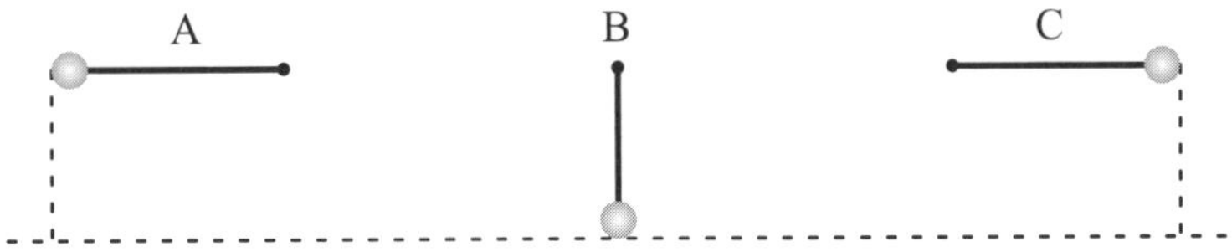

As the pendulum swings from position A to position B, it gains 4 000J of kinetic energy. The pendulum has a mass of 20kg.

14.1 Sketch B shows the lowest point reached by the pendulum during the swing. Calculate the speed of the pendulum when it is at position B. (3)

14.2 Calculate the pendulum's gain in height, with respect to position B, when it reaches position C. (4)

14.3 On the same set of axes, sketch graphs of potential, kinetic and mechanical energy against time, as the pendulum swings from position A to B to C. Use A as the reference point and include the value of 4 000J on your graph. (6)

[18]

TOC 1 Data Sheet 2 Definitions 3 3 solutions 4 4 solutions 5 5 solutions 6 6 solutions 7 7 solutions 8 8 solutions 9 9 solutions 10 10 solutions

Question 15 (Solutions on page 235)

A skateboarder with a mass of 80 kg who skates down a slope experiences a frictional force of 60 N. The slope makes an angle of 25° with the horizontal. After the skateboarder has covered a distance of 36 m, his velocity is 16 m.s^{-1} as shown in the diagram alongside.

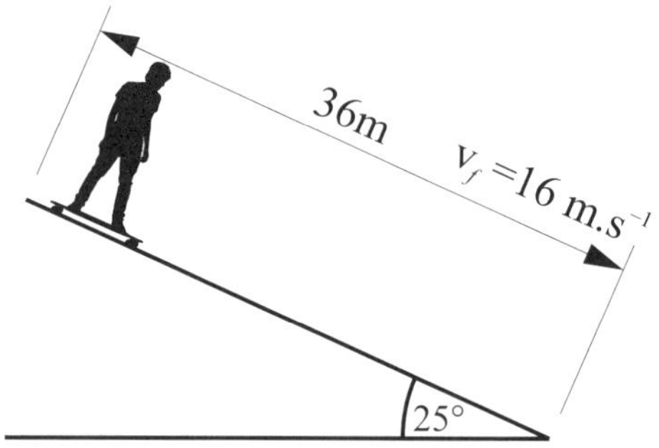

15.1 State the work-energy theorem. (2)

15.2 Calculate the net force acting on the skateboarder. (4)

15.3 Using energy considerations only, calculate the velocity of the skateboarder at the top of the slope. (7)

[13]

Question 16 (Solutions on page 236)

Lula and Adam are performing a motorbike stunt. Adam of mass 50 kg is driving a motorbike at a constant velocity of 4m.s^{-1} while Lula, of mass 45kg, stands on the back of the Bike. Lula loses her balance and jumps backwards off the motorbike making a perfect landing on the pavement with a speed of 3,5 m.s^{-1}. Unfortunately, at the instant Lula jumps off, Adam loses control and crashes into a tree. Luckily, he is wearing protective equipment and escapes injury.

16.1 Calculate the magnitude of Adam's velocity just before he crashes into the tree. (4)

16.2 Name and state the principle used in question 16.1 above. (2)

16.3 If Adam hits the tree head on and it takes 0,8 seconds for him to come to rest, determine the magnitude of the force that Adam experiences. (3)

16.4 The crash helmet Adam is wearing is padded. Use physics principles and relative equations to explain how this helped Adam escape injury. (4)

[13]

Question 17 (Solutions on page 236)

Tim (mass 50kg) moves from rest down a curved slide of height 3m. The lowest point of the slide (point B) is curved and the slide ends 1m above the ground at point C. While moving along the slide 600 J of work is done against friction.

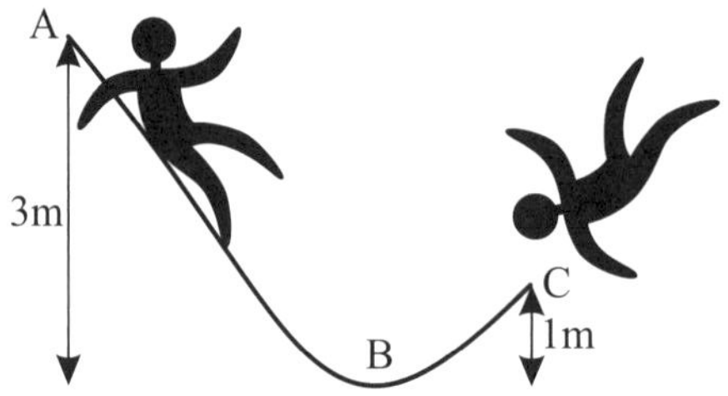

17.1 Is mechanical energy conserved? Give a reason for your answer. (2)

17.2 Calculate Tim's mechanical energy at A. (3)

17.3 What is Tim's mechanical energy at C? (2)

17.4 What is the magnitude of Tim's velocity at C, the moment he exits the slide? (4)

[13]

Question 18 (Solutions on page 236 and 237)

A bullet of mass 2g travelling horizontally at 1 000 $m.s^{-1}$ to the right, hits a wooden block of mass 0,5 kg which is stationary on a rough horizontal surface. The bullet passes through the block and emerges with a reduced velocity of 200 $m.s^{-1}$ in the same direction. As a result of the impact the block slides 0,4 m along the rough surface before coming to rest.

18.1 Calculate the velocity of the block immediately after the bullet emerges. (5)

18.2 Using Energy considerations only, calculate the magnitude of the frictional force which brings the block to rest. (5)

[10]

Question 19 (Solutions on page 237)

A pellet gun is fired at an apple which is suspended from a light string. The pellet gets stuck in the apple when it is fired. The apple and the pellet swing away to the right, and reach a height of 15 cm.

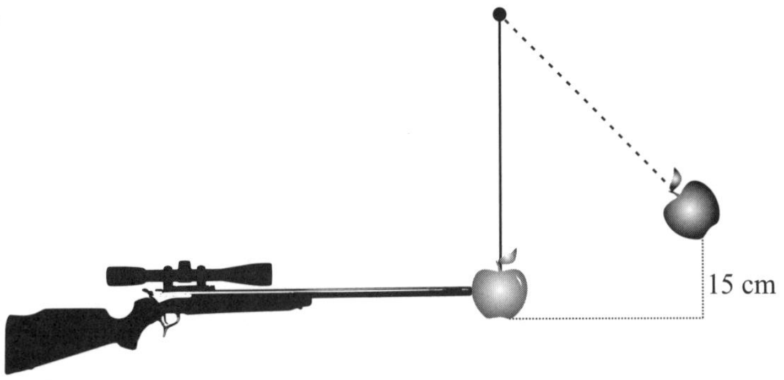

19.1 Calculate the velocity of the apple and pellet combination immediately after impact. (5)

19.2 Calculate the impact speed of the pellet if the pellet has mass of 1g and the apple has a mass of 100g. (4)

[9]

Question 20 (Solutions on page 237)

While doing repair work on the International Space Station, an astronaut's tether breaks, and he gets separated from the space station. The astronaut is moving away from the space station at a constant speed of $3m.s^{-1}$ to the right and has a mass of 80kg. He is also carrying a toolkit which has a mass of 65kg. The astronaut attempts to fire his thrusters to return to the space station. Unfortunately, the thrusters malfunction and do not fire.

When the astronaut is 12m from the space station, he comes up with an idea to get back to the station. He has one minute to return to the space station before an asteroid shower.

20.1 The astronaut throws his toolkit to the right in order to return to the station. Explain why this will help him to return to the space station. (2)

20.2 Determine the velocity at which the toolkit must be thrown for the astronaut to make it back to the space station in time. (8)

[10]

TOC | 1 Data Sheet | 2 Definitions | 3 | 3 solutions | 4 | 4 solutions | 5 | 5 solutions | 6 | 6 solutions | 7 | 7 solutions | 8 | 8 solutions | 9 | 9 solutions | 10 | 10 solutions

Question 21 (Solutions on page 237 and 238)

On an alien planet, with no atmosphere, a science student conducts an experiment. She places a large ball on an inclined frictionless plane. She then records the potential energy of the ball at the top of the slope and releases the ball from rest and records the balls velocity at the bottom of the slope. The experiment is repeated 8 times, increasing the height of the slope by 2 metres each time.

The results of her experiment are tabulated below:

Measurement Number	Height (m)	Potential Energy (J) (top of the slope)	Velocity Squared ($m^2.s^{-2}$) (bottom of the slope)
1	2	60	12
2	4	120	22
3	6	180	38
4	8	240	65
5	10	300	60
6	12	360	72
7	14	420	84
8	16	480	92

When answering the questions below you may ignore all forces of friction:

21.1 State the law of conservation of mechanical energy. (2)

21.2 The student suspects that one of his measurements is incorrect. Which measurement, if any, is incorrect? (1)

21.3 On the axes below sketch a graph of kinetic energy against velocity squared of the ball at the bottom of the incline. (4)

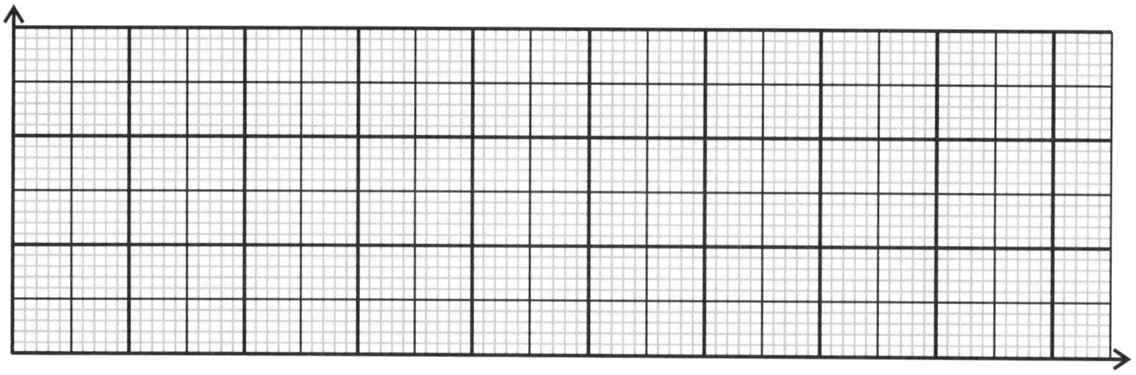

21.4 Determine the gradient of the graph. Include the appropriate unit in your answer. (4)

21.5 Use your answer in 21.4 above to determine the mass of the ball and hence the value of gravitational acceleration on the alien planet. (6)

[17]

Question 22 (Solutions on page 238)

A bullet of mass 20 g is fired at a wooden block of mass 5 kg hanging on a light inextensible string. The bullet lodges in the block and they swing to a maximum height of 12 cm above the block's rest position.

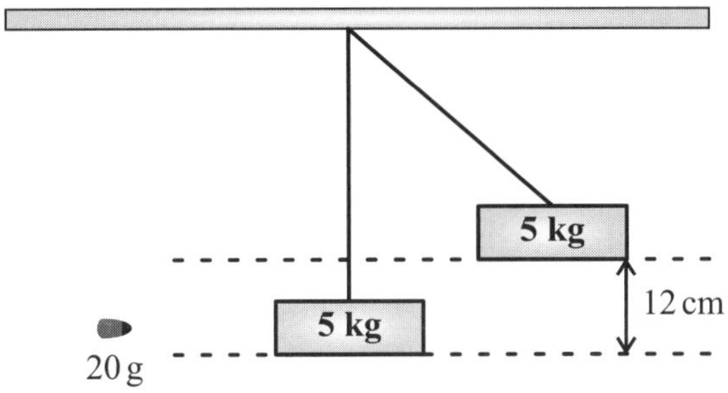

22.1 Calculate the increase in gravitational potential energy of the block-bullet system between the block's rest position and its maximum height. (3)

22.2 Calculate the initial speed of the block-bullet system before it swings upward. (4)

22.3 Calculate the initial speed of the bullet before it hits the block. (4)

[11]

Question 23 (Solutions on page 239)

In a grain processing plant empty carts with a mass of 100kg are loaded with 220kg of grain from a chute vertically above the cart. At the instant the grain is loaded, the cart is traveling at a constant velocity of 4 $m.s^{-1}$ over a frictionless surface. The loaded cart then moves down a rough inclined plane. The work done against friction on the plane is 1250 J. At the bottom of the incline a loaded cart (A) collides with a stationary cart (B) which is also fully loaded.

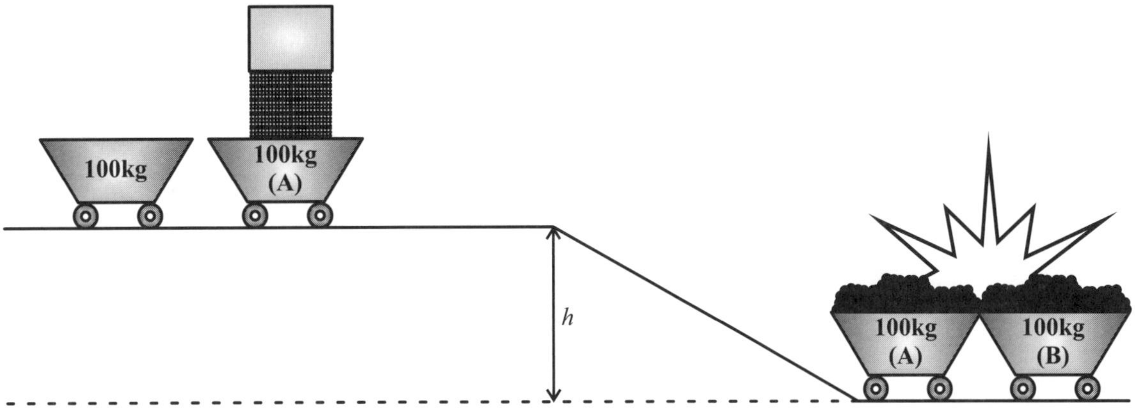

After the collision , cart B moves off with a velocity of 1$m.s^{-1}$, whilst cart A continues in the same direction at 6,25$m.s^{-1}$

23.1 Determine the magnitude of the velocity of cart A immediately after it is loaded with grain. (4)

23.2 State the law used to determine your answer above in question 23.1. (2)

23.3 Determine *h*, the height of the incline. (7)

[13]

Question 24 (Solutions on page 239)

A 500W motor is used to pump water through a pipe from a borehole 10m below the surface. The water exits the pipe with a velocity of $3 m.s^{-1}$. Determine the number of litres of water that the motor can pump in 10 minutes if the motor is 70% efficient. (1 litre of water = 1kg)

[8]

Question 25 (2014 IEB Final Examination) (Solutions on page 239 and 240)

Two different balls A and B of masses 250 g and 300 g respectively have a head-on collision. Ball A is moving to the right at $4 m.s^{-1}$ before the collision and ball B is moving to the left at $6 m.s^{-1}$ before the collision. During the collision ball A experiences an impulse of 1,5 $kg.m.s^{-1}$ to the left.

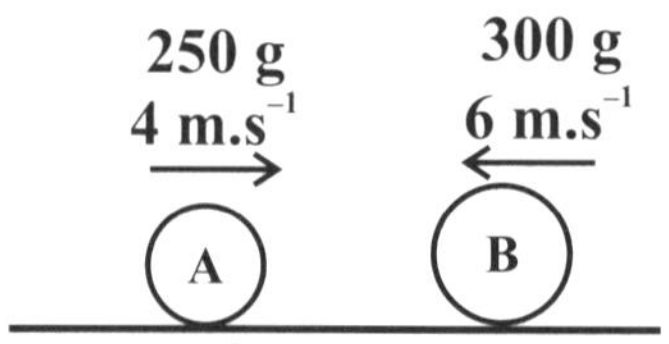

Before collision

25.1 Define momentum. (2)

25.2 Calculate the magnitude and direction of the velocity of ball A immediately after the collision. (5)

25.3 Calculate the magnitude and direction of the velocity of ball B immediately after the collision. (5)

[12]

Question 26 (2015 IEB Supplementary Examination) (Solutions on page 240)

26.1 Railway carriage X, of mass 21 000 kg, crashes into the back of railway carriage Y. which is travelling in the same direction as X on a straight level track. The graph shows how the velocity of each railway carriage varies with time.

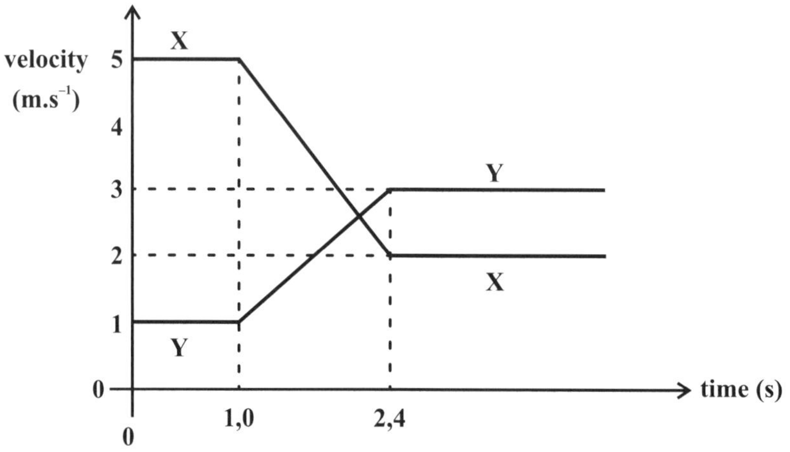

Ignore frictional forces between the railway carriages and the track during the collision. Ignore air resistance.

26.1.1 Calculate the distance travelled by carriage Y between 1,0 s and 2,4 s. (4)

26.1.2 Calculate the magnitude of the change in momentum of railway carriage X between 1,0 s and 2,4 s. (4)

26.1.3 Calculate the net force experienced by railway carriage X between 1,0 s and 2,4 s. (4)

26.1.4 Calculate the mass of railway carriage Y. (4)

26.2 After the collision railway carriage X (mass 21 000 kg) is taken to the repair yard where it is pulled up a track inclined at 20° to the horizontal. It is pulled up the track at a constant speed of 1,4 $m.s^{-1}$ by means of a cable attached to a motor. The gain in vertical height is 8 m.

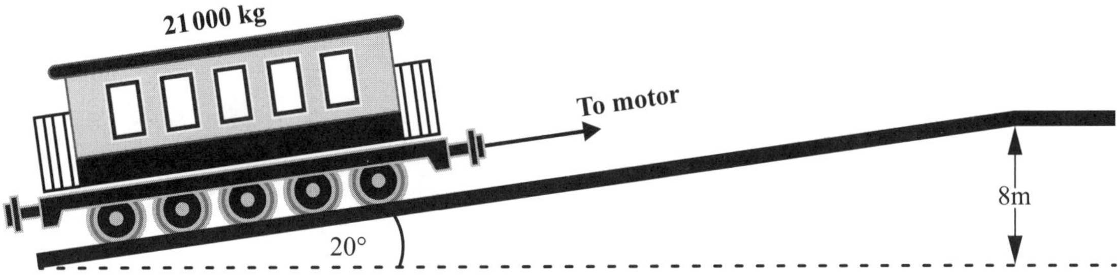

26.2.1 Calculate the gain in gravitational potential energy of the carriage when it moved from the bottom to the top of the slope. (3)

26.2.2 Calculate the magnitude of the force applied by the cable to the carriage if the frictional force between the carriage and the track is a constant 21 kN. (5)

26.2.3 Calculate the output power of the motor. (4)

26.2.4 Explain why the work done by the cable on the carriage between the bottom and top of the slope is greater than the gain in gravitational potential energy of the carriage. (2)

[30]

Question 27 (2016 IEB Final Examination) (Solutions on page 240 and 241)

27.1 A student is experimenting with two carts on a frictionless surface. Cart X has a mass of 0,5 kg and is initially at rest. Cart Y has a mass of 1,2 kg and collides with cart X. Cart Y is initially travelling at 8 $m \cdot s^{-1}$ east and travels at 4 $m \cdot s^{-1}$ east after colliding with cart X. The velocity of cart Y is represented on the velocity time graph below.

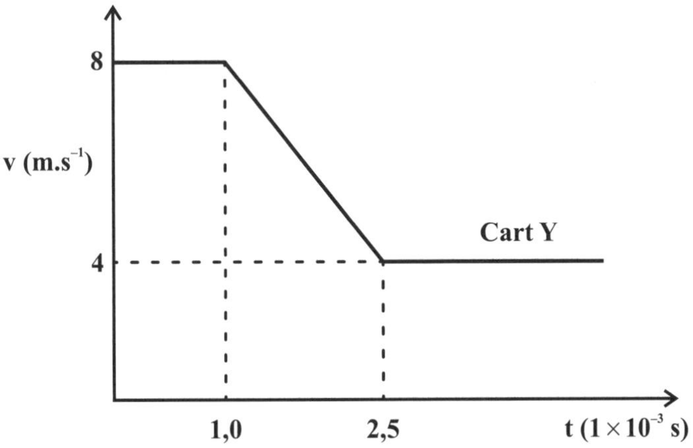

27.1.1 State the law of conservation of momentum. (2)

27.1.2 Calculate the magnitude of the final velocity of cart X. (4)

27.1.3 Calculate the change in momentum of cart Y. (4)

27.1.4 Calculate the magnitude of the force that cart X exerts on cart Y. (4)

27.2 A cyclist is travelling at 15 $m{\cdot}s^{-1}$ at the top of a 450 m long slope that is 30 m high. The cyclist and her bicycle have a combined mass of 70 kg. A constant frictional force of 12 N acts on her all the way to the bottom of the slope.

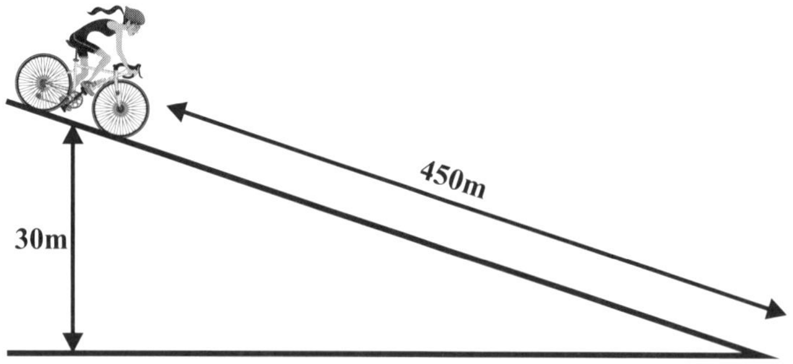

27.2.1 Calculate the kinetic energy of the cyclist at the top of the slope. (3)

27.2.2 Calculate the gravitational potential energy of the cyclist at the top of the slope. (3)

27.2.3 Calculate the work done by the frictional force. (3)

27.2.4 Calculate the cyclist's speed at the bottom of the slope. (4)

[27]

Question 28 (2016 IEB Supplementary Examination) (Solutions on page 241 and 242)

28.1 A truck of mass 2 500 kg was being driven at 25 $m.s^{-1}$. Unfortunately, the driver did not see the low overhead bridge and drove straight into the bridge, peeling open the top of his truck. The truck was stopped by the bridge in a distance of 1,8 m.

28.1.1 Calculate the magnitude of the change in momentum of the truck during the accident. (3)

28.1.2 State the work-energy theorem. (2)

28.1.3 Use the work-energy theorem to calculate the average resultant force that brought the truck to rest. (4)

28.1.4 Use your answers from Questions 28.1.1 and 28.1.3 to calculate how long it took the truck to come to rest. (3)

28.1.5 Fortunately, the driver, who was wearing a seatbelt, was not injured during the accident. Explain why the driver would have been more seriously hurt if the same truck had stopped almost instantly. Use a relevant formula to help you in your explanation. (4)

28.2 A small car of mass 1 084 kg was travelling east at a speed of 33 m·s^{-1}. A large SUV of mass 3 437 kg was travelling west at a speed of 28 m·s^{-1}. The two vehicles collided head on with each other.

Immediately after the collision, the small car was moving west at 5 m·s^{-1}.

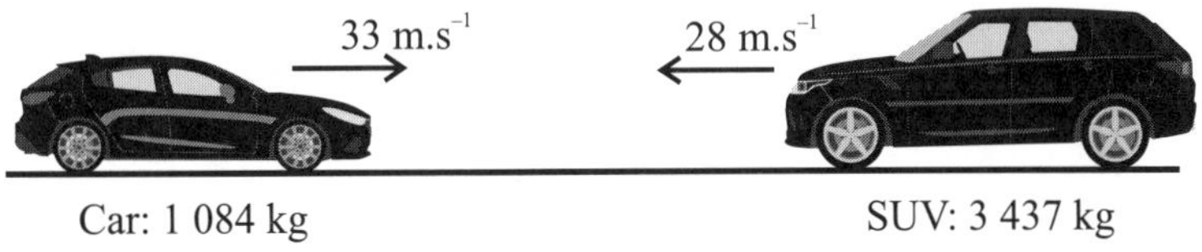

28.2.1 Name the law you would use to calculate the velocity of the SUV immediately after the collision. (2)

28.2.2 Determine the velocity of the SUV immediately after the collision. (5)

28.2.3 Define an elastic collision (2)

28.2.4 Use a calculation to determine if the collision was an elastic collision. (5)

[30]

Question 29 (2017 IEB Final Examination) (Solutions on page 242 and 243)

29.1 A box of mass 2 kg has an initial speed of V_1. The box travels across a rough surface and has a speed of 1,5 m.s^{-1} after it has travelled 0,7 m. The frictional force acting on the box is 26 N.

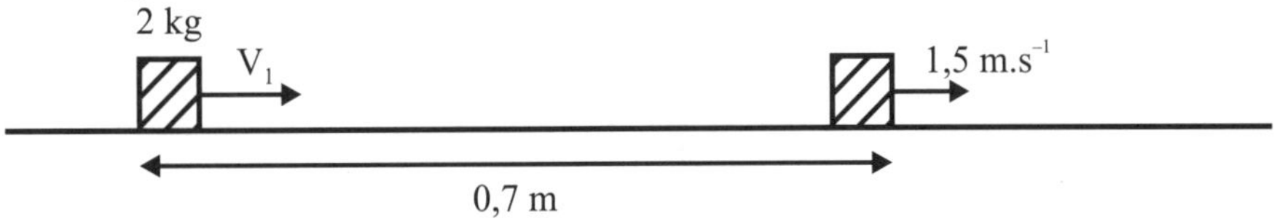

29.1.1 Define frictional force. (2)

29.1.2 Calculate the kinetic energy of the box while it is travelling at 1,5 m.s^{-1}. (3)

29.1.3 Calculate the work done on the box by the frictional force. (3)

29.1.4 State the work energy theorem (2)

29.1.5 Calculate the initial speed V_1 of the box. (4)

29.2 A 1,2 kg crate is attached to a long string as shown in the diagram. A block of mass 0,4 kg collides with the stationary crate with a velocity V_b and rebounds with a velocity of 0,36 m.s^{-1} causing the crate to swing up through a vertical height of 65cm. (frictional forces are negligible)

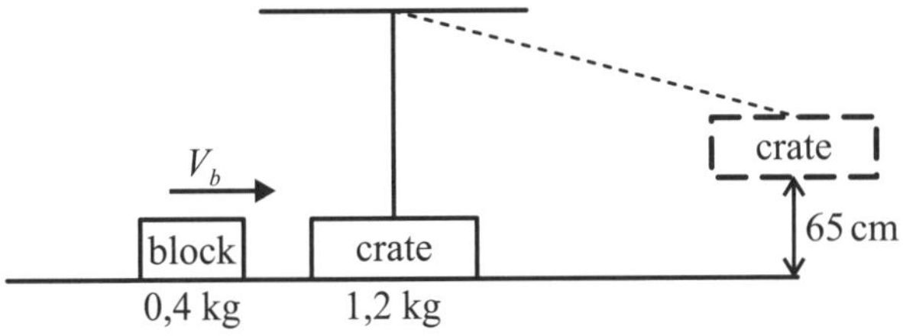

29.2.1 State the principle of conservation of mechanical energy. (2)

29.2.2 Calculate the magnitude of the velocity of the crate immediately after the block collided with the crate. (4)

29.2.3 State the law of conservation of linear momentum. (2)

29.2.4 Calculate the magnitude of the velocity of the block, V_b, just before it collides with the crate. (4)

[26]

TOC | 1 Data Sheet | 2 Definitions | 3 | 3 solutions | 4 | 4 solutions | 5 | 5 solutions | 6 | 6 solutions | 7 | 7 solutions | 8 | 8 solutions | 9 | 9 solutions | 10 | 10 solutions

Question 30 (2017 IEB Supplementary Examination) (Solutions on page 243 and 244)

A reverse bungee is a thrill ride where passengers are strapped into a capsule and are shot into the air by using a pair of strong bungee cords (thick, elastic cables with negligible mass).

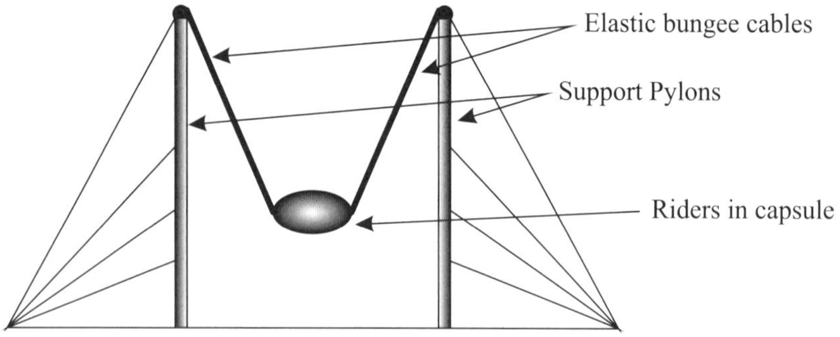

Consider the cables at the bottom of the bungee, i.e. at the lowest point. The cables exert a maximum tension at this point of 7 000 N per cable and the cables are angled at 65° to the horizontal at this point. (See the diagram below.)

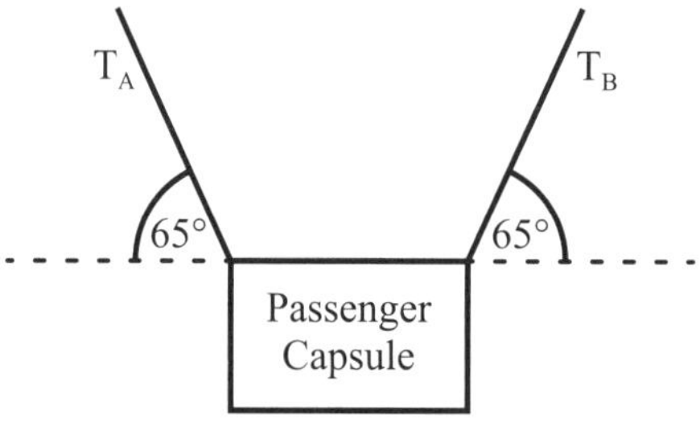

T_A: The tension exerted by cable A

T_B: The tension exerted by cable B

30.1 Calculate the total upward force that the bungee cables exert on the passenger capsule at this point. (3)

30.2 Define resultant vector. (2)

30.3 Calculate the mass of a capsule if it experiences a net force of 4 000 N upwards at this point as it is released. (5)

At a height of 25 m above the release point, a different capsule of mass 320 kg has a speed of 19 $m.s^{-1}$.

30.4 State the work energy theorem (2)

30.5 Calculate the work done by the net force on the capsule to get the capsule to this point. (3)

30.6 Calculate the increase in mechanical energy of the capsule at this point. (5)

30.7 Calculate the average applied force that the cables exerted on the capsule to accelerate it to the speed of 19 $m.s^{-1}$. (4)

30.8 Calculate the maximum height from the release position that the capsule will reach if the cable exerts no further force on the capsule, i.e. the capsule is free to move upwards from the 25 m position. (4)

30.9 Sketch a position vs time graph for the upward motion of the capsule from its release position to its maximum height. Show on the graph the height 25 m and the maximum height reached. (4)

[32]

Question 31 (2018 IEB Final Examination) (Solutions on page 244)

31.1 Students are performing an experiment in the lab. A 0,9 kg trolley is travelling with a constant velocity of 2,4 $m.s^{-1}$ on a long frictionless track when a metal cylinder of mass m is dropped vertically onto the trolley. The trolley with the metal cylinder continues to move with velocity v as shown in the diagram.

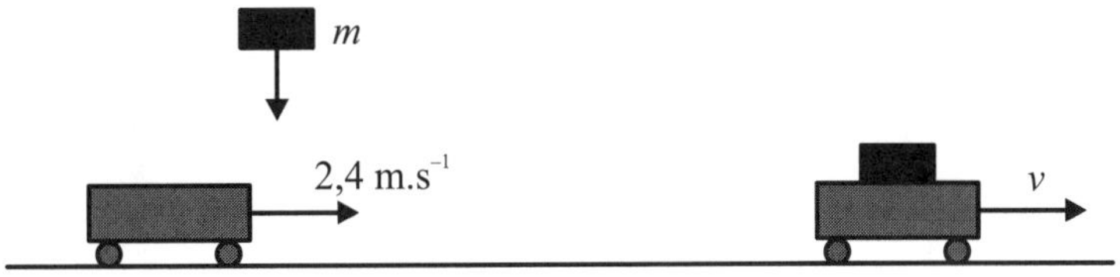

The students use video analysis to plot the following position vs time graph of the trolley.

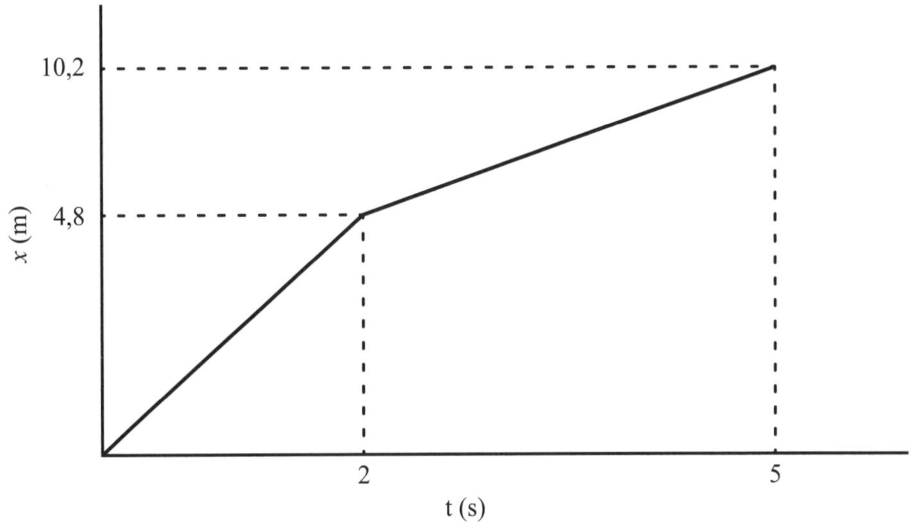

31.1.1 Use the graph to determine the magnitude of the velocity (v) of the trolley after the metal cylinder is dropped on the trolley. (3)

31.1.2 The law of conservation of momentum is a consequence of which of Newton's laws? (2)

31.1.3 Calculate the mass (m) of the metal cylinder. (4)

31.1.4 Why is the vertical velocity of the falling metal cylinder not taken into consideration? (2)

31.2 A steel hammer with a mass of 600 kg is used to drive an iron beam into the ground. The steel hammer falls a distance of 3,5 m from rest under gravity before contacting the beam. The beam is driven a distance of 16 cm into the ground before coming to rest. Ignore air resistance.

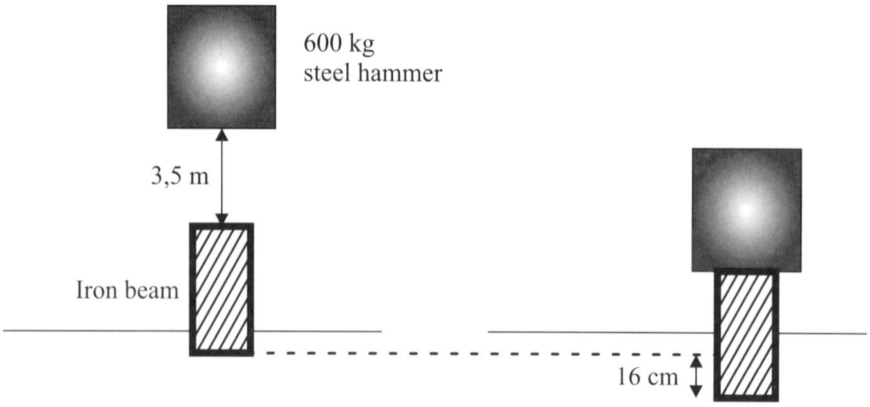

31.2.1 State the principle of the conservation of mechanical energy. (3)

31.2.2 Calculate the magnitude of the velocity of the steel hammer **as it strikes** the iron beam. (4)

31.2.3 State the work-energy theorem. (2)

31.2.4 Calculate the magnitude of the average net force the beam exerts on the hammer while the hammer is brought to rest on the beam (4)

The machine that is used to raise the hammer, so that it can be used again, has a power output of 180W.

31.2.5 Calculate the time the machine will take to lift the hammer through a height of 3,5m. (4)

[27]

Question 32 (2015 IEB Final Examination) (Solutions on page 245)

A rocket of total mass (m) is in deep space travelling at a speed of 1 000 $m.s^{-1}$.

32.1 State Newton's first law of motion. (2)

The rocket fires its engine. The burnt fuel has an exhaust speed of 500 $m.s^{-1}$ in the opposite direction to the rocket.

32.2 Explain why firing the engine changes the speed of the rocket. Use one of Newton's laws to help you in your explanation. (3)

32.3 State the law of conservation of linear momentum. (2)

32.4 Calculate the rocket's final speed if one third of its mass is lost due to the burnt fuel being ejected in a single short burn. (5)

[12]

Question 33 (2015 IEB Final Examination) (Solutions on page 245 and 246)

A block of mass 10 kg is sliding along a uniform rough surface. The surface is horizontal from A to B and inclined at 35° to the horizontal from B to C.

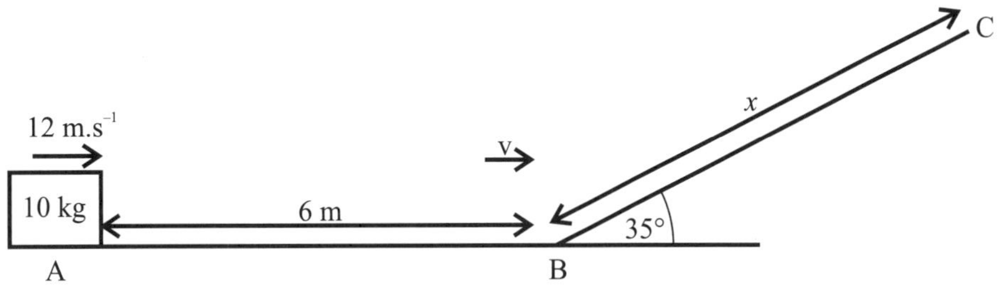

The block is travelling at a speed of 12 $m.s^{-1}$ as it passes A.

33.1 Define the term kinetic energy. (2)

33.2 Calculate the kinetic energy of the block as it passes A. (3)

The frictional force acting on the block as it slides from A to B is 54,9 N.

33.3 State the work energy theorem. (2)

33.4 Calculate the speed of the block (v) as it reaches B. (4)

The block slides up the incline from B and comes to rest at C. The frictional force acting on the block as it slides from B to C is 45,0 N.

33.5 Write an expression for the potential energy of the block at C in terms of x (the distance along the slope from B to C). (2)

33.6 Calculate the distance, x, that the block slides up the slope before coming to rest at C. (5)

33.7 The frictional force experienced by the block on the inclined plane is less than the frictional force experienced on the horizontal surface even though the surfaces are made of the same material. Explain by making use of a relevant equation. (3)

At point C, the object only just manages to remain at rest.

33.8 Draw a labelled free-body diagram of the block at rest at C. (3)

33.9 Calculate the frictional force acting on the block at C. (3)

33.10 Hence calculate the coefficient of friction. (3)

33.11 Explain why the frictional force calculated in Question 33.9 is greater than the frictional force of 45,0 N acting while the block was sliding. (2)

[32]

Question 34 (2018 IEB Supplementary Examination) (Solutions on page 246 and 247)

34.1 A lead bullet of mass 5 g is shot vertically upwards into a wooden block of mass 195 g which is at rest over a hole in a table. Ignore air resistance.

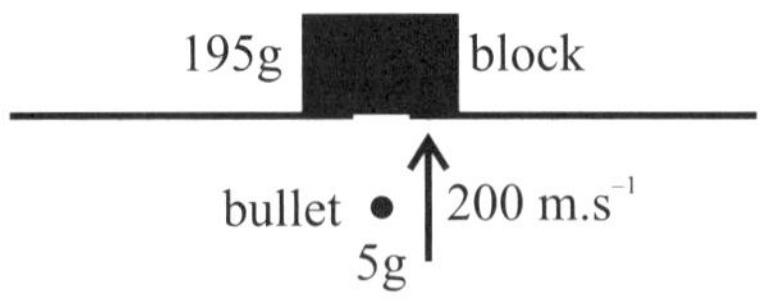

The bullet hits the block with a velocity of 200 $m.s^{-1}$. The bullet embeds itself in the block.

34.1.1 State the law of conservation of momentum. (2)

34.1.2 Calculate the speed of the block and bullet immediately after the bullet has embedded in the block. (4)

34.1.3 Calculate how high the block will rise above the block's original position. (4)

34.2 A crate of mass 70 kg slides down a rough incline which is at an angle of 20° to the horizontal. The crate experiences a constant frictional force of 190 N.

34.2.1 Draw a labelled free-body diagram of all the forces acting on the crate. (3)

34.2.2 Which force in your free-body diagram does no work on the crate? (2)

The crate passes point K on the incline at a speed of 4 $m.s^{-1}$ before passing point L 18m lower down the incline.

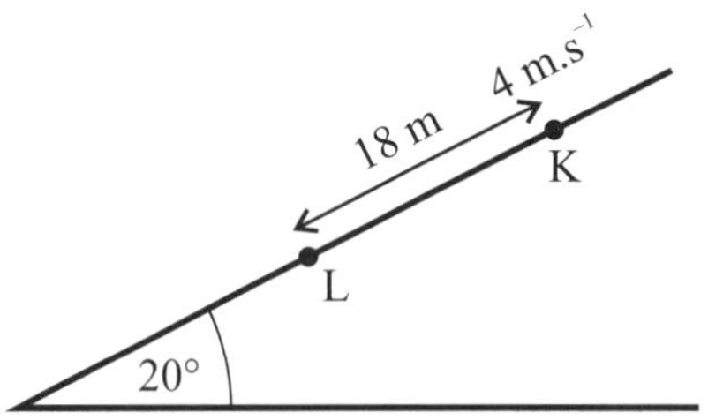

34.2.3 Calculate the kinetic energy of the crate as it passes point K. (3)

34.2.4 Calculate the magnitude of the resultant force acting on the crate between point K and point L. (3)

34.2.5 State the work energy theorem. (2)

34.2.6 Use the work-energy theorem to calculate the speed of the crate as it passes point L. (5)

[28]

Question 35 (2019 IEB Supplementary Examination) (Solutions on page 247)

35.1 A box of mass **m** is pushed, from rest, with a constant applied force of 20 N over a horizontal surface which has three different regions, A, B and C. Each region is 5 m long and exerts a different frictional force on the box as it moves through. The regions are A, B and C as illustrated in the diagram below.

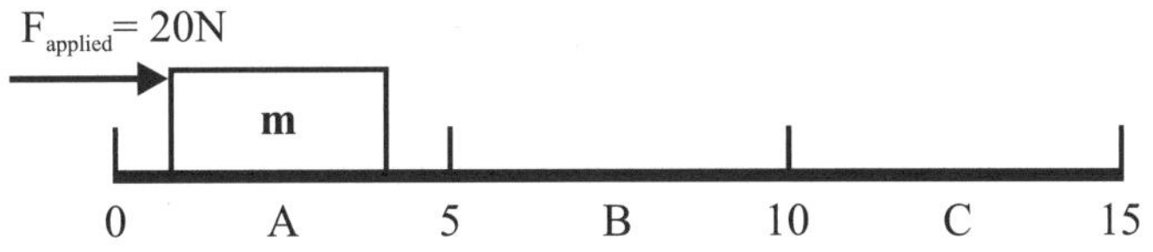

The graph below shows the kinetic energy of the object as a function of the distance from the starting position as the object experiences the constant applied force of 20 N.

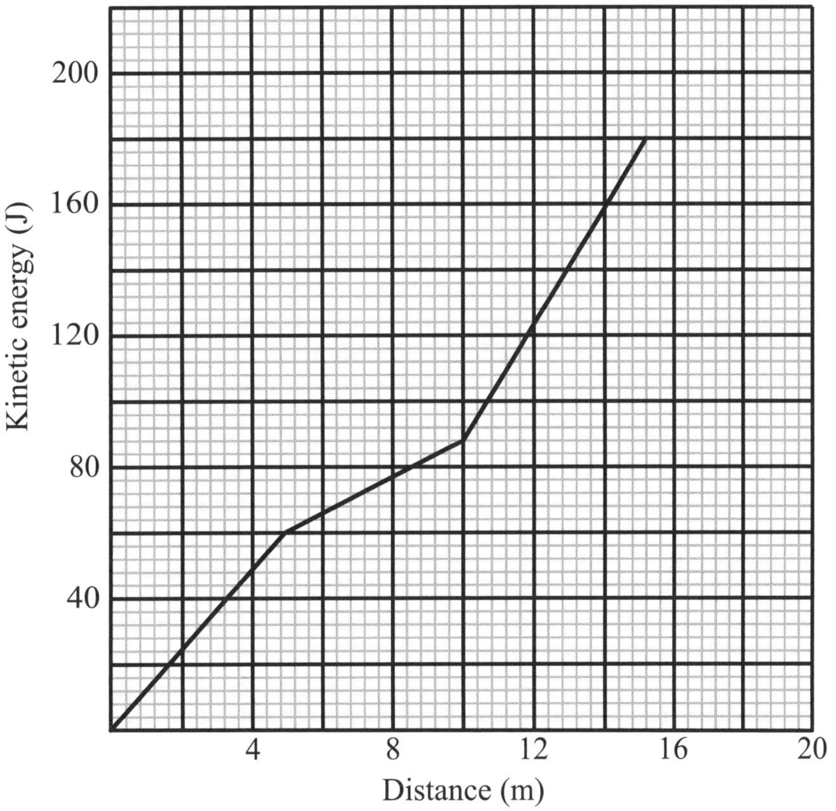

35.1.1 State the work energy theorem. (2)

35.1.2 Use the work-energy theorem to show that the gradient (slope) of the graph represents the net force experienced by the object. (3)

35.1.3 Calculate the net force experienced by the object in region C. (4)

35.1.4 Hence, determine the magnitude of the friction force experienced by the block as it moves over region C. (3)

35.1.5 Which region, A, B or C offers the largest friction force? (1)

35.1.6 Justify your answer in Question 35.1.5 (2)

35.1.7 Assuming that the box starts from rest, and accelerates at 1 $m.s^{-2}$ while moving over region A, calculate the mass of the box. (4)

35.2 A car engine dissipates a power of 60 000 W while the car is travelling at a constant velocity of 60 km.h^{-1}.

35.2.1 Define power. (2)

35.2.2 Convert 60 km.h^{-1} to m.s^{-1}. (2)

35.2.3 Explain what it means for the car to dissipate power at 60 000 W. (2)

35.2.4 Calculate the force applied by the engine under these conditions. (3)

35.3 The car of mass 1 500 kg travelling to the right at 70 km.h^{-1} runs into the back of a stationary van of unknown mass. The two vehicles lock together and move to the right at 7 m.s^{-1}.

Calculate the mass of the van. (4)

[32]

Question 36 (2019 IEB Final Examination) (Solutions on page 248 and 249)

36.1 A student conducts an investigation to establish if the initial velocity of a model car determines the time taken for the car to stop when experiencing a constant resultant force. The student organises for model cars to start with different initial velocities (v). The car then brakes and the student measures the time taken for the car to stop (Δt) and tabulates the results.

36.1.1 State the **independent** variable in the investigation. (2)

The results that the student obtained is recorded in the table.

v (m.s^{-1})	Δt (s)
8	4,8
13	8,2
18	10,7
24	14,8
30	17,8
34	21,0

36.1.2 Plot a graph of time taken to stop, Δt (on the y-axis) vs initial velocity, v (on the x-axis) on the graph paper provided on the next page. (6)

36.1.3 Calculate the gradient of your graph. Show the values you used on your graph and include the appropriate unit in your answer. (5)

36.1.4 Rearrange the equation $F_{net}\,\Delta t = m\Delta v$ to write Δt in terms of v for the experiment described. (1)

The resultant force experienced by the car was kept constant at –140 N for each velocity.

36.1.5 Hence, use your answers to Question 36.1.3 and Question 36.1.4 to calculate the mass of the model car. (3)

36.1.2 Graph paper for question 36.1.2

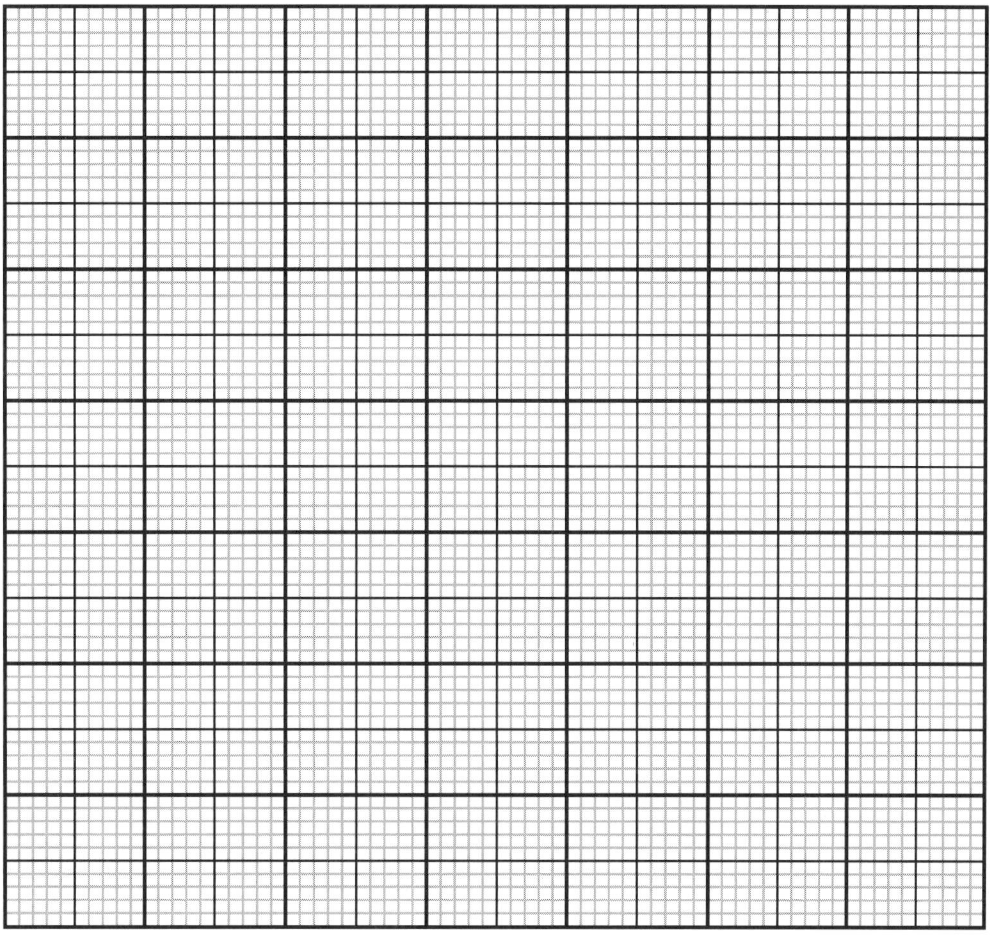

36.2 A cart with a mass of 60 kg is travelling at a speed of 7,5 $m.s^{-1}$ at the bottom of a rough slope inclined at 25° to the horizontal. The cart comes to rest after travelling up the slope to a vertical height of 2,8 m.

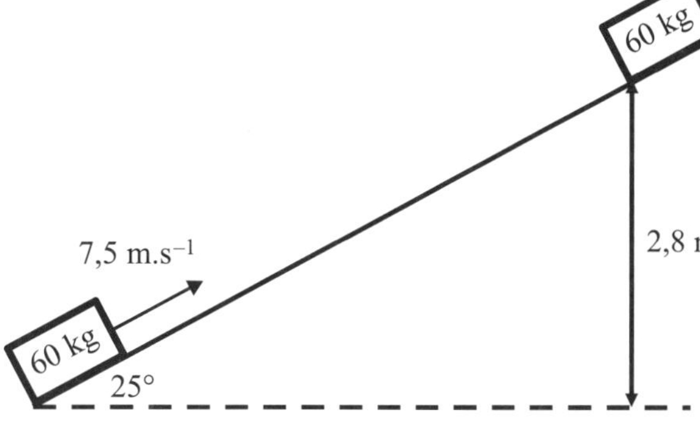

36.2.1 Define *kinetic energy.* (2)

36.2.2 Calculate the kinetic energy of the cart at the bottom of the slope. (3)

36.2.3 Calculate the gain in gravitational potential energy of the cart at the highest point. (3)

36.2.4 Calculate the work done against the frictional force as the cart moves up the slope. (2)

36.2.5 Hence, calculate the magnitude of the frictional force acting on the cart as it moves up the slope. (4)

[31]

TOC | 1 Data Sheet | 2 Definitions | 3 | 3 solutions | 4 | 4 solutions | 5 | 5 solutions | 6 | 6 solutions | 7 | 7 solutions | 8 | 8 solutions | 9 | 9 solutions | 10 | 10 solutions

6. MOMENTUM AND ENERGY (SOLUTIONS)

Question 1

1.1	C	(2)
1.2	C	(2)
1.3	C	(2)
1.4	A	(2)
1.5	B	(2)
1.6	D	(2)
1.7	B	(2)
1.8	D	(2)
1.9	A	(2)
1.10	C	(2)
1.11	A	(2)
1.12	D	(2)
1.13	C	(2)
1.14	D	(2)
1.15	B	(2)
1.16	A	(2)
1.17	C	(2)
1.18	B	(2)
1.19	D	(2)
1.20	D	(2)
1.21	A	(2)
1.22	B	(2)
1.23	D	(2)
1.24	D	(2)
1.25	A	(2)
1.26	A	(2)
1.27	B	(2)
1.28	D	(2)
1.29	A	(2)
1.30	B	(2)
1.31	B	(2)
1.32	C	(2)
1.33	D	(2)
1.34	B	(2)
1.35	D	(2)

[42]

Question 2

$$v_i = 80 \div 3{,}6$$
$$= 22{,}22\,\text{m.s}^{-1}$$
$$F_{net} = \frac{\Delta p}{\Delta t}$$
$$= \frac{m\left(v_f - v_i\right)}{\Delta t}$$
$$= \frac{2500\left(0 - 22{,}22\right)}{0{,}18}$$
$$= -308\,611$$
$$= 308{,}611\text{ kN in opposite direction of original motion}$$

308,611kN < 350 kN, therefore the driver cabin will not be compromised.

[19]

Question 3

3.1
$$W_f = F_f \Delta x$$
$$= (-33)(12)$$
$$= -396\text{ J}$$
(3)

3.2 By the principle of conservation of total energy:

$$E_{Mtop} = E_{Mbot} + W_f$$
$$mgh + \frac{1}{2}mv^2 = mgh + \frac{1}{2}mv^2 + W_f$$
$$(18)(9{,}8)h + 0 = 0 + \frac{1}{2}(18)(2)^2 + 396$$
$$h = 2{,}45\text{ m}$$
(5)

3.3 $v_f{}^2 = v_i^2 + 2a\Delta x$

$0^2 = 3^2 + 2(-0,8)\Delta x$

$\Delta x = 5,63\,\text{m}$ (3)

3.4 The total linear momentum of an isolated system remains constant. (2)

3.5 $p_{bef} = p_{aft}$

$m_1 v_{1i} + m_2 v_{2i} = m_1 v_{1f} + m_2 v_{2f}$

$18(2) + 0 = 18(-1,7) + m_2(3)$

$m_2 = 22,2\,\text{kg}$

$\text{mass of boxes} = 22,2 - 18$

$= 4,2\,\text{kg}$ (5)

3.6 The product of the net force and the contact time. (2)

3.7 $F_{net} = \dfrac{\Delta p}{\Delta t}$

$= \dfrac{18(-1,7-2)}{0,2}$

$= -333$

$= 333\,\text{N}$

[23]

Question 4

4.1 The total linear momentum of an isolated system remains constant. (2)

4.2 $p_{bef} = p_{aft}$

$m_1 v_{1i} + m_2 v_{2i} = (m_1 + m_2) v_f$

$(0,04)(720) + 0 = (0,04 + 0,8) v_f$

$v_f = 34,29\ \text{m.s}^{-1}$ (5)

4.3 $E_{kbefore} = \dfrac{1}{2} m v^2$

$= \dfrac{1}{2}(0,04)(720)^2$

$= 10368\,\text{J}$

$E_{kafter} = \dfrac{1}{2} m v^2$

$= \dfrac{1}{2}(0,04 + 0,8)(34,29)^2$

$= 493,84\ \text{J}$

$E_{kbefore} \neq E_{kafter}$

$\therefore$ The collision is inelastic (4)

4.4 The work done by a net force on an object is equal to the change in the kinetic energy of the object. (2)

4.5 $W_{net} = \Delta E_k$

$-W_f = \dfrac{1}{2} m\left(v_f{}^2 - v_i^2\right)$

$-F_f \Delta x = \dfrac{1}{2} m\left(v_f{}^2 - v_i^2\right)$

$-F_f(0,3) = \dfrac{1}{2}(0,04 + 0,8)\left(0^2 - 34,29^2\right)$

$F_f = 1646,13\,\text{N}$ (5)

[17]

Question 5

5.1 The work done by a net force on an object is equal to the change in the kinetic energy of the object. (2)

5.2 **Method 1: Using the work energy theorem**

$W_{net} = \Delta E_k$

$-W_f = \frac{1}{2}m\left(v_f^2 - v_i^2\right)$

$-F_f \Delta x = \frac{1}{2}m\left(v_f^2 - v_i^2\right)$

$-5(11,5) = \frac{1}{2}(0,15+0,006)\left(0^2 - v_i^2\right)$

$v_i^2 = 737,18$

$v_i = 27,15\,\text{m.s}^{-1}$

Method 2: Using equations of motion

$F_f = ma$

$-5 = (0,15+0,006)a$

$a = -32,05$

$v_f^2 = v_i^2 + 2a\Delta x$

$0^2 = v_i^2 + 2(-32,05)(11,5)$

$v_i^2 = 737,15$

$v_i = 27,15\,\text{m.s}^{-1}$

(4)

5.3 The total linear momentum of an isolated system remains constant. (2)

5.4 First calculate the velocity that the bullet strikes the block

$p_{bef} = p_{aft}$

$m_1 v_{1i} + m_2 v_{1i} = (m_1 + m_2) v_f$

$0,006 v_{1i} + 0 = (0,15+0,006)(27,15)$

$v_{1i} = 705,9\ \text{m.s}^{-1}$ → velocity of the bullet when it strikes the block

Now calculate the recoil velocity of the rifle

$p_{bef} = p_{aft}$

$(m_1 + m_2) v_i = m_1 v_{1f} + m_2 v_{1f}$

$0 = (1,5) v_{1f} + (0,006)(705,9)$

$v_{1f} = -2,82$

$= 2,82\,\text{m.s}^{-1}$ left

(7)

[15]

Question 6

6.1 The total linear momentum of an isolated system remains constant. (2)

6.2 $p_{bef} = p_{aft}$ → taking right as positive for this question

$\therefore m_1 v_{1_i} + m_2 v_{2_i} = v_f(m_1 + m_2)$

$\therefore 4(-2) + 0,15 v_{2_i} = 5,3(4,15)$

$\therefore v_{2_i} = 199,97\,m.s^{-1}$ right

(4)

6.3 **Method 1: Using the work energy theorem**

$W_{net} = \Delta E_k$

$-W_g = \frac{1}{2}m\left(v_f^2 - v_i^2\right)$

$-mgh = \frac{1}{2}m\left(v_f^2 - v_i^2\right)$

$-4,15(9,8)h = 0,5(4,15)\left(2,5^2 - 5,3^2\right)$

$h = 1,11\,\text{m}$

(7)

6.3 **Method 2: Using conservation of total energy**

$$E_{M_{bef}} = E_{M_{aft}} + W_f$$

$$\therefore \left(E_p + E_k\right)_{bef} = \left(E_p + E_k\right)_{aft} + 0$$

$$\therefore mgh + \frac{1}{2}mv^2 = mgh + \frac{1}{2}mv^2 \rightarrow \text{note that you can divide both sides by } m$$

$$\therefore 0 + 0,5(4,15)(5,3)^2 = (4,15)(9,8)h + 0,5(4,15)(2,5)^2$$

$$\therefore h = 1,11\text{m}$$ (7)

[14]

Question 7

7.1 $W_f = F_f \Delta x$

$= 15(50)$

$= 750\text{ J}$ (3)

7.2 $h = 50\sin 20°$

$= 17,1\text{m}$

$E_p = mgh$

$= 25(9,8)(17,1)$

$= 4189,75\text{ J}$ (5)

7.3 $W_{motor} = W_f + E_P \rightarrow$ constant velocity no work is done to change the kinetic energy

$= 750 + 4189,75$

$= 4939,75$

$$P_{motor} = \frac{W_{motor}}{t}$$

$$= \frac{4939,75}{22}$$

$= 224,53\text{ W}$ (4)

7.4 $$\%\text{ Efficiency} = \frac{P_{out}}{P_{in}} \times 100\ \%$$

$$75 = \frac{224,53}{P_{in}} \times 100\ \%$$

$P_{in} = 299,37\text{ W}$ (2)

[14]

Question 8

$p_{bef} = p_{aft}$

$m_1v_{1i} + m_2v_{1i} + m_3v_{3i} = (m_1 + m_2 + m_3)v_f$

$(55)(-1) + (75)(1,5) + (4,5)(0) = (55 + 75 + 4,5)v_f$

$v_f = 0,43\text{ m.s}^{-1}$ West **[5]**

Question 9

9.1 The total linear momentum of an isolated system remains constant. (2)

9.2 $p_{bef} = p_{aft}$

$m_1 v_{1i} + m_2 v_{1i} = m_1 v_{1f} + m_2 v_{1f}$

$(3)v_{1i} + (6)(0) = (3)(-0,5) + (6)(2,25)$

$v_{1i} = 4 \text{ m.s}^{-1}$ (4)

9.3 $E_{M_{top}} = E_{M_{bot}}$

$\therefore (E_p + E_k)_{top} = (E_p + E_k)_{bot}$

$\therefore mgh + \frac{1}{2}mv^2 = mgh + \frac{1}{2}mv^2$ → note that you can divide both sides by m

$\therefore 3(9,8)h + 0 = 0 + 0,5(3)(4)^2$

$\therefore h = 0,82 \text{ m}$ (4)

9.4 $F_{net} = \frac{\Delta p}{\Delta t}$

$= \frac{m(v_f - v_i)}{\Delta t}$

$= \frac{6(2,25 - 0)}{0,01}$

$= 1350 \text{ N}$ (3)

9.5 The work done by a net force on an object is equal to the change in the kinetic energy of the object. (2)

9.6 $W_{net} = \Delta E_k$

$-W_g - W_f = \frac{1}{2}m(v_f^2 - v_i^2)$

$-mgh - F_f \Delta x = \frac{1}{2}m(v_f^2 - v_i^2)$

$-6(9,8)(12 \times 10^{-2}) - 20,5\Delta x = \frac{1}{2}(6)(0^2 - 2,25^2)$

$\Delta x = 0,4 \text{ m}$

$\sin\theta = \frac{h}{\Delta x}$

$\sin\theta = \frac{12 \times 10^{-2}}{0,4}$

$\theta = 17,46^\circ$ → if Δx is not rounded off $\theta = 17,61^\circ$ (8)

[23]

Question 10

10.1 The total linear momentum of an isolated system remains constant. (2)

10.2 $p_{bef} = p_{aft}$

$m_1 v_{1i} + m_2 v_{1i} = m_1 v_{1f} + m_2 v_{2f}$

$(2,5 \times 10^{-3})(450) + (1,5)(0) = (2,5 \times 10^{-3})(105) + (1,5)v_{2f}$

$v_{2f} = 0,575 \text{ m.s}^{-1}$ east (2)

10.3

$$E_{kbefore} = \frac{1}{2}mv^2$$
$$= \frac{1}{2}(2,5\times10^{-3})(450)^2$$
$$= 253,125\text{ J}$$

$$E_{kafter} = \frac{1}{2}mv^2$$
$$= \frac{1}{2}(2,5\times10^{-3})(105)^2 + \frac{1}{2}(1,5)(0,575)^2$$
$$= 14,03\text{ J}$$

$E_{kbefore} \neq E_{kafter}$

∴ The collision is inelastic (3)

10.4 **Method 1: Using the work energy theorem**

$$W_{net} = \Delta E_k$$
$$-W_f = \frac{1}{2}m\left(v_f^2 - v_i^2\right)$$
$$-F_f\Delta x = \frac{1}{2}m\left(v_f^2 - v_i^2\right)$$
$$-F_f\left(20\times10^{-2}\right) = \frac{1}{2}(1,5)\left(0^2 - 0,575^2\right)$$
$$F_f = 1,24\text{ N}$$

Method 2: Using equations of motion

$$v_f^2 = v_i^2 + 2a\Delta x$$
$$0^2 = 0,575^2 + 2a\left(20\times10^{-2}\right)$$
$$a = -0,83\text{ m.s}^{-2}$$
$$F_f = ma$$
$$F_f = (1,5)(-0,83)$$
$$= -1,25$$
$$= 1,25\text{ N} \rightarrow 1,24\text{ N with no rounding}$$

(5)

[12]

Question 11

11.1

$$E_{M_{bef}} = E_{M_{aft}} + W_f$$
$$\therefore \left(E_p + E_k\right)_{bef} = \left(E_p + E_k\right)_{aft} + 0$$
$$\therefore mgh + \frac{1}{2}mv^2 = mgh + \frac{1}{2}mv^2 \rightarrow \text{note that you can divide both sides by } m$$
$$\therefore 0 + \frac{1}{2}(25+30)v^2 = (25+30)(9,8)(5) + 0$$
$$\therefore v = 9,9\text{ m.s}^{-1}$$

(5)

11.2

$$p_{bef} = p_{aft}$$
$$m_1v_{1i} + m_2v_{2i} = \left(m_1 + m_2\right)v_f$$
$$(25)v_{1i} + (30)(0) = (25+30)(9,9)$$
$$v_{1i} = 21,78\text{ m.s}^{-1} \rightarrow \text{this is the velocity of Bob as he collides with Sam}$$
$$E_{M_{bef}} = E_{M_{aft}} + W_f$$
$$\therefore \left(E_p + E_k\right)_{bef} = \left(E_p + E_k\right)_{aft} + 0$$
$$\therefore mgh + \frac{1}{2}mv^2 = mgh + \frac{1}{2}mv^2 \rightarrow \text{note that you can divide both sides by } m$$
$$\therefore (25)(9,8)h + 0 = 0 + \frac{1}{2}(25)(21,78)^2 + 0$$
$$\therefore h = 24,2\text{ m}$$

(8)

11.3

$$E_{kbefore} = \frac{1}{2}mv^2$$
$$= \frac{1}{2}(25)(21,78)^2$$
$$= 5929,61\text{ J}$$

$$E_{kafter} = \frac{1}{2}mv^2$$
$$= \frac{1}{2}(25+30)(9,9)^2$$
$$= 2695,28\text{ J}$$

$E_{kbefore} \neq E_{kafter}$

∴ The collision is inelastic (4)

[17]

Question 12

12.1 $F_{net} = \dfrac{\Delta p}{\Delta t}$

$F_A - F_f = \dfrac{m(v_f - v_i)}{\Delta t}$

$3800 - 0,4 = \dfrac{(46\times10^{-3})(v_f - 0)}{0,8\times10^{-3}}$ → convert milliseconds to seconds

$v_f = 66,08\,\text{m.s}^{-1}$ (5)

12.2 The total linear momentum of an isolated system remains constant. (2)

12.3 $p_{bef} = p_{aft}$

$m_1v_{1i} + m_2v_{1i} = m_1v_{1f} + m_2v_{2f}$

$(46\times10^{-3})(22) + (0,6)(0) = (46\times10^{-3})(-6) + (0,6)v_{2f}$

$v_{2f} = 2,15\ \text{m.s}^{-1}$ (5)

12.4 $E_{k\,before} = \dfrac{1}{2}mv^2$

$= \dfrac{1}{2}(46\times10^{-3})(22)^2$

$= 11,13\,\text{J}$

$E_{k\,after} = \dfrac{1}{2}mv^2$

$= \dfrac{1}{2}(46\times10^{-3})(-6)^2 + \dfrac{1}{2}(0,6)(2,15)^2$

$= 2,21\ \text{J}$

$E_{k\,before} \neq E_{k\,after}$

∴ The collision is inelastic (5)

[17]

Question 13

13.1 **Method 1: Using conservation of Energy and taking Q as zero height**

$E_{M_{bef}} = E_{Maft} + W_f$

$\therefore (E_p + E_k)_{bef} = (E_p + E_k)_{aft} + 0$

$\therefore mgh + \dfrac{1}{2}mv^2 = mgh + \dfrac{1}{2}mv^2$ → note that you can divide both sides by m

$\therefore 0 + 0,5(0,5)(10)^2 = 0,5(9,8)h + 0$ → velocity is 0 at max height

$\therefore h = 5,1\ m$ above point Q

Method 2: Using conservation of Energy and taking ground as zero

$E_{M_{bef}} = E_{Maft} + W_f$

$\therefore (E_p + E_k)_{bef} = (E_p + E_k)_{aft} + 0$

$\therefore mgh + \dfrac{1}{2}mv^2 = mgh + \dfrac{1}{2}mv^2$ → note that you can divide both sides by m

$\therefore 0,5(9,8)(1,5) + 0,5(0,5)(10)^2 = 0,5(9,8)h + 0$ → velocity is 0 at max height

$\therefore h = 6,6$

∴ Height above Q is $6,6 - 1,5 = 5,1\ m$ above point Q

Method 3: Using equations of motion

$v_f{}^2 = v_i{}^2 + 2a\Delta x$

$0 = 10^2 + 2(-9,8)(\Delta x)$

$\therefore \Delta x = 5,1\ \text{m}$ (3)

13.2 In an **isolated system** mechanical energy remains constant. (2)

13.3 **Method 1: Using conservation of Energy and taking Q as zero height**

$E_{M_{bef}} = E_{M_{aft}} + W_f$

$\therefore \left(E_p + E_k\right)_{bef} = \left(E_p + E_k\right)_{aft} + 0$

$\therefore mgh + \frac{1}{2}mv^2 = mgh + \frac{1}{2}mv^2 \rightarrow$ note that you can divide both sides by m

$\therefore 0 + 0,5(0,5)(10)^2 = 0,5(9,8)(2) + 0,5(0,5)v^2 \rightarrow$ the branches are 2m above Q

$\therefore v = 7,80\ m.s^{-1}$

Method 2: Using conservation of Energy and taking ground as zero height

$E_{M_{bef}} = E_{M_{aft}} + W_f$

$\therefore \left(E_p + E_k\right)_{bef} = \left(E_p + E_k\right)_{aft} + 0$

$\therefore mgh + \frac{1}{2}mv^2 = mgh + \frac{1}{2}mv^2 \rightarrow$ note that you can divide both sides by m

$\therefore 0,5(9,8)(1,5) + 0,5(0,5)(10)^2 = 0,5(9,8)(3,5) + 0,5(0,5)v^2$

$\therefore v = 7,80\ m.s^{-1}$ (5)

13.4 **Method 1: Using the work energy theorem**

$W_{net} = \Delta E_k$

$\therefore -W_b - F_g = \frac{1}{2}m\left(v_f{}^2 - v_i{}^2\right)$

$\therefore -W_b = \frac{1}{2}m\left(v_f{}^2 - v_i{}^2\right) + F_g$

$\therefore -W_b = \frac{1}{2}m\left(v_f{}^2 - v_i{}^2\right) + mgh$

$\therefore -W_b = 0,5(0,5)\left(5^2 - 7,8^2\right) + 0,5(9,8)(0,1) \rightarrow$ the ball moved 0,1m up in the branches

$\therefore W_b = 8,47$ J

Method 2: Using conservation of energy principles

$W_{branches} = E_{M_{before\ the\ branches}} - E_{M_{after\ the\ branches}}$

$= \left(E_p + E_k\right)_b - \left(E_p + E_k\right)_a$

$= \left(mgh + \frac{1}{2}mv^2\right)_b - \left(mgh + \frac{1}{2}mv^2\right)_b$

$= 0,5(9,8)(3,5) + 0,5(0,5)(7,8)^2 - 0,5(9,8)(3,6) - 0,5(0,5)(5)^2$

$= 8,47$ J (4)

13.5 **Method 1: Using conservation of Energy and taking ground as zero height**

$E_{M_{bef}} = E_{Maft} + W_f$

$\therefore \left(E_p + E_k\right)_{bef} = \left(E_p + E_k\right)_{aft} + 0$

$\therefore mgh + \frac{1}{2}mv^2 = mgh + \frac{1}{2}mv^2 \rightarrow$ note that you can divide both sides by m

$\therefore 0,5(9,8)(3,6) + 0,5(0,5)(5)^2 = 0,5(9,8)h + 0 \rightarrow$ at max height $v = 0$

$\therefore$ h = 4,88 m above the ground

$\therefore$ She can't catch the ball as she is 5m above the ground

Method 2: Using equations of motion

$0 = 5^2 + 2(-9,8)(\Delta x) \rightarrow v_f{}^2 = v_i^2 + 2a\Delta x$

$\therefore \Delta x = 1,28$ m

$\therefore$ max height above the ground $= 1,28 + 3,6 = 4,88$ m above the ground

$\therefore$ She can't catch the ball as she is 5m above the ground

[20]

TOC | 1 Data Sheet | 2 Definitions | 3 | 3 solutions | 4 | 4 solutions | 5 | 5 solutions | 6 | 6 solutions | 7 | 7 solutions | 8 | 8 solutions | 9 | 9 solutions | 10 | 10 solutions

Question 14

14.1 $\Delta E_k = \frac{1}{2}m\left(v_f^{\,2} - v_i^{\,2}\right)$

$\therefore 4000 = \frac{1}{2}(20)\left(v_f^{\,2} - 0\right)$

$\therefore v_f = 20\,\text{m.s}^{-1}$ (3)

14.2 $E_{M_{bef}} = E_{M_{aft}} + W_f$

$\therefore \left(E_p + E_k\right)_{bef} = \left(E_p + E_k\right)_{aft} + 0$

$\therefore E_p + E_k = mgh + E_k$

$\therefore 0 + 4000 = 20(9,8)h + 0 \rightarrow$ at max height $v = 0$

$\therefore h = 20,41\text{ m}$ (4)

14.3

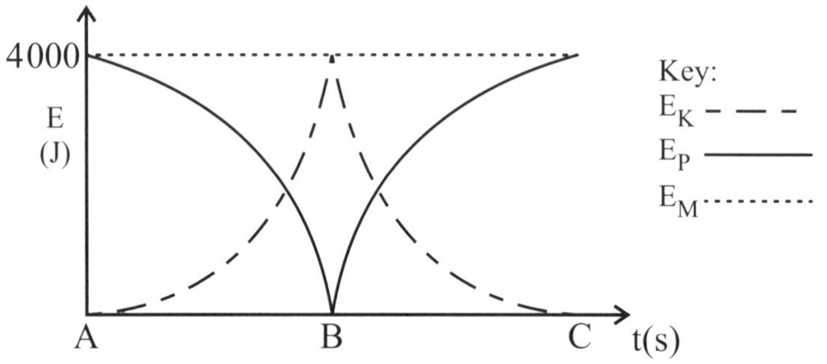

Marks awarded:
Correct shape of graphs
E_M constant
Axes labelled correctly
When kinetic energy is zero potential energy is 4 000 J and vice versa

(6)

[18]

Question 15

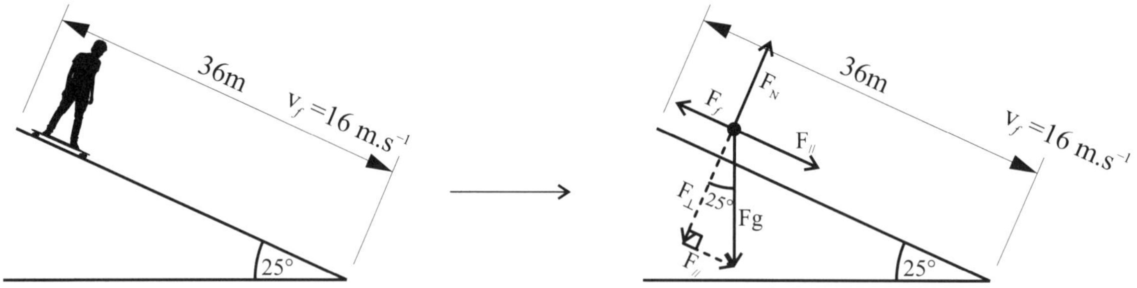

15.1 The work done by a net force on an object is equal to the change in the kinetic energy of the object. (2)

15.2 $F_{net} = F_{//} - F_f$

$= F_g \sin 25^\circ - 60$

$= 80(9,8)\sin 25^\circ - 60$

$= 271,33$ N down the plane (4)

15.3 $W_{net} = \Delta E_k$

$F_{net}\Delta x = \frac{1}{2}m\left(v_f^{\,2} - v_i^{\,2}\right)$

$(271,33)(36) = \frac{1}{2}(80)\left(16^2 - v_i^{\,2}\right)$

$v_i^{\,2} = 11,8$

$v_i = 3,44\,\text{m.s}^{-1}$ down the slope (7)

[13]

Question 16

16.1 $p_{bef} = p_{aft}$

$$(m_1 + m_2)v_i = m_1 v_{1f} + m_2 v_{2f}$$

$$\therefore (50+45)(4) = (45)(-3{,}5) + 50v_{2_f}$$

$$v_{2f} = 10{,}75 \text{ m.s}^{-1}$$ (1)

16.2 Law of conservation of linear momentum. The total linear momentum of an isolated system remains constant (is conserved). (3)

16.3

$$F_{net} = \frac{\Delta p}{\Delta t}$$

$$= \frac{m(v_f - v_i)}{\Delta t}$$

$$= \frac{(50)(0-10{,}75)}{0{,}8}$$

$$= -671{,}88$$

$$= 671{,}88 \text{ N}$$ (2)

16.4 The padding in the helmet increase the time taken to come to rest.

$F_{net}\ \alpha \frac{1}{\Delta t}$ since mass and change in momentum is constant.

If time increases the force exerted on Adam's will decrease. (4)

[10]

Question 17

17.1 No, there is an external force of friction. (1)

17.2

$$E_{M_A} = E_p + E_k$$

$$= mgh + E_k$$

$$= 50(9{,}8)(3)$$

$$= 1470 \text{ J}$$ (3)

17.3

$$E_{M_C} = 1470 - 600$$

$$= 870 \text{ J}$$ (2)

17.4

$$E_{M_C} = E_p + E_k$$

$$870 = mgh + \frac{1}{2}mv^2$$

$$870 = 50(9{,}8)(1) + \frac{1}{2}(50)v^2$$

$$v = 3.9 \text{m.s}^{-1}$$ (4)

[10]

Question 18

18.1 $p_{bef} = p_{aft}$

$$m_1 v_{1i} + m_2 v_{2i} = m_1 v_{1f} + m_2 v_{2f}$$

$$\therefore (2\times10^{-3})(1000) + 0 = (2\times10^{-3})(200) + 0{,}5v_{2_f}$$

$v_{2f} = 3{,}2 \text{ m.s}^{-1}$ right (5)

18.2 $W_{net} = \Delta E_k$

$$-W_f = \frac{1}{2}m\left(v_f^{\ 2} - v_i^{\ 2}\right)$$
$$-F_f \Delta x = \frac{1}{2}(0,5)\left(0^2 - 3,2^2\right)$$
$$-F_f(0,4) = -2,56$$

$F_f = 6,4$ N $\rightarrow$ don't put direction as the question asked for magnitude (5)

[10]

Question 19

19.1 $E_{M_{bef}} = E_{M_{aft}} + W_f$

$$\left(E_p + E_k\right)_{bef} = \left(E_p + E_k\right)_{aft} + 0$$
$$mgh + \frac{1}{2}mv^2 = mgh + \frac{1}{2}mv^2$$
$$0 + \frac{1}{2}mv^2 = m(9,8)\left(15\times10^{-2}\right) \rightarrow \text{divide both sides by } m$$

$v = 1,71\text{m.s}^{-1}$ right (5)

19.2 $p_{bef} = p_{aft}$

$$m_1v_{1i} + m_2v_{1i} = (m_1 + m_2)v_f$$
$$\left(1\times10^{-3}\right)v_{1i} + 0 = \left(101\times10^{-3}\right)(1,71)$$

$v_{1i} = 172,71\text{ m.s}^{-1} \rightarrow v_{1i} = 173,18\text{ m.s}^{-1}$ without any rounding (4)

[9]

Question 20

20.1 According to the law of conservation of momentum, total momentum must be conserved. By throwing the toolkit to the right, the astronaut's velocity must decrease. If the velocity of the toolkit is large enough, the velocity of the astronaut will be to the left for momentum to remain constant. (2)

20.2 First calculate the velocity required by the astronaut to make it back in time:

$$v = \frac{\Delta x}{t} = \frac{12}{60} = 0,2\text{m.s}^{-1}\text{ left}$$

$$p_{bef} = p_{aft}$$
$$(m_1 + m_2)v_i = m_1v_{1f} + m_2v_{2f}$$
$$(80 + 65)(3) = (80)(-0,2) + (65)v_{2f}$$

$v_{2f} = 6,94\text{ m.s}^{-1}$ right (8)

[10]

Question 21

21.1 In the absence of air resistance or any external forces, the mechanical energy of an object is constant. (2)

21.2 Measurement 4. (1)

21.3 Due to conservation of mechanical energy potential energy at the top of the slope is equal to the kinetic energy at the bottom of the incline.

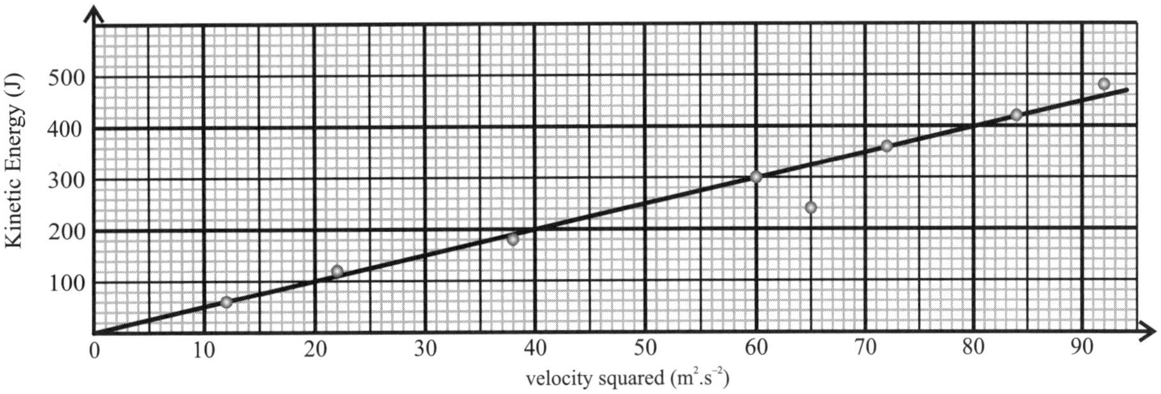

(4)

21.4 $y = \dfrac{400-100}{80-20} \rightarrow$ values from the given table must not be used

$= 5\,\text{kg}$ (4)

21.5 $E_k = \dfrac{1}{2}mv^2 \rightarrow y = mx + c$

gradient $= \dfrac{1}{2}m$

$5 = \dfrac{1}{2}m$

$m = 10\,\text{kg}$

$E_p = mgh$

$60 = (10)(g)(2) \rightarrow$ any value for E_p from the table could be used

$g = 3\,\text{m.s}^{-2}$ (6)

[17]

Question 22

22.1 $E_p = mgh$

$= \left(5 + 20\times10^{-3}\right)(9,8)\left(12\times10^{-2}\right)$

$= 5,9\,\text{J}$ (3)

22.2 $E_{k_{bottom}} = E_{p_{top}}$

$\dfrac{1}{2}mv^2 = 5,9$

$\dfrac{1}{2}\left(5 + 20\times10^{-3}\right)v^2 = 5,9$

$v = 1,53\,\text{m.s}^{-1}$ (4)

22.3 $p_{bef} = p_{aft}$

$m_1 v_{1i} + m_2 v_{1i} = (m_1 + m_2)v_f$

$\left(20\times10^{-3}\right)v_{1i} + 0 = \left(5 + 20\times10^{-3}\right)(1,53)$

$v_{1i} = 384,03\,\text{m.s}^{-1}$ (4)

[17]

TOC | 1 Data Sheet | 2 Definitions | 3 | 3 solutions | 4 | 4 solutions | 5 | 5 solutions | 6 | 6 solutions | 7 | 7 solutions | 8 | 8 solutions | 9 | 9 solutions | 10 | 10 solutions

Question 23

23.1 $p_{bef} = p_{aft}$

$m_1v_{1i} + m_2v_{1i} = (m_1 + m_2)v_f$

$(100)(4) + (220)(0) = (100 + 220)v_f$

$v_f = 1,25 \text{ m.s}^{-1}$ (4)

23.2 The total linear momentum of an isolated system remains constant. (2)

23.3 $p_{bef} = p_{aft}$

$m_1v_{1i} + m_2v_{1i} = m_1v_{1f} + m_2v_{2f}$

$(320)v_{1i} + (320)(0) = (320)(6,25) + (320)(1)$

$v_{1i} = 7,25 \text{ m.s}^{-1}$ right

$\text{W}_{net} = \Delta E_k$

$\text{W}_g - \text{W}_f = \frac{1}{2}m\left(v_f^{\ 2} - v_i^{\ 2}\right)$

$mgh - 1250 = \frac{1}{2}(320)\left(7,25^2 - 1,25^2\right)$

$h = \frac{9410}{9,8(320)}$

$= 3\text{m}$ (7)

[13]

Question 24

$\text{P}_{output} = 500(0,7)$

$= 350 \text{ W}$

$\text{W}_m = \text{Pt}$

$= 350(10 \times 60)$

$= 210 \times 10^3 \text{ J}$

$\text{W}_{net} = \Delta E_k$

$\text{W}_m - \text{W}_g = \frac{1}{2}m\left(v_f^{\ 2} - v_i^{\ 2}\right)$

$210 \times 10^3 - mgh = \frac{1}{2}m\left(3^2 - 0^2\right)$

$210 \times 10^3 = 4,5m + m(9,8)(10)$

$m = 2048,78 \text{kg}$

$\therefore 2048,78$ litres of water in 10 minutes **[8]**

Question 25 (2014 IEB Final Examination)

25.1 The product of the mass and velocity of an object. (2)

25.2 $\Delta p = m\left(v_f - v_i\right)$

$-1,5 = 0,25\left(v_f - 4\right)$

$= -2$

$= 2 \text{m.s}^{-1}$ left (5)

25.3 $p_{before} = p_{after}$

$$m_1v_{1i} + m_2v_{2i} = m_1v_{1f} + m_2v_{2f}$$
$$(0,25)(4)+(0,3)(-6)=(0,25)(-2)+0,3v_{2f}$$
$$v_{2f} = -1$$
$$= 1\,\text{m.s}^{-1}\text{ left}$$ (5)

[12]

Question 26 (2015 IEB Supplementary Examination)

26.1.1 distance = area under graph

$$= \left(\frac{1}{2}\times 1,4\times 2\right)+(1\times 1,4)$$
$$= 2,8\,\text{m}$$ (4)

26.1.2 $\Delta p = m(v_f - v_i)$

$$= 21000(2-5)$$
$$= -63\,000$$
$$= 63\,000\,\text{kg.m.s}^{-1}$$ (4)

26.1.3 $F_{net} = \dfrac{\Delta p}{\Delta t}$

$$= \frac{-63\,000}{1,4}$$
$$= 45\,000\,\text{N in the opposite direction to motion}$$ (5)

26.1.4 $\Delta p = m(v_f - v_i)$

$$63\,000 = m(3-1)$$
$$m = 31500\,\text{kg}$$ (4)

26.2.1 $E_p = mgh$

$$= 21000 \times 9,8 \times 8$$
$$= 1646\,400\,\text{J}$$ (3)

26.2.2 $F_A = mg\sin\theta + F_f$

$$= 21000(9,8)\sin 20^\circ + 21\times 10^3$$
$$= 91387,75\,\text{N}$$ (5)

26.2.3 $P = Fv$

$$= 91387,75(1,4)$$
$$= 127\,942,84\,\text{W}$$ (4)

26.2.4 The cable must do work again gravity as well friction. A portion of the work done by the cable is the work done against friction and the rest is the work done against gravity. (2)

[30]

Question 27 (2016 IEB Final Examination)

27.1.1 The total linear momentum of an isolated system remains constant. (2)

27.1.2 $p_{before} = p_{after}$

$$m_1v_{1i} + m_2v_{2i} = m_1v_{1f} + m_2v_{2f}$$
$$(1,2)(8)+0=(1,2)(4)+0,5v_{2f}$$
$$v_{2f} = 9,6\,\text{m.s}^{-1}$$ (4)

27.1.3
$$\Delta p = m\left(v_f - v_i\right)$$
$$= 1{,}2(4-8)$$
$$= -4{,}8$$
$$= 4{,}8\,\text{kg.m.s}^{-1}\ \text{West}$$
(4)

27.1.4
$$F_{net} = \frac{\Delta p}{\Delta t}$$
$$= \frac{4{,}8}{1{,}5\times10^{-3}}$$
$$= 3\,200\,\text{N}$$
(4)

27.2.1
$$E_k = \frac{1}{2}mv^2$$
$$= \frac{1}{2}(70)(1{,}5)^2$$
$$= 7875\,\text{J}$$
(3)

27.2.2
$$E_p = mgh$$
$$= (70)(9{,}8)(30)$$
$$= 20\,580\,\text{J}$$
(3)

27.2.3
$$W_f = F_f\Delta x$$
$$= 12(450)$$
$$= 5\,400\,\text{J}$$
(3)

27.2.4 Method 1:
$$E_{M_{top}} = E_{M_{bot}} + W_f$$
$$\left(E_p + E_k\right)_{top} = \left(E_p + E_k\right)_{aft} + W_f$$
$$20580 + 7875 = 0 + \frac{1}{2}(70)v^2 + 5400$$
$$v^2 = 658{,}71$$
$$v = 25{,}67\,\text{m.s}^{-1}$$

Method 2:
$$W_{net} = \Delta E_k$$
$$W_g - W_f = \frac{1}{2}m\left(v_f^2 - v_i^2\right)$$
$$20580 - 5400 = \frac{1}{2}(70)\left(v_f^2 - 15^2\right)$$
$$v_f^2 = 658{,}71$$
$$v = 25{,}67\,\text{m.s}^{-1}$$
(4)

[27]

Question 28 (2016 IEB Supplementary Examination)

28.1.1
$$\Delta p = m\left(v_f - v_i\right)$$
$$= 2\,500(0-25)$$
$$= -62\,500$$
$$= 62\,500\,\text{kg.m.s}^{-1}$$
(3)

28.1.2 The work done by a net force on an object is equal to the change in the kinetic energy of the object. (2)

28.1.3
$$-W_{net} = \Delta E_k$$
$$-F_{net}\Delta x = \Delta E_k$$
$$-F_{net}(1{,}8) = \frac{1}{2}(2\,500)\left(0 - 25^2\right)$$
$$F_{net} = 434\,027{,}78\,\text{N}$$ in opposite direction of motion
(4)

28.1.4 $\Delta t = \frac{\Delta p}{F_{net}}$

$= \frac{62\,500}{434\,027,78}$

$= 0,14\,s$ (3)

28.1.5 $F_{net}\ \alpha \frac{1}{\Delta t}$ as impulse remains constant.

If the truck stops instantly the time taken will decrease.
If time decreases the force acting on the driver will increase.
A larger force increases the chance of possible injury to the driver. (4)

28.2.1 The law of conservation of linear momentum (2)

28.2.2 $p_{before} = p_{after}$

$m_1 v_{1i} + m_2 v_{2i} = m_1 v_{1f} + m_2 v_{2f}$

$(1084)(33) + (3437)(-28) = (1084)(-5) + 3437 v_{2f}$

$v_{2f} = -16,02$

$= 16,02\,m.s^{-1}$ West (5)

28.2.3 A collision in which both momentum and kinetic energy are conserved. (2)

28.2.4 $E_{k_{bef}} = \frac{1}{2}m_1 v_1^2 + \frac{1}{2}m_2 v_2^2$

$= \frac{1}{2}(1084)(33)^2 + \frac{1}{2}(3437)(-28)^2$

$= 1\,937\,542\,J$

$E_{k_{aft}} = \frac{1}{2}m_1 v_1^2 + \frac{1}{2}m_2 v_2^2$

$= \frac{1}{2}(1084)(-5)^2 + \frac{1}{2}(3437)(-16,02)^2$

$= 454\,587\,J$

Collision is inelastic as kinetic energy is not conserved. (5)

[30]

Question 29 (2017 IEB Final Examination)

29.1.1 The force that opposes the motion of an object and acts parallel to the surface with which the object is in contact. (2)

29.1.2 $E_k = \frac{1}{2}mv^2$

$= \frac{1}{2}(2)(1,5)^2$

$= 2,25\,J$ (3)

29.1.3 $-W_f = F_f \Delta x$

$-W_f = (26)(0,7)$

$W_f = -18,2$

$= 18,2\,J$ (3)

29.1.4 The work done by a net force on an object is equal to the change in the kinetic energy of the object. (2)

29.1.5 $W_{net} = \Delta E_k$

$W_f = \frac{1}{2}m\left(v_f^2 - v_i^2\right)$

$-18,2 = \frac{1}{2}(2)\left(1,5^2 - v_i^2\right)$

$v_i = 4,52\,m.s^{-1}$ (4)

29.2.1 In the absence of air resistance or any external forces, the mechanical energy of an object is constant. (2)

29.2.2 $E_{M_{bot}} = E_{M_{top}} + W_f$

$\frac{1}{2}mv^2 + mgh = \frac{1}{2}mv^2 + mgh + 0$

$\frac{1}{2}(1,2)v^2 + 0 = 0 + (1,2)(9,8)(0,65)$

$v = 3,57\,\text{m.s}^{-1}$ (4)

29.2.3 The total linear momentum of an isolated system remains constant (is conserved). (2)

29.2.4 $p_{before} = p_{after}$

$m_1v_{1i} + m_2v_{2i} = m_1v_{1f} + m_2v_{2f}$

$(0,4)v_{1i} + 0 = 0,4(-0,36) + 1,2(3,57)$

$v_{1i} = 10,35\,\text{m.s}^{-1}$ (4)

[26]

Question 30 (2017 IEB Supplementary Examination)

30.1 $F_{upward} = 2T\sin 65^\circ$

$= 2(7\,000)\sin 65^\circ$

$= 12\,688,31\,\text{N}$ (3)

30.2 The single vector which has the same effect as the original vectors acting together. (2)

30.3 $F_{net} = F_{upward} - F_g$

$4\,000 = 12\,688,31 - m(9,8)$

$m = 886,56\,\text{kg}$ (5)

30.4 The work done by a net force on an object is equal to the change in the kinetic energy of the object. (2)

30.5 $W_{net} = \Delta E_k$

$= \frac{1}{2}(m)(v_f^2 - v_i^2)$

$= \frac{1}{2}(320)(19^2 - 0^2)$

$= 57\,760\,\text{J}$ (3)

30.6 $E_{mech} = \Delta E_p + \Delta E_k$

$= (320)(9,8)(25) + 57\,760$

$= 136160\,\text{J}$ (5)

30.7 The work done by the applied force is equal to the increase in the capsule's mechanical energy

$W_A = F_A\Delta x$

$136160 = F_A(25)$

$F_A = 5\,446,4\,\text{N}$ (4)

30.8 $E_{M_{bot}} = E_{M_{top}} + W_f$

$\frac{1}{2}mv^2 + mgh = \frac{1}{2}mv^2 + mgh + 0$

$\frac{1}{2}(320)(19)^2 + 320(9,8)(25) = 0 + (320)(9,8)h$

$h = 43,42\,\text{m}$ (4)

30.9

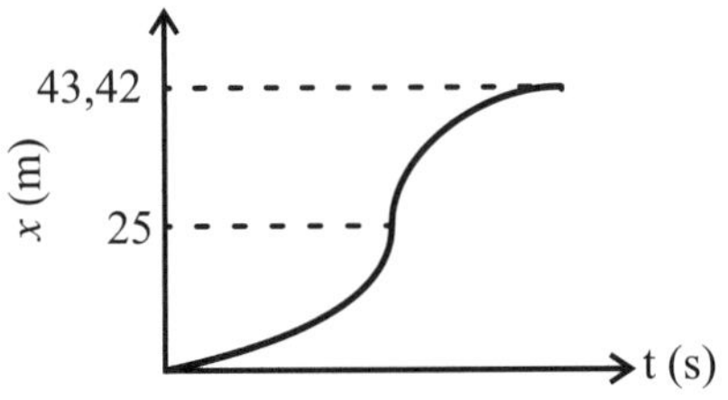

(4)

[32]

Question 31 (2018 IEB Final Examination)

31.1.1 Velocity is the slope of a displacement time graph:

$$v = \frac{10,2-4,8}{5-2}$$
$$= 1,8\,\text{m.s}^{-1}$$ (3)

31.1.2 Newton's 3rd law (2)

31.1.3
$$p_{before} = p_{after}$$
$$m_1 v_{1i} + m_2 v_{2i} = (m_1 + m_2) v_f$$
$$(0,9)(2,4) + 0 = (0,9 + m)(1,8)$$
$$m = 0,3\,\text{kg}$$ (4)

31.1.4 Momentum is a vector and the velocity of *m* has no horizontal component. (2)

31.2.1 In the absence of air resistance or any external forces, the mechanical energy of an object is constant. (3)

31.2.2 Method 1:
$$E_{M_{top}} = E_{M_{bot}}$$
$$\frac{1}{2}mv^2 + mgh = \frac{1}{2}mv^2 + mgh$$
$$0 + 600(9,8)(3,5) = \frac{1}{2}(600)v^2 + 0$$
$$v = 8,28\,\text{m.s}^{-1}$$

Method 2:
$$v_f^2 = v_i^2 + 2a\Delta x$$
$$= 0 + 2(9,8)(3,5)$$
$$= 8,28\,\text{m.s}^{-1}$$ (2)

31.2.3 The work done by a net force on an object is equal to the change in the kinetic energy of the object. (3)

31.2.4 Method 1:
$$\text{W}_{net} = \Delta \text{E}_k$$
$$\text{F}_{net}\Delta x = \frac{1}{2}(m)\left(v_f^2 - v_i^2\right)$$
$$\text{F}_{net}(0,16) = \frac{1}{2}(600)\left(0 - 8,28^2\right)$$
$$\text{F}_{net} = \frac{1}{2}(600)\left(0 - 8,28^2\right)$$
$$= -128\,547$$
$$= 128\,547\,\text{N}$$

Method 2:
$$v_f^2 = v_i^2 + 2a\Delta x$$
$$0 = 8,28^2 + 2a(0,16)$$
$$a = -214,25\,\text{m.s}^{-1}$$
$$\text{F}_{net} = ma$$
$$= 600(-214,25)$$
$$= -128\,547$$
$$= 128\,547\,\text{N}$$ (4)

31.2.5
$$\text{P} = \frac{\text{W}_g}{t}$$
$$\text{P} = \frac{\text{mgh}}{t}$$
$$180 = \frac{600(9,8)(3,5)}{t}$$
$$t = 114,33\,\text{s}$$ (4)

[27]

TOC 1 Data Sheet 2 Definitions 3 3 solutions 4 4 solutions 5 5 solutions 6 6 solutions 7 7 solutions 8 8 solutions 9 9 solutions 10 10 solutions

TOC 1 Data Sheet 2 Definitions 3 3 solutions 4 4 solutions 5 5 solutions 6 6 solutions 7 7 solutions 8 8 solutions 9 9 solutions 10 10 solutions

Question 32 (2015 IEB Final Examination)

32.1 An object continues in a state of rest or uniform (moving with constant) velocity unless it is acted upon by a net or resultant force. (2)

32.2 When the engine fires, it produces a force on the gases. By Newton III, the gases exert a force equal in magnitude but opposite in direction on the rocket. This causes a resultant force to act on the rocket and by Newton II, it will accelerate the rocket in the direction of the net force. (3)

32.3 The total linear momentum of an isolated system remains constant (is conserved). (2)

32.4 $p_{before} = p_{after}$

$m_1 v_{1i} = m_1 v_{1f} + m_2 v_{2f}$

$m(1000) = \frac{2}{3}mv + \frac{1}{3}m(-500) \rightarrow$ divide both sides by m

$v = 1750\ \text{m.s}^{-1}$

(5)

[12]

Question 33 (2015 IEB Final Examination)

33.1 The energy an object has as a result of the object's motion. (2)

33.2

$$\Delta E_k = \frac{1}{2}mv^2$$
$$= \frac{1}{2}(10)(12)^2$$
$$= 720\ \text{J}$$

(3)

33.3 The work done by a net force on an object is equal to the change in the kinetic energy of the object. (2)

33.4 $W_{net} = \Delta E_k$

$F_f \Delta x = \frac{1}{2}(m)(v_f^2 - v_i^2)$

$(-54{,}9)(6) = \frac{1}{2}(10)(v^2 - 12^2)$

$v^2 = 78{,}12$

$v = 8{,}84\ \text{m.s}^{-1}$

(4)

33.5 $\sin 35^\circ = \frac{h}{x}$

$h = x \sin 35^\circ$

$E_p = mgh$

$= (10)(9{,}8)x \sin 35^\circ$

$= 56{,}21x$

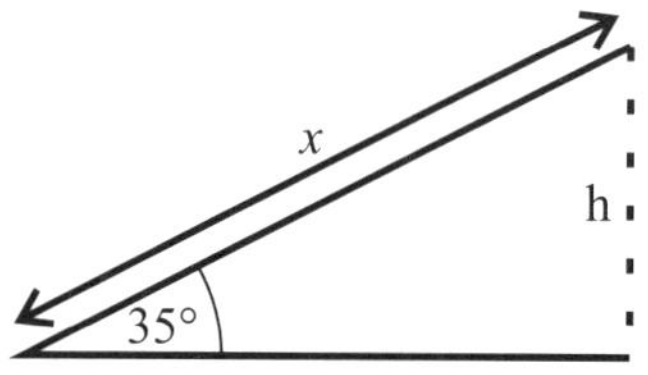

(2)

33.6 Method 1:

$E_{M_B} = E_{M_C} + W_f$

$E_{p_B} + E_{k_B} = E_{p_C} + E_{k_C} + W_f$

$0 + \frac{1}{2}mv^2 = E_{p_C} + 0 + W_f$

$\frac{1}{2}(10)(8{,}84)^2 = 56{,}21x + 45x$

$x = 3{,}86\ \text{m}$

Method 2:

$W_{net} = \Delta E_k$

$-W_g - W_f = \Delta E_k$

$-56{,}21x - 45x = \frac{1}{2}(10)(0 - 8{,}84^2)$

$-101{,}21x = -390{,}728$

$x = 3{,}86\ \text{m}$

(5)

33.7 $F_f = \mu F_N$

$F_N = mg\cos\theta$

As θ increases, the normal force decreases.

If the normal force decreases the force of friction also decreases. (3)

33.8

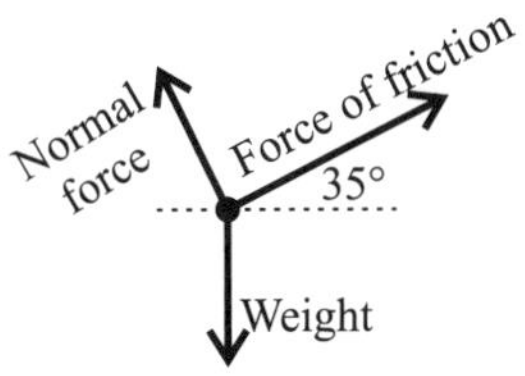

(3)

33.9 $F_f = F_{g//}$

$= mg\sin\theta$

$= 10(9,8)\sin 35^\circ$

$= 56,21\,\text{N}$ (3)

33.10 $F_f = \mu F_N$

$56,21 = \mu mg\cos\theta$

$56,21 = \mu 10(9,8)\cos 35^\circ$

$\mu = 0,7\,\text{N}$ (3)

33.11 Static friction is greater than kinetic friction. (2)

Question 34 (2018 IEB Supplementary Examination)

34.1.1 The total linear momentum of an isolated system remains constant (is conserved). (2)

34.1.2 $p_{before} = p_{after}$

$m_1v_{1i} + m_2v_{2i} = (m_1 + m_2)v_f$

$(0,005)(200) + 0 = (0,195 + 0,005)v_f$

$v_f = 5\,\text{m.s}^{-1}$ (4)

34.1.3 $E_{M_{before}} = E_{M_{after}}$

$(E_p + E_k)_{before} = (E_p + E_k)_{after}$

$0 + \frac{1}{2}mv^2 = mgh + 0$

$\frac{1}{2}(0,2)(5)^2 = (0,2)(9,8)h + 0$

$h = 1,28\,\text{m}$ (4)

34.2.1

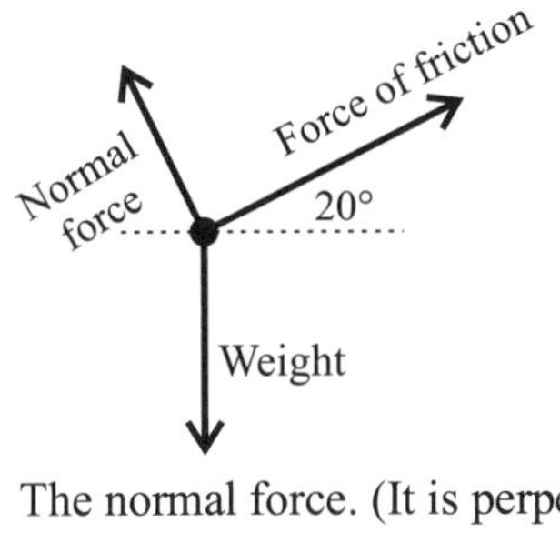

(3)

34.2.2 The normal force. (It is perpendicular to the direction of motion) (2)

34.2.3 $\Delta E_k = \frac{1}{2}mv^2$

$= \frac{1}{2}(70)(4)^2$

$= 560\,\text{J}$ (3)

34.2.4 $F_{net} = mg\sin\theta - F_f$

$= (70)(9,8)\sin 20^\circ - 190$

$= 44,63\,\text{N}$ (3)

34.2.5 The work done by a net force on an object is equal to the change in the kinetic energy of the object. (2)

34.2.6 $W_{net} = \Delta E_k$

$F_{net}\Delta x = E_{k_{final}} - E_{k_{initial}}$

$F_{net}\Delta x = \frac{1}{2}mv_f^2 - E_{k_{initial}}$

$(44,63)(18) = \frac{1}{2}(70)v_f^2 - 560$

$v_f^2 = 38,95$

$v = 6,24\,\text{m.s}^{-1}$ (5)

[28]

Question 35 (2019 IEB Supplementary Examination)

35.1.1 The work done by a net force on an object is equal to the change in the kinetic energy of the object. (2)

35.1.2 $W_{net} = \Delta E_k$

$F_{net}\Delta x = \Delta E_k$

$F_{net} = \frac{\Delta E_k}{\Delta x} \rightarrow$ gradient (slope) of the graph (3)

35.1.3 $C: F_{net} = \frac{180-88}{15-10}$

$= 18,4\text{ N}$ (4)

35.1.4 $F_f = F_A - F_{net}$

$= 20 - 18,4$

$= 1,6\text{ N}$ (3)

35.1.5 B (2)

35.1.6 The net force is smallest when the force of friction is largest. B has the smallest gradient which means that it has the smallest net force. (4)

35.1.7 $F_{net} = \frac{60-0}{5-0}$

$= 12\text{ N}$

$12 = m(1)$

$m = 12\text{ kg}$ (4)

35.2.1 The rate at which work is done or the rate at which energy is transferred. (2)

35.2.2 $v = 60 \div 3,6$

$= 16,67\,\text{m.s}^{-1}$ (2)

35.2.3 The engine of the car converts energy at a rate of 60000 Joules per second (2)

35.2.4 $P = Fv$

$60\,000 = F(16,67)$

$F = 3600\text{ N}$ (3)

35.3 $p_{before} = p_{after}$

$m_1v_{1i} + m_2v_{2i} = (m_1 + m_2)v_f$

$(1500)(19,44) + 0 = (1500 + m_2)(7)$

$m_2 = 2\,665,71\text{ kg}$ (4)

[32]

Question 36 (2019 IEB Final Examination)

36.1.1 Velocity (2)

36.1.2

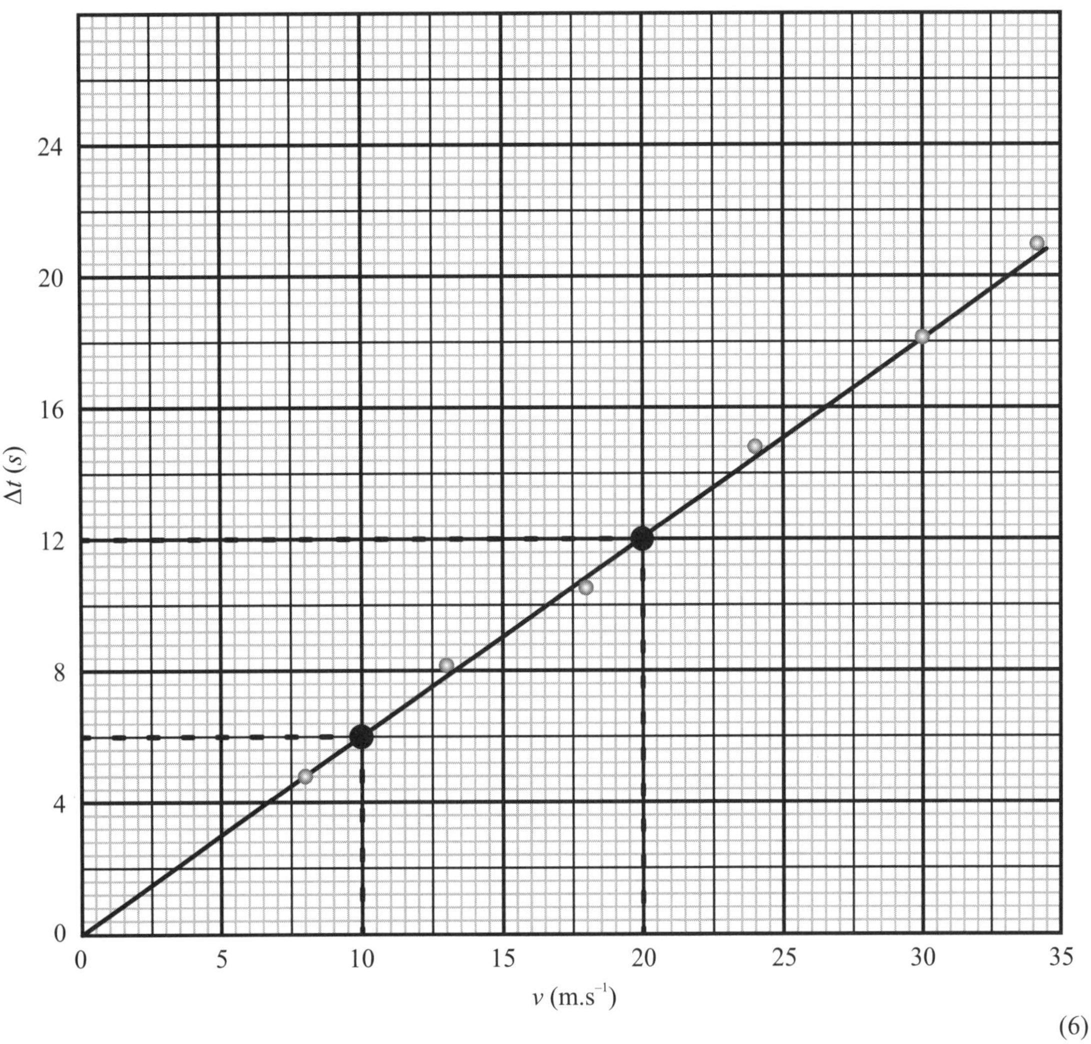

(6)

36.1.3 $\text{Gradient} = \frac{\Delta y}{\Delta x}$

$= \frac{12-6}{20-10} \rightarrow$ points must lie on the line of best fit

$= 0,6\ s^2.m^{-1} \rightarrow$ any answer between 0,57 and 0,66 is acceptable (5)

36.1.4 $F_{net}\ \Delta t = m\Delta v$

$F_{net}\ \Delta t = m(0-v)$

$\Delta t = -\frac{m}{F_{net}}v$ (1)

36.1.5 $\text{Gradient} = -\frac{m}{F_{net}}$

$0,6 = -\frac{m}{-140}$

$m = 86\ kg$ (3)

TOC 1 Data Sheet 2 Definitions 3 3 solutions 4 4 solutions 5 5 solutions 6 6 solutions 7 7 solutions 8 8 solutions 9 9 solutions 10 10 solutions

36.2.1 The energy an object has as a result of the object's motion. (2)

36.2.2 At the bottom:

$$E_k = \frac{1}{2}mv^2$$
$$= \frac{1}{2}(60)(7,5)^2$$
$$= 1687,5\text{ J}$$

(3)

36.2.3 At the top:

$$E_p = mgh$$
$$= (60)(9,8)(2,8)$$
$$= 1646,4\text{ J}$$

(3)

36.2.4

$$W_f = E_{k_{bot}} - E_{p_{top}}$$
$$= 1687,5 - 1646,4$$
$$= 41,1\text{ J}$$

(2)

36.2.5 First calculate the distance (Δx) that the cart moves up the slope:

$$\sin 25^\circ = \frac{2,8}{\Delta x}$$
$$\Delta x = 6,63\text{ m}$$
$$W_f = F_f \Delta x$$
$$41,1 = F_f(6,63)$$
$$F_f = 6,20\text{ N}$$

(4)

[31]

7. ELECTRIC CIRCUITS

AMMETERS AND VOLTMETERS:

Ammeters	Voltmeters
• Measures current strength (I) • Units are amperes (A) • Have negligible resistance • Must be connected in series	• Measures potential difference (V) • Units are volts (V) • Have very high resistance so that the current flowing through them is negligible • Must be connected in parallel

To convert millivolts (mV) or (mA) to volts or amperes divide by 1000 or multiply by 10^{-3}.

RESISTORS IN SERIES AND PARALLEL:

Series

If resistors are connected so that there is only **one path** which the current can take, then the resistors are connected in **series**.

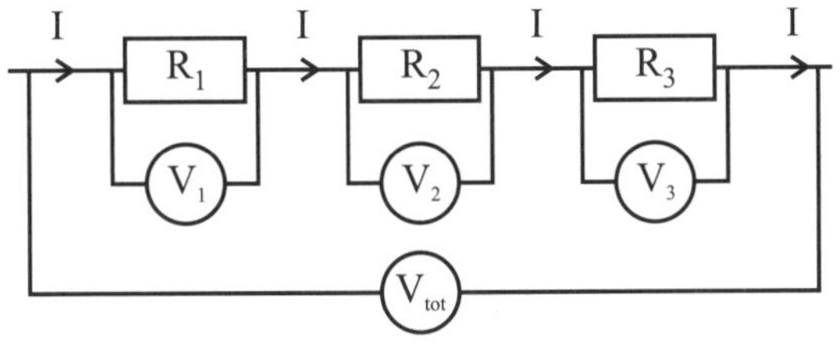

- Current in series is constant
- $V_{total} = V_1 + V_2 + V_3$
- $R_{total} = R_1 + R_2 + R_3$

Resistors in series are voltage dividers.

Parallel

If resistors are connected so that there is **more than one path** which the current can take, then the resistors are connected in **parallel**.

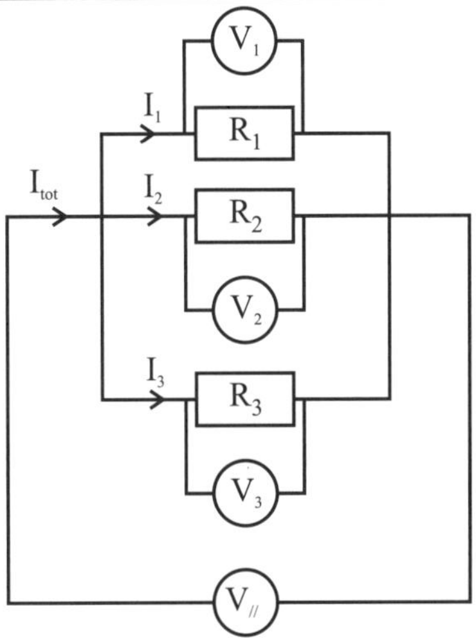

- Current in parallel divides
  $I_{total} = I_1 + I_2 + I_3$
- $V_{//} = V_1 = V_2 = V_3$
- $\frac{1}{R_{//}} = \frac{1}{R_1} + \frac{1}{R_2} + \frac{1}{R_3}$
- The total resistance of a parallel combination of resistors is always less than the smallest resistor in parallel.
- For n **identical** resistors of resistance R connected in parallel, the parallel resistance will be:

  $$R_{//} = \frac{1}{n} \times R$$

- If all resistors in parallel are identical the current will divide equally in each branch.

Resistors in parallel are current dividers.

<u>**Circuit Calculation Tips**</u>:

1) Fill in all information and values you calculate in pencil on the diagram.
2) Don't waste time redrawing the diagram, use the given diagram.
3) When performing calculations, use subscripts for the section of the circuit you are working in.
   In other words, if are working with resistor R_1, label the voltage as V_1 and the current as I_1, unless other subscripts have already been provided in the question.

CURRENT IN PARALLEL

Current will always take the path of least resistance. When resistors are connected in parallel the smaller resistor will receive the larger current.

If all parallel resistors are known in the diagram below, there are three methods that can be used to determine the current (I_1) through resistor R_1:

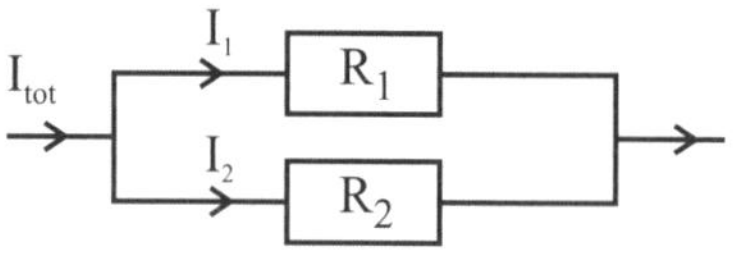

Method 1:

Step1: Calculate the parallel voltage using the equation $\mathbf{V_{//} = I_{tot} \times R_{//}}$

Step 2: Calculate I_1 using the equation: $\mathbf{I_1 = \dfrac{V_{//}}{R_1}}$

Method 2:

To calculate the current (I_x) in resistor R_x (in this case x is 1 or 2) use the equation:

$$\mathbf{I_x = \frac{I_{tot} \times R_{//}}{R_x}}$$

Method 3: This method only works for TWO resistors in parallel

To calculate the current in resistor (R_1) use the equation:

$$\mathbf{I_1 = \frac{R_2}{R_1 + R_2} \times I_{tot}}$$

To calculate the current in resistor (R_2) use the equation:

$$\mathbf{I_2 = \frac{R_1}{R_1 + R_2} \times I_{tot}}$$

<u>Illustrative Example 1</u>:

In the diagram below, determine the current in resistor R_1, R_2 and R_3 if the total current in the circuit is 8A.

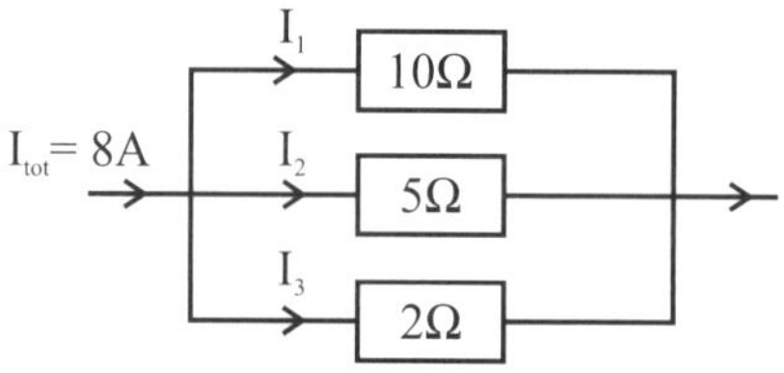

Method 1:	Method 2:
$\frac{1}{R_{//}} = \frac{1}{R_1} + \frac{1}{R_2} + \frac{1}{R_3}$	$\frac{1}{R_{//}} = \frac{1}{R_1} + \frac{1}{R_2} + \frac{1}{R_3}$
$= \frac{1}{10} + \frac{1}{5} + \frac{1}{2}$	$= \frac{1}{10} + \frac{1}{5} + \frac{1}{2}$
$= 0,8$	$= 0,8$
$R_{//} = 1,25$	$R_{//} = 1,25$
$V_{//} = IR_{//}$ $= 8(1,25)$ $= 10\text{ V}$	$\mathbf{I_x = \frac{I_{tot} \times R_{//}}{R_x}}$
$I_1 = \frac{V_{//}}{R_1} = \frac{10}{10} = 1\text{ A}$	$I_1 = \frac{8(1,25)}{10} = \frac{10}{10} = 1\text{ A}$
$I_2 = \frac{V_{//}}{R_2} = \frac{10}{5} = 2\text{ A}$	$I_2 = \frac{8(1,25)}{5} = \frac{10}{5} = 2\text{ A}$
$I_3 = \frac{V_{//}}{R_3} = \frac{10}{2} = 5\text{ A}$	$I_3 = \frac{8(1,25)}{2} = \frac{10}{2} = 5\text{ A}$

Method 3 cannot be used as there are more than 2 resistors.

EQUATIONS:

Equations			
$I = \frac{q}{t}$	$V = \frac{W}{q}$	$R = \frac{V}{I}$	$\text{emf} = I(R_{ext} + r)$
$R_s = R_1 + R_2 + ...$	$\frac{1}{R_p} = \frac{1}{R_1} + \frac{1}{R_2} + ...$	$P = \frac{W}{t}$	$W = Pt$
$W = VIt$	$W = I^2Rt$	$W = \frac{V^2}{R}t$	$N_{e-} = \frac{Q}{q_{e-}}$ **(not on data sheet)**
$P = VI$	$P = I^2R$	$P = \frac{V^2}{R}$	

Illustrative Example 2:

In the circuit shown below the 48 V battery has a negligible resistance.

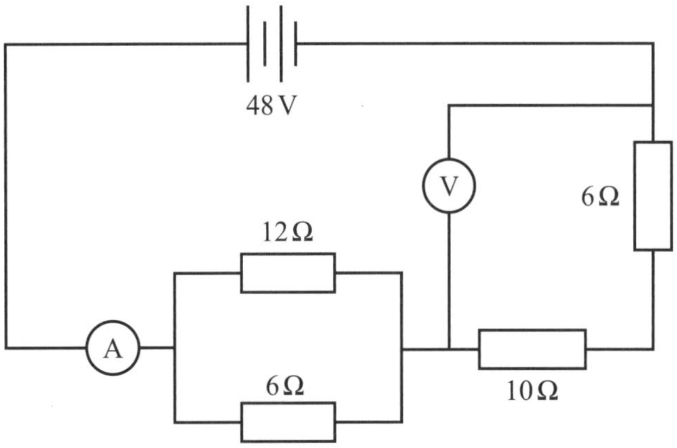

a) In which direction does conventional current flow?
b) In which direction do electrons flow?
c) Calculate the total resistance of the circuit.
d) Determine the reading on the ammeter.
e) Determine the reading on the voltmeter.
f) What would happen to the voltmeter and ammeter readings if the 10Ω resistor were to burn out? Explain your answer.
g) What would happen to the voltmeter and ammeter readings if the 12Ω resistor were to burn out? Explain your answer.
h) Calculate the power dissipated in the 10Ω resistor.
i) Calculate the energy transferred to the 12Ω resistor in 5 minutes.
j) Determine the number of electrons that pass through the 12Ω resistor in 5 minutes.

a) From positive to negative.

b) From negative to positive.

c) $\frac{1}{R_{//}} = \frac{1}{12} + \frac{1}{6}$

$R_{//} = 4\Omega$

$R_{tot} = 10 + 6 + 4$

$= 20\Omega$

d) $I = \frac{V}{R}$

$= \frac{48}{20}$

$= 2,4\,A$

e) $V = IR$

$= 2,4(10 + 6)$

$= 38,4\,V$

f) There would be an open circuit and no current would flow. Both the voltmeter and ammeter would read 0V and 0A respectively.

g) A resistor in parallel is removed and total resistance would increase. Current is inversely proportional to resistance $\left(I \alpha \frac{1}{R}\right)$. If total resistance increases, total current will decrease. Therefore, the ammeter reading would decrease. The resistance across the voltmeter is constant. If resistance is constant, voltage is directly proportional to current $(V \alpha I)$.

If current decreases the reading on the voltmeter will decrease.

h) $V_{10\Omega} = IR$

$= 2{,}4(10)$

$= 24\,V$

$P_{10\Omega} = VI$

$= 24(2{,}4)$

$= 57{,}6\,W$

i) $V_{//} = 48 - 38{,}4$

$= 9{,}6\,V$

$W_{12\Omega} = Pt$

$= \frac{V^2}{R}t$

$= \frac{9{,}6^2}{12}(5\times 60) \rightarrow$ time is in seconds

$= 2304\,J$

j) $I_{12\Omega} = \frac{V}{R}$

$= \frac{9{,}6}{12}$

$= 0{,}8\,A$

$Q_{12\Omega} = It$

$= 0{,}8(5\times 60) \rightarrow$ time is in seconds

$= 240\,C$

$N_{e-} = \frac{Q}{q_{e-}} \rightarrow$ this formula is not on the data sheet

$= \frac{240}{1{,}6\times 10^{-19}}$

$= 1{,}5\times 10^{21}$ electrons

INTERNAL RESISTANCE

All **batteries have internal resistance**. **Internal resistance is an additional resistor placed in series with the battery**. **EMF** is the **total energy supplied per coulomb of charge by the cell**. A **voltmeter across a battery**, or an **open switch** in series, will **read the EMF** if **no current** is flowing in the circuit.

A voltmeter placed over a battery reads the **EMF** of the battery **less** the **voltage 'lost'** to the internal resistance. This is the **voltage** available to the **external circuit**.

When dealing with internal resistance the formula below may be used:

$$\mathbf{EMF = I(R_{ext} + r_{int})}$$

EMF ⇒ EMF of the battery (V)

I ⇒ Total current (A)

R_{ext} ⇒ External circuit resistance (Ω)

r_{int} ⇒ Internal resistance (Ω)

All other circuit equations can still be used when dealing with internal resistance.

Illustrative Example 3:

In the circuit below the cell has an EMF of 12 V. When switch S is closed, the voltmeter across the battery reads 10 V. Determine the internal resistance of the battery.

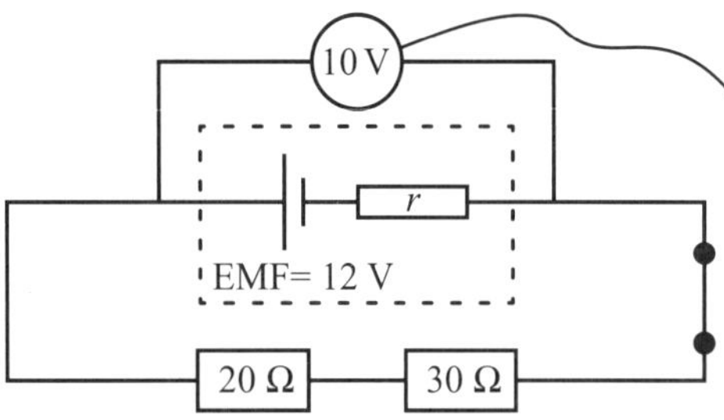

voltmeter reads EMF – V_{lost}
this means the voltage across the internal resistor is 2 V (12 – 10).
10 V is also the voltage available to the external circuit.
(the combined voltage across the 20Ω and 30Ω resistors)

Method 1:

$I = \frac{V}{R} = \frac{10}{50}$

$= 0{,}2\,A$

$r = \frac{V_r}{I}$

$= \frac{2}{0{,}2}$

$= 10\Omega$

Method 2:

$I = \frac{V}{R} = \frac{10}{50}$

$= 0{,}2\,A$

$EMF = I(R_{ext} + r_{int})$

$12 = 0{,}2(50 + r_{int})$

$12 = 10 + 0{,}2r_{int}$

$r_{int} = 10\Omega$

Illustrative Example 4:

In the circuit below the internal resistance of the cell is 0,4 Ω. The reading on the ammeter is 5 A and the resistors have the values shown on the diagram.

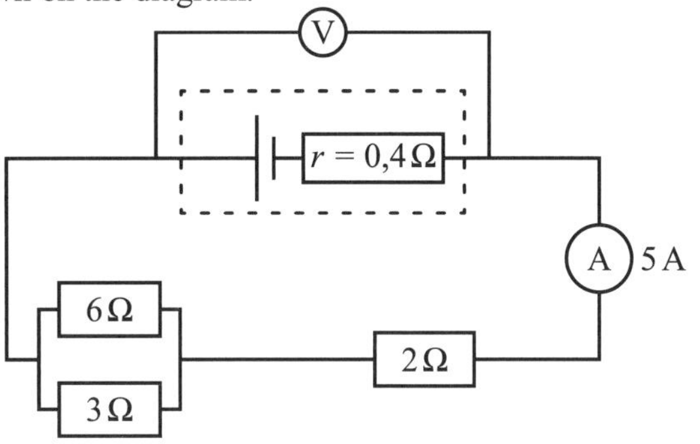

Determine:

a) The reading on the voltmeter.

b) The EMF of the battery.

a) $\frac{1}{R_{//}} = \frac{1}{6} + \frac{1}{3}$

$= 0,5$

$R_{//} = 2\,\Omega$

$V = IR$

$= 5(2+2)$

$= 20\,V$

This is the reading on the voltmeter as it is the voltage of the external circuit.

b) $EMF = I(R_{ext} + r_{int})$

$= 5(4 + 0,4)$

$= 22\,V$

OHM'S LAW EXPERIMENT

Ohm's Law states the current through a conductor is directly proportional to the potential difference across the conductor at constant temperature.

The circuit diagram below can be used to prove Ohm's Law. The voltmeter measures the change in voltage as current in the circuit changes. The current is changed by adjusting the resistance of the rheostat (variable resistor).

Current is the **independent** variable and **voltage** is the **dependent** variable.

The **temperature** of the resistor must be kept **constant** during the experiment.

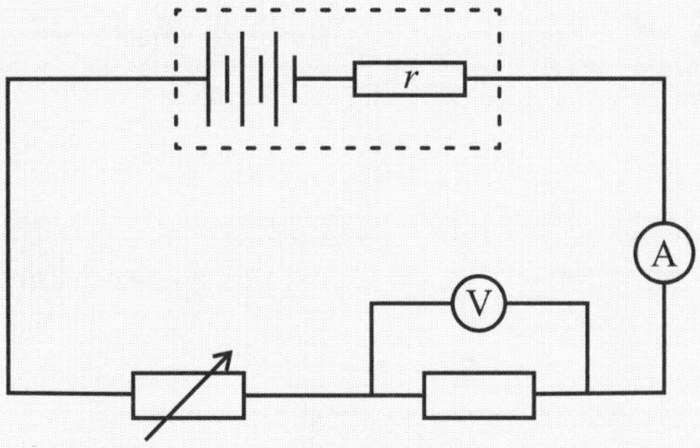

The graph below shows the outcome of the experiment for an Ohmic conductor (a conductor that obeys Ohm's Law). The gradient of the graph represents the change in voltage against the change in current. Therefore, the **gradient** of the graph is the **resistance** of the resistor that the voltmeter is connected across. It cuts the origin as voltage is directly proportional to current at a constant temperature.

Graph of voltage versus current

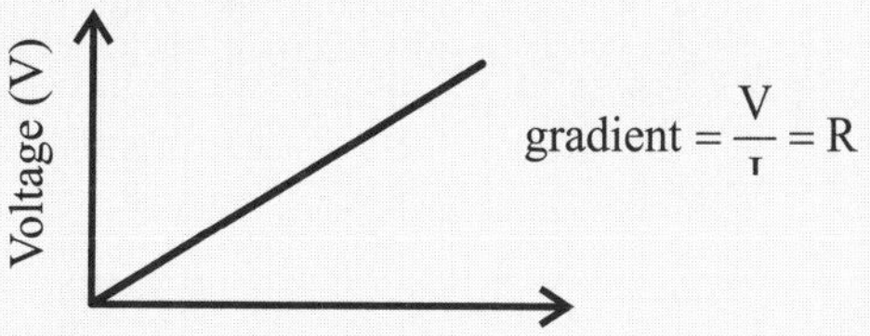

Use points on the line of best fit, not points given in the question, to calculate the gradient.

TOC 1 Data Sheet 2 Definitions 3 3 solutions 4 4 solutions 5 5 solutions 6 6 solutions 7 7 solutions 8 8 solutions 9 9 solutions 10 10 solutions

TOC 1 Data Sheet 2 Definitions 3 3 solutions 4 4 solutions 5 5 solutions 6 6 solutions 7 7 solutions 8 8 solutions 9 9 solutions 10 10 solutions

EXPERIMENT TO DETERMINE EMF AND INTERNAL RESISTANCE

Either of the circuit diagrams below can be used to determine the EMF and internal resistance. The voltmeter measures the change in external voltage as current in the circuit changes. The current is changed by adjusting the resistance of the rheostat (variable resistor).

Current is the **independent** variable and **voltage** is the **dependent** variable.

The **temperature** of the resistor must be kept **constant** during the experiment.

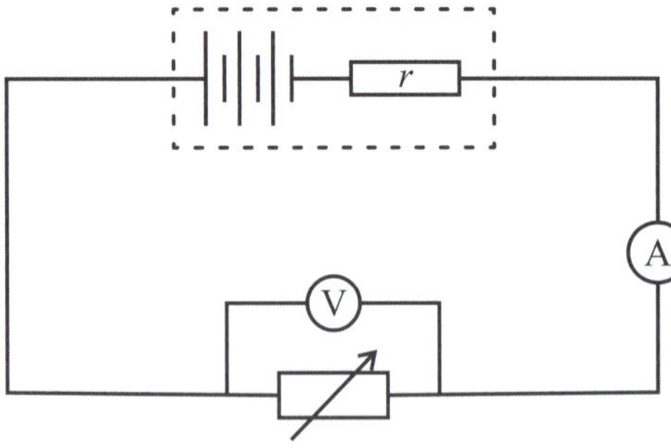

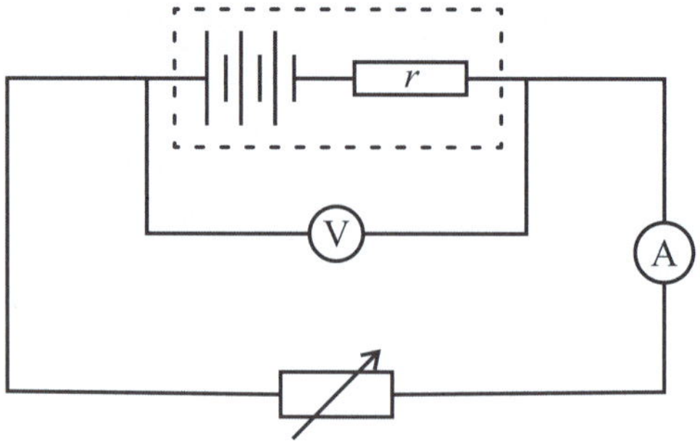

The graph below shows the outcome of the experiment. When current in the circuit is zero the voltmeter read the EMF of the battery. Therefore, the y-intercept of the graph is the EMF.

As current increases the voltage decreases because lost volts to internal resistance increases.

Graph of voltage versus current

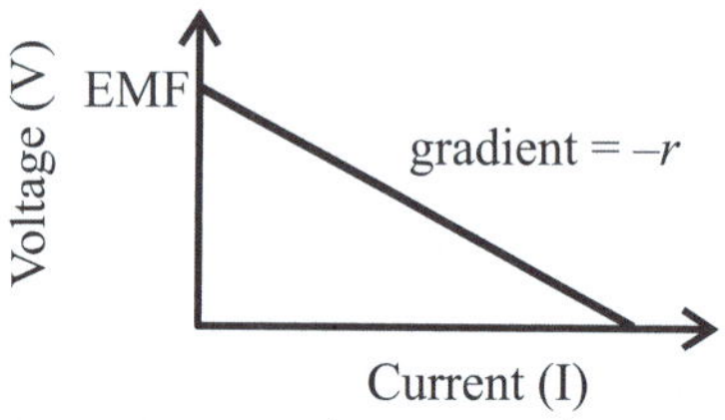

Examine the manipulation of the equation $\text{EMF} = I\left(R_{ext} + r_{int}\right)$ below:

$$\text{EMF} = IR_{ext} + r_{int}$$

$$\text{EMF} = V_{ext} + Ir_{int}$$

$$V_{ext} = \boldsymbol{-r_{int}}\,I + \text{EMF} \rightarrow y = \boldsymbol{m}x + c$$

From the manipulation above, it can be seen that the gradient of the graph is the negative value of internal resistance and the y-intercept is the EMF of the battery.

> **Note that V_{ext} is plotted on the y-axis and current on the x-axis**

ELECTRICITY COST

Electricity is charged according to the number of kilowatt hours (kWh) used.

> **Cost = power × time × cost per kilowatt hour**

> **This is the only formula where power is in kilowatts (kW) and time is in hours (h).**

Illustrative Example 6:

A 60W light bulb is used for an average of 420 minutes a day. Determine the cost of using the lightbulb for a period of 5 days if the electricity is charged at R1,20 per kilowatt hour.

$$\text{cost} = \text{power} \times \text{time} \times \text{cost per kilowatt hour}$$

$$= \left(60 \times 10^{-3}\right)\left(\frac{420}{60} \times 5\right)(1{,}20)$$

$$= \text{R}2{,}52$$

Question 1 (Solutions on page 289)

1.1 In the circuit below, all ammeters have negligible resistance and voltmeters have very high resistance. The internal resistance of the battery may be ignored.

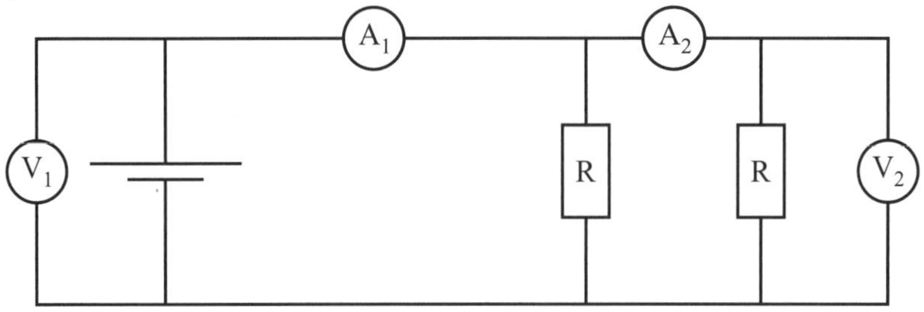

How do the readings on the ammeters and voltmeters compare?

	Ammeter Readings	Voltmeter Readings
A	$A_1 > A_2$	$V_1 > V_2$
B	$A_1 < A_2$	$V_1 = V_2$
C	$A_1 = A_2$	$V_1 > V_2$
D	$A_1 > A_2$	$V_1 = V_2$

(2)

1.2 In the circuit below, all ammeters have negligible resistance and voltmeters have very high resistance. The internal resistance of the battery may be ignored.

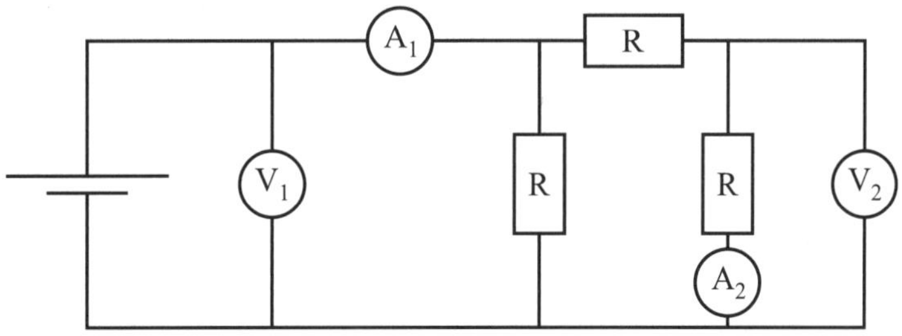

How do the readings on the ammeters and voltmeters compare?

	Ammeter Readings	Voltmeter Readings
A	$A_1 = A_2$	$V_1 = V_2$
B	$A_1 = 3A_2$	$V_1 = 2V_2$
C	$A_1 = 2A_2$	$2V_1 = V_2$
D	$2A_1 = A_2$	$V_1 = V_2$

(2)

1.3 A resistor is connected to a battery and the power dissipated by the resistor is 10W. An identical battery is then placed in series with the first battery. The power dissipated in the resistor is now:

A 5W
B 20W
C 30W
D 40W

(2)

1.4 In the circuit below, voltmeters have very high resistance and the internal resistance of the battery may be ignored.

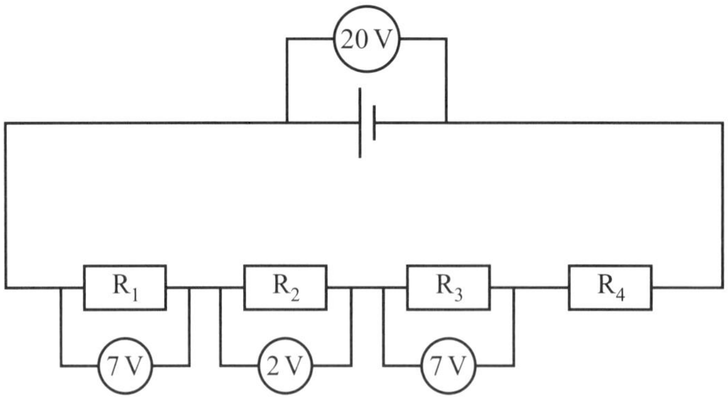

Which of the following are possible values for the resistances of R_1, R_2, R_3 and R_4?

	R_1 (Ω)	R_2 (Ω)	R_3 (Ω)	R_4 (Ω)
A	2	5	2	1
B	4	3	4	1,5
C	3,5	1	3,5	2
D	4	3	4	3

(2)

1.5 In the circuit below, the battery has an EMF of 6,2V.

The internal resistance of the battery is:

A 0,1 Ω
B 0,2 Ω
C 0,4 Ω
D 1,0 Ω

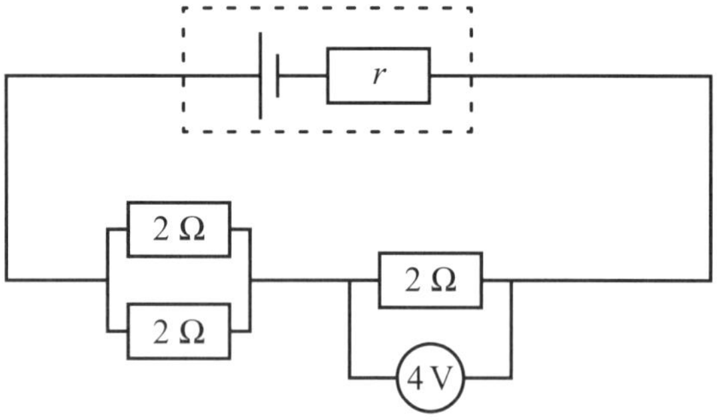

(2)

1.6 In order to minimise losses when transporting power over long distances,

A the current on the line is high and the voltage is low.
B the current and the voltage on the line is high.
C the current on the line is low and the voltage is high.
D the current and the voltage on the line is low. (2)

1.7 In the circuit below the battery has negligible internal resistance and resistor R_1 has 3 times the resistance of R_2. When an amount of charge Q passes through resistor R_1, the work done is W. When the same amount of charge passes through resistor R_2, the work done is:

A W

B $\frac{W}{3}$

C $\frac{W}{9}$

D 3W

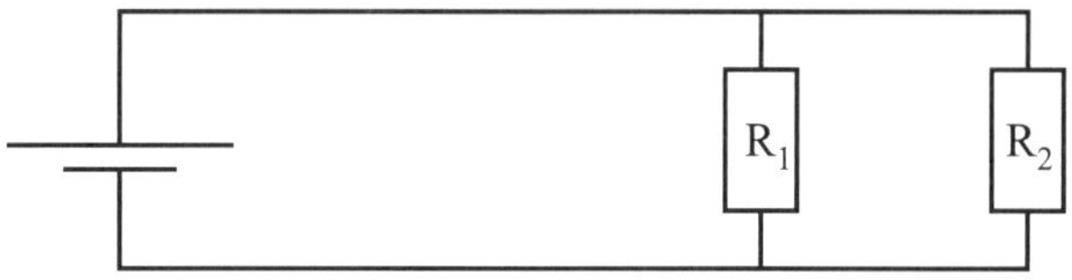

(2)

1.8 Switch S is originally open as shown in the circuit below. How do the readings on the ammeter and voltmeters change when the switch is closed?

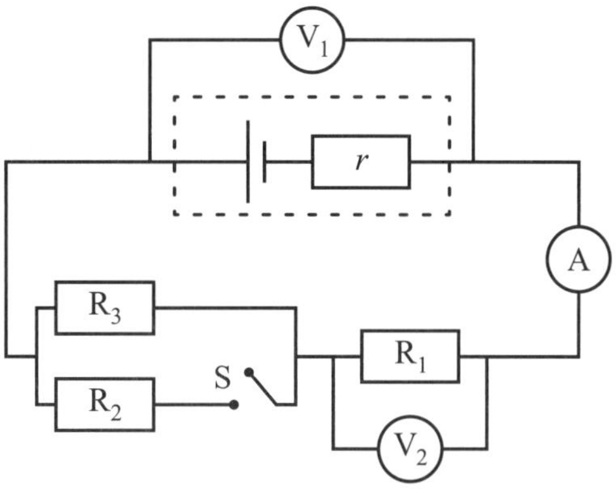

	Ammeter	V_1	V_2
A	Stays the same	Decreases	Decreases
B	Increases	Stays the same	Increases
C	Decreases	Decreases	Increases
D	Increases	Decreases	Increases

(2)

1.9 In the circuit below, the battery has significant internal resistance. The resistance of the connecting wires and ammeters may be ignored while the voltmeter has very high resistance,

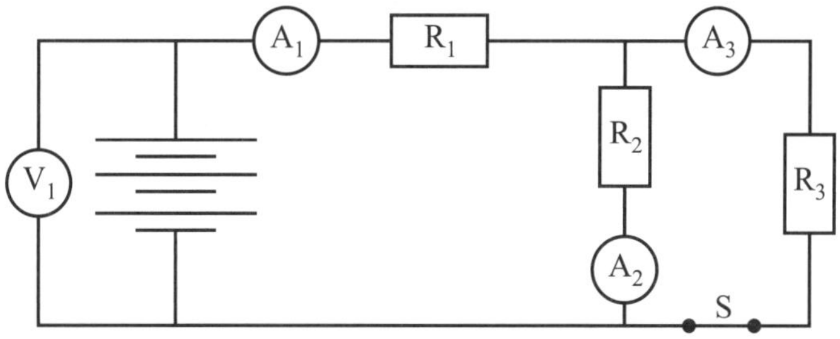

How do the readings on the voltmeters and ammeters change when switch S is opened?

	V_1	A_1	A_2	A_3
A	Decrease	Decrease	Increase	Decrease
B	Increase	Decrease	Increase	Decrease
C	Increase	Increase	Decrease	Increase
D	Decrease	Decrease	Increase	Increase

(2)

1.10 It costs P Rands to use a 500W heater for 15 minutes. What is the cost of electricity per kWh?

A 4P
B 8P
C 2P
D P

(2)

1.11 A special switch controls the heating element of a stove. The stove has 3 heat settings. High, medium and low. Which of the following connections will provide a medium heat?

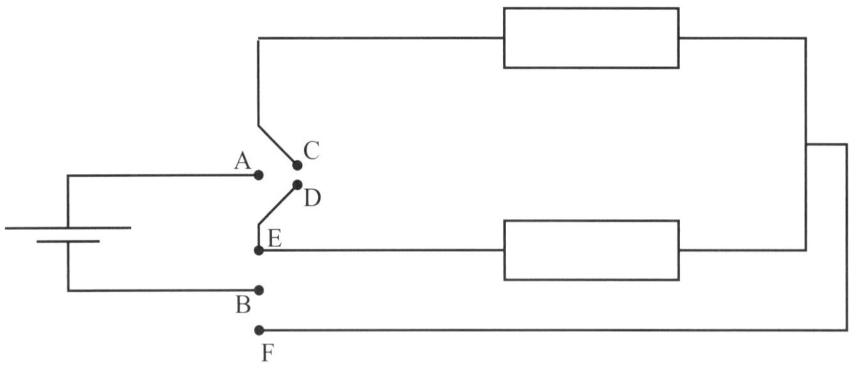

	Connected to A:	Connected to B
A	C and D	F
B	C	E
C	D	E
D	D	F

(2)

1.12 In the diagram below, $R_1 = R_3$ and $R_2 = 2R_1$. The reading on ammeter A is 7,5 A. Resistor R_3 suddenly breaks. Which one of the following correctly describes the readings on the ammeters after R_3 breaks?

	A	A_1	A_2	A_3
A	7,5	3,75	3,75	0
B	4,5	1,5	1	1,5
C	7,5	3	1,5	3
D	4,5	3	1,5	0

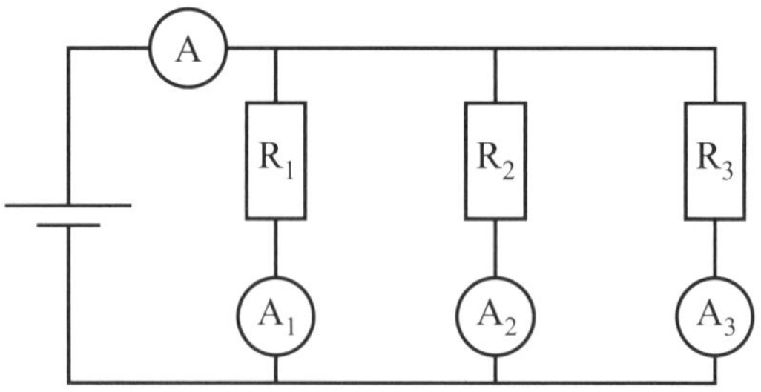

(2)

1.13 Which of the following describes the change in total resistance and reading on the voltmeter when switch S is closed?

	Total Resistance	Voltmeter
A	Increases	Increases
B	Decreases	Decreases
C	Decreases	Increases
D	Increases	Decreases

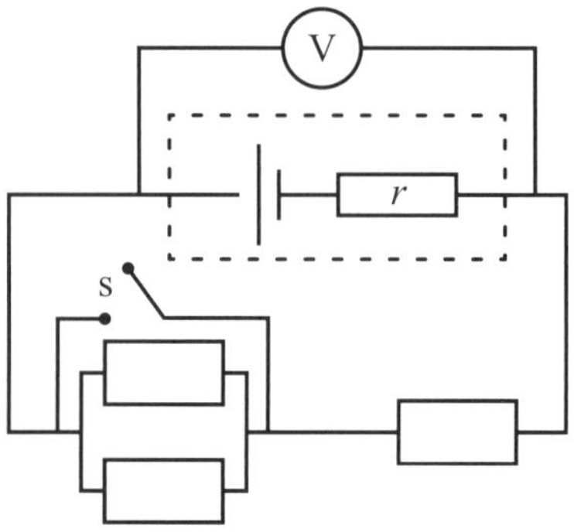

(2)

1.14 Which of the following correctly describes the readings on voltmeter V_1 and V_2 with the switch open and closed?

	Switch open		Switch Closed	
	V_1	V_2	V_1	V_2
A	5	0	0	4
B	0	0	1	4
C	5	0	0	5
D	5	5	1	4

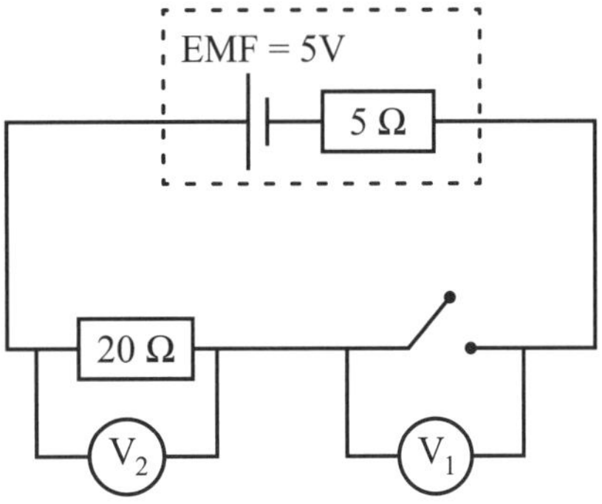

(2)

1.15 At time T_1 switch S_1 is closed and at time T_2 switch S_2 is closed.

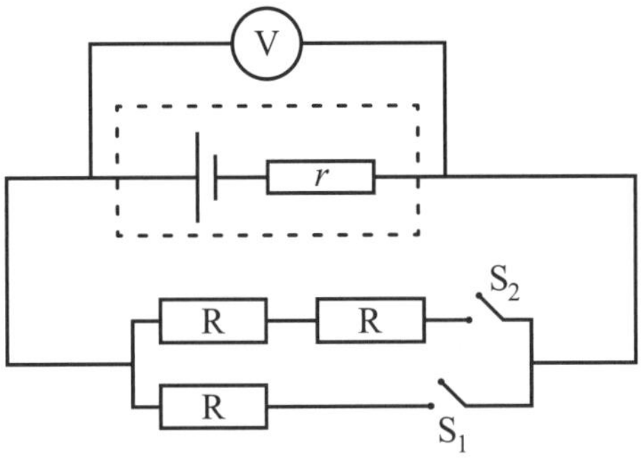

Select the graph which shows the correct variation of the voltmeter reading against time.

A

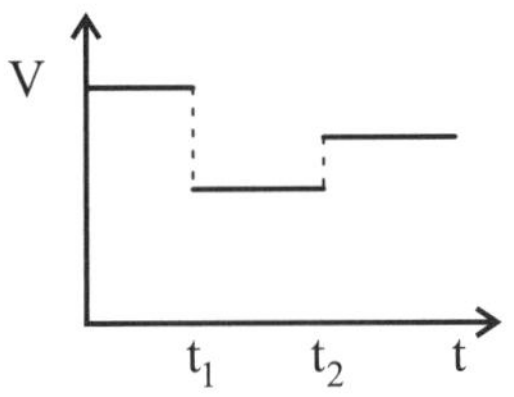

B

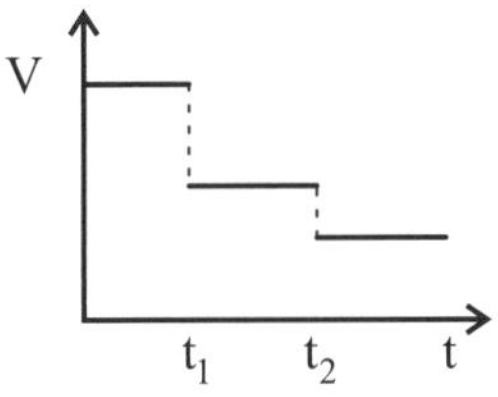

C

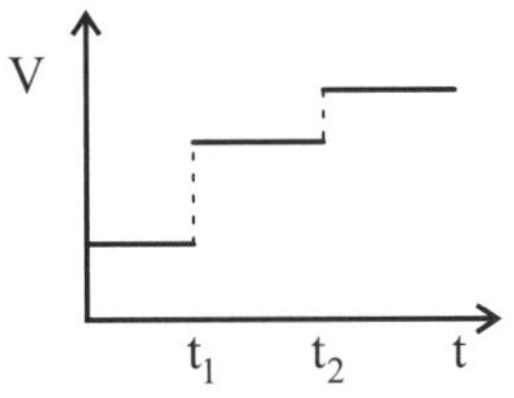

D

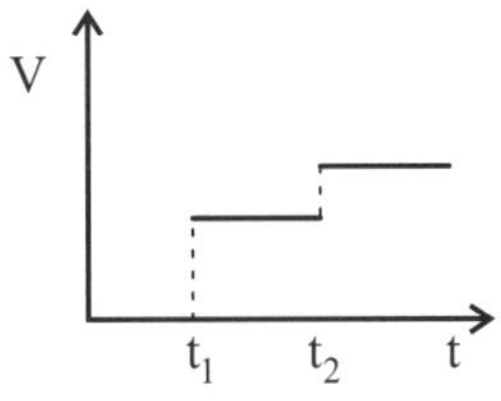

(2)

1.16 In the diagram below, both cells have the same EMF and negligible internal resistance. All resistors have equal resistance. The power dissipated in resistor X in circuit 1 is P.

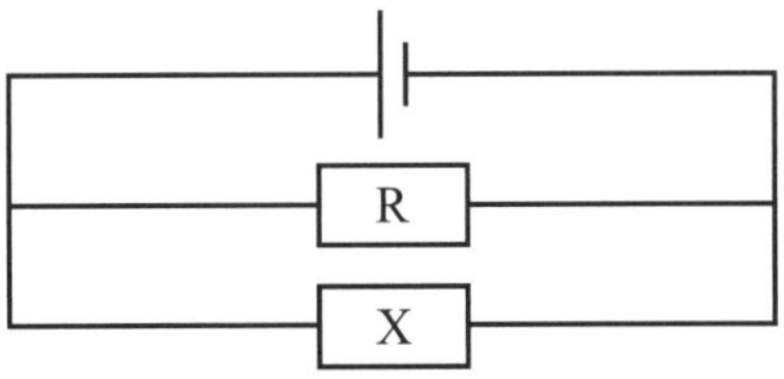

Circuit 1

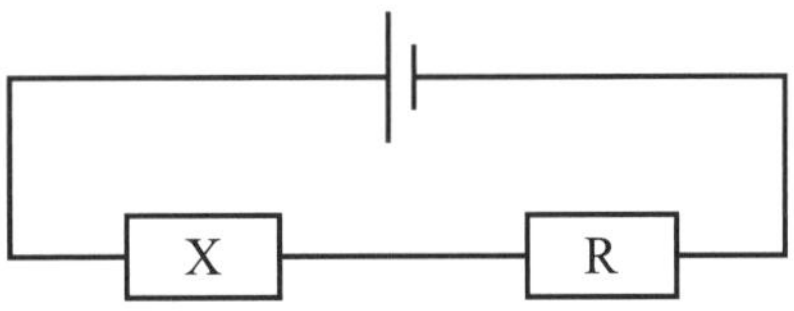

Circuit 2

The power dissipated in resistor X in circuit 2 is:

A P B 4P C 2P D 0,25P (2)

1.17 In the circuit below, all resistors are identical, and the resistance of the connecting wires and cell are negligible. The ratio of power in resistors X, Y and Z is:

A 1 : 1 : 2
B 1 : 1 : 1
C 1 : 1 : 4
D 1 : 2 : 1

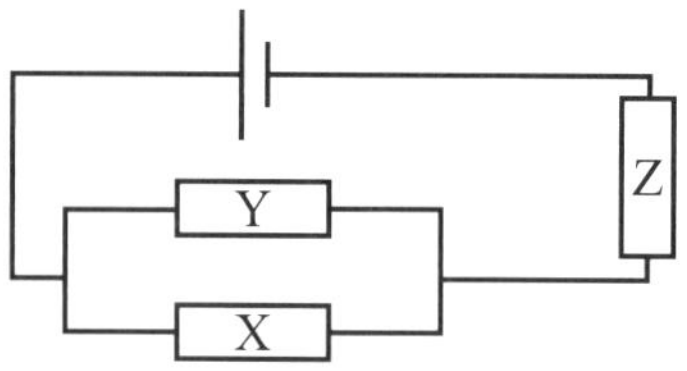

(2)

1.18 In the circuit below, all external resistors are identical. How do the readings on V_1, V_2 and V_3 compare when switch S is open and closed?

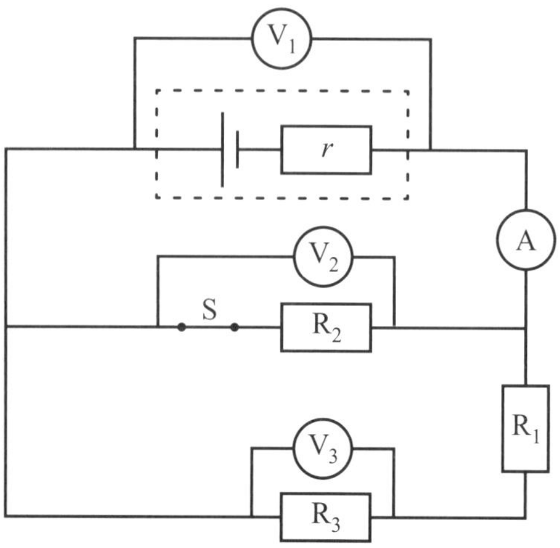

	Switch closed	**Switch open**
A	$V_1 = V_2 = V_3$	$V_1 = V_2 = V_3$
B	$V_1 = V_2 = 2V_3$	$V_1 = V_2 = 2V_3$
C	$V_1 > V_2 = V_3$	$V_1 = \text{EMF}\ \ V_2 = V_3 = 0$
D	$V_1 = V_2 = 2V_3$	$V_1 = \text{EMF}\ \ V_2 = V_3 = 0$

(2)

1.19 Electricity is usually charged at rate per kilowatt hour (kWh). The kilowatt hour is a measure of:

A Charge
B Power
C Energy
D Cost

(2)

1.20 In the circuit below, all resistors are identical. The resistance of the connecting wires and cell are negligible. How does the current through A_1 and A_2 compare?

A $A_1 = A_2$
B $A_1 = 2A_2$
C $\frac{1}{2}A_1 = A_2$
D $2A_1 = A_2$

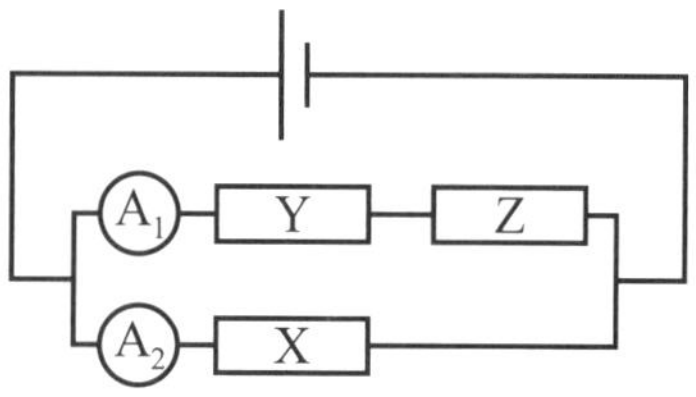

(2)

1.21 In the circuit below the cell has an EMF of 6V and negligible internal resistance. The resistiors have values as shown on the diagram. The voltemeter has very high resistance and the the connecting wires have negligible internal resistance.

The reading on the voltmeter when switch S is open and closed is:

	Switch open	Switch closed
A	0V	2V
B	6V	2V
C	0V	6V
D	6V	4V

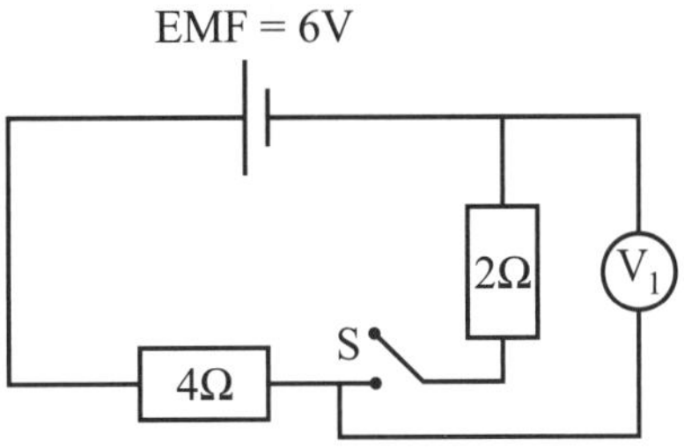

(2)

1.22 In the circuit below V_1 is connected across a variable resistor.

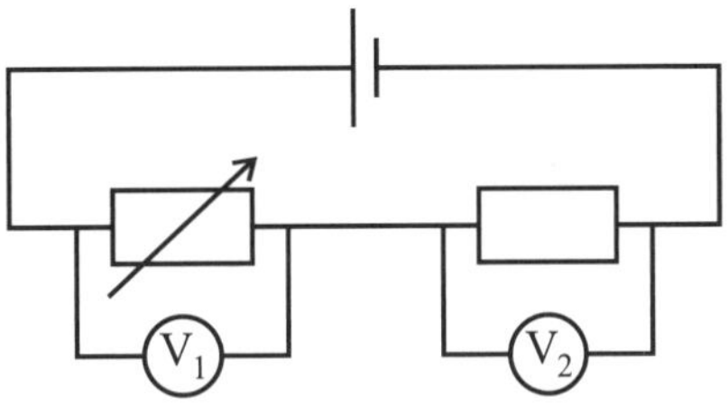

Which one of the following graphs represnts the relationship between the reading on V_1 and V_2 as the resitance of the variable resistior is increased.

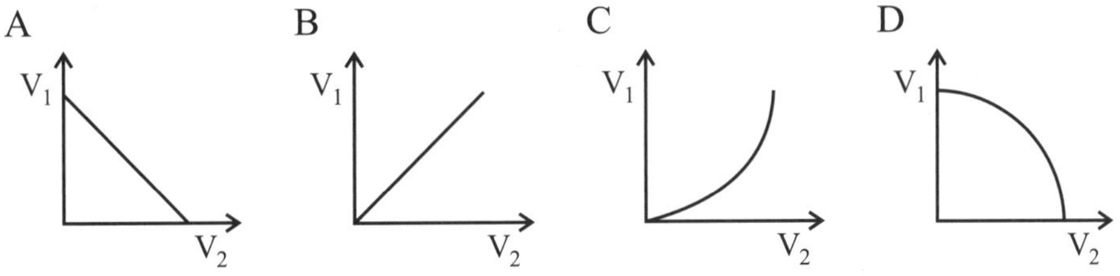

(2)

1.23 Which one of the following graphs best represents the relationship between the potential difference (V) across an ohmic conductor and the current (I) in the conductor at constant temperature?

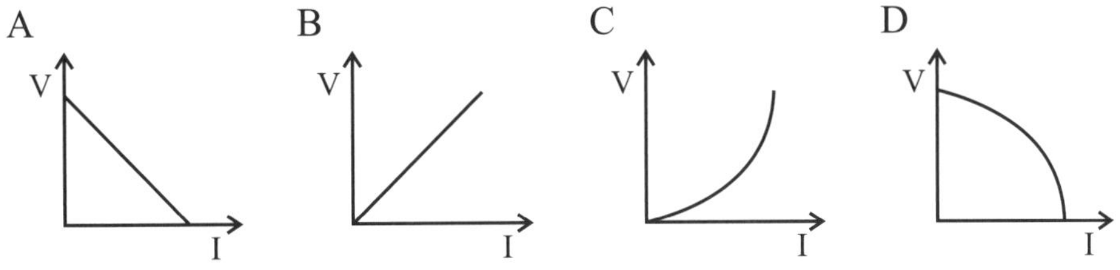

(2)

1.24 The cost of electricity is R2,20 per kWh. The cost of running a 5000W boiler for x minutes is:

A $2,20(5000)(x)$

B $2,20(5)(x)$

C $\dfrac{2,20(5x)}{60}$

D $2,20(5)(60x)$

(2)

TOC 1 Data Sheet 2 Definitions 3 3 solutions 4 4 solutions 5 5 solutions 6 6 solutions 7 7 solutions 8 8 solutions 9 9 solutions 10 10 solutions

1.25 In the circuit shown below the resistances of the battery, switch and connecting wires can be ignored. Both voltmeters have high resistances. The resistors are identical.

How do the readings on V_1, V_2 and the ammeter change when the switch (S) is closed?

	V_1	V_2	A
A	Increase	Decrease	No change
B	No change	Decrease	Increase
C	Decrease	Increase	Decrease
D	Increase	Decrease	Increase

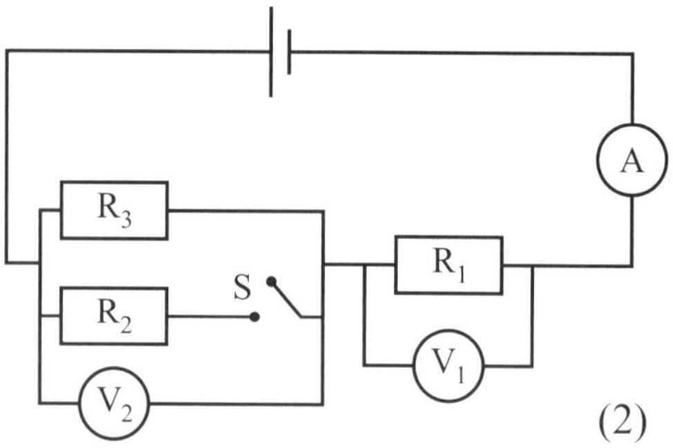

(2)

1.26 Consider the circuit diagram below. Which of the following would describe the ammeter and voltmeter readings when S_2 is opened? The internal resistance of the cell cannot be ignored.

	A_1	A_2	V
A	Increase	Decrease	Increase
B	Increase	Decrease	Decrease
C	Decrease	Increase	Increase
D	Decrease	Decrease	Increase

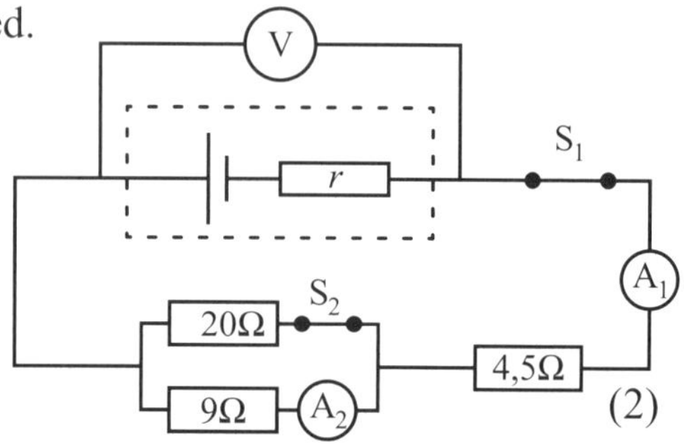

(2)

1.27 Three resistors of resistance 2R, 4R and 4R are connected to form a circuit. A battery of negligible internal resistance and a voltmeter are connected to the resistors as shown in the circuit diagram below.
The reading on the voltmeter is 2V.
What is the emf of the battery?

A 10 V
B 6 V
C 4 V
D 12 V

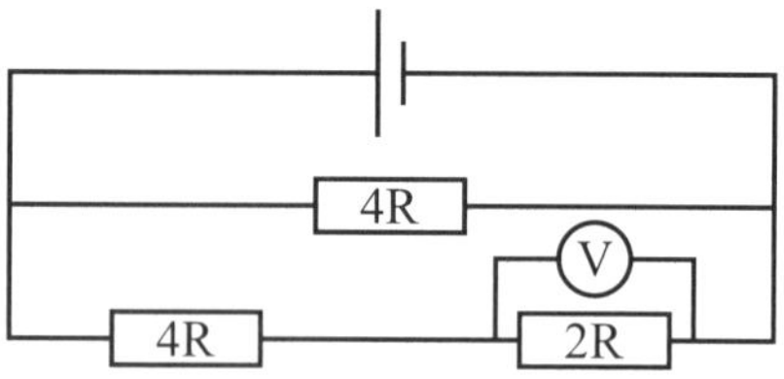

(2)

1.28 The graphs alongside show the results of an experiment. Which graph (A, B, C or D) represents the resistor with the highest resistance?

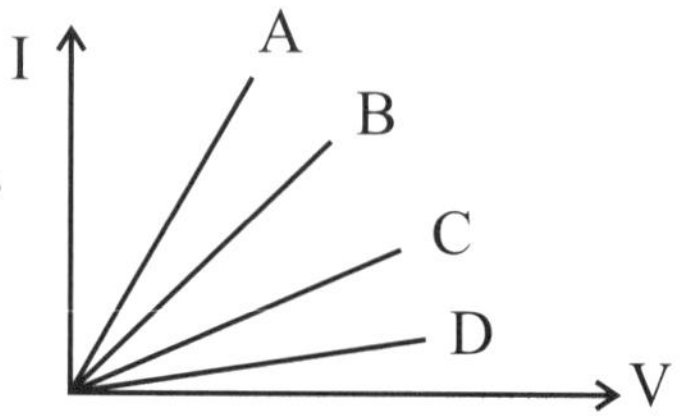

(2)

1.29 Consider the circuit diagram below. Which of the following would describe the ammeter and voltmeter readings when switch S is opened? The internal resistance of the cell cannot be ignored.

	Ammeter	Voltmeter
A	Decrease	Increase
B	Increase	Decrease
C	Decrease	Decrease
D	Increase	Increase

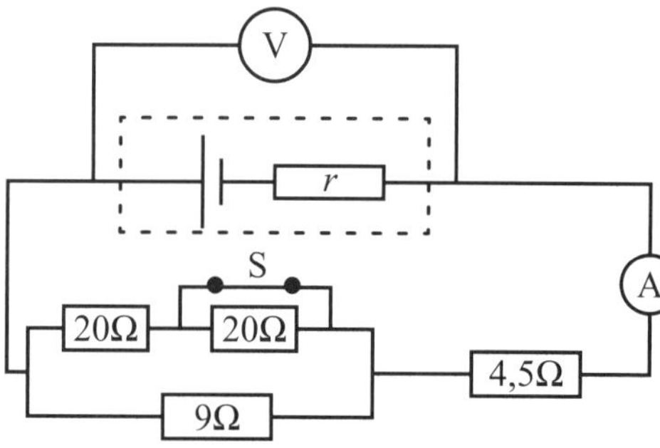

(2)

[58]

Question 2 (Solutions on page 289)

A battery supplies a current of 1 A when connected to a 1,8 Ω resistor and a current of 2 A when connected to a 0,8 Ω resistor. Calculate the internal resistance and emf of the cell.

[7]

Question 3 (Solutions on page 289 and 290)

Gabriel and Judd are conducting an experiment to determine the EMF and internal resistance of a battery. They have access to an ammeter but do not have a voltmeter. They setup the circuit shown below.

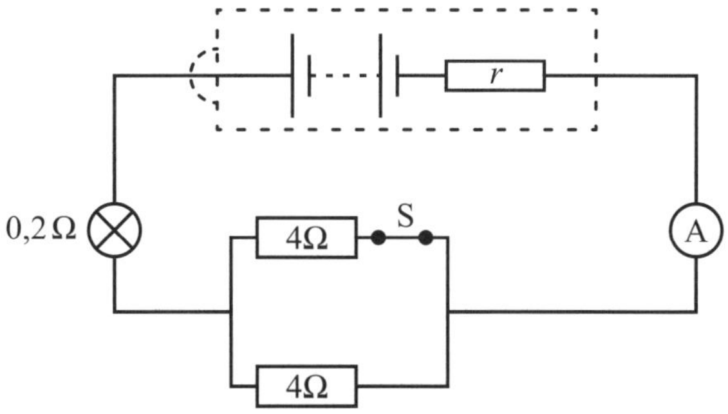

3.1 What is the purpose of placing the switch next to the 4Ω resistor? (2)

3.2 The results of the experiment are shown below:

	Ammeter Reading
Switch open	2 A
Switch closed	3 A

Use the results from the experiment to determine the EMF and internal resistance of the battery. (7)

3.3 Determine the power dissipated in the battery when the switch is closed. (2)

3.4 What is the rate that energy is dissipated in the bulb when the switch is open? (2)

3.5 Calculate the energy dissipated in the bulb in 3 minutes when the switch is open. (3)

3.6 How is the brightness of the bulb affected when the switch is opened? Answer only brighter, dimmer or no change. (1)

3.7 Explain your answer to 3.6 above referring to relevant formula. (3)

[20]

TOC 1 Data Sheet 2 Definitions 3 3 solutions 4 4 solutions 5 5 solutions 6 6 solutions 7 7 solutions 8 8 solutions 9 9 solutions 10 10 solutions

Question 4 (Solutions on page 290)

A circuit consists of a battery with an emf of 30 V and an internal resistance of 2 Ω. A lightbulb, a variable resistor R (rheostat) which can be set at different values, a 5 Ω resistor and a ammeter which reads 2,25 A are connected as shown in the circuit below.

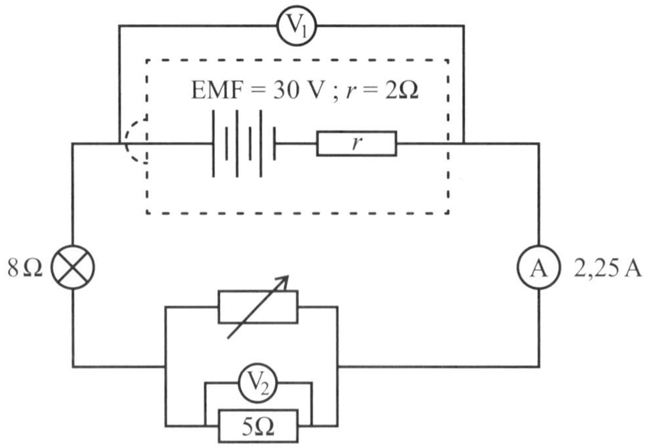

4.1 Define current. (2)

4.2 Calculate the power dissipated in the lightbulb. (3)

4.3 What is the reading on voltmeter V_1? (3)

4.4 What is the reading on voltmeter V_2? (3)

4.5 Determine the resistance that the rheostat is set. (4)

4.6 If the resistance of the rheostat is increased, how will the brightness of the bulb be affected? Explain your answer making reference to relevant formula. (4)

4.7 The rheostat is now adjusted to a resistance of 20Ω. Determine the new reading on V_1. (8)

[27]

Question 5 (Solutions on page 291)

In the circuit shown in the accompanying diagram below, the resistance of the ammeter, voltmeter and battery can be ignored.

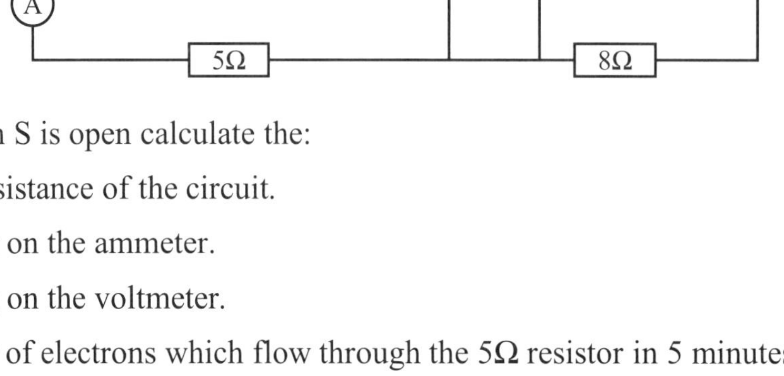

5.1 If switch S is open calculate the: (1)

5.1.1 Total resistance of the circuit. (1)

5.1.2 Reading on the ammeter. (2)

5.1.3 Reading on the voltmeter. (2)

5.1.4 Number of electrons which flow through the 5Ω resistor in 5 minutes. (5)

5.2 Switch S is now closed

5.2.1 What will happen to the readings on the voltmeter and ammeter? Write down only increase, decrease or remains the same. (2)

5.2.2 Explain your answers to question 5.2.1. (3)

5.2.3 Verify your answer above by calculating the readings on the ammeter and voltmeter. (5)

[20]

Question 6 (Solutions on page 291 and 292)

The battery in the circuit diagram below has an emf of 12 V and an unknown internal resistance, r. Voltmeter, V_1, is connected across the battery and voltmeter, V_2, is connected across the 2 Ω resistor. The resistance of the wires and ammeter is negligible. R_1 and R_2 are connected in parallel. R_1 has twice the resistance of R_2.

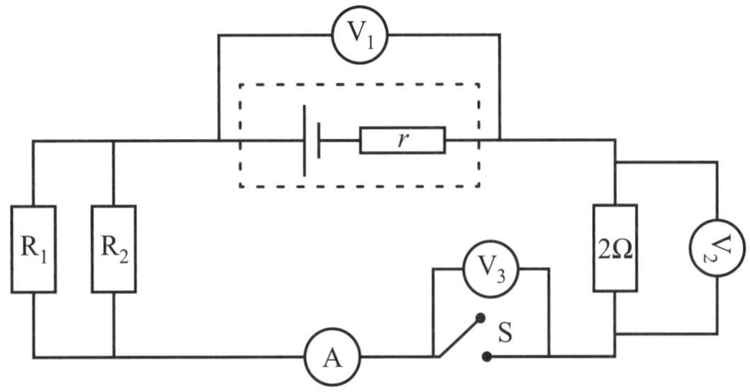

6.1 Write down the reading on voltmeters V_1, V_2 and V_3 when switch S is open. (2)

Switch S is now closed. The reading on V_1 changes to 11 V and the reading on V_2 changes to 2V.

6.2 Determine the internal resistance of the battery. (3)

6.3 Calculate the resistance of R_1. (5)

6.4 Calculate the energy dissipated in resistor R_2 in 10 minutes. (4)

[14]

Question 7 (Solutions on page 292)

An experiment is conducted to determine the EMF (E) and internal resistance (r) of a battery. A battery is connected to a rheostat (variable resistor), a low-resistance ammeter and a high-resistance voltmeter as shown in the diagram below.

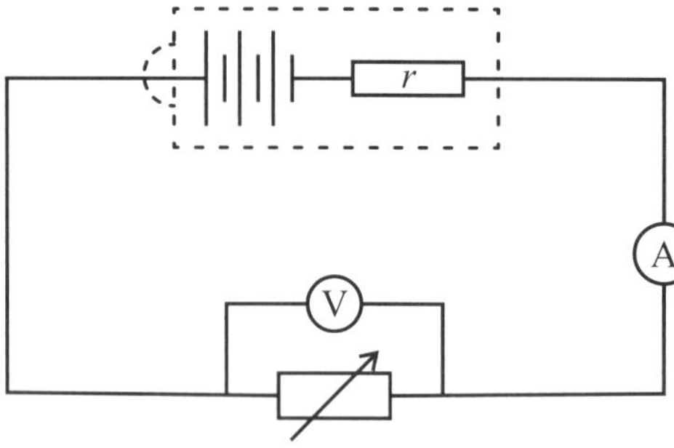

The data obtained from the experiment is shown in the table below.

Voltmeter Reading (V)	Ammeter Reading (A)
10	0,11
9	0,13
8	0,22
7	0,25
6	0,3

7.1 Why is it important that the resistance of the rheostat is always a high value relative to the internal resistance of the battery? (3)

7.2 Using the information in the table above, plot the points and draw a line of best fit on the grid below.

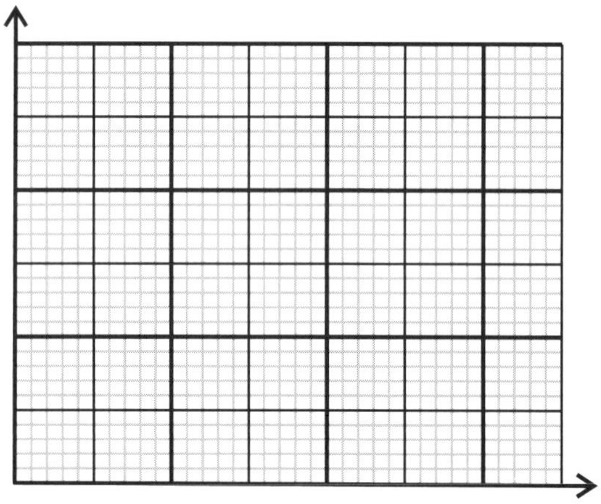

(5)

7.3 Determine the gradient of the line of best fit. (2)

7.4 Use your answer from question 7.3, your knowledge of the equation $EMF = I(R_{ext} + r_{int})$ and that the equation $y = mx + c$ describes a straight line to determine internal resistance of the battery. (4)

[14]

Question 8 (Solutions on page 293)

A science learner is tasked with determining the resistance of an unknown resistor. The learner sets up the circuit shown below.

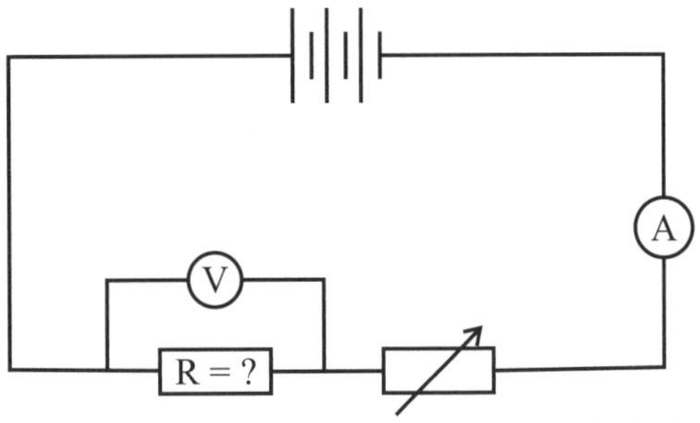

The data obtained from the experiment is shown in the table below.

Voltmeter Reading (V)	Ammeter Reading (A)
2	0,02
10	0,08
14	0,16
25	0,24
35	0,36

8.1 State Ohm's Law. (2)

8.2 Why is there a rheostat (variable resistor) in the circuit? (1)

8.3 What is the dependent variable in the experiment? (1)

8.4 Using the information in the table above, plot a graph of potential difference against current and draw a line of best fit.

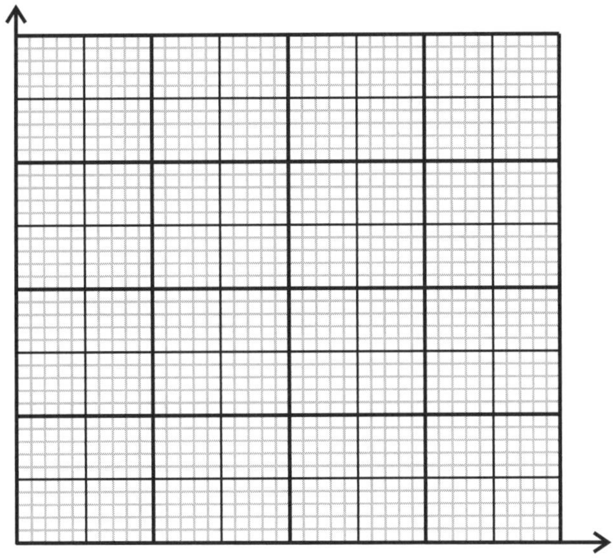

(5)

8.5 Use the graph to determine the resistance of the unknown resistor. (4)

[13]

TOC | 1 Data Sheet | 2 Definitions | 3 | 3 solutions | 4 | 4 solutions | 5 | 5 solutions | 6 | 6 solutions | 7 | 7 solutions | 8 | 8 solutions | 9 | 9 solutions | 10 | 10 solutions

Question 9 (Solutions on page 293)

In the circuit below the battery consists of 3 cells each of 15V and internal resistance *r*. The reading on A_1 is 8A and the reading on A_2 is 4A.

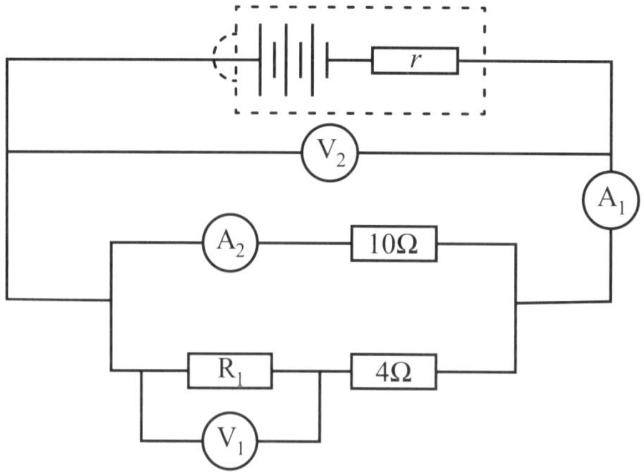

9.1 What is the value of resistor R_1? (1)

9.2 Determine the reading on voltmeter V_2. (3)

9.3 Determine the reading on voltmeter V_1. (3)

9.4 Determine the internal resistance, *r*, of each cell. (4)

9.5 If resistor R_1 breaks What will happen to the readings on A_1, A_2 and V_2. Explain your answer making reference to relevant formula. (6)

[17]

Question 10 (Solutions on page 294)

In the circuit below the battery has negligible internal resistance. When switch S is open the voltmeter reads 20V. When the switch is closed, the voltmeter reads 16V.

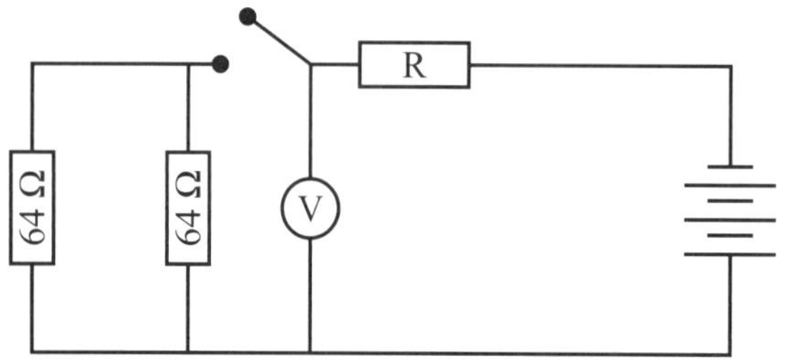

10.1 What does the reading of 20V on the voltmeter represent when the switch is open? (2)

10.2 Determine the resistance of resistor R. (5)

[7]

Question 11 (Solutions on page 294 and 295)

A science learner has a circuit component which requires a voltage of 3V in order to function. He has a voltage source which has an EMF of 12V and internal resistance of 10Ω, a variable resistor and a 300Ω resistor. He sets up the circuit as shown below and adjusts the variable resistor until a voltmeter across the 300Ω resistor reads 3V.

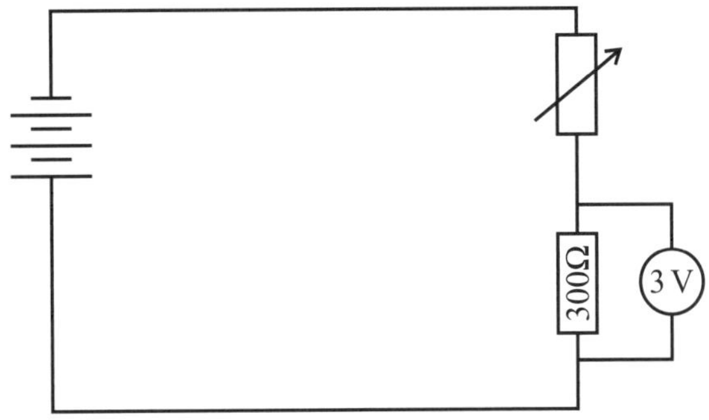

11.1 What resistance is the variable resistor set at when the voltmeter reads 3V? (6)

11.2 The learner now connects the circuit component in parallel across the 300Ω resistor and is surprised that the component does not work. He measures the voltage across the 300Ω resistor and sees that it has changed to 1,2V. The learner then places the voltmeter over the battery and sees that the voltmeter only reads 11,88V.

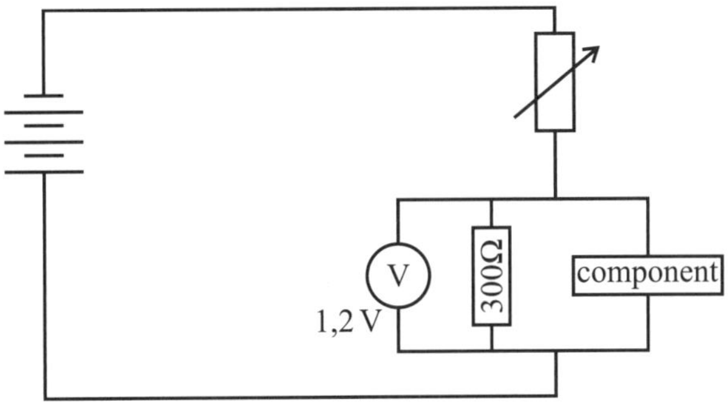

11.2.1 Explain the reason for the decrease in voltage from 3V to 1,2V. (4)

11.2.2 Determine the current in the circuit with the component connected. (2)

11.2.3 Determine the resistance of the component. (5)

11.2.4 What should the variable resistor be set to so that the component functions as intended? (6)

[23]

Question 12 (Solutions on page 295)

In the circuit shown in the diagram below the resistances of the connecting wires, switch and ammeter is negligible. The cell has an internal resistance of 2 Ω.

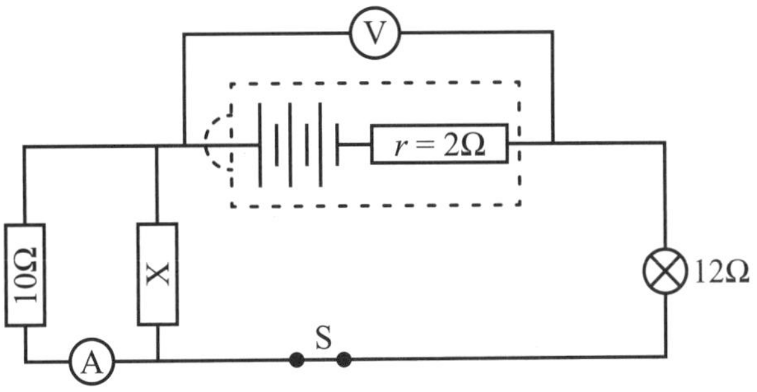

When switch S is closed, the reading on voltmeter, V, decreases from 24V to 21,6V.

12.1 Calculate the reading on the ammeter. (6)

12.2 Calculate the resistance of resistor X. (4)

12.3 How would the brightness of the bulb change if resistor X burns out? Explain your answer referring to a relevant power formula. (4)

12.4 The cost of electricity is R1,30 per kWh. If the bulb is used for 40 minutes per day how much would it cost to run the bulb for 1 year? You may assume there are 365 days per year. (6)

[20]

Question 13 (Solutions on page 296)

Two resistors, P and Q, are connected to a 24 V battery with internal resistance *r* as shown in the circuit diagram below. The power rating of each of the resistors P and Q are indicated on the diagram.

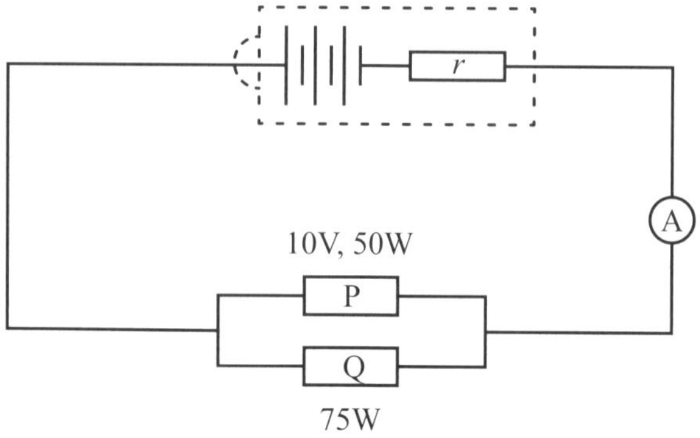

13.1 If the power rating of resistor P is 50 W and the potential difference across resistor P is 10 V, calculate the current flowing through resistor P. (3)

13.2 Determine the current flowing through resistor Q. (3)

13.3 Determine the internal resistance of the battery. (3)

[9]

Question 14 (Solutions on page 296 and 297)

A science learner is trying to determine the EMF and internal resistance of a battery. The learner has an ammeter, five identical new batteries and a box of resistors ranging between 0,1KΩ to 2,2KΩ. The learner sets up the circuit as shown below.

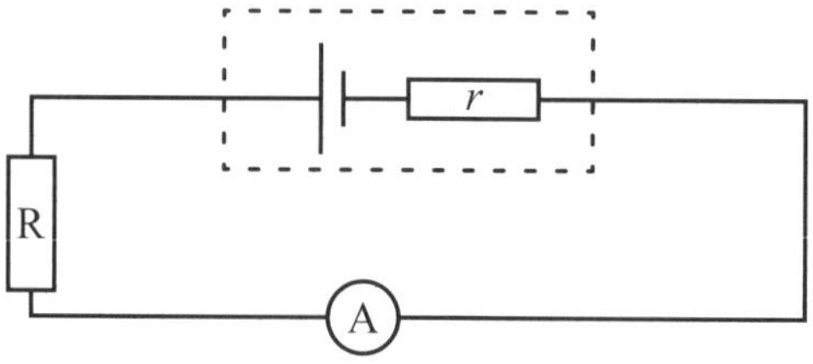

The learner conducts 5 experiments each time replacing the resistor as well as the battery.

14.1 Why is it necessary that the battery is replaced each time the experiment is performed? (1)

14.2 The learner's results are tabulated below. Complete the table. (4)

Resistance (KΩ)	Current (A)	$\frac{1}{I}\left(A^{-1}\right)$
0,1	0,08	
0,4	0,04	
1	0,02	
1,3	0,016	
2,2	0,01	

14.3 Plot a graph of $\frac{1}{I}\left(A^{-1}\right)$ against resistance (KΩ) on the grid below. Draw a line of best fit. (4)

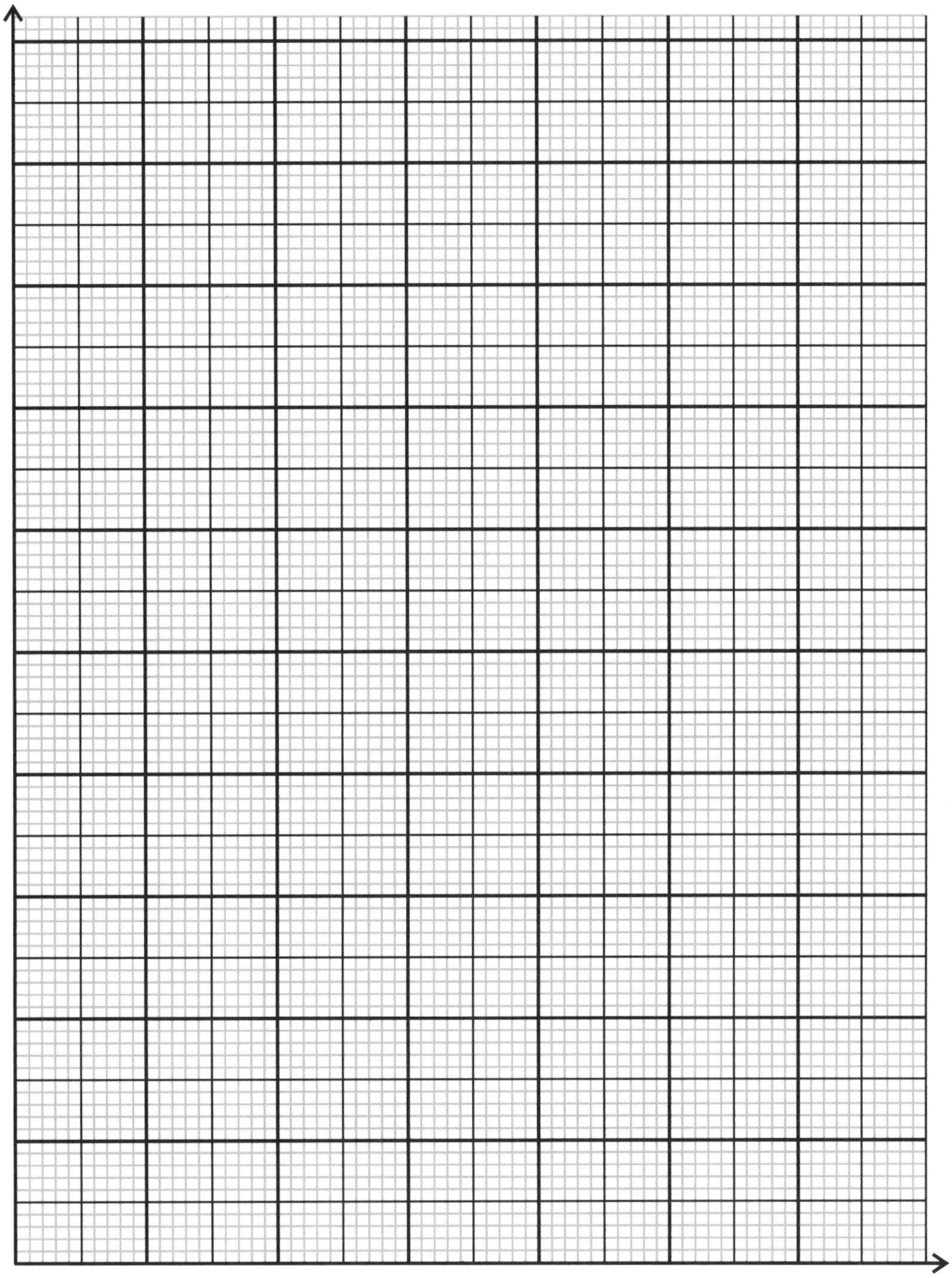

14.4 Show that the equation $EMF = I(R + r)$ can be rewritten as $\frac{1}{I} = \frac{1}{EMF}R + \frac{r}{EMF}$ and use it to determine the EMF and internal resistance of the cell. (8)

14.5 Use a dotted line on the same set of axes to show what the graph would look like if a battery with double the EMF and double the internal resistance of the original cell were used. (3)

[20]

TOC 1 Data Sheet 2 Definitions 3 3 solutions 4 4 solutions 5 5 solutions 6 6 solutions 7 7 solutions 8 8 solutions 9 9 solutions 10 10 solutions

TOC 1 Data Sheet 2 Definitions 3 3 solutions 4 4 solutions 5 5 solutions 6 6 solutions 7 7 solutions 8 8 solutions 9 9 solutions 10 10 solutions

Question 15 (Solutions on page 298)

In the circuit below the resistance of the connecting wires, ammeter and switch can be ignored. The voltmeter has a very high resistance and the battery has significant internal resistance. The emf of the cell is 34V and resistors R_1 and R_2 have resistances of 10Ω and 6Ω respectively. The internal resistance and R_3 are unknown.

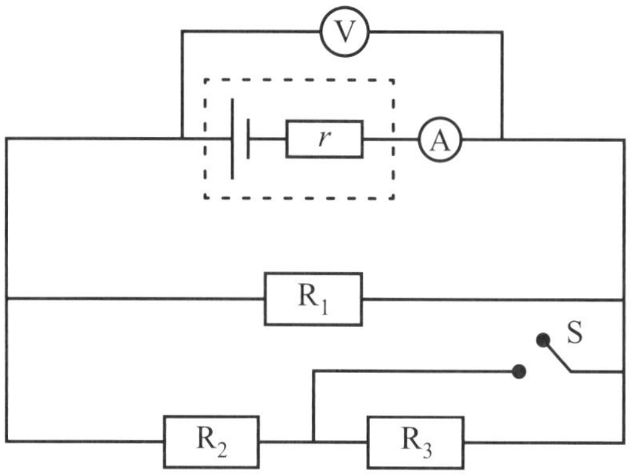

When switch S is open, the ammeter reads 4A and when closed, the ammeter reads 8A.

15.1 State Ohm's Law. (2)

15.2 Fully explain the reason for the increase in the ammeter reading when the switch is closed (4)

15.3 Determine the external resistance of the circuit when the switch is closed. (3)

15.4 Determine the internal resistance of the cell. (5)

15.5 Calculate the reading on the voltmeter when the switch is open. (4)

15.6 Determine the external resistance of the circuit when the switch is open. (3)

15.7 Determine the resistance of R_3. (4)

15.8 Calculate the number of electrons that flow through resistor R_3 in 10 minutes. (6)

[31]

Question 16 (Solutions on page 299)

An experiment to compare and determine the resistance of two pieces of wire, X and Y was conducted. The results of the experiment are graphed below.

Graph of Voltage versus Current for resistors X and Y

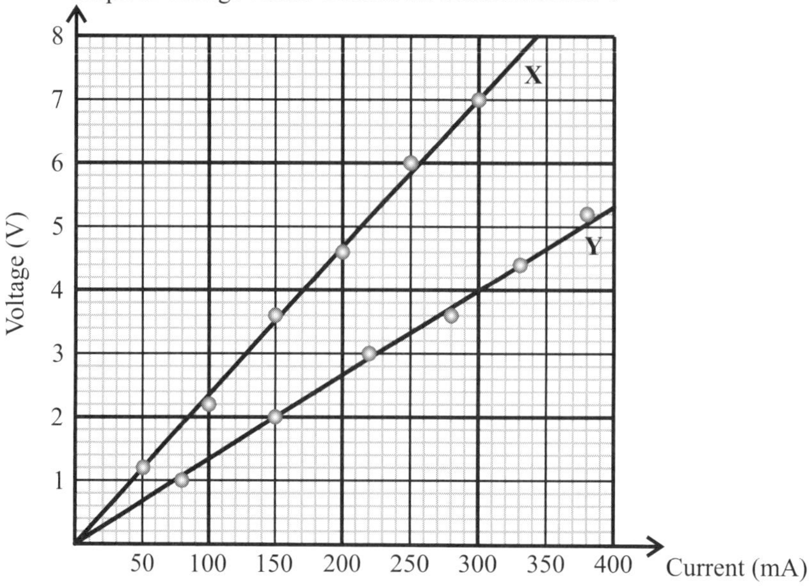

16.1 State Ohm's Law. (2)

16.2 What 3 factors need to be kept constant in the experiment? (3)

16.3 Which wire has the greater resistance? Give a reason for your answer. (2)

16.4 Determine the resistance of each wire, X and Y. (5)

16.5 Which wire would be most suitable to use in a power transmission line? Use a suitable equation to justify your answer. (3)

[15]

Question 17 (Solutions on page 299)

An ambitious science learner wants to make a circuit that will turn on a red LED outside his bedroom when he is studying so he is not disturbed. He purchases a box of LED's which come with a data sheet. He connects the LED to a 6V source with negligible internal resistance. As soon as he connects the LED, he hears a loud popping sound and sees that the LED has broken. He turns to the data sheet and finds the following information.

Introduction:
These diffused LEDs are perfect for a variety of applications. The diffused lenses, wide viewing and medium luminous intensity make them ideal for indicators (e.g. Power, status etc).

Technical information:

Forward Voltage:	2,1V
Angle:	60 deg
Luminous intensity:	275 mCd (@20mA rated current)
Max forward current:	20 mA
Lens type:	Diffused

17.1 Using the above information explain why the LED broke. (2)

The learner then connects a resistor in series with another LED from the box, as shown in the diagram below, and finds that it functions as expected.

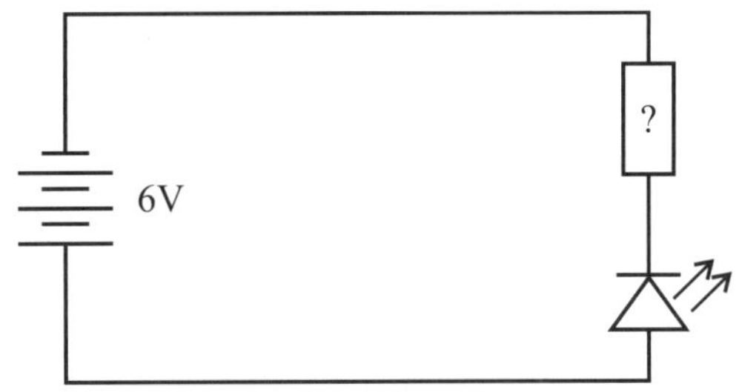

17.2 What is the value of the resistor that must be used in the circuit? (5)

17.3 Calculate the resistance of the LED. (3)

17.4 Determine the power rating of the resistor. (3)

[13]

Question 18 (2014 IEB Exemplar Examination) (Solutions on page 299 and 300)

18.1 In the following circuit the resistances of the ammeters, cells and connecting wires are negligible.

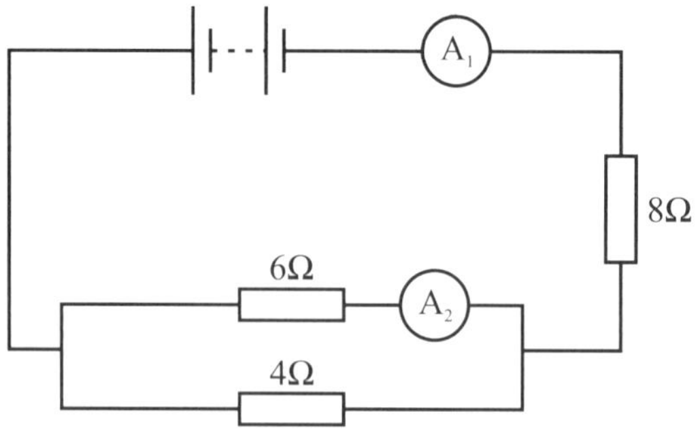

The reading on the ammeter A_1 is 2 A.

18.1.1 State Ohm's Law. (2)

18.1.2 Determine the potential difference across the 8Ω resistor (3)

18.1.3 Calculate the current measured by the ammeter A_2. (3)

18.2 A cell has an emf *E* and internal resistance *r* and is connected to an external circuit. There is a current *I* in the circuit when the potential difference across the terminals of the cell is *V*.

18.2.1 Define *emf.* (2)

The graph below shows the variation of *V* with *I* for the cell.

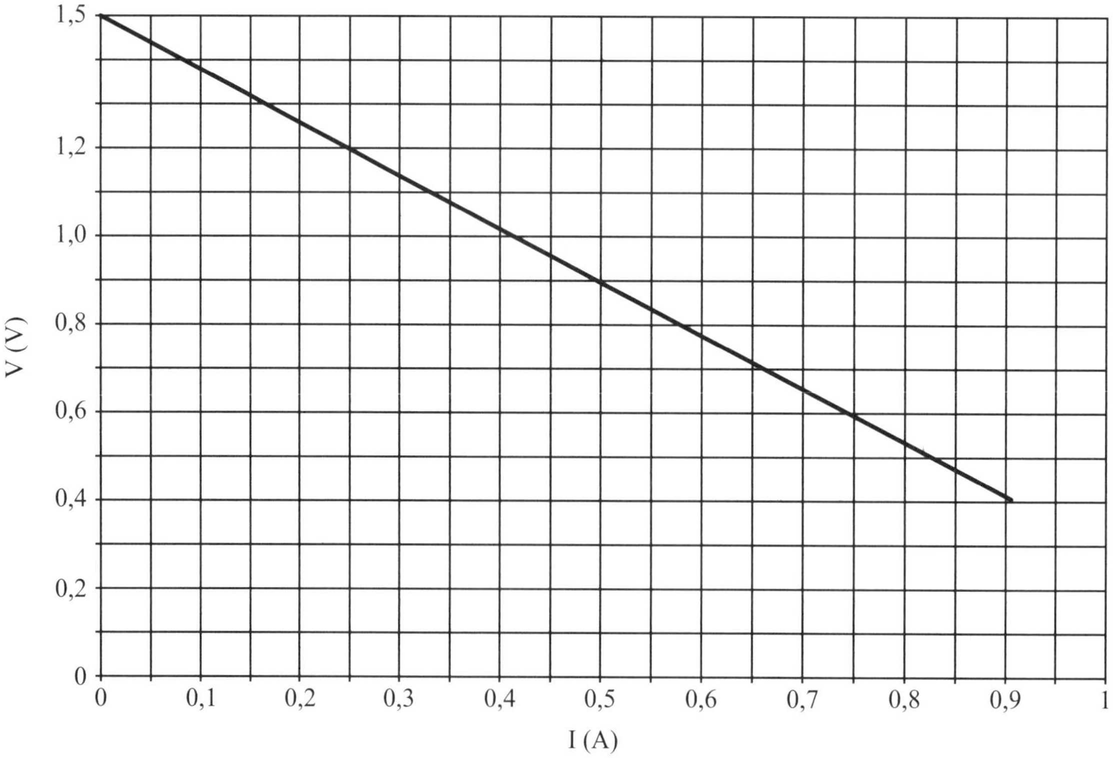

18.2.2 Sketch a diagram of the circuit that could have been used to obtain the data used to plot the above graph. (3)

TOC 1 Data Sheet 2 Definitions 3 3 solutions 4 4 solutions 5 5 solutions 6 6 solutions 7 7 solutions 8 8 solutions 9 9 solutions 10 10 solutions

18.2.3 Use the graph to determine the emf of the cell. Explain how you obtained your answer. (2)

18.2.4 a) Use the equation $V = emf - Ir$, together with the graph, to determine the physical quantity represented by the gradient of the graph. Clearly indicate your reasoning. (2)

b) Calculate the magnitude of the physical quantity represented by the gradient of the graph. (3)

18.3 A motor is used to raise a concrete statue of mass 350 kg through a height of 2,5 m onto the top of a building. It takes 5 minutes to lift the statue into position.

18.3.1 Calculate the power required to lift the statue. (4)

The motor is connected to a 24 V supply and has a resistance of 15Ω.

18.3.2 Calculate the percentage efficiency of the motor. (5)

[29]

Question 19 (2014 IEB Final Examination) (Solutions on page 300 and 301)

19.1 An electric circuit is set up as shown in the diagram below. The resistances of the switch, ammeters and connecting wires are negligible. The voltmeters have very high resistance. The battery has an emf (ε) of 12 V and has significant internal resistance (r).

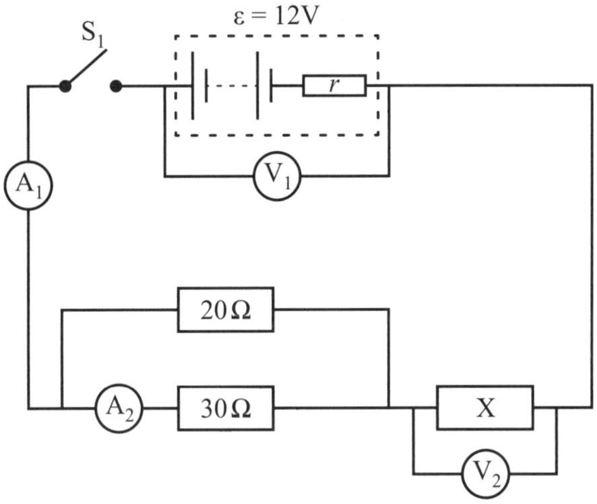

The switch S_1 is CLOSED. The ammeter A_2 reads 0,2 A and the voltmeter V_2 reads 5,5 V.

19.1.1 Define *emf.* (2)

19.1.2 Calculate the reading on ammeter A_1. (4)

19.1.3 Calculate the resistance of resistor **X**. (3)

19.1.4 Calculate the total external resistance of the circuit. (3)

19.1.5 Calculate the internal resistance (r) of the battery. (4)

19.1.6 Resistor **X** is replaced by a new resistor of greater resistance than that of **X**.

a) Will the reading on the voltmeter $\mathbf{V_1}$ connected across the terminals of the battery *increase, decrease or remain the same?* (1)

b) Explain your answer to Question 19.1.6 (a), making reference to relevant formulae. (4)

19.2 An electric kettle is rated 240 V; 1 800 W.

19.2.1 What does 'rated 240 V; 1 800 W' mean in regard to how this kettle works? (2)

19.2.2 Calculate the current drawn by the kettle when connected to a 240 V source. (3)

19.2.3 Calculate the cost of using the kettle for 15 minutes if electricity costs R1,40 per kWh. (3)

[29]

Question 20 (2015 IEB Supplementary Examination) (Solutions on page 301 and 302)

Ayanda and Cindy conduct an experiment to determine how the potential difference across the terminals of a battery is affected by the size of the current through the battery. They set up the circuit shown below. They change the current through the battery by adjusting the resistance of the rheostat (variable resistor). They record the potential difference across the terminals of the battery as given by the reading on the voltmeter. The battery has significant internal resistance. The resistances of the wires and ammeter is negligible. The voltmeter has high resistance.

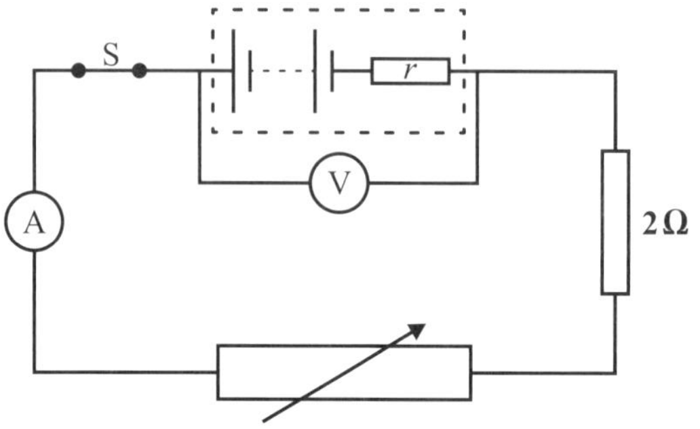

Results

Current (A)	Potential Difference (V)
0,0	15,0
0,6	13,5
1,2	12,0
2,0	10,0
2,6	8,5
3,2	7,0

20.1 Define *emf*. (2)

20.2 What is the emf of the battery used in this experiment? (1)

20.3 What is the dependent variable in this experiment? (2)

20.4 Using the grid on the next page, plot a graph to show the relationship between the potential difference across the terminals of the battery and the current through the battery. The *x*-axis has been labelled for you. (6)

20.5 Use the graph to determine the reading on the voltmeter when the current is 2,3A. (1)

20.6 Determine the internal resistance of the battery. (4)

20.7 Explain why the potential difference across the battery decreases as the current through the battery increases. Make reference to one or more suitable formulae to support your answer. No calculations are required. (3)

20.8 Define resistance. (2)

20.9 Calculate the resistance of the rheostat when the current is 2,0 A. (4)

[25]

20.4

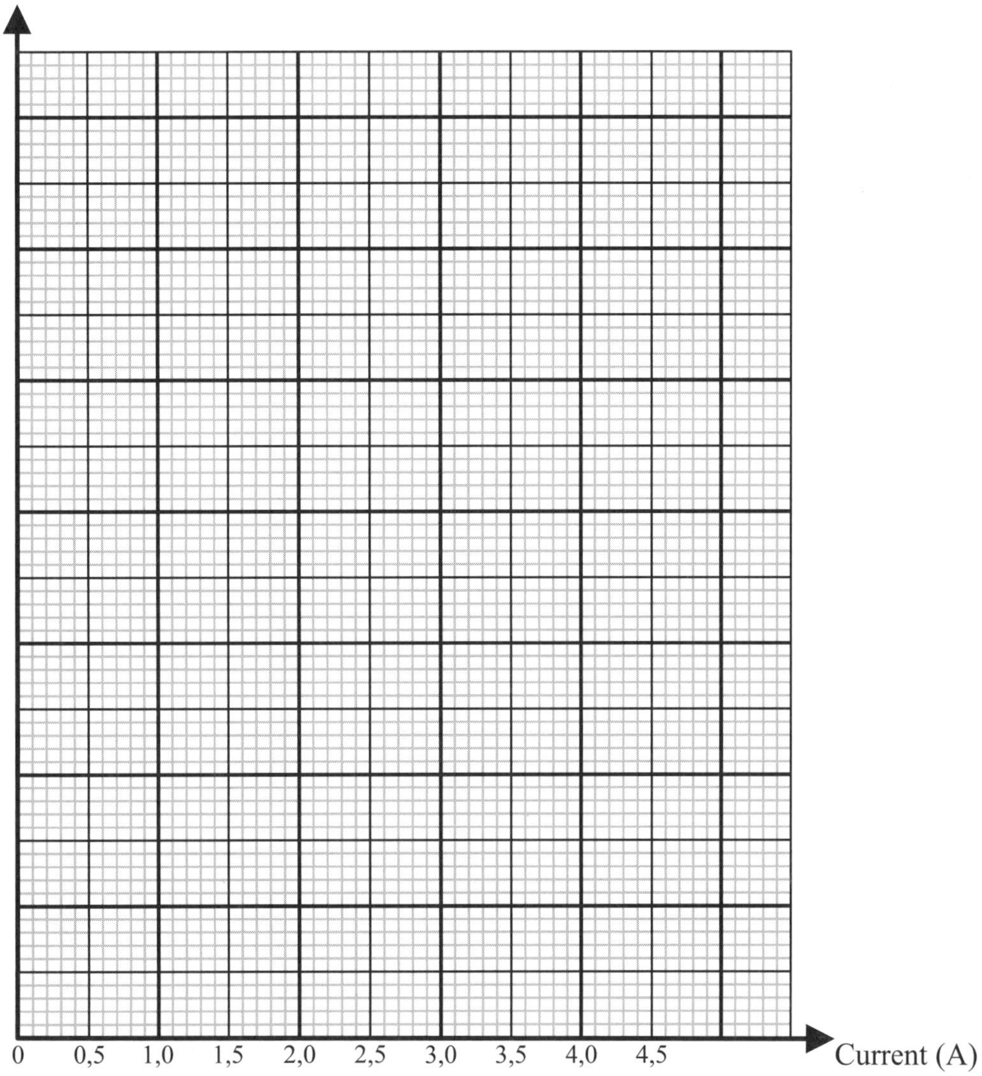

Question 21 (2015 IEB Final Examination) (Solutions on page 303 and 304)

Lauren's dad complains when she does not turn off the lights when she is not in the room. He says it is a waste of power and money.

21.1 Electricity costs R1,40 per kWh. Calculate the cost of having a 100 W light bulb on for six hours. (3)

21.2 The light bulb is labelled '240 V, 100 W'. Calculate the resistance of the light bulb. (3)

Lauren decides to carry out an experiment to determine how the number of identical bulbs in use affects the power consumed. She connects two bulbs in parallel to a power supply, determines the effective resistance (R) of the bulbs in parallel and measures the power consumption (P). She repeats the experiment adding another identical bulb in parallel each time and obtains the following results:

No of bulbs	R (Ω)	P (W)	$\frac{1}{R}\left(\times 10^{-3}\,\Omega^{-1}\right)$
2	288	168	3,47
3	192	252	**(21.5.1)**
4	144	336	6,94
5	115	420	8,70
6	96	504	**(21.5.2)**
7	82	588	12,2

21.3 Name the independent variable. (2)

21.4 Explain why the effective resistance of the parallel circuit decreases as more bulbs are added. (2)

Lauren decides it would be useful to calculate the $\frac{1}{R}$.

21.5 All but two values of $\frac{1}{R}$ have been calculated in the last column. Calculate the values shown as **(21.5.1)** and **(21.5.2)** in the table. (2)

21.6 Plot a graph of P on the y-axis vs. $\frac{1}{R}$ on the *x*-axis on the graph paper provided below. (6)

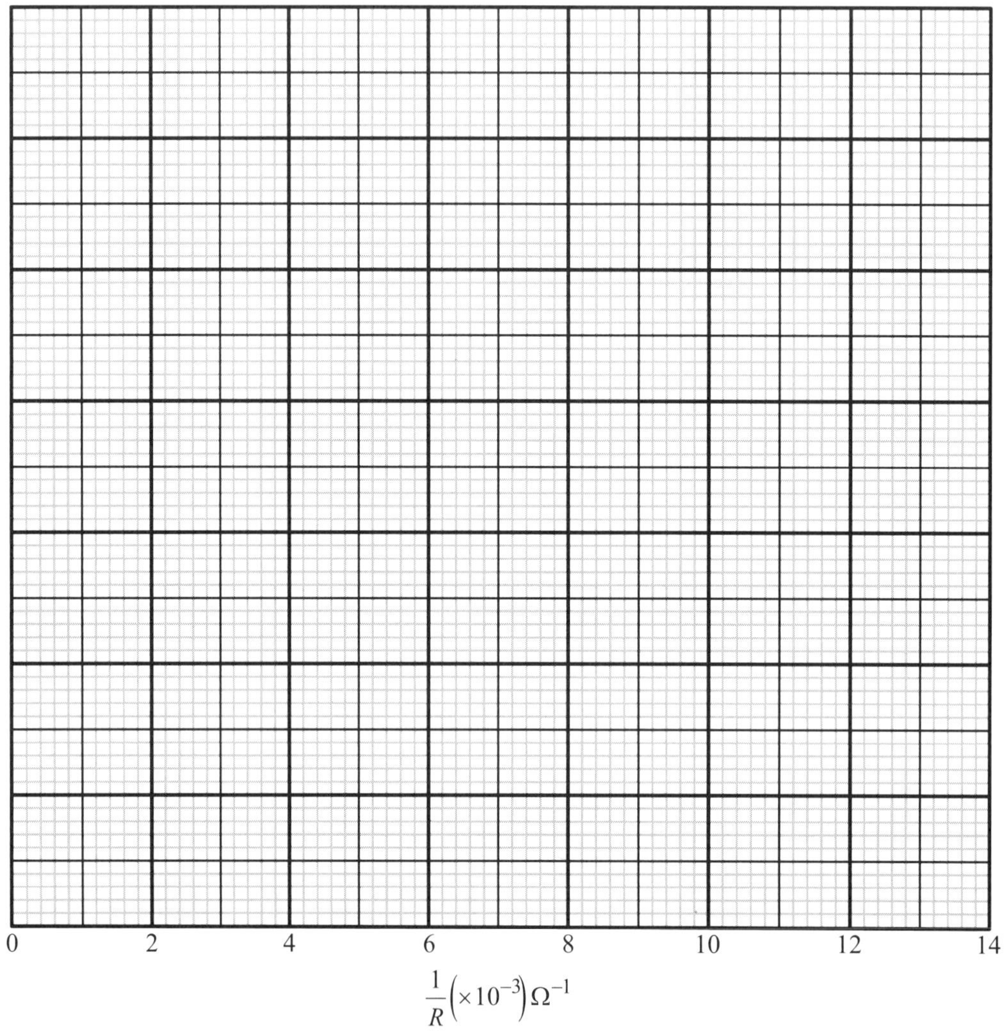

21.7 Use your graph to state the relationship between Power and Resistance. What **two** features of the graph led you to your conclusion? (3)

21.8 Calculate the gradient of the graph. Indicate the values you used for this calculation on your graph. (4)

21.9 Use your answer from Question 21.8 to determine the potential difference of the power supply that the bulbs are actually connected to. You are reminded that $P = V^2.\frac{1}{R}$ and that the equation $y = mx + c$ describes a straight line. (3)

[28]

Question 22 (2016 IEB Supplementary Examination) (Solutions on page 304)

22.1 A battery powers a torch that has a bulb with a resistance of 6 Ω. The potential difference across the bulb is 3 V.

22.1.1 Define potential difference (2)

22.1.2 Calculate the current in the bulb. (3)

22.1.3 Calculate the amount of charge that passes through the bulb in 10 minutes. (3)

22.2 The circuit illustrated was set up by a group of students. The emf of the battery was 12V. When the switch, S, was closed, the ammeter read 2A and the voltmeter read 10V.

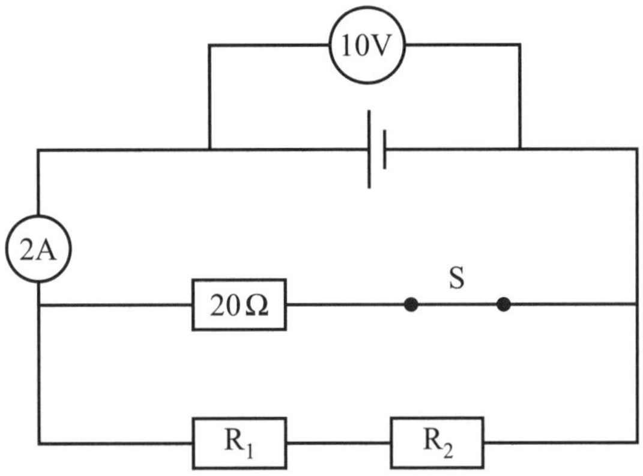

22.2.1 Define *emf.* (2)

22.2.2 Calculate the internal resistance of the battery. (3)

22.2.3 Calculate the current in the 20 Ω resistor. (3)

The power dissipated in the resistor labelled R_1 is 5,85 W.

22.2.4 Determine the resistance of the resistor labelled R_1. (4)

22.2.5 Determine the resistance of resistor R_2. (4)

22.2.6 Will the reading on the voltmeter across the battery increase, decrease or stay the same when the switch, S, is opened? Use an equation to explain your answer. (4)

[28]

Question 23 (2016 IEB Final Examination) (Solutions on page 305)

23.1 A circuit that consists of a battery with an emf of 26 V and an unknown internal resistance, three resistors, an ammeter and a voltmeter is set up as shown in the diagram below.

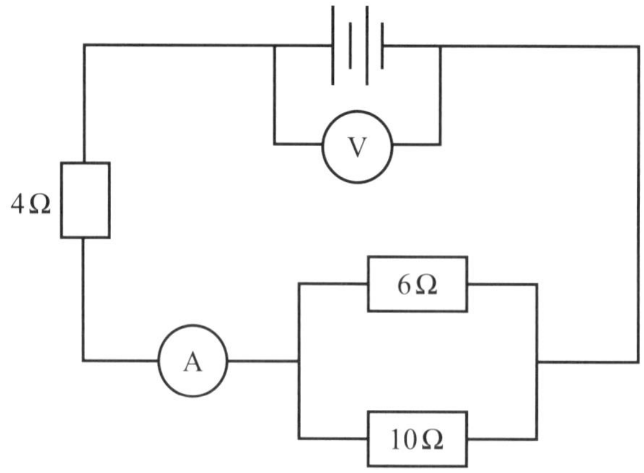

23.1.1 Define *resistance.* (2)

23.1.2 Calculate the effective resistance of the circuit. (5)

The ammeter measures a current of **3 A** with the circuit connected as shown.

23.1.3 Define *current.* (2)

23.1.4 Calculate the potential difference that will be recorded by the voltmeter. (3)

23.1.5 Hence, determine the internal resistance of the battery. (3)

Sometimes, resistors burn out while in operation.

23.1.6 Describe what would happen to the reading on the voltmeter if the 6 Ω resistor burnt out. Use a suitable equation in your explanation. (4)

23.1.7 Predict what the reading on the voltmeter would be if the 4 Ω resistor burnt out. Briefly explain your answer. (3)

23.2 Chris finds an unlabelled battery in the lab and needs to use it in a circuit. However, it is necessary to determine the emf and the internal resistance to decide if the battery is suitable.

Chris connects the unlabelled battery to a 2,0 Ω resistor and measures a current of 2,0 A through the resistor. He then connects the battery to a 1,0 Ω resistor and measures a current of 3,0 A.

Calculate the emf and internal resistance of the unlabelled battery. (5)

[27]

Question 24 (2017 IEB Supplementary Examination) (Solutions on page 305 and 306)

24.1 Older torches have bulbs that are filament light bulbs.

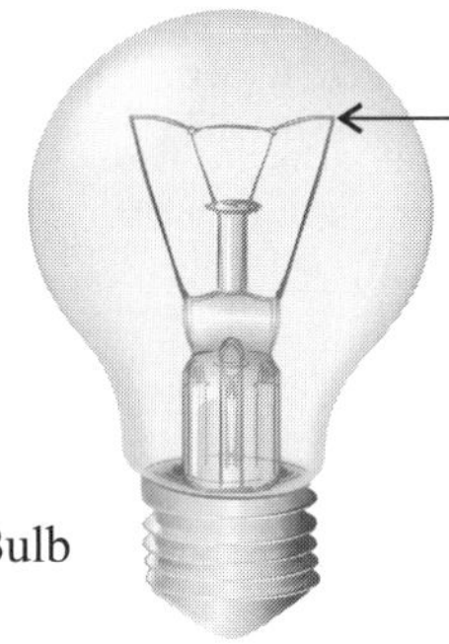

Filament Light Bulb

24.1.1 Is the filament light bulb an ohmic conductor? Explain your answer. (3)

24.1.2 Draw a sketch graph of V (y-axis) vs I (x-axis) for a filament light bulb. (2)

24.1.3 When used in a torch, the filament light bulb gets hot while the wires connecting the bulb to the battery do not, even though the current in both is the same. Explain the difference in temperature by making use of a relevant equation. (5)

24.2 Three resistors are connected to a 24 V battery of negligible internal resistance as shown in the diagram. The battery supplies 60 W of power to the circuit. The value of the resistance of resistor R is unknown.

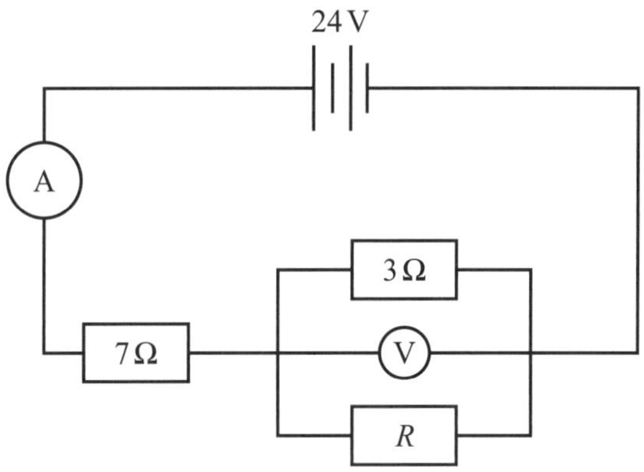

24.2.1 Define power. (2)

24.2.2 Calculate the reading on the ammeter. (3)

24.2.3 State *Ohm's law.* (2)

24.2.4 Calculate the potential difference across the 7 Ω resistor. (3)

24.2.5 Calculate the reading on the voltmeter. (2)

24.2.6 Determine the current flowing through resistor R. (5)

24.2.7 Hence calculate the value of the resistance of resistor R. (3)

[28]

Question 25 (2017 IEB Final Examination) (Solutions on page 306 and 307)

25.1 A circuit consists of a battery with an emf of 16,5 V and an unknown internal resistance, three resistors, an ammeter and a voltmeter. The circuit is connected as shown in the diagram below. The voltmeter measures a potential difference of **12 V**.

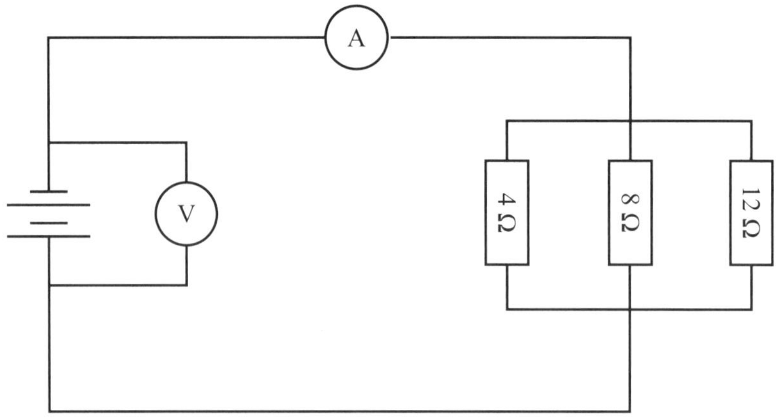

25.1.1 State *Ohm's Law*. (2)

25.1.2 Calculate the current in the 8 Ω resistor. (3)

25.1.3 Calculate the effective resistance of the resistors connected in parallel. (3)

25.1.4 Calculate the current measured by the ammeter. (3)

25.1.5 Calculate the internal resistance of the battery. (3)

25.2 An electrical heater which has a resistance of 50 Ω is operated by connecting the heater to a potential difference of 220 V.

25.2.1 Define *power*. (2)

25.2.2 Calculate the power output of the heater. (3)

Electricity costs R1,24 per kWh.

25.2.3 For how long can you operate the heater with R80 of prepaid electricity? (4)

[23]

Question 26 (2018 IEB Supplementary Examination) (Solutions on page 307 and 308)

26.1 A battery with an emf of 28 V and an internal resistance of 7 Ω is connected in a circuit as shown.

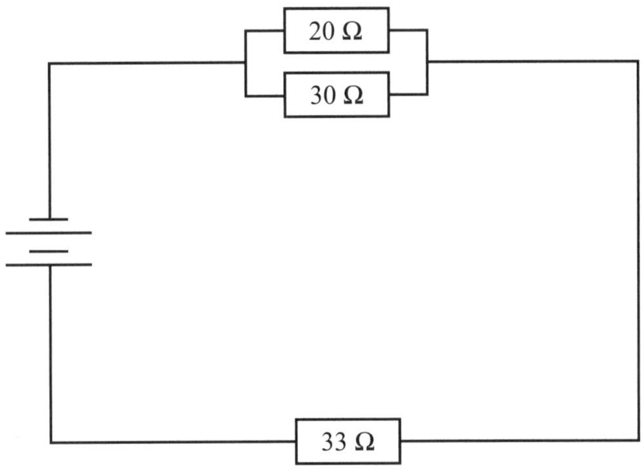

26.1.1 Define *emf.* (2)

26.1.2 Calculate the total resistance of the external circuit. (5)

26.1.3 Calculate the total current drawn from the battery. (3)

26.1.4 Determine the potential difference across the terminals of the battery. (3)

26.1.5 On the circuit diagram above, draw a voltmeter symbol and an ammeter symbol that would enable the potential difference across the 20 Ω resistor and the current through the 20 Ω to be measured. (4)

26.2 Students realise that the potential difference across the terminals of a battery and the current drawn from the battery change as the resistance in a circuit changes.

The students decided to experiment and changed the external resistance of a circuit and recorded the following set of data.

Current (A)	Terminal Potential Difference (V)
0,15	11,75
0,35	11,10
0,55	10,52
0,75	10,23
0,95	9,64
1,15	9,15

26.2.1 Define *potential difference.* (2)

26.2.2 Plot a graph of the terminal potential difference (on the y-axis) vs current (on the x-axis) on the graph paper provided on the next page. (6)

26.2.3 Calculate the gradient of the graph. Indicate the values you used for this calculation on your graph. (4)

26.2.4 Use your answer for Question 26.2.3 to determine the internal resistance of the battery. (2)

26.2.5 What quantity does the y-intercept represent? (2)

[33]

26.2.2 Graph paper

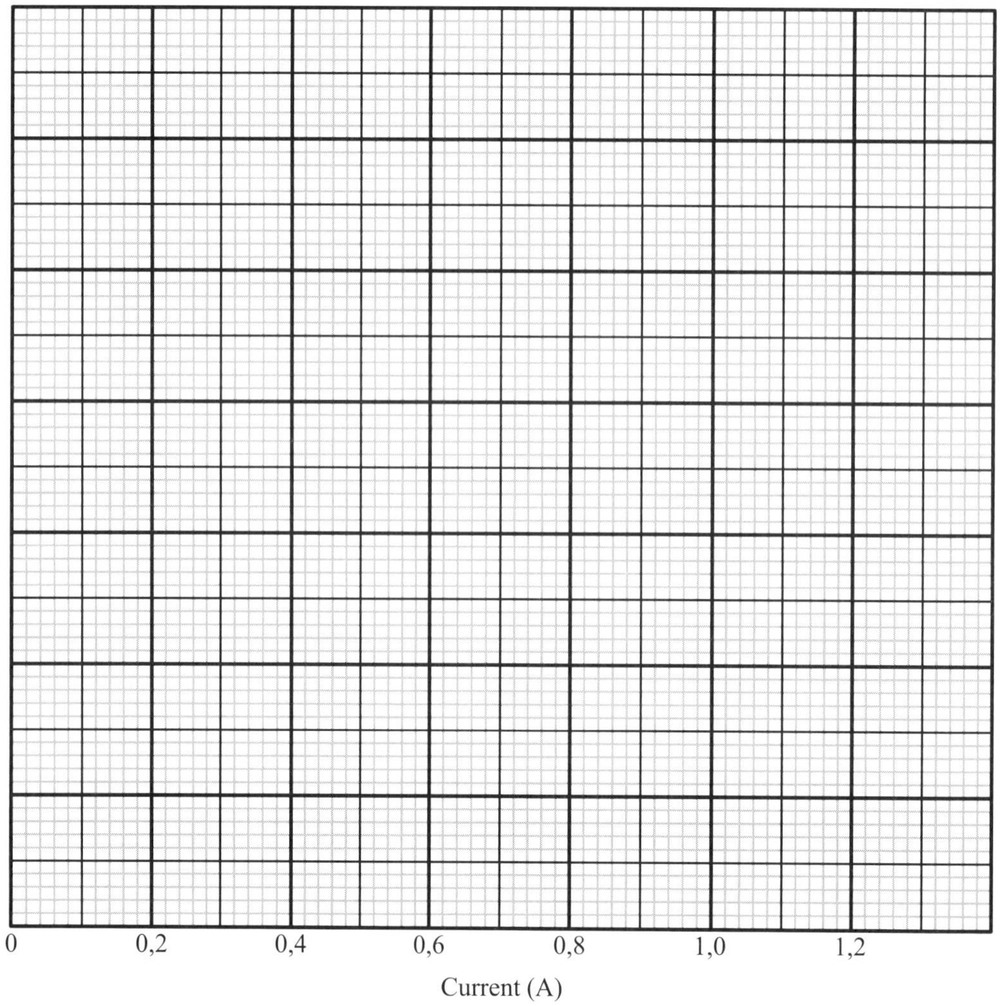

Question 27 (2018 IEB Final Examination) (Solutions on page 309)

27.1 A battery with emf 6 V and an internal resistance r is connected in series to two resistors, each of constant resistance R as shown in diagram 27a.

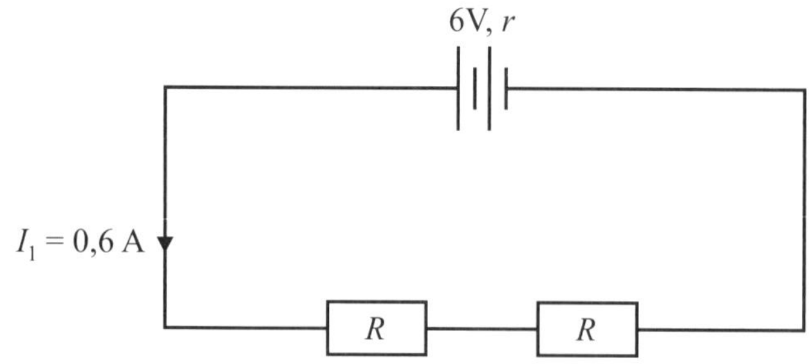

Diagram 27a

The current I_1 supplied by the battery is 0,6 A.
The same battery is now connected to two resistors, also of constant resistance R, connected in parallel as shown in diagram 27b on the next page.

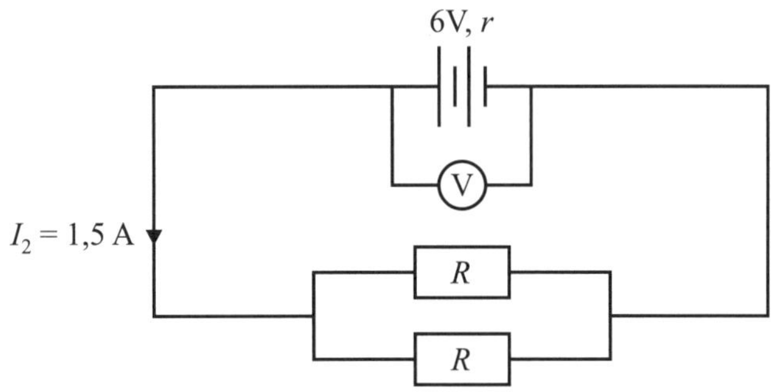

Diagram 27b

The current I_2 supplied by the battery is 1,5 A.

27.1.1 Define *resistance.* (2)

27.1.2 Define emf. (2)

27.1.3 Consider the circuit in diagram 27a and write an equation to express the emf in terms of I_1, r and R. (2)

27.1.4 Consider the circuit in diagram 27b and write an equation to express the emf in terms of I_2, r and R. (2)

27.1.5 Use your equations in Question 27.1.3 and Question 27.1.4 to calculate the resistance of R. (3)

27.1.6 Define *Power.* (2)

27.1.7 Calculate the power dissipated by one resistor R in diagram 27b. (3)

A third resistor R is connected in parallel with the existing resistors in diagram 27b.

27.1.8 State whether the reading of the voltmeter would increase, decrease or stay the same. Use a suitable equation to help you explain your answer. (4)

27.2 Two different bulbs A and B are connected in parallel to a potential difference of 12 V. Bulb A glows more brightly than bulb B.

27.2.1 Define *potential difference.* (2)

For the following questions, answer bulb A, bulb B, or neither.

27.2.2 Which bulb has the greater potential difference across it? (2)

27.2.3 Which bulb carries the greater current? (2)

27.2.4 Which bulb has the greatest resistance? (2)

[28]

Question 28 (2019 IEB Supplementary Examination) (Solutions on page 309 and 310)

A circuit consists of a battery with an emf of 30 V and an internal resistance of 1 Ω. A motor M, a variable resistor (rheostat) which can be set at different values R, a 5 Ω resistor and a switch S are connected as shown in the diagram below.

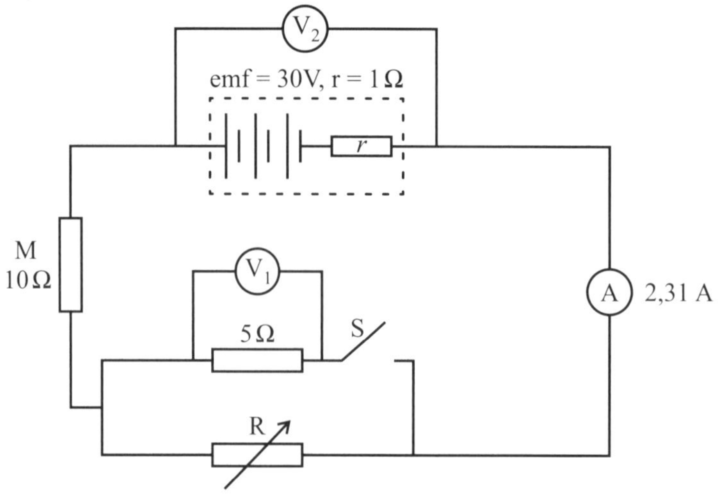

The reading on the ammeter is 2,31 A with the switch open:

28.1 Define *current*. (2)

28.2 Calculate the power dissipated in the motor M. (3)

28.3 Calculate the resistance at which the rheostat is set, R. (4)

28.4 What is the reading on the voltmeter V_1? (1)

28.5 What is the reading on the voltmeter V_2? (2)

28.6 Define *resistance*. (2)

28.7 Suppose the rheostat is now adjusted so that it has a higher resistance.

28.7.1 Will the power dissipated in the motor increase, decrease or remain the same? (1)

28.7.2 Justify your answer in Question 28.7.1 making reference to two relevant formulae. (3)

28.8 The rheostat is adjusted so that its resistance is 10 Ω **and the switch is now closed**.

28.8.1 Calculate the reading on the ammeter. (5)

28.8.2 Calculate the reading on the voltmeter V_1. (3)

[26]

TOC | 1 Data Sheet | 2 Definitions | 3 | 3 solutions | 4 | 4 solutions | 5 | 5 solutions | 6 | 6 solutions | 7 | 7 solutions | 8 | 8 solutions | 9 | 9 solutions | 10 | 10 solutions

Question 29 (2019 IEB Final Examination) (Solutions on page 310 and 311)

29.1 In the circuit represented below, the battery has an emf of 15V and an unknown internal resistance. Voltmeter V_1 is connected across the battery and voltmeter V_2 is connected across an open switch S. The resistance of the ammeter is negligible.

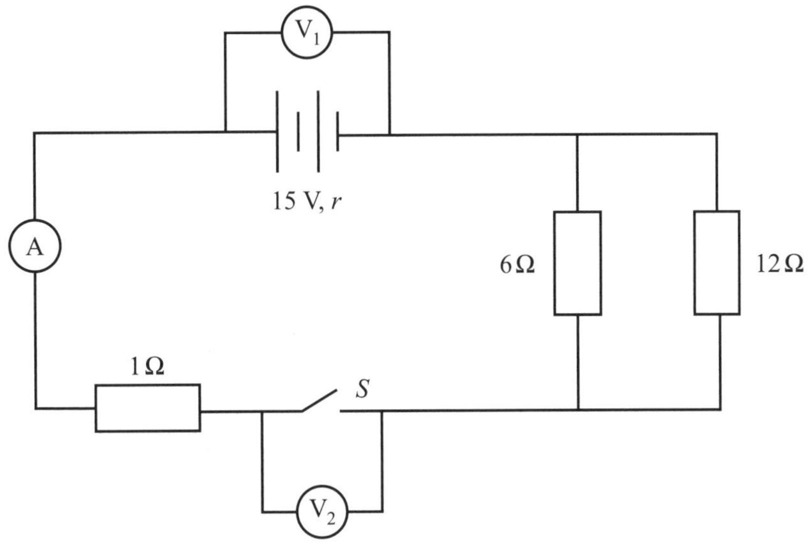

The **switch S is open**

29.1.1 Define *potential difference.* (2)

29.1.2 Determine the reading on voltmeter V_1. (2)

29.1.3 Determine the reading on voltmeter V_2. (2)

The **switch S is now closed**. The reading on voltmeter V_1 drops to 10,5 V.

29.1.4 Use a suitable equation to explain why the reading on V_1 drops. (3)

29.1.5 Calculate the effective resistance of the resistors in parallel. (3)

29.1.6 Calculate the reading on the ammeter. (3)

29.1.7 Calculate the internal resistance of the battery. (3)

29.2 An electrician needs to replace a bulb that has a 220 V supply. Unfortunately, the only working lightbulb in stock is rated 50 V, 100 W.

29.2.1 Calculate the resistance of the 50 V, 100 W light bulb. (3)

29.2.2 Calculate the current that should flow through the working lightbulb. (3)

The electrician uses the 50 V, 100 W light bulb and connects a resistor in series with the light bulb to ensure that the bulb operates at its correct rating when connected to the 220 V supply.

29.2.3 What should the resistance of the resistor be that the electrician connects in series with the light bulb? (3)

[27]

TOC | 1 Data Sheet | 2 Definitions | 3 | 3 solutions | 4 | 4 solutions | 5 | 5 solutions | 6 | 6 solutions | 7 | 7 solutions | 8 | 8 solutions | 9 | 9 solutions | 10 | 10 solutions

7. ELECTRIC CIRCUITS (SOLUTIONS)

Question 1

1.1	D	(2)	1.16	D	(2)
1.2	B	(2)	1.17	C	(2)
1.3	D	(2)	1.18	B	(2)
1.4	C	(2)	1.19	C	(2)
1.5	A	(2)	1.20	D	(2)
1.6	C	(2)	1.21	B	(2)
1.7	A	(2)	1.22	A	(2)
1.8	D	(2)	1.23	B	(2)
1.9	B	(2)	1.24	C	(2)
1.10	B	(2)	1.25	D	(2)
1.11	D	(2)	1.26	C	(2)
1.12	D	(2)	1.27	B	(2)
1.13	B	(2)	1.28	D	(2)
1.14	A	(2)	1.29	A	(2)
1.15	B	(2)			

[58]

Question 2

$EMF = I(R_{ext} + r_{int})$

$EMF = 1(1{,}8 + r_{int})$

$EMF = 1{,}8 + r_{int}$

$EMF = I(R_{ext} + r_{int})$

$EMF = 2(0{,}8 + r_{int})$

$EMF = 1{,}6 + 2r_{int}$

$\therefore 1{,}6 + 2r_{int} = 1{,}8 + r_{int}$

$r_{int} = 0{,}2\ \Omega$

$EMF = 2\ V$

[7]

Question 3

3.1 To control the current in the circuit by changing the resistance. (2)

3.2 Switch open:

$EMF = I(R_{ext} + r_{int})$

$EMF = 2(4{,}2 + r_{int})$

$EMF = 8{,}4 + 2r_{int}$

Switch closed:

$EMF = I(R_{ext} + r_{int})$

$EMF = 3(2{,}2 + r_{int})$

$EMF = 6{,}6 + 3r_{int}$

$\therefore 8{,}4 + 2r_{int} = 6{,}6 + 3r_{int}$

$r_{int} = 1{,}8\ \Omega$

$EMF = 12\ V$ (7)

3.3 $P = I^2R$

$= 3^2(1{,}8)$

$= 16{,}2\ W$ (2)

3.4 $P = I^2R \rightarrow$ rate of energy transfer is power

$= 2^2(0{,}2)$

$= 0{,}8\ W$ (2)

3.5 $W = P.t = 0{,}8(3 \times 60)$

$= 144\,J$ (3)

3.6 Dimmer. (1)

3.7 When the switch is opened total resistance increases.

$I \,\alpha\, \frac{1}{R}$ (current is inversely proportional to resistance)

If resistance increases the current in the circuit will decrease.

$P \,\alpha\, I^2$ (power is directly proportional to current squared)

If current decreases the power dissipated by the bulb will decrease. (3)

[20]

Question 4

4.1 The rate of flow of charge. (2)

4.2 $P = I^2R$

$= 2{,}25^2(8)$

$= 40{,}5\,W$ (3)

4.3 $V_1 = EMF - V_r$

$= 30 - 2{,}25(2)$

$= 25{,}5\,V$ (3)

4.4 $V_2 = V_1 - V_{lightbulb}$

$= 25{,}5 - 2{,}25(8)$

$= 7{,}5\,V$ (3)

4.5 $I_{5\Omega} = \frac{V}{R} = \frac{7{,}5}{5}$

$= 1{,}5\,A$

$\therefore I_{rheostat} = 2{,}25 - {,}15$

$= 0{,}75\,A$

$R_{rheostat} = \frac{V}{I} = \frac{7{,}5}{0{,}75}$

$= 10\,\Omega$ (4)

4.6 If the resistance of the rheostat is increased, total resistance increases. $I \,\alpha\, \frac{1}{R}$ (current is inversely proportional to resistance). Therefore, the current in the circuit will decrease. $P \,\alpha\, I^2$ (power is directly proportional to current squared) if current decreases the power in the bulb will decreases and it will be dimmer. (4)

4.7 $\frac{1}{R_{//}} = \frac{1}{5} + \frac{1}{20}$

$R_{//} = 4\Omega$

$R_{tot} = 4 + 8 + 2$

$= 14\Omega$

$I = \frac{EMF}{R_{tot}} = \frac{30}{14}$

$= 2{,}14\,A$

$V_1 = EMF - V_r$

$= 30 - 2{,}14(2)$

$= 25{,}71\,V$ (8)

[27]

TOC | 1 Data Sheet | 2 Definitions | 3 | 3 solutions | 4 | 4 solutions | 5 | 5 solutions | 6 | 6 solutions | 7 | **7 solutions** | 8 | 8 solutions | 9 | 9 solutions | 10 | 10 solutions

Question 5

5.1.1 $R_{tot} = 25 + 5 + 8 + 12$

$= 50\,\Omega$ (1)

5.1.2 $I = \frac{V}{R} = \frac{20}{50}$

$= 0,4\text{ A}$ (2)

5.1.3 $V = IR = 0,4(20)$

$= 8\text{ V}$ (2)

5.1.4 $Q = It = 0,4(5 \times 60)$

$= 120\text{ C}$

$N_{e-} = \frac{Q}{q_{e-}} = \frac{120}{1,6 \times 10^{-19}}$

$= 7,5 \times 10^{20}$ electrons (5)

5.2.1 Ammeter: Increase
Voltmeter: Decrease (2)

5.2.2 When the switch is closed total resistance decreases.

$I \,\alpha\, \frac{1}{R}$ (current is inversely proportional to resistance). Therefore, the current in the circuit will increase.

$V \,\alpha\, I$ (Voltage is directly proportional to current)

As current in circuit increases, the voltage across the lightbulb and 5Ω resistor will increase and the reading on the voltmeter will decrease. (3)

5.2.3 $\frac{1}{R_{//}} = \frac{1}{20} + \frac{1}{12+8}$

$R_{//} = 10\,\Omega$

$I = \frac{V}{R}$

$= \frac{20}{10+5+25}$

$= 0,5\text{ A}$

$V_{//} = IR_{//}$

$= 0,5(10)$

$= 5\text{ V}$ (5)

[20]

Question 6

6.1 $V_1 = 12\text{ V}$ $V_2 = 0\text{ V}$ $V_3 = 12\text{ V}$ (2)

6.2 $I = \frac{V}{R} = \frac{2}{2}$

$= 1\text{ A}$

$r = \frac{V}{I} = \frac{1}{1}$

$= 1\,\Omega$ (3)

6.3 $V_{//} = 11 - 2$

$= 9V$

$R_{//} = \frac{V_{//}}{I} = \frac{9}{1}$

$= 9\Omega$

$\frac{1}{R_{//}} = \frac{1}{R_1} + \frac{1}{R_2}$

$\frac{1}{9} = \frac{1}{2x} + \frac{1}{x}$

$\frac{1}{9} = \frac{3}{2x}$

$x = 13{,}5\Omega$

$R_1 = 27\Omega$ (5)

6.4 $W = P.t$

$= \frac{V^2}{R}t = \frac{9^2}{13{,}5}(10 \times 60)$

$= 3600\ J$ (4)

[14]

Question 7

7.1 A high resistance ensures that the current in the circuit is low. This ensures that the battery doesn't heat up and keeps that the temperature of the battery remains relatively constant. (3)

7.2 Graph of voltage versus current

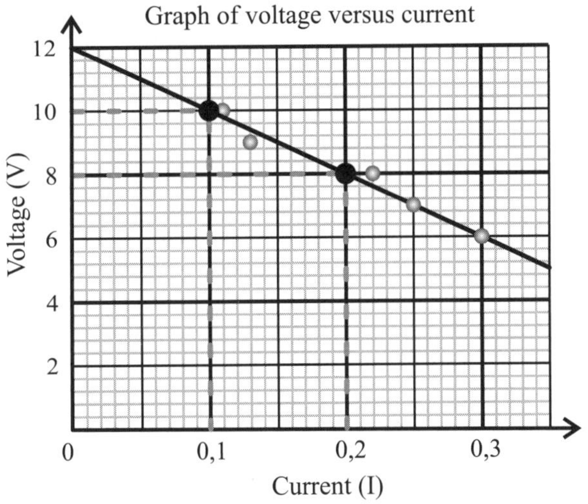

(5)

7.3 gradient $= \frac{10 - 8}{0{,}1 - 0{,}2}$

$= -20$ (2)

7.4 $EMF = I(R_{ext} + r_{int})$

$EMF = I.R_{ext} + I.r_{int} \rightarrow I.R_{ext} = V$

$V = -r_{int}.I + EMF \rightarrow y = mx + c$

$\therefore$ gradient $= -r_{int}$

$-r_{int} = -20$

$r_{int} = 20\Omega$ (4)

[14]

TOC
1 Data Sheet
2 Definitions
3
3 solutions
4
4 solutions
5
5 solutions
6
6 solutions
7
7 solutions
8
8 solutions
9
9 solutions
10
10 solutions

Question 8

8.1 The current through a conductor is directly proportional to the potential difference across the conductor at constant temperature. (2)

8.2 To change the current in the circuit. (by changing the resistance the current will change) (1)

8.3 Potential difference. (1)

8.4

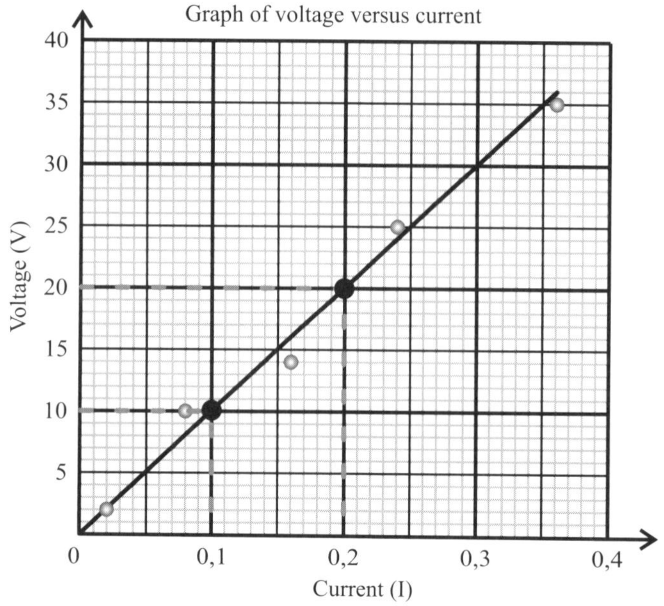

(5)

8.5

$$\text{gradient} = R = \frac{20-10}{0,2-0,1}$$
$$= 100\,\Omega$$

(4)

[13]

Question 9

9.1 6 Ω. As current splits equally the resistance in each branch must be the same (10Ω) (1)

9.2

$$V_2 = I_2R$$
$$= 4(10) = 40\,\text{V}$$

(3)

9.3

$$V_1 = IR_1$$
$$= 4(6) = 24\,\text{V}$$

(3)

9.4

$$V_r = 45 - 40$$
$$= 5\,\text{V}$$
$$r = \frac{V}{I}$$
$$= \frac{5}{8}$$
$$= 0,625\,\Omega$$
$$\therefore r_{\text{cell}} = 0,625 \div 3$$
$$= 0,21\,\Omega$$

(4)

9.5 If resistor R_1 breaks total resistance in the circuit increases. $I \alpha \frac{1}{R}$, If resistance increases current will decrease and A_1 will decrease. If current decreases lost volts will decrease and V_2 will increase. V_1 will read 0V as no current will flow in R_1. As V_2 increases the current in A_2 will increase (6)

[23]

Question 10

10.1 The EMF. (2)

10.2 $I = \frac{V_{//}}{R_{//}} = \frac{16}{32}$

$= 0,5\,A$

$R = \frac{V}{I} = \frac{4}{0,5}$

$= 8\,\Omega$ (5)

[7]

Question 11

11.1 $I = \frac{V}{R} = \frac{3}{300}$

$= 0,01\,A$

$V_{int} = Ir = 0,01(10)$

$= 0,1\,V$

$V_{rheostat} = 12 - 3 - 0,1$

$= 8.9\,V$

$R = \frac{V}{I} = \frac{8,9}{0,01}$

$= 890\,\Omega$ (6)

11.2.1 A resistor has been added in parallel which lowers the total resistance. Current is inversely proportional to resistance. By decreasing the resistance in the circuit current will increase causing a larger voltage drop across the variable resistor and internal resistor. (4)

11.2.2 $V_{rheostat} = 11,88 - 1,2$

$= 10,68\,V$

$I = \frac{V}{R} = \frac{10,68}{890}$

$= 0,012\,A$ (2)

11.2.3 $I_{300\Omega} = \frac{V}{R} = \frac{1,2}{300}$

$= 0,004$

$I_{component} = 0,012 - 0,004$

$= 0,008\,A$

$R = \frac{V}{I} = \frac{1,2}{0,008}$

$= 150\,\Omega$ (5)

11.2.4 $\frac{1}{R_{//}} = \frac{1}{300} + \frac{1}{150}$

$R_{//} = 100\,\Omega$

$I = \frac{V}{R} = \frac{3}{100}$

$= 0,03\,A$

$V_r = Ir = 0,03(10)$

$= 0,3\,V$

$V_{rheostat} = 12 - 0,3 - 3$

$= 8,7\,V$

$R = \frac{V}{I} = \frac{8,7}{0,03}$

$= 290\,\Omega$

[23]

Question 12

12.1 $I_{tot} = \frac{V}{R}$

$= \frac{2,4}{2}$

$= 1,2\,A$

$V_{12\Omega} = IR$

$= 1,2(12)$

$= 14,4\,V$

$V_{10\Omega} = 21,6 - 14,4$

$= 7,2\,V$

$I_{10\Omega} = \frac{V}{R}$

$= \frac{7,2}{10}$

$= 0,72\,A$

(6)

12.2 $I_X = 1,2 - 0,72$

$= 0,48\,A$

$R_X = \frac{V}{I}$

$= \frac{7,2}{0,48}$

$= 15\,\Omega$

(4)

12.3 It will be dimmer. If resistor X burns out, total resistance in the circuit increases. $I\,\alpha\,\frac{1}{R}$, If resistance increases current will decrease. $P\,\alpha\,I^2$. If current decreases the power in the bulb will be less.

(4)

12.4 $P = I^2R$

$= (1,2)^2(12)$

$= 17,28\,W$

$\text{Cost} = \left(\frac{17,28}{1000}\right)\left(\frac{40}{60} \times 365\right)(1,30)$

$= R5,47$

(6)

[20]

Question 13

13.1 $P = VI$

$50 = 10I$

$I = 5\,A$ (3)

13.2 $P = VI$

$75 = 10I$

$I = 7{,}5\,A$ (3)

13.3 $V_r = 24 - 10$

$= 14\,V$

$r = \frac{V_r}{I}$

$= \frac{14}{12{,}5}$

$= 1{,}12\,\Omega$ (3)

[9]

Question 14

14.1 To ensure that the EMF remains constant each time the resistor is changed. (1)

14.2

Resistance (KΩ)	Current (A)	$\frac{1}{I}\left(A^{-1}\right)$
0,1	0,08	12,5
0,4	0,04	25
1	0,02	50
1,3	0,016	62,5
2,2	0,01	100

14.3 Graph of I^{-1} versus Resistance (KΩ)

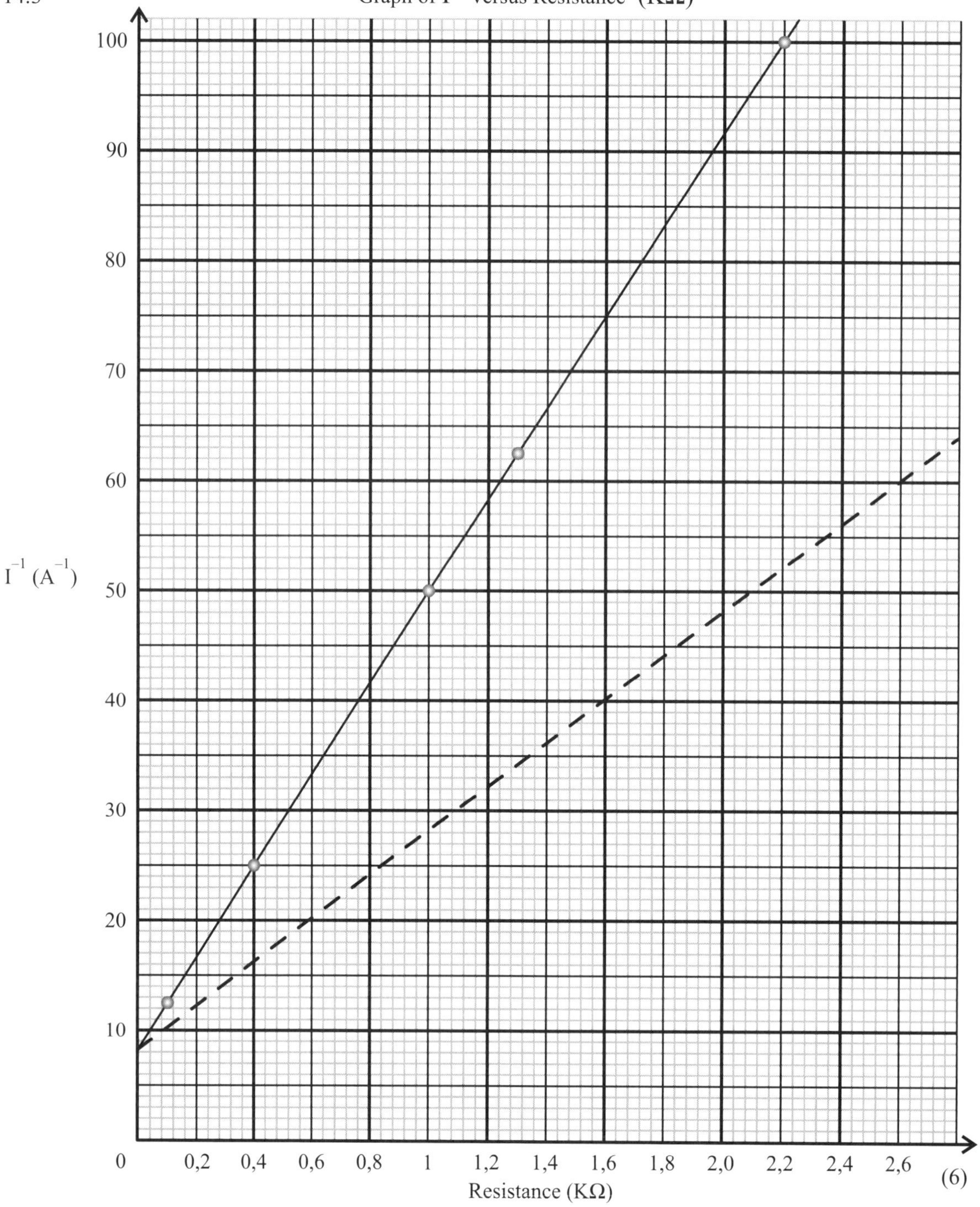

(6)

14.4 $\text{EMF} = I(R + r)$

$$\frac{\text{EMF}}{I} = R + r$$

$$\frac{1}{I} = \frac{1}{\text{EMF}}R + \frac{r}{\text{EMF}}$$

$$\text{gradient} = \frac{75 - 70}{1600 - 1480} = \frac{1}{24}$$

$\text{EMF} = 24\,\text{V}$

$$\frac{r}{\text{EMF}} = 8{,}3 \rightarrow y\text{-intercept}$$

$r = 8{,}3(24)$

$= 199{,}2\,\Omega \rightarrow$ accept any answer between $194{,}4\,\Omega$ and $206{,}4\,\Omega$

14.5 On the graph above.

(3)

[20]

Question 15

15.1 The Current through a conductor is directly proportional to the potential difference across the conductor at constant temperature. (2)

15.2 When the switch is closed a resistor in the parallel branch is short circuited which removes the resistor from the branch. This decreases the total resistance in the circuit. Current is inversely proportional to resistance. By decreasing resistance current increases. (4)

15.3 $\frac{1}{R_{//}} = \frac{1}{10} + \frac{1}{6}$

$R_{//} = 3,75\,\Omega$ (3)

15.4 $V_{ext} = IR = 8(3,75)$

$= 30\,V$

$r = \frac{V}{I} = \frac{4}{8}$

$= 0,5\,\Omega$ (5)

15.5 $V_r = Ir = 4(0,5)$

$= 2\,V$

$V_{ext} = 34 - 2$

$= 32\,V$ (4)

15.6 $R_{ext} = \frac{V}{I} = \frac{32}{4}$

$= 8\,\Omega$ (3)

15.7 **Method 1:**

$I_1 = \frac{V}{R_1}$

$= \frac{32}{10}$

$= 3,2\,A$

$I_{R2} = 4 - 3,2$

$= 0,8$

$V_{R_2} = IR_2$

$= 0,8(6)$

$= 4,8\,V$

$R_3 = \frac{V}{I}$

$= \frac{32 - 4,8}{0,8}$

$= 34\,\Omega$

Method 2:

$\frac{1}{8} = \frac{1}{10} + \frac{1}{6 + R_3}$

$10(6 + R_3) = 8(6 + R_3) + 80$

$R_3 = 34\,\Omega$ (4)

15.8 $Q = It$

$= (0,8)(10 \times 60)$

$= 480\,C$

$Q = N_{e-} \cdot q_{e-}$ → this is not on the data sheet

$N_{e-} = \frac{480}{1,6 \times 10^{-19}}$

$= 3 \times 10^{21}$ electrons (6)

[31]

Question 16

16.1 The Current through a conductor is directly proportional to the potential difference across the conductor at constant temperature. (2)

16.2 Temperature.
Thickness of the wires.
Length of the wires. (3)

16.3 X, as it has the steepest (largest) gradient. (2)

16.4
$$R_X = \frac{7-5{,}6}{350\times10^{-3}-240\times10^{-3}} = 23{,}33\,\Omega \qquad R_Y = \frac{4-2}{300\times10^{-3}-150\times10^{-3}} = 13{,}33\,\Omega$$
(5)

16.5 Wire Y. From $P = I^2R$, if current is constant, power is directly proportional to resistance. Therefore, the lower the resistance of the line the less power is lost on the line. (3)

[15]

Question 17

17.1 The voltage across the LED was 6V where it should have been 2,1V. (2)

17.2
$$\begin{aligned} R &= \frac{V}{I} \\ &= \frac{6-2{,}1}{20\times10^{-3}} \\ &= 195\,\Omega \end{aligned}$$
(5)

17.3
$$\begin{aligned} R &= \frac{V}{I} \\ &= \frac{2{,}1}{20\times10^{-3}} \\ &= 105\,\Omega \end{aligned}$$
(3)

17.4
$$\begin{aligned} P &= VI \\ &= 3{,}9\left(20\times10^{-3}\right) \\ &= 0{,}078\,\text{W} \end{aligned}$$
(3)

[13]

Question 18

18.1.1 The current through a conductor is directly proportional to the potential difference across the conductor at constant temperature. (2)

18.1.2
$$\begin{aligned} V &= IR \\ &= 8(2) \\ &= 16\,\text{V} \end{aligned}$$
(3)

18.1.3 Method 1:
$$\frac{1}{R_{//}} = \frac{1}{6} + \frac{1}{4}$$
$$R_{//} = 2{,}4\,\Omega$$
$$\begin{aligned} V_{//} &= R_{//}I \\ &= 2{,}4(2) \\ &= 4{,}8\,\text{V} \end{aligned}$$
$$\begin{aligned} I_1 &= \frac{V_{//}}{R} \\ &= \frac{4{,}8}{6} \\ &= 0{,}8\,\text{A} \end{aligned}$$

Method 2: Using a ratio for two resistors
$$\begin{aligned} I_1 &= \frac{4}{4+6}(2) \\ &= 0{,}8\,\text{A} \end{aligned}$$
(3)

18.2.1 EMF is the total energy supplied per coulomb of charge by the cell. (2)

18.2.2

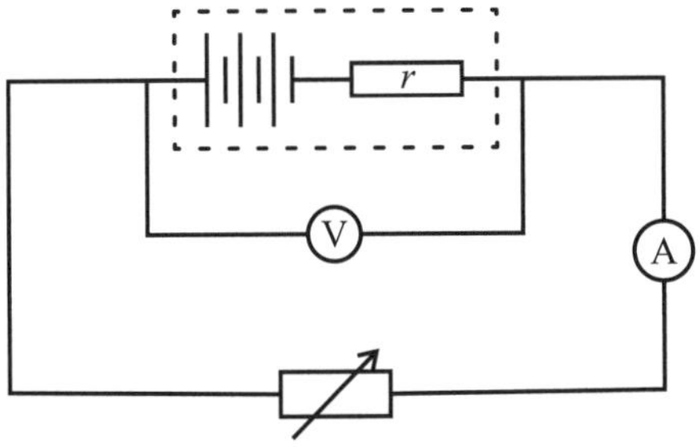

Marks are awarded for:

- Voltmeter across cells or rheostat
- Ammeter in series
- Circuit contains a rheostat

(3)

18.2.3 V = EMF – lost volts. Lost volts = 0 when I = 0. Therefore, EMF = 1,5 V. (2)

18.2.4 a) $V = -rI + EMF$

This is in the form $y = mx + c$

$\therefore -r = \text{gradient of the graph}$ (2)

b) $-r = \dfrac{0,6-1,5}{0,75-0}$

$= -1,2$

$r = 1,2\,\Omega$ (3)

18.3.1 $P = \dfrac{W}{t} = \dfrac{mgh}{t}$

$= \dfrac{350(9,8)(2,5)}{5(60)}$

$= 28,58\text{ W}$ (4)

18.3.2 $P = \dfrac{V^2}{R}$

$= \dfrac{24^2}{15}$

$= 38,4\text{ W}$

$\%\,efficiency = \dfrac{power\ out}{power\ in} \times 100$

$= \dfrac{28,58}{38,4} \times 100$

$= 74,4\%$

[29]

Question 19 (2014 IEB Final Examination)

19.1.1 The total energy supplied per coulomb of charge by the cell. (2)

19.1.2 Method 1:

$\dfrac{1}{R_{//}} = \dfrac{1}{20} + \dfrac{1}{30}$

$R_{//} = 12\,\Omega$

$V_{//} = R_{30\Omega} I$

$= 30(0,2)$

$= 6\text{ V}$

$I_{20\Omega} = \dfrac{V_{//}}{R_{20\Omega}}$

$= \dfrac{6}{20}$

$= 0,3\text{ A}$

$I_1 = 0,5\text{ A} \rightarrow 0,2 + 0,3$ (4)

Method 2: Using a ratio for two resistors

$I_{30\Omega} = \dfrac{20}{20+30} I_1$

$0,2 = \dfrac{20}{20+30} I_1$

$I_1 = 0,5\text{ A}$

19.1.3 $R_x = \frac{V_x}{I} = \frac{5,5}{0,5} = 11\Omega$ (3)

19.1.4 $R_{ext} = 12 + 11 \rightarrow R_{//} + R_{series}$
$= 23\Omega$ (3)

19.1.5 Method 1:
$V_{ext} = 6 + 5,5$
$= 11,5$
$r = \frac{V_r}{I} = \frac{12 - 11,5}{0,5} = 1\Omega$

Method 2: Using a ratio for two resistors
$EMF = I(R_{ext} + r_{int})$
$12 = 0,5(23 + r_{int})$
$r_{int} = 1\Omega$ (4)

19.1.6 a) Increase (2)

b) Total resistance increases. Current is inversely proportional to resistance. Therefore current in the circuit and the battery will decrease.
$V_1 = EMF - V_{lost}$
$V_{lost} = Ir$
If current (I) decreases lost volts will decrease and V_1 will increase. (4)

19.2.1 When the kettle is connected to a voltage source of 240 V, the power used by the kettle is 1 800 W. (2)

19.2.2 $P = VI$
$1800 = 240I$
$I = 7,5\,A$ (3)

19.2.3 $\text{Cost} = (1,8)\left(\frac{15}{60}\right)(1,4)$
$= R0,63$ (3)

[29]

Question 20 (2015 IEB Supplementary Examination)

20.1 The total energy supplied per coulomb of charge by the cell. (2)

20.2 15 V (1)

20.3 Potential difference. (2)

20.4 (6)

Graph to show the relationship between the potential difference across the terminals of a battery and the current through the battery.

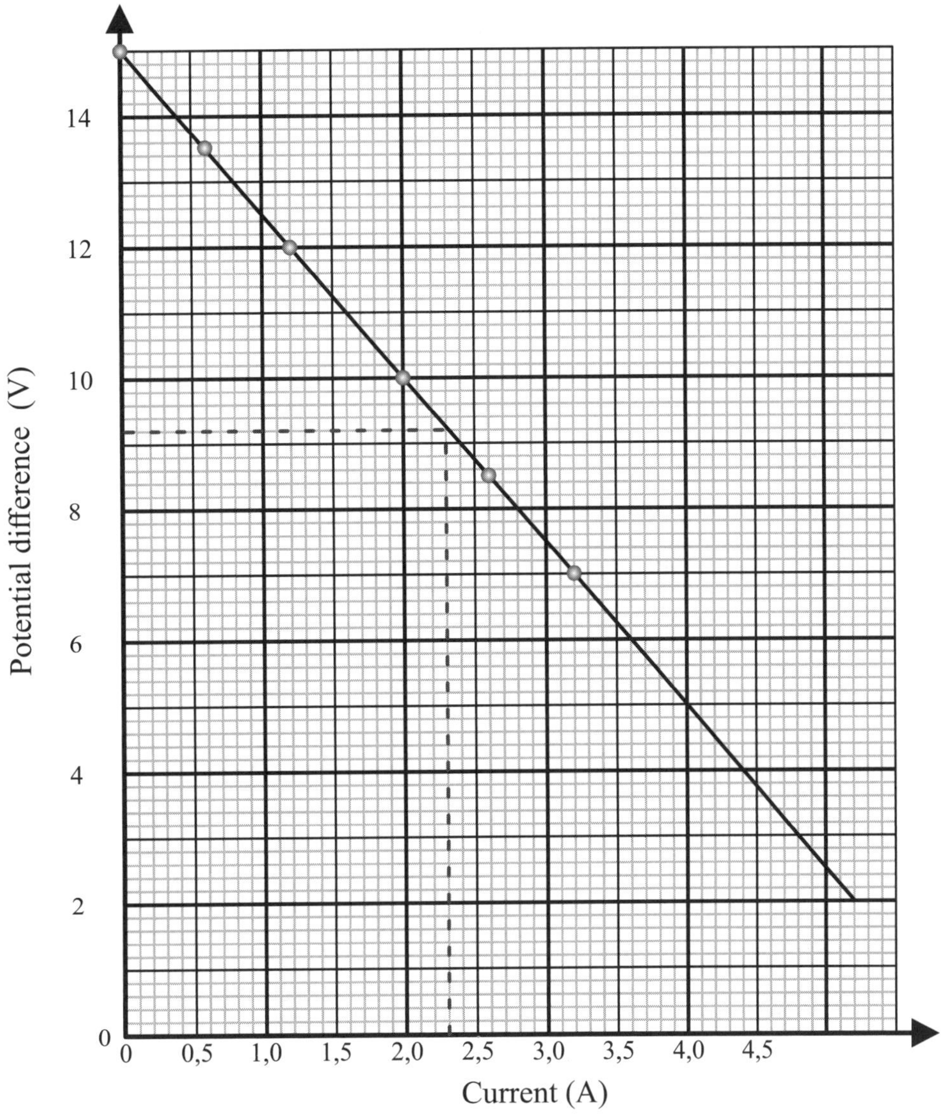

20.5 9,2 V (1)

20.6 $-r = \dfrac{5-15}{4-0}$

$r = 2,5\,\Omega$ (4)

20.7 $V = EMF - V_{lost}$

$V_{lost} = Ir$

If current (I) increases lost volts will increase and V will decrease. (3)

20.8 Resistance is a material's opposition to the flow of electric current. (2)

20.9 $R_{ext} = \dfrac{V}{I}$

$= \dfrac{10}{2}$

$= 5\,\Omega$

$R_{ext} = R_{2\Omega} + R_{rheostat}$

$5 = 2 + R_{rheostat}$

$R_{rheostat} = 3\,\Omega$ (4)

[25]

Question 21 (2015 IEB Final Examination)

21.1 Cost $= (0,1)(6)(1,4)$

$= R0,84$ (2)

21.2 $R = \frac{V^2}{P} = \frac{240^2}{100}$

$= 576\,\Omega$ (3)

21.3 Resistance (number of bulbs is also acceptable) (2)

21.4 As resistors are added in parallel more pathways for current to flow are added. This makes it easier for charge to flow. (2)

21.5 21.5.1 5,21 (1)

21.5.2 10,42 (1)

21.6 Marks are awarded as follows:

- Heading
- *y*-axis title and unit
- *y*-axis scale (plotted points greater than half the graph paper, scale in sensible multiples)
- plotted points (all 6 points plotted within half small block)
- line of best fit (with a ruler)

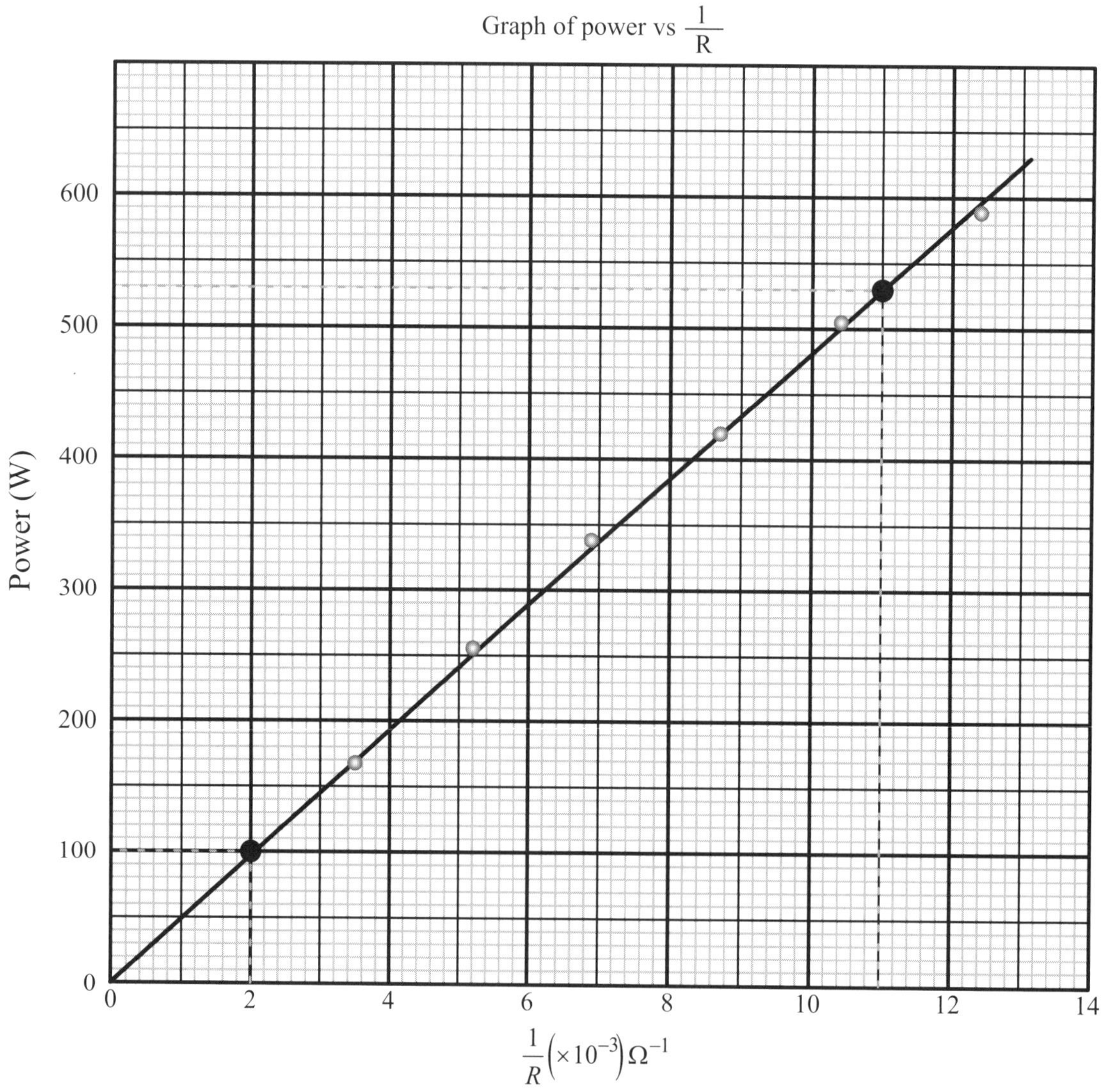

(6)

21.7 Power is inversely proportional to resistance.

1. Straight line graph with a **constant gradient**
2. The line of best fit **passes through the origin**. (3)

21.8 Gradient $= \dfrac{530-100}{11\times10^{-3}-2\times10^{-3}}$

$= 47\,777,78 \rightarrow$ any value between 45 790 and 50 610 is acceptable (4)

21.9 Power is plotted on the y-axis and $\dfrac{1}{R}$ on the x-axis. Therefore, the gradient of the graph is V^2.

$V^2 = 47\,777,78$

$\therefore V = 218,58\ V \rightarrow$ any value between 213,99 V and 224,97 V is acceptable (3)

[28]

Question 22 (2016 IEB Supplementary Examination)

22.1.1 Potential difference is the work done per unit positive charge. (2)

22.1.2 $V = IR$

$3 = I(6)$

$I = 0,5\,A$ (3)

22.1.3 $q = It$

$= (0,5)(10\times60)$

$= 300\,C$ (3)

22.2.1 EMF is the total energy per coulomb of charge supplied by the cell (2)

22.2.2 $V_r = 2\,V \rightarrow 12-10$

$r = \dfrac{V}{I} = \dfrac{2}{2}$

$= 1\,\Omega$ (3)

22.2.3 $V = IR$

$10 = I(20)$

$I = 0,5\,A$ (3)

22.2.4 $I_{R_1} = 1,5\,A \rightarrow 2-0,5$

$P = I^2R_1$

$5,85 = (1,5)^2 R_1$

$R_1 = 2,6\,\Omega$ (4)

22.2.5 $V_{//} = 10\,V$

$V_{R_1} = IR_1$

$= 1,5(2,6)$

$= 3,9\,V$

$V_{R_2} = 6,1\,V$

$R_2 = \dfrac{V}{I} = \dfrac{6,1}{1,5}$

$= 4,07\,\Omega$ (4)

22.2.6 When the switch opens total resistance increases. Current is inversely proportional to resistance. Therefore, current in the circuit will decrease.

$V = EMF - V_{lost}$

$V_{lost} = Ir$

If current (I) decreases lost volts will decrease and V will increase. (4)

[28]

Question 23 (2016 IEB Final Examination)

23.1.1 Resistance is a material's opposition to electric current. (2)

23.1.2 $\frac{1}{R_{//}} = \frac{1}{6} + \frac{1}{10}$

$R_{//} = 3,75\,\Omega$

$R_{tot} = 3,75 + 4$

$= 7,75\,\Omega$ (5)

23.1.3 Current is the rate of flow of charge. (2)

23.1.4 $V = IR$

$= 3(7,75)$

$= 23,25\,V$ (3)

23.1.5 $V_r = 2,75\,V \rightarrow 26 - 23,25$

$r = \frac{V}{I}$

$= \frac{2,75}{3}$

$= 0,92\,\Omega$ (3)

23.1.6 Total resistance increases. Current is inversely proportional to resistance. Therefore, current in the circuit will decrease.

$V = EMF - V_{lost}$

$V_{lost} = Ir$

If current (I) decreases lost volts will decrease and V will increase. (4)

23.1.7 26 V. If the 4 Ω resistor burns out no current will flow in the circuit and there will be lost volts. Therefore, the voltmeter will read the EMF. (3)

23.2

$EMF = I(R_{ext} + r_{int})$ | $EMF = I(R_{ext} + r_{int})$

$EMF = 2(2 + r_{int})$ | $EMF = 3(1 + r_{int})$

$EMF = 4 + 2r_{int}$ | $EMF = 3 + 3r_{int}$

$\therefore 4 + 2r_{int} = 3 + 3r_{int}$

$r_{int} = 1\,\Omega$

$EMF = 6\,V$ (5)

[27]

Question 24 (2017 IEB Supplementary Examination)

24.1.1 No, a filament light bulb is non-ohmic. The current through the filament is not directly proportional to the potential difference across the filament (or does not obey Ohm's law) as resistance changes with temperature. (3)

24.1.2 Voltage vs Current for a filament lightbulb

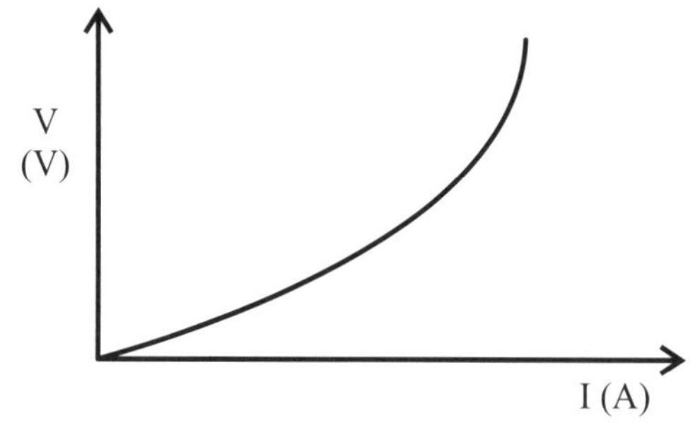

(5)

24.1.3 The resistance of the bulb is much greater than the resistance of the wires.

$P = I^2R$, if current is constant, power is directly proportional to resistance. Therefore, the power of the bulb is much greater than that of the wires and therefore the bulb heats up. (3)

24.2.1 Power is the rate at which work is done. (2)

24.2.2 $P = VI$

$60 = 24I$

$I = 2,5\,A$

24.2.3 Ohm's law states that the current through a conductor is directly proportional to the potential difference across the conductor at constant temperature. (2)

24.2.4 $V = IR$

$= 2,5(7)$

$= 17,5\,V$ (3)

24.2.5 $V_{//} = 6,5\,V \rightarrow 24 - 17,5$ (2)

24.2.6 $I_{3\Omega} = \frac{V_{//}}{R}$

$= \frac{6,5}{3}$

$= 2,17\,A$

$I_R = 0,33\,A \rightarrow 2,5 - 2,17$ (5)

24.2.7 $R = \frac{V}{I}$

$= \frac{6,5}{0,33}$

$= 19,70\,\Omega$ (3)

[28]

Question 25 (2017 IEB Final Examination)

25.1.1 Ohm's law states that the current through a conductor is directly proportional to the potential difference across the conductor at constant temperature. (2)

25.1.2 $I_{8\Omega} = \frac{V_{//}}{R}$

$= \frac{12}{8}$

$= 1,5\,A$ (3)

25.1.3 $\frac{1}{R_{//}} = \frac{1}{4} + \frac{1}{8} + \frac{1}{12}$

$R_{//} = 2,18\,\Omega$ (3)

25.1.4 $I = \frac{V}{R}$

$= \frac{12}{2,18}$

$= 5,50\,A$ (3)

25.1.5 $V_r = 4,5\,V \rightarrow 16,5 - 12$

$r = \frac{V}{I}$

$= \frac{4,5}{5,5}$

$= 0,82\,\Omega$ (3)

25.2.1 Power is the rate at which work is done. (2)

25.2.2 $P = \frac{V^2}{R}$

$= \frac{220^2}{50}$

$= 968\ W$ (3)

25.2.3 $80 = (0,968)(t)(1,24)$

$t = 66,64$ hours $\rightarrow$ you cannot round the anser up to 66,65 hours

(4)

[23]

Question 26 (2018 IEB Supplementary Examination)

26.1.1 EMF is the total energy supplied per coulomb of charge by the cell. (2)

26.1.2 $\frac{1}{R_{//}} = \frac{1}{20} + \frac{1}{30}$

$R_{//} = 12\,\Omega$

$R_{ext} = 45\,\Omega \rightarrow 12 + 33$ (5)

26.1.3 $EMF = I(R_{ext} + r_{int})$

$28 = I(45 + 7)$

$I = 0,54\ A$ (3)

26.1.4 Method 1:

$V_{ext} = IR_{ext}$

$= 0,54(45)$

$= 24,3\ V$

Method 2:

$V = EMF - V_{lost}$

$= EMF - Ir$

$= 28 - 0,54(7)$

$= 24,22\ V$

The difference in the answers between method 1 and 2 is due to the rounding of current in 26.1.3, both answers are acceptable. The answer using an non-rounded figure is 24,23. This answer is also acceptable.

26.1.5

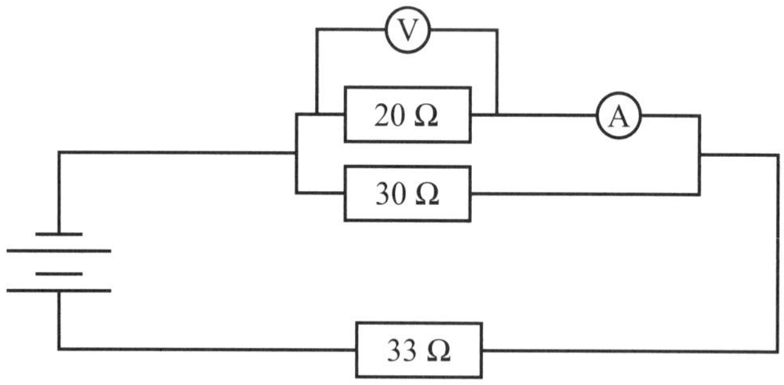

- Ammeter must be in series with the 20Ω
- Voltmeter must be in parallel with the 20 Ω or 30 Ω resistor.

(4)

26.2.1 Potential difference is the work done per unit positive charge. (2)

26.2.2 • Marks are awarded as follows:

- Heading
- *y*-axis title and unit
- *y*-axis scale (plotted points greater than half the graph paper, scale in sensible multiples)
- plotted points (all 6 points plotted within half small block)
- line of best fit (with a ruler) (6)

Graph of Terminal Potential Difference vs Current

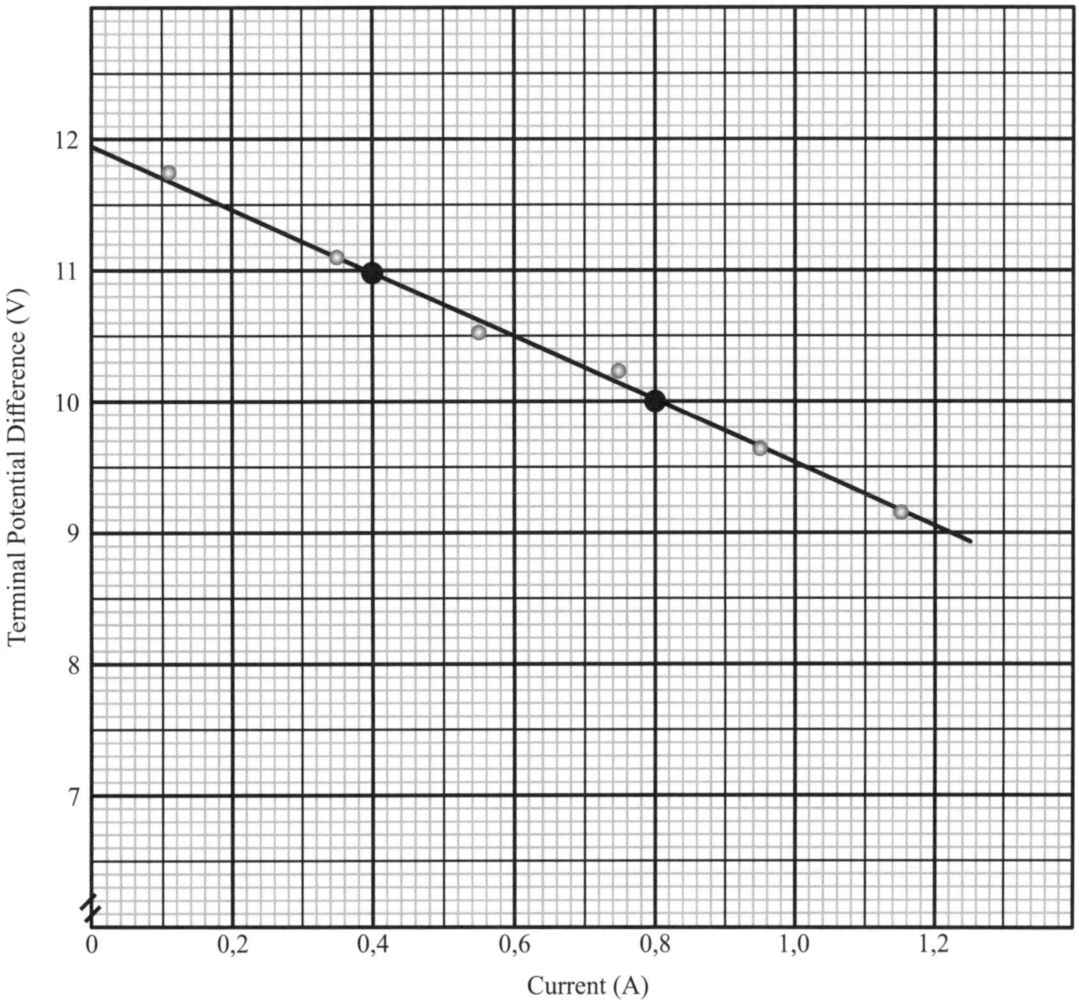

26.2.3 Gradient $= \dfrac{10-11}{0,8-0,4}$

$= -2,5 \rightarrow$ any value between $-2,67$ and $-2,37$ is acceptable (4)

26.2.4 $\text{EMF} = \text{IR}_{ext} + r_{int}$

$\text{EMF} = \text{V}_{ext} + \text{I}r_{int}$

$\text{V}_{ext} = -\boldsymbol{r_{int}}\,\text{I} + \text{EMF} \rightarrow y = \boldsymbol{m}x + c$

$-r = \text{gradient}$

$r = 2,5\,\Omega$ (2)

26.2.5 The EMF of the battery. (2)

[33]

TOC
1 Data Sheet
2 Definitions
3
3 solutions
4
4 solutions
5
5 solutions
6
6 solutions
7
7 solutions
8
8 solutions
9
9 solutions
10
10 solutions

Question 27 (2018 IEB Final Examination)

27.1.1 Resistance is a materials opposition to the flow of electric current (2)

27.1.2 EMF is the total energy supplied per coulomb of charge by the cell (2)

27.1.3 $\text{EMF} = I_1(R_{ext} + r_{int})$

$6 = 0{,}6(2R + r)$ (2)

27.1.4 $\text{EMF} = I_2(R_{ext} + r_{int})$

$6 = 1{,}5(0{,}5R + r)$ (2)

27.1.5 $6 = 0{,}6(2R + r)$

$10 = 2R + r$

$r = 10 - 2R$

$6 = 1{,}5(0{,}5R + r)$

$4 = 0{,}5R + r$

$r = 4 - 0{,}5R$

$10 - 2R = 4 - 0{,}5R$

$R = 4\,\Omega$ (3)

27.1.6 Power is the rate at which work is done. (2)

27.1.7 $P = I^2R$

$= (0{,}75)^2(4)$

$= 2{,}25\text{ W}$ (3)

27.1.8 Total resistance decreases. Current is inversely proportional to resistance. Therefore, current in the circuit will increase.

$V = \text{EMF} - V_{lost}$

$V_{lost} = Ir$

If current (I) increases lost volts will increase and V will decrease. (4)

27.2.1 Potential difference is the work done per unit positive charge (2)

27.2.2 Neither (Voltage is the same in parallel) (2)

27.2.3 Bulb A (2)

27.2.4 Bulb B (2)

[28]

Question 28 (2019 IEB Supplementary Examination)

28.1 Current is the rate of flow of charge. (2)

28.2 $P = I^2R$

$= (2{,}31)^2(10)$

$= 53{,}36\text{ W}$

28.3 Method 1:

$V_r = Ir = 2{,}31(1)$

$= 2{,}31\text{ V}$

$V_M = IR_M = 2{,}31(10)$

$= 23{,}1\text{ V}$

$V_R = 30 - 23{,}1 - 2{,}31$

$= 4{,}59\text{ V}$

$R = \frac{V}{I} = \frac{4{,}59}{2{,}31}$

$= 1{,}99\,\Omega$

Method 2:

$\text{EMF} = I(R_{ext} + r_{int})$

$30 = 2{,}31(R + 10 + 1)$

$R = 1{,}99\,\Omega$

28.4 0 V (1)

28.5 $27,69\,V \rightarrow 30-2,31$ (2)

28.6 Resistance is a material's opposition to the flow of electric current. (2)

28.7.1 Decrease. (2)

28.7.2 $I=\frac{V}{R}$, Therefore, current is inversely proportional to Resistance.

Total resistance increases. Therefore, current in the circuit will decrease.

$P=I^2R$, Therefore, power is directly proportional to current.

If current decreases power will decrease.

28.8.1 Method 1:

$$\frac{1}{R_{//}}=\frac{1}{10}+\frac{1}{5}$$

$$R_{//}=3,33\,\Omega$$

$$EMF=I(R_{ext}+r)$$

$$30=I(10+3,33+1)$$

$$I=2,09\,A$$

Method 2:

$$\frac{1}{R_{//}}=\frac{1}{10}+\frac{1}{5}$$

$$R_{//}=3,33\,\Omega$$

$$I=\frac{V}{R}=\frac{30}{3,33+10+1}=2,09\,A$$

(5)

28.8.2

$$V_{//}=IR_{//}=2,09(3,33)=6,96\,V$$

(3)

[26]

Question 29 (2019 IEB Final Examination)

29.1.1 Potential difference is the work done per unit positive charge (2)

29.1.2 15 V (2)

29.1.3 15 V (2)

29.1.4 $V_1=EMF-V_{lost}$

$V_{lost}=Ir$

When the switch closes current flows in the battery and there is a voltage drop over the internal resistance causing the voltmeter reading to decrease. (3)

29.1.5 $\frac{1}{R_{//}}=\frac{1}{6}+\frac{1}{12}$

$R_{//}=4\,\Omega$ (3)

29.1.6

$$I=\frac{V}{R}=\frac{10,5}{4+1}=2,1\,A$$

(3)

29.1.7

$$r=\frac{V}{I}=\frac{15-10,5}{2,1}=2,14\,\Omega$$

(3)

29.2.1 $P = \frac{V^2}{R}$

$100 = \frac{50^2}{R}$

$R = 25\,\Omega$ (3)

29.2.2 Method 1:

$I = \frac{V}{R}$

$= \frac{50}{25}$

$= 2\,\text{A}$

Method 2:

$P = I^2R$

$100 = I^2(25)$

$I = 2\,\text{A}$ (3)

29.2.3 $R = \frac{V}{I}$

$= \frac{220-50}{2}$

$= 85\,\Omega$ (3)

[27]

8. ELECTROSTATICS

PRINCIPLE OF CONSERVATION OF CHARGE

Conservation of charge is the principle that the total electric charge in an isolated system never changes.
If **two objects touch** and separate the **new charge on each object** will be **the sum** of the original charge on each object divided by 2.
The formula below can be used to determine the charge on two objects after they have touched:

$$Q_{new} = \frac{Q_1 + Q_2}{2}$$

$Q_{new} \rightarrow$ New charge on each object (C)
$Q_1 \rightarrow$ Original charge on first object (C)
$Q_2 \rightarrow$ Original charge on second object (C)

The above formula is the only formula that takes into account the sign of charge in the electrostatics section.

TRANSFER OF ELECTRONS

When **two charged objects touch electrons transfer** from the object with **the most negative** object **to** the **most positive** object.

To calculate the number of electrons transferred use the formula below:

$$N_{e-} = \frac{Q}{q_{e-}}$$

$N_{e-} \rightarrow$ Number of electrons transferred
$Q \rightarrow$ Charge transferred (C)
$q_{e-} \rightarrow$ Charge of an electron $(1{,}6 \times 10^{-19}\ \text{C})$

The formula to calculate number of electrons is not on the data sheet.

Illustrative Example 1:

Sphere A, with a charge of 3C and sphere B with a charge of –5C touch each other and are then separated.

a) Determine the charge on each sphere after they touch.
b) Were electrons transferred from A to B or B to A?
c) Calculate the number of electrons transferred when the spheres touch.

a) $$Q_{new} = \frac{Q_A + Q_B}{2} = \frac{3-5}{2} = -1\text{C}$$

b) B to A. (B is more negative than A)

c) First calculate the charge transferred:
Charge transferred:

$$Q_{transferred} = Q_{orignal} - Q_{new} = 3-(-1) = 4\text{C}$$

or

$$Q_{transferred} = Q_{orignal} - Q_{new} = -1-(-5) = 4\text{C}$$

$$N_{e-} = \frac{Q}{q_{e-}} = \frac{4}{1{,}6\times10^{-19}} = 2{,}5\times10^{19}\ \text{electrons}$$

TOC | 1 Data Sheet | 2 Definitions | 3 | 3 solutions | 4 | 4 solutions | 5 | 5 solutions | 6 | 6 solutions | 7 | 7 solutions | 8 | 8 solutions | 9 | 9 solutions | 10 | 10 solutions

COULOMB'S LAW

Two point charges in free space or air exert forces on each other. The force is directly proportional to the product of the charges and inversely proportional to the square of the distance between the charges.

The formula below is used to calculate the electrostatic force between two charges:

$$\mathbf{F} = \frac{\mathbf{k}Q_1Q_2}{r^2}$$

$F \rightarrow$ force between charged objects (N)

$k \rightarrow$ coulomb's constant $\left(9\times10^{9}\ \mathrm{N.m^2.C^{-2}}\right)$

$Q_1 \rightarrow$ charge on first object (C)

$Q_2 \rightarrow$ charge on second object (C)

$r \rightarrow$ distance between charges (m)

According to Newton's 3rd law both objects will always experience the same force irrespective of their charges.
Force is a vector. Therefore, you need to include direction in your answers.
Opposite charges attract and like charges repel.

Table of Conversion for Units of Charge

Prefix	Conversion
centi – (cC)	$\times10^{-2}$
milli – (mC)	$\times10^{-3}$
micro – (μC)	$\times10^{-6}$

Prefix	Conversion
nano – (nC)	$\times10^{-9}$
pico – (pC)	$\times10^{-12}$

Illustrative Example 2:

Sphere A with a charge of 2μC and sphere B with a charge of –4μC are separated by a distance of 10mm as shown on the diagram below. Determine the electrostatic force sphere B experiences due to sphere A.

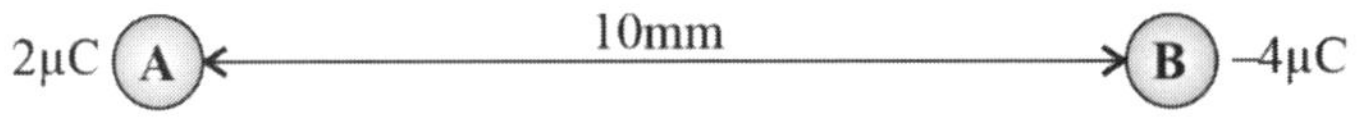

$$F = \frac{kQ_1Q_2}{r^2}$$

$$= \frac{9\times10^{9}\left(2\times10^{-6}\right)\left(4\times10^{-6}\right)}{\left(10\times10^{-3}\right)^2} \rightarrow \text{do not include the sign of the charges}$$

$= 720\,\mathrm{N}$ Left

Illustrative Example 3:

Sphere A with a charge of 5μC, sphere B with a charge of –1μC and sphere C with a charge of 2 μC are separated as shown on the diagram below. Determine the resultant force sphere B experiences due to A and C.

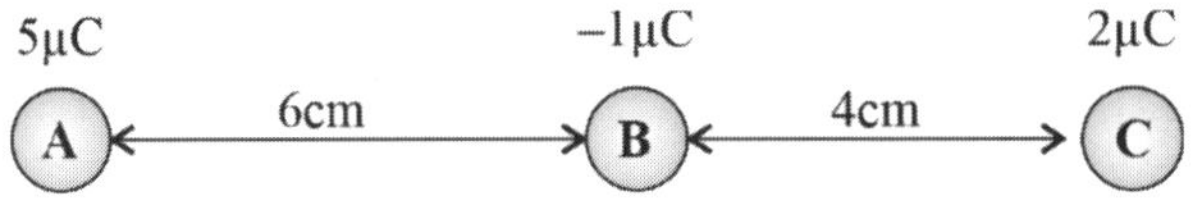

$$F_{\mathrm{AonB}} = \frac{kQ_1Q_2}{r^2} = \frac{9\times10^{9}\left(5\times10^{-6}\right)\left(1\times10^{-6}\right)}{\left(6\times10^{-2}\right)^2}$$

$= 12{,}5\,\mathrm{N}$ left

$$F_{\mathrm{ConB}} = \frac{kQ_1Q_2}{r^2} = \frac{9\times10^{9}\left(2\times10^{-6}\right)\left(1\times10^{-6}\right)}{\left(4\times10^{-2}\right)^2}$$

$= 11{,}25\,\mathrm{N}$ right

$F_{net} = 12{,}5 - 11{,}25 \rightarrow$ taking left as postive

$= 1{,}25\,\mathrm{N}$ left

ELECTRIC FIELDS

An electric field is the region around an electric charge where another charge (or charged object) will experience an electrostatic force. The **direction** of the electric field at a point is **the direction that a positive test charge** (+1C) **would move** if placed at that point.
An **electric field line** always **travels from positive to negative**.

The **electric field** due to **a positive charge** always moves out and **away from the charge**.
The **electric field** due to a **negative charge** always moves in **and towards the negative charge**.

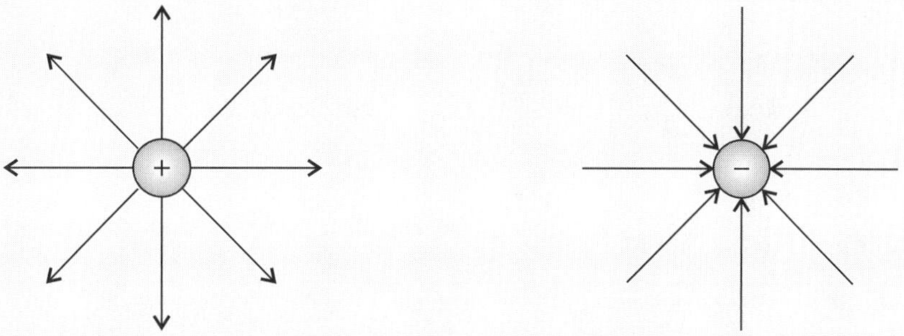

- The **number of field lines** indicate the **strength of the charge**. The more field lines the greater the charge.
- Field lines **move** out or into the charge **at right angles to the surface of the charge**.

The electric field pattern for two oppositely charged particles is shown below:

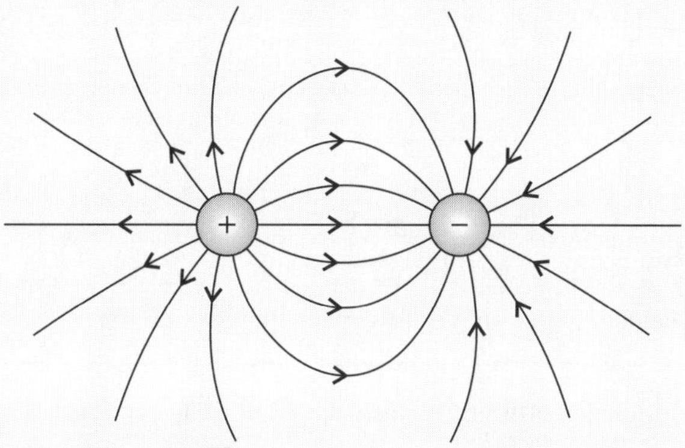

- The electric field lines move from the positive charge to the negative charge.
- If one charge is greater than the other, the larger charge will have more field lines.

The electric field pattern for two like charges particles is shown below:

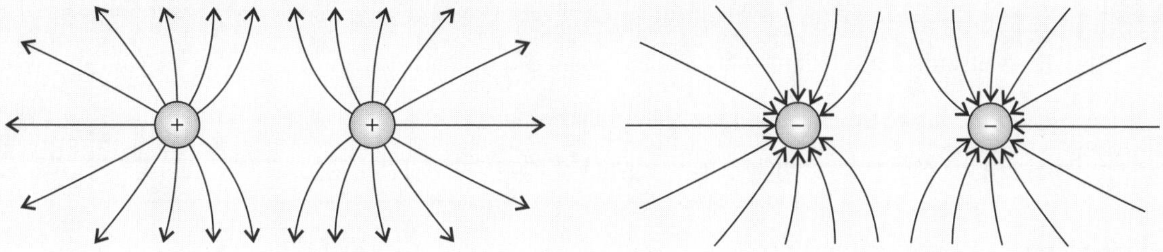

- There is a cancellation of electric field between two like charges.
- If the charges are of different magnitude the cancellation area will be closer to the smaller charge
- The cancellation area occurs at the point where the electric field from each charge is equal.

The electric field between parallel plates is shown below:

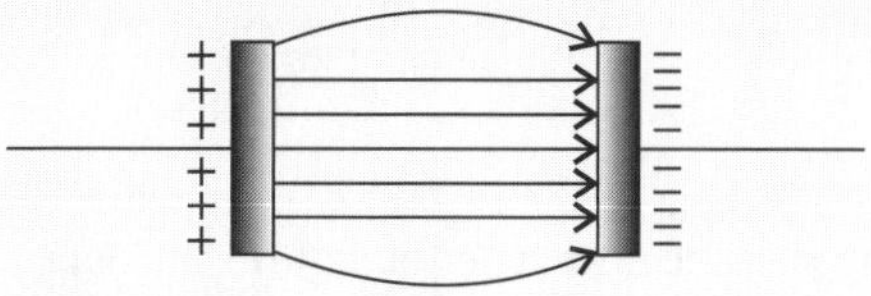

- The electric field between parallel plates is uniform everywhere except at the edges
- The electric field lines move from the positive plate to the negative plate.

ELECTRIC FIELD STRENGTH

Electric field strength at any point in space is the force per unit charge experienced by a positive test charge at that point.

The electric field strength can be calculated using the formula below:

$$\mathbf{E} = \frac{\mathbf{k}Q}{r^2}$$

$E \rightarrow$ electric field strength $\left(\text{N.C}^{-1}\right)$

$k \rightarrow$ coulomb's constant $\left(9\times10^{9}\ \text{N.m}^2.\text{C}^{-2}\right)$

$Q \rightarrow$ charge on object (C)

$r \rightarrow$ distance from charge (m)

Illustrative Example 4:

Determine the electric field at point X, 40mm to the East of a charge of –80nC.

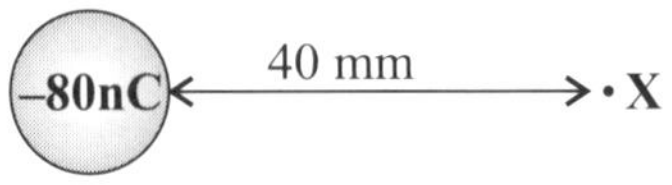

$$\begin{aligned} E &= \frac{kQ}{r^2} \\ &= \frac{9\times10^{9}\left(80\times10^{-9}\right)}{\left(40\times10^{-3}\right)^2} \end{aligned}$$

$= 450\,000\ \text{N.C}^{-1}$ **West** $\rightarrow$ electric field moves towards a negative charge

Note that the above formula only considers the distance from a single charge.

The electric field strength can also be calculated using the formula:

$$\mathbf{E} = \frac{\mathbf{F}}{q}$$

$E \rightarrow$ electric field strength $\left(\text{N.C}^{-1}\right)$

$F \rightarrow$ the force that charge q experiences in the electric field (N)

$q \rightarrow$ the charge of an object placed in the electric field (C)

CHARGE IN AN ELECTRIC FIELD

An **electric field** always **travels from positive to negative**.

A **positive charge** will **move in the same direction as the electric field (towards negative)**.

A **negative charge** will **move in the opposite direction as the electric field (towards positive)**.

$+q$ The charge will experience a force to the right (in the same direction as the electric field)

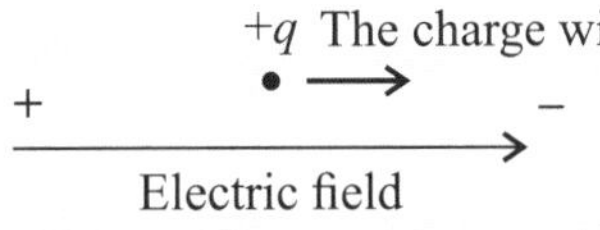

$-q$ The charge will experience a force to the left (in the opposite direction as the electric field)

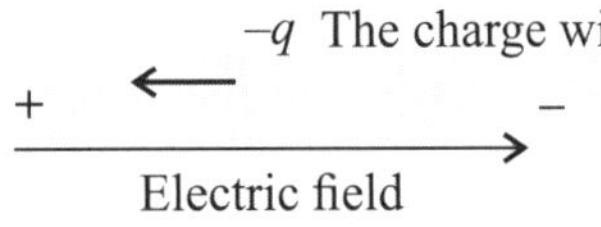

Illustrative Example 5:

A charge of –20μC placed at a distance of 30 mm from an unknown charge experiences a force of 20 N to the **right**. Determine the unknown charge.

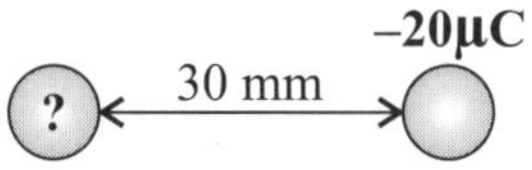

Note that as the negative charge experiences a force to the right, the electric field is to the left. Therefore, the unknown charge is also negative.

$$E = \frac{F}{q}$$

$$= \frac{20}{20\times10^{-6}}$$

$= 1000\,000\ \text{N.C}^{-1}$ left $\rightarrow$ this is the electric field due to the unknown charge Q

$$E = \frac{kQ}{r^2}$$

$$1000\,000 = \frac{9\times10^9 Q}{\left(30\times10^{-3}\right)^2}$$

$Q = -1\times10^{-7}\ \text{C} \rightarrow$ note that the charge is negative

Illustrative Example 6:

Sphere A, with a charge of 5μC, is separated from sphere C with a charge of 2 μC, by a distance of 10cm. Point X lies 4 cm to the left of point C.

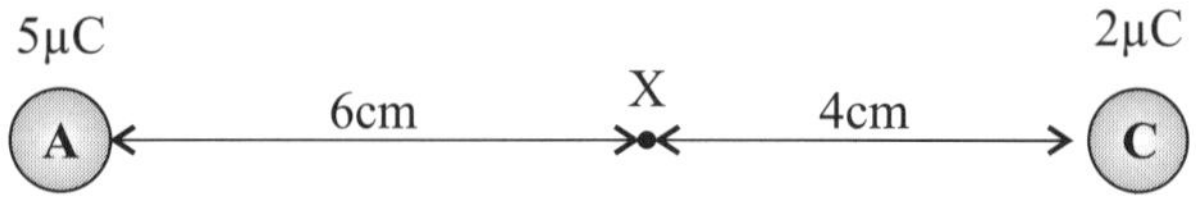

a) Determine the resultant electric field at point X.
b) A charge of –1μC is placed at point X. Determine the resultant force this charge experiences.

a)

$$E_A = \frac{kQ_A}{r^2} = \frac{9\times10^9\left(5\times10^{-6}\right)}{\left(6\times10^{-2}\right)^2} = 12\,500\,000\ \text{N.C}^{-1}\ \text{right}$$

$$E_C = \frac{kQ_C}{r^2} = \frac{9\times10^9\left(2\times10^{-6}\right)}{\left(4\times10^{-2}\right)^2} = 11\,250\,000\ \text{N left}$$

$E_{net} = 12\,500\,000 - 11\,250\,000 \rightarrow$ taking right as postive

$= 1\,250\,000\ \text{N.C}^{-1}$ right

b) $F = Eq$

$= 1\,250\,000\left(1\times10^{-6}\right)$

$= 1,25\ \text{N}$ left $\rightarrow$ as the charge is negative it will move in the opposite direction of the field

Note that this is the same answer as in illustrative example 3 on page 313.

TOC 1 Data Sheet 2 Definitions 3 3 solutions 4 4 solutions 5 5 solutions 6 6 solutions 7 7 solutions 8 8 solutions 9 9 solutions 10 10 solutions

WORKING WITH RATIOS

When dealing with ratios you are considering the factor that each charge or distance is changed by.

Illustrative Example 1:

Two charges of magnitude Q and q are separated by a distance of r. At this distance they exert a force of F on each other. If the distance between them is doubled what force will they exert on each other?

$$F_{new} = F\left[\frac{(1)(1)}{(2)^2}\right] \rightarrow \text{from } \frac{kQ_1Q_2}{r^2} \rightarrow \text{the distance is increased by a factor of 2}$$

$$= \frac{F}{4}$$

Illustrative Example 2:

Sphere A has a charge of Q and sphere B has a charge of 3Q are separated by a distance of x. At this distance they exert a force of F on each other. If the distance between the objects is halved and the charge of A is doubled what is the new force experienced between the spheres?

$$F_{new} = F\left[\frac{(2)(1)}{\left(\frac{1}{2}\right)^2}\right] \rightarrow \text{from } \frac{kQ_1Q_2}{r^2}$$

$$= 8F$$

The numbers used in the formula are not the distances between the charges or the actual charges of the objects. It is the factor that the distance between the charged objects or the charges of the objects changes by.

Illustrative Example 3:

A sphere with charge Q generates an electric field with strength E at a distance r from the sphere.
What is the strength of the electric field generated by a sphere with charge 2Q at a distance $2r$?

$$E_{new} = E\left[\frac{(2)}{(2)^2}\right] \rightarrow \text{from } \frac{kQ}{r^2}$$

$$= \frac{E}{2}$$

Illustrative Example 4:

Two charged spheres are separated by distance r. At this distance, they exert a force of F on each other. The distance is changed so that the force that they exert on each other is 3 times greater. By what factor was the distance changed by?

$$F_{new} = 3F$$

$$3F = F\left[\frac{(1)(1)}{x^2}\right] \rightarrow \text{from } \frac{kQ_1Q_2}{r^2}$$

$$3F = \frac{F}{x^2}$$

$$x = \frac{1}{\sqrt{3}} \rightarrow \text{this is the same } \frac{3}{\sqrt{3}}$$

$\therefore$ The distance between the spheres was **decreased** by a factor of $\sqrt{3}$

TWO DIMENSIONAL VECTORS

Electrostatic **forces and fields** can also **act** in **two dimensions.**
Electrostatic **forces and fields** are **vectors** and **direction must be given** in your solution unless the question asks for magnitude.

Illustrative Example 1:

Three charged spheres are arranged as shown in the diagram below. Sphere A has a charge of –10μC, sphere B has a charge of 5μC and sphere C has a charge of –15μC. Sphere A is 8mm directly South of sphere B. Sphere C is 15mm to the East of sphere B.

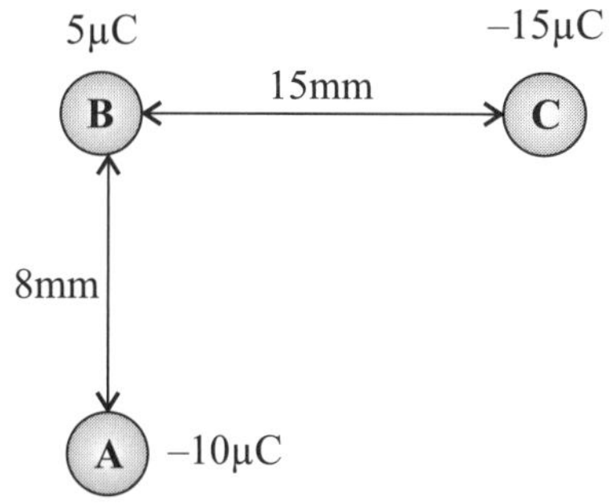

Determine the resultant force that sphere B experiences due to sphere A and C.

$$F_{AonB} = \frac{kQ_AQ_B}{r^2} = \frac{9\times10^9\left(10\times10^{-6}\right)\left(5\times10^{-6}\right)}{\left(8\times10^{-3}\right)^2} = 7\,031,25\,\text{N South}$$

$$F_{ConB} = \frac{kQ_CQ_B}{r^2} = \frac{9\times10^9\left(15\times10^{-6}\right)\left(5\times10^{-6}\right)}{\left(15\times10^{-3}\right)^2} = 3\,000\,\text{N East}$$

Now draw a vector diagram:

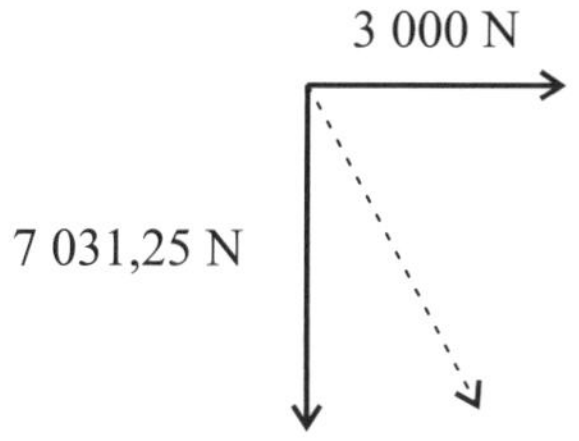

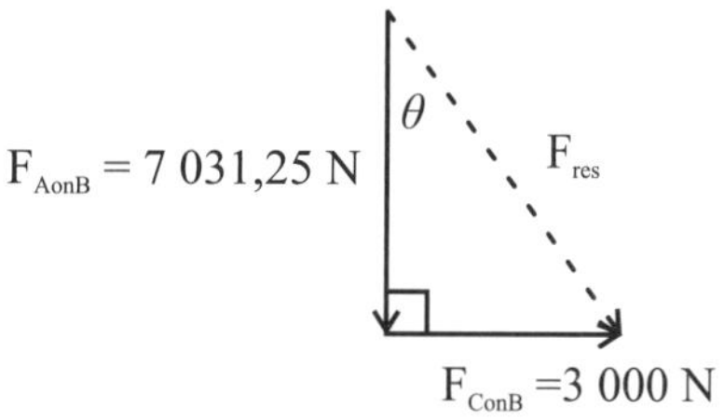

Magnitude of resultant force:

$$F_{res}{}^2 = 7\,031,25^2 + 3000^2$$

$$F_{res} = 7\,644,51\,\text{N}$$

Direction:

$$\tan\theta = \frac{3000}{7\,031,25}$$

$$\theta = 23,11^\circ$$

$$\therefore F_{res} = 7\,644,51\,\text{N on a bearing of } 156,89^\circ \rightarrow 180^\circ - 23,11^\circ$$

TOC 1 Data Sheet 2 Definitions 3 3 solutions 4 4 solutions 5 5 solutions 6 6 solutions 7 7 solutions 8 8 solutions 9 9 solutions 10 10 solutions

Question 1 (Solutions on page 341)

1.1 Two identically charged objects are separated by a distance r. They exert a force F on each other. If you halve the distance between the two charged objects, what will be the new force that the charged objects exert on each other?

A $\frac{F}{2}$

B 2F

C $\frac{F}{4}$

D 4F (2)

1.2 Two identical metal spheres on insulated stands placed a distance, r, from each other, carry different charges of x and y respectively, as indicated in the diagram. Both spheres experience a force, F. Which one of the following options describes the strength of the electric field of x at position y.

A $\frac{F}{x}$

B $\frac{ky}{r^2}$

C $\frac{F}{y}$

D Fy (2)

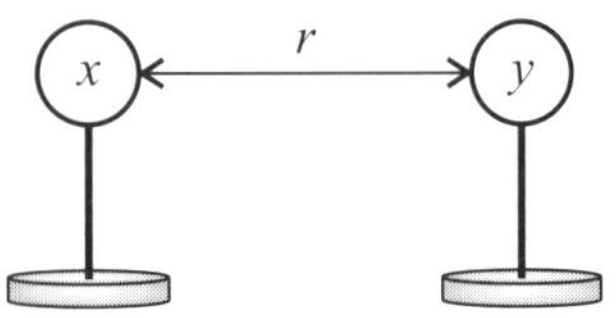

1.3 Two particles are at distance d apart. One particle has charge +2Q and the other –3Q. The two particles exert an electrostatic force of attraction, F, on each other. Each particle is then given an additional charge +Q and their separation distance remains unchanged.

Which of the following gives the force that now acts between the two particles?

A an attractive force of F
B an attractive force of 2F
C a repulsive force of F
D a repulsive force of 2F (2)

1.4 Two spheres, A and B, are at a distance x apart. Sphere A has a charge of 5Q and sphere B has a charge of –10Q. Sphere A exerts a force of magnitude F on particle B. The magnitude of the force that sphere B exerts on A is:

A 2F

B $\frac{F}{2}$

C F

D $\frac{F}{3}$ (2)

1.5 Two identical metal spheres, A and B, carrying charges of + 12 nC and + 18 nC respectively are brought into contact. At the moment of contact…

A $1{,}875 \times 10^{10}$ electrons are transferred from A to B.
B $1{,}875 \times 10^{19}$ electrons move from A to B.
C 3 electrons are transferred from A to B.
D Electrons do not move as both spheres are positively charged. (2)

1.6 An electron is placed at point X in a uniform electric field as shown in the diagram below. In which direction will the electron accelerate?

A East
B West
C North
D South

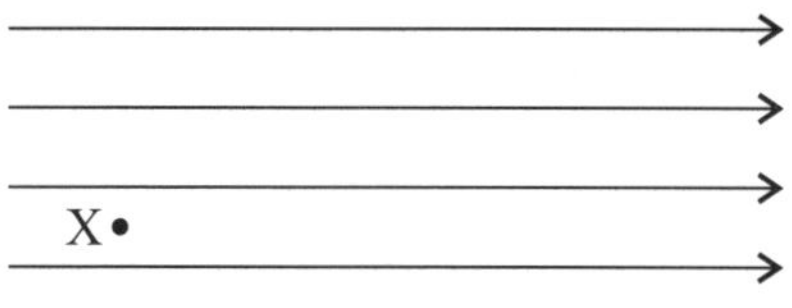

(2)

1.7 Three point charges of magnitude –6μC, +6μC and +4μC are placed at the three corners of an isoceles triangle, as shown in the diagram below.

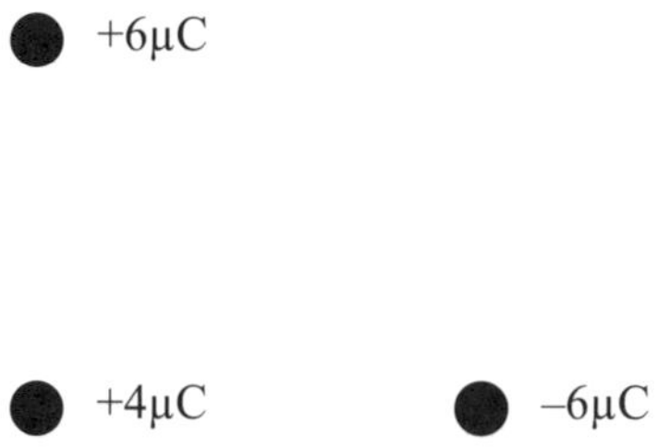

Which of the following best represents the direction of the resultant force exerted on the +4μC charge by the other two charges?

A ← B → C ↘ D ↗ (2)

1.8 A positively charged sphere with a charge of +8Q is separated from a negatively charged sphere with a charge of –2Q by a distance of *r* and as a result an attractive force, F, is exerted on each. The spheres touch each other and are then moved back to their original positions. What is the new force on each sphere in terms of F?

A $\frac{9}{16}$F B $\frac{16}{9}$F C $\frac{9}{4}$F D $\frac{4}{9}$F (2)

1.9 The diagram shows two equal and opposite charges that are fixed in place.

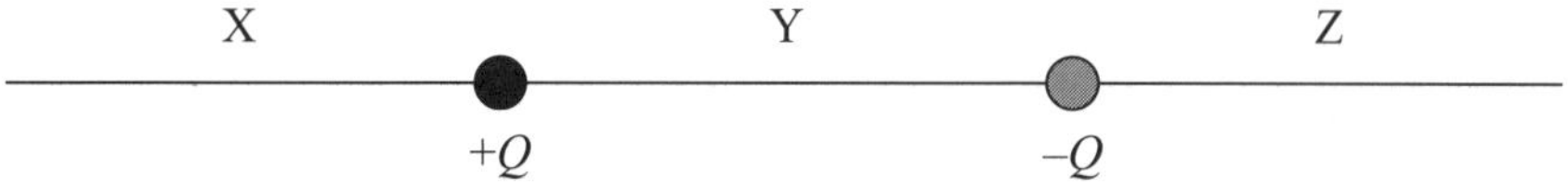

At which point(s) is the resultant electric field directed to the left?

A X and Y only
B X and Z only
C Y only
D X, Y and Z

(2)

TOC 1 Data Sheet 2 Definitions 3 3 solutions 4 4 solutions 5 5 solutions 6 6 solutions 7 7 solutions 8 8 solutions 9 9 solutions 10 10 solutions

1.10 The diagram shows two charges that are fixed in place.

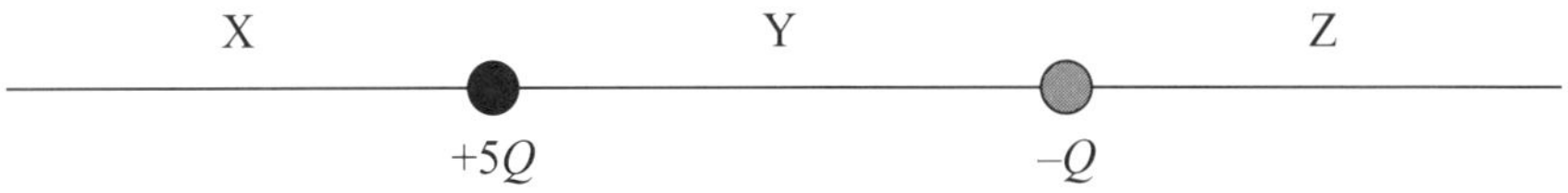

At which point(s) is it possible for the resultant electric field to be zero?

A Y only
B X only
C X and Z only
D Z only (2)

1.11 Two identically charged objects are separated by a distance r. They exert a force F on each other. If you halve the distance between the two charged objects and double the charge on each object, what will be the new force that the charged objects exert on each other?

A 8F
B 16F
C 4F
D F (2)

1.12 The diagram shows two particles at distance d apart. One particle has charge $+2Q$ and the other $-2Q$. The two particles exert an electrostatic force of attraction, F, on each other. Each particle is then given an additional charge $+Q$ and their separation is increased to distance $2d$. The new electrostatic force will be…

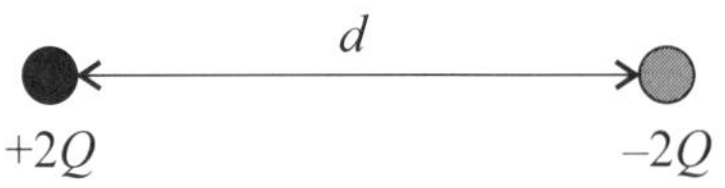

A F B $\frac{3}{16}$F C $\frac{3}{4}$F D 16F (2)

1.13 Two point charges (A and B) are placed a distance ***d*** apart as shown on the diagram below. The resultant electric field intensity at point P is zero.

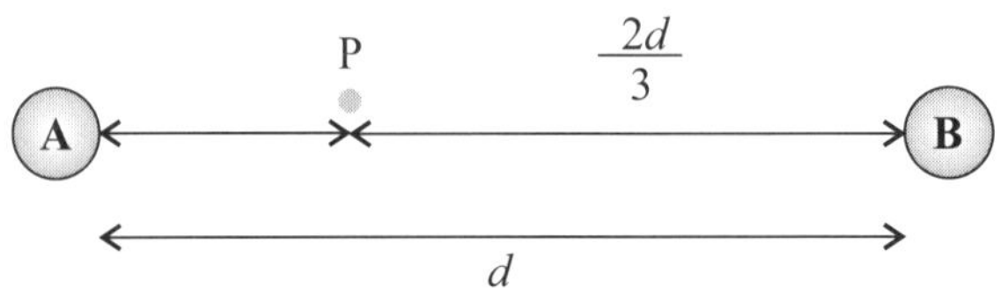

Which of the following statements regarding X and Y is correct?

	Charge on A	Charge on B	
A	Positive	Positive	Charge on A > charge on B
B	Negative	Positive	Charge on A < charge on B
C	Positive	Negative	Charge on A > charge on B
D	Negative	Negative	Charge on A < charge on B

(2)

1.14 Two charges experience a force F when held a distance r apart. How would this force be affected if one charge is doubled, the other charge is tripled and the distance between the charges is halved?

A 12F
B 10F
C 20F
D 24F (2)

1.15 A metal sphere K has a charge of 4 nC and an identical sphere L has a charge of –8 nC. When the spheres are 10 mm apart, sphere K exerts a force ***F*** on sphere L. The spheres are touched and returned to their original positions. Sphere L now exerts a force of ________ on sphere K

A $\frac{F}{8}$ B $\frac{F}{4}$ C $\frac{3F}{4}$ D $16F$ (2)

1.16 Two small, oppositely charged spheres on an insulated surface are held a distance r apart.

When the spheres are released simultaneously, they each experience a force F, they roll towards each other due to this electrostatic force of attraction.

Which one of the graphs below represents the magnitude of the force experienced by each sphere as a function of the distance r between the spheres?

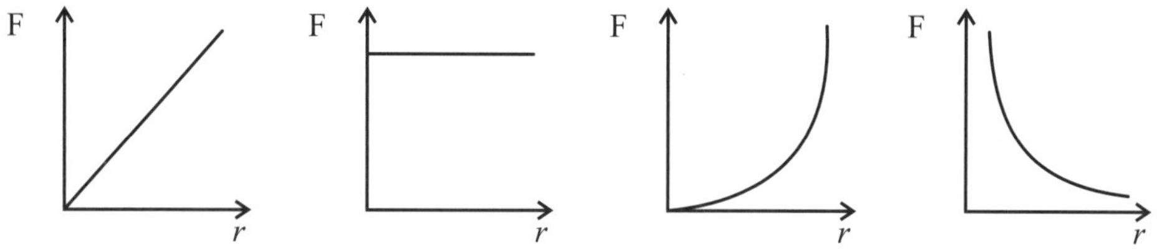

A   B   C   D (2)

1.17 The magnitude of the electric field at a point P from a positive point charge q is E N.C^{-1}.
Which ONE of the following statements below regarding the electrostatic force is correct?

A The force on a +2 C charge placed at P will have a magnitude $2E$ N directed away from q.

B The force on a +2 C charge placed at P will have a magnitude $\frac{E}{4}$ N directed away from q.

C The force on a +1 C charge placed at P will have a magnitude E N directed towards q.

D The force on a +2 C charge placed at P will have a magnitude $\frac{E}{4}$ N directed towards q. (2)

1.18 The electric field diagram for two point charges, X and Y, is shown below.

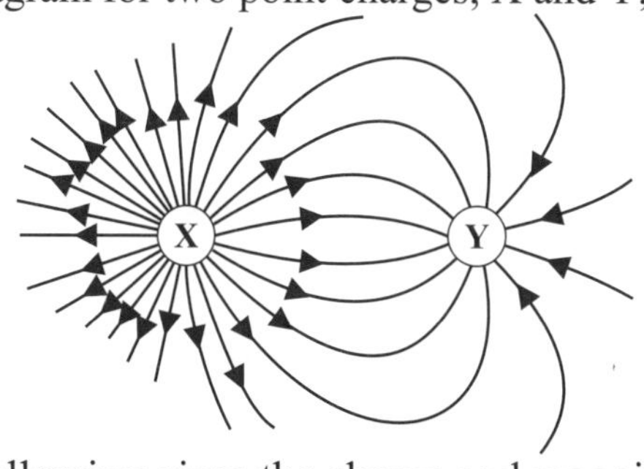

Which one of the following gives the charge and magnitudes of X and Y.

	Charge on X	Charge on Y	Size of charge
A	positive	negative	$Q_X < Q_Y$
B	positive	negative	$Q_X > Q_Y$
C	negative	positive	$Q_X < Q_Y$
D	negative	positive	$Q_X > Q_Y$

(2)

1.19 Conducting sphere P carries a charge of +6 nC and conducting sphere Q carries a charge of +14 nC. They are brought together and touch and then are separated to the same distance again. Which of the following statements is true?

A The force of repulsion between the charges was greater before touching then it is after touching.

B Electrons flow from sphere Q to P.

C The force of repulsion between the charges is greater after touching then it was before touching.

D Protons flow from sphere P to Q. (2)

1.20 Two charged objects, Q_1 and Q_2, are attracting each other at a separation distance of r. If the charge Q_1 is reduced by a factor of 4, then which of the following changes should be made to r to keep the force of attraction unchanged?

A Decrease r by a factor of 4
B Increase r by a factor of 4
C Decrease r by a factor of 2
D Increase r by a factor of 2 (2)

1.21 A sphere X has a charge of –5μC. P is a positive sphere with a charge of 3μC situated 2m to the right of X.

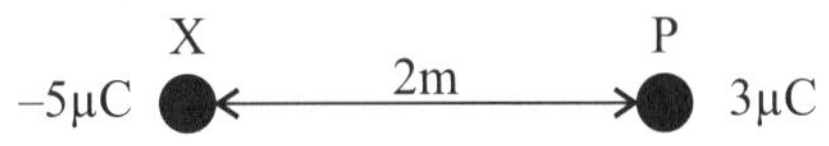

What is the electric field at point P due to X?

A 0,03375 $N.C^{-1}$ left
B 0,03375 $N.C^{-1}$ right
C 11 250 $N.C^{-1}$ right
D 11 250 $N.C^{-1}$ left (2)

1.22 Two identical conducting spheres *X* and *Y* carry charges of +3,2nC and –5,2nC respectively. The spheres are allowed to touch.

During touching, sphere *X* gains:

A 2×10^{-9} electrons
B 1×10^{-9} electrons
C $4{,}2 \times 10^{-9}$ electrons
D $2{,}625 \times 10^{10}$ electrons (2)

1.23 When two identical metal spheres X and Y are brought into contact and then separated again, it is found that the charge on each sphere is –12nC. Which row in the table supplies the possible charges, in nC, which could have been on the spheres before they made contact?

	Charge on X (nC)	Charge on Y (nC)
A	–22	–10
B	–22	2
C	–24	Neutral
D	10	14

(2)

1.24 The force of repulsion between two positive conducting spheres with charges of $2Q$ and $6Q$ separated by a distance, r, is F. The spheres are momentarily touched and then separated to a distance of $2r$. What will the new force between the charges be?

A $\frac{F}{3}$

B F

C $\frac{F}{4}$

D $\frac{4F}{3}$

(2)

1.25 The diagram below shows two point charges, A and B. A carries a charge of Q and B carries a charge of $2Q$. A third point charge C carrying a charge is inserted between A and B.

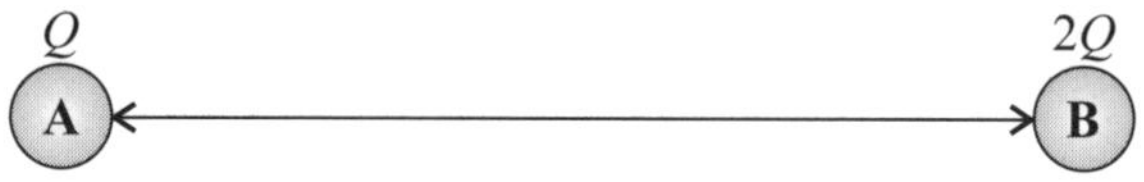

At what point along the line between A and B must C be inserted so the resultant electrostatic force on C is zero?

A It is not possible to be zero at any point between A and B.
B Halfway between A and B.
C Closer to A than B.
D Closer to B than A.

(2)

1.26 The force between two small charged conducting objects P and Q, on insulated stands is F. The charges on P and Q are 4nC and –2nC respectively and they are a distance r apart.

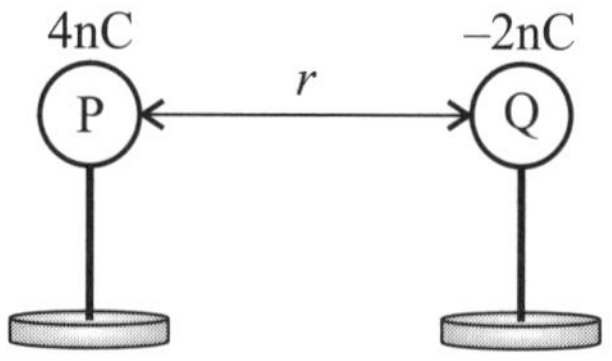

The objects are now allowed to touch each other and then placed at the original positions. The magnitude of the repulsive force between P and Q is now:

A F

B $\frac{1}{2}F$

C $\frac{1}{4}F$

D $\frac{1}{8}F$

(2)

TOC
1 Data Sheet
2 Definitions
3
3 solutions
4
4 solutions
5
5 solutions
6
6 solutions
7
7 solutions
8
8 solutions
9
9 solutions
10
10 solutions

1.27 Three point charges of magnitudes Q, Q and $-5Q$ are placed at the three corners of an equilateral triangle as shown in the diagram below.

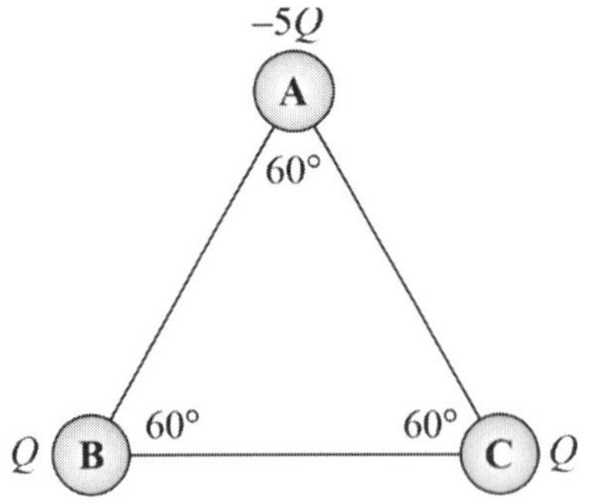

Which one of the following vectors best represents the direction of the resultant force exerted on A by B and C?

A $\leftarrow$ B $\rightarrow$ C $\uparrow$ D $\downarrow$ (2)

1.28 Three identical spheres, A, B and C on insulated stands are charged as shown in the diagram below. Charged sphere B is moved to touch A and then moved to touch C.

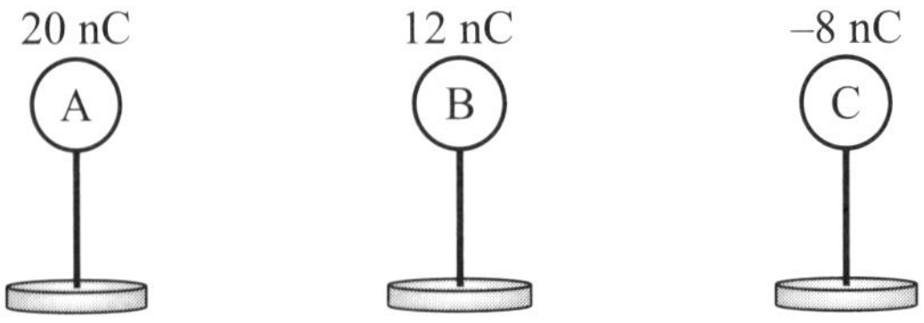

The charge on B will now be:

A –4 nC
B 4 nC
C 8 nC
D 24 nC

(2)

1.29 Two small charged conducting spheres on insulated stands are placed a distance $2r$ apart from each other. One carries a positive charge $3Q$, and the other has a negative charge $-3Q$.

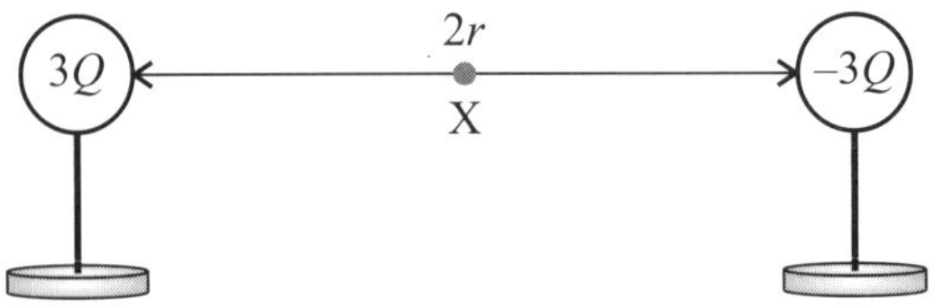

The spheres are brought together so that they touch each other. They are then separated and placed back in their original positions.

Which of the following pairs give the correct magnitude of the electric field at point X, midway between the two charges?

	Before Touching each other	**After touching each other**
A	0	0
B	$\frac{6kQ}{r^2}$	0
C	0	$\frac{6kQ}{r^2}$
D	$\frac{9kQ}{r^2}$	0

(2)

1.30 Two charges of +5 nC and –5 nC are located on a straight line. P and R are two points that lie on the same straight line as shown in the diagram below.

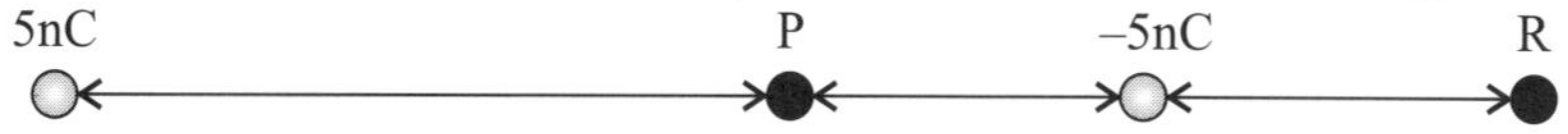

Which one of the following correctly represents the directions of the resultant electric fields at P and at R?

	Direction of resultant field at P	Direction of resultant field at R
A	Right	Left
B	Left	Left
C	Right	Right
D	Left	Right

(2)

1.31 Two charged particles, X and Y exert repulsive forces on each other. The charge on X is + 6q while the charge on Y is +q. The magnitude of the force on particle Y is

A The same size as the force on X.
B Six times larger than the force on X.
C Three times as large as the force on X.
D One third the size of the force on X. (2)

1.32 The following diagrams illustrate the size of the charge on a particle and point P a certain distance away from the charge. In which diagram will the electric field be the largest at P?

A 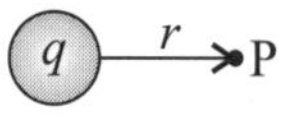

B 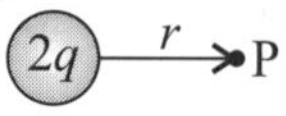

C 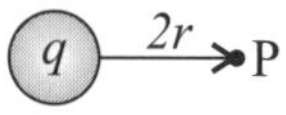

D 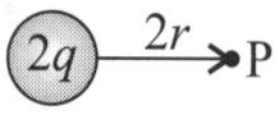

(2)

1.33 Questions 1.33 and 1.34 relate to the diagram and information below. Two charges, Q and q are held in place a distance d apart. The magnitude of the charge on Q is twice that of the charge on q. When released, charge Q accelerates to the left and experiences a force F whilst charge q accelerates to the right.

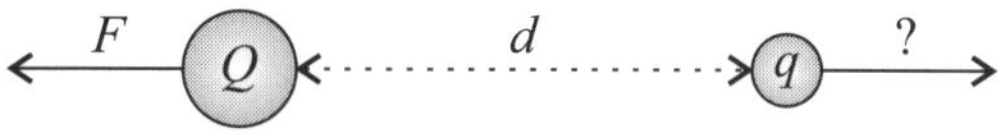

Which one of the following correctly represents the charge on Q and q as well as the force that charge q experiences?

	Charge on Q	Charge on q	Force on q
A	positive	positive	0,5F
B	negative	positive	2
C	positive	negative	F
D	negative	negative	F

(2)

1.34 What is the correct expression for the magnitude of the electric field of charge Q at the position of charge q?

A $\frac{kQq}{d^2}$ B $\frac{kq}{d^2}$ C $\frac{F}{q}$ D $\frac{F}{Q}$ (2)

1.35 Determine which charge in the table below is in the smallest electric field:

	Charge	Force charge experiences
A	8q	20 N
B	30q	50 N
C	20q	40 N
D	50q	30 N

(2)

[70]

TOC 1 Data Sheet 2 Definitions 3 3 solutions 4 4 solutions 5 5 solutions 6 6 solutions 7 7 solutions 8 8 solutions 9 9 solutions 10 10 solutions

TOC
1 Data Sheet
2 Definitions
3
3 solutions
4
4 solutions
5
5 solutions
6
6 solutions
7
7 solutions
8
8 solutions
9
9 solutions
10
10 solutions

Question 2 (Solutions on page 341)

Two charged objects, A and B, are separated by a distance of 6 mm. The charge on A is 2 nC and the force of repulsion between charge A and B is 1,5 mN

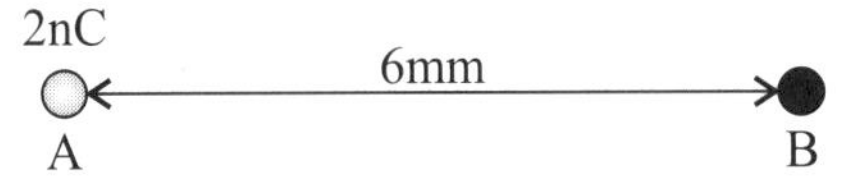

2.1 If the magnitude of charge B is greater than that of A, draw an electric field line diagram to represent the field set up by charges A and B. (3)

2.2 State Coulomb's Law. (2)

2.3 Calculate the charge on B. (5)

2.4 How many electrons did A lose to obtain a charge of 2 nC? (2)

[12]

Question 3 (Solutions on page 342)

Three small, identical metal spheres, A, B and C, are placed on insulating stands. Each sphere carries a charge of – 8 nC. The spheres are arranged so that A is 6 mm from B and C is 4 mm from B as shown in the diagram below.

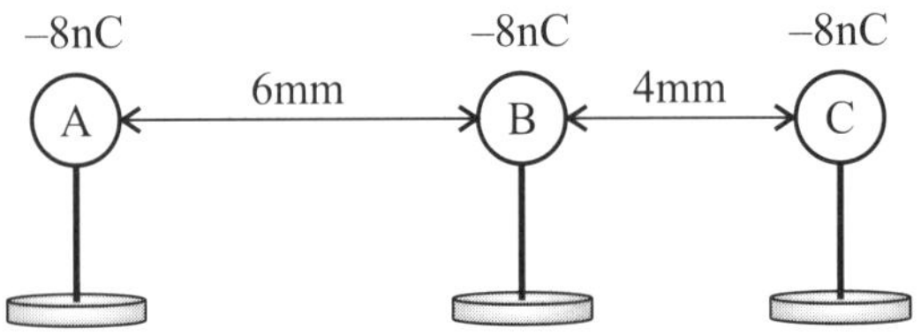

3.1 State Coulomb's Law. (2)

3.2 Calculate the force exerted on B by A. (4)

3.3 Draw a free-body diagram showing the electrostatic forces exerted on B by A and C. (3)

3.4 Determine the resultant force acting on B. (5)

[14]

Question 4 (Solutions on page 342)

Two insulated point charges (A and B) are fixed in position in line with each other along the dashed line as shown. X, Y and Z are areas or positions along the dashed line and are not charges. X is an area to the left of A. Point Y is a fixed position equidistant between A and B. Z is a point 2mm to the right of B. A and B are 0,5cm apart.

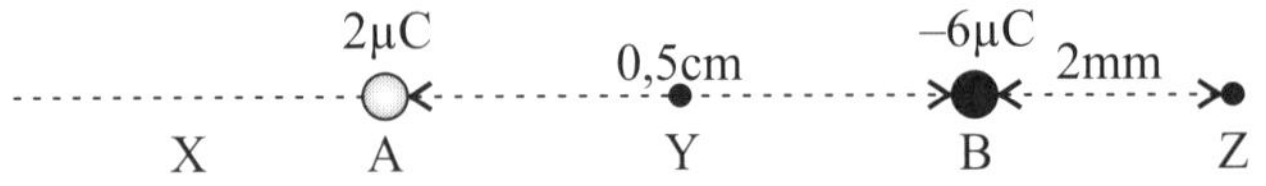

4.1 Define an electric field (2)

4.2 Determine the resultant electric field at Y. Take the top of the page as North. (5)

4.3 What is the direction of the electric field due to B at X. (1)

4.4 What is the resultant electric field at point Z? (6)

4.5 Determine the acceleration of a sphere with a mass of 100g and a charge of –3μC that is placed at Z. (5)

[19]

Question 5 (Solutions on page 343)

Two point charges Q_1 and Q_2 are placed 20cm apart. Q_1 has charge of $+3\mu C$ and Q_2 has charge of $+6{,}48\mu C$. An unknown charge is moved between Q_1 and Q_2 until it experiences no electrostatic force. At what distance, in centimetres, from Q_1 will this occur?

[10]

Question 6 (Solutions on page 343)

Two identical spheres have a mass of 100g and are suspended from insulated strings. At a distance of 10mm, the spheres attract each other as shown in the diagram below. At this point the tension in each string is 3,08 N. The charge on the spheres are equal in magnitude.

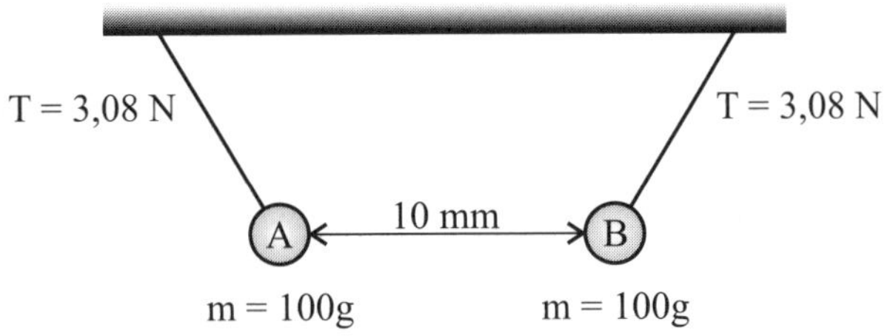

6.1 State Coulomb's Law. (2)

6.2 Draw a fully labelled free body diagram showing all of the forces acting on sphere A. (3)

6.3 Determine the magnitude of the electrostatic force of attraction acting on sphere A. (5)

6.4 Hence, determine the charge on sphere A, if the charge on B is positive. (5)

[15]

Question 7 (Solutions on page 343 and 344)

Two identical spheres, A and B, are attached to non-conducting threads and suspended from a ceiling. The balls are given the same positive charge and they hang as shown in the diagram below. The mass of each ball is 50g. The distance between the spheres is 20 cm.

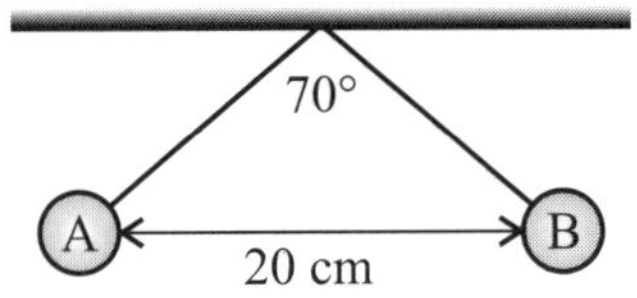

7.1 State Coulomb's Law. (2)

7.2 Draw a fully labelled free body diagram showing all of the forces acting on sphere A. include one angle that is not 90° on your diagram. (3)

7.3 Determine the magnitude of the electrostatic force that ball B exerts on ball A. (5)

7.4 Hence, calculate the charge on each sphere. (4)

[14]

TOC
1 Data Sheet
2 Definitions
3
3 solutions
4
4 solutions
5
5 solutions
6
6 solutions
7
7 solutions
8
8 solutions
9
9 solutions
10
10 solutions

Question 8 (Solutions on page 344)

Two spheres are placed in an insulated cylindrical container. Sphere P has a charge of –60nC and Q has a charge of –10μC. The mass of Sphere Qis 2,5 times the mass of P. When the spheres are released P levitates above Q at a height of 3,5cm without touching each other.

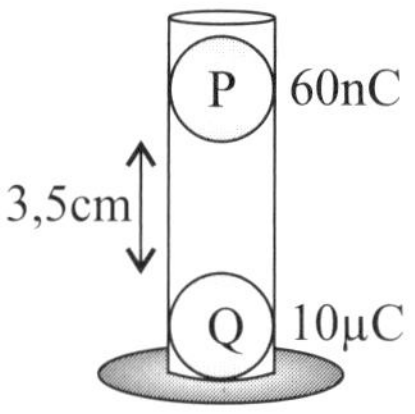

8.1 State Coulomb's Law. (2)

8.2 Draw a fully labelled free body diagram showing all of the forces acting on sphere P. (2)

8.3 Calculate the mass of sphere Q. (6)

[10]

Question 9 (Solutions on page 344 and 345)

Justin is performing an experiment to investigate electric fields. He suspends two identical spheres of unknown mass from insulated threads. One sphere carries a charge of +1,1pC whilst the other has a charge of +1,8pC. Justin places the spheres 150mm apart.

9.1 State Newton's law of universal gravitation. (2)

9.2 Justin attempts to measure the force of electrostatic repulsion between the spheres. However, he finds that the spheres exert no force on each other. He takes his finding to his science teacher who suggests that another one of Newton's laws may be the reason. Explain the science teacher's reasoning. (4)

9.3 Determine the mass of the spheres. (6)

[12]

Question 10 (Solutions on page 345)

Two metal spheres, sphere A and sphere B, on insulating stands are positioned 60 cm from each other as shown below. The spheres may be treated as point charges.

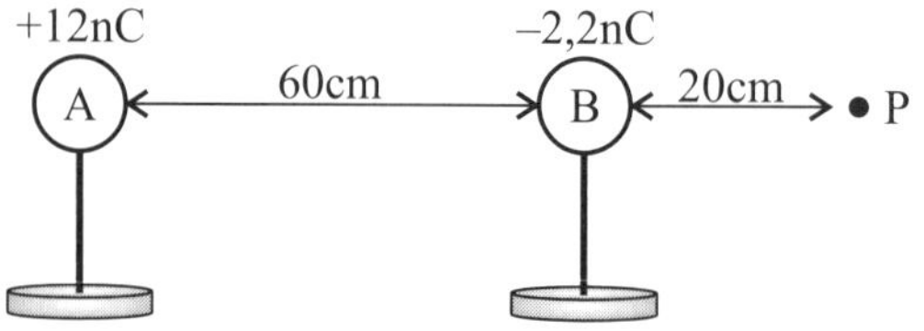

Sphere A carries a charge of +12,0 nC, while sphere B carries a charge of –2,2 nC.

10.1 Draw the electric field pattern that is produced by the spheres. (3)

10.2 Define the magnitude of the electric field at a point. (2)

10.3 Calculate the net electric field strength at point P, which lies 20 cm to the right of sphere B along the straight line connecting the two spheres' centres. (5)

10.4 Calculate the net electric force that an electron would experience at point P. (3)

10.5 When the electron is placed at point P it will accelerate. Will the acceleration increase, decrease or remain constant? Explain your answer. (4)

[17]

Question 11 (Solutions on page 346)

An electron is placed 30mm from a charged sphere on an insulated table. At the instant the electron begins to accelerate, the sphere is neutralised. It takes the electron $4{,}13 \times 10^{-9}$ s to reach the sphere.

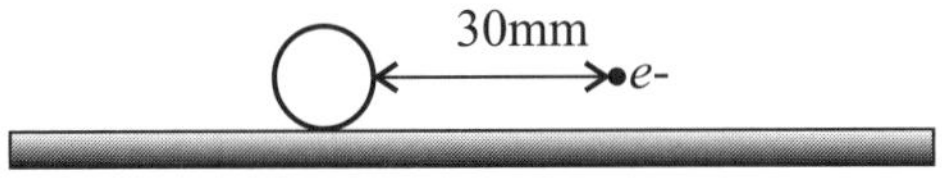

11.1 State Coulomb's Law. (2)

11.2 Determine the magnitude of the force acting on the electron at a distance of 30mm from the sphere. (5)

11.3 Why is it important that the sphere is neutralised at the instant the electron begins to accelerate? (3)

11.4 Is the sphere positively or negatively charged? Give a reason for your answer. (2)

11.5 Hence, calculate the charge on the sphere. Give your answer in nanocoulombs. (6)

[17]

Question 12 (Solutions on page 346)

Three small, identical metal spheres, Q_1, Q_2 and Q_3, are placed on insulating stands. Sphere Q_1 carries a charge of – 8 μC, sphere Q_2 carries a charge of – 4 μC and sphere Q_3 carries a charge of +2 μC. The spheres are arranged in such a way that Q_2 and Q_3 are each 6 mm from Q_1 as shown in the diagram below.

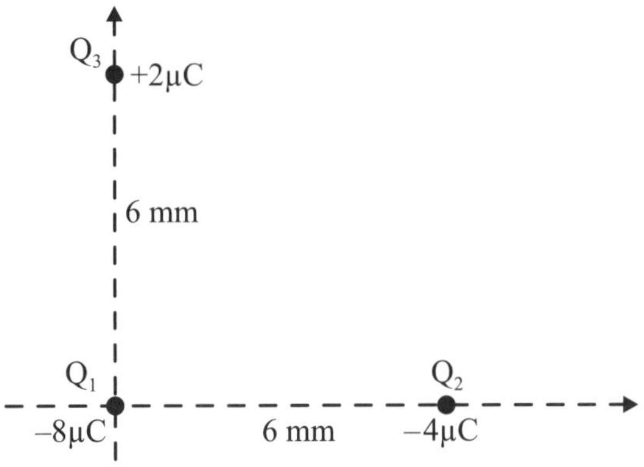

12.1 Calculate the magnitude of the force exerted on Q_1 by Q_2. (4)

12.2 Draw a free-body diagram showing the electrostatic forces exerted on Q_1 by Q_2 and Q_3. Refer to the top of your page as north (3)

12.3 Determine the resultant force acting on Q_1. (8)

[15]

TOC 1 Data Sheet 2 Definitions 3 3 solutions 4 4 solutions 5 5 solutions 6 6 solutions 7 7 solutions 8 8 solutions 9 9 solutions 10 10 solutions

Question 13 (Solutions on page 347)

Two positively charged metal spheres each with a mass of 4 g are suspended from the same point by light, inextensible strings of equal length, making an angle of 20° with each other as shown in the diagram 1 below. The spheres are then forced together until they make contact and are then released. Once released they now make a new angle, θ, with each other.

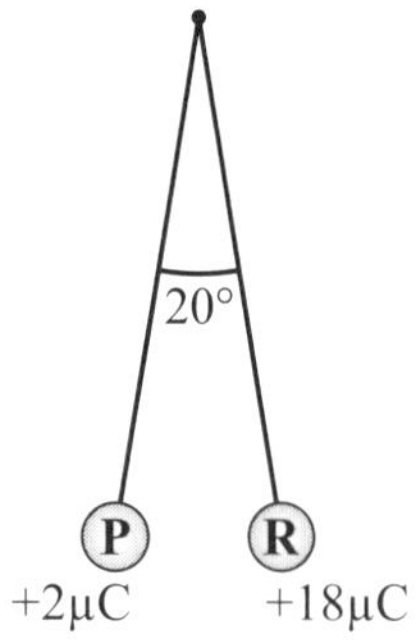

Diagram 1

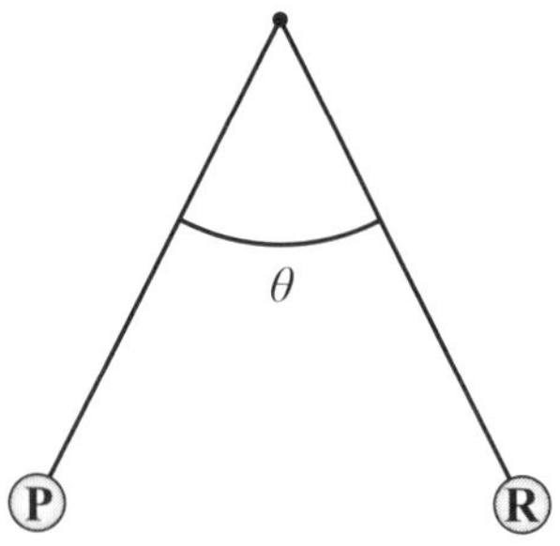

Diagram 2

13.1 Sketch the combined field pattern between charges P and R in diagram 1. (4)

13.2 State Coulomb's Law. (2)

13.3 Draw a labelled free body diagram of the forces acting on sphere R in diagram 1. (3)

13.4 Calculate the magnitude of the electrostatic force of repulsion between the charges in diagram 1. (4)

13.5 Hence, calculate the distance between the charges in diagram 1. (4)

13.6 Calculate the new charge on each sphere after touching in diagram 2. (2)

13.7 Were electrons transferred From P to R or R to P when they touch? (1)

13.8 How many electrons were transferred when P and R touch? (3)

13.9 Determine the value of θ, the new angle in diagram 2 if the spheres are now 8,66m apart. (7)

[30]

Question 14 (Solutions on page 348)

The distance between the electron and proton in a hydrogen atom is separated by a distance of approximately 53pm. Determine the electrostatic force of attraction between the proton and electron in a hydrogen atom.

[7]

Question 15 (Solutions on page 348)

A and B are two small spheres separated by a distance of 0,70 m. Sphere A carries a charge of +3 μC and sphere B carries a charge of –4 μC.

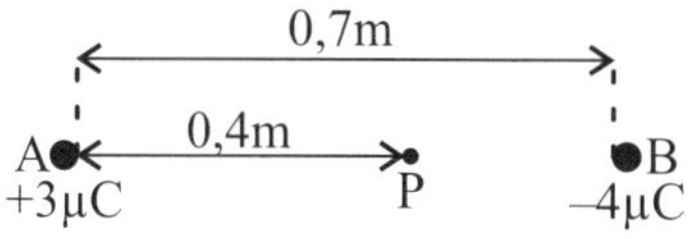

P is a point between spheres A and B and is 0,40 m from sphere A, as shown in the diagram above.

15.1 Define electric field strength. (2)

15.2 Calculate the magnitude of the net electric field strength at point P. (5)

15.3 A point charge of magnitude 3 nC is now placed at point P. Calculate the magnitude of the electrostatic force experienced by this charge. (3)

[10]

TOC 1 Data Sheet 2 Definitions 3 3 solutions 4 4 solutions 5 5 solutions 6 6 solutions 7 7 solutions 8 8 solutions 9 9 solutions 10 10 solutions

Question 16 (Solutions on page 348)

A sphere Q, with a charge of 3 μC, is placed 1 m away from a second sphere R, with a charge of –4 μC. The spheres lie along a straight line, as shown in the diagram below. Point P is located a distance of 0,3 m to the left of sphere Q, while point X is located between Q and R. Point Z is located an unknow distance from point Q.

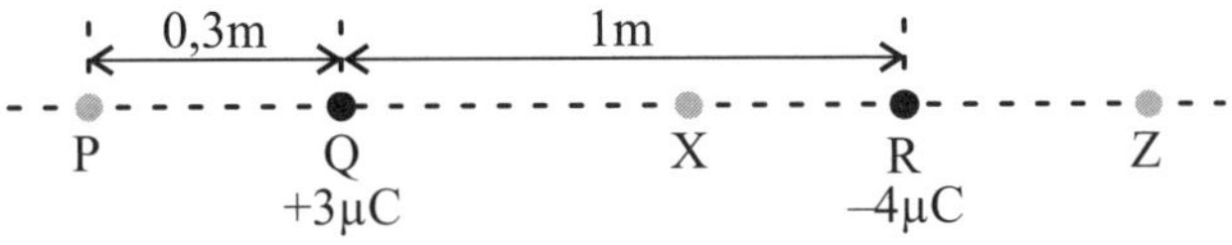

16.1 At which point or points is it not possible for the electric field to be zero? Explain your answer. (4)

16.2 Calculate the net electric field at point P, due to the two charged spheres Q and R. (6)

16.3 An alpha particle (a helium nucleus with no electrons) is placed at point P. Calculate the resultant force the alpha particle would experience. (4)

16.4 Where must an electron be placed to experience no force? (7)

[20]

Question 17 (Solutions on page 349)

A small charged sphere on the end of an insulated handle carries a charge of –8 μC. It is brought close to a piece of tissue paper of mass 0,5 g with a charge of +2 μC.

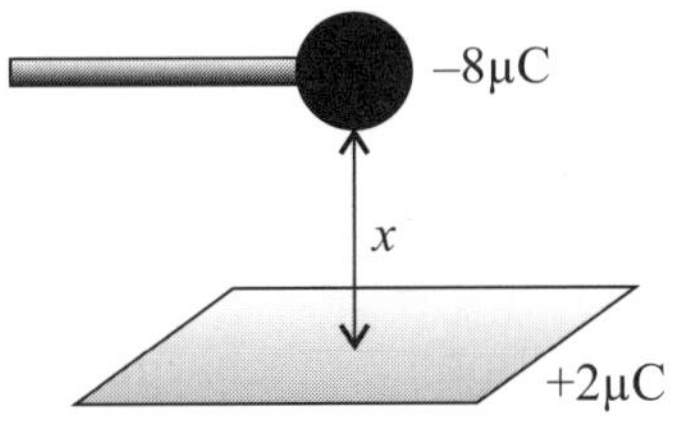

17.1 State Coulomb's Law. (2)

17.2 Calculate the value of x, the maximum distance at which the sphere would be able to lift the tissue paper. You may assume that the force of attraction due to the mass of the objects is negligible. (8)

17.3 State Newton's Universal Law of Gravitation. (2)

17.4 Using calculations, prove that the assumption in 17.2 is true at the distance you calculated, if the mass of the sphere and handle is 60g. (5)

[17]

TOC
1 Data Sheet
2 Definitions
3
3 solutions
4
4 solutions
5
5 solutions
6
6 solutions
7
7 solutions
8
8 solutions
9
9 solutions
10
10 solutions

Question 18 (Solutions on page 349)

Two point charges are placed at two of the corners of a right angled triangle as shown in the diagram below. The distance between the point charges is shown on the diagram. X is a point at the third corner of the right angled triangle.

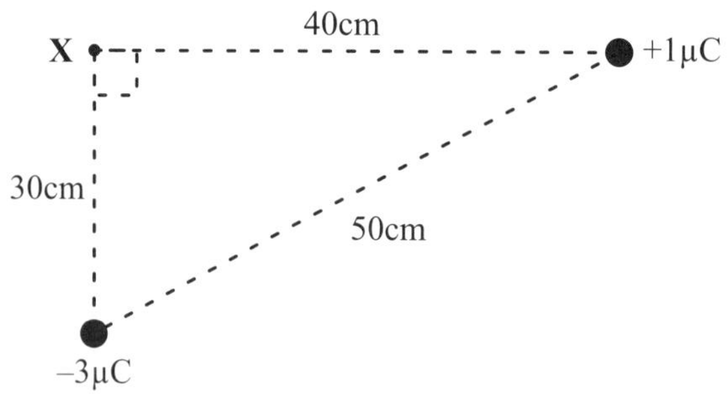

18.1 Define electric field strength. (2)

18.2 Calculate the magnitude of the net electric field strength at point X. (5)

18.3 Determine the direction of net electric field at point X. (4)

18.4 An electron is placed at point X. Calculate the force acting on the electron at this point. (6)

[17]

Question 19 (Solutions on page 350)

A hollow metal sphere, A, of mass 150g with a charge of +85nC is fixed onto an insulated table. Another hollow metal sphere, B, with a mass of 40g is placed at a distance of 40mm from sphere A. At the instant sphere B is released it experiences an acceleration of 2,87 $m.s^{-2}$. (Ignore gravitational forces of attraction for this question)

19.1 State Coulomb's Law. (2)

19.2 Calculate the magnitude of the charge on sphere B (6)

19.3 The graph below shows the velocity of charge B after it is released as a function of time.

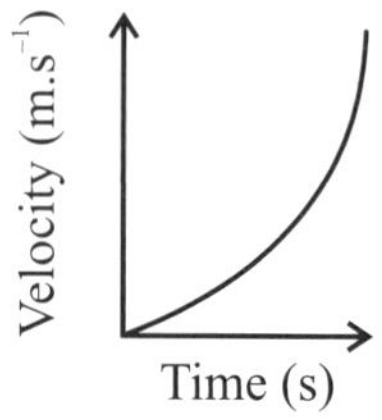

Use the graph to determine the sign of the charge on B. Explain your answer. (4)

[12]

Question 20 (Solutions on page 350)

Two charged particles are placed 200 mm apart at points A and B as shown.
X is a point midway between points A and B. The charge at point A is unknown while the charge at point B is +1 nC.

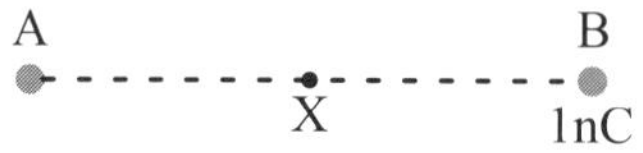

The resultant electric field strength at point X due to the charges is 2 700 $N.C^{-1}$ towards the charge at point A.

20.1 Determine the charge of the particle at point A. Give your answer in nC. (8)

20.2 Calculate the electrostatic force a charge of –2 nC would experience if it were placed at point X. (3)

[11]

Question 21 (Solutions on page 351)

Two identical metal spheres with equal and opposite charges of 150 nC are placed on insulated stands with their centres 10 cm apart from each other.

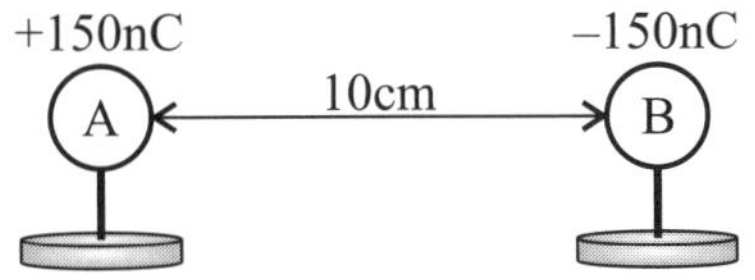

The table below shows the resultant electric field as a function of distance from the positive charge between A and B. The graph is a sketch of the results in the table.

Net Electric Field $N.C^{-1}$ ($\times 10^6$)	Distance from positive charge (cm)
13,67	1
3,59	2
1,78	3
1,22	4
21.5.1	5
1,22	6
21.5.2	7
3,59	8
21.5.3	9

Graph of the magnitude of the resultant electric field against distance from positive charge

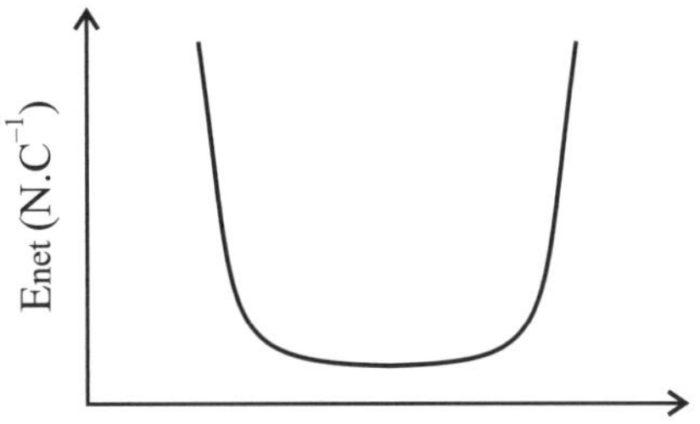

21.1 State Coulomb's Law. (2)

21.2 Calculate the magnitude of the force which sphere B exerts on sphere A. (5)

21.3 Define electric field strength. (4)

21.4 Draw a diagram of the resultant electric field between and around the charges. (3)

21.5 Complete the values that have been labelled 21.5.1, 21.5.2 and 21.5.3 in the table. (9)

21.6 On the graph below, label where you would expect 1cm, 5cm and 9cm to be with the letters X, Y and Z respectively. Labels must be on the graph not the axis.

Graph of the magnitude of the resultant electric field against distance from positive charge

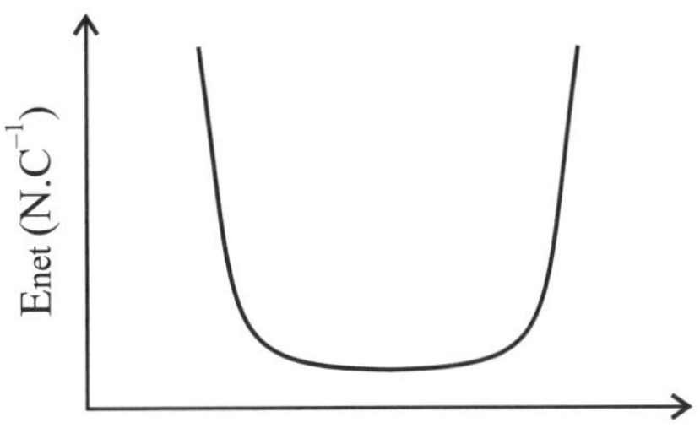

(3)

21.7 With reasons, use the table and the graph to explain how the magnitude of the resultant electric field changes between A and B. (4)

[30]

TOC 1 Data Sheet 2 Definitions 3 3 solutions 4 4 solutions 5 5 solutions 6 6 solutions 7 7 solutions 8 8 solutions 9 9 solutions 10 10 solutions

Question 22 (2014 IEB Final Examination) (Solutions on page 352)

Two positive point charges, A and B, are separated by a distance of 8 mm. The charge on A is 1 nC and the charge on B is 9 nC.

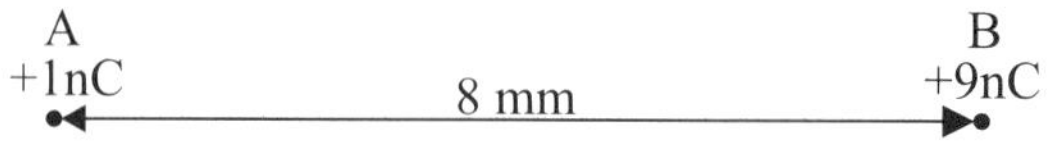

22.1 Draw an electric field line diagram to represent the field set up by charges A and B. (3)

22.2 State *Coulombs law.* (2)

22.3 Calculate the force exerted by charge A on charge B. (5)

22.4 Calculate the number of electrons that charge A lost when it obtained its charge of 1 nC. (2)

22.5 At a distance '*x*' from charge A the magnitude of the resultant electric field due to charges A and B is zero. Point '*x*' lies on the straight line joining charges A and B.

22.5.1 Define resultant vector. (2)

22.5.2 Define the magnitude of the electric field at a point. (2)

22.5.3 Determine the distance '*x*' from charge A. Show all working/reasoning in support of your answer. (4)

[20]

Question 23 (2015 IEB Supplementary Examination) (Solutions on page 352 and 353)

The diagram shows a conducting sphere X of radius 40 mm carrying a charge of $6{,}4 \times 10^{-8}$ C. The sphere is at the top of an insulated stand which is placed on a digital balance. The weight of the sphere and stand is $9{,}54 \times 10^{-3}$ N as shown by the reading on the balance.

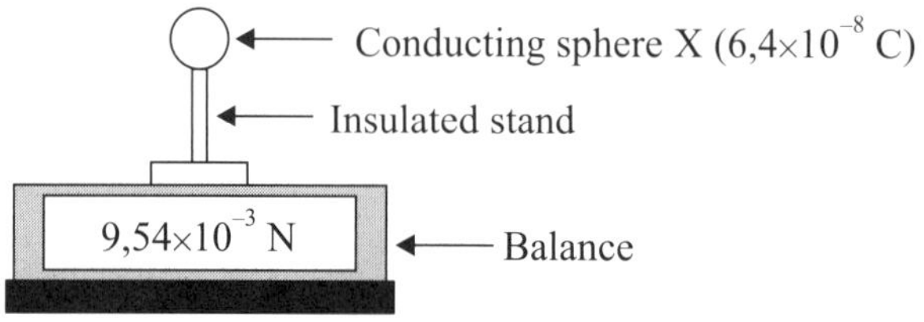

23.1 Draw an electric field line diagram to represent the field set up by sphere X. (3)

23.2 Calculate the magnitude of the electric field strength at the surface of the sphere X. (4)

23.3 Another sphere, Y, carrying a charge of $-4{,}8 \times 10^{-8}$ C is held so that its centre is 60 mm vertically above the centre of sphere X.

a) Calculate the magnitude of the electric force of sphere X on sphere Y. (4)

b) Calculate the new reading on the balance. (2)

[13]

Question 24 (2015 IEB Final Examination) (Solutions on page 353)

A charged particle of charge 25 nC is placed in an electric field of strength $4{,}8 \times 10^5\ N \cdot C^{-1}$.

24.1 Calculate the magnitude of the force experienced by the charge while in the electric field. (3)

24.2 A uniform electric field could be established by a parallel plate system connected to a source of potential difference as shown.

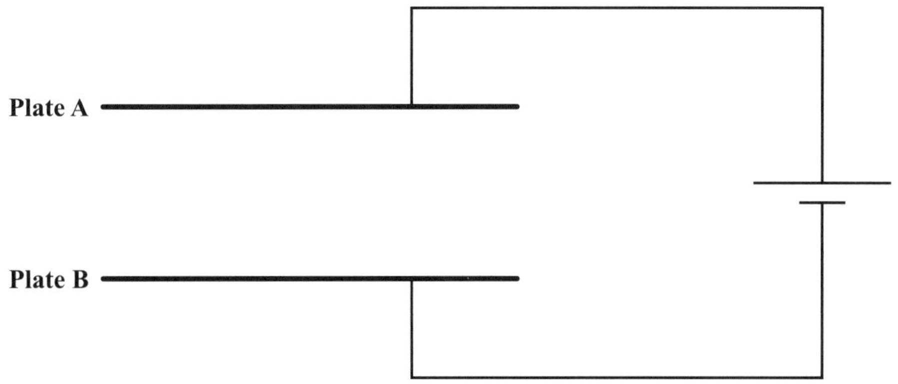

On the diagram above sketch the electric field pattern between the parallel plates. You must also label the positive and negative plates. (3)

[6]

Question 25 (2016 IEB Supplementary Examination) (Solutions on page 353)

25.1 Define *the magnitude of an electric field at a point.* (2)

25.2 The diagram below represents an electric field in a region of space. It can be seen that the field lines are parallel and evenly spaced on the left-hand side and then spread out on the right-hand side.

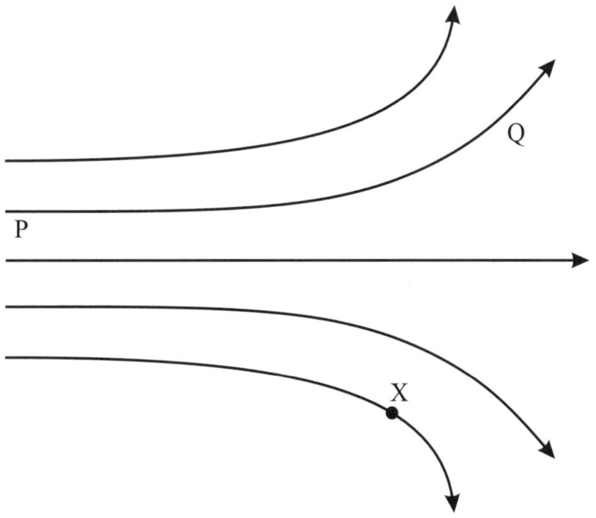

25.2.1 Compare the strength of the electric field at the positions labelled P and Q. Use evidence from the diagram to explain your answer. (2)

25.2.2 An **electron** is placed at position X as shown. On diagram, draw an arrow starting on the electron to indicate the force experienced by the electron in the electric field. Label the arrow F. (2)

[6]

TOC 1 Data Sheet 2 Definitions 3 3 solutions 4 4 solutions 5 5 solutions 6 6 solutions 7 7 solutions 8 8 solutions 9 9 solutions 10 10 solutions

Question 26 (2016 IEB Final Examination) (Solutions on page 353 and 354)

David is curious as to how the electric field at a fixed distance away from a charged sphere depends on the magnitude of the charge on the sphere.

David charges the sphere positively and measures the electric field (E) at a fixed distance from the centre of the sphere. During his investigation, he repeats the experiment, each time changing the magnitude of the charge on the sphere (Q). The results are recorded in the table below.

Q (nC)	**E (kN.C^{-1})**
2	6
5	19
7	25
9	34
12	41
14	52

26.1 Define *electric field.* (2)

26.2 Draw the electric field lines around a positively charged sphere. (2)

26.3 State an hypothesis for this investigation. (2)

26.4 Plot a graph of electric field (on the y-axis) vs charge (on the *x*-axis) on the graph paper below. (6)

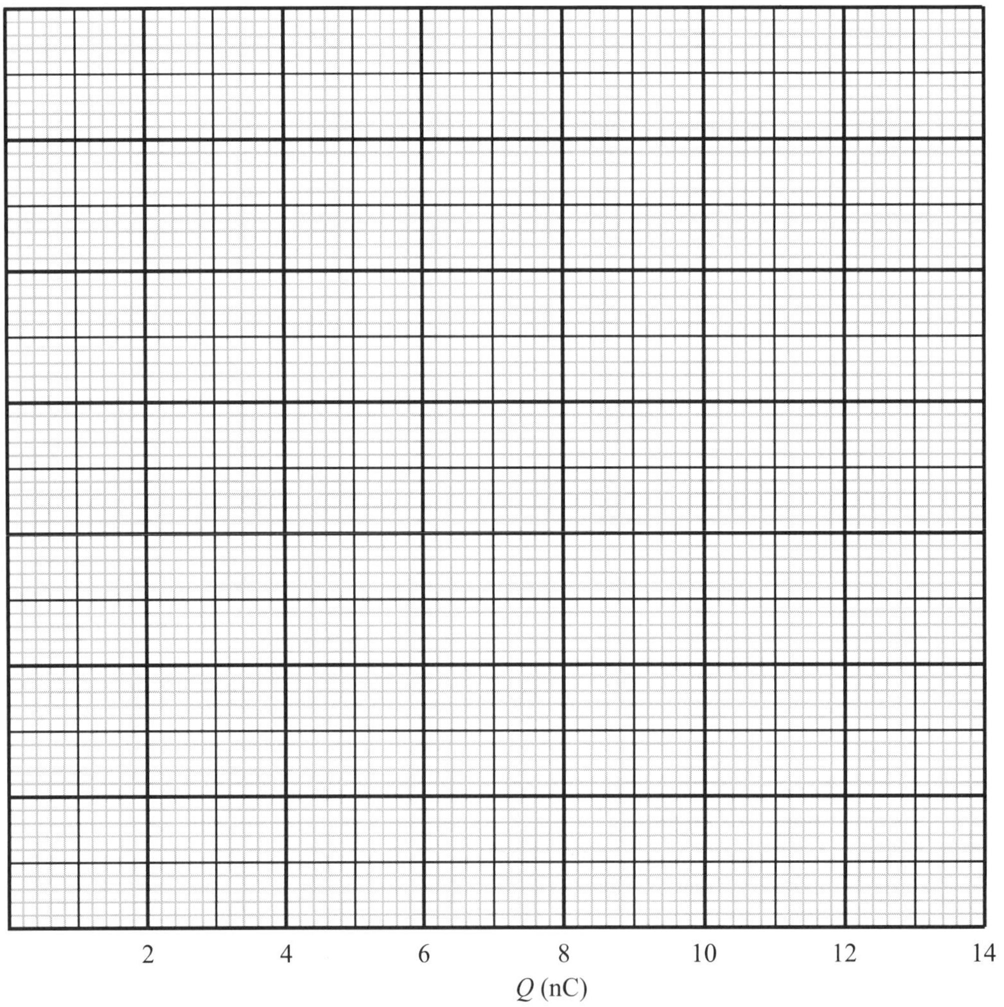

26.5 Calculate the gradient of the graph. Indicate the values you used for this calculation on your graph. (4)

26.6 Use your answer from Question 26.5, your knowledge of electric fields and that the equation $y = mx + c$ describes a straight line to determine the distance from the charge at which David made all the measurements of electric field. Express your answer to three decimal places. (3)

[19]

Question 27 (2017 IEB Supplementary Examination) (Solutions on page 354)

A small metal sphere has a charge of +5 nC. The electric field is measured to have a magnitude of 312 500 $N \cdot C^{-1}$ at an unknown distance from the charge.

27.1 Define *electric field.* (2)

27.2 Calculate the distance from the charge where the electric field strength was measured (3)

[5]

Question 28 (2017 IEB Final Examination) (Solutions on page 354 and 355)

A small test charge of mass 20 g and charge 1 nC, is released from rest 0,6 m from a charge *Q* in empty space. The test charge takes 3,3 s to reach charge *Q*.

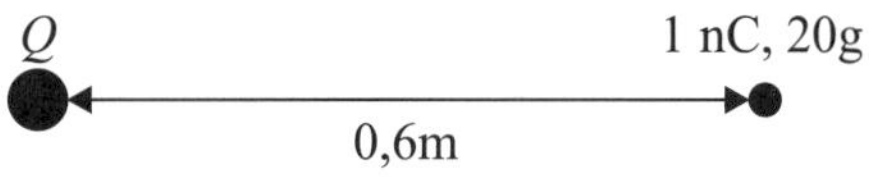

28.1 Calculate the magnitude of the average acceleration experienced by the test charge. (3)

28.2 Calculate the magnitude of charge *Q*. Assume the acceleration calculated in Question 28.1 is the acceleration 0,6 m from charge *Q*. (4)

28.3 Why was it necessary in Question 28.2 to specify the acceleration at 0,6 m from the charge *Q*? Briefly explain your answer. (3)

[10]

Question 29 (2018 IEB Supplementary Examination) (Solutions on page 355)

Two identical isolated metal spheres, R and T, carry charges of + 6 nC and + 10 nC as shown in the diagram.

29.1 Sketch the electric field lines around the two charged spheres. (3)

The two spheres are brought together and allowed to touch each other. The spheres are then separated to a distance of 1,8 m apart.

29.2 Calculate the new charge on each sphere. (2)

29.3 Calculate the number of electrons transferred while the spheres were touching. (2)

29.4 Did the electrons move from sphere R to T or from sphere T to R while the spheres were touching? (2)

A third sphere S with a charge of –5 nC is placed between the original spheres R and T at a distance of 0,7 m from sphere R.

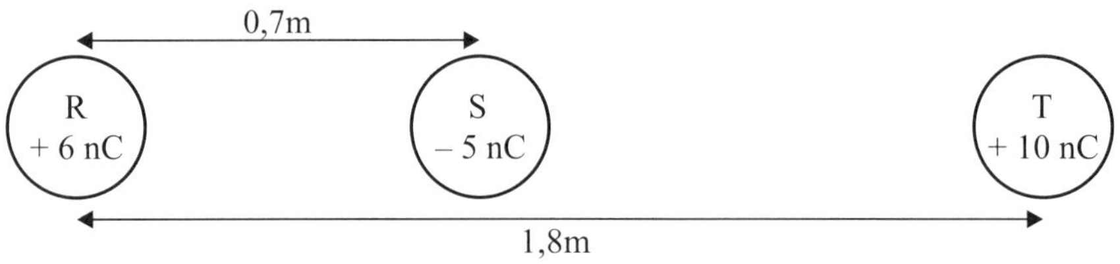

29.5 State *Coulomb's Law.* (2)

29.6 Calculate the magnitude of the net force acting on sphere S due to spheres R and T. (6)

[17]

Question 30 (2019 IEB Supplementary Examination) (Solutions on page 356)

Two small identical polystyrene balls, A and B, each of mass 2 g are hung by insulating threads from a support. Each ball is given an identical negative charge. The balls repel each other so that they reach equilibrium 10 cm apart with the threads at angles of 70° to the horizontal as shown in the diagram below.

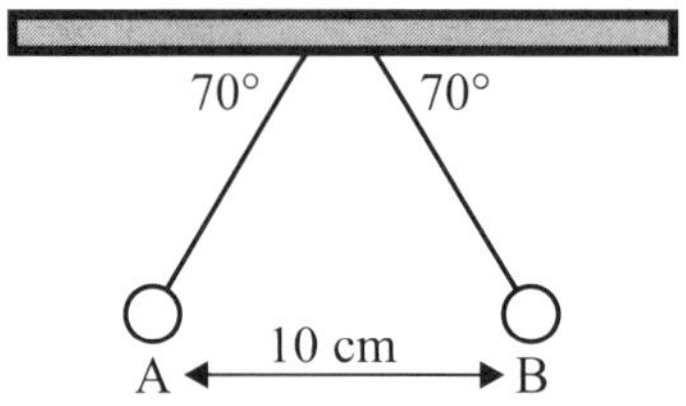

30.1 Draw the electric field pattern around the two negative charges. (2)

30.2 Define *weight.* (2)

30.3 Calculate the weight of one of the polystyrene balls. (2)

30.4 Define a *vector quantity.* (2)

30.5 Draw a labelled free body diagram for polystyrene ball A. (3)

30.6 State *Coulomb's law.* (2)

30.7 Calculate the magnitude of the negative charge on each polystyrene ball. (6)

[19]

TOC 1 Data Sheet 2 Definitions 3 3 solutions 4 4 solutions 5 5 solutions 6 6 solutions 7 7 solutions 8 8 solutions 9 9 solutions 10 10 solutions

Question 31 (2019 IEB Final Examination) (Solutions on page 357)

31.1 In a demonstration of electrostatics, a small ball on an insulating rod is given a charge of + 30 nC.

31.1.1 Draw a diagram showing the electric field around a + 30 nC charge. (2)

The + 30 nC charge is now held directly above a similar ball having a charge of – 100 nC and a mass of 1,5 g, which lies on an insulating table.
The upper ball is brought closer to the lower ball in order to pick it up.

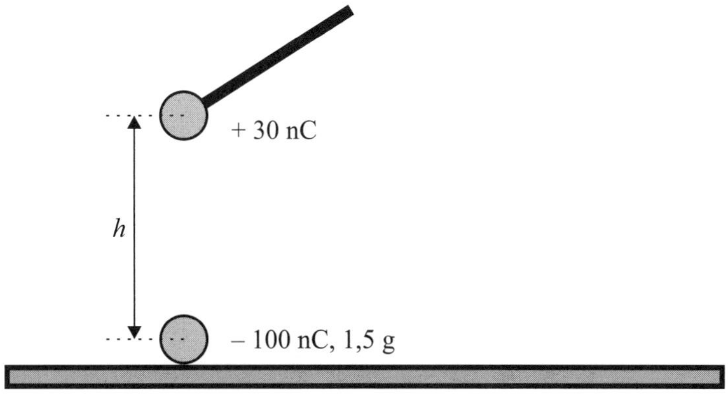

31.1.2 State *Coulomb's Law.* (2)

31.1.3 Calculate the distance h at which the 1,5 g ball will just be lifted off the table by the electrostatic force. (6)

31.2 Charged particles of –2 μC and + 6 μC are placed 5 cm apart as shown in the diagram.

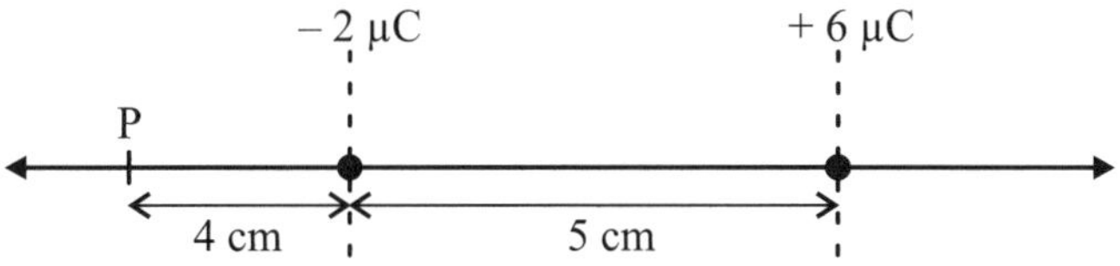

31.2.1 Calculate the magnitude of the electric field due to the + 6 μC charge at point P. (4)

31.2.2 Hence, Calculate the net electric field at point P. (5)

[19]

8. ELECTROSTATICS (SOLUTIONS)

Question 1

1.1	D	(2)
1.2	C	(2)
1.3	A	(2)
1.4	C	(2)
1.5	A	(2)
1.6	B	(2)
1.7	C	(2)
1.8	A	(2)
1.9	B	(2)
1.10	D	(2)
1.11	B	(2)
1.12	B	(2)
1.13	D	(2)
1.14	D	(2)
1.15	A	(2)
1.16	D	(2)
1.17	A	(2)
1.18	B	(2)
1.19	C	(2)
1.20	C	(2)
1.21	D	(2)
1.22	D	(2)
1.23	C	(2)
1.24	A	(2)
1.25	C	(2)
1.26	D	(2)
1.27	D	(2)
1.28	B	(2)
1.29	B	(2)
1.30	A	(2)
1.31	A	(2)
1.32	B	(2)
1.33	D	(2)
1.34	C	(2)
1.35	D	(2)

[70]

Question 2

2.1

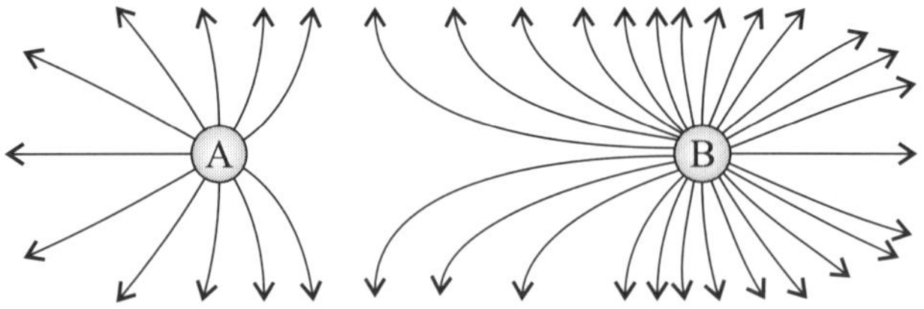

- More field lines on B
- Charge moving out of A and B
- Point of cancellation closer to A than to B

(3)

2.2 Two point charges in free space or air exert forces on each other. The force is directly proportional to the product of the charges and inversely proportional to the square of the distance between the charges. (2)

2.3 $F = \dfrac{kQ_AQ_B}{r^2}$

$$1,5\times10^{-3} = \frac{9\times10^{9}\left(2\times10^{-9}\right)Q_B}{\left(6\times10^{-3}\right)^2}$$

$Q_B = 3\times10^{-9}$ C (5)

2.4 $N_{e-} = \dfrac{Q}{q_{e-}}$

$$= \frac{2\times10^{-9}}{1,6\times10^{-19}}$$

$= 1,25\times10^{10}$ electrons (2)

[12]

Question 3

3.1 Two point charges in free space or air exert forces on each other. The force is directly proportional to the product of the charges and inversely proportional to the square of the distance between the charges. (2)

3.2

$$F = \frac{kQ_AQ_B}{r^2} = \frac{9\times10^9\left(8\times10^{-9}\right)\left(8\times10^{-9}\right)}{\left(6\times10^{-3}\right)^2}$$

$= 0,016\,\text{N right (East is also acceptable)}$ (4)

3.3 

(3)

3.4

$$F_{C\text{ on }B} = \frac{kQ_CQ_B}{r^2} = \frac{9\times10^9\left(8\times10^{-9}\right)\left(8\times10^{-9}\right)}{\left(4\times10^{-3}\right)^2}$$

$= 0,036\,\text{N Left (West is also acceptable)}$

$$F_{net} = 0,036 - 0,016$$
$$= 0,02\,\text{N Left}$$

(5)

[14]

Question 4

4.1 The force per unit positive charge. (2)

4.2

$$E_Y = \frac{kQ_A}{r^2} = \frac{9\times10^9\left(2\times10^{-6}\right)}{\left(0,25\times10^{-2}\right)^2} = 2,88\times10^9\ \text{N.C}^{-1}\ \text{East}$$

$$E_Y = \frac{kQ_B}{r^2} = \frac{9\times10^9\left(6\times10^{-6}\right)}{\left(0,25\times10^{-2}\right)^2} = 8,64\times10^9\ \text{N.C}^{-1}\ \text{East}$$

$$E_{net} = 2,88\times10^9 + 8,64\times10^9$$
$$= 1,15\times10^{10}\ \text{N.C}^{-1}\ \text{East}$$

(5)

4.3 East (1)

4.4

$$E_Z = \frac{kQ_A}{r^2} = \frac{9\times10^9\left(2\times10^{-6}\right)}{\left(0,5\times10^{-2}+2\times10^{-3}\right)^2} = 367,35\times10^6\ \text{N.C}^{-1}\ \text{East}$$

$$E_Z = \frac{kQ_B}{r^2} = \frac{9\times10^9\left(6\times10^{-6}\right)}{\left(2\times10^{-3}\right)^2} = 1,35\times10^{10}\ \text{N.C}^{-1}\ \text{West}$$

$$E_{net} = 1,35\times10^{10} - 367,35\times10^6$$
$$= 1,31\times10^{10}\ \text{N.C}^{-1}\ \text{West}$$

(6)

4.5

$$F = Eq$$
$$= 1,31\times10^{10}\left(3\times10^{-6}\right)$$

$= 39\,397,95\,\text{N East} \rightarrow$ charge is negative and electric field is to the West

$$a = \frac{F}{m} = \frac{39\,397,95}{0,1}$$
$$= 393\,979,5\,\text{m.s}^{-2}\ \text{East}$$

(5)

[19]

Question 5

$$E_{Q_1} = \frac{kQ_1}{r^2} = \frac{9\times10^9\left(3\times10^{-6}\right)}{r^2} \qquad E_{Q_1} = \frac{kQ_2}{r^2} = \frac{9\times10^9\left(6,48\times10^{-6}\right)}{(0,2-r)^2}$$

$$E_{Q_1} = E_{Q2}$$

$$\frac{9\times10^9\left(3\times10^{-6}\right)}{r^2} = \frac{9\times10^9\left(6,48\times10^{-6}\right)}{(0,2-r)^2}$$

$$(0,2-r)^2\left(3\times10^{-6}\right) = r^2\left(6,48\times10^{-6}\right)$$

$$(0,2-r)^2 = 2,16r^2$$

$$0,2-r = r\sqrt{2,16}$$

$$r + r\sqrt{2,16} = 0,2$$

$$r\left(1+\sqrt{2,16}\right) = 0,2$$

$$r = 0,08$$

$$= 8\,\text{cm}$$

[10]

Question 6

6.1 Two point charges in free space or air exert forces on each other. The force is directly proportional to the product of the charges and inversely proportional to the square of the distance between the charges. (2)

6.2

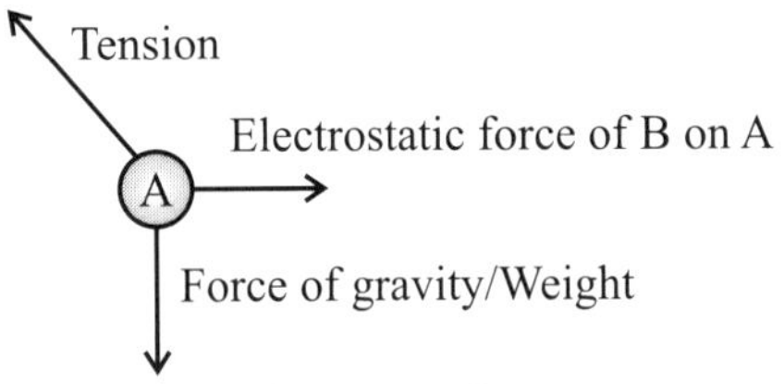

(3)

6.3 $3,08^2 = 0,98^2 + F_{B\text{ on }A}{}^2$

$F_{B\text{ on }A} = 2,92\,\text{N}$

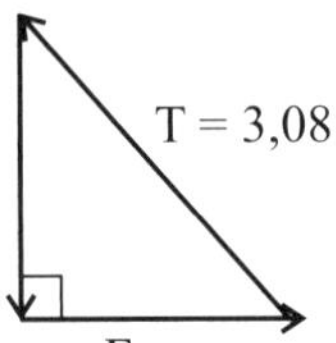

(5)

6.4 $F = \frac{kQ_AQ_B}{r^2}$

$$2,92 = \frac{9\times10^9 Q^2}{\left(10\times10^{-3}\right)^2}$$

$$Q = -1,8\times10^{-7}\text{ C}$$

(5)

[15]

Question 7

7.1 Two point charges in free space or air exert forces on each other. The force is directly proportional to the product of the charges and inversely proportional to the square of the distance between the charges. (2)

7.2

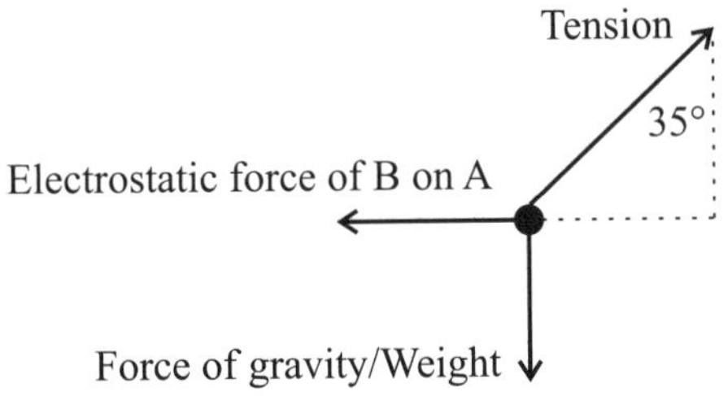

or

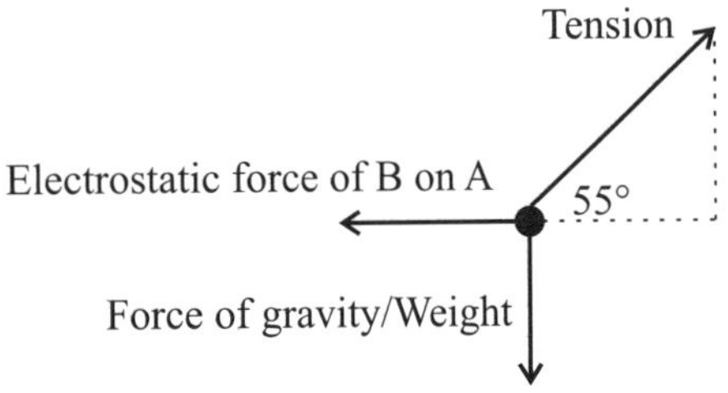

(4)

7.3 $\tan 35^\circ = \dfrac{F_{B\ on\ A}}{F_g}$

$F_{B\ on\ A} = 0,49 \tan 35^\circ$

$= 0,34\,N$

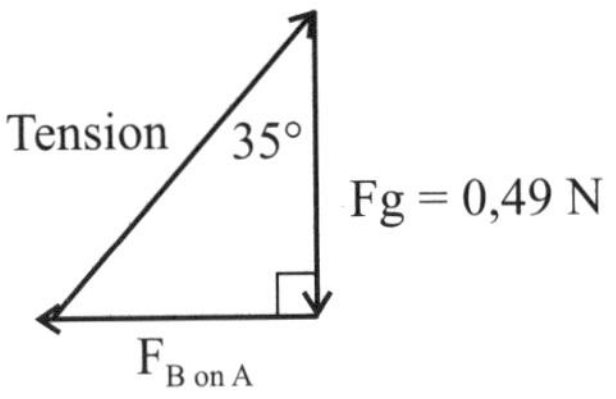

(5)

7.4 $F = \dfrac{kQ_AQ_B}{r^2}$

$0,34 = \dfrac{9\times10^9 Q^2}{\left(20\times10^{-2}\right)^2}$

$Q = 1,23\times10^{-6}\ C$

(4)

[14]

Question 8

8.1 Two point charges in free space or air exert forces on each other. The force is directly proportional to the product of the charges and inversely proportional to the square of the distance between the charges. (2)

8.2

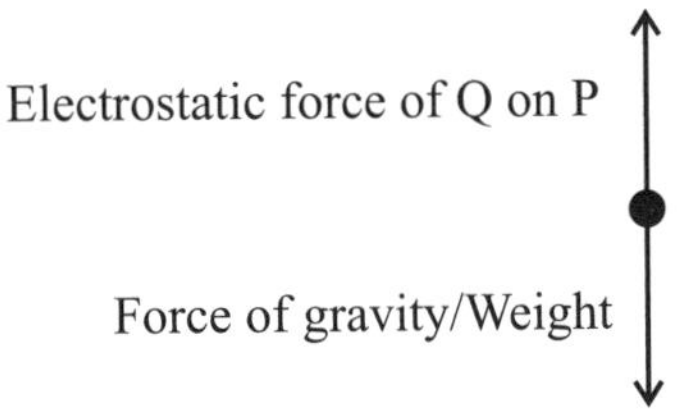

(2)

8.3 $F = \dfrac{kQ_QQ_P}{r^2}$

$= \dfrac{9\times10^9\left(60\times10^{-9}\right)\left(10\times10^{-6}\right)}{\left(3,5\times10^{-2}\right)^2}$

$= 4,41\,N$

$F_g = m_p a$

$4,41 = m_p\left(9,8\right)$

$m_p = 0,45\,kg$

$m_Q = 1,13\,kg \rightarrow$ if no rounding was performed tha answer would be $1,12\,kg$

(6)

[10]

Question 9

9.1 Every particle with mass in the universe attracts every other particle with a force which is directly proportional to the product of their masses and inversely proportional to the square of the distance between their centres. (2)

9.2 Although the spheres exert an electrostatic force of repulsion on each other due to their charge, according to Newton's Law of Universal Gravitation, they also exert a force of attraction on each other due to their mass. If these forces are equal, they will experience a zero resultant force. (4)

TOC
1 Data Sheet
2 Definitions
3
3 solutions
4
4 solutions
5
5 solutions
6
6 solutions
7
7 solutions
8
8 solutions
9
9 solutions
10
10 solutions

TOC 1 Data Sheet 2 Definitions 3 3 solutions 4 4 solutions 5 5 solutions 6 6 solutions 7 7 solutions 8 **8 solutions** 9 9 solutions 10 10 solutions

9.3 $F = \dfrac{k\,Q_1Q_2}{r^2}$

$$= \frac{9\times10^9\left(1{,}1\times10^{-12}\right)\left(1{,}8\times10^{-12}\right)}{\left(150\times10^{-3}\right)^2}$$

$$= 7{,}92\times10^{-13}\ \text{N}$$

$$F = \frac{G\,m_1m_2}{r^2}$$

$$7{,}92\times10^{-13} = \frac{6{,}7\times10^{-11}m^2}{\left(150\times10^{-3}\right)^2}$$

$m = 0{,}02\ \text{kg}$ (6)

[12]

Question 10

10.1

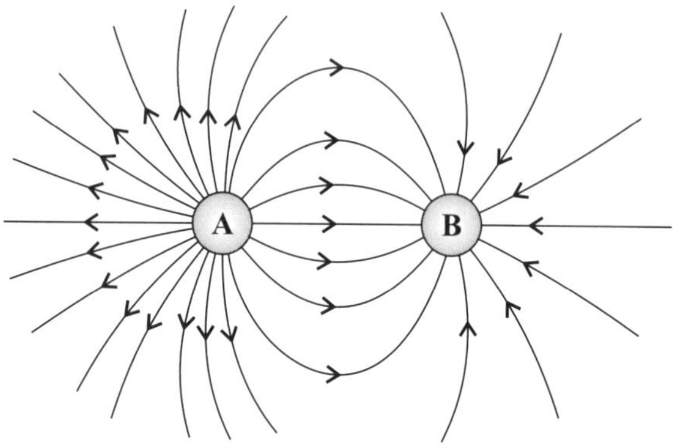

(3)

10.2 The force per unit positive charge. (2)

10.3 $E_{Q_A} = \dfrac{kQ_A}{r^2}$

$$= \frac{9\times10^9\left(12\times10^{-9}\right)}{\left(80\times10^{-2}\right)^2}$$

$= 168{,}75\ \text{N.C}^{-1}$ right

$E_{Q_B} = \dfrac{kQ_B}{r^2}$

$$= \frac{9\times10^9\left(2{,}2\times10^{-9}\right)}{\left(20\times10^{-2}\right)^2}$$

$= 495\ \text{N.C}^{-1}$ left

$E_{net} = 495 - 168{,}75$

$= 326{,}25\ \text{N.C}^{-1}$ left (5)

10.4 $F = Eq$

$= 326{,}25\left(1{,}6\times10^{-19}\right)$

$= 5{,}22\times10^{-17}$ N right (3)

10.5 Decrease. The strength of the electric field is inversely proportional to the square of the distance from a charge. As the electron moves away to the right the electric field will decrease. Force is directly proportional to the electric field and acceleration is directly proportional to acceleration. As the electric field decreases so does the force and the acceleration. (4)

[17]

Question 11

11.1 Two point charges in free space or air exert forces on each other. The force is directly proportional to the product of the charges and inversely proportional to the square of the distance between the charges. (6)

11.2 $\Delta x = v_i \Delta t + \frac{1}{2} a \Delta t^2$

$30 \times 10^{-3} = 0 + \frac{1}{2} a \left(4,13 \times 10^{-9}\right)^2$

$a = 3,52 \times 10^{15}\ \text{m.s}^{-2}$

$F_{net} = ma$

$= 9,1 \times 10^{-31}\left(3,52 \times 10^{15}\right)$

$= 3,2 \times 10^{-15}\ \text{N}$ (4)

11.3 If the sphere was not neutralised, as the electron approached it the force on the electron would increase because force is inversely proportional to the distance between the charged objects. If the force increases the acceleration would not be uniform. (2)

11.4 Positively charged. The electron accelerates towards the sphere. (2)

11.5 $F = \frac{k Q_1 Q_2}{r^2}$

$3,2 \times 10^{-15} = \frac{9 \times 10^9 \left(1,6 \times 10^{-19}\right) Q_2}{\left(30 \times 10^{-3}\right)^{-2}}$

$= 2 \times 10^{-9}$

$= 2\,\text{nC}$ (6)

[17]

Question 12

12.1 $F = \frac{k Q_1 Q_2}{r^2}$

$= \frac{9 \times 10^9 \left(8 \times 10^{-6}\right)\left(4 \times 10^{-6}\right)}{\left(6 \times 10^{-3}\right)^2}$

$= 8000\,\text{N}$ (4)

12.2

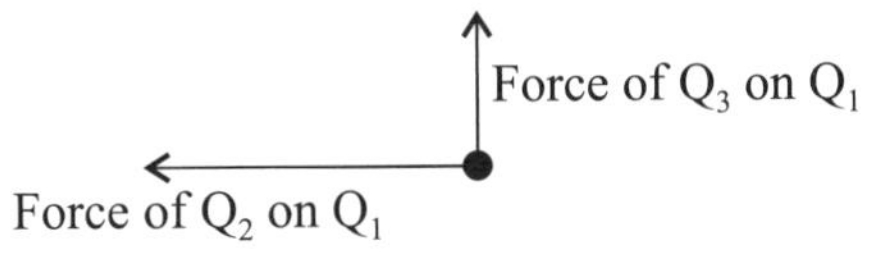

- Labels
- Correct direction of forces
- Horizontal component must be longer than vertical component (3)

12.3 $F_{Q_3 \text{ on } Q_1} = \frac{k Q_1 Q_3}{r^2}$

$= \frac{9 \times 10^9 \left(8 \times 10^{-6}\right)\left(2 \times 10^{-6}\right)}{\left(6 \times 10^{-3}\right)^{-2}}$

$= 4000\,\text{N North}$

$F_{net}^2 = 4000^2 + 8000^2$

$F_{net} = 8944,27$ N on a bearing of $296,57^\circ$

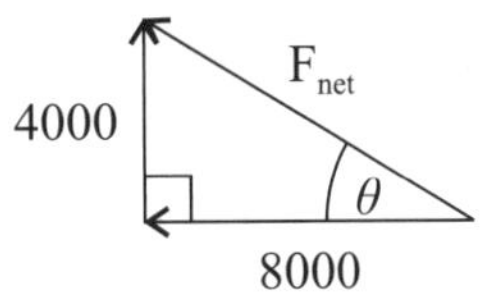

$\tan\theta = \frac{4000}{8000}$

$\theta = 26,57^\circ$ (8)

[15]

TOC 1 Data Sheet 2 Definitions 3 3 solutions 4 4 solutions 5 5 solutions 6 6 solutions 7 7 solutions 8 8 solutions 9 9 solutions 10 10 solutions

Question 13

13.1

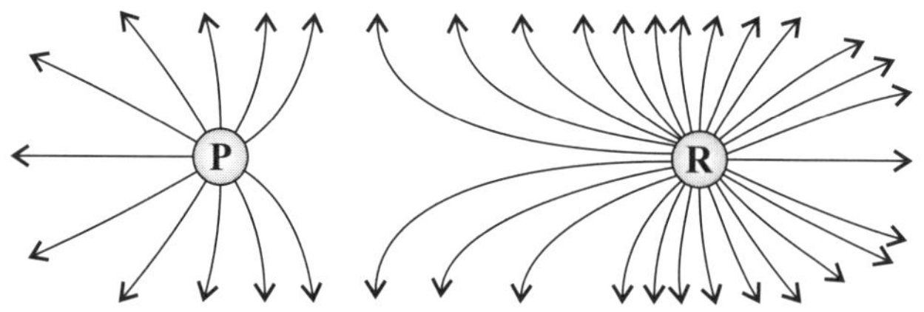

(4)

13.2 Two point charges in free space or air exert forces on each other. The force is directly proportional to the product of the charges and inversely proportional to the square of the distance between the charges. (2)

13.3

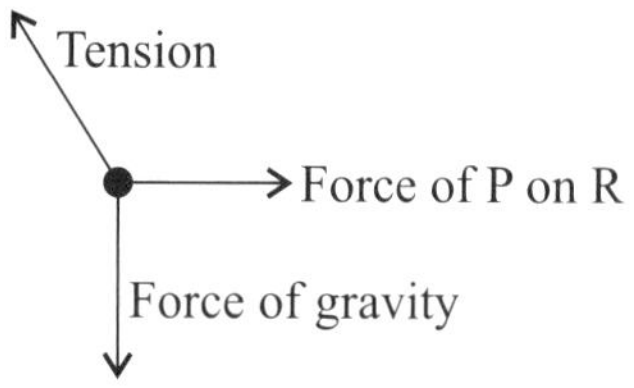

(3)

13.4 $\tan 10^\circ = \dfrac{F_{P\text{ on }R}}{0{,}0392}$

$F_{P\text{ on }R} = 6{,}91\times10^{-3}\text{ N}$

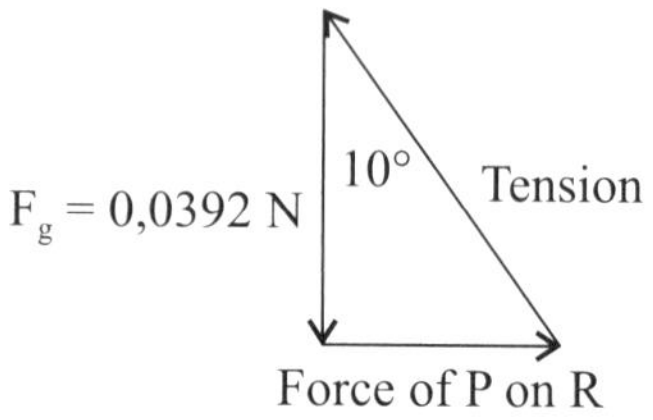

(4)

13.5 $F = \dfrac{kQ_1Q_2}{r^2}$

$6{,}91\times10^{-3} = \dfrac{9\times10^9\left(2\times10^{-6}\right)\left(18\times10^{-6}\right)}{r^2}$

$r = 6{,}85\text{ m}$

(4)

13.6 $\text{New charge} = \dfrac{Q_1+Q_2}{2} = \dfrac{2\times10^{-6}+18\times10^{-6}}{2}$

$= 1\times10^{-5}\text{ C}$

(2)

13.7 P to R (1)

13.8 $\text{Charge transferred} = 18\times10^{-6} - 1\times10^{-5}$

$= 8\times10^{-6}\text{ C}$

$N_{e-} = \dfrac{Q}{q_{e-}}$

$= \dfrac{8\times10^{-6}}{1{,}6\times10^{-19}}$

$= 5\times10^{13}$ electrons

(3)

13.9 $F = \dfrac{kQ_1Q_2}{r^2}$

$= \dfrac{9\times10^9\left(1\times10^{-5}\right)^2}{\left(8{,}66\right)^2}$

$= 0{,}012\text{ N}$

$\tan\left(\dfrac{\theta}{2}\right) = \dfrac{0{,}012}{0{,}0392}$

$\theta = 34{,}04^\circ$

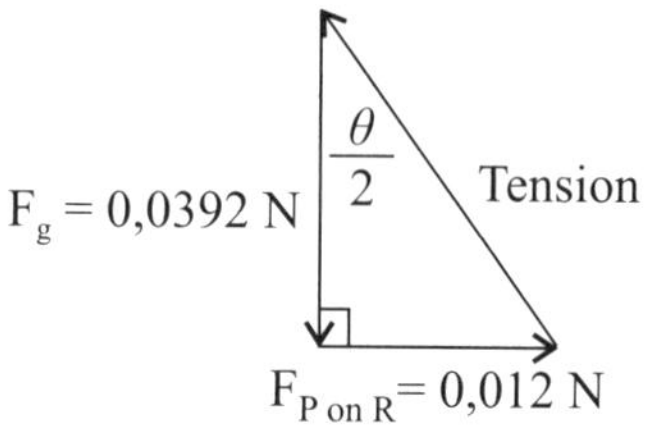

(7)

[30]

Question 14

$$F = \frac{kQ_1Q_2}{r^2} = \frac{9\times10^9\left(1,6\times10^{-19}\right)^2}{\left(53\times10^{-12}\right)^2} \rightarrow \text{the charge on a proton and electron is the same}$$

$$= 8,20\times10^{-8}\text{ N}$$ **[7]**

Question 15

15.1 The force per unit positive charge. (2)

15.2 $E_A = \frac{kQ_A}{r^2} = \frac{9\times10^9\left(3\times10^{-6}\right)}{(0,4)^2} = 168\,750\text{ N.C}^{-1}\text{ right}$

$E_B = \frac{kQ_B}{r^2} = \frac{9\times10^9\left(4\times10^{-6}\right)}{(0,3)^2} = 400\,000\text{ N.C}^{-1}\text{ right}$

$E_{net} = 168\,750 + 400\,000$

$= 568\,750\text{ N.C}^{-1}$ (5)

15.3 $F = Eq = 568\,750\left(3\times10^{-9}\right)$

$= 1,71\times10^{-3}\text{ N right}$ (3)

[10]

Question 16

16.1 X: The field from both charges are in the same direction. Therefore, would be added together and cannot sum to zero.

Z: Electric field is inversely proportional to square of the distance from the charged object. At Z charge R is closer than Q and has a greater magnitude of charge. Although the fields from the charges are in opposite direction the field from R will always be greater than the field from Q and they cannot sum to zero.

16.2 $E_Q = \frac{kQ_Q}{r^2} = \frac{9\times10^9\left(3\times10^{-6}\right)}{(0,3)^2} = 300\,000\text{ N.C}^{-1}\text{ left}$

$E_R = \frac{kQ_R}{r^2} = \frac{9\times10^9\left(4\times10^{-6}\right)}{(1,3)^2} = 21301,78\text{ N.C}^{-1}\text{ right}$

$E_{net} = 300\,000 - 21301,78$

$= 278\,698,22\text{ N.C}^{-1}\text{ left}$ (6)

16.3 $F = Eq = 278\,698,22\left(2\times1,6\times10^{-19}\right)$

$= 8,92\times10^{-14}\text{ N left}$

16.4 $E_Q = E_R$

$$\frac{9\times10^9\left(3\times10^{-6}\right)}{(x)^2} = \frac{9\times10^9\left(4\times10^{-6}\right)}{(1+x)^2}$$

$$1 + 2x + x^2 = \frac{4x^2}{3}$$

$x = 6,46\text{ m}$ or $x \neq -0,46\text{ m} \rightarrow$ not applicable

The electron must be placed 6,46 m to the left of Q.

[20]

TOC
1 Data Sheet
2 Definitions
3
3 solutions
4
4 solutions
5
5 solutions
6
6 solutions
7
7 solutions
8
8 solutions
9
9 solutions
10
10 solutions

Question 17

17.1 Two point charges in free space or air exert forces on each other. The force is directly proportional to the product of the charges and inversely proportional to the square of the distance between the charges. (2)

17.2 $F_g = ma$

$= 0,5\times10^{-3}(9,8)$

$= 4,9\times10^{-3}$ N

$$F = \frac{kQ_1Q_2}{r^2}$$

$$4,9\times10^{-3} = \frac{9\times10^9\left(8\times10^{-6}\right)\left(2\times10^{-6}\right)}{x^2}$$

$x = 5,42$ m (5)

17.3 Every particle with mass in the universe attracts every other particle with a force which is directly proportional to the product of their masses and inversely proportional to the square of the distance between their centres. (2)

17.4 $$F = \frac{Gm_1m_2}{r^2}$$

$$= \frac{6,7\times10^{-11}\left(60\times10^{-3}\right)\left(0,5\times10^{-3}\right)}{(5,42)^2}$$

$= 6,84\times10^{-17}$ N

The force of atraction due to the masses of objects is negligible compared to the force of attraction due to their charge. (5)

[17]

Question 18

18.1 The force per unit positive charge. (2)

18.2 $$E_{1\mu} = \frac{kQ_A}{r^2} = \frac{9\times10^9\left(1\times10^{-6}\right)}{\left(40\times10^{-2}\right)^2}$$

$= 56\,250$ N.C^{-1} left

$$E_{-3\mu} = \frac{kQ_B}{r^2} = \frac{9\times10^9\left(3\times10^{-6}\right)}{\left(30\times10^{-2}\right)^2}$$

$= 300\,000$ N.C^{-1} down

$E_{net}{}^2 = 56\,250^2 + 300\,000^2$

$E_{net} = 305\,227,89$ N.C^{-1} (5)

18.3 $$\tan\theta = \frac{56\,250}{300\,000}$$

$\theta = 10,62^\circ$ West of South

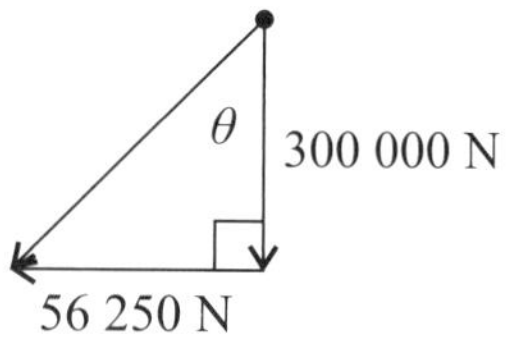

(4)

18.4 $F = Eq$

$= 305\,227,89\left(1,6\times10^{-19}\right)$

$= 4,88\times10^{-14}$ N on a bearing of $10,62^\circ \rightarrow 10,62^\circ$ East of North

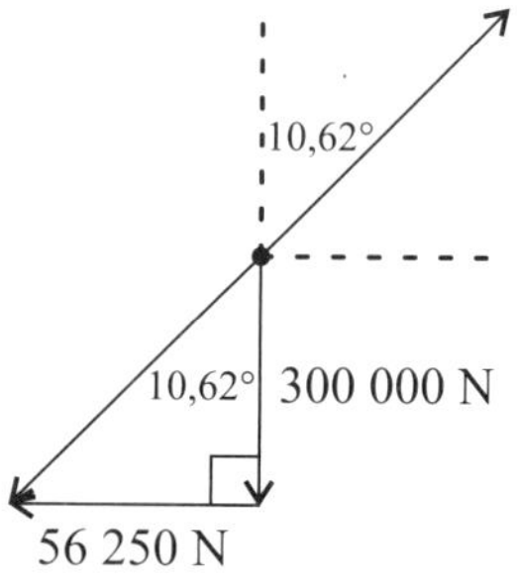

(6)

[17]

Question 19

19.1 Two point charges in free space or air exert forces on each other. The force is directly proportional to the product of the charges and inversely proportional to the square of the distance between the charges. (2)

19.2 $F = ma$

$$= (40\times10^{-3})(2{,}87)$$

$$= 0{,}11\,\text{N}$$

$$F = \frac{k\,Q_A Q_B}{r^2}$$

$$0{,}11 = \frac{(9\times10^{9})(85\times10^{-9})Q_B}{(40\times10^{-3})^2}$$

$$Q_B = 2{,}3\times10^{-7}\,\text{C}$$ (6)

19.3 Negative. The gradient of the graph is increasing. Therefore, the acceleration is increasing. Acceleration is directly proportional to force. Therefore, the force on the particle is increasing. As Force is inversely proportional to the square of the distance, the sphere must be accelerating towards A. Therefore the charge is negative as unlike charges attract. (4)

[12]

Question 20

20.1 $E_A = \frac{kQ_A}{r^2}$

$$= \frac{9\times10^{9} Q_A}{(100\times10^{-3})^2}$$

$$= 9\times10^{11} Q_A\ \text{N.C}^{-1}$$

$E_B = \frac{kQ_B}{r^2}$

$$= \frac{9\times10^{9}(1\times10^{-9})}{(100\times10^{-3})^2}$$

$$= 900\,\text{N.C}^{-1}$$

$$E_{net} = E_A + E_B$$

$$2700 = 9\times10^{11} Q_A + 900$$

$$Q_A = 2\times10^{-9}\,\text{C}$$

$$\therefore Q_A = -2\,\text{nC}$$ (8)

20.2 $F = Eq$

$$= 2700(2\times10^{-9})$$

$$= 5{,}4\times10^{-6}\ \text{right}$$ (3)

[11]

TOC
1 Data Sheet
2 Definitions
3
3 solutions
4
4 solutions
5
5 solutions
6
6 solutions
7
7 solutions
8
8 solutions
9
9 solutions
10
10 solutions

Question 21

21.1 Two point charges in free space or air exert forces on each other. The force is directly proportional to the product of the charges and inversely proportional to the square of the distance between the charges. (2)

21.2 $F = \frac{kQ_1Q_2}{r^2}$

$= \frac{9\times10^9\left(150\times10^{-9}\right)^2}{\left(10\times10^{-2}\right)^2}$

$= 0,02\ \text{N}$ (5)

21.3 The force per unit positive charge. (2)

21.4

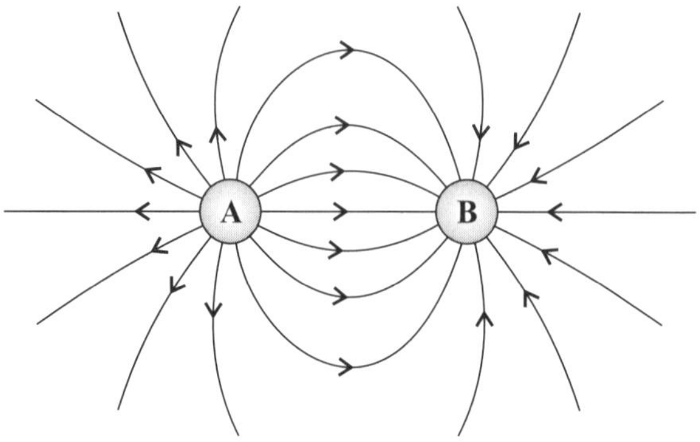

- Same number of field lines on each charge
- Field lines symmetrical
- Field must be from A to B

(3)

21.5.1 $E_A = \frac{kQ_A}{r^2}$

$= \frac{9\times10^9\left(150\times10^{-9}\right)}{\left(5\times10^{-2}\right)^2}$

$= 540\,000\ \text{N.C}^{-1}$ right

$E_B = 540\,000\ \text{N.C}^{-1}$ right $\rightarrow$ 5 cm is halfway and the charges are the same

$E_{net} = E_A + E_B$

$= 540\,000 + 540\,000$

$= 1,08\times10^6$

$\therefore$ missing value in the table is 1,08 (7)

21.5.2 1,78 → by symmetry (1)

21.5.3 13,67 → by symmetry (1)

21.6 Graph of the magnitude of the resultant electric field against distance from positive charge

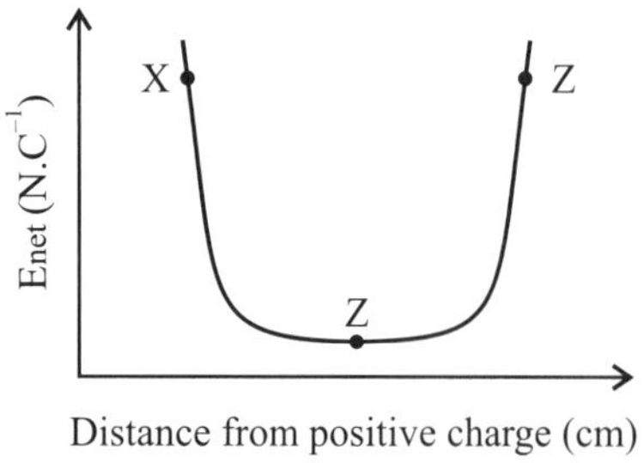

(3)

21.7 The closer you move towards either charge A or B, the stronger the electric field. As you move away from the positive charge the electric field will decrease until you reach halfway between the charges. At this point the field is weakest because it is furthest away from both charges. Once you cross halfway (5cm) you start getting closer to B where the charge will increase again. As the charges are the same the magnitude of the electric field will be exactly the same at any position on either side of 5cm between the charges. (4)

[30]

Question 22 (2014 IEB Final Examination)

22.1

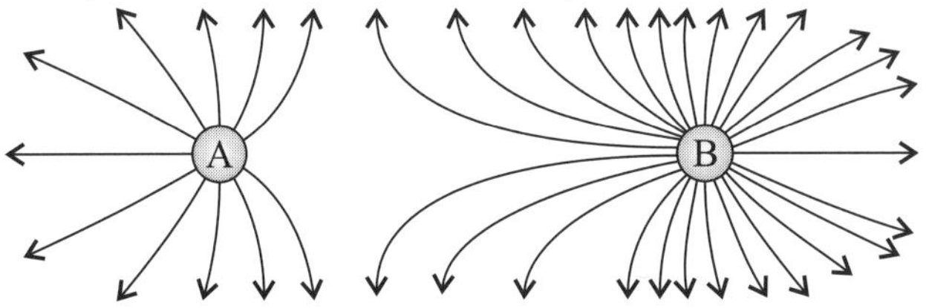

(3)

22.2 Two point charges in free space or air exert forces on each other. The force is directly proportional to the product of the charges and inversely proportional to the square of the distance between the charges. (2)

22.3
$$F = \frac{kQ_1Q_2}{r^2} = \frac{9\times10^9\left(1\times10^{-9}\right)\left(9\times10^{-9}\right)}{\left(8\times10^{-3}\right)^2}$$
$$= 1{,}27\times10^{-3}\ \text{N right}$$
(5)

22.4
$$N_{e-} = \frac{Q}{q_{e-}}$$
$$= \frac{1\times10^{-9}}{1{,}6\times10^{-19}}$$
$$= 6{,}25\times10^9\ \text{electrons}$$
(2)

22.5.1 A single vector which has the same effect as the original vectors acting together. (2)

22.5.2 The force per unit positive charge. (2)

22.5.2
$$E_A = E_B$$
$$\frac{kQ_A}{r_A^2} = \frac{kQ_B}{r_B^2} \rightarrow \text{didvide both sides by k}$$
$$\frac{1\times10^{-9}}{x^2} = \frac{9\times10^{-9}}{\left(8\times10^{-3} - x\right)^2}$$
$$\left(8\times10^{-3} - x\right)^2 = 9x^2$$
$$8\times10^{-3} - x = 3x$$
$$x = 2\times10^{-3}\ \text{m to the right of A}$$
(4)

[20]

Question 23 (2015 IEB Supplementary Examination)

23.1

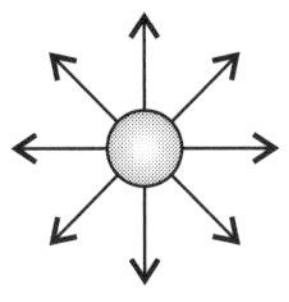

(3)

23.2
$$E_A = \frac{kQ_A}{r^2}$$
$$= \frac{9\times10^9\left(6{,}4\times10^{-8}\right)}{\left(40\times10^{-3}\right)^2}$$
$$= 360000\ \text{N.C}^{-1}$$
(4)

23.3 a)
$$F = \frac{kQ_1Q_2}{r^2} = \frac{9\times10^9\left(6{,}4\times10^{-8}\right)\left(4{,}8\times10^{-8}\right)}{\left(60\times10^{-3}\right)^2}$$
$$= 7{,}68\times10^{-3}\ \text{N}$$
(4)

b) Balance reading $= 9,54\times10^{-3} - 7,68\times10^{-3}$

$= 1,86\times10^{-3}$ N (2)

[13]

Question 24 (2015 IEB Final Examination)

24.1 $F = Eq$

$= \left(4,8\times10^{5}\right)\left(25\times10^{-9}\right)$

$= 0,012$ N (3)

24.2

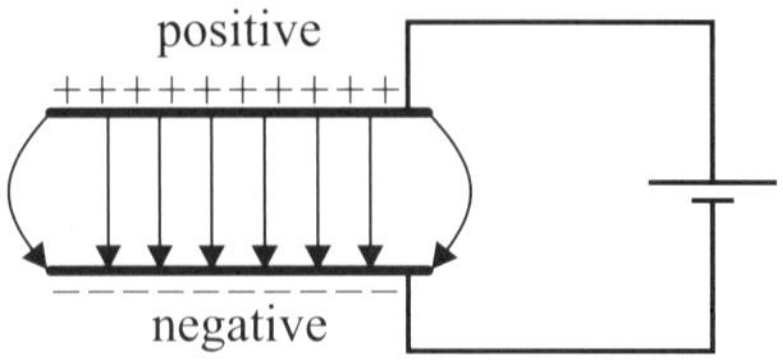

(3)

[6]

Question 25 (2016 IEB Supplementary Examination)

25.1 The force per unit positive charge. (2)

25.2.1 At P the field lines are closer to each other than at Q. Therefore, the strength of the electric field at P is greater than at Q. (2)

25.2.2

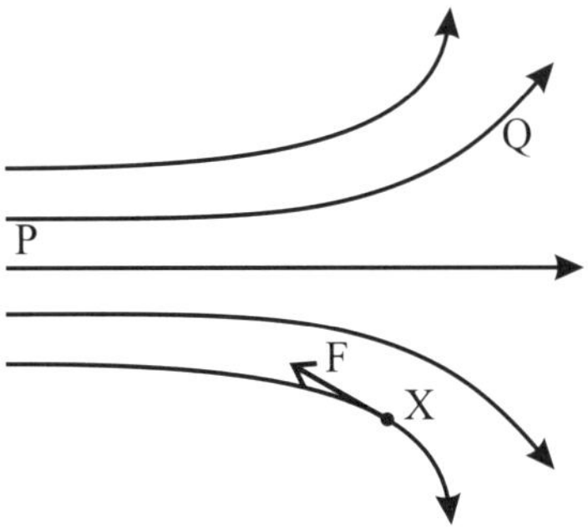

- Arrow must be in the opposite direction to the field
- Force must be a tangent to the electric field line

(2)

Question 26 (2016 IEB Final Examination)

26.1 The force per unit positive charge. (2)

26.2

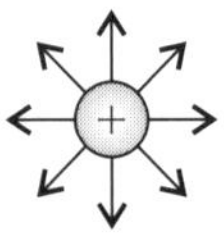

(2)

26.3 Electric field is directly proportional to the charge. (2)

26.4 Shown on the next page.

26.5 Gradient $= \dfrac{\Delta y}{\Delta x}$

$= \dfrac{36\times10^{3} - 47\times10^{3}}{10\times10^{-9} - 13\times10^{-9}}$

$= 3,67\times10^{12}\ \text{N.C}^{-1} \rightarrow$ any answer between $3,30\times10^{12}$ and $4,04\times10^{12}$ is acceptable (4)

26.6 $E = \dfrac{k}{r^2}Q + 0 \rightarrow y = mx + c$

gradient $= \dfrac{k}{r^2}$

$r = \sqrt{\dfrac{9\times10^{9}}{3,67\times10^{12}}}$

$= 0,050\,\text{m}$ (3)

26.4 (4)

Graph showing Electric Field vs Charge

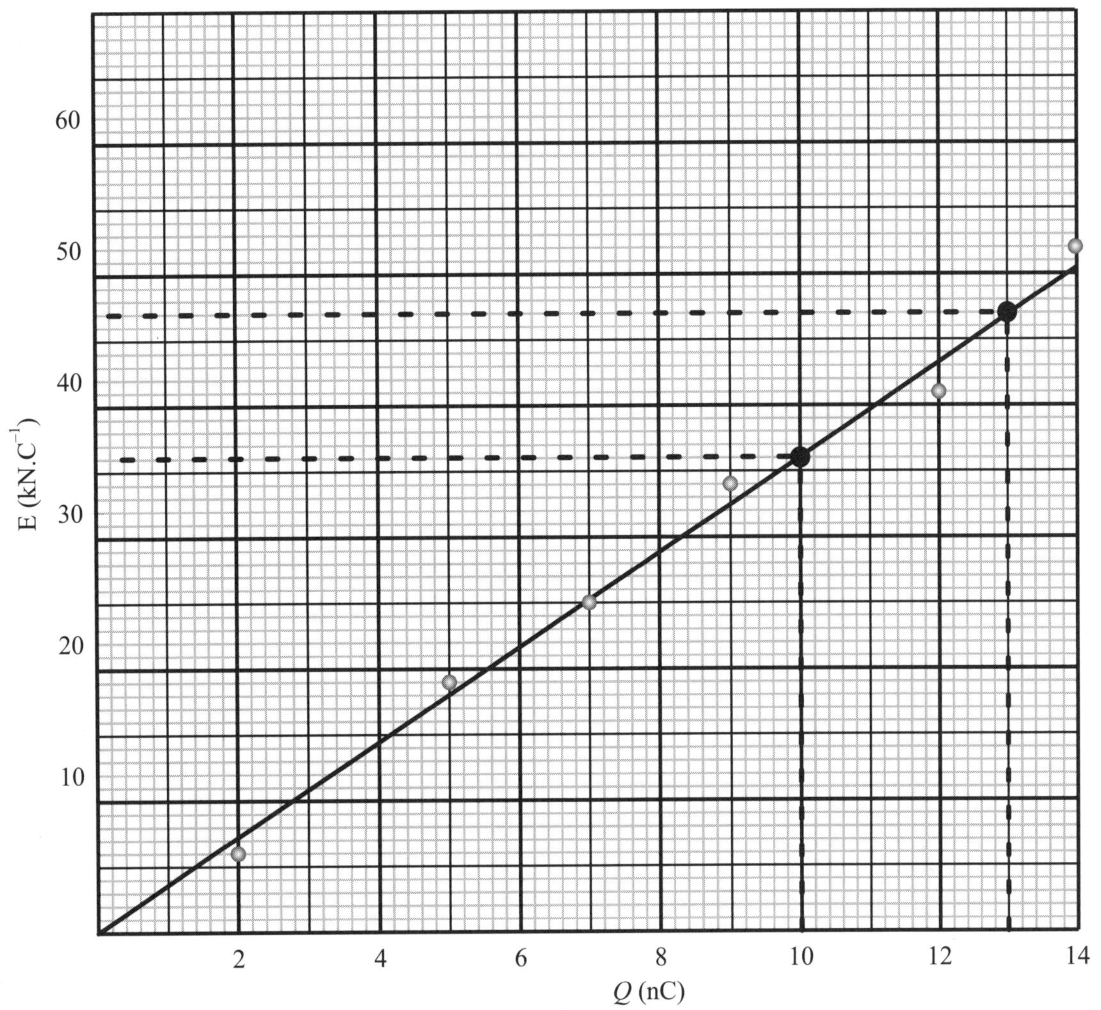

Question 27 (2017 IEB Supplementary Examination)

27.1 The force per unit positive charge. (2)

27.2

$$E = \frac{kQ}{r^2}$$

$$312\,500 = \frac{9\times10^9\left(5\times10^{-9}\right)}{r^2}$$

$$r = 0{,}012 \text{ m}$$

(3)

[5]

Question 28 (2017 IEB Final Examination)

28.1

$$\Delta x = v_i\Delta t + \frac{1}{2}a\Delta t^2$$

$$0{,}6 = 0 + \frac{1}{2}a\left(3{,}3\right)^2$$

$$a = 0{,}11 \text{m.s}^{-1}$$

(3)

TOC | 1 Data Sheet | 2 Definitions | 3 | 3 solutions | 4 | 4 solutions | 5 | 5 solutions | 6 | 6 solutions | 7 | 7 solutions | 8 | 8 solutions | 9 | 9 solutions | 10 | 10 solutions

28.2 $F = ma$

$= 0,02(0,11)$

$= 2,2 \times 10^{-3}$ N

$F = \dfrac{kQ_1Q_2}{r^2}$

$2,2 \times 10^{-3} = \dfrac{9 \times 10^9 (1 \times 10^{-9}) Q}{(0,6)^2}$

$Q = 8,8 \times 10^{-5}$ C (4)

28.3 Acceleration is not constant. Electric field and hence the force depend on the distance from charge Q. (3)

[10]

Question 29 (2018 IEB Supplementary Examination)

29.1

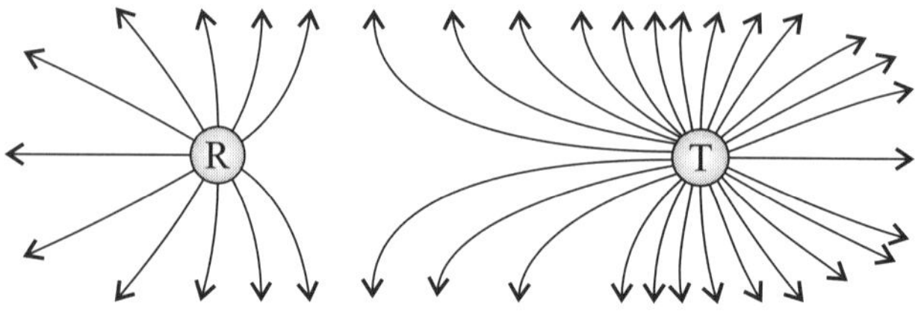

(3)

29.2 $Q_{new} = \dfrac{Q_1 + Q_2}{2}$

$= \dfrac{6 \times 10^{-9} + 10 \times 10^{-9}}{2}$

$= 8 \times 10^{-9}$ C (2)

29.3 $Q_{transferred} = 8 \times 10^{-9} - 6 \times 10^{-9}$

$= 2 \times 10^{-9}$ C

$N_{e-} = \dfrac{Q_{transferred}}{q_{e-}}$

$= \dfrac{2 \times 10^{-9}}{1,6 \times 10^{-19}}$

$= 1,25 \times 10^{10}$ electrons (2)

29.4 From R to T. (2)

29.5 Two point charges in free space or air exert forces on each other. The force is directly proportional to the product of the charges and inversely proportional to the square of the distance between the charges. (2)

29.6 $F_R = \dfrac{kQ_RQ_S}{r^2}$

$= \dfrac{9 \times 10^9 (6 \times 10^{-9})(5 \times 10^{-9})}{(0,7)^2}$

$= 5,51 \times 10^{-7}$ N left

$F_T = \dfrac{kQ_TQ_S}{r^2}$

$= \dfrac{9 \times 10^9 (10 \times 10^{-9})(5 \times 10^{-9})}{(1,8 - 0,7)^2}$

$= 3,72 \times 10^{-7}$ N right

$F_{net} = 5,51 \times 10^{-7} - 3,72 \times 10^{-7}$

$= 1,79 \times 10^{-7}$ N (6)

[17]

Question 30 (2019 IEB Supplementary Examination)

30.1

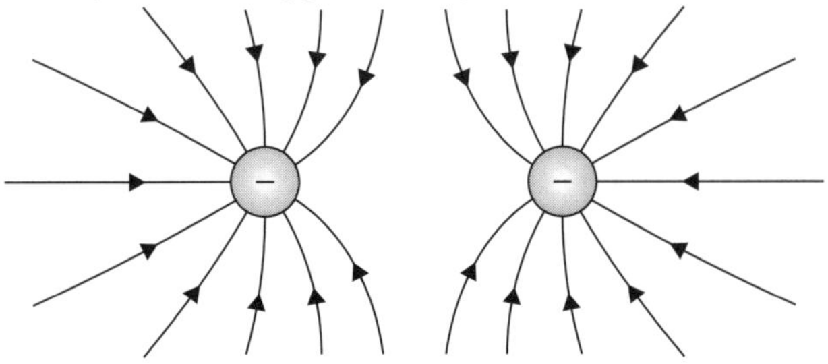

(2)

30.2 The gravitational force the Earth exerts on any object on or near its surface. (2)

30.3 $W = mg$

$= (2\times10^{-3})(9,8)$

$= 0,0196$ N downwards (2)

30.4 A physical quantity that has both magnitude and direction. (2)

30.5

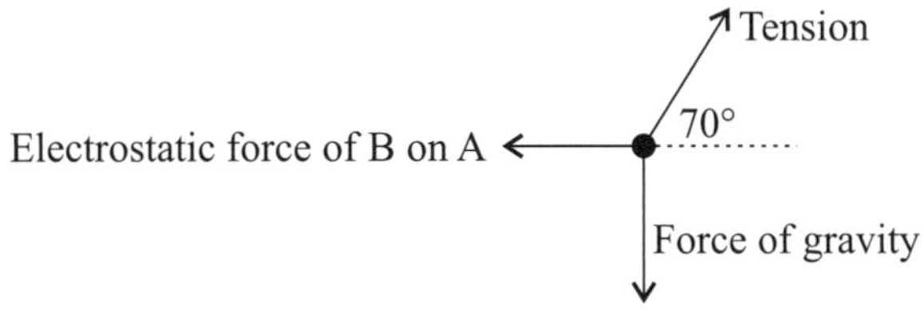

(3)

30.6 Two point charges in free space or air exert forces on each other. The force is directly proportional to the product of the charges and inversely proportional to the square of the distance between the charges. (2)

30.7 Calculate the magnitude of the negative charge on each polystyrene ball. (6)

Method 1:

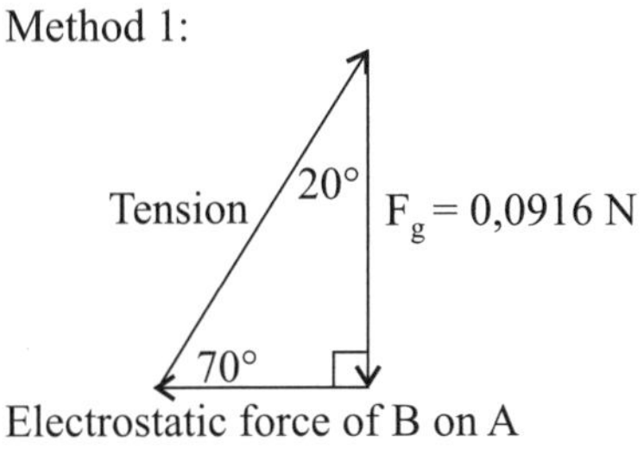

$$\tan 20^\circ = \frac{F_{B\,on\,A}}{F_g}$$

$$F_{B\,on\,A} = 0,0916\tan 20^\circ$$

$$= 7,13\times10^{-3}\ \text{N}$$

$$F = \frac{kQ_1Q_2}{r^2}$$

$$7,13\times10^{-3} = \frac{9\times10^9 Q^2}{(10\times10^{-2})^2}$$

$$Q = 8,9\times10^{-8}\ \text{C}$$

Method 2:

The vertical component of tension is equal to the force of gravity.

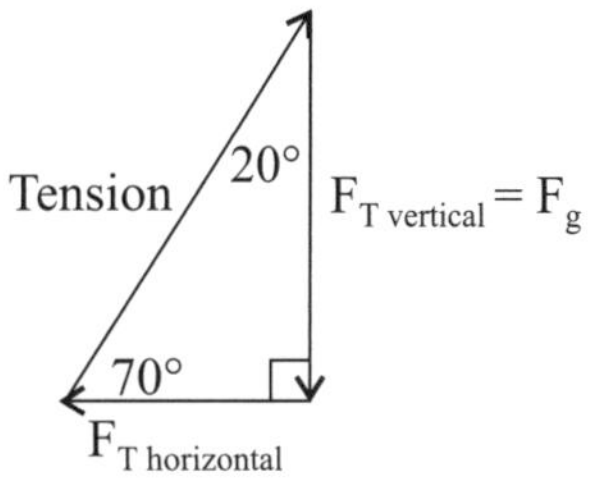

$$\tan 20^\circ = \frac{F_{T_{horizontal}}}{F_{T_{vertical}}}$$

$$F_{T_{horizontal}} = 0,0916\tan 20^\circ$$

$$= 7,13\times10^{-3}\ \text{N}$$

$$F = \frac{kQ_1Q_2}{r^2}$$

$$7,13\times10^{-3} = \frac{9\times10^9 Q^2}{(10\times10^{-2})^2}$$

$$Q = 8,9\times10^{-8}\ \text{C}$$

[19]

TOC | 1 Data Sheet | 2 Definitions | 3 | 3 solutions | 4 | 4 solutions | 5 | 5 solutions | 6 | 6 solutions | 7 | 7 solutions | 8 | 8 solutions | 9 | 9 solutions | 10 | 10 solutions

Question 31 (2019 IEB Final Examination)

31.1.1

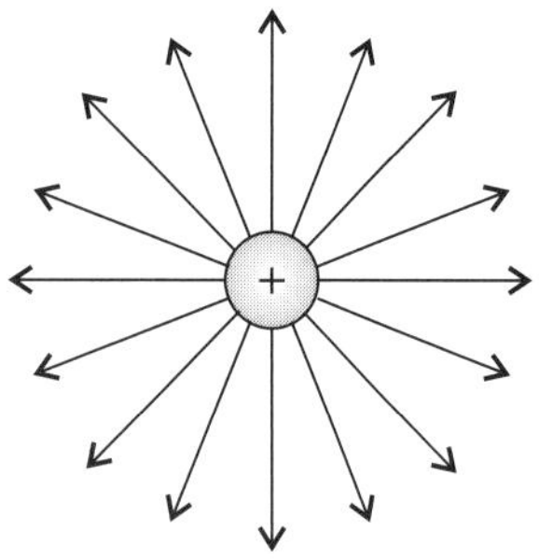

(2)

31.1.2 Two point charges in free space or air exert forces on each other. The force is directly proportional to the product of the charges and inversely proportional to the square of the distance between the charges. (2)

31.1.3 $F_g = ma$

$= 1,5 \times 10^{-3}(9,8)$

$= 14,7 \times 10^{-3}$ N

$F = \dfrac{kQ_1Q_2}{r^2}$

$14,7 \times 10^{-3} = \dfrac{9 \times 10^9 (30 \times 10^{-9})(100 \times 10^{-9})}{h^2}$

$h = 4,29 \times 10^{-2}$ m (6)

31.2.1 $E = \dfrac{kQ}{r^2}$

$= \dfrac{9 \times 10^9 (6 \times 10^{-6})}{(9 \times 10^{-2})^2}$

$= 6,67 \times 10^6$ N.C^{-1} (4)

31.2.2 $E_{-2\mu C} = \dfrac{kQ}{r^2}$

$= \dfrac{9 \times 10^9 (2 \times 10^{-6})}{(4 \times 10^{-2})^2}$

$= 11,25 \times 10^6$ N.C^{-1} right

$E_{net} = 11,25 \times 10^6 - 6,67 \times 10^6$

$= 4,58 \times 10^6$ N.C^{-1} right (5)

[19]

9. ELECTROMAGNETISM

INDUCTION OF A MAGNETIC FIELD

When current passes through a conductor, a magnetic field is induced around the wire.

THE RIGHT-HAND THUMB RULE

The **direction of the magnetic field** in a conductor can be determined by **the right-hand thumb rule**. For a straight, single wire, point the **thumb of your right hand in the direction of the conventional current** and your **fingers will curl in the direction of the induced magnetic field** as shown in diagram 1 below.

The same rule can be used for the magnetic field around a conductor where the current is flowing into or out of the page. Place your thumb in the direction of the current and your fingers will curl in the direction of the magnetic field (either clockwise or anticlockwise).

A **solid** (closed) **circle** denotes **current** flowing **out of the page** (like the point of an arrow) towards you while a circle with a **cross** (like the back of an arrow) denotes current flowing **into the page** away from you.

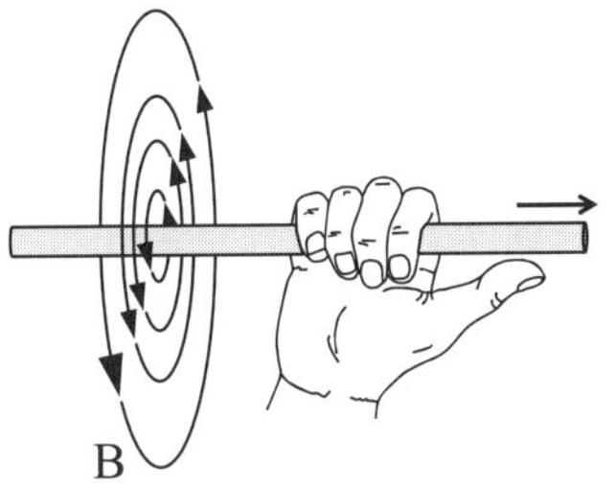

Diagram 1

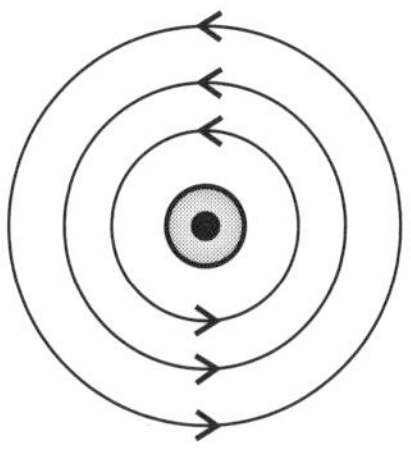

Diagram 2
Current flowing out of the page
(arrow coming towards you)

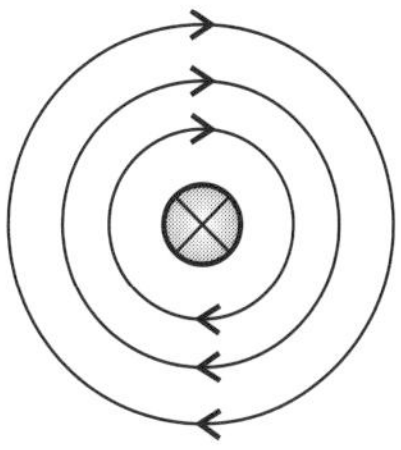

Diagram 3
Current flowing into the page
(arrow moving away from your)

THE RIGHT-HAND SOLENOID RULE

When **current flows** in a solenoid, a **magnetic field is induced** in the solenoid.
The **right-hand solenoid rule** can be used to determine the direction of the current in a solenoid or the direction of the magnetic field.

To use the right-hand solenoid rule, **curl your fingers** around the solenoid **in the direction of the current**. Your **thumb will point towards** the **North** pole. Diagram 1 and 2 below show how the right-hand solenoid rule is used. Diagram 3 shows a cross section of a solenoid and how the magnetic field runs through the solenoid.

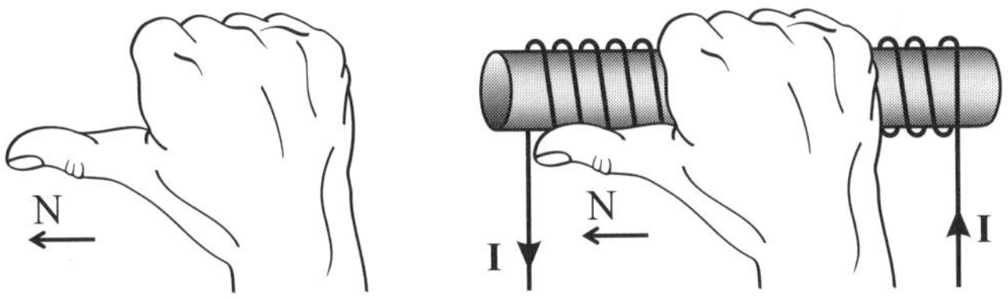

Diagram 1
Right hand solenoid Rule

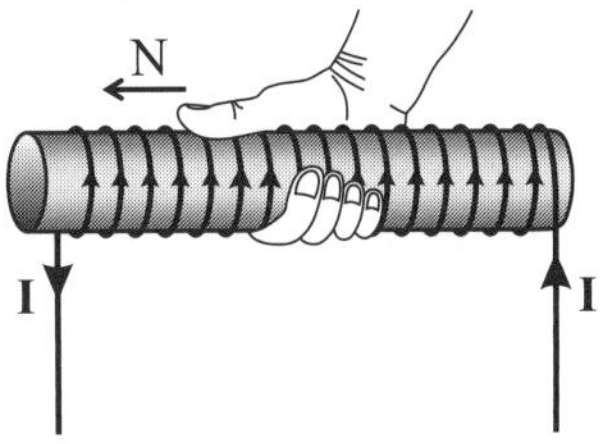

Diagram 2
Right hand solenoid Rule

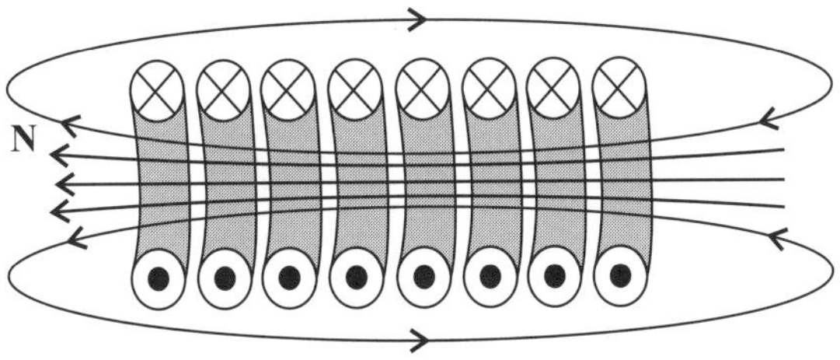

Diagram 3
Magnetic field through a solenoid

FORCE ON A CURRENT CARRYING CONDUCTOR (THE MOTOR EFFECT)

When the magnetic field around a current carrying conductor interacts with another magnetic field, the **conductor will experience a force**.

In diagram 1 below, **current is flowing out of the page**. There is a **cancellation of fields on top** of the conductor where the field from the magnet is in the opposite direction to the field from the conductor.
At the **bottom of the conductor**, there is a **build up of magnetic field** where the fields from the magnets and the conductor are in the same direction. This causes a **force upwards** on the conductor.

In diagram 2 below, **current is flowing out the page**. There is a **cancellation of fields on the bottom** of the conductor where the field from the magnet is in the opposite direction to the field from the conductor.
At the **top of the conductor**, there is a **build up of magnetic field** where the fields from the magnets and the conductor are in the same direction. This causes a **force downwards** on the conductor.

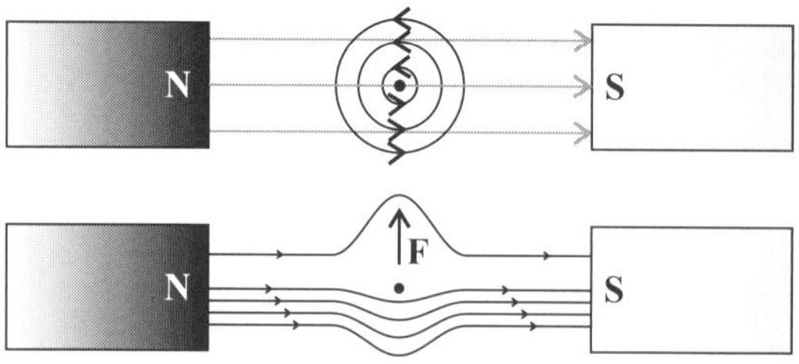

Diagram 1

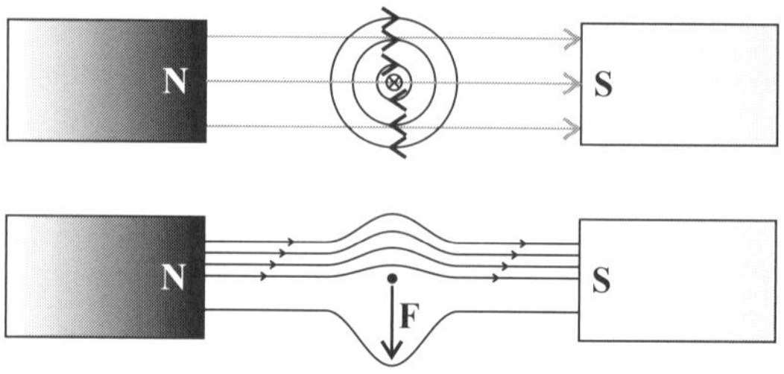

Diagram 2

Force on a current carrying conductor

$$\mathbf{F = I\ell B\sin\theta}$$

$F \rightarrow$ Force on current carrying conductor (N)

$I \rightarrow$ Magnitude of Current in the conductor (A)

$\ell \rightarrow$ Length of the conductor (m)

$B \rightarrow$ Magnetic flux density (Tesla)

$\theta \rightarrow$ the angle between the conductor and the magnetic field $(\mathrm{degrees})$

Calculations with the above formula are not required.
You only have to state and interpret relationships between the variables.

To increase the force on the conductor:

- **Increase the length of the conductor between the magnetic field (add loops)**
- **Increase the current in the conductor**
- **Increase the emf across the conductor**
- **Increase the strength of magnetic field**
- **The force will be a maximum when θ is 90°**

THE DIRECT CURRENT (DC) MOTOR

A motor converts electrical energy to mechanical energy.
When a **current flows through the armature** (coil windings) in **a magnet field**, it **will experience a turning force** (torque). However, the coil can only **rotate continually in one direction if the direction of the current is reversed for each half turn of the coil**. This keeps the direction of the turning force on the armature constant.

The **split ring commutator reverses the direction of the current in the armature every half turn.** Diagram 1 below shows a simple DC motor and diagram 2 shows a cross section of the motor and the force on each side of the coil.

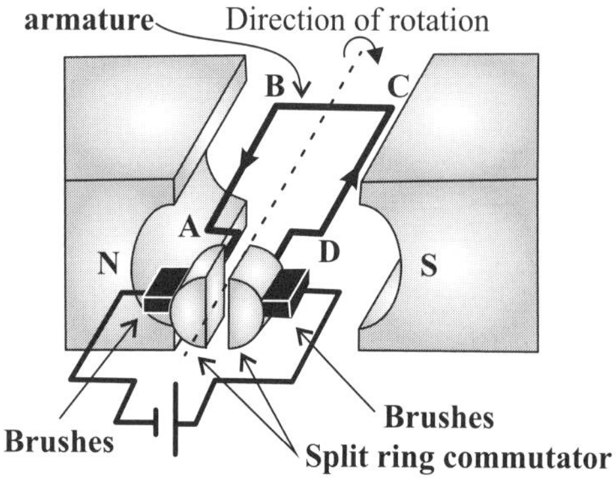

Diagram 1

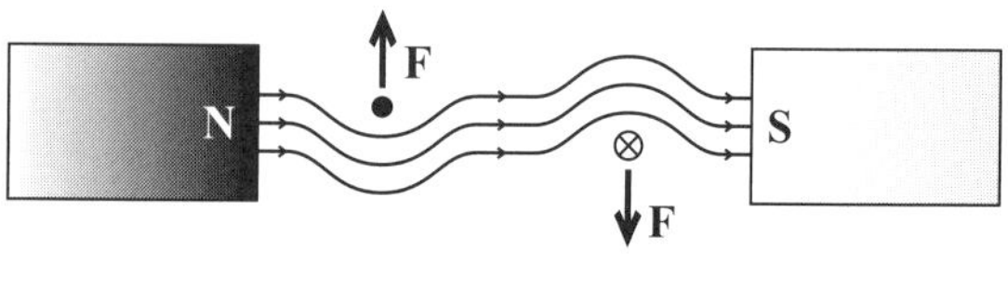

Cross section looking in from the split ring

Diagram 2

FLEMMING'S LEFT HAND MOTOR RULE

Flemming's left hand motor rule is used to determine direction of either the force, current or magnetic field when a current carrying conductor is in a magnetic field.

Using this rule, you hold your **left hand** with your **thumb, index finger and middle finger at right angles** to each other.

- The **thumb** will point in the **direction of the force**.
- The **index finger** will point in the direction of the **magnetic field** (the finger points from North to South)
- The **middle finger** will point in the direction of the **current**

This is shown in diagram 1 below.

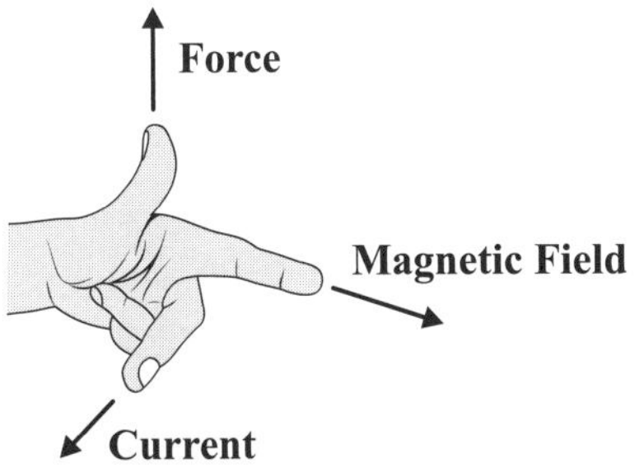

Diagram 1:
Flemming's Left Hand Motor Rule

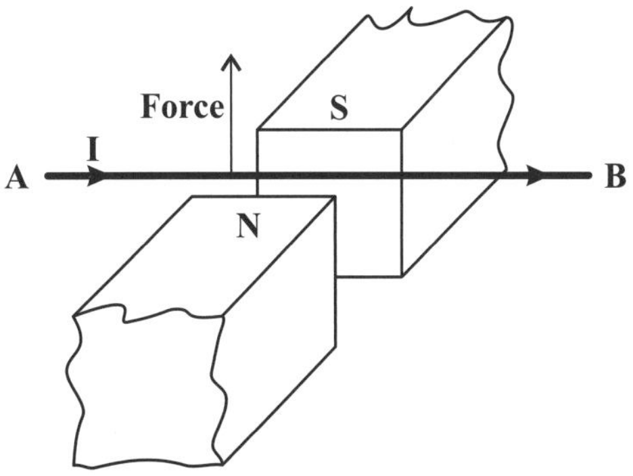

Diagram 2

Using Flemming's left hand motor rule in diagram 2 above, the **force on AB is upwards**.

Illustrative Example:

The diagram below shows a simple direct current (DC) motor.
Use Flemming's left hand motor rule to determine the direction of rotation of the motor.

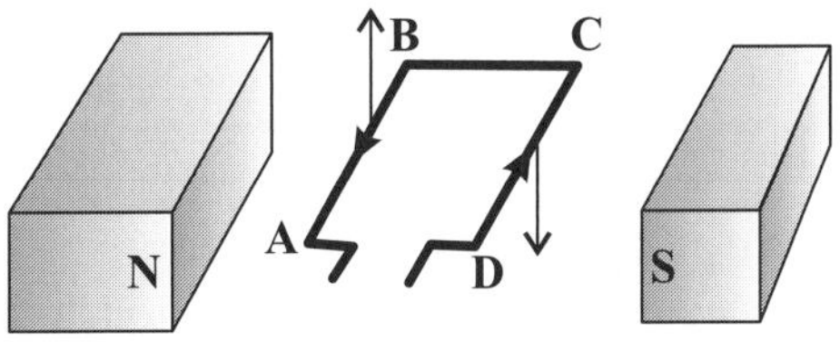

Using Flemming's left hand motor, the **force on segment AB is upwards** and **the force on segment CD is downwards**. Therefore, the motor will **rotate clockwise**.

> **The left-hand rule is used when a conductor in a magnetic field experiences a force due to the current in the conductor.**
> **The left hand is used for the motor and the right hand for all other rules.**

THE SPLIT RING COMMUTATOR

Examine the diagrams below **without a split ring commutator**:

- Diagram 1 starts with current flowing B to A in the loop (armature).
- Using Flemming's left hand motor rule, segment AB will experience a force upwards.
- Once the motor has rotated through 180°, current is still flowing B to A (diagram 2).
- This means that when segment BA is on the right-hand side, the force will still be up.
- The motor will then begin to rotate anticlockwise.
- The motor will not rotate continuously and will get stuck in the vertical position

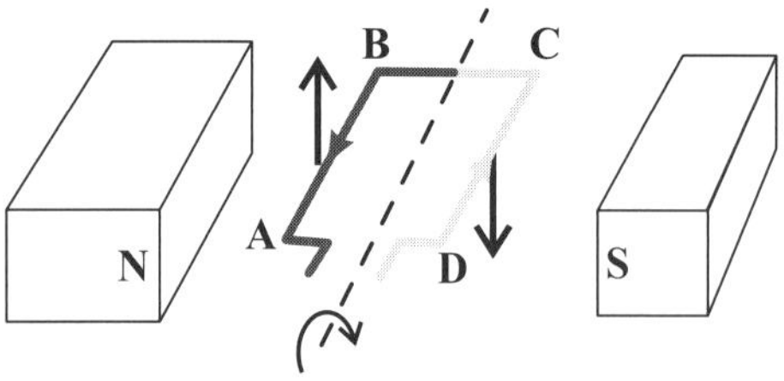

Clockwise rotation

Diagram 1:
Motor rotates clockwise

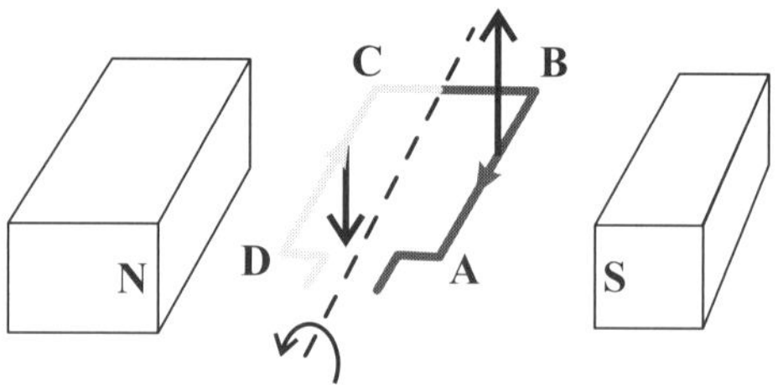

Anti-clockwise rotation

Diagram 2:
After rotating through the vertical position (90°) rotation will be anticlockwise as there is no split ring

The function of the **split ring** commutator is to **reverse the direction of the current** in the armature **every half rotation**. The diagram below shows how this is achieved.

(1) At the start side AB is connected to the negative terminal and the force on AB is upwards. DC is connected to the positive terminal and the force on DC is downwards

(2) The coil will rotate clockwise

(3) When the coil rotates 90° the split ring loses connection with the brushes and the battery. At this point current stops flowing. Momentum carries the coil over.

(4) AB is now connected to the positive terminal of the battery and DC is connected to the negative terminal of the battery. Current now flows ABCD instead of DCBA

(5) Once the coil has rotated through a half a turn the force on side AB is now downwards and the force on DC is upwards allowing the motor to rotate continuously in one direction.

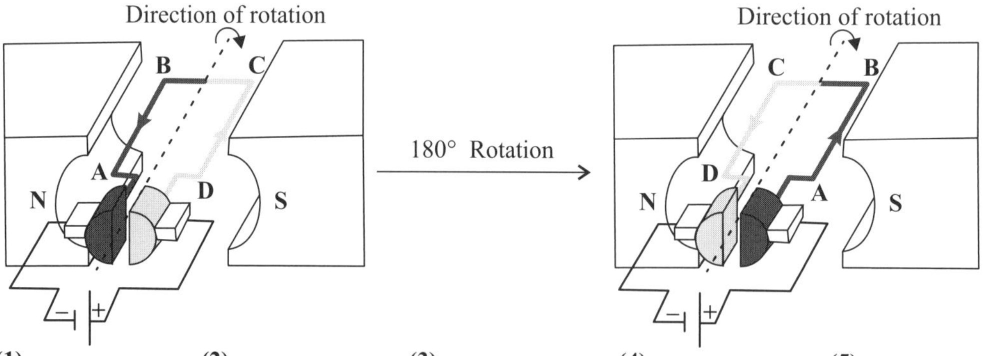

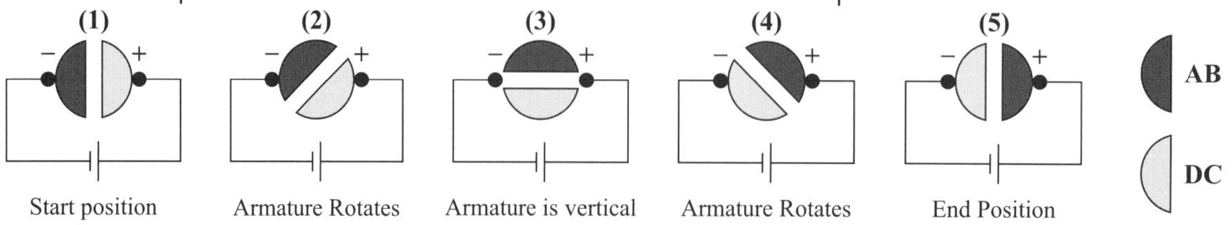

Start position	Armature Rotates	Armature is vertical	Armature Rotates	End Position
AB connected to negative brush	AB connected to negative brush	AB is not connected DC is not connected	AB connected to positive brush	AB connected to positive brush
DC Connected to positive brush	DC Connected to positive brush	Momentum carries the armature over	DC Connected to negative brush	DC Connected to negative brush
Current is flowing DCBA	Current is flowing DCBA	Current is not flowing in the armature	Current is flowing ABCD	Current is flowing ABCD

MAGNETIC FLUX DENSITY (B)

Magnetic flux density (B) is a representation of the magnitude and direction of the magnetic field.
The unit of magnetic flux density is the Tesla.

MAGNETIC FLUX (ϕ)

For a loop of area (A) in the presence of a uniform magnetic flux density (B), the formula for magnetic flux (ϕ) passing through the loop is shown below:

Magnetic flux

$$\phi = BA\cos\theta$$

$\phi \rightarrow$ Magnetic flux (Wb)

B $\rightarrow$ Magnetic flux density (Tesla)

A $\rightarrow$ Area (m^2)

θ $\rightarrow$ Angle between the magnetic flux density and the normal to the coil

Calculations with the above formula are not required.
You only have to state and interpret relationships between the variables.

INDUCTION OF AN ELECTRIC CURRENT

A change in magnetic flux causes a current to be induced in a conductor.

Faraday's law of electromagnetic inductions states that:
The emf induced is directly proportional to the rate of change of magnetic flux.

Lenz's Law states that:
The induced current flows in a direction so as to set up a magnetic field to oppose the change in magnetic flux.

Examine the diagrams below. When the magnet enters the coil there is a change in magnetic flux. According to Faraday's law, this induces an emf and hence a current in the coil.

To determine the direction of the current use the right-hand solenoid rule (page 358) and Lenz's law.

- Your **thumb points** towards the end of the solenoid where a **North pole will be induced**
- Your **fingers then curl in the direction of the current** around the solenoid

Diagram 1: Magnet pushed into the solenoid

- As the magnets North pole moves towards the solenoid there is a **change in magnetic flux**
- According to Lenz's law, a **current will be induced** to setup a magnetic field to **oppose the change in magnetic flux**
- A current is induced to create a North pole on the left hand-side of the solenoid. This repels the North pole of the magnet to stop it from entering the solenoid.
- The current flows up the face of the solenoid and the galvanometer will deflect. Once the magnet is inside the solenoid there is no change in flux and the galvanometer will read zero.

Diagram 1

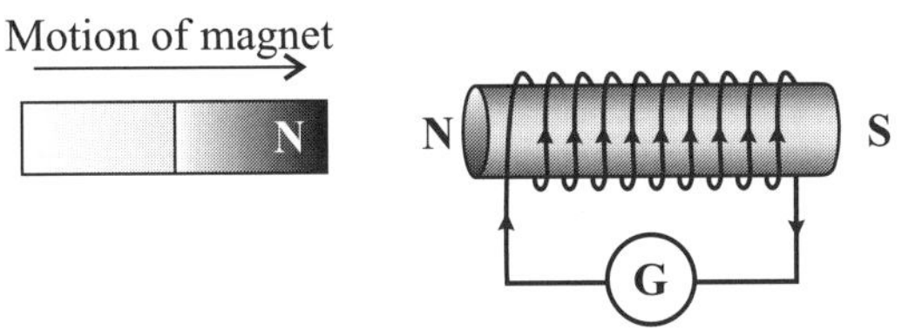

Diagram 2: Magnet pulled out of the solenoid

- As the magnets North pole moves away from the solenoid there is a **change in magnetic flux**
- According to Lenz's law, a **current will be induced** to setup a magnetic field **to oppose the change in magnetic flux**
- A current is induced to create a South pole on the left hand-side (this means a North pole is created on the right hand side). This attracts the North pole of the magnet to stop it from exiting the solenoid.
- The current flows down the face of the solenoid and the galvanometer will deflect in the opposite direction to when the magnet was pushed in.

Diagram 2

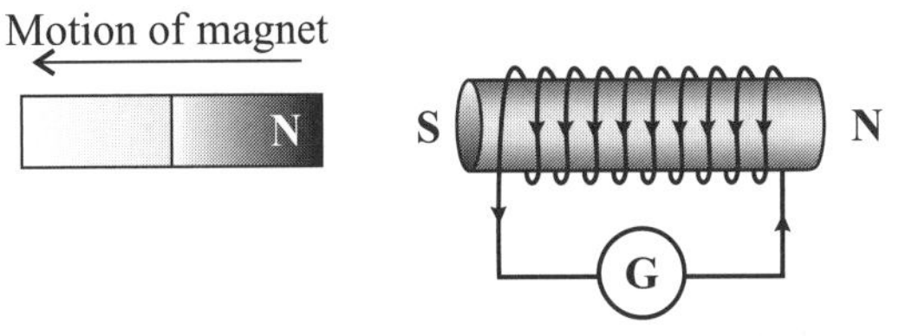

THE AC GENERATOR

A simple AC generator is shown in the diagram below.
Generators convert **mechanical energy to electrical energy**
When **a coil is rotated through a magnetic field**, there is a **change in flux**.
According to Faraday's Law, if there is a change in flux an emf will be induced in the coil which induces a current.

FLEMMING'S RIGHT HAND DYNAMO (GENERATOR) RULE

Flemming's right hand dynamo rule is used to determine direction of either the force, current or magnetic field when a coil is rotated in a magnetic field.

Using this rule, you hold your **right hand** with your **thumb, index finger and middle finger at right angles** to each other.

- The **thumb** will point in the **direction of the force**.
- The **index finger** will point in the direction of the **magnetic field** (the finger points from North to South)
- The **middle finger** will point in the direction of the **current**

This is shown in the diagram below.

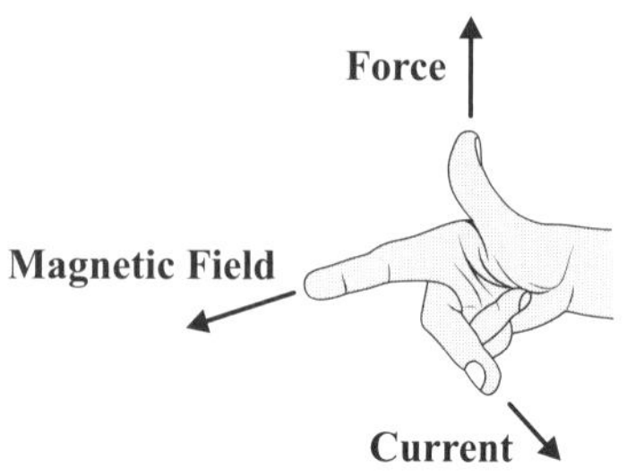

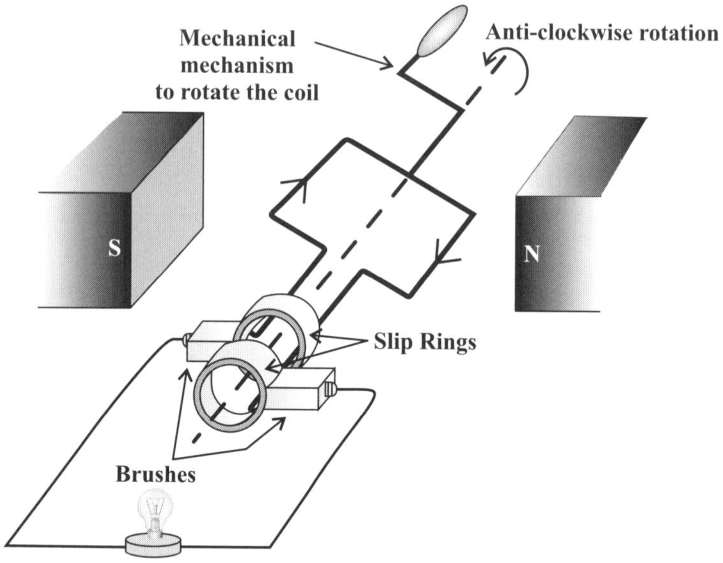

As slip rings are used in the AC generator, the current is reversed every half turn.

THE NORMAL TO A COIL (LOOP)

The **normal line** is the line **perpendicular to a surface**. Examine the diagrams below.

- **Diagram 1** shows a **coil horizontal in the field**. At this point the **angle** between the normal to the coil and magnetic flux density is **90°**. This means that flux is **zero** in this position (cos90° = 0).
- **Diagram 2** shows a **coil vertical in the field**. At this point the **angle** between the normal to the coil and magnetic flux density is **0°**. This means that flux is a maximum in this position (cos0° = 1)

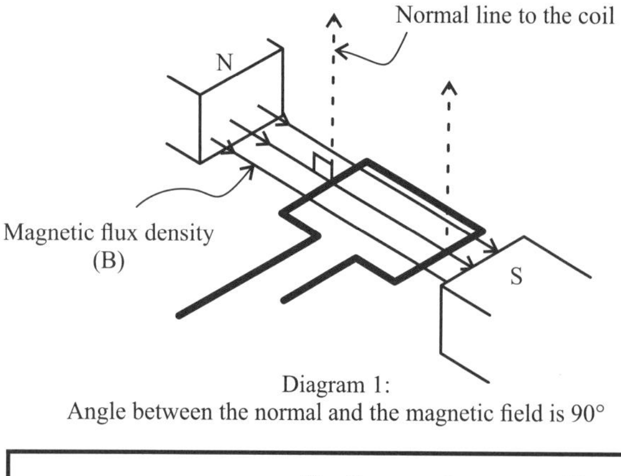

Diagram 1:
Angle between the normal and the magnetic field is 90°

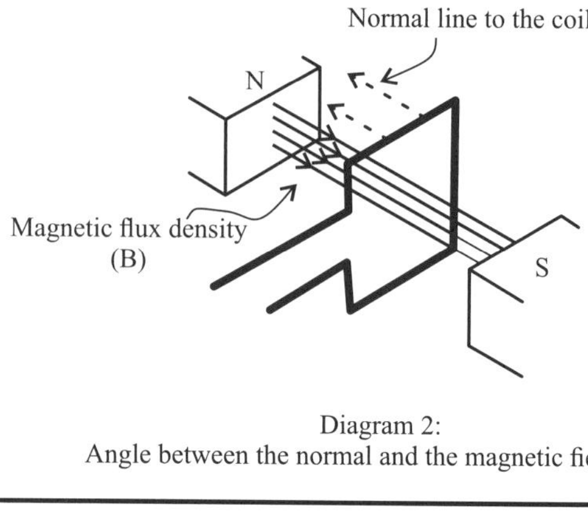

Diagram 2:
Angle between the normal and the magnetic field is 0°

On the previous page it was shown that $\phi = BA\cos\theta$.
When $\theta = 90°$, Cos90° = 0 and flux is zero.
When $\theta = 0°$, cos0° = 1 and flux is a maximum

EMF AND FLUX IN AN AC GENERATOR

From Faraday's law of electromagnetic induction, **the emf induced is directly proportional to the rate of change of magnetic flux**.

The induced emf in a coil is given by:

Induced emf

$$\textbf{emf} = -N\frac{\Delta\phi}{\Delta t}$$

$emf \rightarrow$ induced voltage (V)

N $\rightarrow$ number of turns in the coil

$\frac{\Delta\phi}{\Delta t} \rightarrow$ rate of change of flux $(Wb.\text{s}^{-1})$

The graphs below show how the flux, rate of change of flux and emf vary as an AC generator is rotated in a magnetic field. The graphs start in the position shown in diagram 1.

Note that the **rate of change of flux** $\left(\frac{\Delta\phi}{\Delta t}\right)$ is the **gradient of a flux graph** and **EMF is the negative gradient of the flux graph**.

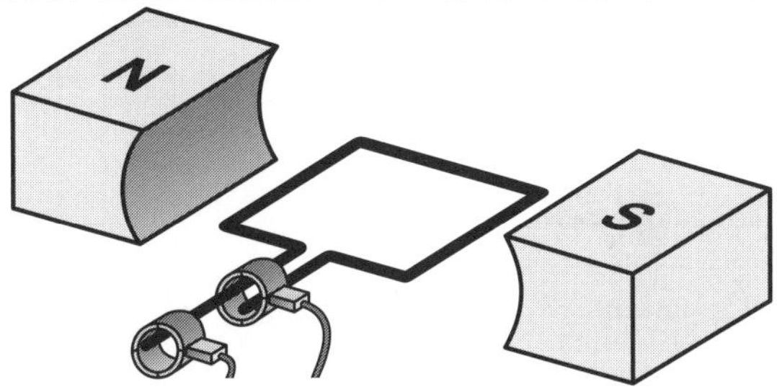

Diagram 1:
Flux is zero
Rate of change of flux is a maximum

Diagram 2:
Flux is a maximum
Rate of change of flux is zero

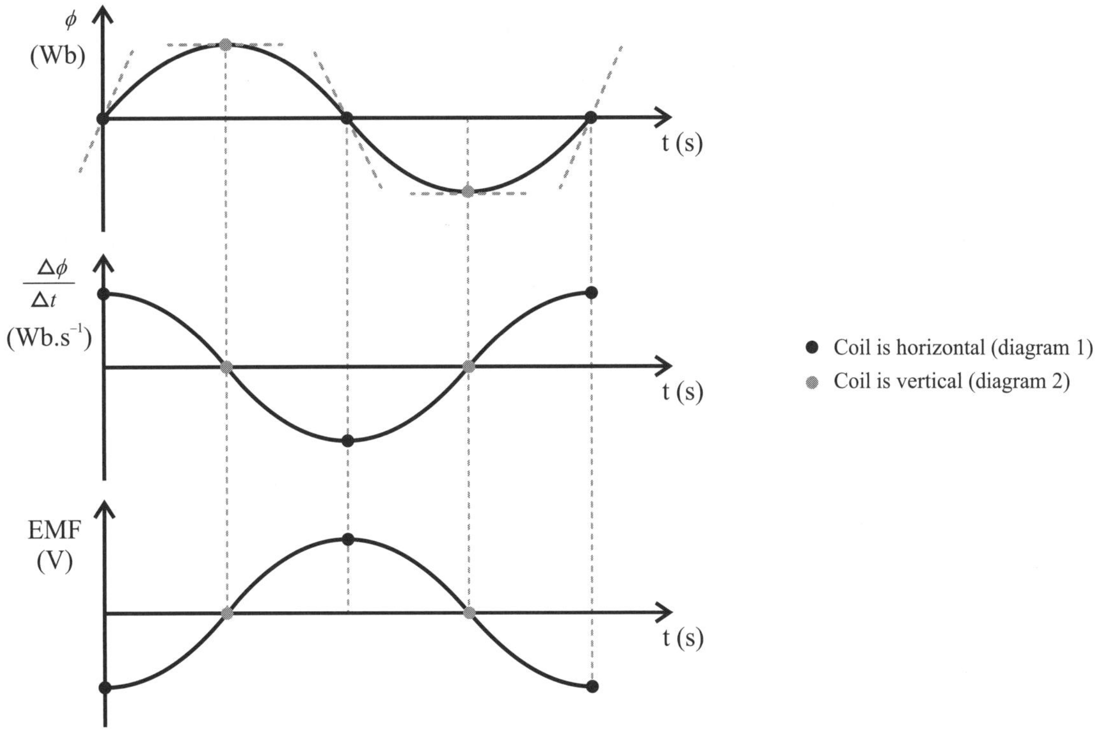

Magnetic flux linkage is the product of the number of turns on a coil and the flux through the coil $(N\Delta\phi)$**. No calculations are required for emf in this section.**

The EMF graph is the rate of change of flux graph reflected over the time axis.

This is due to the negative in the equation $\textbf{emf} = -N\frac{\Delta\phi}{\Delta t}$.

TRANSFORMERS

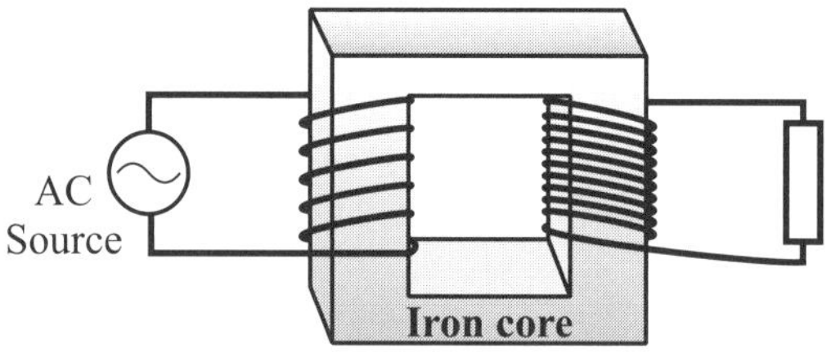

Diagram 1:
Step-up Transformer

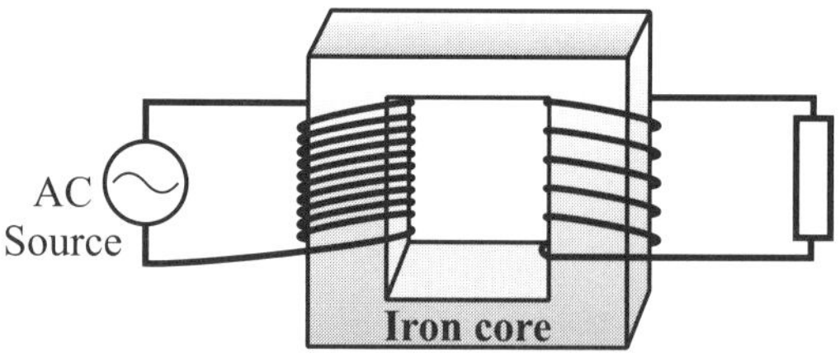

Diagram 2:
Step-down Transformer

Transformers are used to **step up** (increase) or **step down** (decrease) the **voltage** of **alternating current**.

- When alternating current flows through the primary coil, a changing magnetic field is induced.
- The changing magnetic field is transferred through the iron core to the secondary coil.
- This creates a changing electric field in the secondary coil. According to Faraday's law, this change in flux due to the changing magnetic field will induce a changing EMF and current in the secondary coil.

In an ideal transformer the **power input into the primary coil is equal to the power output on the secondary coil.**

Transformer Power Equations

$$P_{primary} = P_{secondary}$$

$$V_{primary} I_{primary} = V_{secondary} I_{secondary}$$

$$\frac{V_{primary}}{V_{secondary}} = \frac{N_{primary}}{N_{secondary}}$$

(N is the number of turns)

From the equations it can be seen that:

- If **voltage** is **stepped up**, **current** must be **stepped down**.
- If **voltage is stepped down, current must be stepped up**.
- The ratio between the number of **windings in the primary and secondary coil** is **equal to the ratio of the voltage across the primary and secondary coil**.
- **Transformers only work with alternating current**. A transformer relies on a change in flux. This occurs because of the AC current. If direct current was used there would be no change in flux and no induced voltage or current in the secondary coil of the transformer.

Illustrative Example:

A transformer has an input voltage of 25V. The secondary coil is connected to a resistor which draws a current of 5A. The ratio of turns on the primary coil to the secondary coil is 5000: 25 000.

a) Determine the voltage on the secondary side of the coil.
b) Determine the current in the primary coil.

a)

$$\frac{V_{primary}}{V_{secondary}} = \frac{N_{primary}}{N_{secondary}}$$

$$\frac{25}{V_{secondary}} = \frac{5000}{25000}$$

$$\frac{V_{secondary}}{25} = \frac{25000}{5000}$$

$$V_{secondary} = 125\,V$$

b)

$$V_{primary} I_{primary} = V_{secondary} I_{secondary}$$

$$25(I_{primary}) = (125)(5)$$

$$I_{primary} = 25\,A$$

The symbol for a transformer in a circuit diagram is 

POWER TRANSMISSION

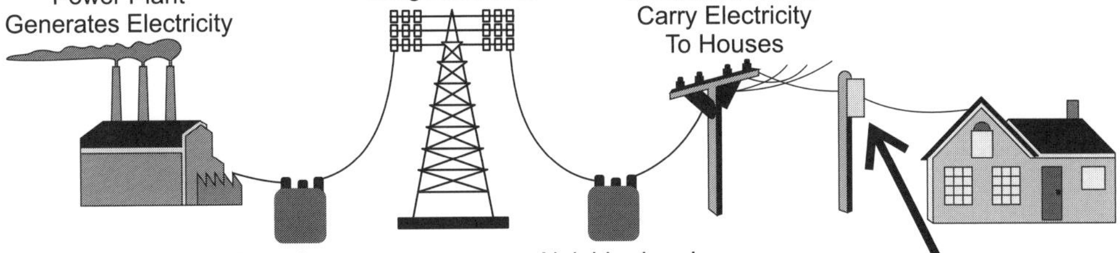

Transmission of power from power plants to homes uses transmission lines which generally stretch for very long distances. The longer the transmission line, the greater its resistance (R).

When current flows in the transmission line it heats up the wire and power is converted to heat energy.
From the equation $P = I^2R$, power is directly proportional to the square of the current (I).
This means the greater the current in the line, the more power is lost in transmitting it.
Power is transmitted at a high voltage and low current to minimise power loss on the transmission line.

Electricity is generated as alternating current so that transformers can be used to step-up and step-down the voltage as it is transmitted from the power plants to homes and businesses.

DIODES

A **diode** is a component that **only allows current to flow in one direction**.
The circuit symbol for a diode is shown below.

When the positive end of a voltage source is connected to the positive end of a diode (and in turn the negative end of the source is connected to the negative end of the diode) the diode is said to be **forward biased**.

When a diode is forward biased the diode will turn on and allow current to flow. When the diode is reverse biased (positive end of the source connected to negative end of the diode) the diode will turn off and current will not flow through it.

HALF-WAVE RECTIFICATION (CONVERTING AC TO DC)

The circuit in diagram 1 below shows how half-wave rectification is achieved. Diagram 2 shows the input voltage from the alternating current source and diagram 3 shows the output voltage across the resistor.

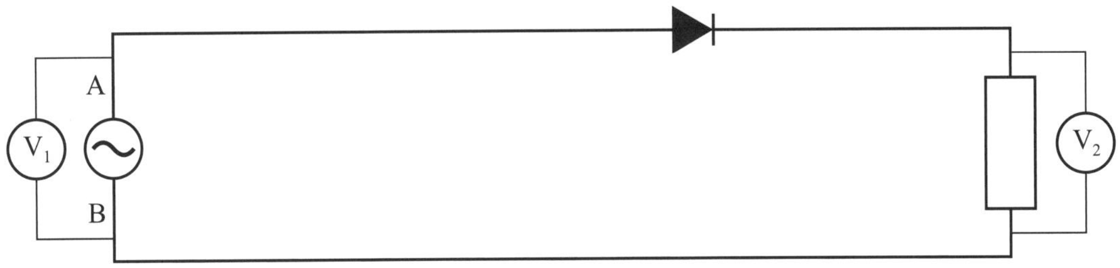

Diagram 1:
Half-wave rectification circuit

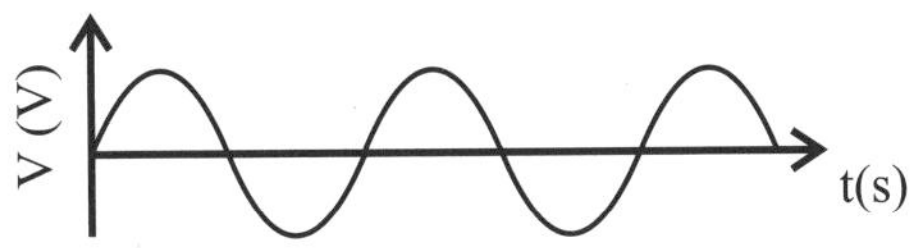

Diagram 2:
Input Voltage (V_1)

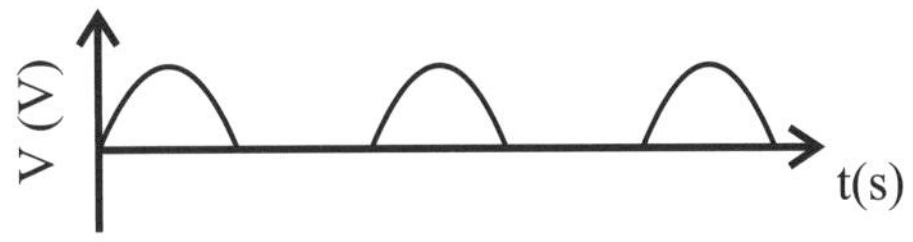

Diagram 3:
output voltage (V_2)

- When terminal A of the voltage source is positive, the diode is forward biased, and current flows.
- When terminal A of the voltage source is negative, the diode is reverse biased, and current does not flow.
- Half-wave rectification is inefficient as half the input power is not used (wasted).

FULL-WAVE RECTIFICATION

Diagram 1 below shows the circuit diagram for a full-wave rectifier. Diagram 2 shows the input voltage from the alternating current source. Diagram 3 shows output voltage after passing through the bridge rectifier. The diodes on the same side of the rectifier are always drawn back to back (D2 and D4) and front to front (D1 and D3).

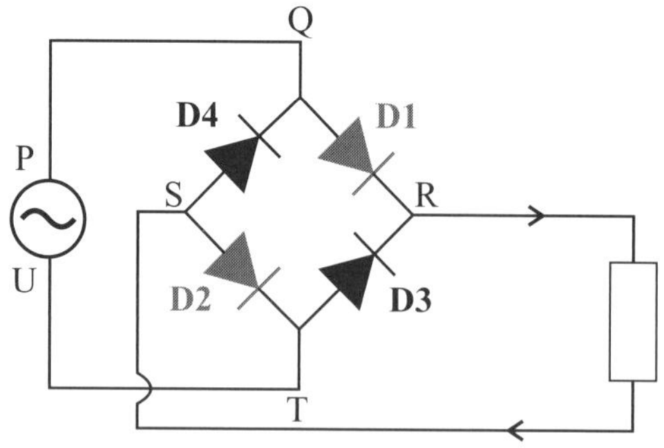

Diagram 1:
full-wave rectification circuit

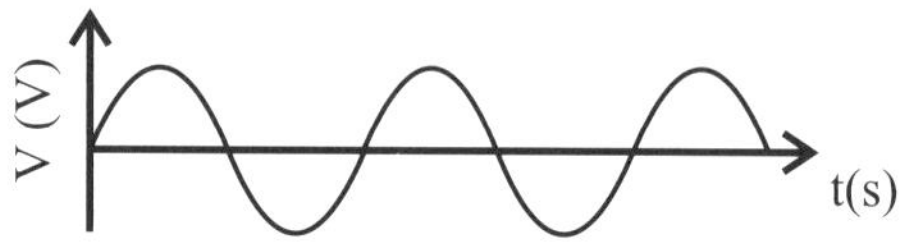

Diagram 2:
Input Voltage (V_1)

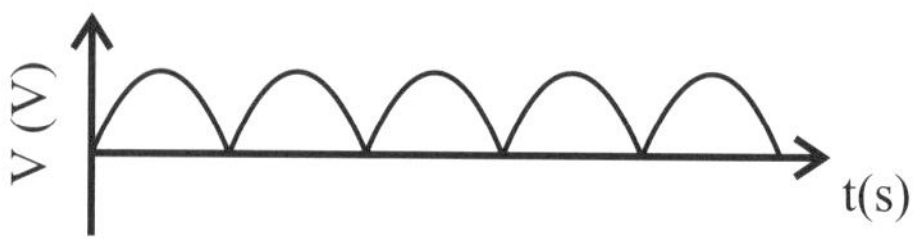

Diagram 3:
output voltage (V_2)

- When **P is positive**, diodes **D1 and D2** are **forward biased** and current flows PQRSTU.
- When **U is positive**, diodes **D3 and D4** are **forward biased** and current flows UTRSQP.
- In this way the **current flowing through the external circuit** (in this case the resistor) is always in the **same direction** (R to S),

The graphs of current and voltage have the exact same shape.

Question 1 (Solutions on page 417)

1.1 Two conductors are placed between magnets as shown in diagram 1 and 2 below. The current in the conductor in diagram 1 is out of the page and the force on the conductor in diagram 2 is downwards. Use the relevant rule(s) to choose the correct answer.

Diagram 1 — Diagram 2

	Force on conductor in diagram 1	Direction of current in conductor in diagram 2
A	Down	Into the page
B	Up	Out of the page
C	Out of the page	Down
D	Into the page	Up

(2)

1.2 A transformer has 2300 turns on the primary coil and 1000 turns on the secondary coil. The primary coil draws a current of 0,52 A from a 230 V, AC supply. The current in the secondary coil is 1 A. Determine the efficiency of the transformer.

A 100%

B 42%

C 84%

D 95% (2)

1.3 A transformer has an input voltage to the primary coil of x V. The coil ratio of primary to secondary is 5:2.

	Type of Transformer	Secondary Output Voltage (V)
A	Step up	$\frac{2x}{5}$
B	Step down	$\frac{5x}{2}$
C	Step up	$\frac{5x}{2}$
D	Step down	$\frac{2x}{5}$

(2)

1.4 The graph shows the variation of the magnetic flux ϕ through a coil with time t that is rotating in a uniform magnetic field.

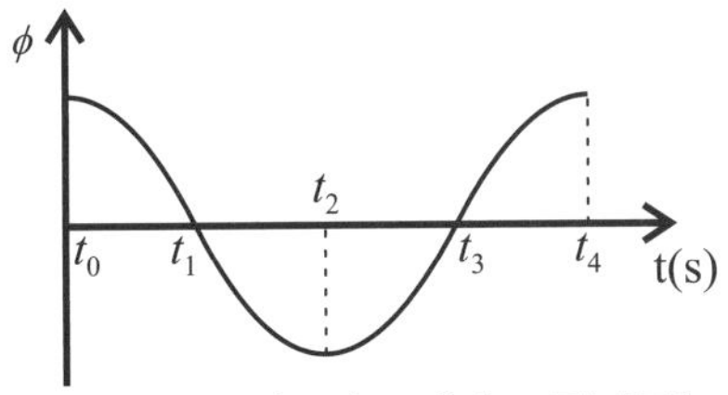

At which time(s) would the magnitude of the EMF be a maximum?

A t_0, t_2 and t_4

B t_0 and t_4

C t_1 and t_3

D t_2 only (2)

1.5 Question 1.5 and 1.6 refer to the information given below
A wire is placed between two magnets with current in the direction shown. The wire experiences a force of magnitude F.

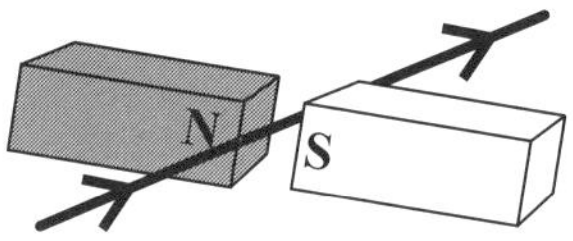

Three other arrangements, X, Y and Z, of an identical wire which is twice the length of that above and magnets are set up as shown below.

X Y Z

Choose the option which correctly describes the direction of the force the wire experiences in the original arrangement as well as the magnitude of the force in each arrangement X, Y and Z.

	Direction of force in original arrangment	Magnitude of force in arrangement X, Y and Z
A	Up	0,5F
B	Down	2F
C	Up	2F
D	Down	4F

(2)

1.6 In which arrangement(s) will the force be in the same direction as the original arrangement.

A X, Y and Z
B X and Y only
C Y and Z only
D Z only (2)

1.7 Which one of the following changes will lead to an increase in the emf of an AC generator without changing its frequency?

A Decrease the resistance of the coil
B Increase the resistance of the coil
C Increase the speed of rotation of the coil
D Increase the area of the coil (2)

1.8 The graph below is a flux versus time graph for an AC generator.

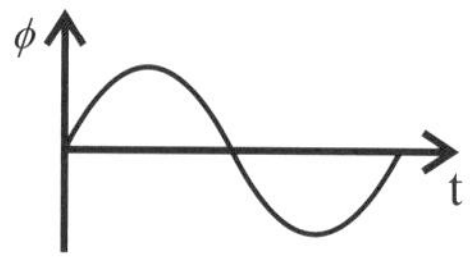

Which of the graphs below represent the voltage against time for the same generator?

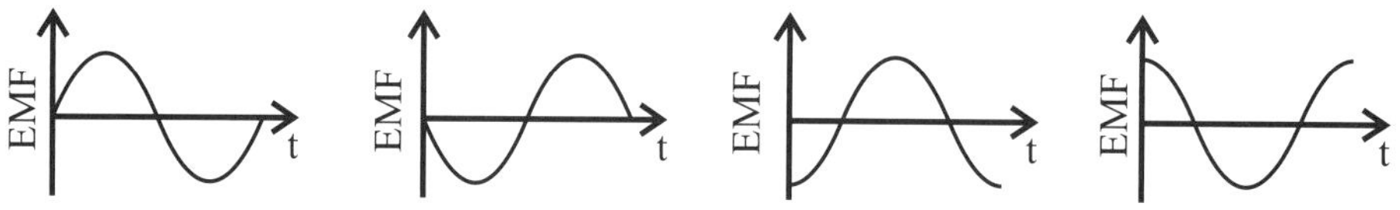

A B C D

TOC 1 Data Sheet 2 Definitions 3 3 solutions 4 4 solutions 5 5 solutions 6 6 solutions 7 7 solutions 8 8 solutions 9 9 solutions 10 10 solutions

1.9 The diagram below shows a full wave bridge rectifier connected to an alternating (AC) source.

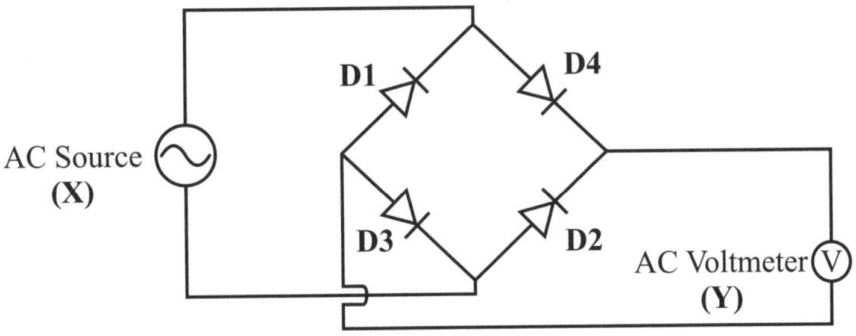

Which one of the following options gives the correct output of the AC voltmeter and the correct path of current through the diode bridge for one full cycle?

	Output	Direction of current
A	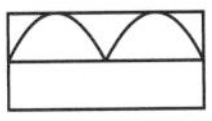	X→D2→Y→D1→X→D4→Y→D3→X
B	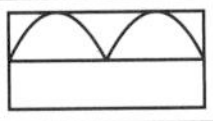	X→D4→Y→D3→X→D2→Y→D1→X
C	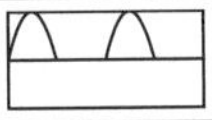	X→D4→Y→D3→X→D2→Y→D1→X
D	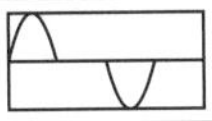	X→D2→Y→D1→X→D4→Y→D3→X

(2)

1.10 The diagram shows a conductor in a uniform magnetic field. The conductor is moved through the field to the right as shown by the arrow on the diagram. The direction of the induced current in the conductor is:

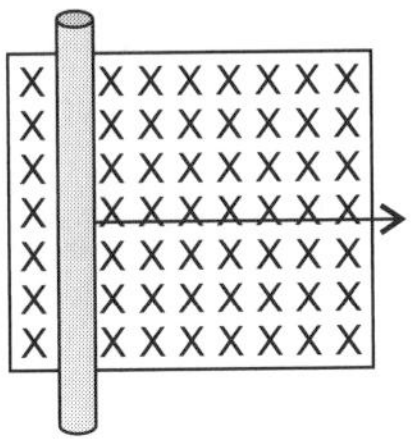

A Down the page
B Up the page
C There is no induced current as the magnetic field is constant
D There is no induced current as there is no change in magnetic flux (2)

1.11 A transformer is connected to a battery in series with a switch. The switch is closed momentarily and then opened.

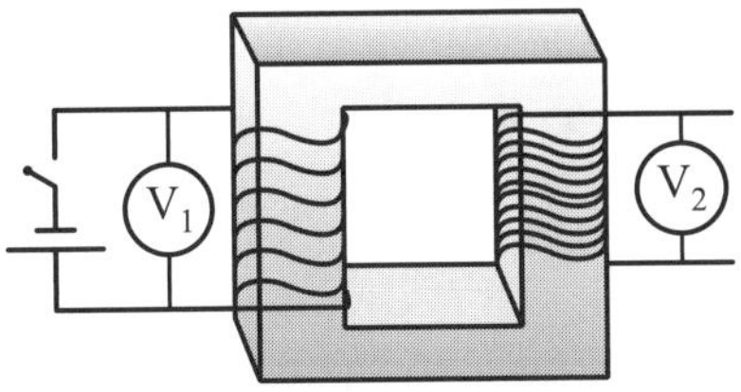

Which of the graphs correctly shows the variations against time of the readings on V_1 and V_2 respectively?

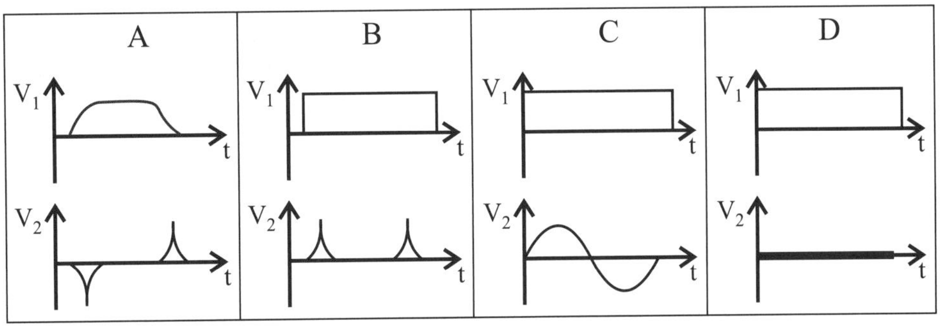

(2)

1.12 The diagram below shows the cross-section of a current-carrying conductor placed in a uniform magnetic field.

In which direction will the conduction experience a force?

A A
B B
C C
D D

(2)

1.13 A magnet is moved such that it creates the current direction shown in the solenoid below:

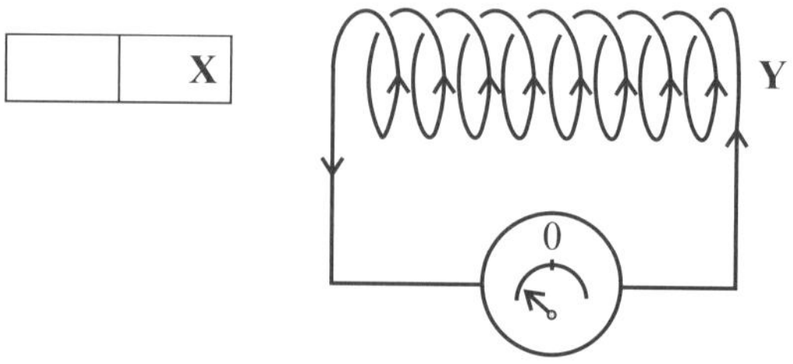

Which of the options below would produce this current?

	Polarity of X	Polarity at Y	Direction of magnet movement
A	South	South	Towards the solenoid
B	North	North	Away from solenoid
C	North	South	Towards solenoid
D	South	North	Away from the solenoid

(2)

1.14 The diagram below shows a copper coil wrapped a around a plastic conduit. A magnet is moved in the direction as shown on the diagram.

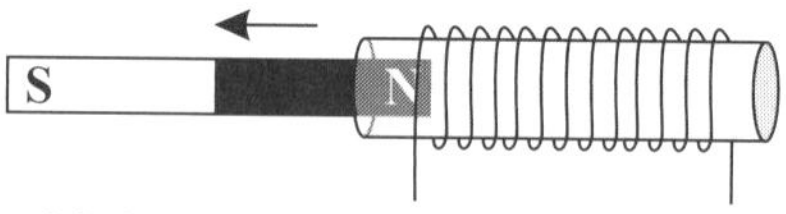

Choose the diagram which correctly shows the direction of the induced current in the coil and the correct polarity of the coil.

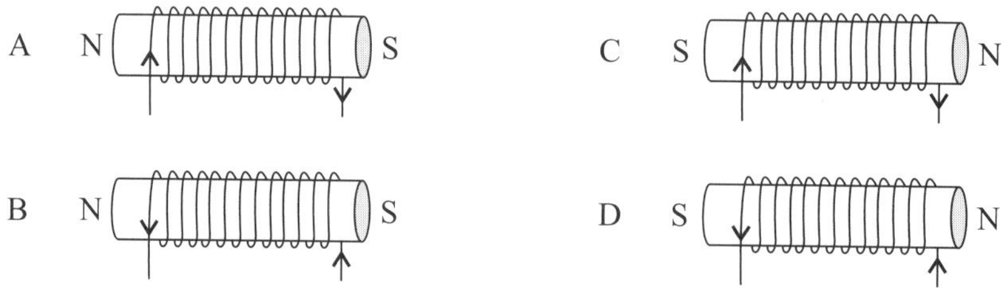

(2)

1.15 A current flows in a conductor placed between two magnets as shown in the diagram alongside.

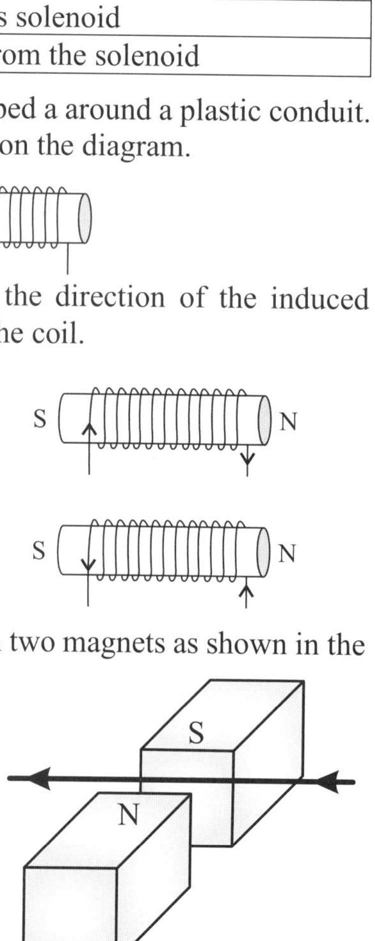

In which direction will the wire experience a force when the current is moving in the directions shown?

A Upwards
B Downwards
C Towards the South pole
D Towards the North pole

1.16 In an AC generator, a loop of wire is rotated in a magnetic field causing the lightbulb to glow.

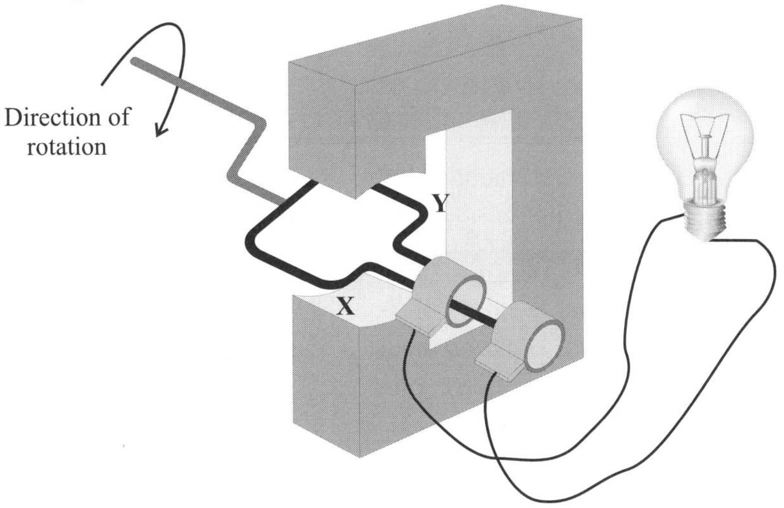

The solid dark line in the following diagrams illustrates the orientation of the plane XY of the loop.

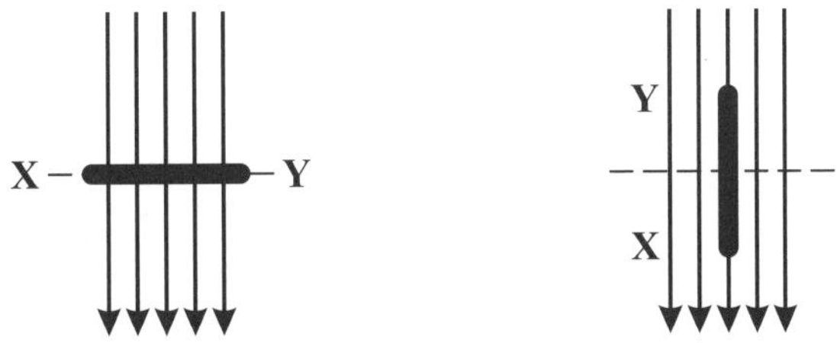

diagram 1 diagram 2

Which option below correctly describes the magnetic flux and induced EMF for Diagram 1 and 2.

	Diagram 1		Diagram 2	
	EMF (V)	Flux (ϕ)	EMF (V)	Flux (ϕ)
A	Maximum	Maximum	Zero	Zero
B	Zero	Zero	Maximum	Maximum
C	Maximum	Zero	Zero	Maximum
D	Zero	Maximum	Maximum	Zero

(2)

1.17 The diagram below shows two solenoids near each other.

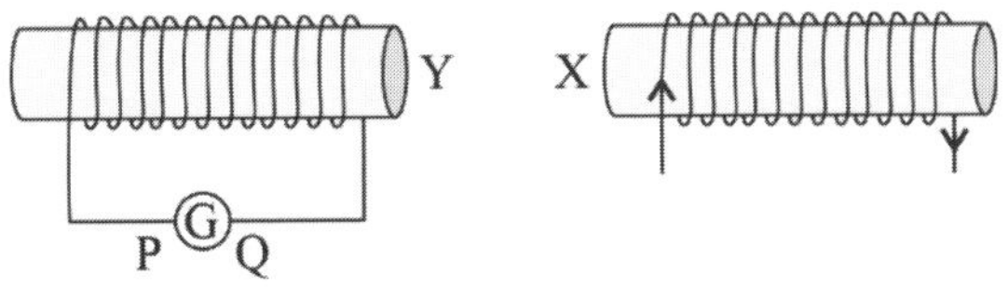

Choose the option which correctly describes the polarity of X and Y as well as the direction of the induced current through the galvanometer at the instant shown in the diagrams.

	Polarity at X	Polarity at Y	Direction of current through the galvanometer
A	North	North	P to Q
B	South	South	Q to P
C	North	South	P to Q
D	North	North	Q to P

(2)

TOC 1 Data Sheet 2 Definitions 3 3 solutions 4 4 solutions 5 5 solutions 6 6 solutions 7 7 solutions 8 8 solutions 9 9 solutions 10 10 solutions

1.18 Two parallel current-carrying conductors are placed a distance d apart from each other. Conductor A carries a current of I and conductor B carries a current of $10I$. Conductor B is in the magnetic field due to conductor A. (2)

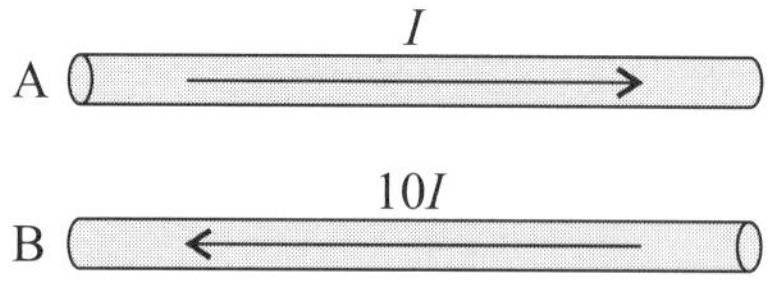

Which of the following statements about the force that current-carrying conductor A exerts on current-carrying conductor B is correct?

	Magnitude of Force of A on B	Direction of Force on B
A	Equal to the force that B exerts on A	Downwards
B	Equal to the force that B exerts on A	Upwards
C	Less than the force that B exerts on A	Upwards
D	Less than the force that B exerts on A	Downwards

1.19 A loop of wire connected to a d.c. power source at P and Q is placed into a magnetic field as shown below.

Which one of the following combinations will result in the wire swinging as shown?

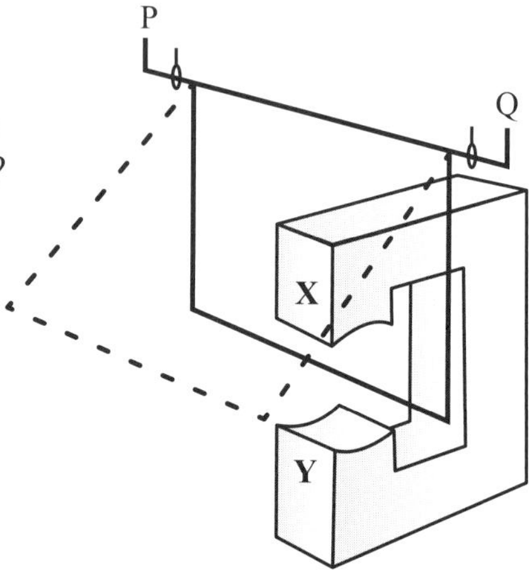

	Polarity at P	Polarity at Q	Polarity at X	Polarity at Y
A	Positive	Negative	North	South
B	Negative	Positive	South	North
C	Positive	Negative	South	North
D	Negative	Positive	South	North

(2)

1.20 An experiment was carried out to study the effect of a magnetic field on a current carrying conductor Y, placed within a magnetic field. X and Z are poles of magnets.

When a current flows through Y, the conductor moves downwards as shown by the arrow. Which one of the following combinations, regarding the polarities of the magnets and the direction of the current is correct?

	Polarity at X	Polarity at Z	Current direction in Y
A	South	North	Out of the page
B	North	North	Into the page
C	North	South	Out of the page
D	South	North	Into the page

(2)

1.21 Consider an experiment with a permanent magnet and a metal ring. The metal ring is connected to a galvanometer. Initially the magnet is held above the ring (as shown in the diagram below) and the meter shows zero current.

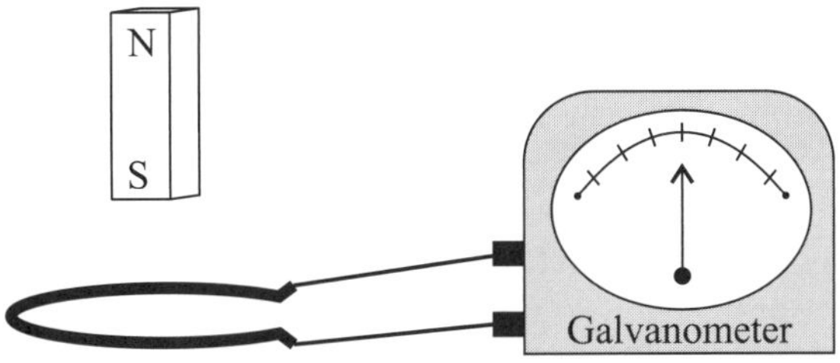

What will be observed on the meter when the magnet is released, and it falls through the ring?

A The needle on the meter is observed to deflect in one direction and does not return to zero.

B The needle on the meter is observed to deflect in one direction and returns to zero.

C The needle on the meter is observed to deflect in one direction and then deflects in the other direction with same magnitude.

D The needle on the meter is observed to deflect in one direction and then deflects in the other direction with a greater magnitude. (2)

1.22 In the diagram below a straight copper, current-carrying conductor, G, experiences a downward force when placed between the two permanent bar magnets, F and H. Which one of the following combinations are correct?

	Direction of magnetic field due to F and H	Direction of current in G	Direction of magnetic field around G
A	H to F	Into the page	Clockwise
B	H to F	Out of the page	Anti-clockwise
C	F to H	Out of the page	Clockwise
D	F to H	Into the page	Anti-clockwise

(2)

1.23 The DC motor shown below has a current through the armature as shown in the diagram.

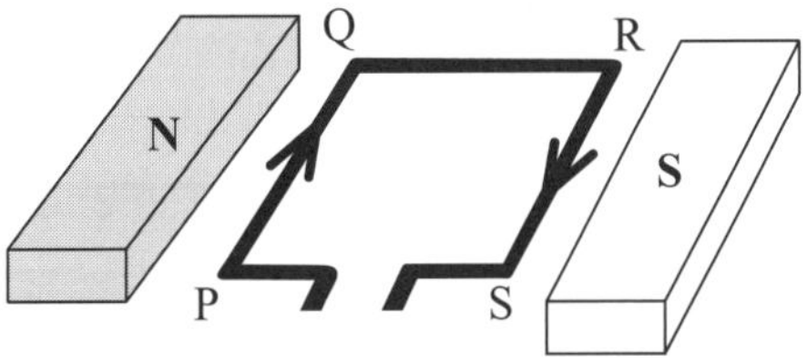

Choose the option which correctly describes the segments which experience a force and the direction of rotation of the coil.

	Segments experiencing a force	Direction of rotation
A	PQ and RS	Clockwise
B	QR and PS	Anti-clockwise
C	PQ and RS	Anti-clockwise
D	QR and PS	Clockwise

(2)

1.24 The diagram below shows a conductor in a uniform magnetic field. The direction of the magnetic field is out of the page as shown. The direction of the conventional current (I) in the conductor is given by the direction of the arrow.

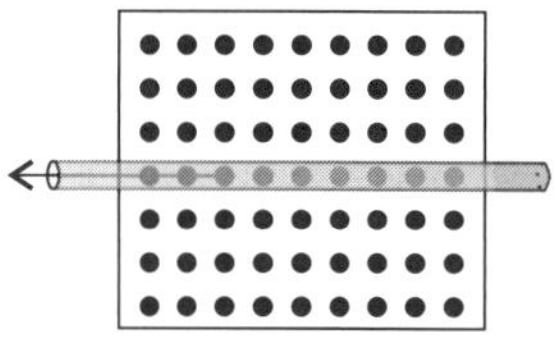

The direction of the force experienced by the conductor is:

A Up

B Down

C Into the page

D Out of the page (2)

1.25 When a magnet is dropped through a stationary coil, which of the following will not increase the maximum induced emf?

A Using a stronger magnet of the same length.

B Increasing the number of turns in the coil.

C Using a longer magnet of the same strength.

D Dropping the magnet from a higher point. (2)

1.26 The primary and secondary coil of a transformer are connected to ammeters. Current in the primary coil is then turned on using a DC source. What would be observed on the ammeter connected to the secondary side of the coil?

A There would be no reading as a DC source is being used.

B The reading reaches a maximum and returns to zero.

C The reading reaches a constant average between the maximum and zero.

D The reading fluctuates between a maximum and minimum in either direction. (2)

1.27 A magnet is moved away from a solenoid. The diagram below is a cross section of the solenoid with the direction of the current in the coil as shown.

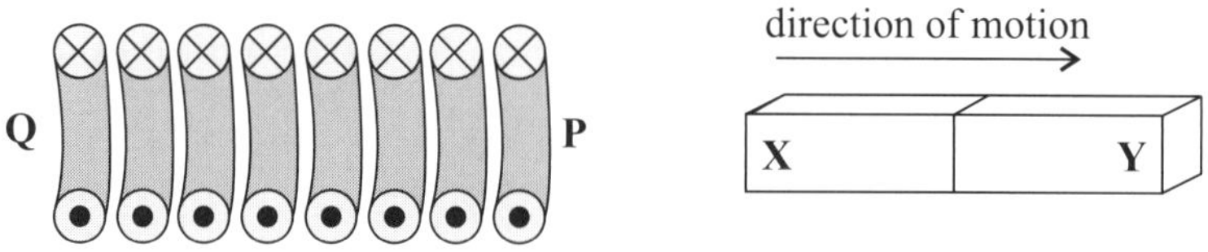

Which of the following are the correct poles of the solenoid and the magnet?

	Q	P	X	Y
A	South	North	North	South
B	North	South	South	North
C	South	North	North	South
D	North	South	North	South

(2)

1.28 The magnetic flux ϕ through a coil having 100 turns varies with time t as shown below.

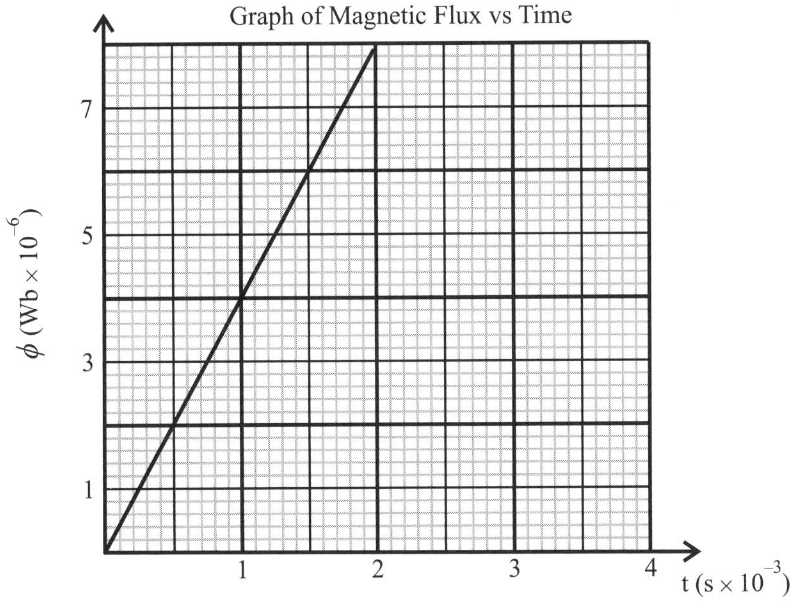

The induced EMF in the coil is:

A – 4 V B 4 V C – 400 V D – 0,4 V (2)

1.29 The diagram below shows a cross section of a DC motor which rotates along axis PQ.

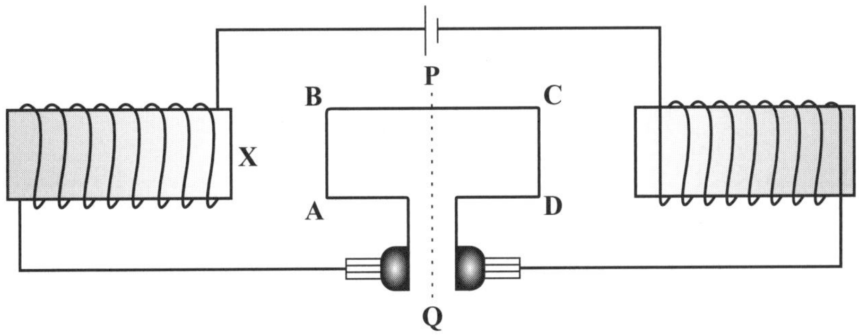

Choose the option which describes the correct polarity of the electromagnet at X, the direction of rotation along the axis and the force on segment CD.

	Polarity at X	Direction of rotation	Direction of force on CD
A	South	Clockwise	Into the page
B	North	Anti-clockwise	Out of the page
C	North	Clockwise	Into the page
D	South	Anti-clockwise	Out of the page

(2)

1.30 A coil is placed in a magnetic field as shown below.

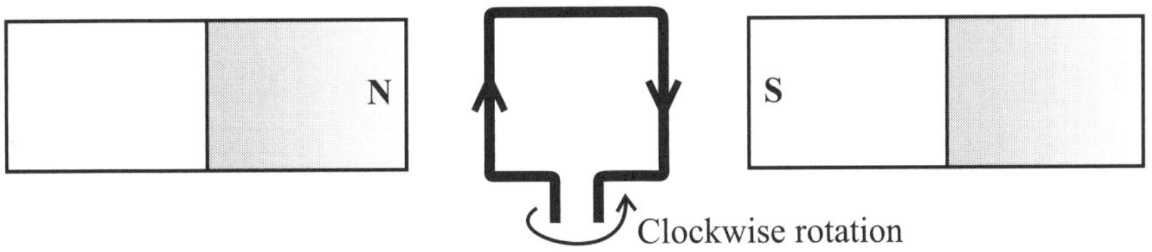

The diagram above is a…

A A motor, where the current is induced by the rotation of the coil.

B A generator, where the current induces a force on the coil.

C A motor, where the current induces a force on the coil.

D A generator, where the current is induced by the rotation of the coil. (2)

1.31 The magnetic flux passing through a coil of wire changes as shown in the graph below. During which time interval(s) will the induced emf in the coil be a maximum?

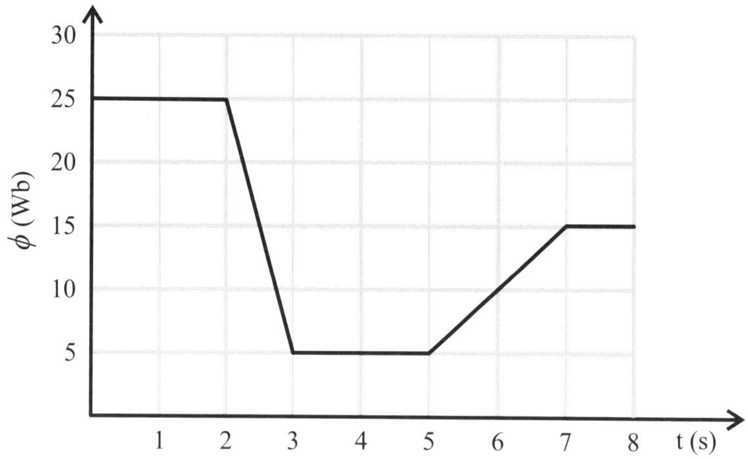

A 0-2 s, 3-5 s and 7-8 s
B 2-3 s
C 5-7 s
D 2-3 s and 5-7 s

(2)

1.32 A coil is rotated in a magnetic field. The graph shows how the induced emf changes with time for one complete rotation of the coil.

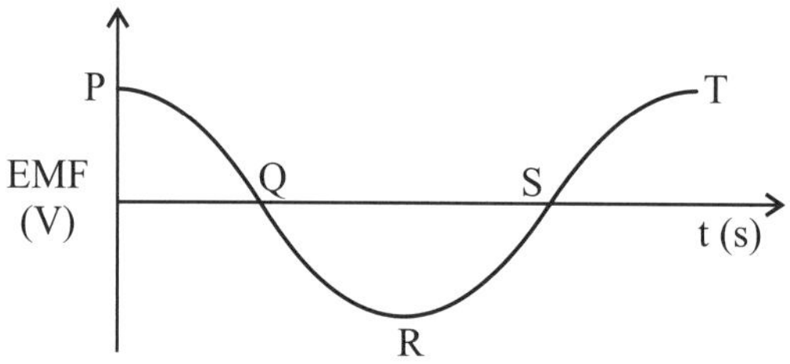

Which one of the following graphs shows the corresponding magnetic flux with time for one complete rotation of the coil?

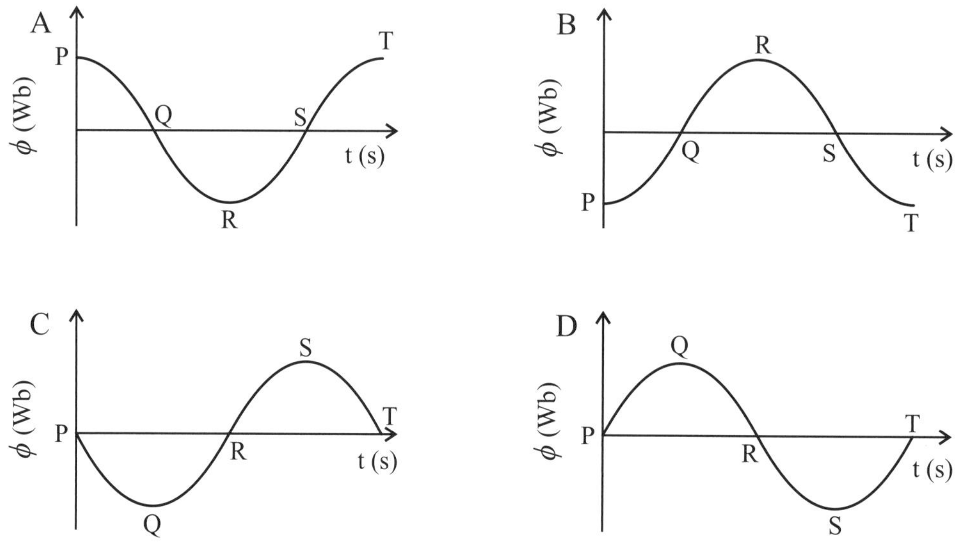

(2)

1.33 The solid line in the graph below represents the output of an AC generator. The dotted line represents the output of the same generator after a change has been made to the generator.

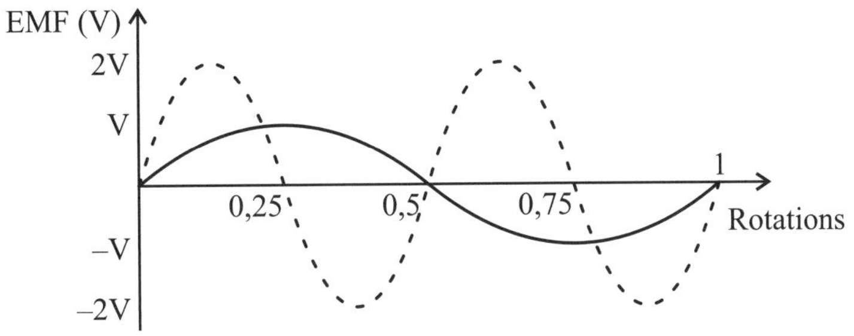

Which one of the following could be the change made to the generator?

A The number of turns on the coil was doubled.

B The strength of the magnetic field was doubled.

C The surface area of the coil was doubled.

D The speed of rotation of the coil was doubled. (2)

1.34 The coils of an AC generator make one complete rotation. The resulting graph for the output emf is shown below.

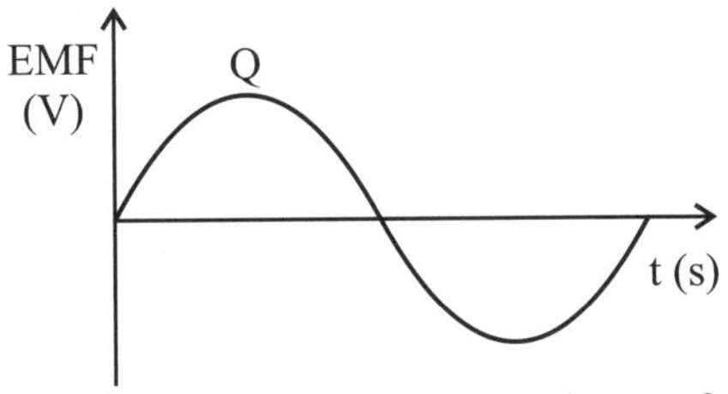

Position Q on the graph is obtained when the plane of the coil is at an angle of __° to the magnetic field and the magnitude of flux is ____

	Coil is at angle of	Flux is
A	0°	Zero
B	45°	Maximum
C	90°	Zero
D	180°	Minimum

(2)

1.35 A magnet is spun on an axis PQ as shown in the diagram below.

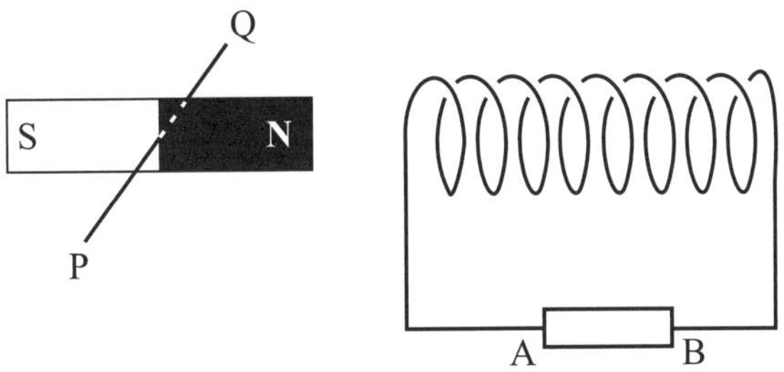

At the instant shown in the diagram…

A The induced current will flow through the resistor from A to B.

B The induced current will flow through the resistor from B to A.

C No current will flow as the magnet does not enter the coil.

D No current will flow as no galvanometer is present. (2)

TOC
1 Data Sheet
2 Definitions
3
3 solutions
4
4 solutions
5
5 solutions
6
6 solutions
7
7 solutions
8
8 solutions
9
9 solutions
10
10 solutions

1.36 A single conducting loop is in a region of magnetic field as shown in the diagram. An anticlockwise current is induced in the loop because the magnetic flux is decreasing.

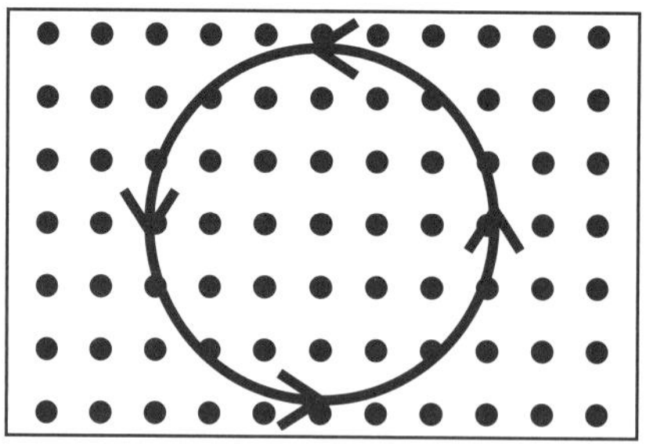

Which of the following changes to the situation would make the induced current larger?

A The magnetic field is increased in magnitude.

B Increase the rate at which the magnetic flux is decreasing.

C Use a loop with a bigger diameter.

D Move the loop sideways, but keep it in the magnetic field

(The above question is from the 2016 IEB Supplementary Examination) (2)

1.37 Two circuits are shown in the diagram.

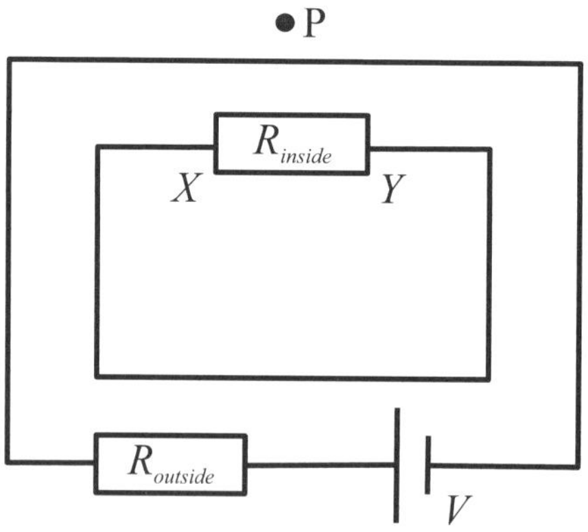

The resistance in the outside circuit, $R_{outside}$, is **decreasing** at a constant rate. In which direction is the magnetic field at point P pointing and in which direction is the conventional current through the resistor, R_{inside}, in the smaller inside circuit?

	Magnetic field at P	Current through R_{inside}
A	Into the page	From X to Y
B	Into the page	From Y to X
C	Out of the page	From X to Y
D	Out of the page	From Y to X

(The above question is from the 2017 IEB Final Examination) (2)

1.38 A conductor carries a current perpendicularly into the page between the poles of two magnets as shown in the diagram. In what direction will the conductor experience a force?

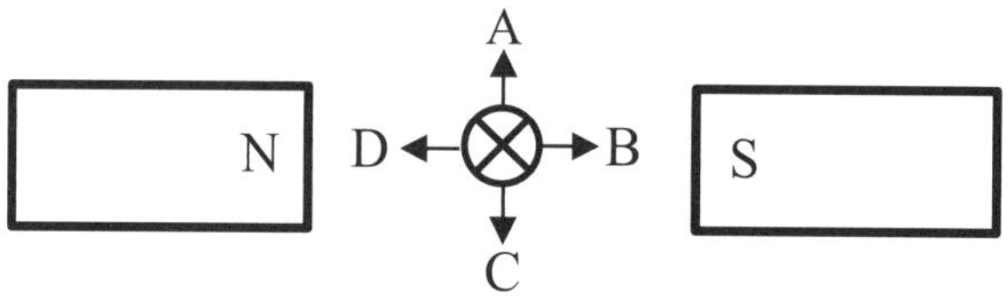

(The above question is from the 2017 IEB Supplementary Examination) (2)

1.39 A coil and a magnet can each move horizontally to the left or to the right simultaneously at the same speed.

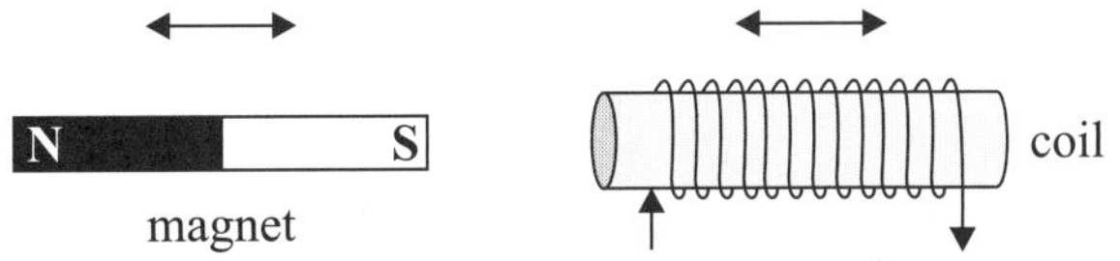

In which of the following will a conventional current be induced in the coil in the direction shown in the diagram when both the magnet and the coil are moving?

	Direction of motion of magnet	Direction of motion of coil
A	To the left	To the right
B	To the left	To the left
C	To the right	To the right
D	To the right	To the left

(The above question is from the 2018 IEB Final Examination) (2)

1.40 A wire has a conventional current *I* directed to the right as shown in the diagram.

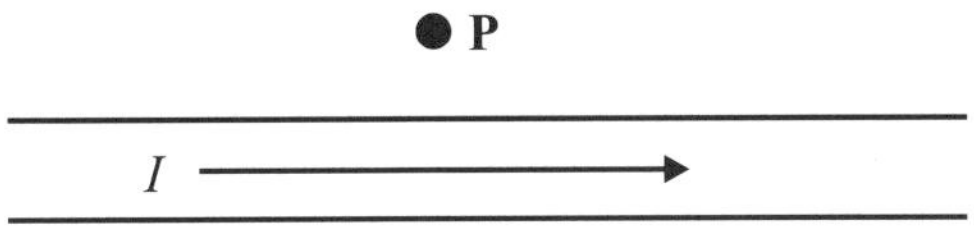

At point P, what is the direction of the associated magnetic field?

A Into the plane of the paper.

B Out of the plane of the paper.

C Towards the top of the page.

D Towards the bottom of the page.

(The above question is from the 2018 IEB Supplementary Examination) (2)

1.41 The name of the law used to determine the direction of the induced current in a conducting coil which experiences a changing magnetic flux is:

A Faraday's law

B Flemming's left hand motor rule

C Flemming's right hand dynamo rule

D Lenz's law

The above question is from the 2018 IEB Supplementary Examination) (3)

1.42 A conducting square coil is placed in a uniform magnetic field. The magnetic field is directed into the page. There is a clockwise current in the coil.

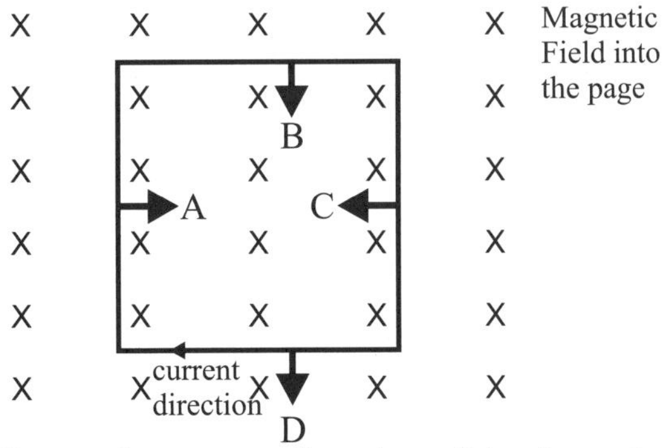

Which arrow indicates the correct direction of the force that acts on the side of the coil?

The above question is from the 2019 IEB Final Examination) (2)

[86]

TOC 1 Data Sheet 2 Definitions 3 3 solutions 4 4 solutions 5 5 solutions 6 6 solutions 7 7 solutions 8 8 solutions 9 9 solutions 10 10 solutions

Question 2 (Solutions on page 417)

A non-rigid flexible wire is connected to a DC power source via a switch. The wire is held in a fixed position by stands at A and B as shown in the diagram below.

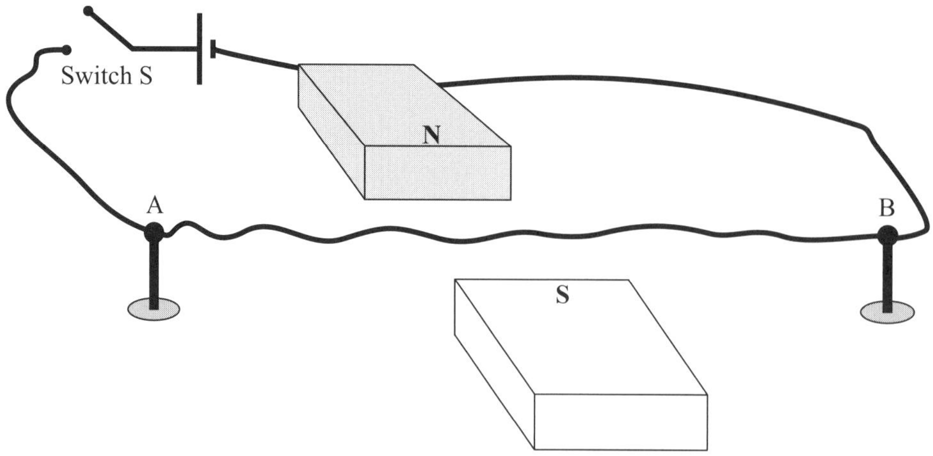

2.1 State the direction of the force on the wire when the switch is closed. (1)

2.2 Name the rule which was used to find the direction of the force in 2.1 above. (2)

2.3 What would be observed if an AC (alternating current) source was used instead of a DC source? Explain why this occurs. (3)

2.4 State two ways in which the force that the conductor experiences could be increased. (2)

[8]

Question 3 (Solutions on page 417 and 418)

The diagram below shows an electrical device used to power a transformer which in turn powers a lamp.

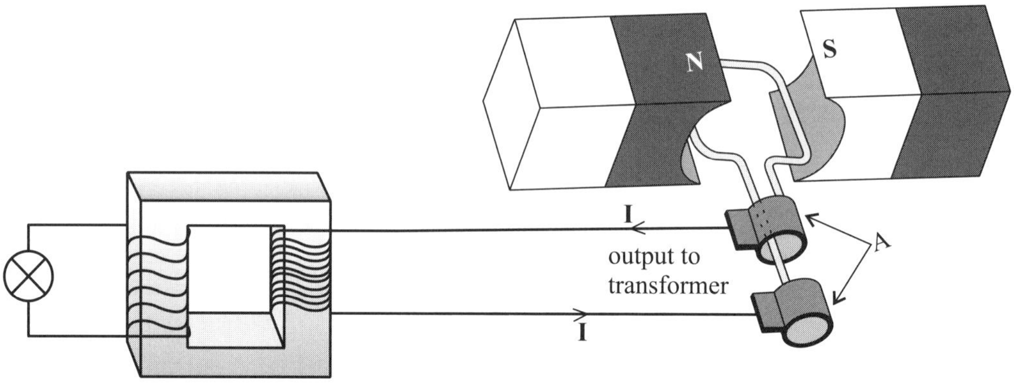

3.1 What type of energy conversion is taking place in the above device? (1)

3.2 Name the components labelled A in the diagram and state their function. (2)

3.3 State the direction of rotation of the coil. (1)

3.4 State two ways in which the EMF of a generator can be increased without changing the frequency. (2)

3.5 The input to the transformer is 230V. The primary side of the transformer has 8000 turns and the secondary has 200 turns. Determine the voltage across the lamp. (4)

3.6 The current in the primary coil is 0,08 A. Determine resistance of the lamp. (4)

[14]

Question 4 (Solutions on page 418)

A bar magnet is dropped through a coil attached to an oscilloscope as shown in the diagram. As the magnet falls through the coil it induces an emf in the coil. The oscilloscope plots the graph shown below of the induced emf against time.

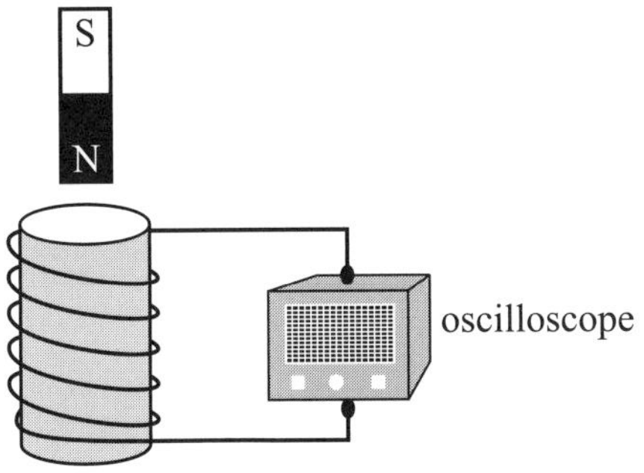

Graph of induced EMF versus time

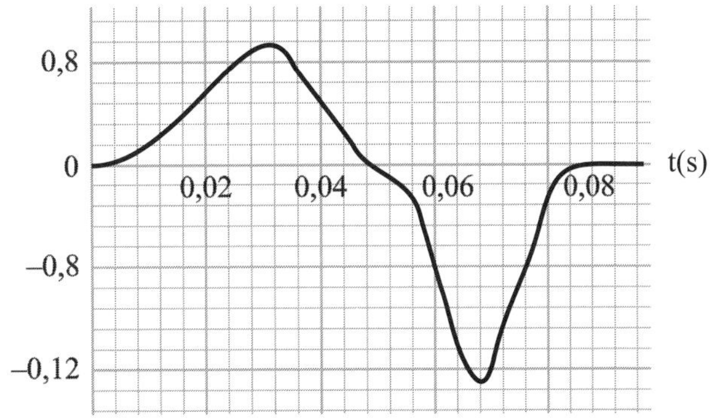

4.1 State Lenz's law (2)

4.2 State the polarity (north or south) of the top of the coil as the magnet enters the coil. (1)

4.3 At what time is the magnitude of the induced EMF a maximum? (2)

4.4 State Faraday's law of electromagnetic induction. (2)

4.5 Why is the magnitude of the maximum induced emf greater as the magnet exits the coil than when it enters the coil? (2)

4.6 Name the energy conversion of the magnet dropping through the coil. (2)

4.7 State what the area under the graph represents and using a suitable formula explain why the area between the time axis and positive section of the graph is equal to the area between the time axis and negative section of the graph. (5)

On the graph below, the dotted line represents the original experiment, sketch how the graph of the induced emf against time will change when each of the following changes is made respectively to the initial experiment.

Graph of induced EMF versus time

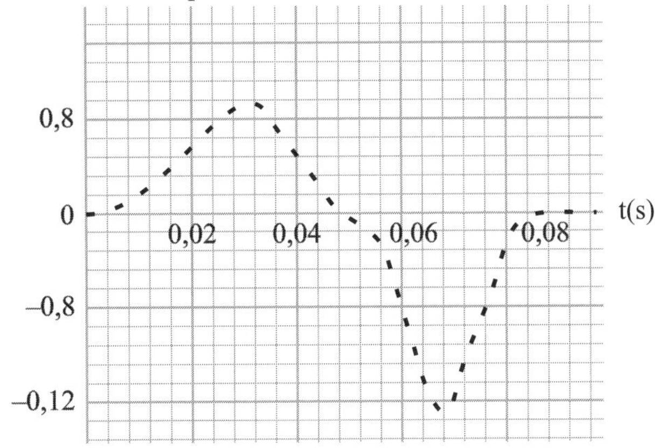

4.8 The same magnet is dropped from the same height through the same coil with the South pole entering the coil first. (2)

4.9 A magnet of the same mass and length, but half the strength is dropped through the same coil from the same height with the North pole entering the coil first. (2)

[15]

Question 5 (Solutions on page 418)

A cross section of a rectangular coil of a generator rotating clockwise in a magnetic field is shown in the diagram below.

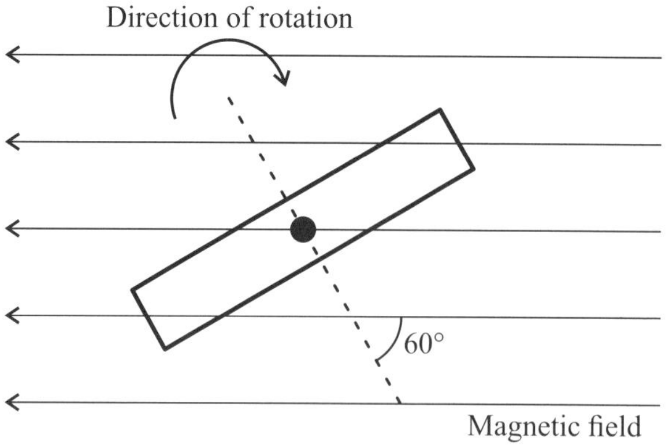

At the instant shown in the diagram, the normal line to the coil is at an angle of 60° to the magnetic field.

5.1 State Faraday's law of electromagnetic induction. (2)

5.2 What is the minimum angle the generator must rotate in order for the EMF to be zero? (2)

The graph below is a plot of the variation in magnetic flux linkage as the coil rotates in the magnetic field.

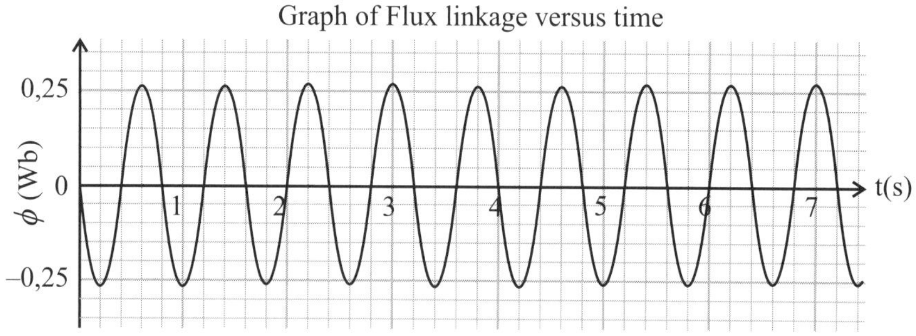

5.3 What is the angle between the normal to the coil and the magnetic field at 0,8 seconds? (2)

5.4 At what time(s) during the first second is the EMF zero? (3)

5.5 State the position of the coil (horizontal or vertical) in the magnetic field at 4,4 seconds. (2)

5.6 Based on the above graph and given that the maximum induced EMF induced by the generator is 0,5V, sketch a graph of induced EMF against time on the grid below for the first two seconds. (5)

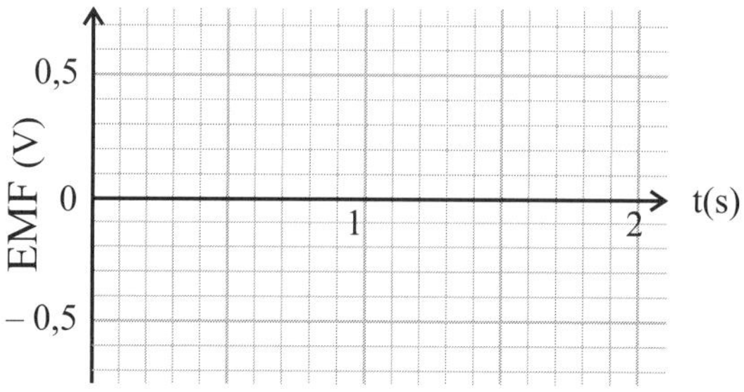

[16]

Question 6 (Solutions on page 419)

The table below shows the results of an experiment to determine the magnetic flux density passing through a conductor. The conductor used in the experiment is a copper rod of length 7cm between the magnets and a mass of 4×10^{-4} kg. The rod is suspended by a spring balance graduated in Newtons. The current is controlled by varying the resistance of the variable resistor in the circuit and connected to a DC source at P and Q.

Force on conductor (mN)	Current (I)	Reading on Spring Balance (mN)
	0,12	3,50
	0,20	3,20
	0,32	2,80
	0,40	2,50
	0,56	2,00
	0,68	1,55
	0,80	1,10
	0,92	0,7
	1,00	0,42
	1,12	0

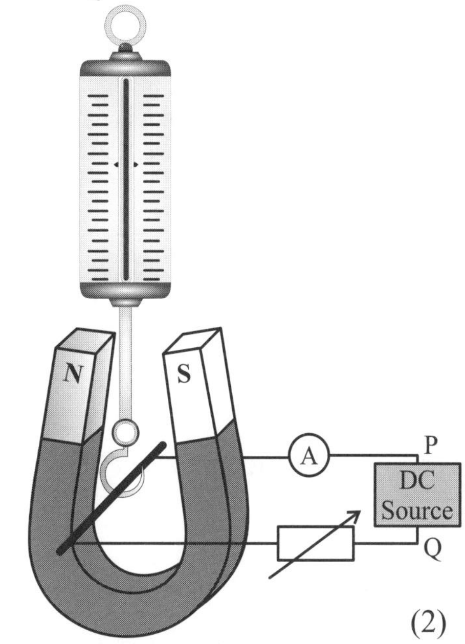

6.1 State the polarity of the DC source at P. (2)

6.2 Determine the weight of the copper rod. (2)

6.3 Complete the column for the force exerted on the conductor. (3)

6.4 On the grid below, plot a graph of force on the conductor against current. (5)

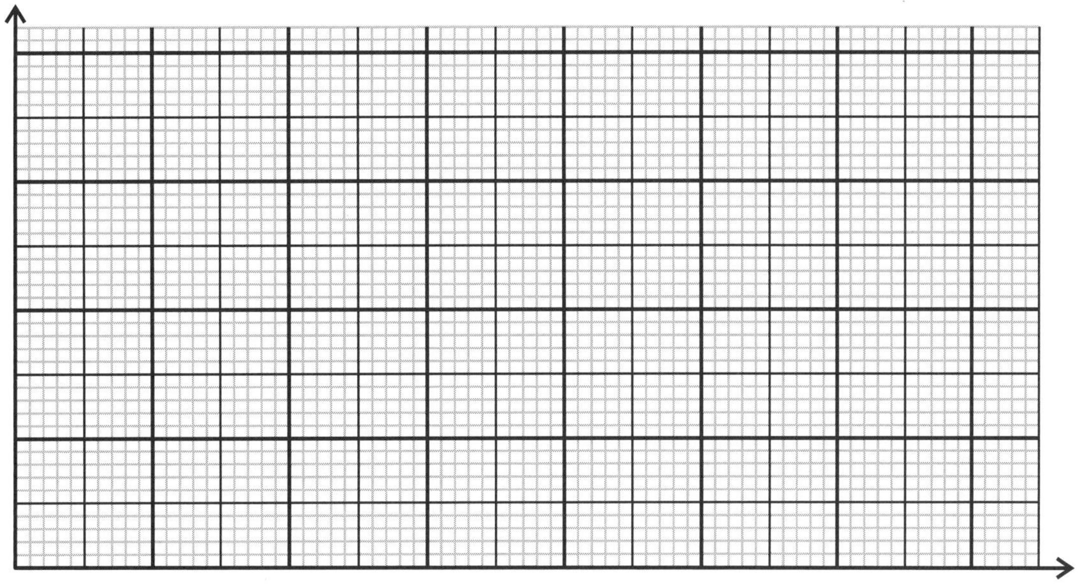

6.5 Determine the gradient of the graph. Units are not necessary (3)

6.6 Using your knowledge of the equation $F = IlB\sin\theta$ and the fact that the equation $y = mx + c$ describes the equation of a straight line to determine the magnetic flux density in the copper rod. (4)

[19]

TOC | 1 Data Sheet | 2 Definitions | 3 | 3 solutions | 4 | 4 solutions | 5 | 5 solutions | 6 | 6 solutions | 7 | 7 solutions | 8 | 8 solutions | 9 | 9 solutions | 10 | 10 solutions

Question 7 (Solutions on page 419 and 420)

Jayden is a very good mathematics learner but does not take science. He attempts to build a device from the notes of a friend who does take science. He constructs the device shown below.

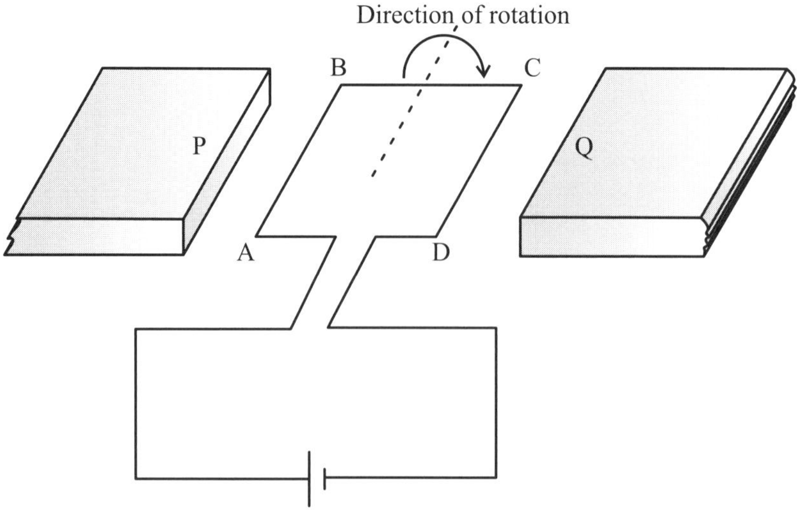

7.1 Is the device pictured above a motor or generator? Give a reason for your answer. (2)

7.2 The coil rotates in a clockwise direction. Is Q the North or South pole of the magnet? (3)

7.3 When the coil rotates 90° from the position shown in the diagram, the coil reaches a vertical position. What direction is the force acting on side AB of the coil? (1)

7.4 Assuming the device shown above functions correctly, on the grid below, draw a graph of flux linkage against degrees of rotation for one full cycle starting at the position shown in the diagram above. The maximum flux linkage in the coil is 1,5 Weber.

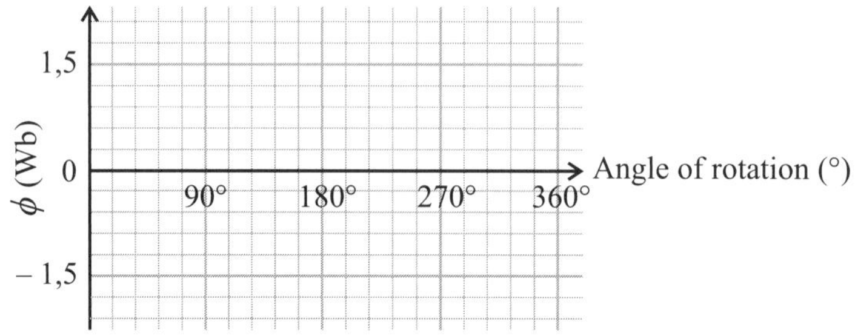

(4)

7.5 Not being a science learner, Jayden has made two critical errors in the design of his device. What are the errors that Jayden has made and what would be observed if the device were turned on without these errors being corrected? (4)

[14]

Question 8 (Solutions on page 420)

An experiment to determine how the force acting on a magnet placed inside a solenoid is conducted using the apparatus shown below. The results of the experiment are shown alongside the diagram.

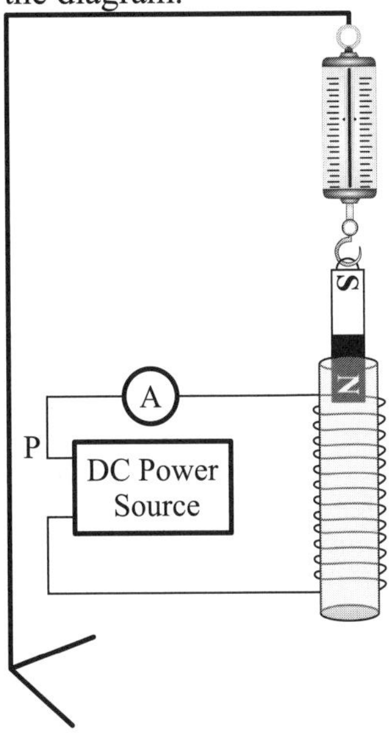

Current (A)	Force (N)
0,5	8
1,0	13,8
1,5	19,6
2,0	25,2
2,5	31

8.1 State Lenz's law. (2)

8.2 Based on the results, is the terminal of the power source labelled P positive or negative? (2)

8.3 Draw a fully labelled free body diagram of the forces acting on the magnet while a current is flowing in the solenoid. (3)

8.4 On the grid below, plot a graph of the results in the table above.

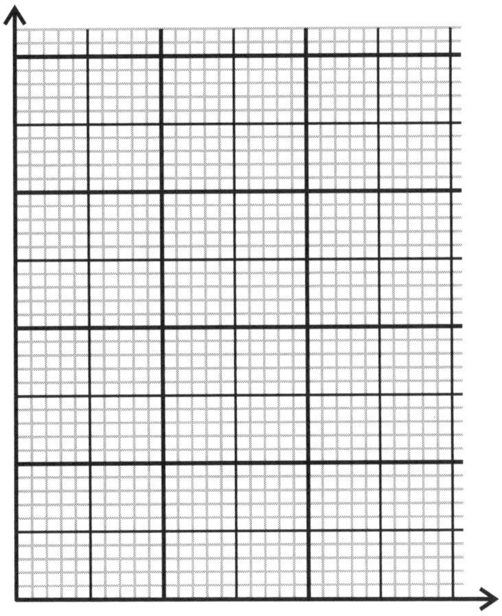

(6)

8.5 Using your graph determine the mass of the magnet. (5)

[19]

Question 9 (Solutions on page 420 and 421)

Rachel finds a 3V DC motor which she would like to use in an experiment. Unfortunately, she has no power source available to drive the motor. Being an innovative science learner, she constructs the generator below to drive the motor.

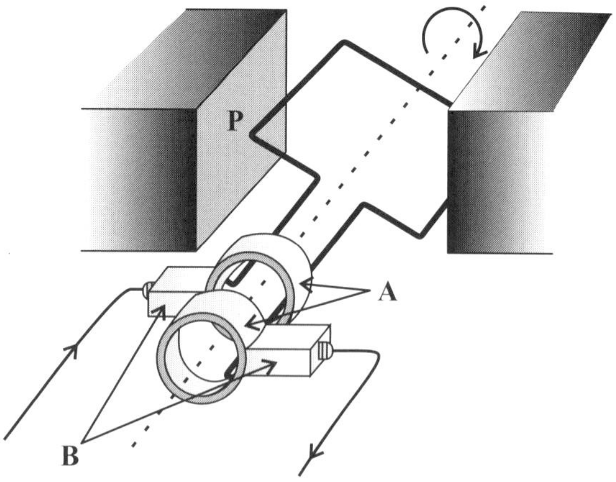

9.1 State Faraday's law of electromagnetic induction (2)

9.2 Provide labels for the parts A and B (2)

9.3 The generator is being rotated clockwise. At the instant shown in the diagram current is flowing as shown. Is P the North or South pole of the magnet? (2)

9.4 Rachel wishes to connect the generator directly to her motor. Would the motor function as intended? Give a reason for your answer (3)

Rachel then constructs the device shown below and connects it between the motor and generator.

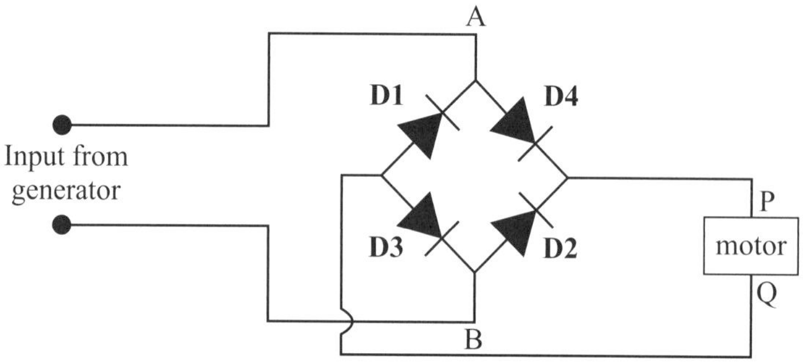

9.5 Name the device in the diagram above and explain how it functions. (5)

9.6 Rachel finds that when she rotates her generator the motor does not switch on. She decides to measure the output voltage of her generator and finds that it is only 1,5V. She decides to build a transformer to obtain the required voltage. She takes a soft iron core and wraps the primary side with 1000 turns. How many turns should be on the secondary side of the transformer? (3)

9.7 The motor is rated at 300mW. What current needs to be induced in the generator in order for the motor to function. (5)

[22]

Question 10 (Solutions on page 421)

Two physical science learners conduct an experiment to determine the relationship between the magnitude of the induced emf in a generator and the number of loops that are wound on the coil. They set up an experiment similar to the generator in the diagram below.

Number of Loops	Induced EMF (V)
200	9,40
300	15,40
400	19,30
500	25,50
600	30,60
700	34,70

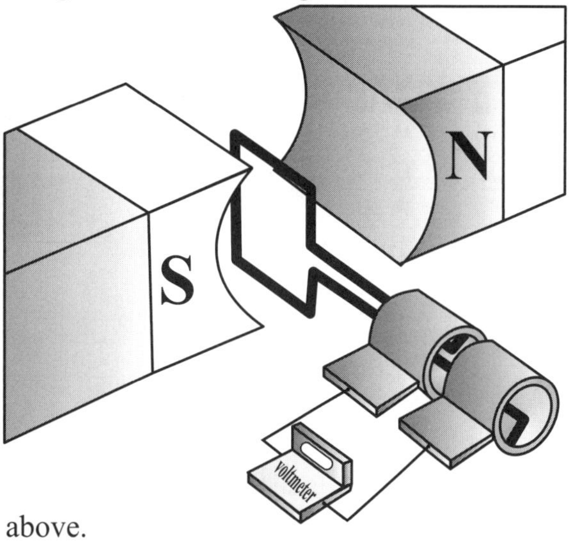

The results obtained are recorded in the table above.

10.1 What is the independent variable in this experiment? (2)

10.2 Name two variables which need to be kept constant in the experiment. (2)

10.3 Plot a graph of induced EMF against the number of loops in the coil.

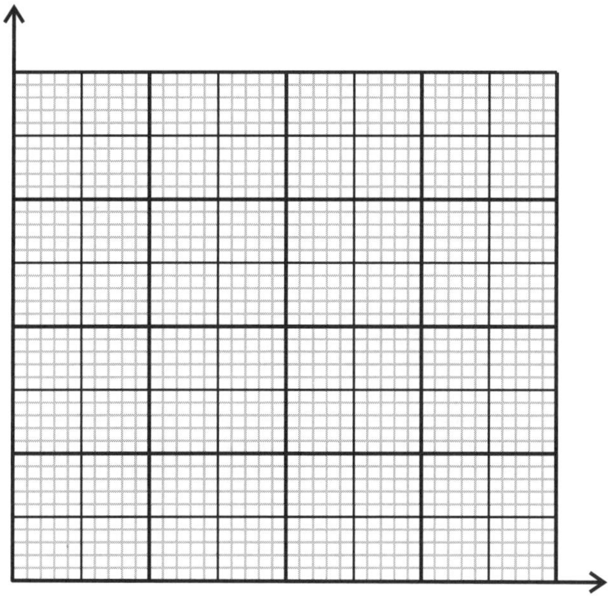

(6)

10.4 Use your knowledge of Faraday's Law and the equation for a straight line graph ($y = mx + c$) to determine the rate of change of flux during this experiment. No units are required. (4)

10.5 Define a diode. (2)

10.6 The output current from the AC generator is passed through a full wave bridge rectifier consisting of 4 diodes. On separate axes, draw a sketch graph of the input current against time from the generator and output current against time for the rectifier. Assume the coil starts in position shown in the diagram above and does two full rotations. (4)

[14]

TOC 1 Data Sheet 2 Definitions 3 3 solutions 4 4 solutions 5 5 solutions 6 6 solutions 7 7 solutions 8 8 solutions 9 9 solutions 10 10 solutions

Question 11 (Solutions on page 422)

A thick copper wire is secured on top of an insulating stand on top of a mass balance. The wire is situated perpendicularly between the poles of two magnets with a flux density *B*. As current is increased in the source the reading on the mass balance increases.
The table below shows the results of the experiment as current is increased.

I (A)	Δm (kg)	Force (N)
0,5	0,25	
1,0	0,40	
1,5	0,70	
2,0	1,00	
2,5	1,10	
3,0	1,40	

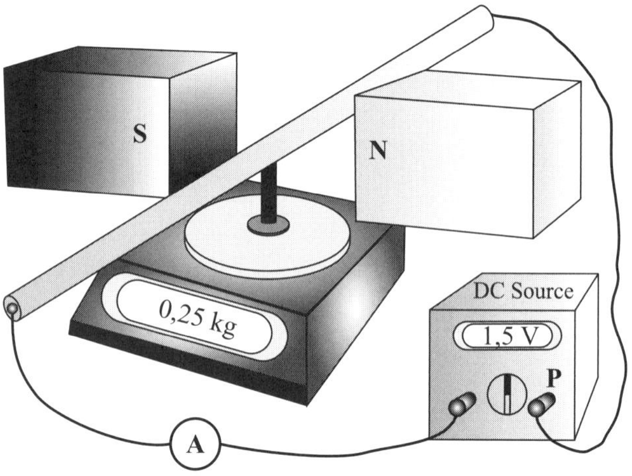

11.1 Is the polarity of terminal P positive or negative? (2)

11.2 State the independent variable. (2)

11.3 Why is the change in mass recorded as opposed to the mass balance reading? (1)

11.4 Fill in the missing values in the column for force experienced by the conductor. (3)

11.5 On the grid below plot a graph of force versus current.

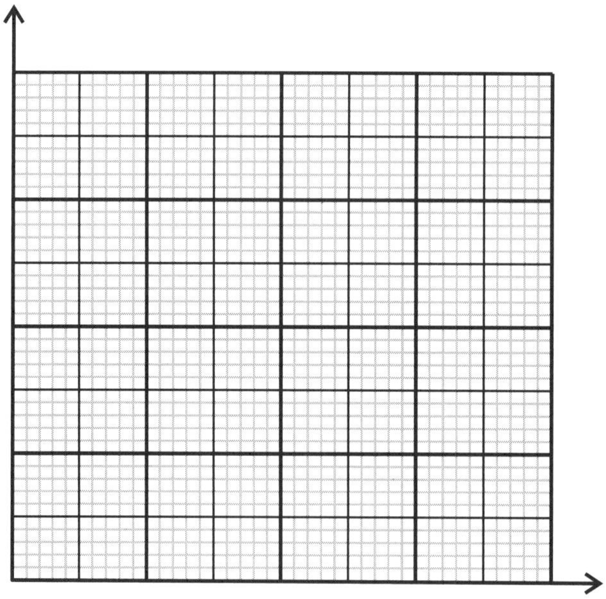

(6)

11.6 Determine the gradient of the graph. Include units in your answer. (4)

11.7 The length of the conductor between the magnets is 2,2 cm. Using your knowledge of the equation $F = IlB\sin\theta$ and the fact that the equation $y = mx + c$ describes the equation of a straight line to determine the magnetic field strength of the magnet. (4)

[17]

Question 12 (Solutions on page 422)

The device illustrated alongside represents an electric motor.

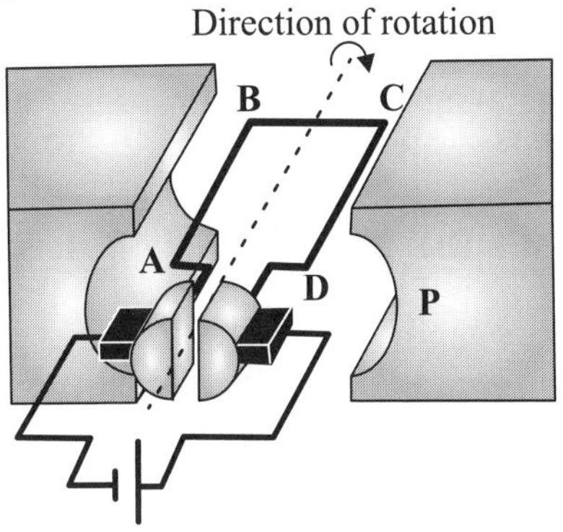

12.1 State Faraday's Law (2)

12.2 What type of energy transformation occurs in the motor? (1)

12.3 State the polarity of the magnet at pole P. (1)

12.4 Describe the function of the split ring commutator in the motor. (2)

12.5 Name two ways in which the turning force of the armature can be increased. (2)

[8]

Question 13 (Solutions on page 423)

The diagram below shows a simplified sketch of how power is delivered to homes from a power station.

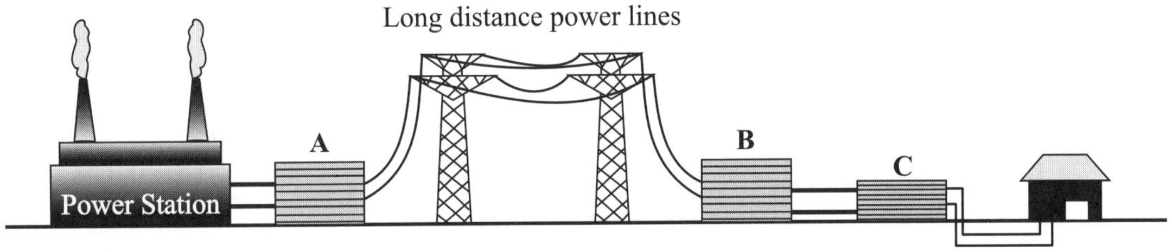

13.1 A, B and C are transformers. For each transformer, state whether the transformer is a step up or step down transformer. (3)

13.2 Why are transformers necessary in the national grid delivering power to our homes? Use an appropriate equation to support your answer. (3)

13.3 Name the principle which transformers operate on. (1)

The South African grid supplies a voltage of 230V. America's electricity grid supplies a voltage of 110V. You wish to import an appliance from America. You build the transformer below to supply your appliance with electricity in South Africa.

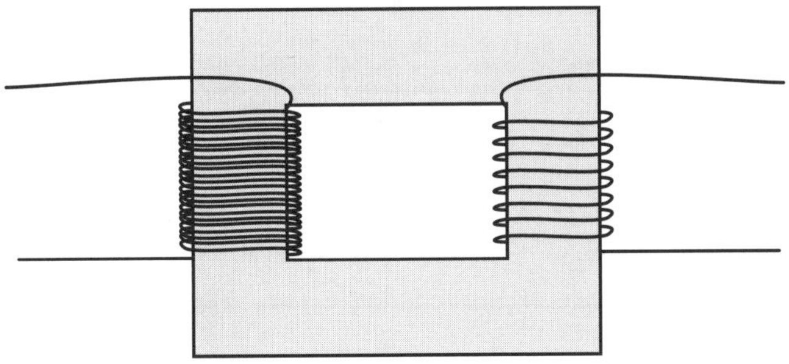

13.4 What type of transformer is shown above? (1)

13.5 If the primary coil has 23 000 turns in the coil, calculate the number of turns in the secondary coil. (3)

13.6 If your appliance is rated at 345W, what current is flowing in the primary coil? (4)

[15]

TOC | 1 Data Sheet | 2 Definitions | 3 | 3 solutions | 4 | 4 solutions | 5 | 5 solutions | 6 | 6 solutions | 7 | 7 solutions | 8 | 8 solutions | 9 | 9 solutions | 10 | 10 solutions

Question 14 (Solutions on page 423)

Nolo wishes to run her geyser using a smart switch to save electricity. The smart switch connects to WI-FI and enables Nolo to switch her geyser on and off using an application on her phone. After some investigation Nolo finds that her geyser is rated at 3,5kW. The switch has the following information printed on it:

WI-FI:	**2.4GHz 802.11 b/g/n**
Input:	**AC 100-240V 50/60Hz 15A** **DC 0-24V 15A**
Output:	**AC 100-240V 50/60Hz 15A** **DC 0-24V 15A**

14.1 Using relevant calculations explain why it would not be safe for Nolo to use the smart switch with her geyser. She plans to use the switch in South Africa where the electricity supply is 230V at 50Hz. (4)

Being a physical science learner, Nolo knows it would not be safe to use the smart switch with the geyser. Instead, she constructs the relay circuit below to isolate the smart switch from the higher voltage AC supply. The relay circuit uses a solenoid with an iron core inside of it.

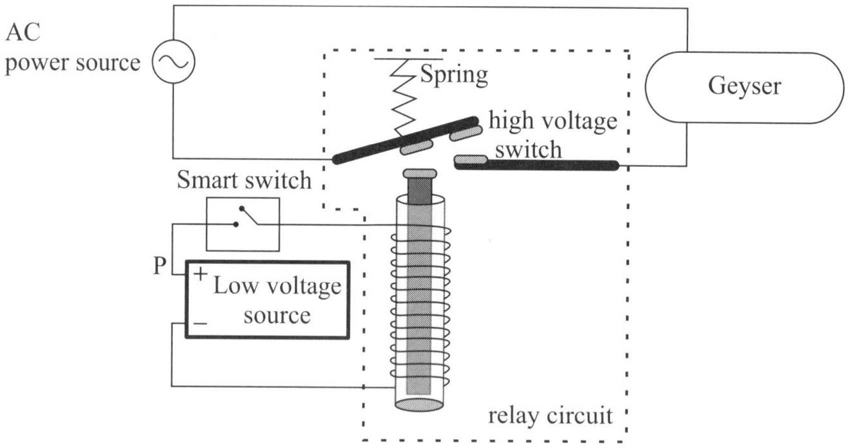

14.2 State Lenz's law (2)

14.3 The relay circuit Nolo designs is energised when the smart switch is closed. Explain using physics principles how the relay circuit functions to isolate the smart switch. (5)

14.4 Is the low voltage power source an AC or DC source? Explain your answer. (3)

[14]

Question 15 (Solutions on page 423)

A square coil of wire consisting of 20 turns passes at a constant speed into, through and out of a magnetic field as shown in the diagram below.

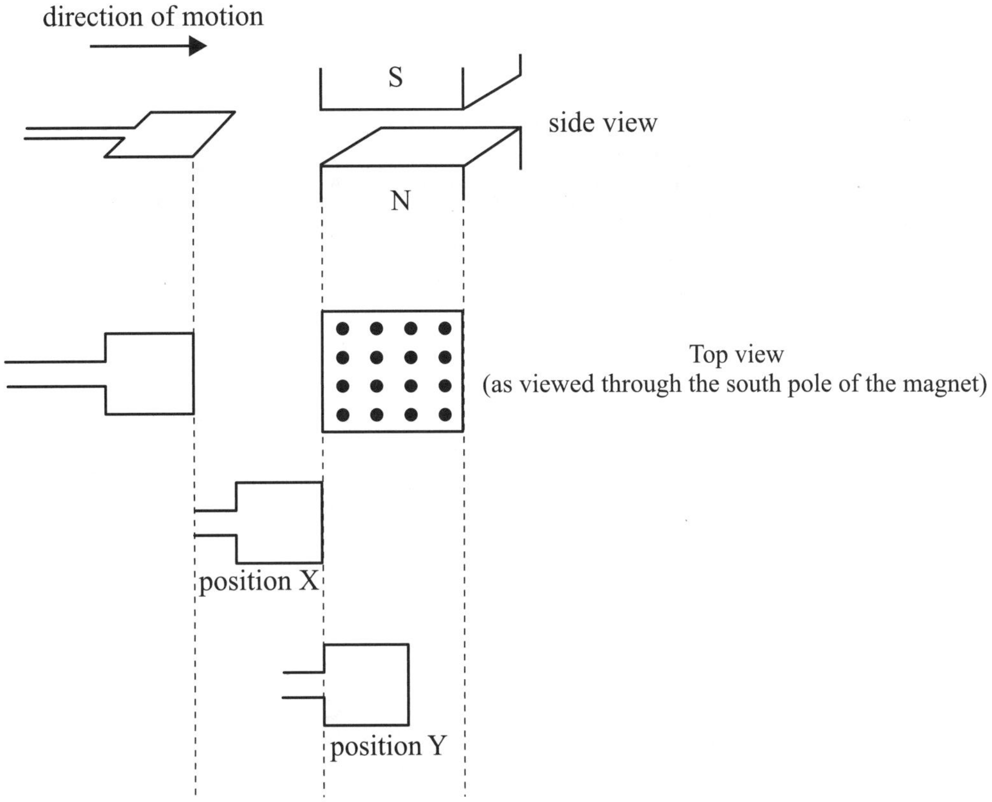

The maximum EMF induced in the coil is 5V. Sketch the EMF induced in the loop as it passes into, through and out of the magnetic field. You do not need to include values on the axes.

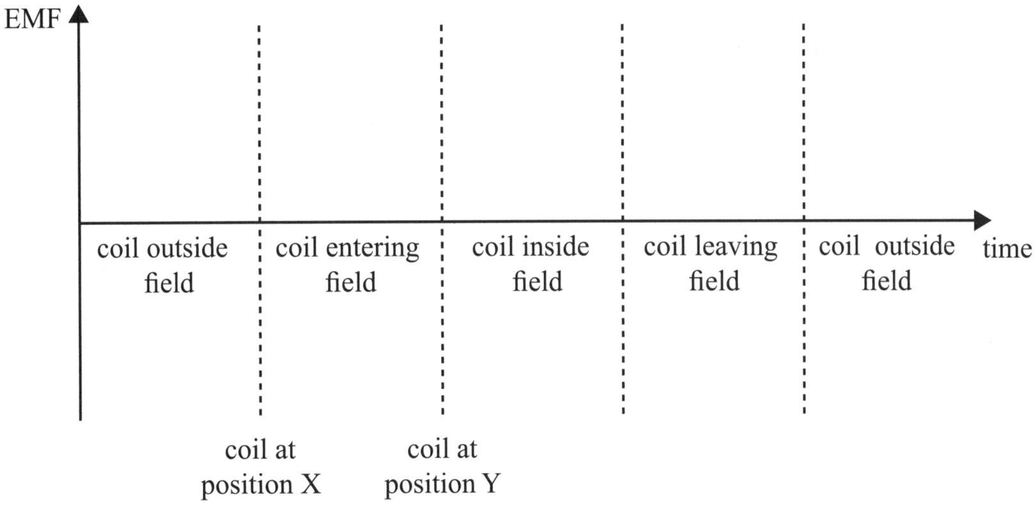

[8]

Question 16 (2008 IEB Final Examination) (Solutions on page 424)

We will remember 2008 as the year of darkness, or if you prefer, the start of the big power crisis. Load shedding was a frequent occurrence, and the sales of generators went sky high. Every day brought a joke or two on load shedding and ESKOM, until the daily papers begged people to stop targeting ESKOM. Perhaps one of the best cartoons of the year was the following:

[redacted]

This cartoon was sponsored by ESKOM

[Source: *The Star*]

A simple generator consists of a coil turning in a magnetic field. The magnetic field is produced by permanent magnets. Look at the diagram.

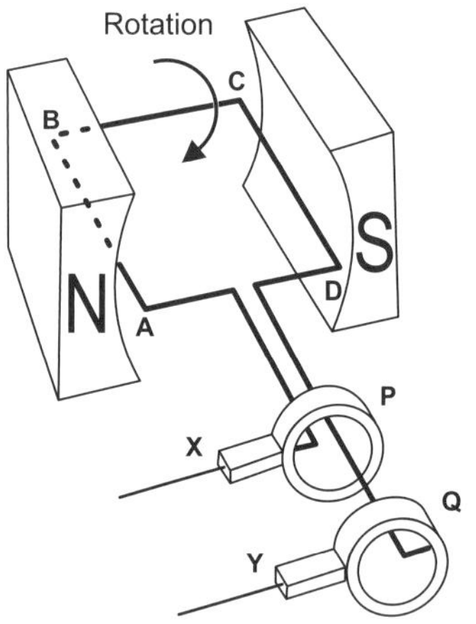

Answer the following questions:

16.1 When a conductor moves in a magnetic field, an emf is induced in the conductor. What is this phenomenon called? (1)

16.2 What energy transfers take place in the generator? (1)

16.3 Name components P and Q. (1)

16.4 What is the function of components P and Q? (1)

16.5 Name components X and Y. (1)

16.6 What is the function of components X and Y? (1)

The following diagrams show the rotation of the coil in the magnetic field.

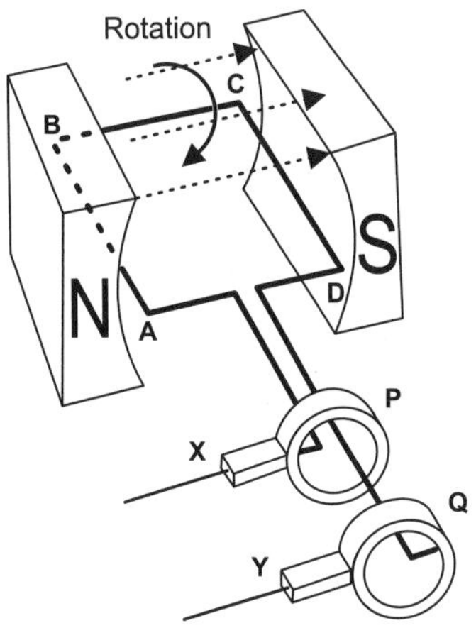

Diagram 1
Start of cycle

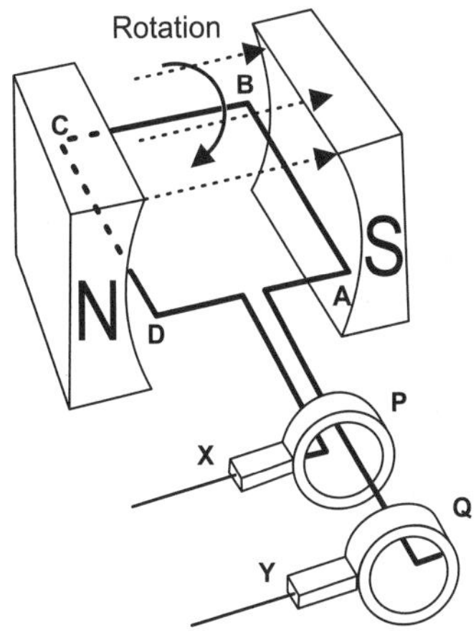

Diagram 2
$\frac{1}{2}$ cycle

The coil is turned mechanically in a clockwise direction, i.e. AB starts moving upwards from the horizontal and CD starts moving downwards (as shown in Diagram 1).

After a $\frac{1}{4}$ cycle the coil has turned through 90°. AB will now be at the top and CD at the bottom (the coil is vertical).

After $\frac{1}{2}$ cycle, AB will now be on the right-hand side and CD on the left-hand side (the coil is horizontal), as shown in Diagram 2.

16.7 The following table shows the position and motion for one complete cycle of the coil, starting with AB on the left-hand side, moving up. Write only the number of the question and the missing value to complete the table. (6)

Position of coil	Motion of Part AB of coil	Magnitude of Current (max or zero)	Direction of current (ABCD or DCBA)
horizontal	moving up, cutting field lines	16.7.1	16.7.2
vertical	parallel to field lines, moving to the right	16.7.3	
horizontal	moving down, cutting field lines	16.7.4	16.7.5
vertical	parallel to field lines, moving to the left		16.7.6
horizontal	moving up, cutting field lines	16.7.7	

16.8 Use the axes below to answer the questions which follow.

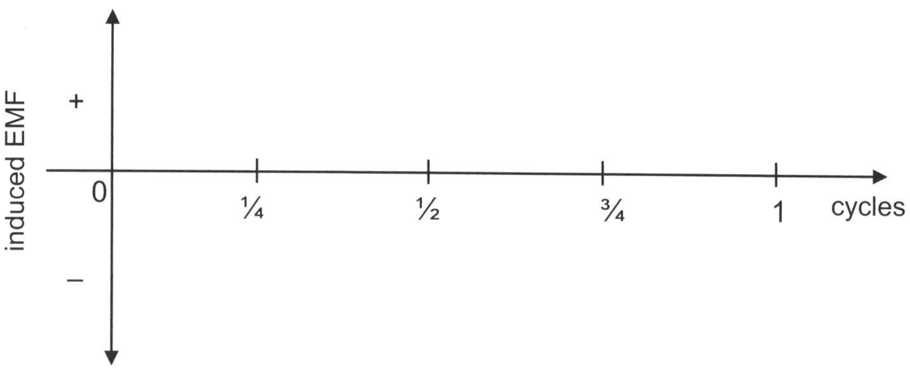

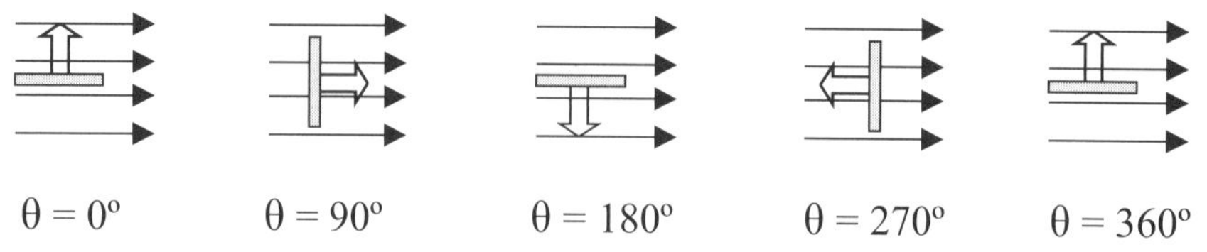

The group of arrows indicates the direction of the magnetic field and the block arrow indicates the direction of motion of AB of the coil. The angle θ indicates the angle through which section AB has turned.

16.8.1 Draw the graph of the induced emf for one complete cycle of section **AB** of the coil, when **AB** starts from the horizontal position. (4)

16.8.2 **On the same set of axes** (as used in 16.8.1) draw the graph of the induced EMF in section **AB** of the coil when the coil is rotated at half its original speed. (4)

[20]

Question 17 (2009 IEB Final Examination) (Solutions on page 424 and 425)

17.1 Asiya and Amy conduct an investigation to help them understand electromagnets. They know that magnetic fields are produced by current-carrying conductors. They started their investigation by studying the following arrangements of coiled conductors.

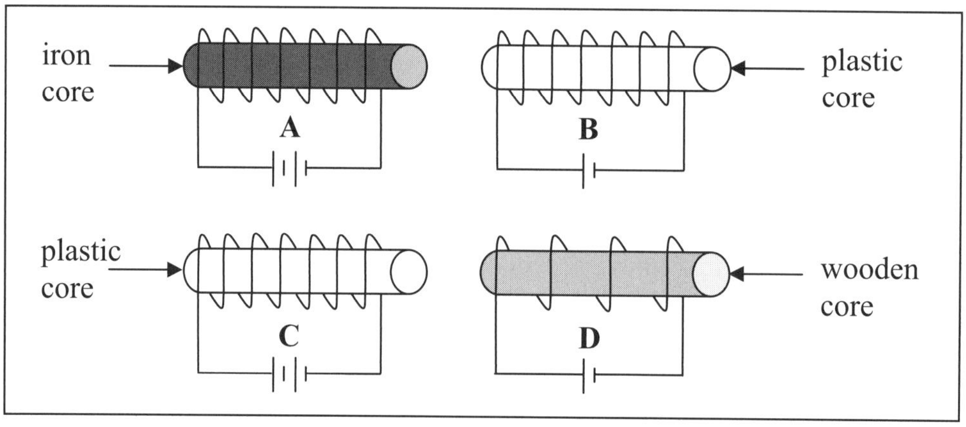

17.1.1 The girls try to predict which arrangement would produce the greatest magnetic field. Make your own prediction and list the arrangements, by writing the appropriate letter, in order from the strongest magnetic field to the weakest magnetic field. (4)

17.1.2 Formulate a hypothesis for an investigation on the effect of the core material on the performance of the electromagnet. (3)

Asiya and Amy are now ready to start experimenting in a more formal manner. They connect each of the electromagnets, A, B, C and D (as on the previous page) to compare the relative strengths of the magnetic fields.

17.1.3 Suggest a method that can be used to compare the relative strengths of the magnetic fields. (2)

Using their method suggested in 17.1.3, they claim that they will be able to determine which material is the best to use for the core of the electromagnet.

17.1.4 What is the independent variable for their experiment? (1)

17.1.5 What is the dependent variable for their experiment? (1)

17.1.6 Would this experiment enable the girls to determine which material is the best to use for the core of the electromagnet? Justify your answer. (5)

17.1.7 Suggest two improvements that can be made to the girls' arrangement of coiled conductors. (2)

17.2 The girls also know that a changing magnetic field can induce an emf in a coil of wire. They experiment with the apparatus below:

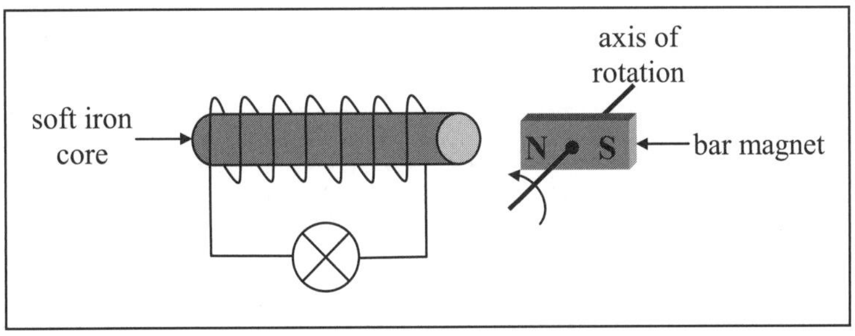

The bar magnet is rotated anti-clockwise, by turning a handle. When the bar magnet rotates, the bulb that is connected to the coil glows. The magnet takes 0,5 s to complete 1 revolution.

17.2.1 Explain why an emf is induced in the coil when the magnet rotates. (4)

17.2.2 Sketch a graph to show how the induced emf varies with time. Provide a suitable scale along the time axis. Let the position of the magnet as shown above correspond with t = 0 s. (3)

17.2.3 State two changes that can be made to this apparatus that will increase the brightness of the bulb. (2)

[27]

Question 18 (2011 IEB Final Examination) (Solutions on page 425)

Mike and Sue have a camping fridge which requires a 24 V d.c. power source. Two 12 V car batteries can be used to provide the required voltage.

18.1 How should the batteries be connected to each other in order to provide the 24 V required by the fridge? (1)

18.2 When the batteries are connected correctly the fridge draws a current of 6 A. Calculate the power input to the fridge. Ignore the internal resistance of the batteries. (3)

18.3 The fridge can also be connected via a transformer and rectifier to a 240 V AC source as shown in the simplified flow chart in Diagram 1 below.

Diagram 1: Flow chart to show how voltage is changed from 240 V AC to 24 V DC

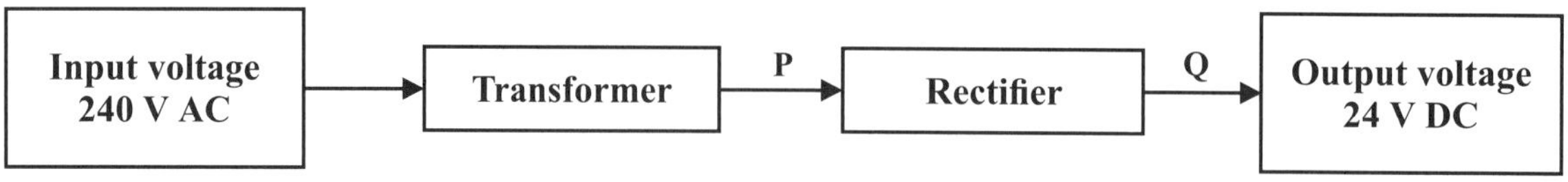

The rectifier consists of a combination of diodes connected as shown in Diagram 2.

Diagram 2: Arrangement of diodes in rectifier

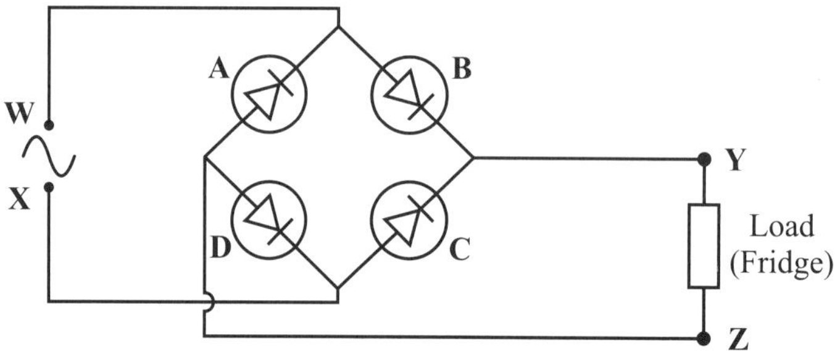

18.3.1 Define a diode. (2)

18.3.2 What is the function of the rectifier? (2)

18.3.3 Describe the path taken by conventional current in the circuit shown in Diagram 2 **when W is positive**. Indicate which diodes (A, B, C, D) the current passes through and the direction of the current through the load (Y to Z or Z to Y). (3)

18.3.4 What type of transformer (step-up or step-down) is required in Diagram 1? (1)

18.3.5 Ignoring actual values of emf and time, draw sketch graphs to represent the change in emf with time

a) immediately **before** the current passes through the rectifier (position P on Diagram 1) and

b) immediately **after** the current passes through the rectifier (position Q on Diagram 1) (4)

[16]

Question 19 (2011 IEB Final Examination) (Solutions on page 425 and 426)

Natalie has a kinetic torch which she finds very useful when she goes camping as it produces electricity when it is shaken. When she shakes the torch a magnet moves back and forth through a hollow solenoid that is connected via a simple circuit to an LED.

She decides to conduct an experiment to determine how the speed at which a magnet moves through a solenoid affects the emf induced across the ends of the solenoid. She makes use of apparatus available in her school science laboratory and follows the method outlined below.

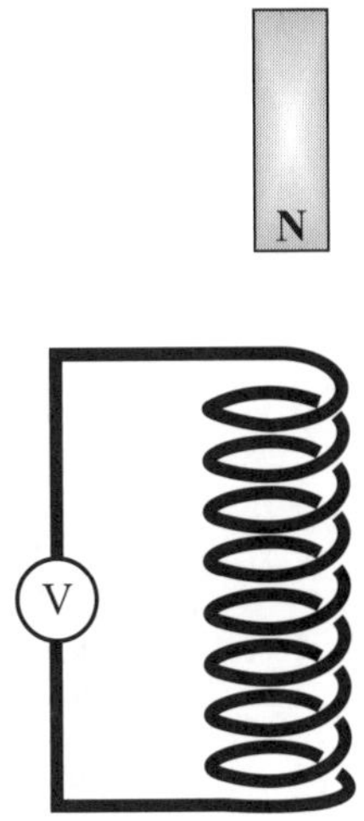

Method

1. Set up the apparatus as shown in the diagram alongside.
2. Release the magnet from a height of 5 cm above the top of the solenoid so that it falls through the centre of the solenoid.
3. Record the maximum induced emf as the magnet enters the solenoid.
4. Repeat steps 1 to 3 dropping the magnet from heights of 10 cm, 15 cm, 20 cm and 25 cm respectively above the top of the solenoid.
5. Calculate the speed of the magnet on entry to the solenoid.

Table to show the magnitude of the maximum induced emf on entry, for a magnet falling through a solenoid at different speeds.

Height (m)	Entry Speed (m.s^{-1})	Maximum induced EMF on entry (V)
0,05	1,00	0,27
0,10	1,41	0,39
0,15	1,73	0,46
0,20	2,00	0,53
0,25	2,23	0,60

19.1 On the **diagram on the next page,** use clear arrows to mark the direction of the current induced in the solenoid as the magnet enters. (2)

19.2 On the **graph paper on the next page,** plot a graph of maximum induced emf on entry against entry speed for the magnet falling through the solenoid. (7)

19.3 Use your graph to determine the maximum induced emf on entry when the magnet enters the solenoid at a speed of 1,30 m.s^{-1}. (2)

19.4 What can you conclude about the relationship between the entry speed of the magnet and the maximum induced EMF? (2)

19.5 Suggest **two** changes that could be made to the design of the kinetic torch to produce a larger EMF. (4)

[17]

TOC 1 Data Sheet 2 Definitions 3 3 solutions 4 4 solutions 5 5 solutions 6 6 solutions 7 7 solutions 8 8 solutions 9 9 solutions 10 10 solutions

19.1

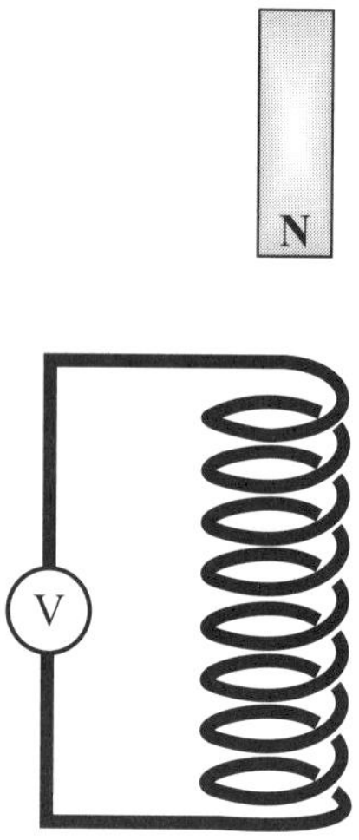

19.2

Graph of maximum induced emf on entry against entry speed for the magnet falling through the solenoid

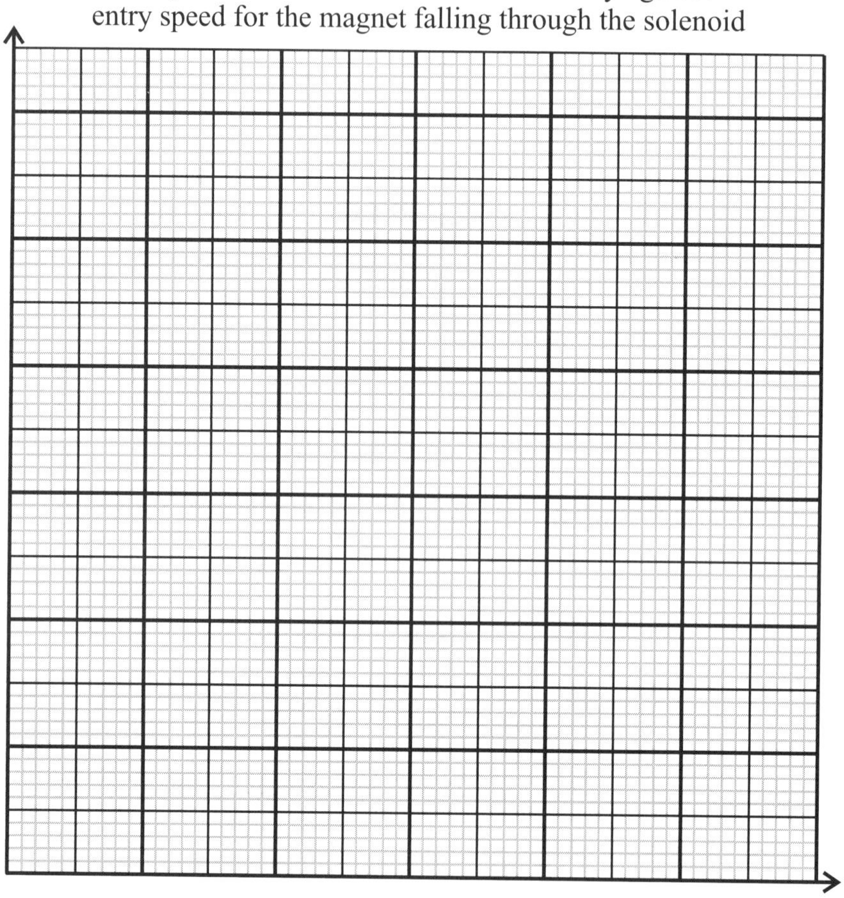

Question 20 (2013 IEB Final Examination) (Solutions on page 426)

Tawanda makes a small wind generator as shown in the diagram below. The plastic blades catch the wind which causes the spindle and magnet to turn. Below the magnet is a copper coil of wire wound around a soft iron rod and attached to a light emitting diode.

Diagram NOT drawn to scale.

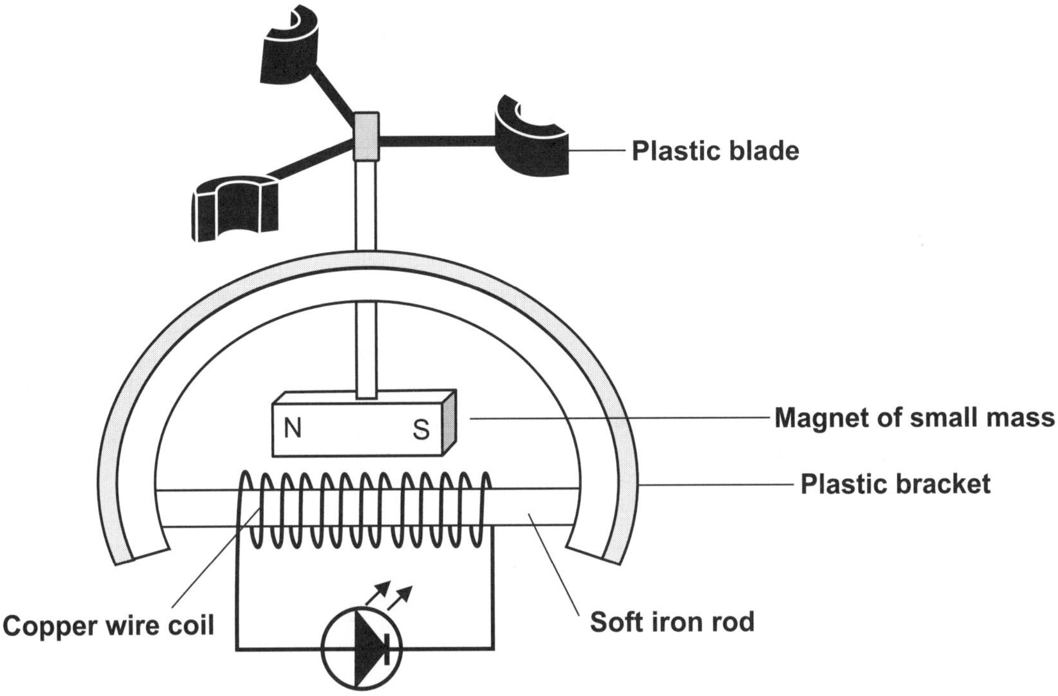

Tawanda makes the following observations:

- As the magnet turns the LED flashes on and off regardless of the speed of rotation.
- When the LED is replaced with a small filament globe,
  - the globe shines brighter when the magnet spins faster.
  - when the magnet rotates fast enough the bulb glows continuously.

20.1 State the energy conversions that take place in this generator. (2)

20.2 Explain why an emf is induced in the coil when the magnet rotates. (2)

20.3 Explain why the LED flashes on and off, regardless of the speed of rotation of the magnet. (4)

20.4 Use Faraday's Law of Electromagnetic Induction to explain why the globe is brighter when the magnet turns faster. (4)

20.5 What is the advantage of using a magnet of **small mass** rather than a **heavy** magnet? (2)

20.6 Suggest TWO more design changes that Tawanda could make to his generator that would cause it to produce a greater emf, other than changing the mass of the magnet. (2)

20.7 Why are wind turbines considered an unreliable source of power generation? (1)

[17]

TOC 1 Data Sheet 2 Definitions 3 3 solutions 4 4 solutions 5 5 solutions 6 6 solutions 7 7 solutions 8 8 solutions 9 9 solutions 10 10 solutions

Question 21 (2014 Exemplar Examination) (Solutions on page 427)

Lauren and Tayla read in their textbook, "a force acts on a current carrying conductor placed in a magnetic field". They decide to carry out an investigation to determine the relationship between the current in the wire and the magnitude of the force experienced.

They set up the following apparatus. Two magnets with their opposite poles facing each other were placed on a scale. A stiff piece of copper wire was **fixed in position** between the poles of the magnets (as shown in the diagram below).

The girls altered the current in the wire and noticed that the scale reading changed. They recorded their results in a table.

Current (A)	Scale Reading (N)	Change in scale reading (mN)
0,0	2,080	0
0,5	2,163	83
1,0	2,338	175
1,5	2,606	268
2,0	2,947	341
2,5	3,382	435
3,0	3,908	526

21.1 Draw a sketch showing the magnetic field around a straight, current carrying conductor. Represent the current as flowing into the page. (2)

21.2 State the independent variable. (1)

21.3 The reading on the scale increases as the current increases. Explain the **origin** of the force being measured. (2)

21.4 Does the current flow 'into the page' or 'out of the page' in the diagram above? Explain your answer. (3)

21.5 Plot a graph of **change in scale reading** in mN against **current** in A.

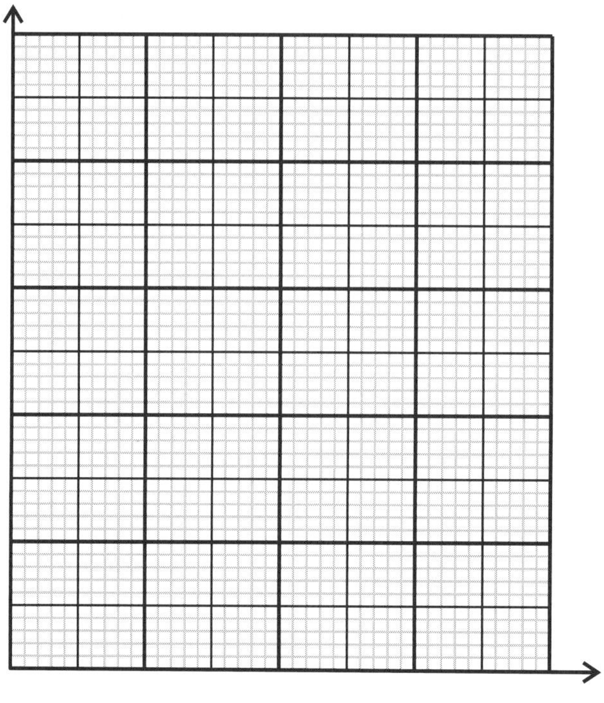

(7)

21.6 Describe the relationship between the force on the wire and the current in the wire. Which features of the graph lead you to your conclusion? (3)

21.7 Why was it more appropriate to plot the change in the scale reading rather than the scale reading itself? (2)

[20]

Question 22 (2014 IEB Supplementary Examination) (Solutions on page 427 and 428)

22.1 The diagram below represents a simplified sketch of a DC electric motor.

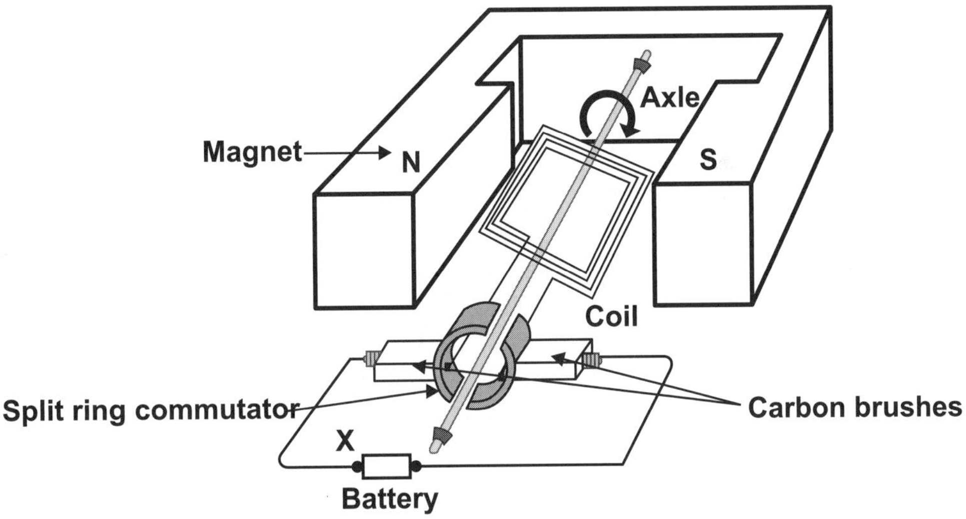

22.1.1 The coil rotates in a clockwise direction as indicated by the solid black arrow. What is the polarity (positive or negative) of the pole of the battery labelled X? (2)

22.1.2 Describe the energy conversion that takes place in the electric motor. (2)

22.1.3 Electric motors have had a great impact on society. Name TWO devices that use electric motors. (2)

22.1.4 The simplified graph below shows the changes in torque (turning force) with time for one complete cycle of rotation of the DC motor shown in the diagram.

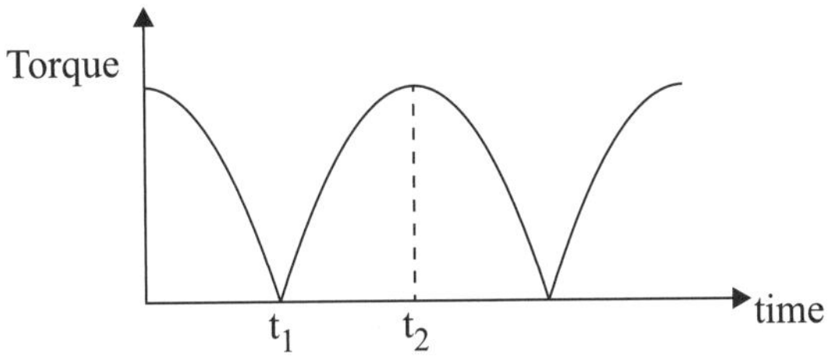

Give the orientation of the coil in the field (*vertical or horizontal*) for time

(a) t_1 (1)

(b) t_2 (1)

22.1.5 Explain why the torque (turning force) changes with time in the manner shown in the graph. (4)

22.2 The diagram below represents a simplified sketch of an AC generator.

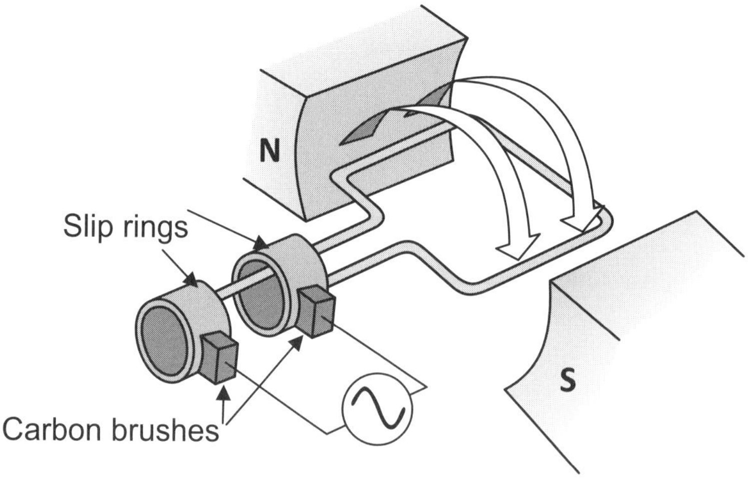

22.2.1 Give TWO structural differences between the DC motor and the AC generator. (4)

22.2.2 State *Faraday's law* of electromagnetic induction. (2)

22.2.3 State TWO ways of increasing the magnitude of the induced emf. (2)

22.2.4 The simplified sketch graph below shows the changes in induced emf with time for two complete cycles of rotation of the AC generator shown in the diagram.

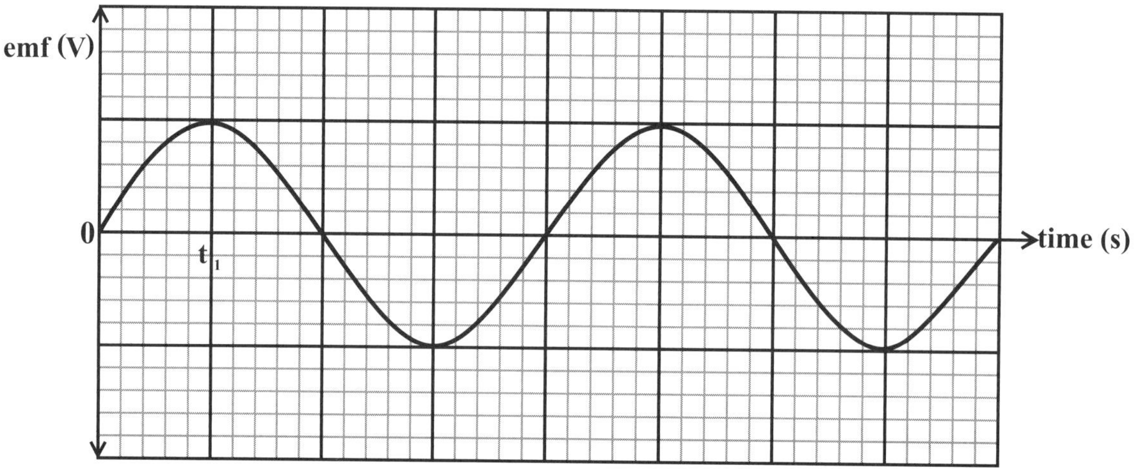

Give the orientation of the coil in the field (*vertical or horizontal*) for times

(a) 0 s (1)

(b) t_1 (1)

(c) On the above diagram, draw a graph of emf against time when the speed of rotation is halved. (4)

22.2.5 Although most of South Africa's electricity is generated by coal-fired power stations, there is a nuclear power station near Koeberg in the Western Cape.

(a) State TWO environmental advantages of the generation of electricity in nuclear power stations over coal-fired power stations. (2)

(b) State TWO environmental disadvantages of the generation of electricity in nuclear power stations. (2)

[30]

Question 23 (2015 IEB Final Examination) (Solutions on page 428)

23.1 A long straight conductor has a current directed into the page as shown.

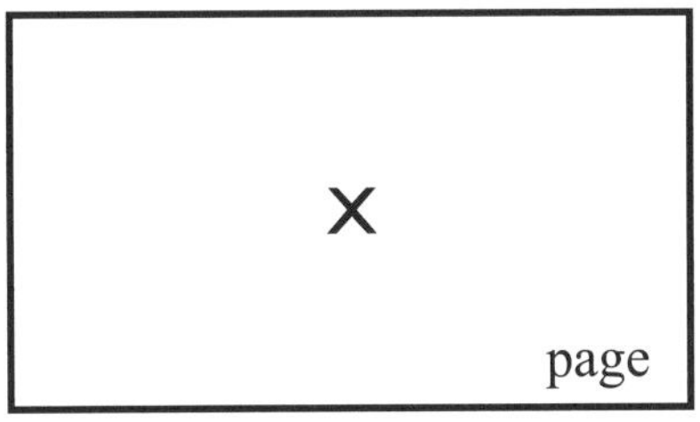

23.1.1 On the diagram above, sketch the magnetic field that is produced around the current carrying conductor. You must draw at least three magnetic field lines. (2)

23.1.2 The long, straight conductor is now placed between the poles of permanent magnets, as shown.

On the diagram above indicate:

- the magnetic field due to the permanent magnets. You must draw at least two field lines between the magnets.
- the direction of the force experienced by the conductor. Label this force, F. (4)

23.1.3 Briefly explain the origin of the force experienced by the conductor. (2)

23.1.4 How would you position the long straight conductor in a magnetic field so that it does not experience a force? (2)

23.2 An electric motor is constructed as part of an experiment by some students. A diagram of their motor with the coil in the horizontal position is shown.

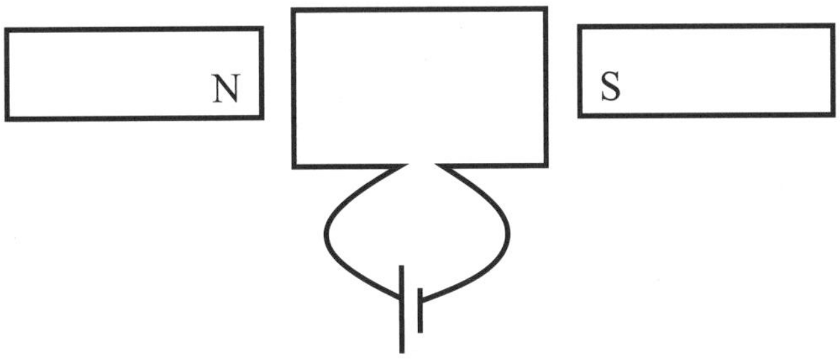

23.2.1 State the energy conversion that occurs while a motor operates. (2)

The motor initially rotates from the horizontal position shown until the coil is just past the vertical. At this position, the coil starts rotating in the opposite direction.

23.2.2 What device have the students forgotten to include in their motor? (2)

23.2.3 Explain the purpose of the forgotten device. (2)

TOC
1 Data Sheet
2 Definitions
3
3 solutions
4
4 solutions
5
5 solutions
6
6 solutions
7
7 solutions
8
8 solutions
9
9 solutions
10
10 solutions

23.3 A microphone is often used when addressing large audiences.

A simple microphone generates electricity from sound waves. The figure below shows the structure of a microphone.

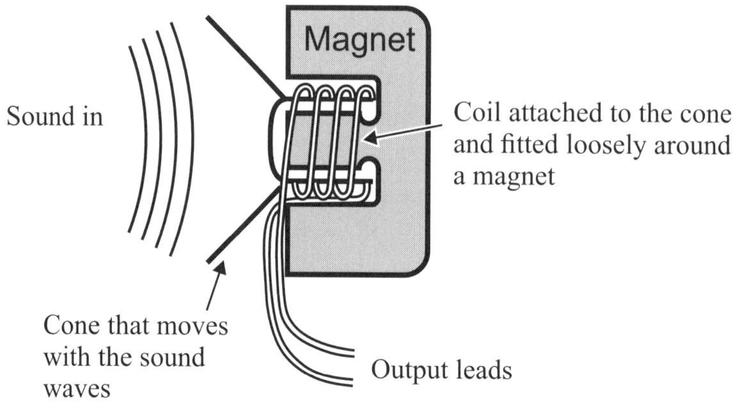

The magnet is fixed to the case inside the microphone. There is a coil that is attached to the cone. The sound waves move the cone backwards and forwards. The leads from the coil are connected to a recording device or an amplifier.

23.3.1 State Faraday's law of electromagnetic induction. (2)

23.3.2 Use the diagram above to help you explain how the microphone converts sound to voltage. Use bullet points in your explanation. (4)

[22]

Question 24 (2015 IEB Supplementary Examination) (Solutions on page 429)

The diagram below represents a simple step-up transformer. An alternating current is supplied to the primary (input) coil.

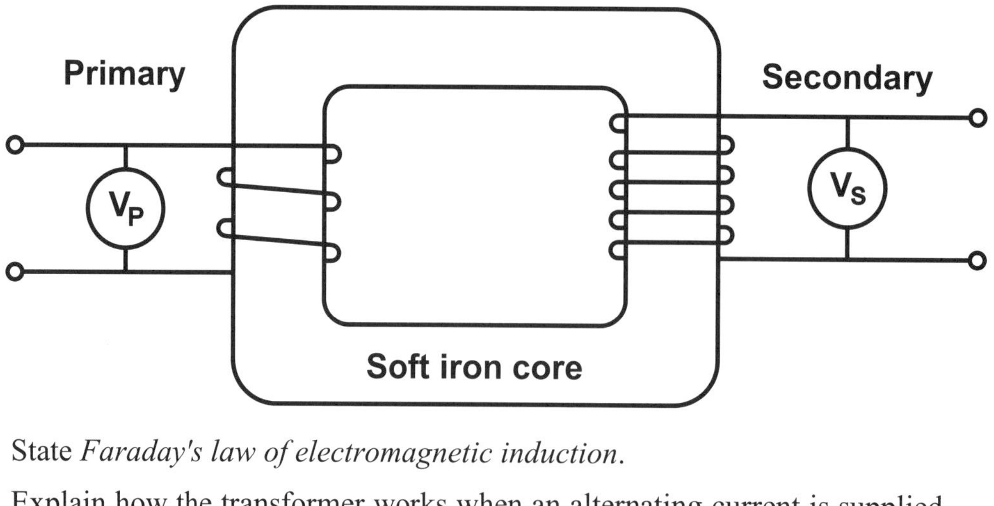

24.1 State *Faraday's law of electromagnetic induction.* (2)

24.2 Explain how the transformer works when an alternating current is supplied to the primary coil. (3)

24.3 Use the equation for Faraday's law to explain how this transformer steps **up** the voltage. (2)

$$\text{emf} = -\frac{N\Delta\phi}{\Delta t}$$

24.4 Power stations produce electricity at 25 000 V. Electricity is sent through the national grid cables at 400 000 V. Transformers are used to step-up the voltage from the power stations to the cables of the national grid.

24.4.1 If the number of turns on the primary coil is 500 then how many turns are required on the secondary coil? (3)

24.4.2 The input current to the primary coil of the transformer is 0,5 A. Calculate the current in the cables of the national grid. Assume no loss of power in the transformer. (4)

24.4.3 Use scientific principles to explain why it is an economic advantage to transmit electrical energy through the national grid at high voltages and low currents. Use a suitable formula to assist your explanation. No calculation is required. (3)

24.5 Consider the diagram below which shows five positions of the coil for one complete rotation of a simple generator. On the diagrams on the next page, draw the corresponding sketch graphs of…

24.5.1 emf (ε) vs time; and (3)

24.5.2 flux (φ) vs time. (3)

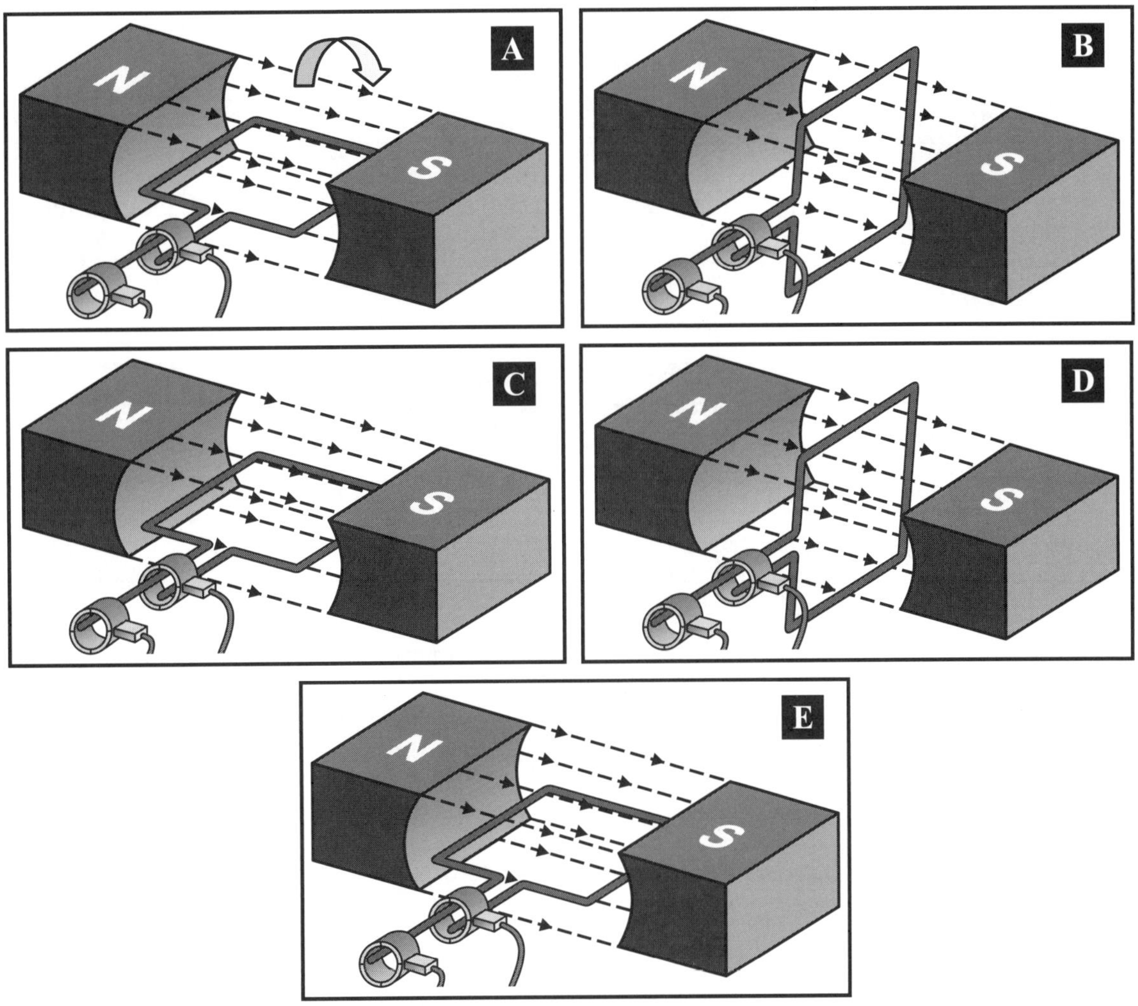

TOC
1 Data Sheet
2 Definitions
3
3 solutions
4
4 solutions
5
5 solutions
6
6 solutions
7
7 solutions
8
8 solutions
9
9 solutions
10
10 solutions

Diagrams sheet for question 24.5 below:

24.5.1

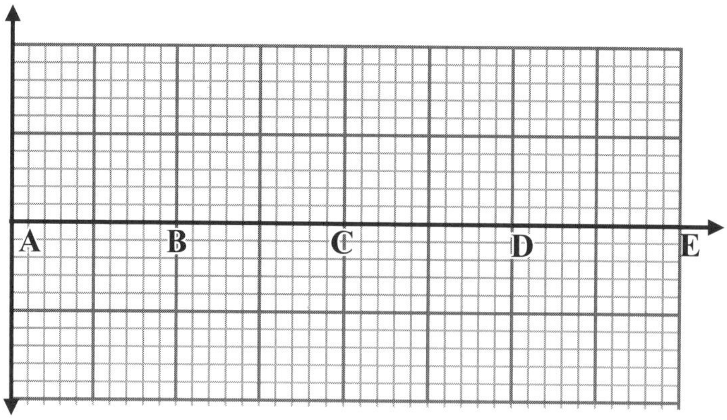

24.5.2

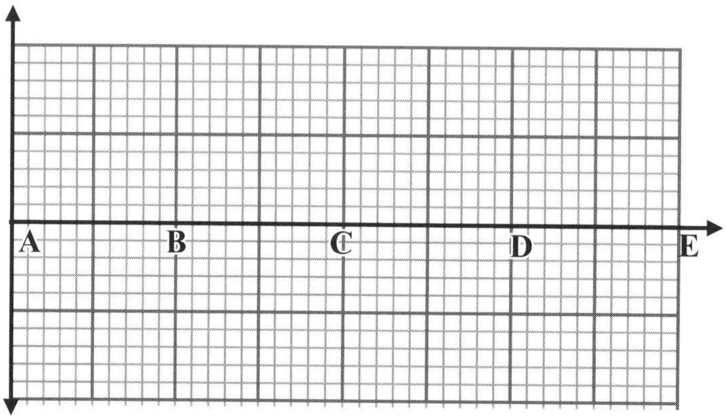

[23]

Question 25 (2016 IEB Final Examination) (Solutions on page 429 and 430)

25.1 A conductor is hanging from the ceiling on two springs in an external magnetic field. The springs and the conductor are shown in the diagram.

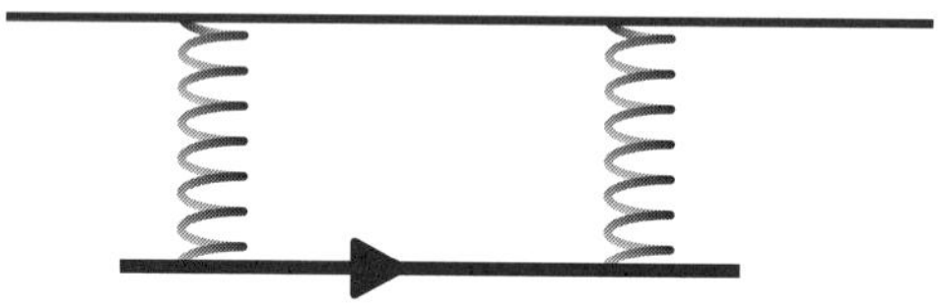

A conventional current is directed from left to right through the conductor.

25.1.1 In which direction must an external magnetic field be directed to increase the tension in the springs supporting the conductor? (2)

25.1.2 Name two factors you could adjust to increase the tension in the springs. (2)

TOC 1 Data Sheet 2 Definitions 3 3 solutions 4 4 solutions 5 5 solutions 6 6 solutions 7 7 solutions 8 8 solutions 9 9 solutions 10 10 solutions

25.2 An iron-core transformer is illustrated below.

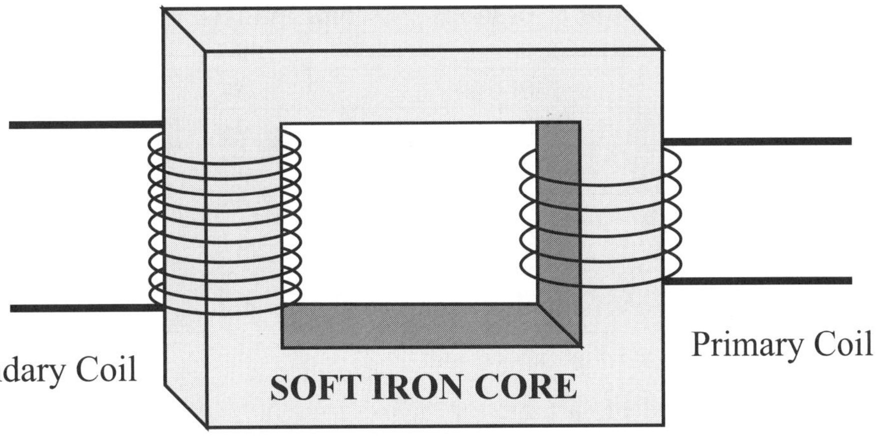

25.2.1 State Faraday's Law of electromagnetic induction. (2)

25.2.2 Explain the operation of an iron-core transformer. Use bullet points in your answer. (4)

Eskom produces electricity at a power station with a potential difference of 20 kV. This electricity is transmitted via a network of cables across the country at a potential difference of 765 kV.

25.2.3 Why does Eskom transmit energy at such a high voltage? Use a suitable equation to help you explain your answer. (4)

25.2.4 Calculate the ratio of the number of turns on the secondary coil to the number of turns on the primary coil needed to change 20 kV to 765 kV. (3)

25.2.5 Name the type of transformer used to change 20 kV to 765 kV. (2)

[19]

Question 26 (2016 IEB Supplementary Examination) (Solutions on page 430)

Two good physics students decide to conduct an experiment to determine how the magnitude of the induced emf in a homemade generator depends on the number of loops that are wound on the coil in their generator. The students set up an experiment similar to the generator in the diagram below. The students make sure that they turn the generator at the same rate for all of their experiments.

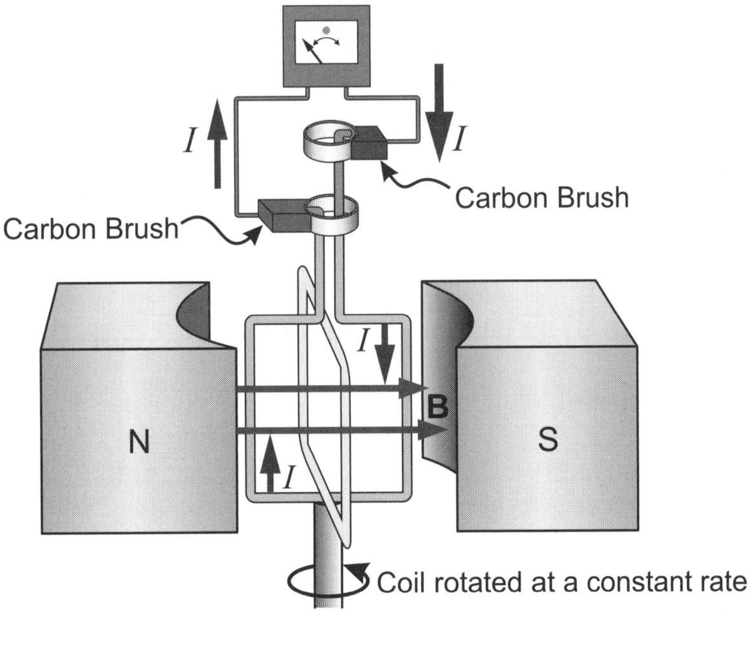

TOC | 1 Data Sheet | 2 Definitions | 3 | 3 solutions | 4 | 4 solutions | 5 | 5 solutions | 6 | 6 solutions | 7 | 7 solutions | 8 | 8 solutions | 9 | 9 solutions | 10 | 10 solutions

The results that the students obtain are recorded in the table below

Number of loops	emf induced (V)
200	0,94
300	1,54
400	1,93
500	2,55
600	3,06
700	3,47

26.1 State the energy conversion that occurs in a generator (2)

26.2 State a hypothesis for the experiment. (2)

26.3 Name the independent variable for the experiment. (2)

26.4 Name one other variable, besides the rate of rotation, which the students had to keep constant during the experiment to ensure a fair test. (2)

26.5 On the graph paper below, plot a graph of induced emf against the number of loops in the coil.

(7)

26.6 Calculate the gradient of the graph. (4)

26.7 Use your answer to Question 26.6, your knowledge that $\text{emf} = -N\dfrac{\Delta\phi}{\Delta t}$ and that the equation $y = mx + c$ describes a straight line to determine the magnitude of the rate of change of flux during the experiment. (2)

[21]

Question 27 (2017 IEB Final Examination) (Solutions on page 431)

27.1 A loudspeaker operates as a force is exerted on a current carrying conductor in a magnetic field.

The diagram below illustrates a cross-section of a simple design of a loudspeaker. It consists of a permanent magnet with a coil of wire, called the voice coil, surrounding the north pole of the magnet. When an electrical signal is sent to the voice coil, a force is experienced by the voice coil. The speaker cone is connected to the voice coil and moves with the voice coil.

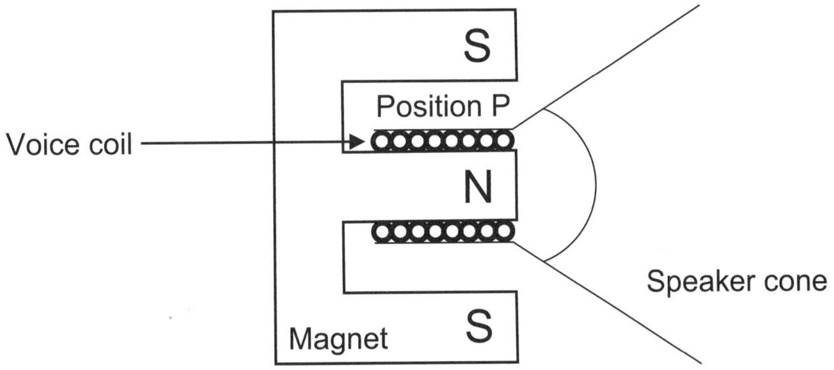

27.1.1 Use a sketch to show the direction of the magnetic field around a single current carrying conductor where the current is directed into the page. The direction of the current must also be shown. At least three field lines must be shown. (3)

27.1.2 In order for the speaker cone to move to the right in the diagram above, in which direction must the current in the coil be directed at position P? (2)

27.1.3 A loudspeaker needs the speaker cone to vibrate. How is this achieved? Briefly explain your answer in point form. (3)

27.2 The diagrams illustrate an electrical generator with a rotating coil shown in a number of different positions labelled A–E between magnetic poles.

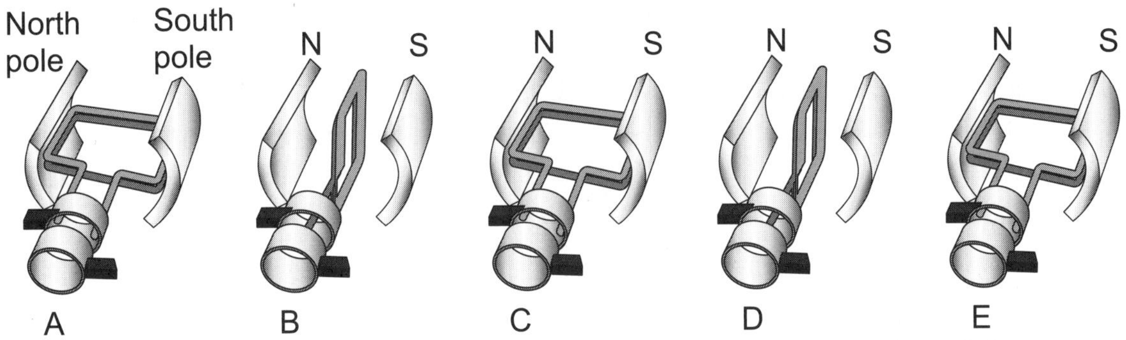

27.2.1 State the energy conversion that takes place during the operation of the generator. (2)

27.2.2 A student states that the diagrams illustrate an a.c. generator. Is this statement correct? Give a reason for your answer. (2)

27.2.3 State *Faraday's Law of electromagnetic induction.* (2)

27.2.4 Draw a sketch graph of the emf output from this generator as a function of time. Position A occurs at 0 s. Label points A–E to correspond to the diagrams. (3)

27.2.5 Briefly explain why you labelled point C in the position shown in your answer to Question 27.2.4. (2)

[19]

Question 28 (2017 IEB Supplementary Examination) (Solutions on page 431)

28.1 A student constructs an electromagnetic device as shown in the diagram. The poles of the magnets are labelled A and B.

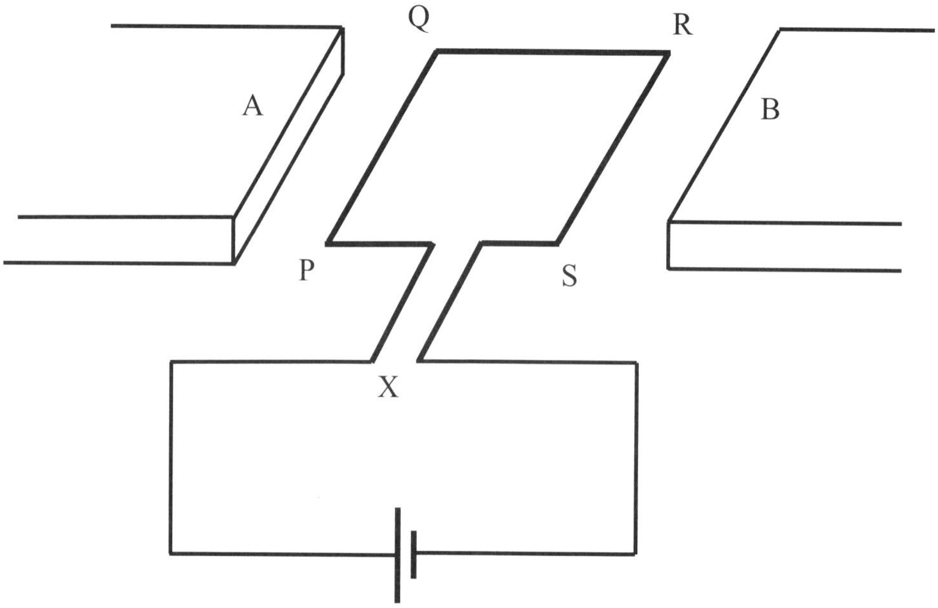

28.1.1 Is the electromagnetic device being used as a motor or a generator? Use energy considerations to motivate your answer. (2)

28.1.2 Is the direction of the conventional current in the coil PQRS or SRQP? (2)

28.1.3 When viewing the coil from position X, the coil rotates anticlockwise. Is the pole labelled A, north or south? (2)

28.1.4 When the coil reaches its vertical direction, state the direction of the force acting on side PQ. (2)

28.1.5 Does the coil rotate continuously in one direction? Briefly explain your answer. (3)

28.2 Two students, Peter and Mark, each drop a magnet from the same height. Peter simply drops the magnet, while Mark drops the magnet through a copper ring. Both students drop the magnet with the south pole facing downwards.

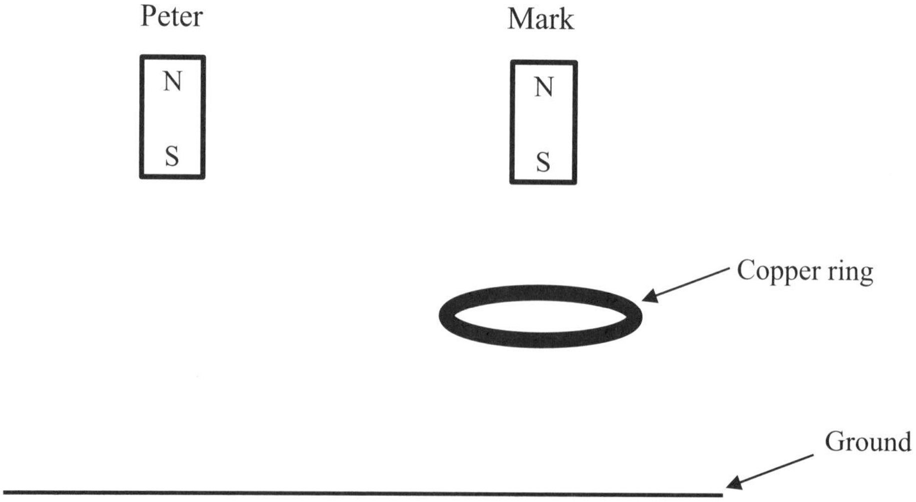

28.2.1 Describe the change in energy when Mark drops the magnet. (3)

28.2.2 State *Lenz's law.* (2)

TOC 1 Data Sheet 2 Definitions 3 3 solutions 4 4 solutions 5 5 solutions 6 6 solutions 7 7 solutions 8 8 solutions 9 9 solutions 10 10 solutions

The diagram below shows the copper ring with the magnet approaching.

28.2.3 State the direction of the current in the copper ring (clockwise or anticlockwise). (2)

28.2.4 Will the magnets reach the ground at the same time if dropped simultaneously? If not, whose magnet will reach the ground first? Explain your answer. (4)

[22]

Question 29 (2018 IEB Final Examination) (Solutions on page 431 and 432)

29.1 A current-carrying wire PQ is placed between the poles of two permanent magnets as shown in the diagram.

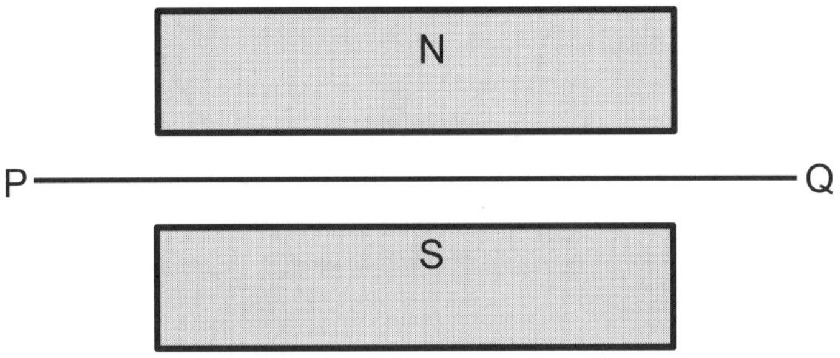

29.1.1 On the diagram above, sketch lines to show the direction of the magnetic field due to the permanent magnets. (2)

29.1.2 The force on the wire PQ is directed into the paper. Is the current direction in the wire from P to Q or from Q to P? (2)

29.2 A rectangular conducting loop travels from left to right at a constant velocity, v, through a magnetic field directed out of the page as shown in the diagrams (a)–(e).

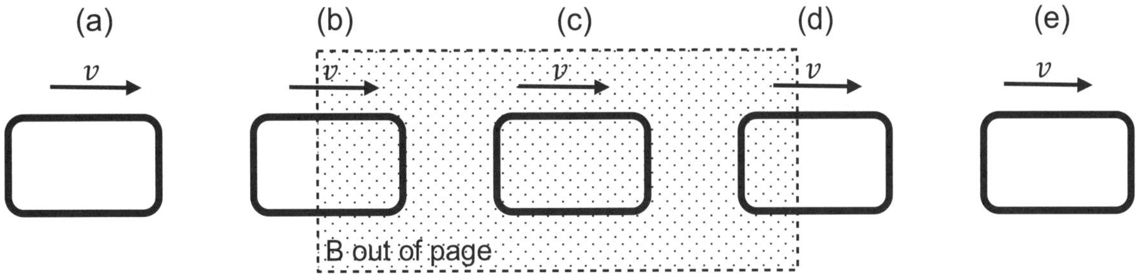

29.2.1 State *Lenz's law.* (2)

29.2.2 During the motion described:

(a) At what positions (a)–(e) is a current induced in the loop? (2)

(b) If there is a current induced in the loop, state the direction of the induced current as clockwise or anti-clockwise. (2)

29.2.3 For diagram (c) briefly explain why there is, or why there is not, an induced current in the loop. (2)

29.3 A long primary solenoid (P) has a secondary coil (S) wound around the middle as shown in the diagram.

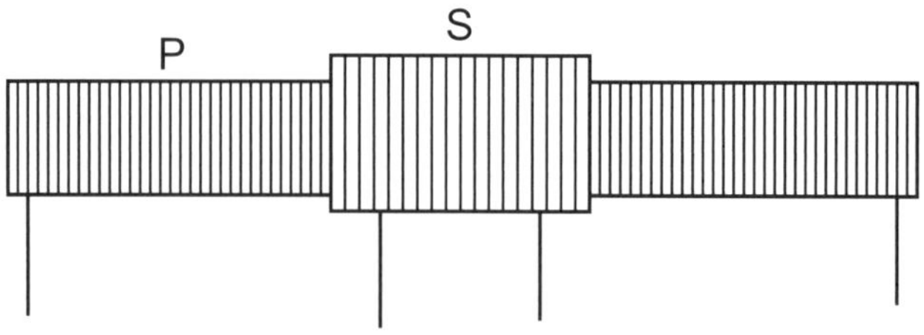

The current in the **primary solenoid** changes with time as shown on the graph below.

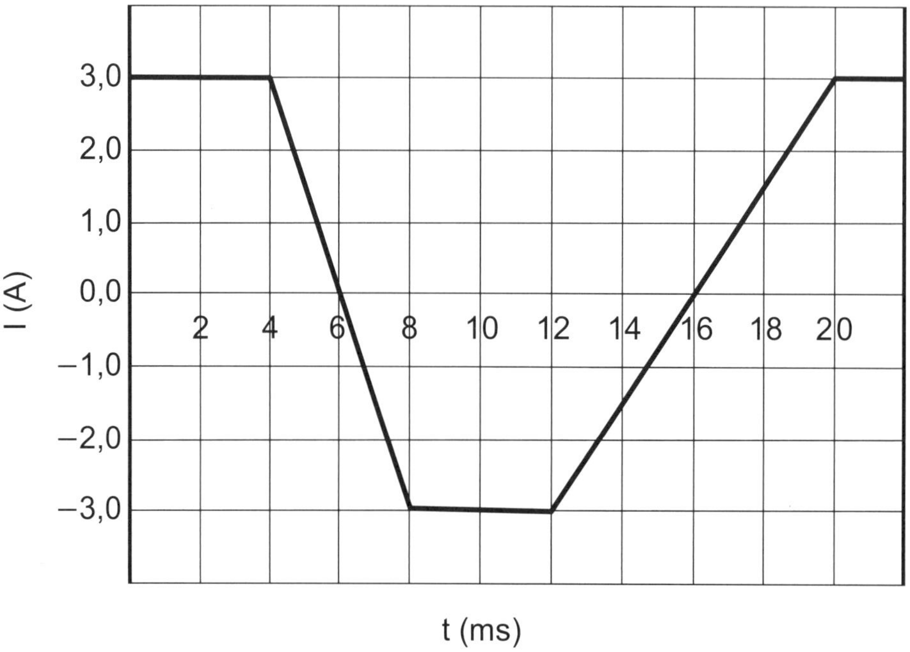

29.3.1 State *Faraday's law of electromagnetic induction.* (2)

The **maximum emf** induced in the secondary solenoid is **4 mV**.

29.3.2 On the graph provided **below**, draw the corresponding induced emf vs time graph for the **secondary coil**. The relative sizes of the emf must be included on the graph.

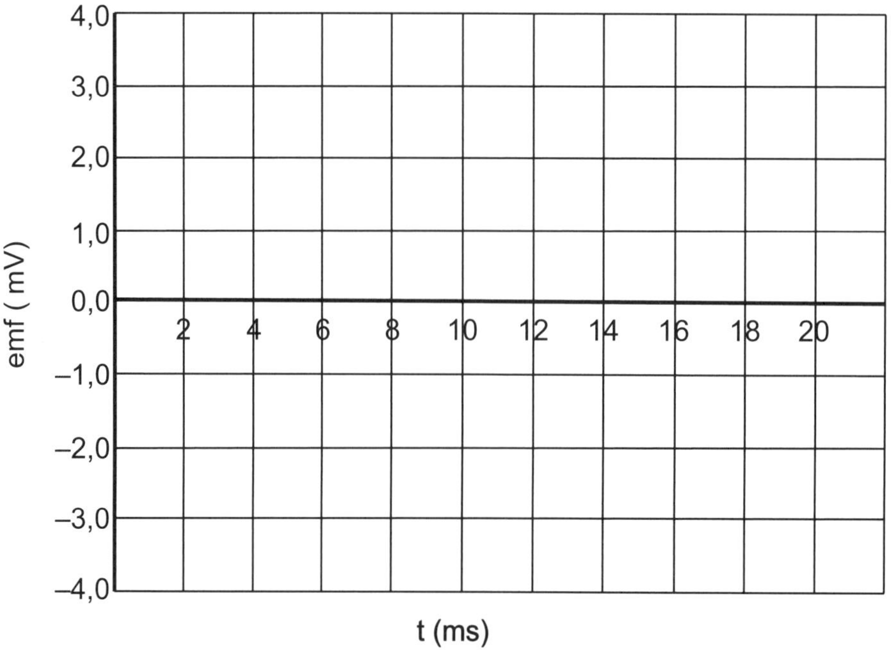

(4)

[18]

Question 30 (2018 IEB Supplementary Examination) (Solutions on page 432)

30.1 The magnetic field lines created by a current in a conductor are shown in the diagram.

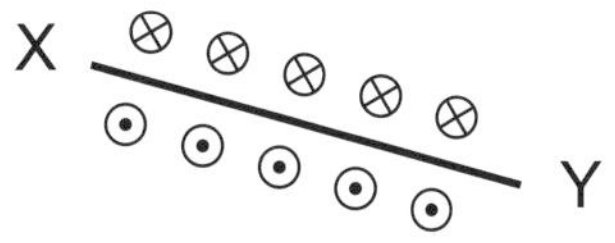

Is the conventional current direction from X to Y or Y to X? (2)

The coil and magnets illustrated in the diagram below could be part of a motor or a generator.

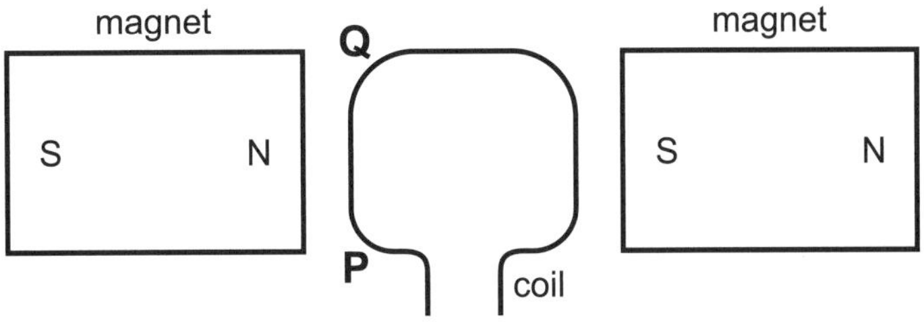

30.2 Compare the motor and generator in terms of energy conversion (2)

30.3 Consider the coil in the above diagram to be part of a motor. The current direction is from **P** to **Q** in the coil. (2)

30.3.1 In which direction would side PQ experience a force? (2)

30.3.2 How would you change two factors in order to increase the magnitude of the force exerted on side PQ? (2)

30.3.3 A current carrying conductor placed in a magnetic field will not always experience a force. Describe a situation in which a current carrying conductor in a magnetic field will not experience a force. (2)

30.4 Consider the coil to be part of a generator. (2)

30.4.1 Define *magnetic flux linkage.* (2)

30.4.2 Use Faraday's Law to explain why a current is induced in the coil as it rotated in the magnetic field. (4)

30.4.3 State *Lenz's Law.* (2)

30.4.4 As side PQ is rotated out of the page, will the current be induced from **P** to **Q** or from **Q** to **P**? (2)

[20]

TOC
1 Data Sheet
2 Definitions
3
3 solutions
4
4 solutions
5
5 solutions
6
6 solutions
7
7 solutions
8
8 solutions
9
9 solutions
10
10 solutions

Question 31 (2019 IEB Final Examination) (Solutions on page 433)

31.1 A uniform magnetic field points upwards along the plane of the paper as shown in the diagram. A wire is perpendicular to the paper. When the wire carries a current, the net magnetic field at point X is zero.

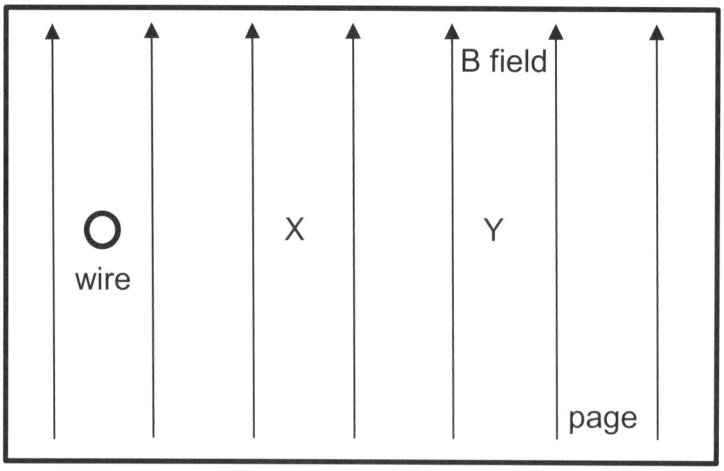

31.1.1 State the direction of the current in the wire (into or out of the page). (2)

Point Y is twice as far from the wire as point X. The magnetic field due to a current in a wire is inversely proportional to the distance from the wire.

31.1.2 Describe the net magnetic field at point Y. Be specific about the direction and magnitude relative to the uniform B field. (4)

31.2 Name two practical examples of electromagnetic induction usage. (2)

31.3 The diagram below represents a solenoid, with a current of 2 A in the direction indicated.

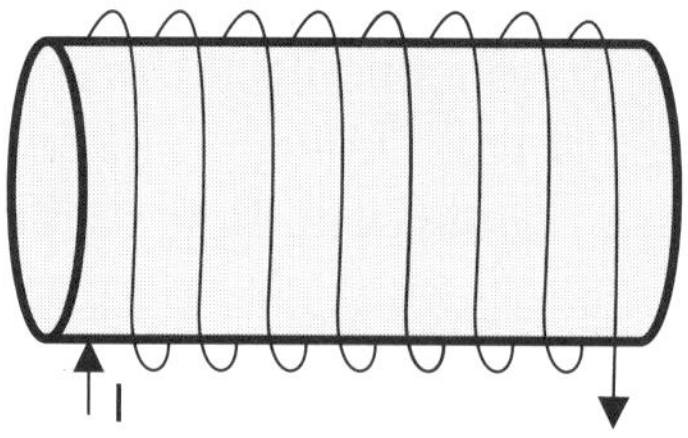

31.3.1 On the diagram **above**, sketch the magnetic field associated with the solenoid **and** indicate which end is the north pole. (3)

A small coil at rest, connected to a sensitive voltmeter is situated near the stationary solenoid as shown.

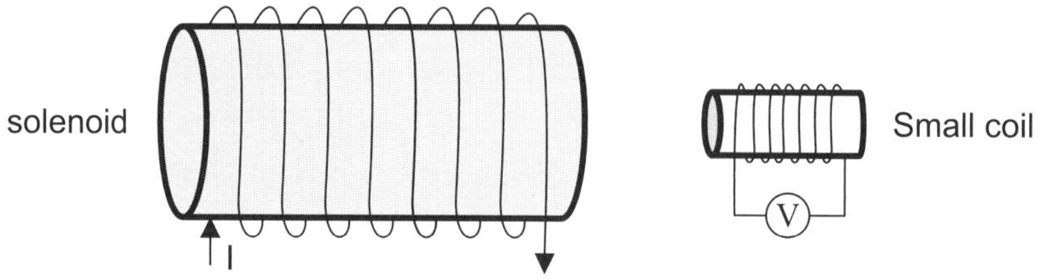

31.3.2 State *Faraday's law of electromagnetic induction.* (2)

31.3.3 Explain why the voltmeter has a zero reading. (2)

31.3.4 State **three** different ways in which an emf could be induced in the small coil. (6)

[21]

Question 32 (2019 IEB Supplementary Examination) (Solutions on page 433)

32.1 Two coils P and Q have diameters d and 2d respectively. The magnetic field in the region of P has magnitude of 1 unit and in the region of Q the magnetic field has a magnitude of 2 units. Both magnetic fields are directed into the page.

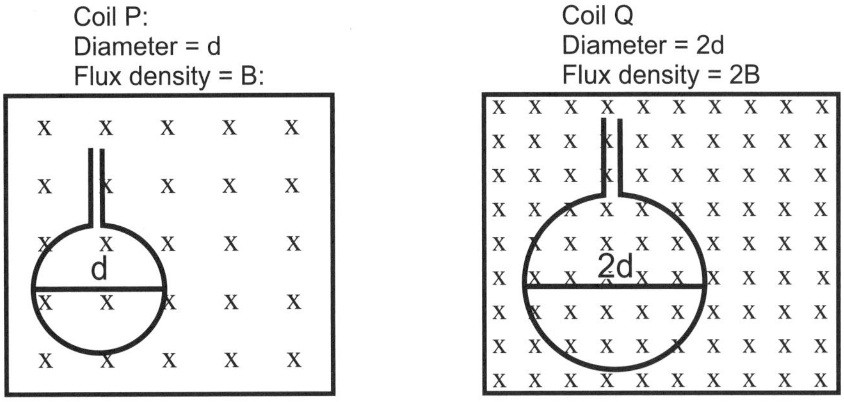

32.1.1 Define *magnetic flux linkage* φ. (2)

32.1.2 Express the ratio $\frac{\varphi_p}{\varphi_q}$ as a decimal. Show your working. (4)

32.2 The coil of an AC generator rotates at a constant rate in a magnetic field as shown below.

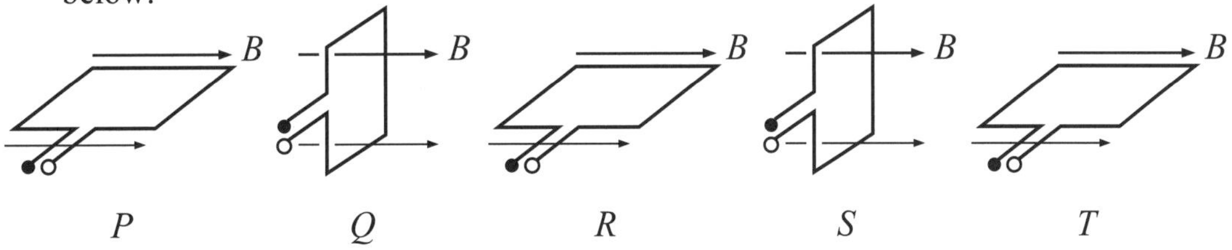

32.2.1 Explain briefly why an emf is induced in the coil. (2)

32.2.2 Draw a sketch graph showing emf against position for the coil, marking P, Q, R, S and T on the x-axis. (3)

32.3 The sketch below shows a simple dc motor.

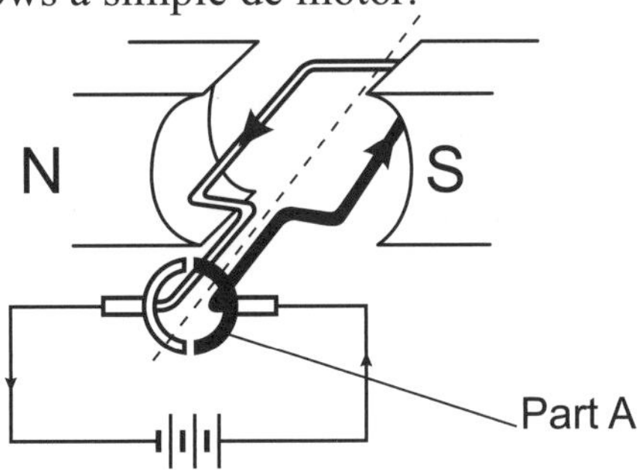

32.3.1 Describe the energy conversion that takes place in the dc motor. (2)

32.3.2 Name the law used to predict the direction of rotation of the coil. (1)

32.3.3 Predict whether the coil will rotate clockwise or anti-clockwise. (2)

32.3.4 Name and state the function of part A, and describe briefly how it achieves this function. (4)

[20]

TOC
1 Data Sheet
2 Definitions
3
3 solutions
4
4 solutions
5
5 solutions
6
6 solutions
7
7 solutions
8
8 solutions
9
9 solutions
10
10 solutions

9. ELECTROMAGNETISM (SOLUTIONS)

Question 1

1.1	B	(2)
1.2	C	(2)
1.3	D	(2)
1.4	C	(2)
1.5	B	(2)
1.6	D	(2)
1.7	D	(2)
1.8	C	(2)
1.9	B	(2)
1.10	B	(2)
1.11	A	(2)
1.12	D	(2)
1.13	C	(2)
1.14	D	(2)
1.15	B	(2)
1.16	D	(2)
1.17	A	(2)
1.18	A	(2)
1.19	C	(2)
1.20	A	(2)
1.21	D	(2)
1.22	B	(2)
1.23	C	(2)
1.24	A	(2)
1.25	C	(2)
1.26	B	(2)
1.27	D	(2)
1.28	D	(2)
1.29	A	(2)
1.30	D	(2)
1.31	B	(2)
1.32	C	(2)
1.33	D	(2)
1.34	C	(2)
1.35	B	(2)
1.36	B	(2)
1.37	D	(2)
1.38	C	(2)
1.39	D	(2)
1.40	B	(2)
1.41	D	(2)
1.42	D	(2)

[86]

Question 2

2.1 Downwards (1)

2.2 Fleming's left hand motor rule. (2)

2.3 The wire would vibrate. As the direction of current changes, the direction of force on the conductor will also change. (3)

2.4 Increase the strength of the magnets (use larger magnets) and increase the current in the conductor. (2)

[8]

Question 3

3.1 Mechanical energy to electrical energy (1)

3.2 Slip rings. To allow the generator to turn. (2)

3.3 Anticlockwise. (1)

3.4 Increase the strength of magnets. Increase the number of turns in the coil. (2)

3.5

$$\frac{V_s}{N_s} = \frac{V_p}{N_p}$$

$$\frac{V_s}{200} = \frac{230}{8000}$$

$$V_s = \frac{230}{8000} \times 200$$

$$= 5,75\,\text{V}$$

(4)

3.6 $P_s = P_p$

$I_s V_s = I_p V_p$

$I_s(5{,}75) = 0{,}08(230)$

$I_s = 3{,}2\ \text{A}$

$R = \frac{V}{I} = \frac{5{,}75}{3{,}2} = 1{,}80\ \Omega$ (4)

[14]

Question 4

4.1 The induced current flows in a direction so as to set up a magnetic field to oppose the change in magnetic flux. (2)

4.2 North (1)

4.3 0,068 seconds (2)

4.4 The emf induced is directly proportional to the rate of change of magnetic flux. (2)

4.5 The magnet is accelerating due to gravity. It exits the coil faster than it entered. Therefore the rate of change of flux is larger when the magnet exits the coil than when it enters. (2)

4.6 Mechanical to electrical. (2)

4.7 The area under the graph represents the change in magnetic flux (magnetic flux linkage). Area under the graph = EMF.Δt

$\text{EMF} = -N\frac{\Delta\phi}{\Delta t}$

$\text{EMF}.\Delta t = -N.\Delta\phi$

As the number of turns and change in flux is constant the area under the graph is the same. (5)

4.8 and 4.9

Graph of induced EMF versus time

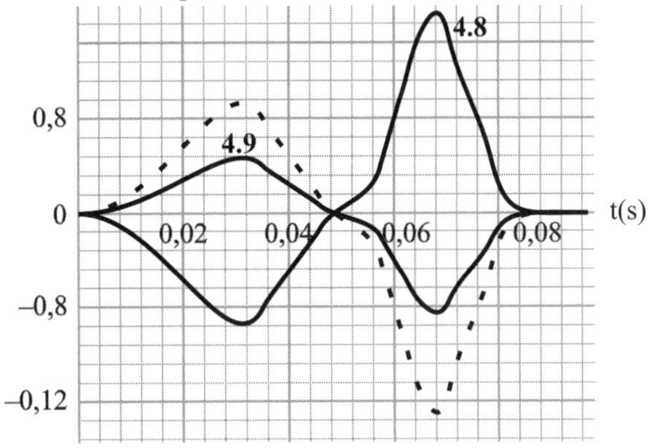

(4)

[20]

Question 5

5.1 The emf induced is directly proportional to the rate of change of magnetic flux. (2)

5.2 120° (2)

5.3 90° (2)

5.4 0,2 ; 0,6 and 1 second (3)

5.5 Horizontal (2)

5.6

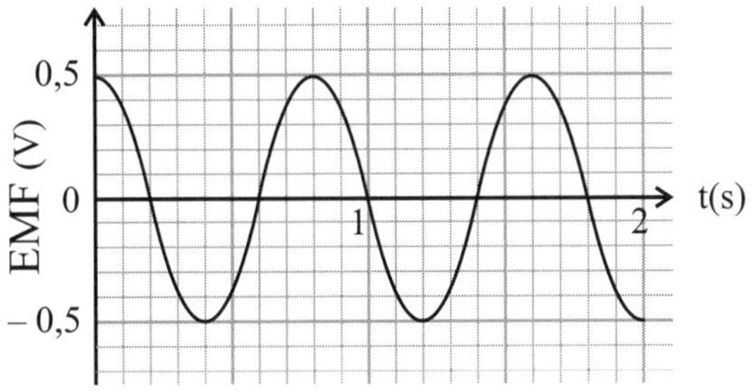

(5)

[16]

Question 6

6.1 Positive (2)

6.2 $F = ma$

$= (4\times10^{-4})(9,8)$

$= 3,92\times10^{-3}$ N (3)

6.3

Force on conductor (mN)	Current (I)	Reading on Spring Balance (mN)
0,42	0,12	3,50
0,72	0,20	3,20
1,12	0,32	2,80
1,42	0,40	2,50
1,92	0,56	2,00
2,37	0,68	1,55
2,82	0,80	1,10
3,22	0,92	0,70
3,50	1,00	0,42
3,92	1,12	0,00

(5)

6.4

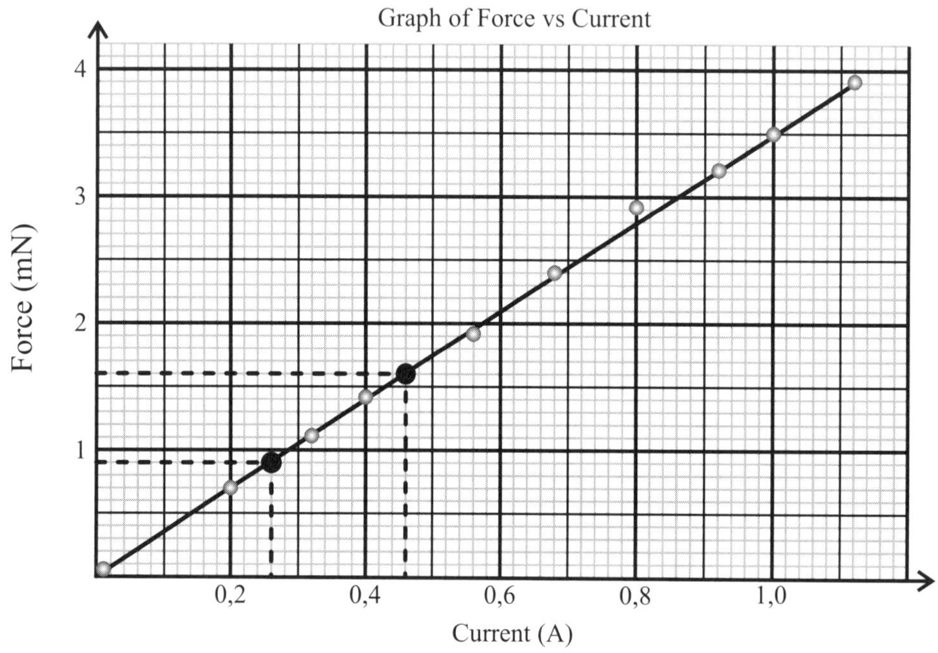

6.5

$$\text{gradient} = \frac{y_2 - y_1}{x_2 - x_1}$$

$$= \frac{1,6\times10^{-3} - 0,9\times10^{-3}}{0,46 - 0,26}$$

$$= 3,5\times10^{-3}$$

(5)

6,6 $\text{gradient} = \ell B \sin\theta \sin 90^\circ$

$3,5\times10^{-3} = (7\times10^{-2})B$

$B = 0,05$ Tesla (4)

[19]

Question 7

7.1 A motor. It is converting electrical to mechanical energy. (There is a DC power source) (2)

7.2 Q is the North pole. (3)

7.3 Downwards. (1)

7.4

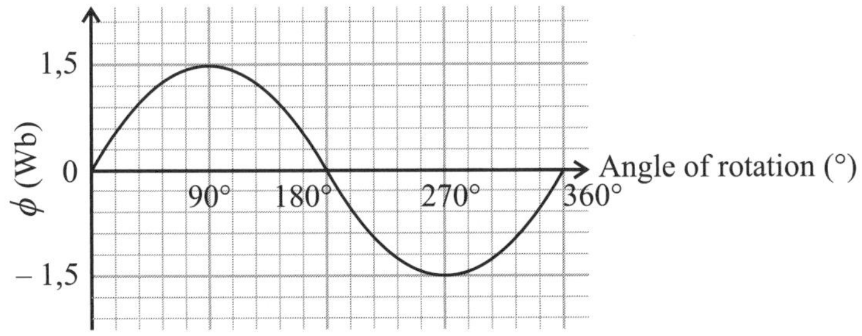

(4)

7.5 He has not included brushes or a split ring commutator. When the motor is turned on without these, the wires would twist and get tangled and the motor would not make a full roataion as the current in the armature would not be reversed every 180°. (4)

[14]

Question 8

8.1 The induced current flows in a direction so as to set up a magnetic field to oppose the change in magnetic flux. (2)

8.2 Negative. (A south pole is induced at the top of the coil) (2)

8.3

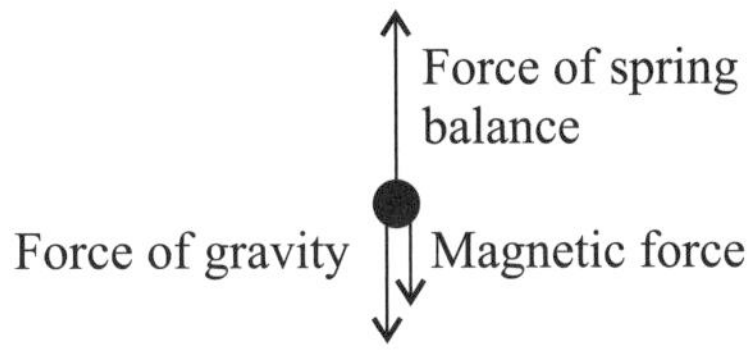

(3)

8.4 Graph of Force against Current

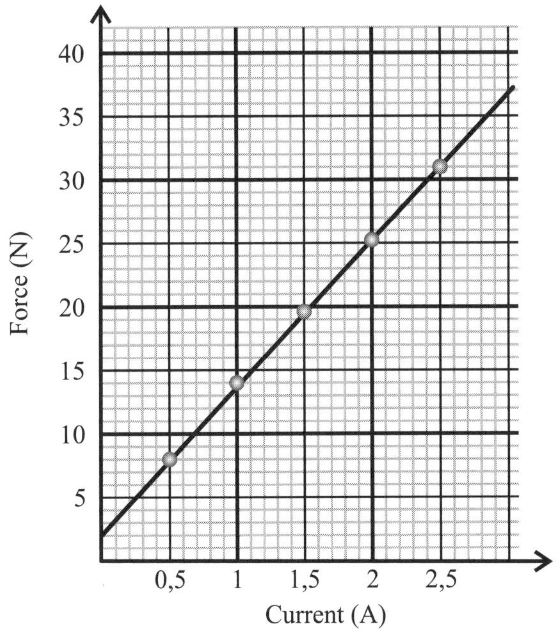

(6)

8.5 When current is zero the force reading is equal to the mass of the magnet.

y-int: (0;2)

$F = mg$

$2 = m(9.8)$

$m = 0{,}2\,\text{kg}$ (5)

[10]

Question 9

9.1 The emf induced is directly proportional to the rate of change of magnetic flux. (2)

9.2 A: Slip Rings
B: Carbon Brushes (2)

9.3 North. (2)

9.4 No. The generator is producing alternating current and the motor requires direct current. (3)

9.5 A full wave bridge rectifier. When point A is positive and B is negative, D4 and D3 are on. Current flows through the motor from P to Q. When current reverses, B becomes positive and A becomes negative. At this point D1 and D2 will turn on and current still flows through the motor from P to Q ensuring that current only flows in one direction in the motor. (5)

9.6
$$\frac{N_s}{N_p} = \frac{V_s}{V_p}$$
$$\frac{N_s}{1000} = \frac{3}{1,5}$$
$$N_s = 2\,000 \text{ turns}$$
(3)

9.7
$$P_{output} = VI$$
$$300 \times 10^{-3} = (3) I_{output}$$
$$I_{output} = 0,1\,A$$
$$P_{input} = VI$$
$$300 \times 10^{-3} = (1,5) I$$
$$I = 0,2\,A$$
(5)

[22]

Question 10

10.1 Number of loops in the coil. (2)

10.2 Speed of rotation
Magnetic field strength (Strength of the magnets) (2)

10.3

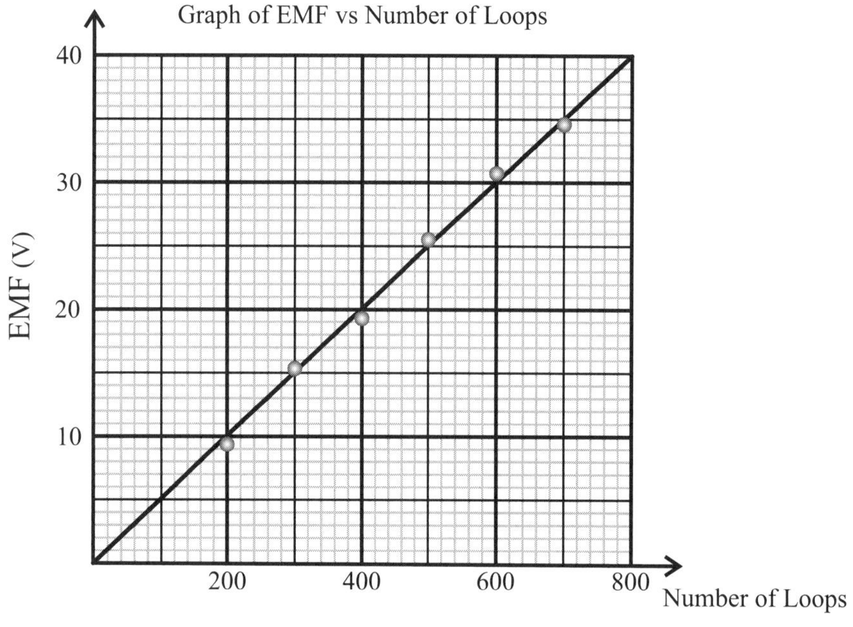

(6)

10.4
$$\text{EMF} = -N\frac{\Delta\phi}{\Delta t} \rightarrow y = mx + c$$
$$\text{gradient} = -\frac{\Delta\phi}{\Delta t} = -\frac{20-5}{400-100}$$
$$= -0,05$$
(4)

10.5 A component that only allows current to flow in one direction. (2)

10.6

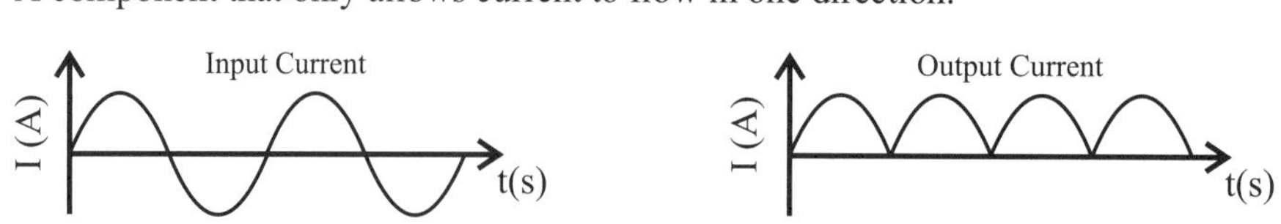

(4)

[20]

Question 11

11.1 Positive (2)

11.2 Current (2)

11.3 The change in mass is representative of the force on the conductor. (1)

11.4

I (A)	Δm (kg)	Force (N)
0,5	0,25	**2,45**
1,0	0,40	**3,92**
1,5	0,70	**6,86**
2,0	1,00	**9,80**
2,5	1,10	**10,78**
3,0	1,40	**13,72**

(3)

11.5

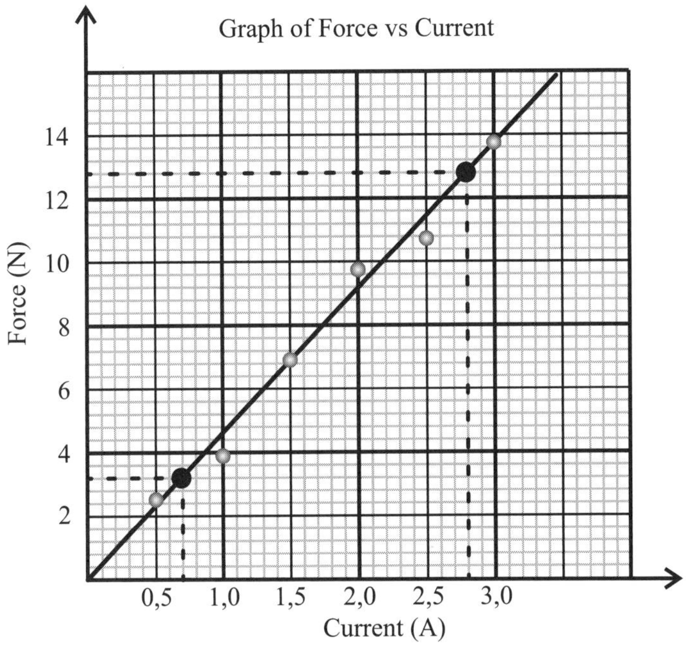

(6)

11.6 $\text{Gradient} = \dfrac{12{,}8 - 3{,}2}{2{,}8 - 0{,}7}$

$= 4{,}57\ \text{N.A}^{-1}$

11.7 $\text{Gradeint} = lB\sin 90^\circ$

$4{,}57 = \left(2{,}2 \times 10^{-2}\right)B$

$B = 207{,}73\ \text{T}$ (4)

[17]

Question 12

12.1 The emf induced is directly proportional to the rate of change of magnetic flux. (2)

12.2 Electrical to mechanical. (1)

12.3 South (1)

12.4 The Split ring reverses the direction of the current every 180°. This allows the armature to rotate continuously in the same direction. (2)

12.5 Any two of the following answers:

- Increase the number of turns in the coil
- Use stronger magnets
- Increase the strength of the current in the armature
- Use a material of less resistance for the armature (2)

Question 13

13.1 A: Step up transformer
B: Step down transformer
C: Step down transformer (3)

13.2 $P = I^2R$

$\therefore P \,\alpha\, I^2$

To minimise power loss on the line during transportation current needs to be low and voltage needs to be high. Transformers are used to step up voltage and step down current. (3)

13.3 Faradays law of electromagnetic induction (mutual induction is also acceptable) (1)

13.4 Step down (1)

13.5 $\frac{N_s}{N_p} = \frac{V_s}{V_p}$

$\frac{N_s}{23000} = \frac{110}{230}$

$N_s = 11000$ turns (3)

13.6 $P_p = P_s$

$V_p I_p = P_s$

$230 I_p = 345$

$I_p = 1{,}5\text{ A}$ (4)

[15]

Question 14

14.1 Max power of switch:

$P = VI$

$= 230(15)$

$= 3450\text{ W}$

The maximum power rating of the switch is 3 450 W. As the geyser is rated at 3 500W it would not be safe to use the switch to power it. (4)

14.2 The induced current flows in a direction so as to set up a magnetic field to oppose the change in magnetic flux. (2)

14.3 When the smart switch is turned on, a current flows in the solenoid. This induces a magnetic North pole at the top of the iron core. This attracts the high voltage switch (which must be made of a magnetic material) causing it to close and turn the geyser on. When the smart switch is opened (turned off) the magnetic field stops, and the spring pulls the high voltage switch open turning off the geyser. This way the smart switch does not directly supply the current to the geyser. (5)

14.4 DC. The source has a negative and positive terminal. (3)

[14]

Question 15

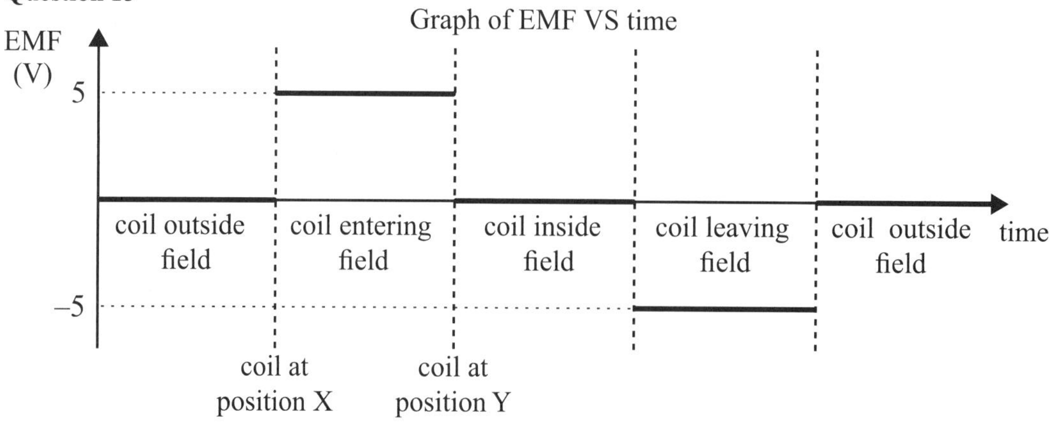

[10]

Question 16 (2008 IEB Final Examination)

16.1 Electromagnetic induction (1)

16.2 Mechanical energy to electrical energy (1)

16.3 Slip rings (1)

16.4 Carries the current in and out of the coil and allows the generator to rotate without tangling the wires. (1)

16.5 Carbon Brushes. (1)

16.6 Maintains continous contact with the slip rings and carries the current from the rings to the external circuit. (1)

16.7 (6)

16.7.1 Max

16.7.2 ABCD

16.7.3 Zero

16.7.4 Max

16.7.5 DCBA

16.7.6 No current

16.7.7 Max

16.8 The graph of 16.8.2 must be half the amplitude of 16.8.1. 16.8.2 must be a full graph as the x-axis gives the coil position and not time. (8)

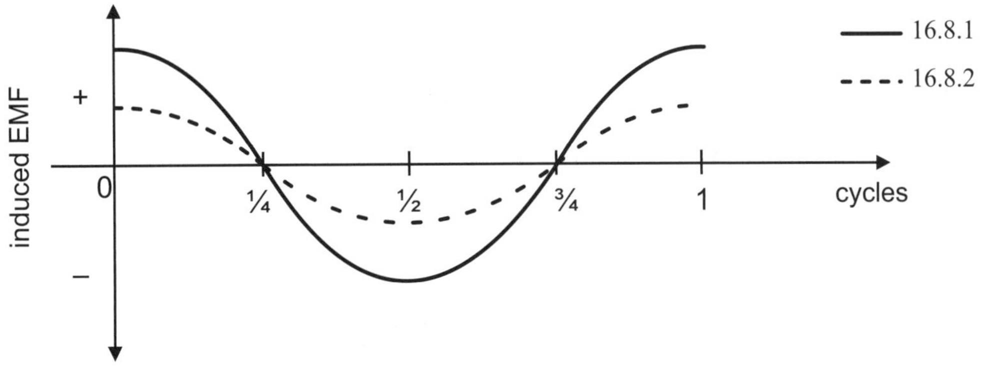

[20]

Question 17 (2009 IEB Final Examination)

17.1.1 A, C, B, D (4)

17.1.2 The iron would produce the greatest magnetic field. (3)

17.1.3 Measure the maximum mass of magnetic material (for example, iron filings) that each magnet can lift. (2)

17.1.4 Material used for the core. (1)

17.1.5 Mass of magnetic mataerial that can be lifted. (1)

17.1.6 No, the experiment described is not a fair test.

- The EMF of the power supply should be the same for all experiments
- Number of windings should be the same for all experiments
- The experiment should be repeated multiple times to verify the results (5)

17.1.7 The same power supply and same number of windings should be used for each experiment. (2)

17.2.1 The rotating magnet produces a changing magnetic field/magnetic flux. This magnetic flux interacts with the particles in the wire inducing an emf. (4)

17.2.2

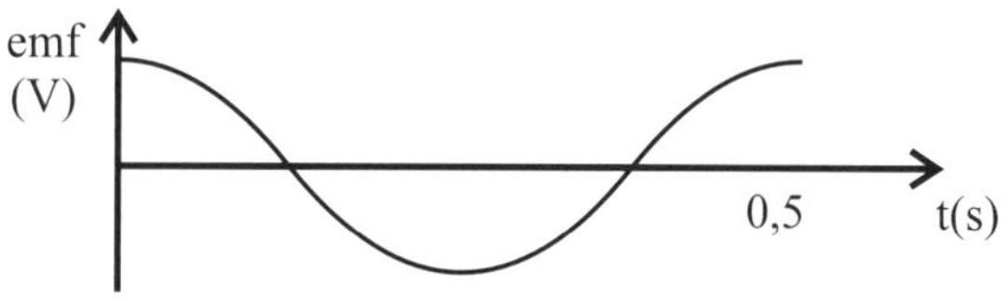

(3)

17.2.3 Any two of the following:

- Increase speed of rotation of the magnet
- Increase the number of coils in the wire
- Place the magnet closer to the coil
- Use a stronger magnet

(2)

Question 18 (2011 IEB Final Examination)

18.1 In series. (1)

18.2 $P = VI$

$= 24(6)$

$= 144\ \text{W}$

(3)

18.3.1 A component that only allows current to flow in one direction. (2)

18.3.2 To change a.c. to d.c. (2)

18.3.3 When W is positive current flows through **diode B** through the load **from Y to Z** and through **diode D** to X. (No current passes through diodes A and C which are in reverse bias.) (1)

18.3.4 Step down (1)

18.3.5

(a)

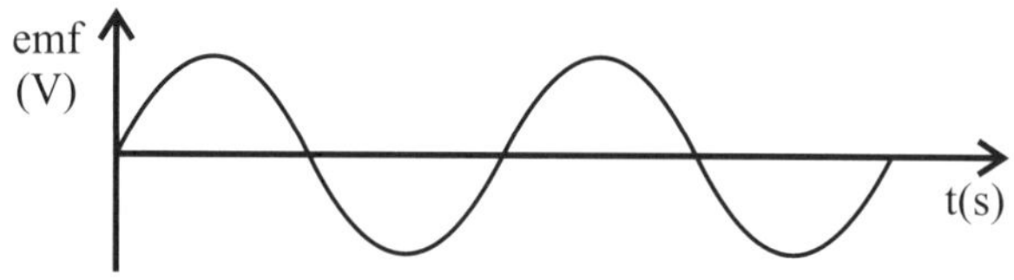

(2)

(b)

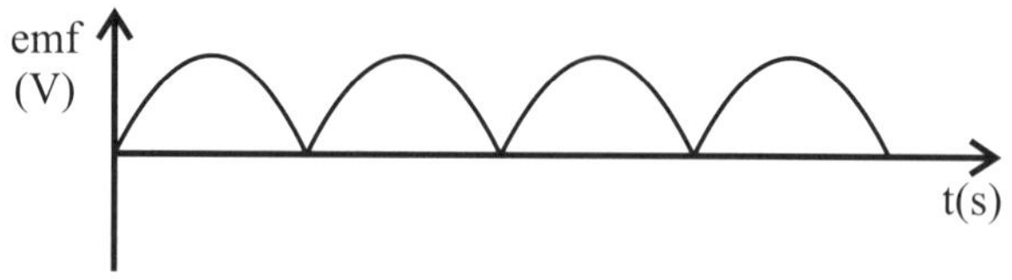

(2)

[16]

Question 19 (2011 IEB Final Examination)

19.1

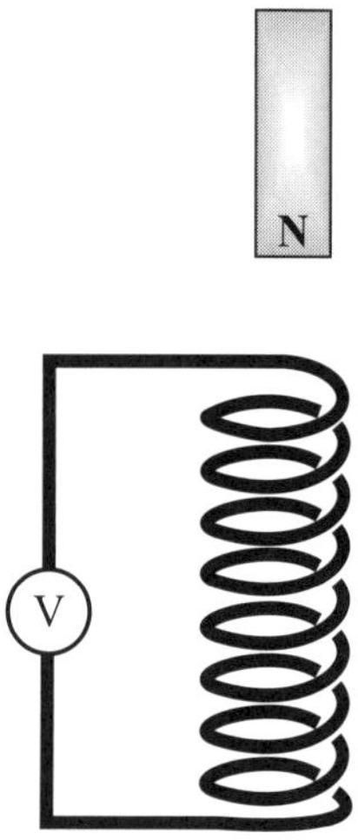

(2)

TOC 1 Data Sheet 2 Definitions 3 3 solutions 4 4 solutions 5 5 solutions 6 6 solutions 7 7 solutions 8 8 solutions 9 9 solutions 10 10 solutions

19.2 Graph of maximum induced emf on entry against entry speed for the magnet falling through the solenoid

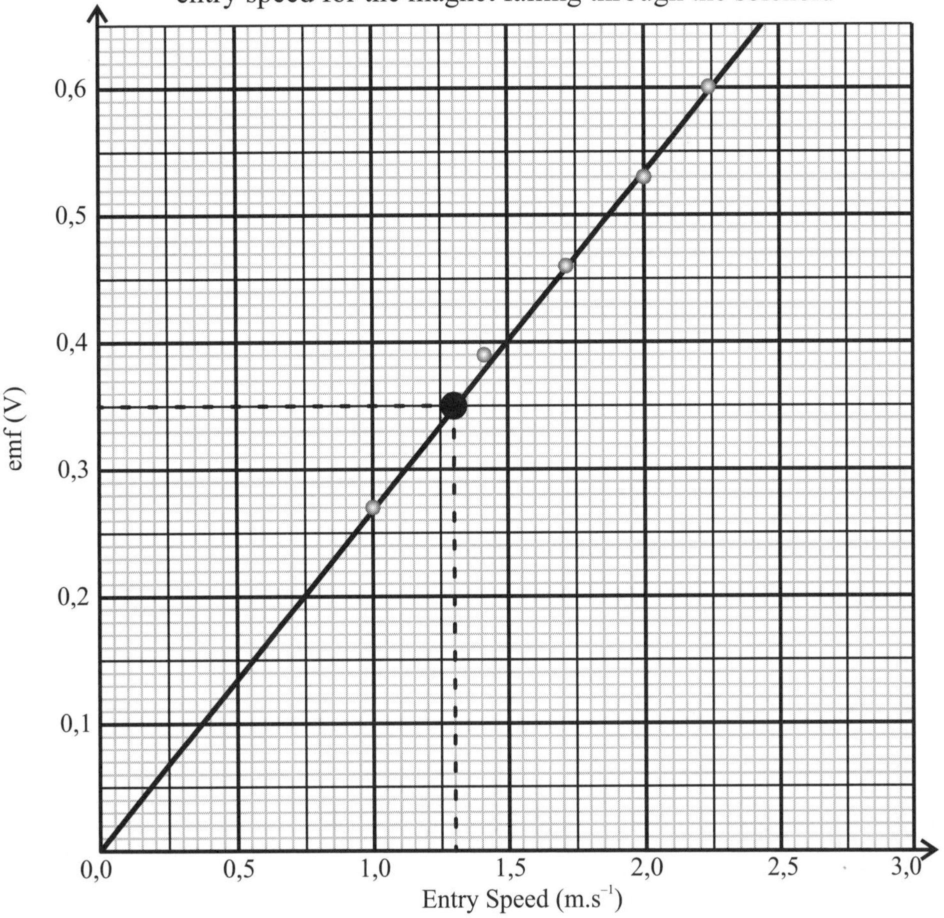

(7)

19.3 0,35 V (read from the graph) (2)

19.4 The maximum induced emf is directly proportional to the speed of the magnet. (2)

19.5 Any two of the following:

- Increase the density of coils on the solenoid (more coils per unit length).
- Use a stronger magnet.
- Make the torch longer (so that falling magnet gains more speed).
- Do not accept: Increase the length of the solenoid. (4)

[17]

Question 20 (2013 IEB Final Examination)

20.1 Mechanical to electrical (2)

20.2 There is **change in magnetic flux (linkage)** between the coils and the magnet as the magnet spins which induces an emf in the coil OR magnetic field (lines) cutting through conductor / coil. (2)

20.3 The wind generator produces an **alternating current.** The LED will only allow current to pass through in **one direction** (left to right) therefore it will only light up for every half revolution of the magnet (OR LED will only conduct current in forward bias OR half-wave rectification through the diode.) (4)

20.4 From EMF $= -\frac{N\Delta\varphi}{\Delta t}$, EMF is inversely proportional to time. The magnet turns faster time decreases and EMF and current will increase causing the globe to shine brighter. (4)

20.5 It can **spin faster** with less wind power, therefore, a greater induced emf (2)

20.6 Add more coils to the solenoid.
Use Stronger magnets. (2)

20.7 Power is only generated when there is wind. (1)

[17]

Question 21

21.1

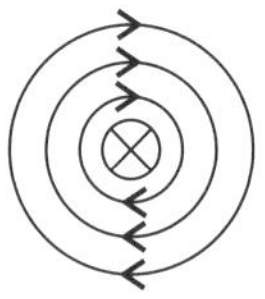

(2)

21.2 Current. (1)

21.3 Magnetic field due to magnet interacts with magnetic field produced by current (2)

21.4 Current flows out of the page. The force on the wire is up, according to Newton's third law the force on the magnets will be down. (3)

21.5 Graph of current against change in scale reading

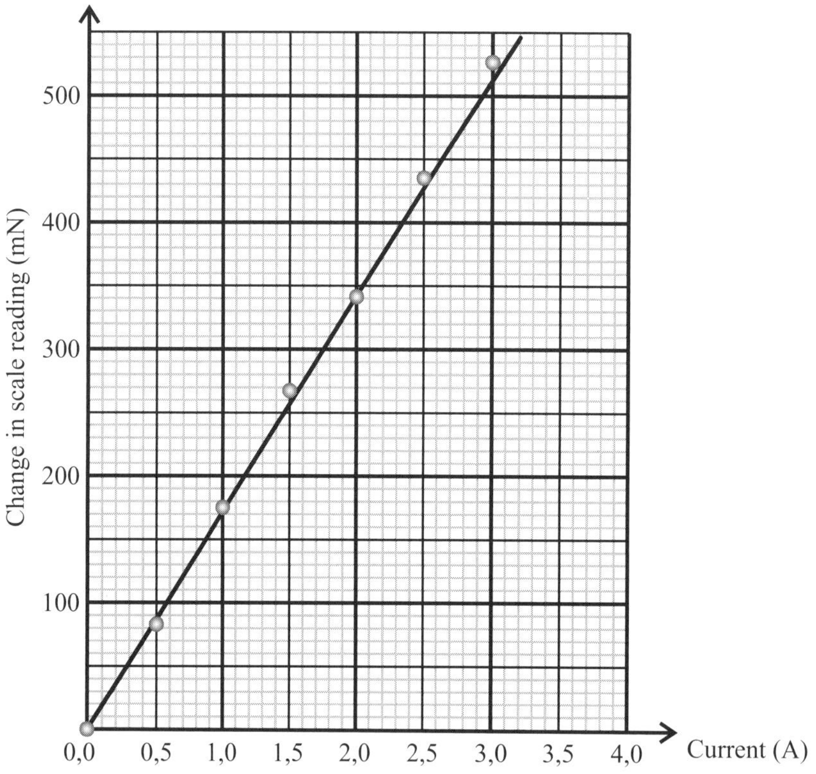

(7)

21.6 Force is directly proportional to the current. The graph is a straight line through the origin. (3)

21.7 You want to measure the force due to the magnetic fields interacting, not the weight of the magnets. (2)

[20]

Question 22 (2014 IEB Supplementary Examination)

22.1.1 Negative (2)

22.1.2 Electrical energy to mechanical energy. (2)

22.1.3 Cars, Fans, Hairdryers, Blow heaters, etc… (2)

22.1.4 (a) Vertical (1)

(a) Horizontal (1)

22.1.5
- When the coil is vertical the **gaps in the split ring commutator are opposite the brushes** therefore there is **no current** though the coil and hence no torque.
- When the coil is horizontal the **current direction is perpendicular to the magnetic field** which results in maximum torque. (4)

22.2.1 The DC motor has a split-ring commutator and the AC generator has slip rings
The DC motor has a power source and the AC generator has no power source (4)

22.2.2 The emf induced is directly proportional to the rate of change of magnetic flux. (2)

22.2.3 Any two of the following:
- Stronger magnets
- More windings on the coil
- Turn the coil faster (2)

22.2.4 (a) Vertical (1)

(b) Horizontal (1)

(c) (4)

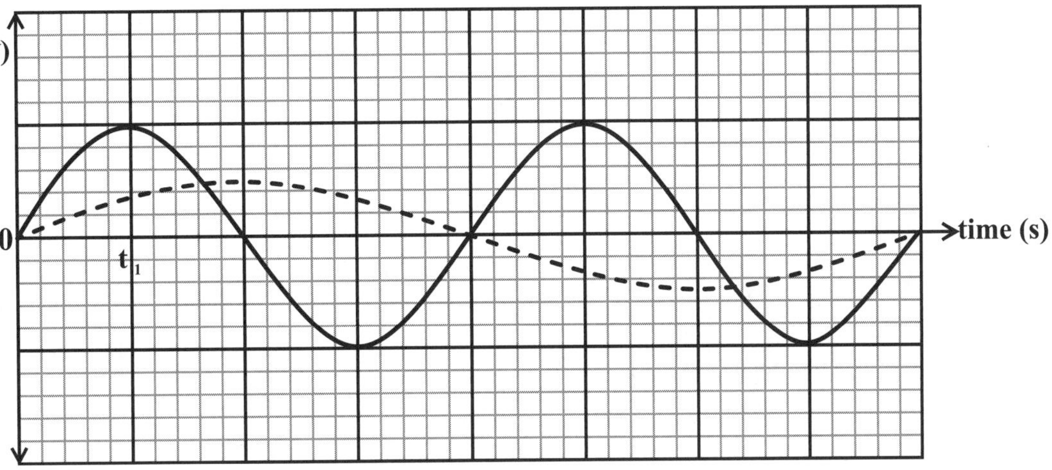

22.2.5 (a) No greenhouse gas emissions (less global warming)
NOT using up non-renewable fossil fuel (2)

(b) Disposal of nuclear waste –remains radioactive for thousands of years – can contaminate groundwater, soil, etc. if it leaks
Risk of meltdown/explosion/earthquake – massive exposure to radiation (2)

[30]

Question 23 (2015 IEB Final Examination)

23.1.1

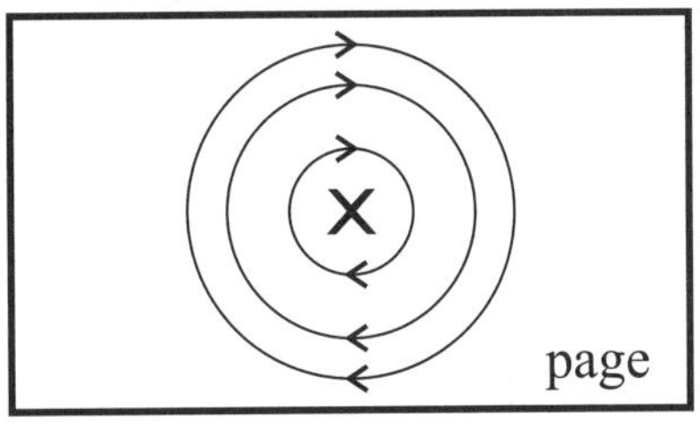

(2)

23.1.2

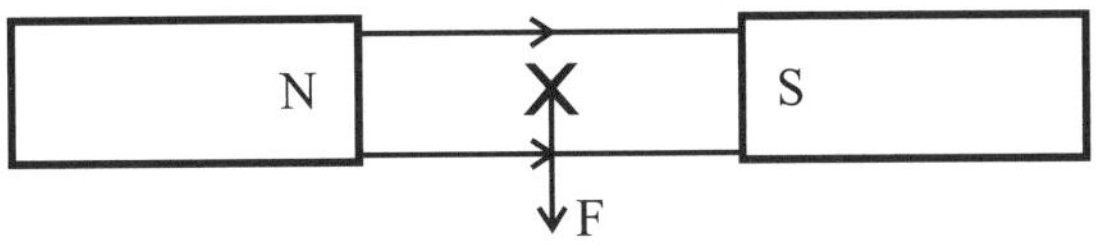

(4)

23.1.3 The magnetic field due to the current interacts with the magnetic field due to the magnets. (2)

23.1.4 The wire must be parallel to the field lines. (2)

23.2.1 Electrical energy to mechanical energy. (2)

23.2.2 Split ring commutator. (2)

23.2.3 Reverse the direction of the current in the coil every half rotation to ensure that coil rotates continuously in the same direction. (2)

23.3.1 The emf induced is directly proportional to the rate of change of magnetic flux. (2)

23.3.2
- As the cone moves, the coil moves relative to the magnet.
- The coil experiences a change in magnetic flux which induces an EMF in the coil. (4)

[22]

Question 24 (2015 IEB Supplementary Examination)

24.1 The emf induced is directly proportional to the rate of change of magnetic flux. (2)

24.2 An alternating current is needed in order to set up a **changing** magnetic field therefore producing a **change in flux** in the secondary coil and hence inducing an emf in the secondary coil. (3)

24.3 The rate of change of magnetic flux linkage in both coils is the same. The induced emf is directly proportional to the number of turns there are **more turns in the secondary coil**. Therefore the voltage in the secondary will be higher than in the primary. (2)

24.4 24.4.1 $\frac{N_s}{N_p} = \frac{V_s}{V_p}$

$N_s = \frac{400\,000}{25\,000} \times 500$

$= 8\,000 \text{ turns}$ (3)

24.4.2 $V_p I_p = V_s I_s$

$25\,000(0,5) = (400\,000) I_s$

$I_s = 0,03125 \text{ A}$ (3)

24.4.3 As power is constant a high voltage means a lower current on the power line. There will be **less energy (power) lost** in the form of heat in the power lines due to the resistance of the power lines, $P = I^2R$ therefore $P \propto I^2$ (when R is constant). The lower the current the less power is lost. (3)

24.5 24.5.1

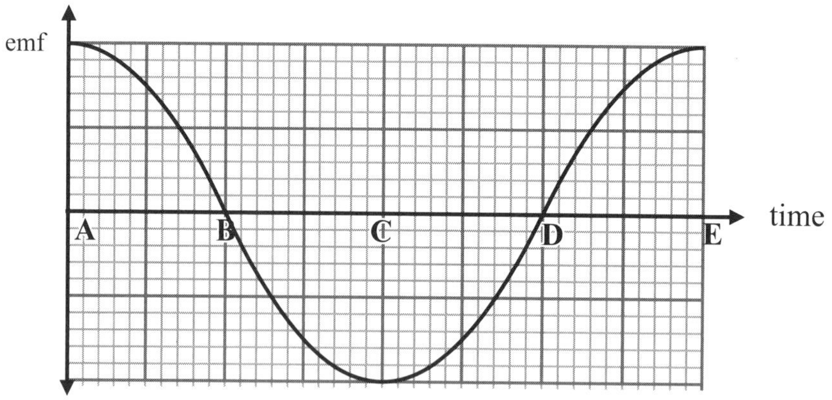

(3)

24.5.2

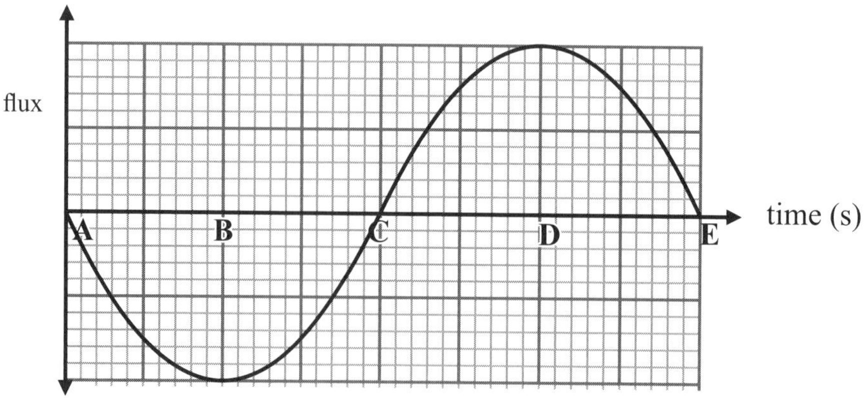

(3)

[23]

Question 25 (2016 IEB Final Examination)

25.1.1 Out of the page (2)

25.1.2 Any two of the following:

- Current
- Magnetic field
- Length of the conductor in the field (2)

25.2.1 The emf induced is directly proportional to the rate of change of magnetic flux. (2)

25.2.2
- Current in primary coil produces a magnetic flux in the core
- As current in primary coil is alternating current, magnetic flux in the core is changing
- The changing magnetic flux is transmitted through the core to the secondary coil.
- By Faraday's law, the changing flux induces an emf in secondary coil. (4)

25.2.3 As power is constant a high voltage means a lower current on the power line. There will be **less energy (power) lost** in the form of heat in the power lines due to the resistance of the power lines, $P = I^2R$ therefore $P \propto I^2$ (when R is constant). The lower the current the less power is lost. (4)

25.2.4 $\frac{N_s}{N_p} = \frac{V_s}{V_p}$

$= \frac{765}{20}$

$= 38,25$ (3)

25.2.5 Step up transformer. (2)

[19]

Question 26 (2016 IEB Final Examination)

26.1 Mechanical energy to electrical energy (2)

26.2 The greater the number of loops in the coil, the greater the emf induced. (2)

26.3 Number of loops. (2)

26.4 Area of coil or magnetic field. (2)

26.5

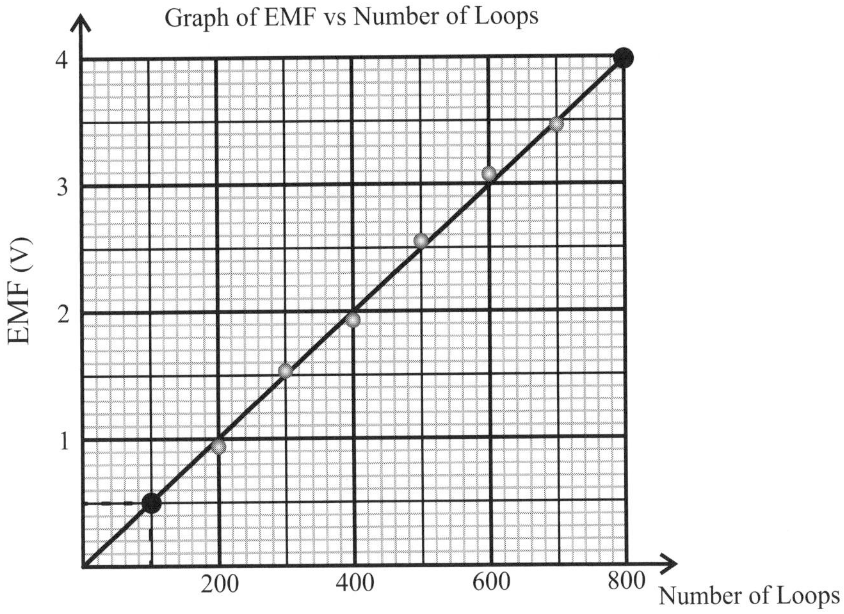

(7)

26.6 $\text{Gradient} = \frac{\Delta y}{\Delta x}$

$= \frac{4 - 0,5}{800 - 100}$

$= 0,005$ (3)

26.7 $\text{EMF} = -N\frac{\Delta\varphi}{\Delta t}$

Plotting EMF on the y-axis and number of loops on the x-axis means that:

$\text{Gradient} = -\frac{\Delta\varphi}{\Delta t}$

$\therefore \frac{\Delta\varphi}{\Delta t} = 0,005\ \text{Wb.s}^{-1}$ (2)

[21]

Question 27 (2017 IEB Final Examination)

27.1.1

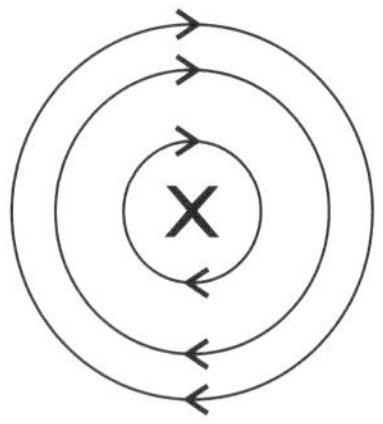

(3)

27.1.2 Into the page (2)

27.1.3 Use AC current as it continually changes direction. This will cause the force on the coil to continually change direction which will cause the wire to vibrate. (3)

27.2.1 Mechanical energy to electrical energy. (2)

27.2.2 Yes, there are slip rings. (2)

27.2.3 The emf induced is directly proportional to the rate of change of magnetic flux. (2)

27.2.4

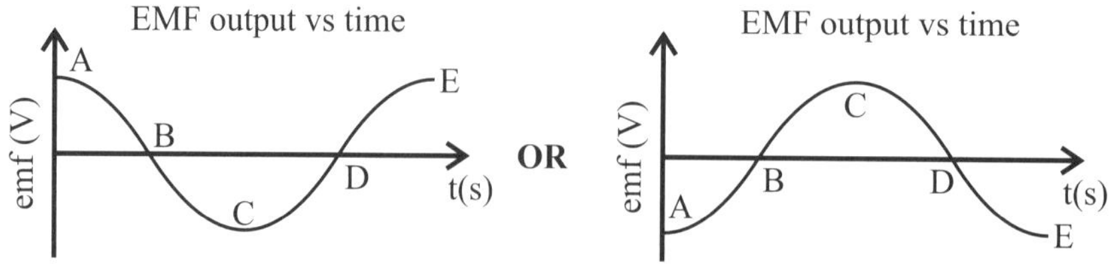

(3)

27.2.5 At point C, the magnitude of the change in flux is a maximum and therefore EMF is a maximum. (2)

[19]

Question 28 (2017 IEB Supplementary Examination)

28.1.1 A motor. Electrical energy is being converted to Mechanical energy. (2)

28.1.2 PQRS (2)

28.1.3 North (2)

28.1.4 Down (2)

28.1.5 No there is no split ring commutator. This means when PQ is next to pole B, the force on the wire is up instead of down. (3)

28.2.1 Gravitational potential energy to kinetic energy AND electrical energy. (3)

28.2.2 The induced current flows in a direction so as to set up a magnetic field to oppose the change in magnetic flux. (2)

28.2.3 Clockwise (2)

28.2.4 No, Peter's magnet will reach the ground first. The induced current in the ring will set up a magnetic field to oppose the magnet falling. The acceleration of the magnet falling through the ring will be less than gravity. (4)

[22]

Question 29 (2018 IEB Final Examination)

29.1.1

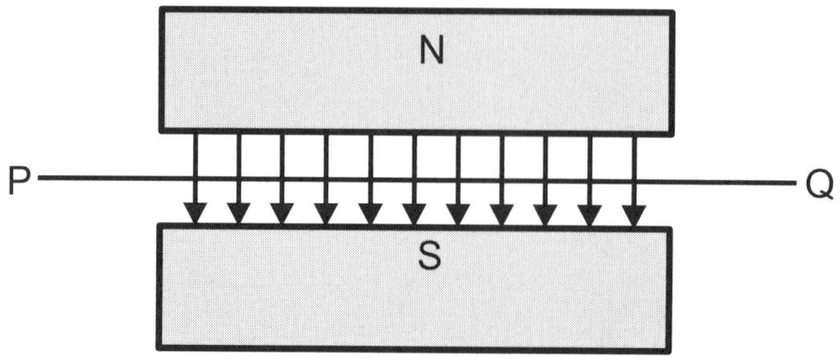

(2)

29.1.2 P to Q. (2)

29.2.1 The induced current flows in a direction so as to set up a magnetic field to oppose the change in magnetic flux. (2)

29.2.2 Diagram b, clockwise
Diagram d, anticlockwise (2)

TOC | 1 Data Sheet | 2 Definitions | 3 | 3 solutions | 4 | 4 solutions | 5 | 5 solutions | 6 | 6 solutions | 7 | 7 solutions | 8 | 8 solutions | 9 | 9 solutions | 10 | 10 solutions

29.2.3 There is no induced current in (c) as the rate of change of magnetic flux is zero. (2)

29.3.1 The emf induced is directly proportional to the rate of change of magnetic flux. (2)

29.3.2

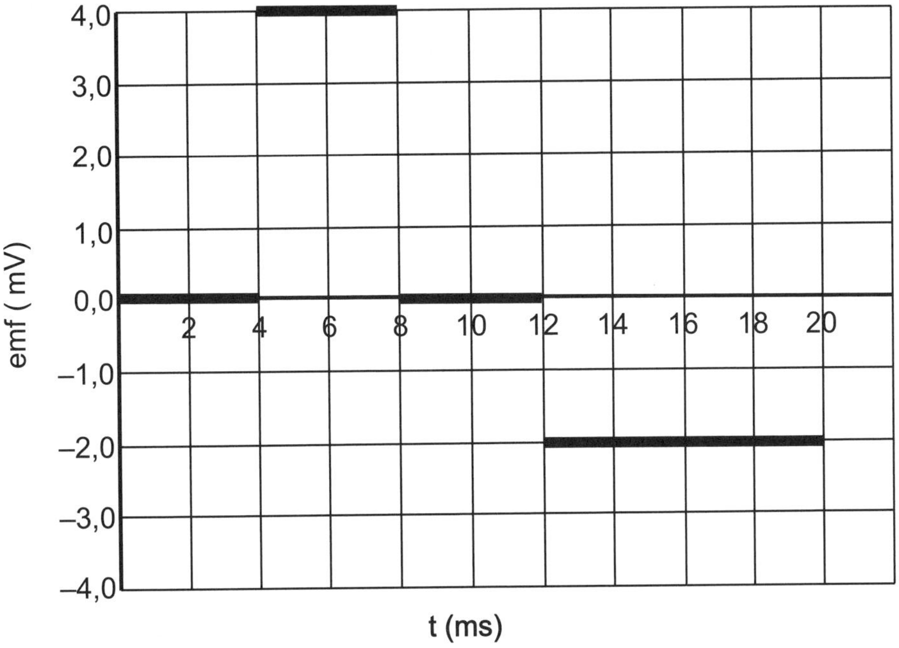

(4)

[18]

Question 30 (2018 IEB Supplementary Examination)

30.1 Y to X (2)

30.2 Motor: Electrical energy to Mechanical energy
Generator: Mechanical energy to electrical energy (2)

30.3 30.3.1 Into the page (2)

30.3.2 Any two of the following:
- Increase current
- Increase strength of magnets
- Increase length of wire in field (2)

30.3.3 When the conductor is parallel to the field lines (2)

30.4 30.4.1 Magnetic flux linkage is the product of the number of turns on the coil and the flux through the coil. (2)

30.4.2
- Magnetic flux changes as the coil rotates.
- Faraday's law states that a changing magnetic flux induces an emf.
- An induced emf in a closed circuit means a current in the circuit. (4)

30.4.3 The induced current flows in a direction so as to set up a magnetic field to oppose the change in magnetic flux. (2)

30.4.4 P to Q (2)

[20]

Question 31 (2019 IEB Final Examination)

31.1.1 Into the page (2)

31.1.2 The magnetic field at point Y will be in the same direction as B but half the magnitude. (4)

31.2 Generators, transformers, Induction stoves, microphones, etc... (2)

31.3.1

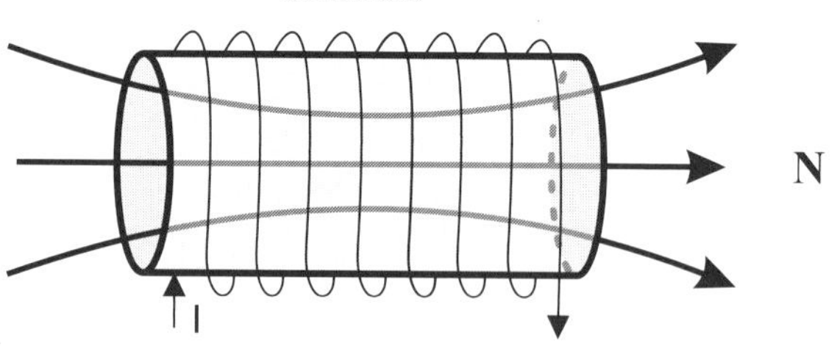

(3)

31.3.2 The emf induced is directly proportional to the rate of change of magnetic flux. (2)

31.3.3 None of the coils are moving. Therefore, there is no change in magnetic flux. (2)

31.3.4
- Move the coil or solenoid relative to each other
- Rotate the coil so the effective area will change
- Use alternating current in the solenoid (continously change the current in the solenoid) (6)

[21]

Question 32 (2019 IEB Supplementary Examination)

32.1.1 Magnetic flux linkage is the product of the number of turns on the coil and the flux through the coil. (2)

32.1.2 $\varphi = BA\cos\theta$

$A = 2\pi r^2$

$\therefore \varphi \,\alpha\, B$ and $\varphi \,\alpha\, r^2$

Coil Q has double the flux density and double the radius

$$\therefore \frac{\varphi_p}{\varphi_q} = \frac{1}{2(2)^2}$$

$$= 0{,}125$$

(4)

32.2.1 There is a changing magnetic flux linkage through the coil. (2)

32.2.2

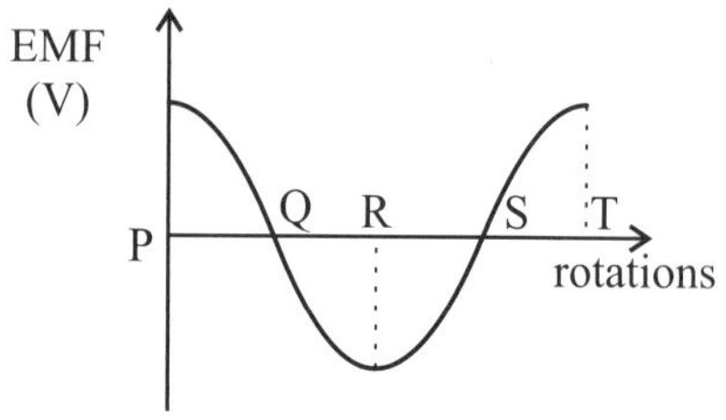

OR

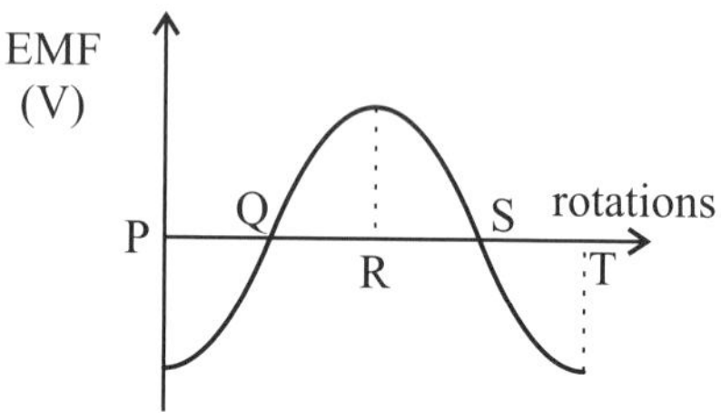

(3)

32.3.1 Electrical energy to Mechanical energy (2)

32.3.2 Flemming's left hand motor rule (1)

32.3.3 Clockwise (2)

32.3.4 Split ring commutator.
It reverses the direction of the current in the coil every 90° (half rotation). This allows the coil (armature) to rotate continuously in one direction. (4)

[20]

10. PHOTONS AND ELECTRONS

THE PARTICLE NATURE OF LIGHT

Light is **electromagnetic radiation. Quantum theory** tells us that **light has wave and particle nature. A particle of light** is a **packet of energy called a photon.**
The **energy of a photon** of light is **directly proportional to the frequency** of light.
The **wavelength and frequency** of light are **inversely proportional.**
As **frequency increases, wavelength decreases** and vice versa.
In a vacuum light travels at a constant speed of 3×10^{8} m.s^{-1}.

Frequency and Wavelength of Light

$$f = \frac{c}{\lambda}$$

Where:

$f \rightarrow$ Frequency of light (Hz)

$c \rightarrow$ speed of light $\left(3\times10^{8}\ \text{m.s}^{-1}\right)$

$\lambda \rightarrow$ wavelength of light (m)

Illustrative Example 1:

The wavelength of red light is 650 nm . Determine the frequency of this red light.

$$f = \frac{c}{\lambda} = \frac{3\times10^{8}}{650\times10^{-9}} = 4,62\times10^{14}\ \text{Hz}$$

Illustrative Example 2:

The frequency of blue light is $6,6\times10^{14}$ Hz. Determine the wavelength of this blue light.

$$f = \frac{c}{\lambda}$$

$$6,6\times10^{14} = \frac{3\times10^{8}}{\lambda}$$

$$\lambda = \frac{3\times10^{8}}{6,6\times10^{14}} = 4,55\times10^{-7}\ \text{m}$$

ENERGY OF A PHOTON

The energy of a photon of light can be calculated using **either** of the equations below:

Energy of a Photon

$$E = hf \quad \text{or} \quad E = \frac{hc}{\lambda}$$

Where:

$E \rightarrow$ Energy of a photon of light (J)

$h \rightarrow$ Planck's constant $\left(6,6\times10^{-34}\ \text{J.s}\right)$

$f \rightarrow$ Frequency of light (Hz)

$c \rightarrow$ speed of light $\left(3\times10^{8}\ \text{m.s}^{-1}\right)$

$\lambda \rightarrow$ wavelength of light (m)

TOC | 1 Data Sheet | 2 Definitions | 3 | 3 solutions | 4 | 4 solutions | 5 | 5 solutions | 6 | 6 solutions | 7 | 7 solutions | 8 | 8 solutions | 9 | 9 solutions | 10 | 10 solutions

Illustrative Example 3:

The frequency of a certain electromagnetic radiation is 3×10^{19} Hz. Determine the energy of this type of electromagnetic radiation.

$$E = hf = (6,6 \times 10^{-34})(3 \times 10^{19})$$
$$= 1,98 \times 10^{-14} \text{ J}$$

Illustrative Example 4:

The wavelength of green light is 530 nm. Determine the energy of green light with this wavelength.

$$E = \frac{hc}{\lambda} = \frac{(6,6 \times 10^{-34})(3 \times 10^{8})}{530 \times 10^{-9}}$$
$$= 3,74 \times 10^{-19} \text{ J}$$

THE ELECTRON VOLT

An **electron volt (eV) is a unit of energy** equivalent to $1,6 \times 10^{-19}$ J.
Both electron volts and joules are suitable energy units.

To convert **electron volts to joules** you **multiply by $1,6 \times 10^{-19}$**.

To convert **joules to electron volts** you **divide by $1,6 \times 10^{-19}$**.

THE PHOTOELECTRIC EFFECT

The **photoelectric effect** is the process that occurs when **light shines on a metal** and **electrons are ejected**. This is illustrated in the diagram below.

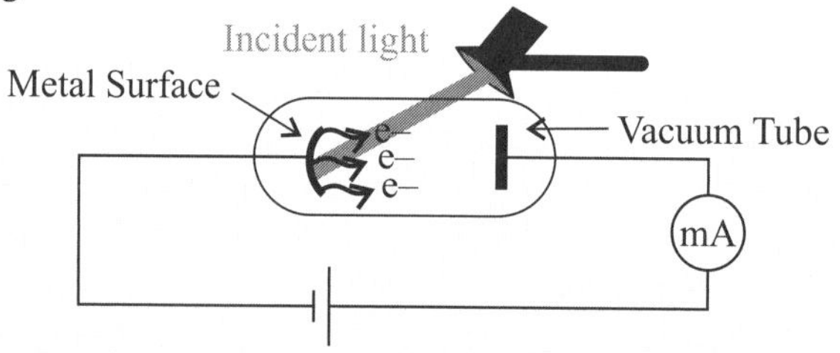

For **electrons to be emitted** when light (electromagnetic radiation) is shone onto a metal, the **light must have sufficient energy**.

The minimum amount of energy needed to emit an electron from the surface of a metal is called the work function (W_o). The work function is specific to each type of material.

The minimum frequency of incident radiation at which electrons will be emitted from a particular metal is called the threshold frequency (f_o).

The **threshold frequency (minimum frequency)** corresponds to the **maximum wavelength (λ_o)** or **threshold wavelength**, which will cause an electron to be emitted.

If the **energy of a photon is greater than the work function** (or the **frequency of the light is greater than the threshold frequency**) of a metal, the photon will cause an **electron** to be **emitted** from the metal.

If the electromagnetic radiation has **energy greater than the work function**, the **excess energy is transferred to the electron in the form of kinetic energy**. This means that **as frequency increases so does E_{Kmax}**.

Photoelectric Equation

$$E = W_o + E_{k_{max}}$$

Where:

E → Energy of a photon of incident radiation (J) Note that $E = hf$ or $E = \frac{hc}{\lambda}$

W_o → Work function of the metal (J) Note that $W_o = hf_o$ and $W_o = \frac{hc}{\lambda_o}$

$E_{k_{max}}$ → Maximum kinetic energy of an emitted electron (J) Note that $E_{k_{max}} = \frac{1}{2} m_{e-} v^2$

m_{e-} → Mass of an electron $(9,1 \times 10^{-31}$ kg$)$

v → velocity of an emitted electron (m.s^{-1})

Illustrative Example 1:

Potassium metal with a work function of 2,3 eV is irradiated with light of wavelength 380 nm. Determine the:

a) Work function of potassium in joules.
b) Maximum kinetic energy of the emitted electron.
c) Maximum velocity of an emitted electron.

a) $W_o = 2,3\left(1,6\times10^{-19}\right)$

$= 3,68\times10^{-19}$ J

b) $E = W_o + E_{k_{max}}$

$\frac{hc}{\lambda} = W_o + E_{k_{max}}$

$\frac{\left(6,6\times10^{-34}\right)\left(3\times10^{8}\right)}{380\times10^{-9}} = 3,68\times10^{-19} + E_{k_{max}}$

$E_{k_{max}} = 1,53\times10^{-19}$ J

c) $E_{k_{max}} = \frac{1}{2}m_{e^-}v^2$

$1,53\times10^{-19} = \frac{1}{2}\left(9,1\times10^{-31}\right)v^2$

$v = 5,8\times10^{5}$ m.s^{-1}

Illustrative Example 2:

When Zinc is irradiated with electromagnetic radiation of frequency 8×10^{15} Hz, the maximum velocity of an electron emitted from the zinc is $3,175\times10^{6}$ m.s^{-1}. Determine the work function of the Zinc in eV.

$E = W_o + E_{k_{max}}$

$hf = W_o + \frac{1}{2}m_{e^-}v^2$

$\left(6,6\times10^{-34}\right)\left(8\times10^{15}\right) = W_o + \frac{1}{2}\left(9,1\times10^{-31}\right)\left(3,175\times10^{6}\right)^2$

$W_o = 6,93\times10^{-19}$ J

$W_o = \frac{6,93\times10^{-19}}{1,6\times10^{-19}}$

$= 4,33$ eV

INTENSITY, FREQUENCY AND CURRENT

As **intensity** (brightness) of the light (incident radiation) **increases**, the **number of photons** arriving on the surface of the metal **increases**.

Each photon of light (with sufficient energy) **will cause one electron to be emitted** from the metal.
Increasing the **intensity** causes **more electrons** to be released.
An **increase** in the number of **electrons** released will cause the **current** in the circuit to **increase**.

As **frequency increases**, the **energy of each photon** of light (incident radiation) **increases**.
Increasing the **frequency** will **increase the kinetic energy of the emitted electrons**.
This means that the **velocity** with which the electrons leave the surface with, **will increase**.
Increasing the frequency does not affect the current in the circuit.
Current is related to the number of electrons emitted, not the energy of the electrons.

- **Increasing intensity increases the number of emitted electrons and increases the current in the circuit.**
- **This only happens if the frequency of the incident light is greater than the threshold frequency.**
- **Increasing frequency increases the kinetic energy and velocity of the emitted electrons. Increasing the frequency does not increase the current.**

TOC | 1 Data Sheet | 2 Definitions | 3 | 3 solutions | 4 | 4 solutions | 5 | 5 solutions | 6 | 6 solutions | 7 | 7 solutions | 8 | 8 solutions | 9 | 9 solutions | 10 | 10 solutions

THE GRAPH OF KINETIC ENERGY (E_K) AGAINST FREQUENCY

The graph of kinetic energy against frequency for a particular metal is shown below.

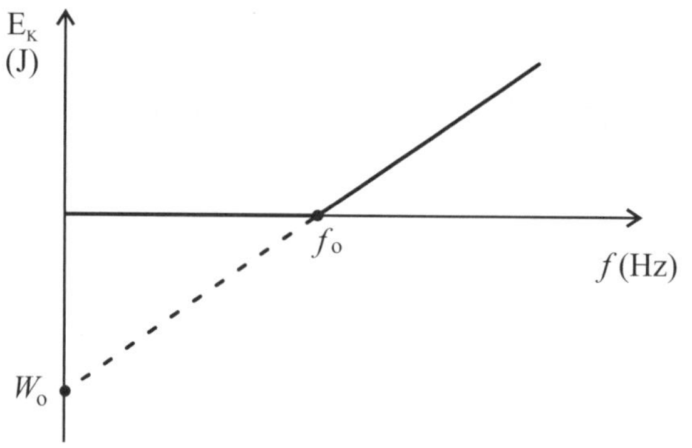

In the graph, for any **frequency below the threshold frequency (f_0)**, the **kinetic energy** of the emitted electrons is **zero**. This is because no electrons are emitted if the energy of the incident radiation is less than the threshold frequency of the metal.

At frequencies above the threshold frequency, kinetic energy increases as frequency increases.
The ***x*-intercept** of the graph is the **threshold frequency** of the metal.

The work function and Planck's constant can also be determined from the graph.
Examine the manipulation of the photoelectric equation to write the equation in the form $y = mx + c$ below:

$$E = W_o + E_{k_{max}}$$

$$hf = W_o + E_{k_{max}}$$

$E_{k_{max}} = \boldsymbol{hf - W_o} \rightarrow y = mx + c$, kinetic energy is plotted on the y-axis and frequency on the x-axis

From the manipulation it can be seen that:

- The **gradient** of the graph is **Planck's constant.**
- The ***y*-intercept** is the **negative work function** of the metal.

> **If the *y*-axis is in joules the gradient of the graph will be Planck's constant in J.s.**
> **If the *y*-axis is in eV the gradient of the graph will be Planck's constant in eV.s.**

THE LIGHT SPECTRUM

The order of colours in the visible light spectrum is **red**, **orange**, **yellow**, **green**, **blue**, **indigo** and **violet**.
To remember the order of the spectrum, use the first letter of each colour to spell the name **ROY G BIV**.
As you move **from red to violet** in the visible spectrum **wavelength decreases** and **energy increases**.
Infra-red radiation falls out of the visible spectrum and has a **lower energy** (**longer wavelength**) than red light.
Ultraviolet (UV) radiation has a **higher energy** (**shorter wavelength**) than violet light and also falls out of the visible spectrum.

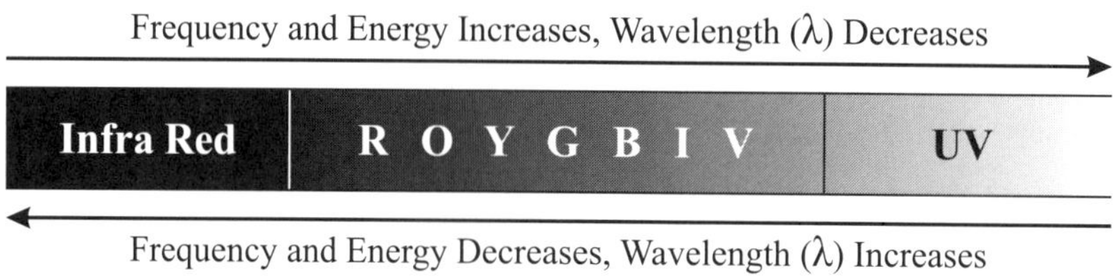

LINE EMISSION SPECTRUM

Electrons in an atom **are arranged** so that the **energy** of the atom **is as low as possible.**
This is known as the **ground state** of the atom.
When those atoms are given energy, the **electrons absorb the energy and move to a higher energy level.**
Every atom has its own **distinct set of energy levels** like every person has their own unique fingerprint.
When a gas is heated, **electrons absorb energy** and move to a **higher energy level, further from the nucleus.**
The atom is then said to be in an unstable **excited state.**
When the **electrons fall back down, they release the energy they absorbed in the form of light.**
This is known as a **line emission spectrum.**
Each transition between energy levels **results in the emission of a photon with a particular wavelength.**
The larger the transition the **more energy** the light has and the **lower** the **wavelength.**
As energy levels are distinct to each atom, the **emission spectrum is unique to the atom.**

The emission spectrum for the hydrogen atom with the corresponding wavelengths the hydrogen atom emits is shown below.

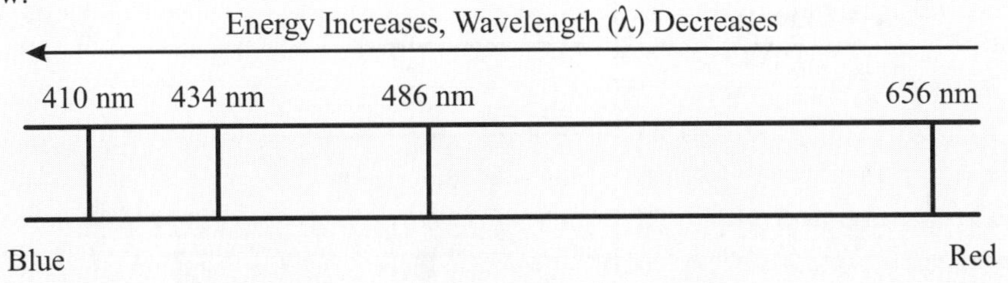

Line Emission Spectrum of the Hydrogen Atom

GAS DISCHARGE TUBES

Gas discharge tubes are tubes filled with a gas at low pressure. When a high enough **voltage is applied** across the tube, the **gas ionises and acts like a conductor**, allowing a current to flow through the circuit. The **current excites the atoms of the ionised gas.** When the **electrons fall back to their ground state, they emit photons to release the excess energy.**

The light given off from a gas discharge tube forms a line emission spectrum. If the tube were filled with Hydrogen gas, the emission spectrum above would be produced.

> **In order to obtain a line emission spectrum the light from a gas discharge tube must be passed through a prism to split the light into its different colours.**

ENERGY LEVEL DIAGRAMS

The diagram below shows an energy level diagram and the energy associated with each level.
Electrons in the **n = 1 energy level are closest to the nucleus** and have the **lowest potential energy. Electrons in the energy level furthest from the nucleus** (n = 3) have the **highest potential energy. Free electrons** have **zero potential energy**. The **potential energy** is given as a **negative value** because **energy is released as electrons move to lower levels.**

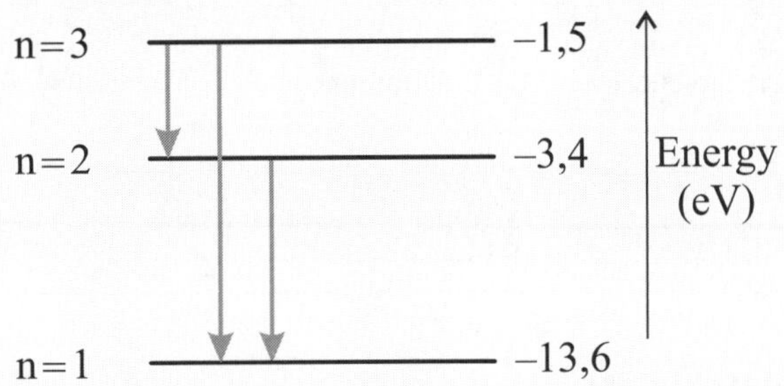

As electrons transition from an excited state back to their ground state the energy released is equal to the difference in potential energy between the energy levels.

The grey **arrows show** the **possible transitions** that an electron can undergo for the three energy levels shown.

CALCULATING THE POTENTIAL ENERGY BETWEEN ENERGY LEVELS

The Formula below is used to calculate the potential energy between energy levels.

Potential Energy Between Energy Levels

$$\Delta E = E_2 - E_1$$

$\Delta E \rightarrow$ difference in potential energy between two energy levels (J or eV)

$E_2 \rightarrow$ Energy of the highest energy level the electron started in

$E_1 \rightarrow$ Energy of the energy level the electron falls to

Illustrative Example:

The diagram below shows some of the energy levels of an atom of a hypothetical element.

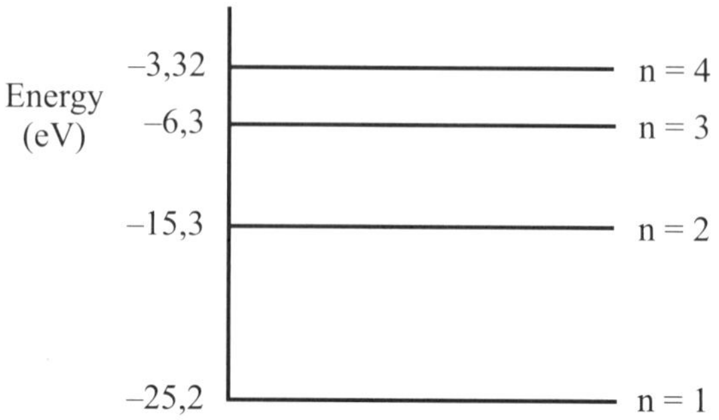

a) How many possible transitions are possible for the element? Show these on the diagram.

b) Calculate the shortest wavelength that can be emitted when an electron transitions between two energy levels for the given element.

c) Calculate the highest frequency of electromagnetic radiation that can be emitted from the element.

a) 6

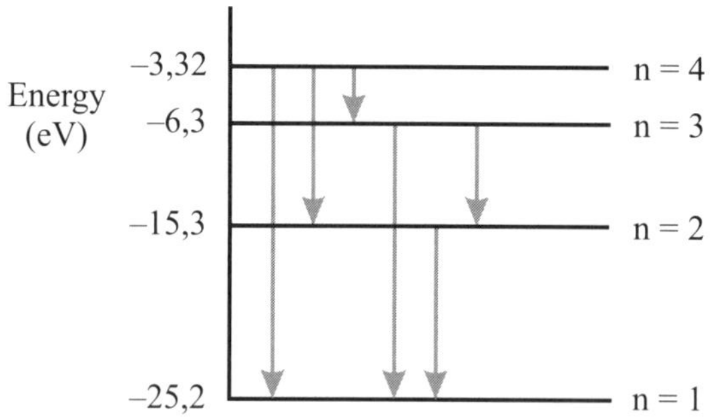

b) The shortest wavelength has the largest energy. This would be a transition between levels n = 4 and n = 1.

$$\Delta E = E_4 - E_1$$
$$= -3,32 - (-25,2)$$
$$= 21,88 \text{ eV}$$

You now have to convert the energy from eV to Joules.

$$\Delta E = 21,88\left(1,6\times10^{-19}\right)$$
$$= 3,50\times10^{-18} \text{ J}$$

$$E = \frac{hc}{\lambda}$$

$$3,50\times10^{-18} = \frac{\left(6,6\times10^{-34}\right)\left(3\times10^{8}\right)}{\lambda}$$

$$\lambda = 5,66\times10^{-8} \text{ m}$$

c) The highest frequency corresponds to the shortest wavelength

$$f = \frac{c}{\lambda} = \frac{3\times10^{8}}{5,66\times10^{-8}}$$
$$= 5,30\times10^{15} \text{ Hz}$$

Question 1 (Solutions on page 472)

1.1 The cathode of a photocell is illuminated with monochromatic light. The energy of the photons is greater than the work function of the metal cathode. Which one of the following graphs best shows the way in which the number of photoelectrons emitted varies with the intensity of the light?

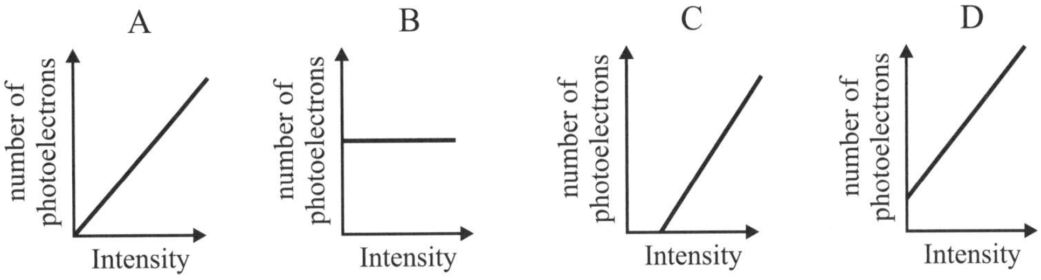

(2)

1.2 The work function of a metal is the:

A maximum energy required to eject a photoelectron from the surface of a metal

B minimum energy required to eject a photoelectron from the surface of a metal

C maximum frequency required to eject a photoelectron from the surface of a metal

D minimum frequency required to eject a photoelectron from the surface of a metal (2)

1.3 Line X on the graphs below shows how the maximum kinetic energy of emitted photoelectrons varies with the frequency of the incident radiation for a certain metal. Which graph shows the results for a metal Y that has a lower work function than X?

Metal X is represented by a solid line and Metal Y is represented by a dotted line.

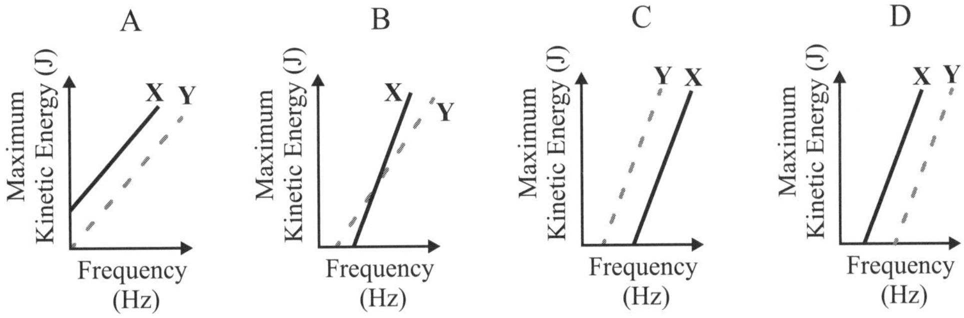

(2)

1.4 A monochromatic light source is shone onto a metal and photoelectrons are emitted. The intensity of light is slowly increased. Which of the following is correct?

	Energy of photoelectron	Number of photoelectrons emitted per second
A	Increases	Increases
B	Remains constant	Remains constant
C	Increases	Remains constant
D	Remains constant	Increases

(2)

1.5 Which one of the following statements about electron transitions in atomic spectra is false?

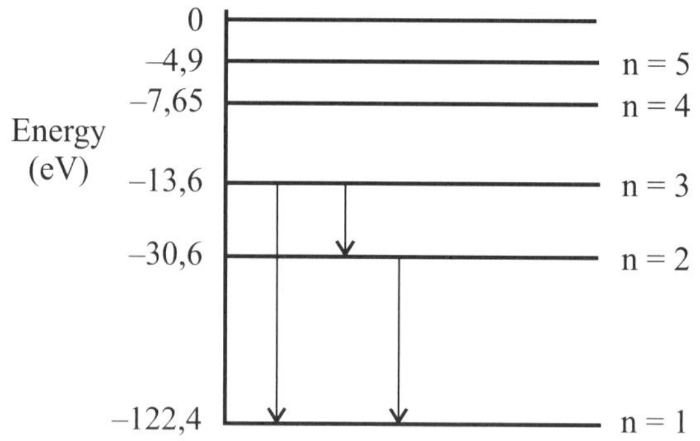

A An electron transition from the n = 2 to the n = 1 energy level will emit a shorter wavelength than a transition from the n = 4 to the n = 3 energy level.

B An electron moving from the n = 1 to the n = 3 energy level absorbs energy.

C An electron emits light when it moves from a higher energy level to a lower energy level.

D An electron transition from the n = 3 to the n = 1 energy level will emit a longer wavelength than a transition from the n = 5 to the n = 3 energy level. (2)

1.6 The diagram below shows the electron transitions P, Q, R and S between different energy levels in an atom.

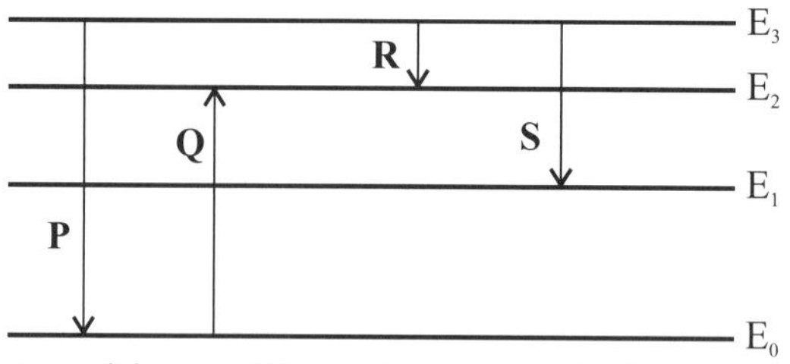

Which one of the transitions will result in an emission of a radiation with the longest wavelength?

A P
B Q
C R
D S (2)

1.7 An energy of 6,4 eV corresponds to a frequency of:

A $1{,}02 \times 10^{-18}$ Hz
B 4×10^{19} Hz
C $6{,}03 \times 10^{52}$ Hz
D $1{,}55 \times 10^{15}$ Hz (2)

1.8 Which statement about atomic line emission spectra is false?

A Emission lines occur when electrons within in an atom lose energy.
B When an electron transitions from a higher energy level to a lower energy level, visible light is always emitted.
C Emission spectra provide evidence that there are discrete energy levels within an atom.
D An element can be identified by its line emission spectrum (2)

1.9 The work functions of metals A and B are in the ratio 1 : 2. Light frequencies f and $2f$ are incident on the surfaces of A and B respectively. Assuming that f is greater than the threshold frequency of A, and $2f$ is greater than the threshold frequency of B, what is the ratio of the maximum kinetic energies of the photoelectrons emitted?

A 1:1
B 1:2
C 1:3
D 1:4 (2)

1.10 The graph below shows the relationship between the kinetic energy of electrons ejected from an aluminium plate and the frequency of light shone on the aluminium plate.

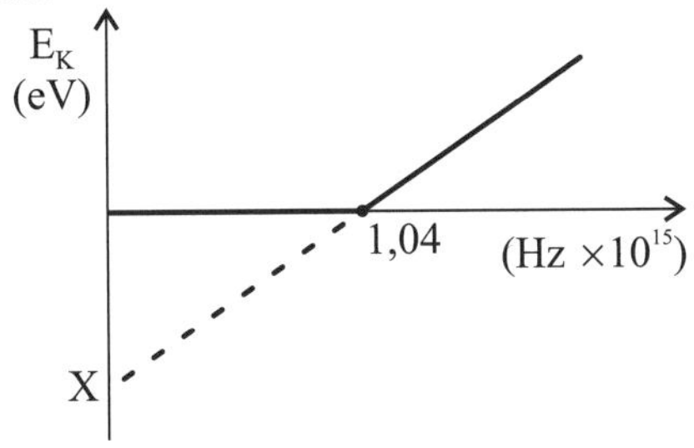

The value of X is:

A $1{,}66 \times 10^{-4}$ J
B $-6{,}86 \times 10^{-19}$ J
C $-4{,}29$ eV
D $-6{,}86 \times 10^{-19}$ eV (2)

1.11 The wavelength of a monochromatic light source P is three times that of a monochromatic light source Q. The energy of a photon from source P will be ___________ of a photon from source Q.

The missing phrase is:

A equal to the energy
B one third of the energy
C three times the energy
D one ninth the energy (2)

1.12 Electron transitions occur in an atom as shown in the diagram. In each transition photons are emitted.

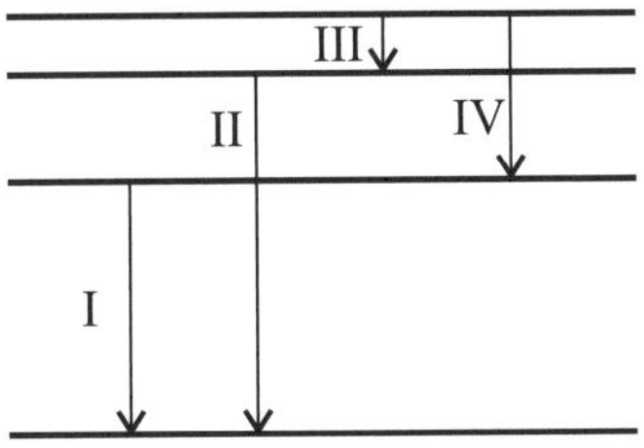

If the emitted photons are all capable of releasing photoelectrons from a certain metal, which photon will release electrons with the lowest kinetic energy?

A I
B II
C III
D IV (2)

1.13 A single photon has 4 times the energy of the work function for metal X. When this photon is incident on metal X,

A It ejects a single electron with energy equivalent to 4 times the work function.
B It ejects 4 electrons with energy equivalent to the work function.
C It ejects a single electron with energy equivalent to 3 times the work function.
D It ejects 3 electrons with energy equivalent to the work function. (2)

1.14 Light incident on a metal surface has a frequency greater than the threshold frequency. Increasing the frequency of the light incident on a metal surface,

A Decreases the threshold frequency of the metal.
B Increases the number of photoelectrons emitted from the metal surface.
C Increases the work function of the metal.
D Increases the kinetic energy of the photoelectrons. (2)

1.15 A line emission spectrum…

A Proves that an atom contains electrons.
B Proves the quantization of the energy of electrons in an atom.
C Can be used to determine the number of electrons in an atom.
D Proves that electrons can only occupy specific orbitals in an atom. (2)

1.16 Monochromatic light of different intensities irradiates the surface of metal X and metal Y. It causes electrons to be emitted from metal X, but not metal Y. This is because…

A Metal X has a smaller work function than metal Y.
B Metal X has a greater work function than metal Y.
C The energy of a photon striking metal X is greater than those striking metal Y.
D The intensity of the light irradiating metal X is greater than the intensity of the light irradiating metal Y. (2)

1.17 A metal with a work function of 4,3 eV is placed on the plate of a negatively charged electroscope.

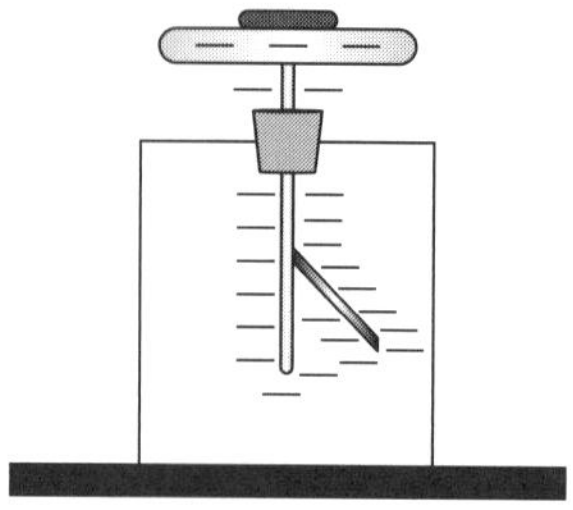

Which of the following would cause the gold leaf to fall most rapidly?

A Shine light on the metal with a frequency of $1{,}05 \times 10^{15}$ Hz
B Shine light on the metal with a wavelength of 240 nm
C Shine high intensity light on the metal with a frequency of $8{,}25 \times 10^{14}$ Hz
D Shine very high intensity light on the metal with a wavelength of 800 nm. (2)

1.18 Electrons are emitted from the surface of a metal plate when it is irradiated with blue light of wavelength 475 nm. The threshold wavelength of the metal is 595 nm. The metal is now irradiated with red light of wavelength 650 nm but with double the intensity of the blue light. How will the current change when the red light is shone on the metal in comparison to the blue light?

The current will…

A stay the same.

B be zero.

C halve.

D double. (2)

1.19 A photocell is connected in a closed circuit with an ammeter, which registers a reading. Which of the following changes will increase the reading on the ammeter?

A Making the incident light brighter.

B Making the incident light dimmer.

C Increasing the wavelength of the incident light.

D Changing the metal in the photocell to one with a higher work function. (2)

1.20 When light of a certain frequency is incident on the cathode of a photocell, the ammeter in the circuit registers a reading.
The intensity of the incident light is now increased while keeping the frequency constant. Which one of the following correctly describes the reading on the ammeter and the reason for this reading?

	Ammeter Reading	Reason
A	Increases	The kinetic energy of the electrons increases
B	No change	The kinetic energy of the electrons does not change
C	Increases	The number of electrons emitted increases
D	No change	The number of electrons emitted does not change

(2)

1.21 When light of a certain wavelength is incident on a metal surface, no electrons are ejected. Which ONE of the following changes may result in electrons being ejected from the metal surface?

A Increase the intensity of the light.

B Use light with much lower frequency.

C Use light with a much shorter wavelength.

D Increase the surface area of the metal. (2)

1.22 In a vacuum, all electromagnetic waves have the same…

A Energy.

B Frequency.

C Wavelength.

D Speed. (2)

1.23 A metal plate with a threshold frequency of 5×10^{14} Hz is resting on a positively charged electroscope. It is irradiated for a long period of time by light with a wavelength of 595 nm. What will be observed?

A The gold leaf will slowly fall as electrons are ejected from the metals surface

B There will be no change to the position of the gold leaf.

C The gold leaf will deflect to a larger angle then before.

D The gold leaf will fall and then rise again. (2)

1.24 The diagram represents 3 energy levels, X, Y and Z, in a certain atom. The energy difference between levels Y and Z is twice the energy difference between levels X and Y. If the wavelength of a photon emitted as a result of transition P, from level X to Y, is λ, then what is the wavelength of the photon emitted during transition Q, from level X to Z?

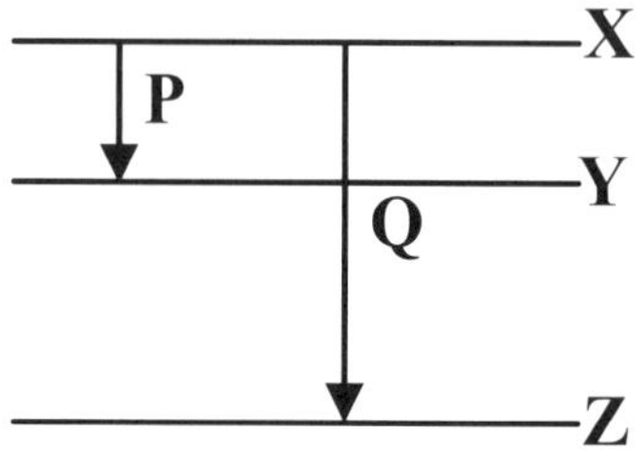

A 2λ.

B 3λ.

C $\lambda/2$.

D $\lambda/3$.

(The above question is from the 2014 IEB Final Examination)

1.25 The diagram represents transitions of electrons in the energy levels in a certain atom. Which one of the following statements is true concerning the emission of photons associated with transitions X and Y?

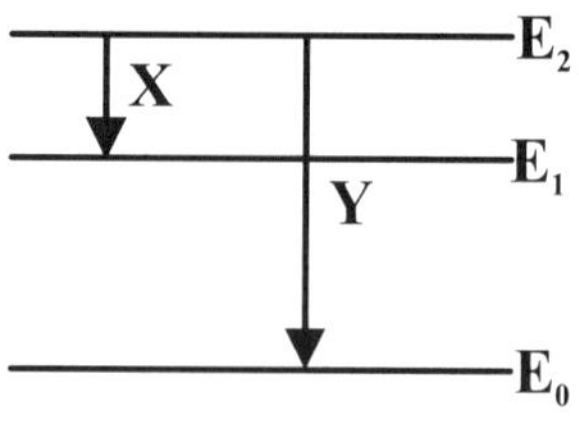

The photon associated with X has a greater …

A frequency than the photon associated with Y.

B wavelength than the photon associated with Y.

C energy than the photon associated with Y.

D intensity than the photon associated with Y.

(The above question is from the 2014 IEB Supplementary Examination) (2)

1.26 The work function of a metal is the ____________ ____________ needed to emit an electron from the surface of a metal.

A maximum frequency.

B minimum frequency.

C minimum energy.

D maximum energy.

(The above question is from the 2015 IEB Supplementary Examination) (2)

[50]

TOC 1 Data Sheet 2 Definitions 3 3 solutions 4 4 solutions 5 5 solutions 6 6 solutions 7 7 solutions 8 8 solutions 9 9 solutions 10 10 solutions

Question 2 (Solutions on page 472)

The diagram shows ultraviolet light falling on the surface of a caesium cathode in a photocell. The work function of caesium is 3,36 x 10^{-19} J. The wavelength of a photon of ultraviolet light is 350 nm.

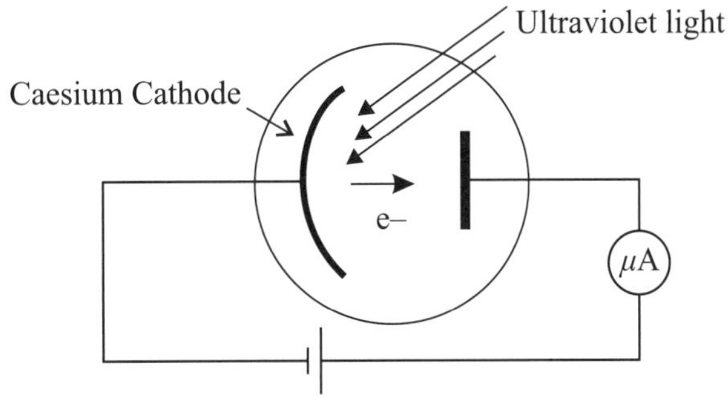

2.1 Define the work function of a metal. (2)

2.2 Calculate the energy of a photon of ultra-violet light. (4)

2.3 Calculate the maximum speed of the photoelectrons emitted. (4)

2.4 The intensity of the ultra-violet light is such that it transfers 8,49 x 10^{-9} J of energy in one second to the caesium cathode. If one photon releases one electron, then calculate the number of electrons released from the cathode in one second. (2)

2.5 How will the number of electrons emitted be affected if:

2.5.1 The intensity of the incident light is increased? (1)

2.5.2 The frequency of the incident light is increased? (1)

[14]

Question 3 (Solutions on page 472 and 473)

When electromagnetic radiation is incident on a metal plate, photoelectrons may be emitted.

3.1 Define threshold frequency. (2)

3.2 Aluminium has a work function of 4,28 eV. Calculate the threshold frequency of aluminium. (3)

3.3 Calculate the maximum velocity of a photoelectron emitted from aluminium when it is irradiated with light that has a frequency of 2×10^{15} Hz (5)

[10]

Question 4 (Solutions on page 473)

The diagram below shows the lowest three energy levels of a hydrogen atom.

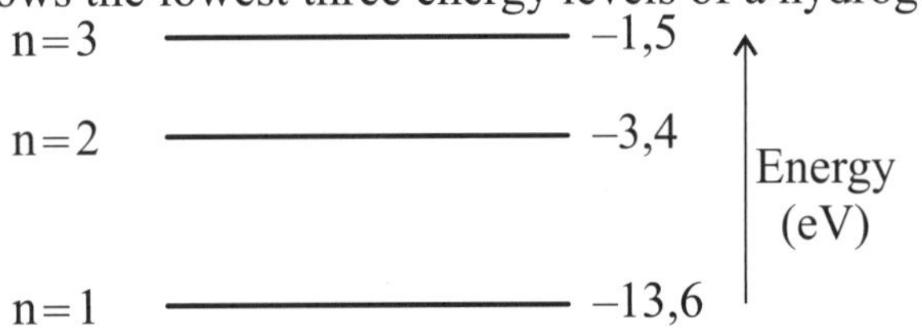

4.1 The hydrogen atom can emit light with wavelength of $6{,}65 \times 10^{-7}$ m when excited. Calculate the frequency of this light. (2)

4.2 The energy of a photon of this frequency is $3{,}04 \times 10^{-19}$ J. By means of a calculation, determine which electron transition emits this photon. (2)

[4]

TOC
1 Data Sheet
2 Definitions
3
3 solutions
4
4 solutions
5
5 solutions
6
6 solutions
7
7 solutions
8
8 solutions
9
9 solutions
10
10 solutions

TOC 1 Data Sheet 2 Definitions 3 3 solutions 4 4 solutions 5 5 solutions 6 6 solutions 7 7 solutions 8 8 solutions 9 9 solutions 10 10 solutions

Question 5 (Solutions on page 473 and 474)

The diagram below shows the lowest four energy levels of a hydrogen atom and the approximate wavelengths for three different spectrums, ultraviolet, visible and infrared light.

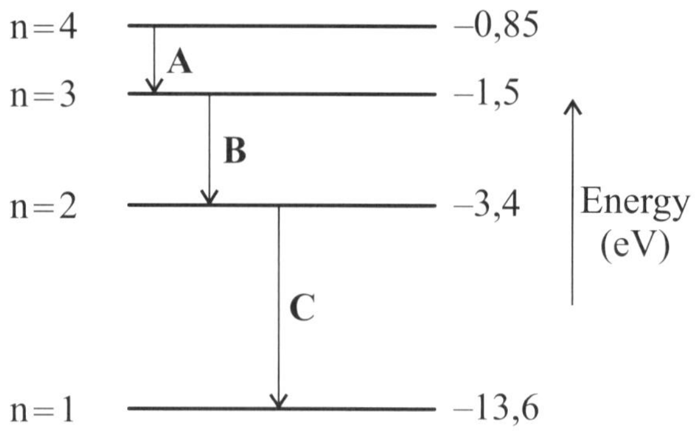

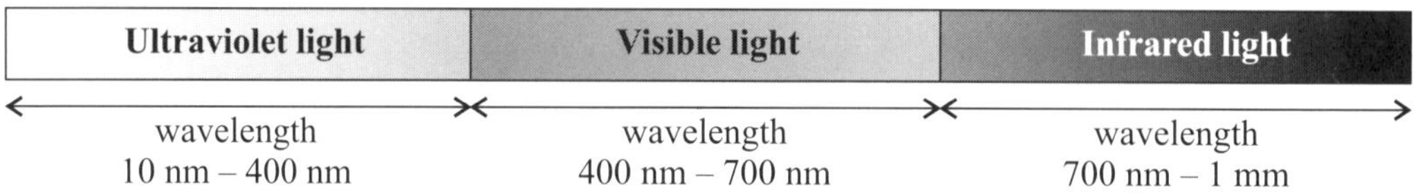

5.1 Each of the transitions, A, B and C belong to one of the above spectrums. Match transitions A, B and C with the most probable region of the spectrum which they are associated with. (3)

5.2 Prove that a transition from the third energy level to ground state would emit light in the UV spectrum. (6)

5.3 Why are the levels in the diagram stated as negative values? (2)

The surface of a sample of caesium is irradiated with photons from each of the three transitions shown above. The threshold frequency for caesium is $5,1 \times 10^{14}$ Hz.

5.4 Which of the transitions (A, B or C) cause photoelectrons to be emitted from the surface of caesium? (4)

5.5 Photons transitioning from the 3rd energy level to the ground state of hydrogen are incident on the surface of the caesium. Calculate the maximum speed of electrons emitted from caesium. (5)

5.6 How many unique wavelengths will be in the emission spectrum of this hydrogen atom if there are only four energy levels? (2)

5.7 Hydrogen gas in a discharge tube emits light of wavelength 485,29 nm.

5.7.1 Calculate the energy (in eV) that corresponds to this wavelength of light. (4)

5.7.2 Which electron transition will result in the emission of light with a wavelength of 485,29 nm? (2)

[28]

Question 6 (Solutions on page 474)

Tintswalo has an unknown metal. She is attempting to determine what the metal is by measuring the maximum kinetic energy of the photoelectrons emitted from the surface of the metal. She irradiates the metal with different frequencies of light. She uses the results of her experiment to plot the graph below. The table alongside the graph shows a table of work functions of different metals which Tintswalo found on the internet.

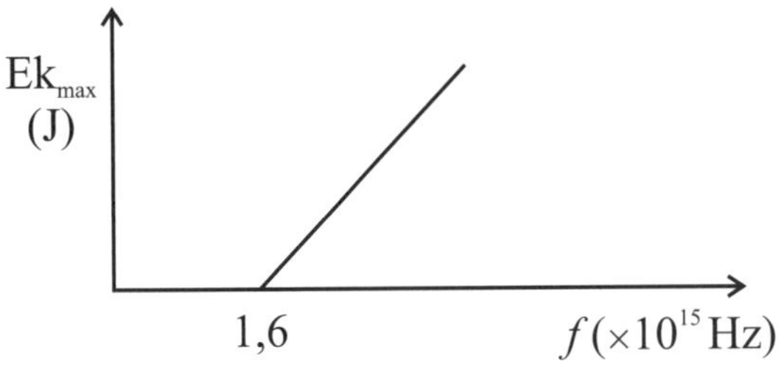

Metal	Work Function (eV)
Sodium	2,39
Calcium	2,99
Zinc	4,33
Copper	4,7
Platinum	6,35

6.1 Define the work function of a metal. (2)

6.2 State the independent variable in this experiment. (2)

6.3 Use the given information to determine what metal is used in the experiment. (4)

6.4 The surface of another metal is irradiated using UV light with a wavelength of 400 nm. The maximum speed of the emitted photoelectrons is 191 000 $m.s^{-1}$. Use the table to determine which metal is being irradiated. (7)

[15]

Question 7 (Solutions on page 475)

The four emission lines P, Q, R and S shown in the diagram below arise from the excitement of a hydrogen atom.

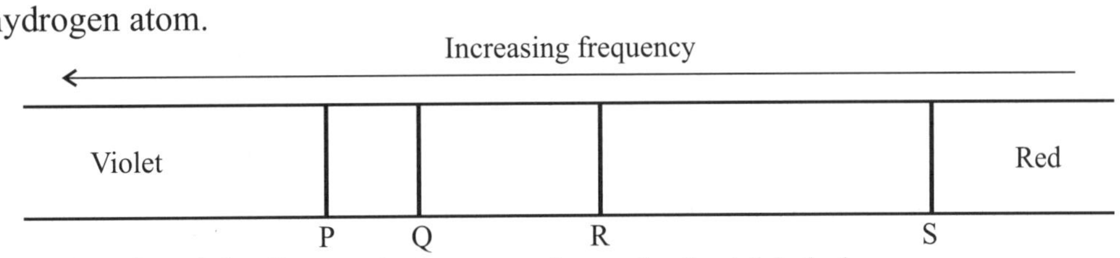

The wavelengths of the four emissions are shown in the table below.

Emission line	Wavelength ($\times 10^{-7}$ m)
	6,58
	4,86
	4,34
	4,10

Frequencies associated with these wavelengths are emitted when electrons move from a higher energy level to the –3,4 eV energy level.

7.1 Fill in the table above placing the emission P, Q, R and S in the correct row. (4)

7.2 Calculate the value of the energy of the light associated with the emission line R. (4)

7.3 To produce emission R, an electron transitions from energy level *x*. Determine the energy (in eV) of energy level *x*. (4)

7.4 The work function of zinc is 4,33 eV. Which of the emissions would cause photoelectrons to be emitted from the surface of zinc? (4)

[16]

TOC | 1 Data Sheet | 2 Definitions | 3 | 3 solutions | 4 | 4 solutions | 5 | 5 solutions | 6 | 6 solutions | 7 | 7 solutions | 8 | 8 solutions | 9 | 9 solutions | **10** | 10 solutions

Question 8 (Solutions on page 475 and 476)

Sodium metal is irradiated by varying frequencies of electromagnetic radiation. The maximum kinetic energy of the photoelectrons emitted is recorded in the table below.

Frequency ($\times 10^{14}$ Hz)	Maximum Kinetic Energy (eV)
6	0,2
7	0,61
8	1,02
9	1,43
10	1,85

8.1 Define threshold frequency. (2)

8.2 Plot a graph of maximum kinetic energy against frequency on the graph paper below.

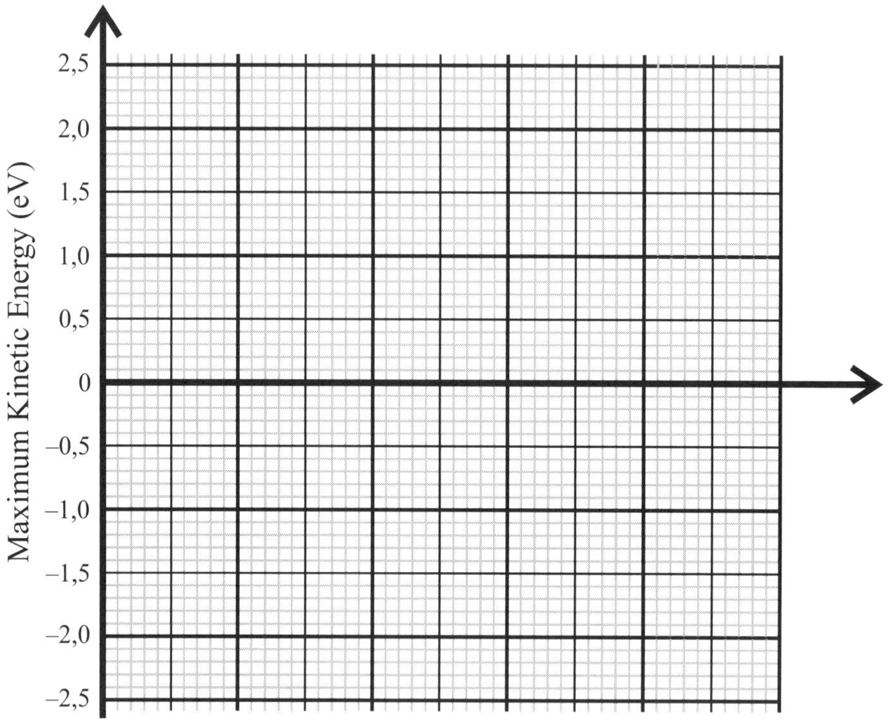

(6)

8.3 Using your graph state the:

8.3.1 Threshold frequency of sodium. (2)

8.3.2 Work function of sodium in joules. (2)

8.4 The experiment is repeated using a new metal instead of sodium. The work function of the new metal is half the work function of sodium. Draw a second line on the graph to illustrate the results of the experiment with the new metal. (3)

8.5 A science learner calculates the gradient of the graph to be $4,1\times10^{-15}$. The learner concludes that there is an error in the data as the gradient of the graph should be equal to $6,6\times10^{-34}$ (Planck's constant). Is the learner correct? Explain your answer fully. (4)

8.6 The maximum kinetic energy of photoelectron emitted from the surface of sodium is $1,92\times10^{-19}$ J.

8.6.1 Use your graph to determine the frequency of the incident radiation. (3)

8.6.2 Calculate the wavelength of the incident radiation. (3)

[25]

Question 9 (Solutions on page 476)

In the circuit below, orange light with a wavelength of 600 nm is incident on the metal surface. The ejected electrons are emitted with zero kinetic energy.

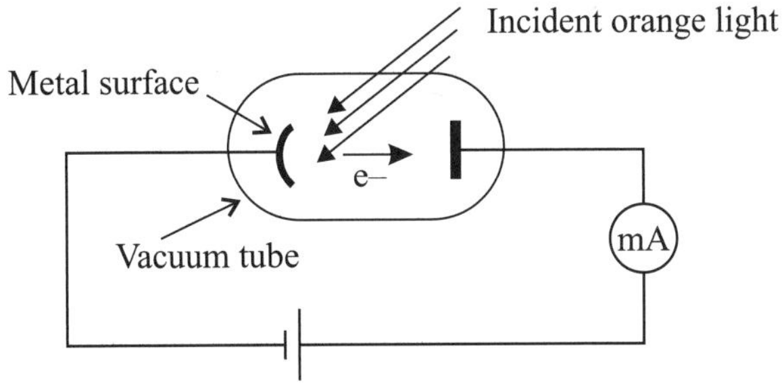

9.1 Describe the photoelectric effect. (2)

9.2 Define the work function of a metal (2)

9.3 Calculate the work function of the metal in the circuit above. (4)

9.4 The orange light is then replaced by a very dim light of wavelength 100 nm. Will the milliammeter in the circuit detect a photocurrent? (1)

9.5 Explain your answer to question 9.4 above. (2)

[11]

Question 10 (Solutions on page 476 and 477)

The diagram below shows an experiment where red light and UV light are shone onto a negatively charged plate of zinc metal.

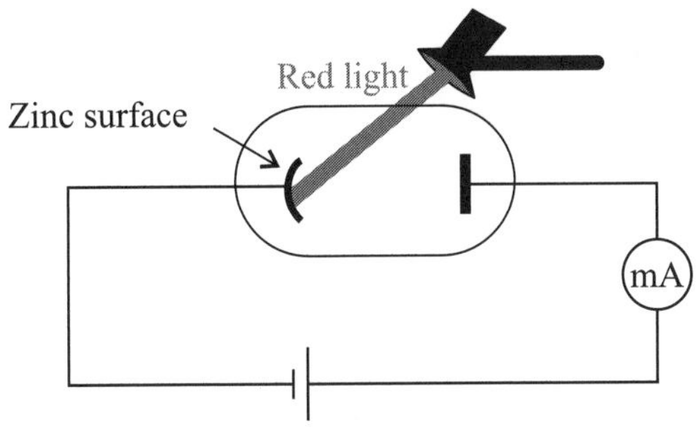

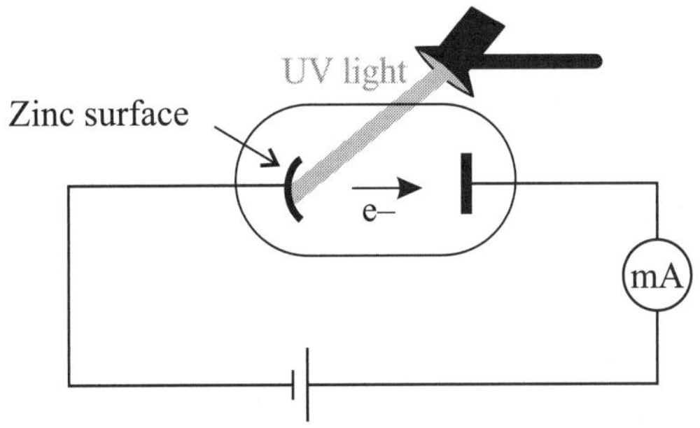

When red light is shone onto the negatively charged plate of the zinc metal, the milliammeter reads 0 mA. When UV light is shone onto the same plate, electrons are emitted, and a reading is seen on the milliammeter.

10.1 What phenomenon is described above? State the significance of this effect. (3)

10.2 Explain why the red light has no effect but the UV light causes electrons to be emitted. (3)

The work function of zinc is 4,33 eV.

10.3 What is the work function of zinc in joules. (1)

10.4 Calculate the maximum kinetic energy of an electron ejected from the zinc metal by a photon of wavelength of 100 nm. (4)

10.5 The intensity of both lights is increased:

10.5.1 For each experiment, state what would happen to the reading on the milliammeter. (state only increase, decrease or remain the same) (2)

10.5.2 Explain your answer to 10.5.1 above. (4)

10.6 Draw a sketch graph of the maximum kinetic energy of the emitted electrons against frequency. On your graph clearly indicate the axes labels and units, the threshold frequency and work function of the metal in electron volts. You must provide the actual value of the work function of zinc but no other values are necessary. (5)

10.7 What are the units of the gradient? (2)

10.8 What is the value of the gradient? (2)

[25]

Question 11 (Solutions on page 477 and 478)

A retail store would like a doorbell to ring as customer walks through the door.
The storeowner sets up the circuit below using a relay switch to ring the doorbell.
A relay is a switch that operates based on current. The relay in the circuit below is known as a normally closed relay. This means when it is not supplied with current the switch will close. When supplied with a current the switch will open.

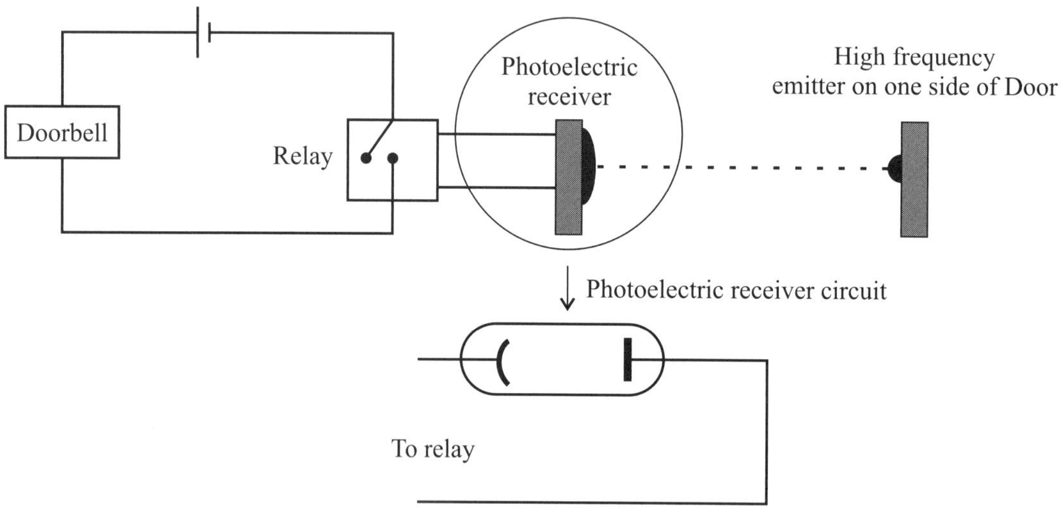

11.1 What phenomenon does the photoelectric receiver make use of? (1)

11.2 Use the diagram and information above to explain why the doorbell will ring when a customer walks through the door. (3)

11.3 The work function of the metal used in the receiver is 1,5 eV. What is the longest wavelength of light that will cause electron to be emitted? (4)

11.4 When the intensity of the emitter is reduced the doorbell starts to ring without the beam being broken. Use physics principles to explain why this occurs. (4)

11.5 The frequency of the light from the emitter is $9{,}5 \times 10^{14}$ Hz. Due to the light incident on the emitter, a current of 928 pA is induced in the circuit to the relay.

11.5.1 Calculate the energy of a photon of the light from the emitter. (3)

11.5.2 Determine the amount of energy transferred to the metal cathode in 10 seconds. You may assume that every photon of light incident on the surface of the metal ejects 1 electron. (7)

[22]

Question 12 (Solutions on page 478)

12.1 The apparatus below is used to demonstrate the photoelectric effect.

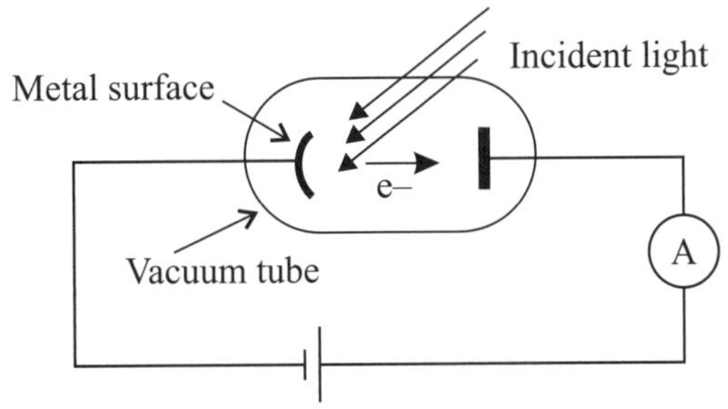

The frequency of a photon in the incident light is 15×10^{15} Hz. The maximum speed of the electrons emitted is $4{,}58 \times 10^{6}$ m.s^{-1}.

12.1.1 Calculate the energy of a photon of the incident light. (3)

12.1.2 Calculate the work function of the metal surface. (4)

12.1.3 The metal is replaced with cesium with a work function of 2,1 eV. Will the maximum speed of the photo electrons emitted by cesium be faster, slower or the same as the original emitter? Give a reason for your answer. (3)

12.1.4 How will the number of electrons emitted per second be affected by increasing the:

(a) Intensity of the incident light on the metal surface? (1)

(b) Frequency of the incident light? (1)

12.2 Diagram 1 below shows some of the possible energy emissions as excited electrons in a hot gas fall to lower energy levels.
Diagram 2 below shows the line emission spectrum produced. The white lines indicate the wavelengths at which light was observed.

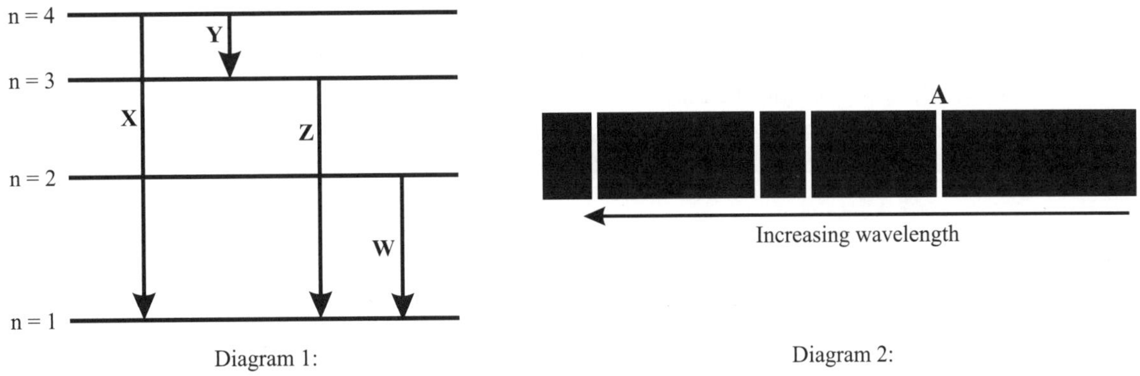

Diagram 1: Diagram 2:

12.2.1 Which of the emissions, X, Y, Z or W in diagram 1 is most likely to correspond to spectral line A in diagram 2? Explain your answer. (4)

12.2.2 The transition shown as Z above, releases red light of frequency $4{,}3 \times 10^{14}$ Hz. What is speed of the light emitted by transition Z? (2)

[18]

Question 13 (Solutions on page 479)

The maximum kinetic energy of electrons which were ejected from the surface of potassium metal was measured. The experiment was repeated using different frequencies of light. The results are shown in the graph below.

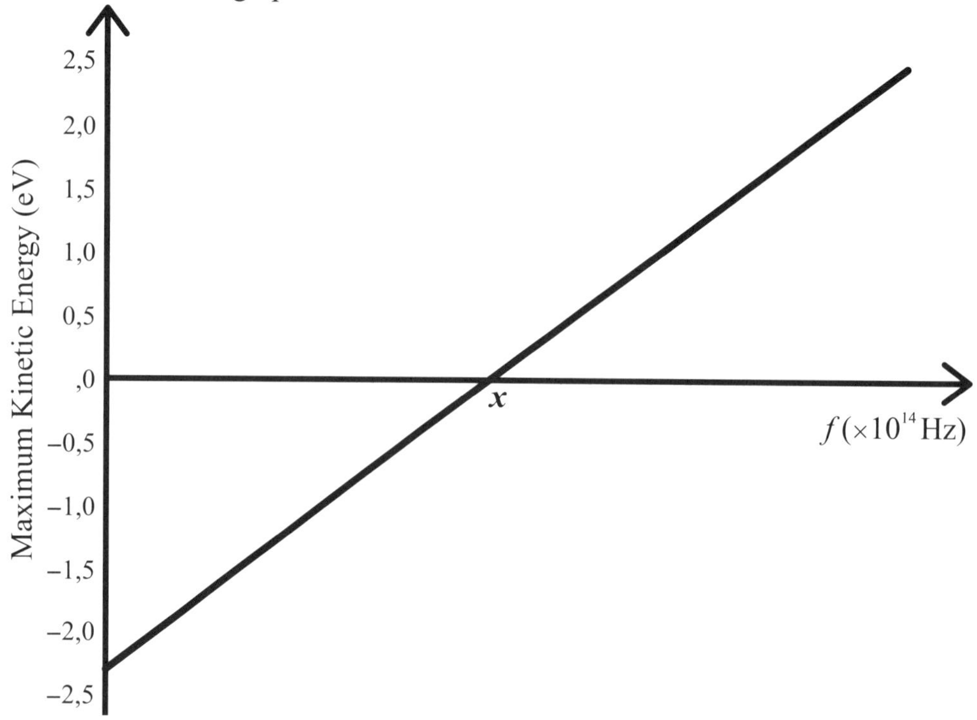

The mathematical equation of the graph is $y = 0,4125x - 2,2$.

13.1 Describe the photoelectric effect (2)

13.2 What does the value of x represent? (1)

13.3 Determine the value of the work function in joules. (2)

13.4 Calculate the value of the gradient in J.s. (calculations must be shown) (4)

13.5 Determine the numerical value of x. (4)

13.6 The exact same experiment is performed using lithium instead of potassium. The work function of lithium is 4×10^{-19} J. Draw the graph which will be obtained for the maximum kinetic energy of electrons ejected lithium against frequency of light on the graph above. The values of the work function and threshold frequency must be clearly shown on the graph. (5)

[18]

Question 14 (Solutions on page 479)

The diagram below shows some of the energy levels of an atom of a hypothetical element. An electron is excited and moves from the ground state to the 4th energy level (n = 4).

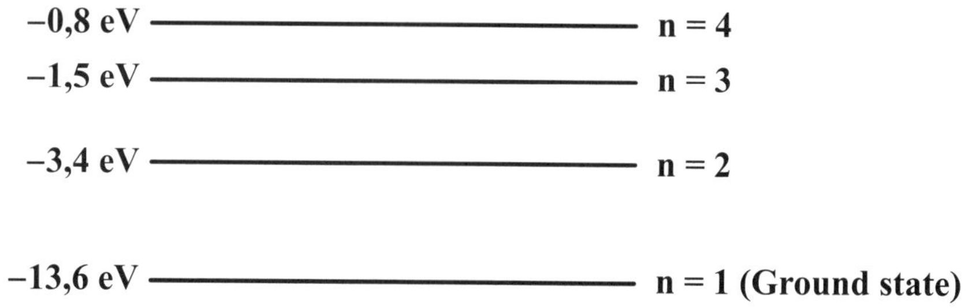

Calculate the longest wavelength of light that could be emitted when the electron transitions to a lower energy level.

[4]

Question 15 (Solutions on page 480)

A component in an alarm system uses high frequency beam of light which is shone onto a photocell. This causes electrons to be released the from the surface of the metal which flow into the alarm system. If the beam is crossed, a signal is sent to the alarm system which sets off a siren.

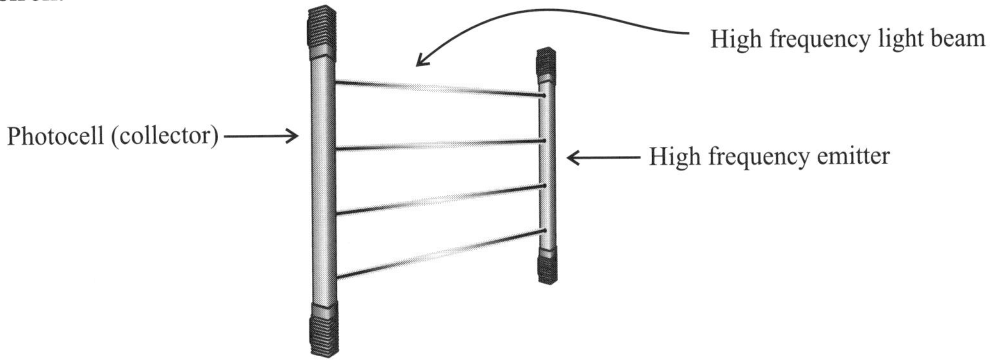

15.1 Describe the photoelectric effect. (2)

15.2 Explain why crossing the beam activates the siren. (2)

15.3 The metal in the photocell has a work function of 5,5 eV. (3)

15.3.1 Define work function. (2)

15.3.2 A science learner that did not study their photoelectric cells claims they can easily bypass the alarm system. The learner takes a torch that emits white light which consists of wavelengths between 400 nm and 700 nm and shines the torch onto the collector of the photocell. The learner then attempts to cross the beam. Use calculations to show why the alarm will still be triggered. (5)

15.3.3 The learner decides to try the experiment using 4 of the same torches as before (quadrupling the brightness of the light). Is it possible for the learner to be successful using this approach? Explain your answer fully. (3)

[17]

Question 16 (Solutions on page 480)

An energy level diagram for a particular element is drawn below. The only positions that the outer electron can occupy are the energy levels E_1, E_2 and E_3.

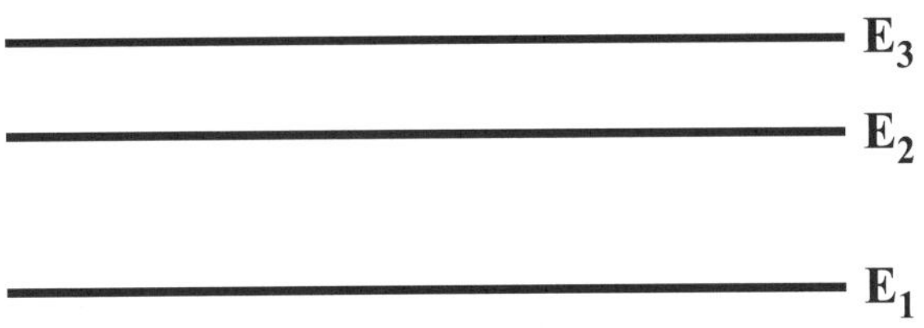

16.1 State three observations that can be deduced about the atomic structure of an atom from the existence of line emission spectra. (3)

16.2 If the longest wavelength of light that can be emitted for this energy level diagram is 532 nm, which transition would be responsible for releasing this wavelength of light? (2)

16.3 Calculate the energy that corresponds to this wavelength of light. (3)

[8]

TOC | 1 Data Sheet | 2 Definitions | 3 | 3 solutions | 4 | 4 solutions | 5 | 5 solutions | 6 | 6 solutions | 7 | 7 solutions | 8 | 8 solutions | 9 | 9 solutions | 10 | 10 solutions

Question 17 (Solutions on page 480 and 481)

17.1 A 0,1 mW bulb emits monochromatic violet light of wavelength 450 nm. Light from the bulb is shone onto a metal plate and electrons are emitted.

17.1.1 If the lightbulb is 20% efficient, calculate the number of photons that will be incident on the metal plate per second. (5)

17.1.2 Hence, write down the number of electrons emitted per second from the metal. (1)

17.2 An investigation was conducted to determine the effects of changes in frequency and intensity on the current generated in a photoelectric cell when light is incident on it.

The apparatus is used in the investigation is shown in the diagram below.

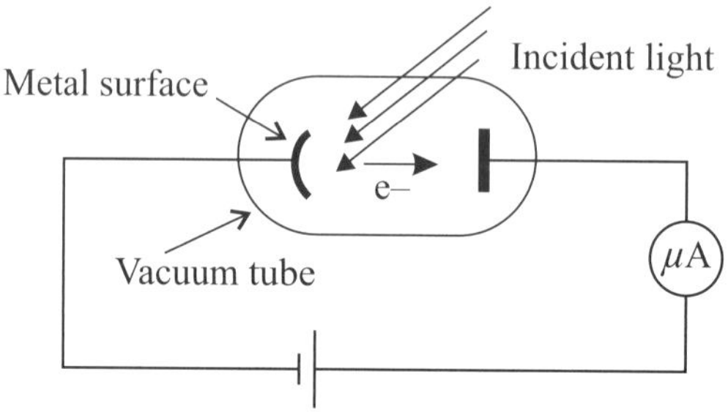

The work function of the metal used in the experiment is 2 eV and some of the results of the experiment is shown below. Complete the missing values in the table.

Experiment	Frequency ($\times 10^{14}$ Hz)	Intensity (lumens per square meter)	Current (μA)
1	4	20	0
2	4,5	40	**(17.2.1)**
3	5	20	15
4	5	40	**(17.2.2)**
5	5,5	60	**(17.2.3)**
5	6	10	**(17.2.4)**
6	8	**(17.2.5)**	150

(14)

[16]

Question 18 (2008 IEB Final Examination) (Solutions on page 481)

18.1 Peter and Avni want to investigate whether electrons are emitted by a metal as a result of light shining on it. They find some sheets of aluminium, copper and iron in their school's laboratory. They also find a piece of apparatus which looks like that which is shown in the diagram below.

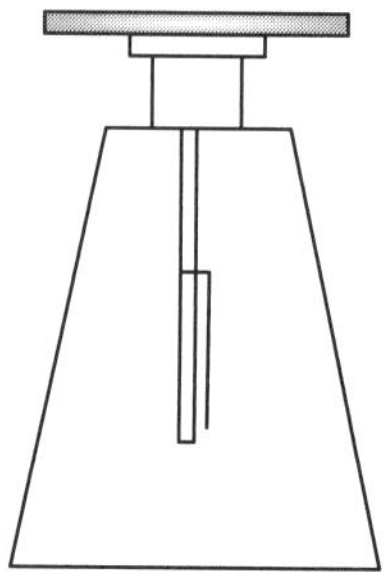

18.1.1 Name this piece of apparatus. (1)

18.1.2 Name the 'effect' that they are discussing. (1)

Peter and Anvi make a list of threshold frequencies for each of these metals.

Metal	Threshold frequency (Hz)
aluminium	$9,85 \times 10^{14}$
copper	$1,13 \times 10^{15}$
iron	$1,09 \times 10^{15}$

18.1.3 Explain what **the threshold frequency** of a metal is. (2)

In the laboratory they find three light sources with the same intensity which are labelled as being the following colours and frequencies:

Light	Frequency
ultra violet	$1,25 \times 10^{15}$ Hz
blue	$6,67 \times 10^{14}$ Hz
infra red	$1,22 \times 10^{13}$ Hz

They put the aluminium sheet on the metal cap of the instrument and give the instrument with the sheet, a negative charge. (Diagram 1).

Then they shine the ultra violet light on the aluminium sheet and observe that the gold leaf falls back slightly. (Diagram 2).

They then discharge the instrument and switch off the light source.

Taking each of the different colours of light in turn, they repeat this procedure and record their results for the aluminium sheet.

Then they repeat the whole procedure using the copper sheet and the three light sources and then the iron sheet with the same sources. They collect their results in a table as shown below.

Diagram 1

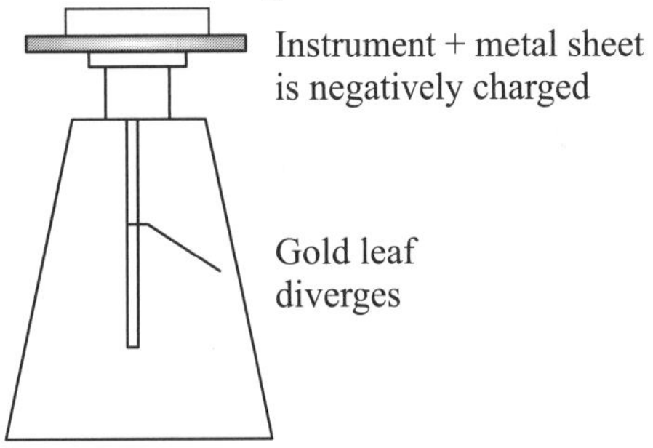

Diagram 2

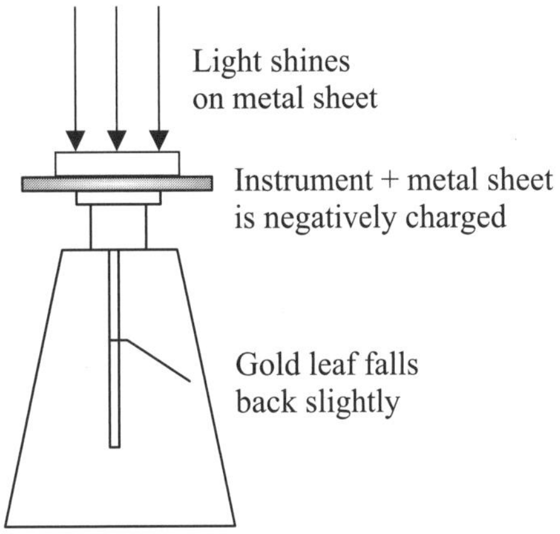

	aluminium	copper	iron
ultra violet	a	b	c
blue	d	e	f
infra red	g	h	i

18.1.4 Use the letters in the table and list **only** those experiments where you think that Peter and Avni **will observe a change in the position of the gold leaf**. Give the letter and state what would be observed. (4)

TOC
1 Data Sheet
2 Definitions
3
3 solutions
4
4 solutions
5
5 solutions
6
6 solutions
7
7 solutions
8
8 solutions
9
9 solutions
10
10 solutions

TOC | 1 Data Sheet | 2 Definitions | 3 | 3 solutions | 4 | 4 solutions | 5 | 5 solutions | 6 | 6 solutions | 7 | 7 solutions | 8 | 8 solutions | 9 | 9 solutions | **10** | 10 solutions

18.1.5 Give a reason for the observation in experiment **a.** (2)

18.1.6 Give a reason for the observation in experiment **h**. (1)

18.1.7 Explain whether it would make any difference to the observations to experiment **a** if they used an ultra violet light source of a higher intensity. (1)

18.1.8 Explain whether they would observe anything different in experiment **a** if light of a higher frequency but with the same intensity was used. (1)

18.1.9 Peter and Avni want to report back in general on what they have learnt from these experiments.
Make use of bullets and **identify at least four general observations** on the results of these experiments. (4)

18.2 Here is a table of the frequencies and wavelengths of various types of electromagnetic radiation:

	wavelength (m)	**frequency (Hz)**
γ - rays	10^{-12} and less	10^{20} and more
X - rays	$10^{-12} - 10^{-9}$	$10^{17} - 10^{20}$
ultra violet light	$10^{-9} - 10^{-7}$	$10^{15} - 10^{17}$
visible light	$10^{-7} - 10^{-6}$	$10^{14} - 10^{15}$
infra red light	$10^{-6} - 10^{-3}$	$10^{11} - 10^{14}$
micro waves	$10^{-3} - 1$	$10^{8} - 10^{11}$
radio waves	$1 - 10^{4}$	$10^{5} - 10^{8}$

18.2.1 State the relationship between wavelength and frequency of electromagnetic radiation **in words**. (2)

18.2.2 Calculate the wavelength of the blue light Peter and Avni used in their experiment. (2)

18.2.3 Where will the following electromagnetic radiations be used in day to day life?

(a) radiation with a frequency of 4×10^{18} Hz (1)

(b) radiation with a wavelength 1 378 m (1)

(c) radiation with a wavelength $4{,}3 \times 10^{-5}$ m (1)

18.2.4

(a) Give the equation relating the energy and frequency for all types of electromagnetic radiation. (1)

(b) Use the relationship written down in (a) to explain why radiation with a frequency of $3{,}12 \times 10^{22}$ Hz can be life threatening. (2)

(c) Give the **name** of this radiation. (1)

[28]

Question 19 (2009 IEB Final Examination) (Solutions on page 482)

The apparatus shown below was used to investigate the Photoelectric Effect. The apparatus allows for the investigation of several variables. The frequency and intensity of the incident radiation can be changed; the type of metal used at the metal surface can be altered; and the emf supplied across the electrodes can be adjusted.

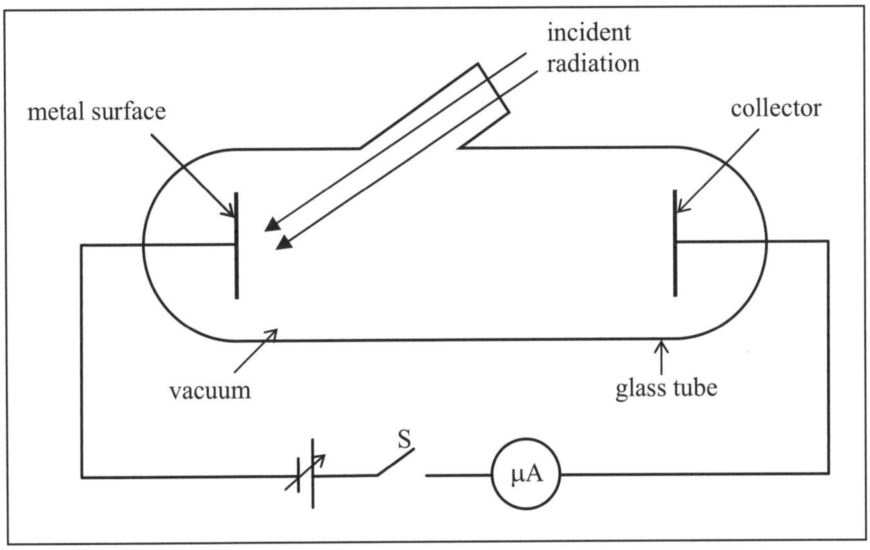

19.1 Early investigators of this effect found that a zinc plate, when negatively charged, would lose its charge when exposed to ultraviolet light, while a positively charged zinc plate showed no such effect. What could the investigators conclude from these observations? (2)

19.2 A source of bright red light and a source of faint blue light are shone in turn on to the metal surface for the same length of time. In both cases, electrons are ejected from the metal surface.

19.2.1 Name the variables that are being adjusted. (2)

19.2.2 The wavelength of blue light is 440 nm. Calculate the energy of a photon from this source. Express the answer in eV. (6)

19.2.3 The maximum kinetic energy of the electrons ejected by the faint blue light is greater than the maximum kinetic energy of the electrons ejected by the bright red light. Explain why this happens. (6)

19.3 The table below shows the work functions of selected metals.

Metal	**W_f: Work function (eV)**
Caesium	2,14
Sodium	2,75
Copper	4,94
Platinum	5,65

Each of these metals is used in turn at the metal surface. The same light source (of the same frequency and intensity) is shone on each metal plate for the same length of time.

19.3.1 Predict which metal will produce the largest reading on the ammeter. (1)

19.3.2 Give a reason for your answer in 19.3.1 (2)

19.3.3 Calculate the threshold frequency of sodium. (5)

[24]

Question 20 (2010 IEB Supplementary Examination) (Solutions on page 482 and 483)
Sarah wants to conduct an investigation on the photoelectric effect. Her aim is to determine the work function of some metals. She uses the apparatus shown below. She places samples of caesium, potassium and sodium in turn at the metal surface and irradiates them with the light emitted from a variety of LEDs. She measures the stopping voltage for each metal under that radiation if there is a reading on the microammeter, by adjusting the voltage until the current stops. The voltage at which the current stops is called the stopping voltage.

Diagram NOT drawn to scale.

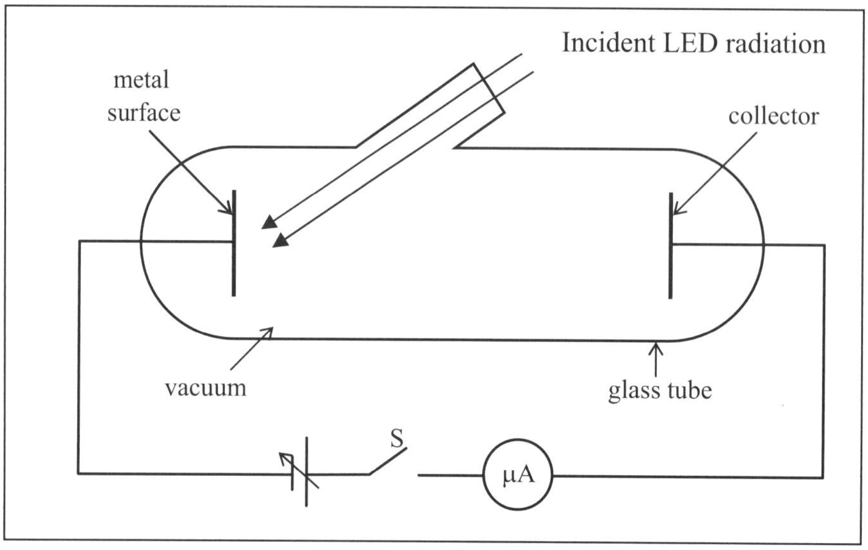

20.1 What is meant by the work function of a metal? (3)

20.2 Why is the metal surface connected to the positive terminal of the battery? (2)

20.3 Sarah's method is listed below, but she has listed the steps in the incorrect order.

Method:

a. Calculate the frequency of the light emitted from the LED and record this in your table.
b. Select the LED that will be used to irradiate the metal. Record its wavelength in your table.
c. If electrons are ejected (i.e. there is a reading on the microammeter), adjust the voltage on the variable voltage supply until current stops flowing. Record the voltage as the Stopping Voltage in your table.
d. Select the metal to be placed at the surface.
e. Convert the kinetic energy from eV to Joules.
f. Repeat the procedure for the other metals.
g. Use the value for Stopping Voltage to determine the values for kinetic in energy in eV.

Provide a correct sequence of steps for the method that Sarah could follow by listing the letters a. to g. in your answer book in the order in which the steps should be followed.

(7)

20.4 Sarah's incomplete table of results for her **experiment with caesium** is shown below.

Colour/range of incident radiation	**Wavelength of incident radiation**	**Frequency (Hz)**	**Stopping Voltage (V)**	**Maximum kinetic energy of electrons (eV)**	**Maximum kinetic energy of electrons (J)**
Green	540 nm	$5{,}56\times10^{14}$	**(b)**	0,15	$2{,}43\times10^{-20}$
Blue	470 nm	$6{,}38\times10^{14}$	0,49	0,49	**(c)**
Indigo	440 nm	**(a)**	0,67	0,67	$1{,}08\times10^{-19}$
Violet	410 nm	$7{,}32\times10^{14}$	0,88	0,88	$1{,}41\times10^{-19}$
Ultraviolet	350 nm	$8{,}57\times10^{14}$	1,40	1,40	$2{,}23\times10^{-19}$

20.4.1 Sarah has not recorded her data in an acceptable manner. What mistake has she made? (1)

20.4.2 Determine the values labelled **a, b** and **c** in the table. (6)

20.4.3 What is the independent variable in this experiment? (1)

20.4.4 Using the axes below, plot a best-fit line graph of E_K (eV) versus frequency ($\times10^{15}$ Hz) for caesium.

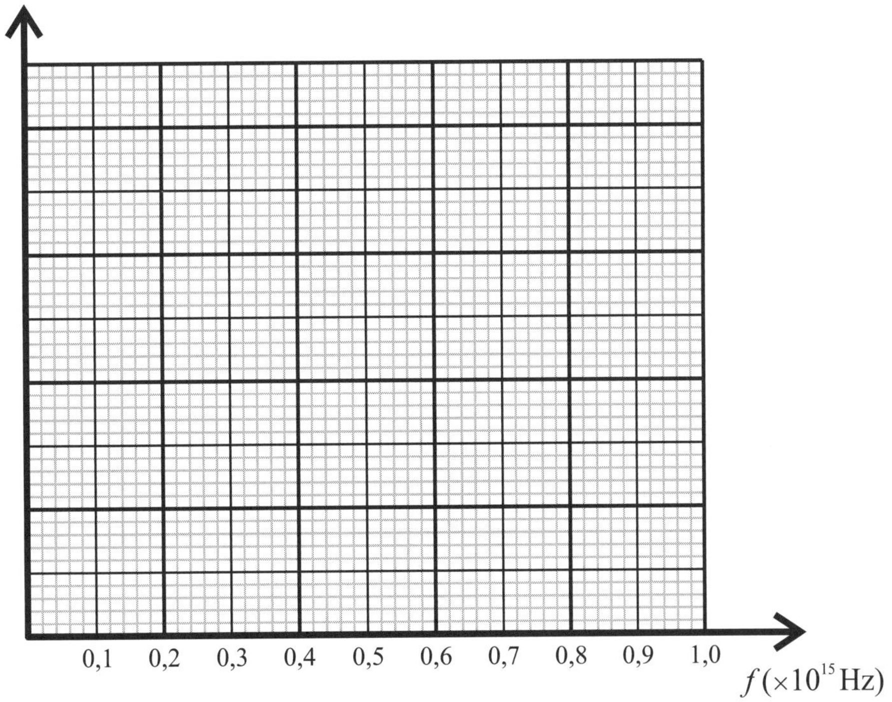

(5)

20.4.5 Determine the gradient of the graph. Show your method clearly. (4)

20.4.6 To what constant does the value in 20.4.5 correspond? (1)

20.4.7 Use the graph to determine the threshold frequency for caesium. (1)

20.4.8 Determine the work function for caesium. (4)

20.4.9 Are Sarah's results reliable? Explain your answer. (3)

TOC | 1 Data Sheet | 2 Definitions | 3 | 3 solutions | 4 | 4 solutions | 5 | 5 solutions | 6 | 6 solutions | 7 | 7 solutions | 8 | 8 solutions | 9 | 9 solutions | 10 | 10 solutions

20.5 Sarah looks up the work functions for potassium and sodium in a textbook and finds the following values:

Metal	**W_f: Work function (eV)**
potassium	2,30
sodium	2,75

Using the information about caesium, Sarah tries to predict what the graph of E_K (in eV) versus frequency for potassium might look like. On the same set of axes as the graph in 20.4.4, show the graph that you predict for **potassium**. (3)

[41]

Question 21 (2012 IEB Final Examination) (Solutions on page 484 and 485)

Electromagnetic radiation of varying frequency is shone on the sodium metal cathode of a photocell. The maximum kinetic energy of the photoelectrons emitted is recorded.

Table to show how the maximum kinetic energy (Ek) of a photoelectron emitted from sodium metal varies with the frequency (f) of the electromagnetic radiation.

Frequency ($\times 10^{14}$ Hz)	**Maximum kinetic energy (eV)**
7	0,59
8	1,00
9	1,42
10	1,83
11	2,24

21.1 Plot a graph of maximum kinetic energy versus frequency as represented by these results for sodium metal. Use the graph paper provided on the next page. The scale on the y-axis has been marked for you. You must fill in your own scale for the *x*-axis which must start at ZERO. (6)

21.2 Define *threshold frequency.* (2)

21.3 Read off the threshold frequency for sodium metal from the graph. (2)

21.4 If the maximum kinetic energy of the photo electrons emitted is 2,0 eV then determine:

21.4.1 the **frequency** of the radiation incident on the sodium metal cathode. (1)

21.4.2 the **wavelength** of the radiation incident on the sodium metal cathode. (3)

21.4.3 the **energy** of the radiation incident on the sodium metal cathode (in joules). (3)

21.5 State and explain how the graph would change (if at all) when the intensity of the light is increased for each of the frequencies used. (3)

21.6 The magnitude of the value given by the ***y*-intercept is equal to the work function (W_f)** of the metal.

21.6.1 Extend your graph backwards to cut the *y*-axis and hence state the work function of the metal (in eV). (1)

21.6.2 Convert your answer to Question 21.6.1 to joules. (1)

21.6.3 Use the photoelectric effect equation $E = W_f + \frac{1}{2}mv^2$, to explain why the *y*-intercept is equal to the work function (W_f). (3)

Graph paper for question 21.1

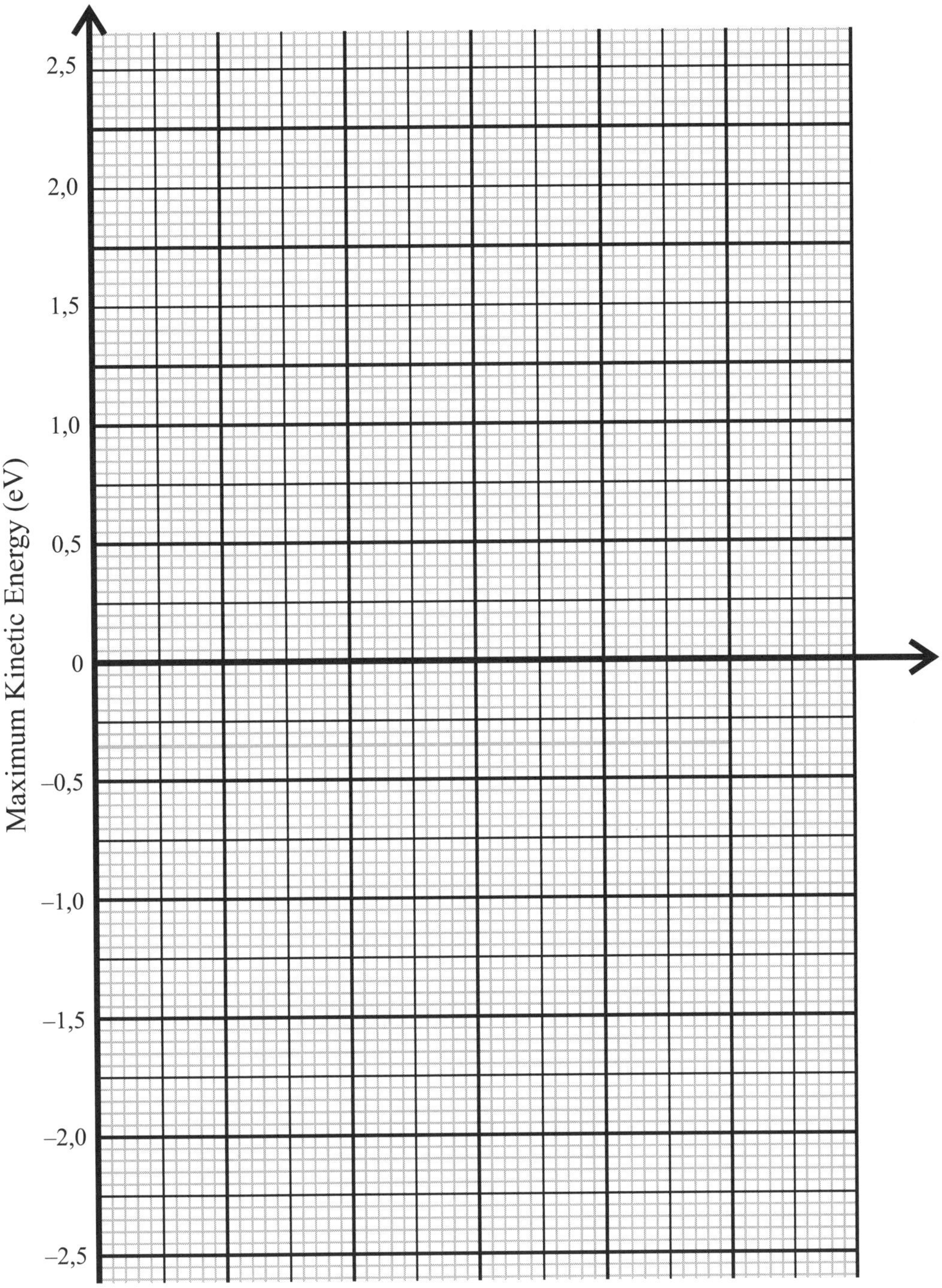

[25]

TOC
1 Data Sheet
2 Definitions
3
3 solutions
4
4 solutions
5
5 solutions
6
6 solutions
7
7 solutions
8
8 solutions
9
9 solutions
10
10 solutions

Question 22 (2013 IEB Final Examination) (Solutions on page 485)

Read the following information regarding the use of light meters in fully automatic cameras.

A fully automatic camera has a built-in light meter. When light comes into the light meter, it strikes a metal object that releases electrons and creates a current. This automatically opens and closes the lens to adjust for high and low lighting conditions.

22.1 What name is given to the physical phenomenon whereby electrons are released from a metal when light strikes the metal? (1)

22.2 **Bright** light (high intensity) produces a greater current than **dim** light (low intensity)

22.2.1 How is the maximum kinetic energy of the electrons that are emitted affected by using brighter light?
(State *increase, decrease* or *no effect)* (1)

22.2.2 How is the number of electrons that are emitted per second affected by using a brighter light? (State *increase, decrease* or *no effect*) (1)

22.2.3 Explain your answers to Question 22.2.1 and Question 22.2.2 and hence explain why bright light produces a greater current than dim light. (4)

22.3 What happens to the maximum speed of the electrons that are emitted, as the frequency of the incident light is increased? (State only *increases, decreases* or *no effect*) Assume that the intensity remains constant. (1)

22.4 Explain your answer to Question 22.3 with reference to one or more suitable formulae. (3)

22.5 A certain metal has a work function of $3{,}8 \times 10^{-19}$ J. Light of wavelength 480 nm strikes the metal surface.

22.5.1 Calculate the frequency of a photon of this light. (4)

22.5.2 Calculate the maximum speed of the electrons emitted when light of wavelength 480 nm strikes the metal surface. (7)

22.5.3 When light of a certain wavelength strikes the metal surface, no electrons are emitted. Suggest a reason why no electrons are emitted. (2)

[24]

Question 23 (2014 IEB Exemplar Examination) (Solutions on page 486)

23.1 Aluminium has a work function of $W_0 = 4{,}08$ eV.

23.1.1 Define the term *work function.* (2)

23.1.2 Calculate the threshold frequency of light that is required to release an electron from an aluminium plate. (4)

There are two sources of light in the laboratory that you can use to shine onto the aluminium surface.

Light Source	Wavelength (nm)
A	400
B	250

23.1.3 Use a calculation to help you decide which light source will be able to release electrons from the aluminium plate. (4)

23.1.4 If you used the light source that ejects electrons, what would you do to ensure more electrons are emitted per second from the metal plate? Explain your answer. (2)

23.2 The Bunsen burner was invented by Robert Bunsen, as he needed a very hot, clean flame to investigate the coloured lights emitted by different elements when they are heated. Bunsen was the first person to study the 'emission spectra' of elements.

23.2.1 Use an energy level diagram to help explain the source of atomic emission spectra. (3)

23.2.2 Emission spectra can be used to identify elements. Why does each element have a unique emission spectrum? (2)

[17]

Question 24 (2014 IEB Final Examination) (Solutions on page 486)

The graph below shows how the maximum kinetic energy of an electron emitted from the metal cathode of a photoelectric cell varies with the wavelength of the incident radiation.

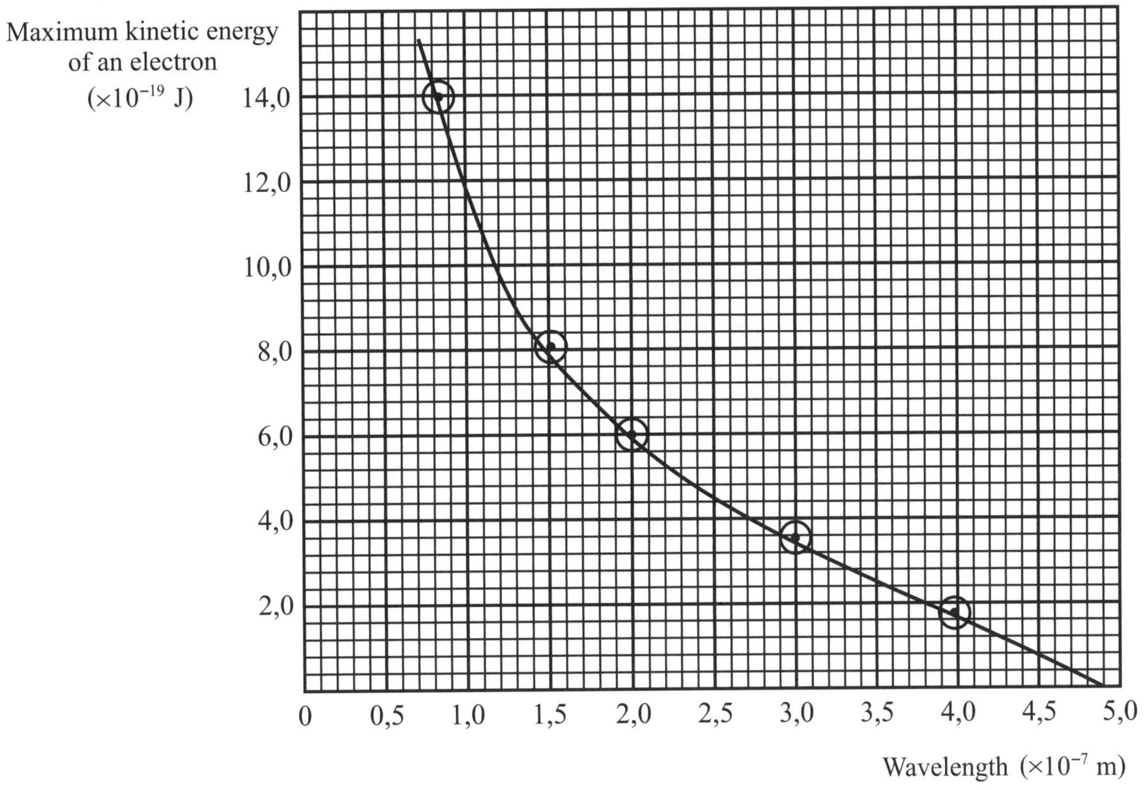

24.1 Use the graph to determine the maximum kinetic energy of the electron emitted when the wavelength of the incident radiation is $1,0 \times 10^{-7}$ m. (1)

24.2 Describe the relationship shown in the graph. (2)

24.3 Use your knowledge of the photoelectric effect to EXPLAIN the relationship shown in the graph. Support your answer with reference to relevant formulae. (3)

24.4 Use the graph to calculate the threshold frequency of the light needed to emit electrons from the metal cathode of the photovoltaic cell. (4)

24.5 Calculate the work function of the metal used for the cathode of the photovoltaic cell. (3)

[13]

Question 25 (2015 IEB Final Examination) (Solutions on page 487)

25.1 An electroscope with a negatively charged zinc plate is shown below. The gold leaf is deflected due to like charges repelling each other.

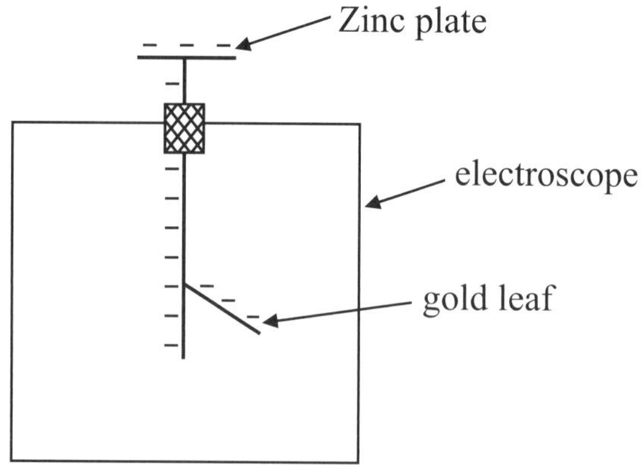

When visible light is shone on the plate, nothing is observed. When ultraviolet light is shone on the negatively charged electroscope, the gold leaf collapses.

25.1.1 Name the phenomenon described. (2)

25.1.2 Explain why visible light has no effect while the ultra-violet light collapses the gold leaf. (3)

25.2 The work-function of caesium is $3,36 \times 10^{-19}$ J.

25.2.1 Define *work-function.* (2)

25.2.2 Calculate the lowest frequency photon that can eject an electron from caesium. (3)

25.2.3 Calculate the maximum kinetic energy of an electron ejected from caesium by a photon of wavelength 400 nm. (4)

[14]

Question 26 (2015 IEB Supplementary Examination) (Solutions on page 487)

The diagram shows some of the energy levels of an isolated hydrogen atom. The arrows, labelled A and B, represent transitions of electrons between the energy levels.

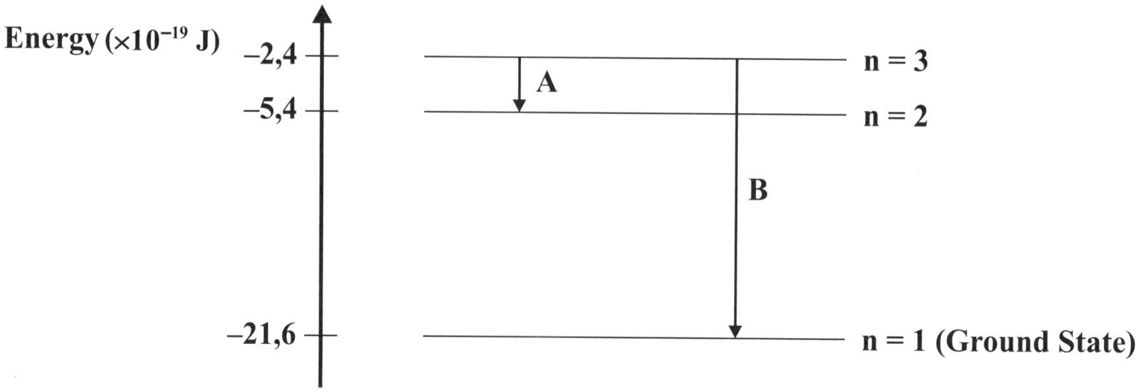

The lowest energy level of an atom is known as the ground state. Each energy level is assigned an integer number n, known as the principal quantum number.

26.1 Calculate the frequency of the photon emitted when an excited electron falls from energy level n = 3 to energy level n = 2. (4)

26.2 Is the wavelength of the photon emitted in transition A ***greater than, less than or equal to*** the wavelength of the photon emitted in transition B? for the experiment. (1)

26.3 Explain your answer to Question 26.2, making reference to one or more suitable formulae. No further calculations are required. (3)

26.4 Use the energy level diagram given for hydrogen to prove that the energy (E) of an energy level is inversely proportional to the principal quantum number squared (n^2). (3)

[11]

Question 27 (2016 IEB Final Examination) (Solutions on page 487)

The work functions of selected metals are recorded in the table below.

Metal	**Work Function ($\times 10^{-19}$ J)**
Sodium	3,94
Aluminium	6,53
Zinc	6,90
Iron	7,20

27.1 Define *work function.* (2)

Light of wavelength 296 nm is incident on a sample of each metal in turn.

27.2 Calculate the energy of a photon of light of 296 nm. (3)

27.3 Which metals listed in the table will emit electrons at this wavelength? (2)

27.4 Calculate the maximum kinetic energy of the electrons ejected from sodium metal when light of 296 nm is incident on the metal. (3)

27.5 The intensity of the 296 nm light is now increased. Will the light now be able to eject electrons from the other metals listed in the table? Briefly explain your answer. (4)

[14]

Question 28 (2016 IEB Supplementary Examination) (Solutions on page 488)

28.1 Describe the photoelectric effect. (2)

28.2 An energy level diagram, for a particular element, is drawn to scale in the diagram below. The only positions that the outer electron can occupy are the energy levels E_1, E_2 and E_3.

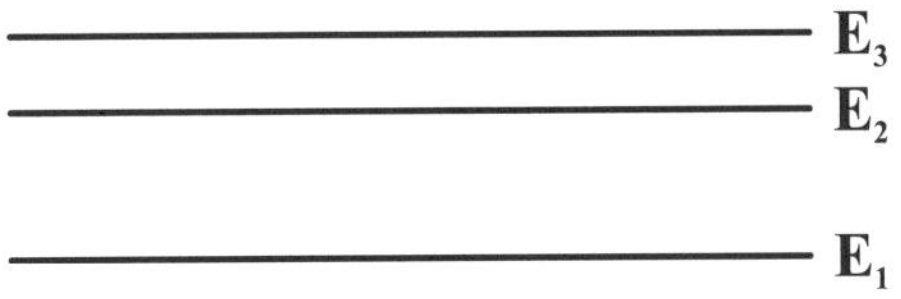

28.2.1 How many spectral lines are possible for this element? (2)

28.2.2 Which transition would release light with the highest frequency? (2)

For this energy-level diagram, the longest wavelength possible is 618 nm.

28.2.3 On the diagram above, show the transition for this wavelength. (2)

28.2.4 Calculate the energy in joules that corresponds to a wavelength of 618 nm. (4)

28.2.5 Explain why a transition between energy levels produces an emission line. (2)

[14]

TOC 1 Data Sheet 2 Definitions 3 3 solutions 4 4 solutions 5 5 solutions 6 6 solutions 7 7 solutions 8 8 solutions 9 9 solutions 10 10 solutions

Question 29 (2017 IEB Final Examination) (Solutions on page 488)

The energy levels for a hydrogen atom are represented on the diagram below.

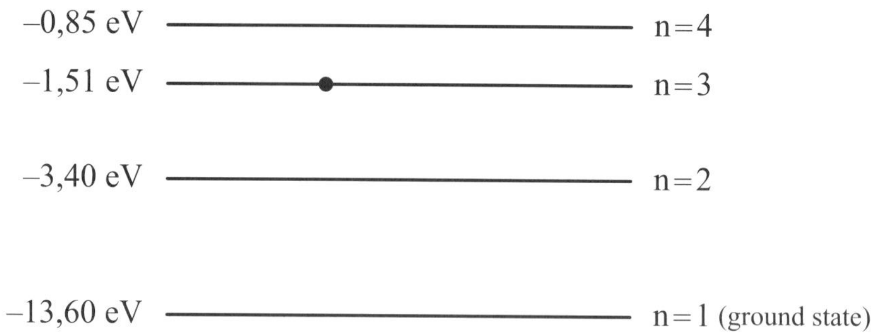

An excited electron is in the 3rd energy level as indicated.

29.1 How many unique frequencies will be in the emission spectrum as the excited electron returns to the ground state? (2)

29.2 Calculate the frequency of the photon emitted when the electron transition is from the $n = 2$ level to the ground state. (4)

29.3 Hydrogen gas in a discharge tube emits light of wavelength 655 nm.

29.3.1 Calculate the energy (in eV) that corresponds to this wavelength of light (4)

29.3.2 On the diagram above, draw an arrow for the transition that will result in a wavelength of 655 nm. (2)

29.4 Why are the energy levels stated as negative values? (2)

[14]

Question 30 (2018 IEB Supplementary Examination) (Solutions on page 488 and 489)

30.1 Ultraviolet light of frequency $9{,}1 \times 10^{14}$ Hz is shone onto a metal surface. The work function of the metal is $3{,}5 \times 10^{-19}$ J. Electrons are ejected from the metal.

30.1.1 Calculate the energy of a photon of ultraviolet light. (3)

30.1.2 Define *work function*. (2)

30.1.3 Calculate the maximum velocity of the ejected electrons. (4)

30.2 Light of wavelength 524 nm is emitted from a certain element when an electron transition occurs between the fifth and second energy level.

30.2.1 Describe a photon. (2)

30.2.2 Calculate the energy of the photon of light that is emitted. (3)

The second energy level has an energy of –2,81 eV.

30.2.3 Calculate the energy of an electron in the fifth orbital. (3)

[17]

Question 31 (2017 IEB Supplementary Examination) (Solutions on page 489)

In experiments to demonstrate the photoelectric effect, a beam of light with a single frequency is shone onto a clean, metal surface. The maximum kinetic energy of the ejected electrons was measured.

The experiment was repeated at different frequencies of light and the graph of maximum kinetic energy vs frequency was obtained for potassium metal.

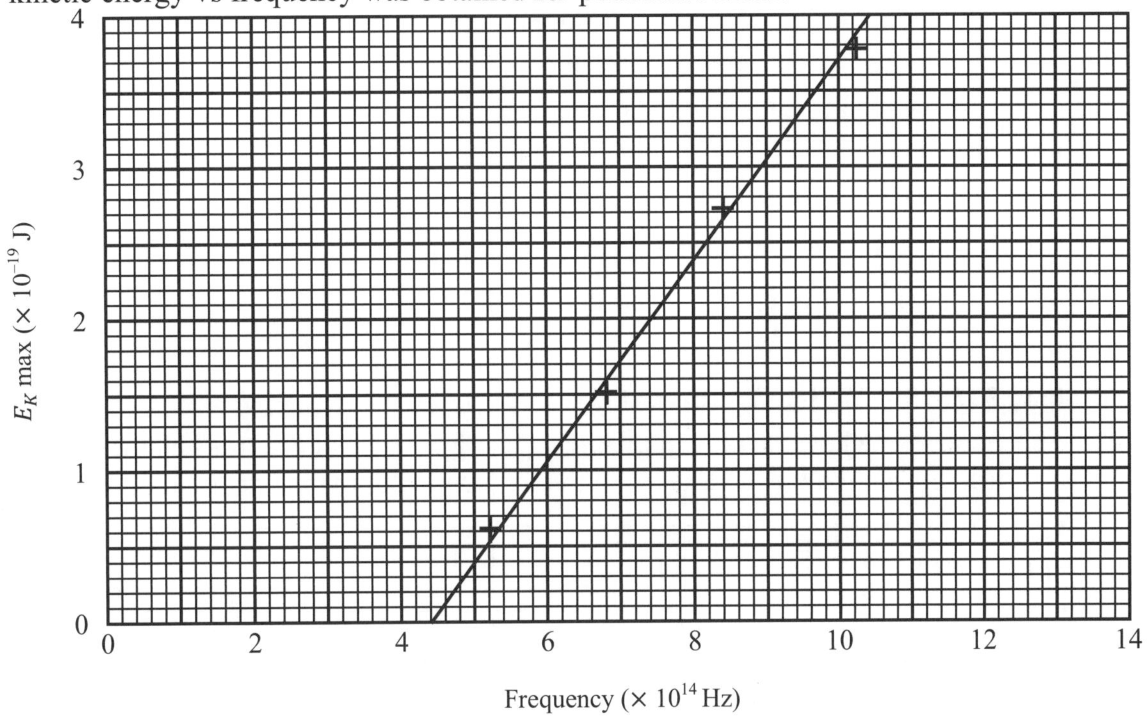

31.1 Define threshold frequency. (2)

31.2 Use the graph to help you determine the minimum energy needed to eject an electron from the surface of potassium. (3)

31.3 Use the graph to describe the relationship between maximum kinetic energy and the frequency of the incident light. (3)

The work function of copper is double the work function of potassium.

31.4 The experiment is repeated with copper instead of potassium. Which one of the graphs below would best represent the results for copper (————)?The graph for potassium (- - - -) has been included for comparison. Explain your choice of answer by referring to relevant features of the graph.

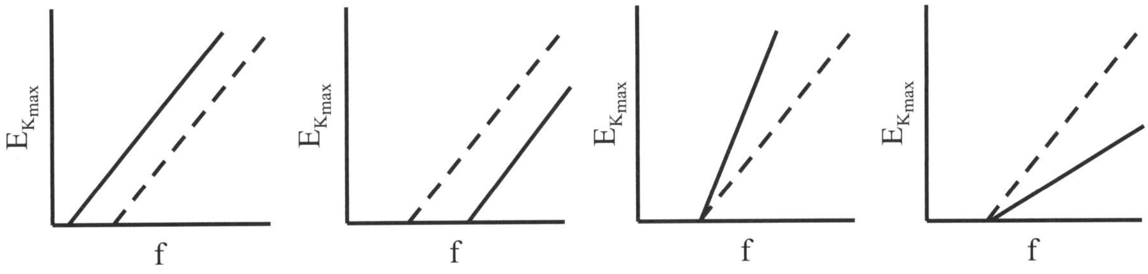

A B C D

(4)

31.5 Light of frequency 15 × 10^{14} Hz is incident on the copper metal. Calculate the kinetic energy of the electrons ejected from **copper**. (4)

[16]

Question 32 (2019 IEB Final Examination) (Solutions on page 489)

The longest wavelength that will cause electrons to be ejected from a sodium metal surface when light is shone on the metal is 583 nm.

32.1 Define *threshold frequency*. (2)

32.2 Calculate the threshold frequency for sodium metal. (3)

32.3 Hence, calculate the work function of sodium metal. (3)

A low intensity light of wavelength of 450 nm is incident on the sodium.

32.4 Calculate the kinetic energy of the ejected electrons. (4)

A higher intensity light, also of wavelength 450 nm, replaces the low intensity light.

32.5 What will the effect be of the higher intensity light on

32.5.1 the kinetic energy of the ejected electrons? (2)

32.5.2 the number of ejected electrons? (2)

[16]

Question 33 (2018 IEB Final Examination) (Solutions on page 490)

33.1 The graph shows how the maximum kinetic energy $E_{K(max)}$ of electrons emitted from a surface of calcium metal varies with the frequency f of the incident radiation.

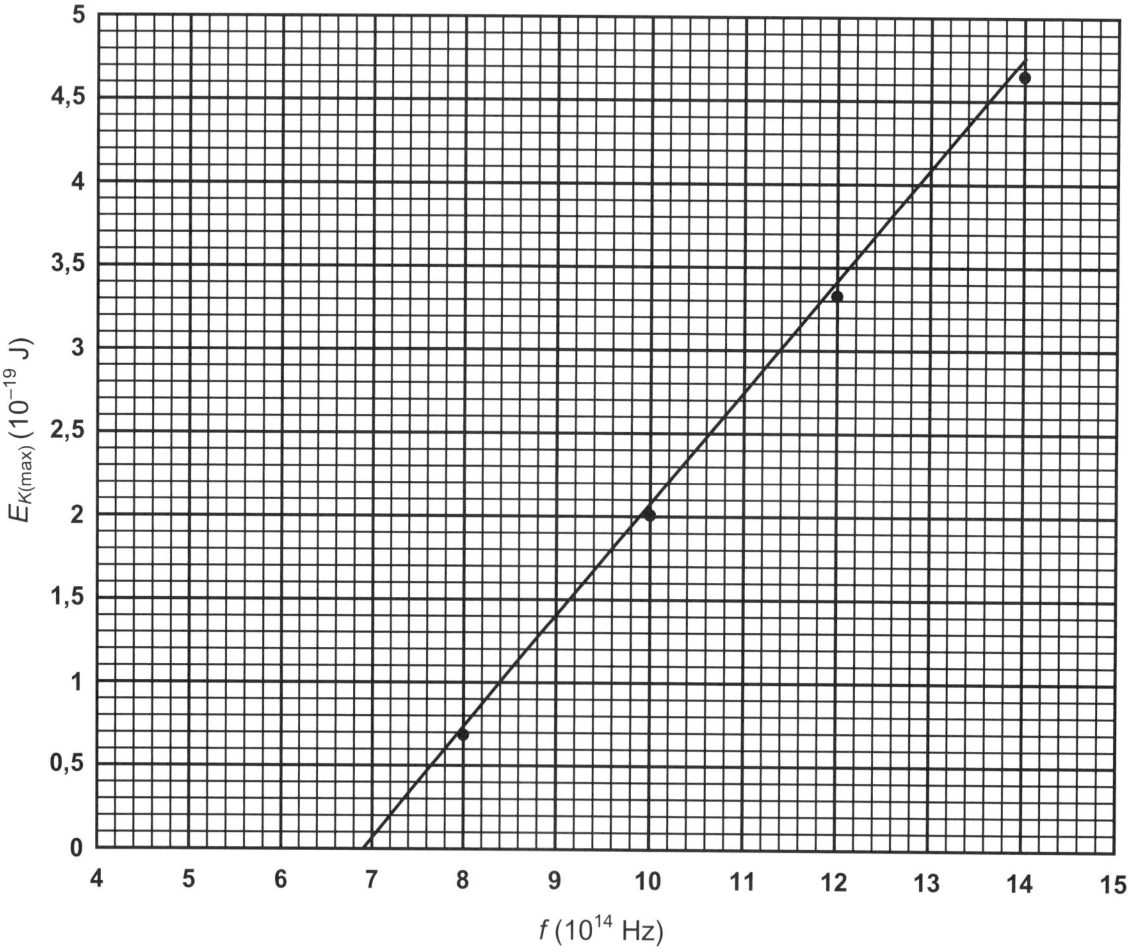

33.1.1 Define work function. (2)

33.1.2 Calculate the work function of calcium. (4)

33.1.3 The experiment is repeated using magnesium instead of calcium metal. The work function of magnesium is 1,3 times the work function of calcium. Draw a second line on the graph above to illustrate the results of the experiment with magnesium. (2)

33.2 The four emission lines P, Q, R and S in the hydrogen spectrum are illustrated in the diagram.

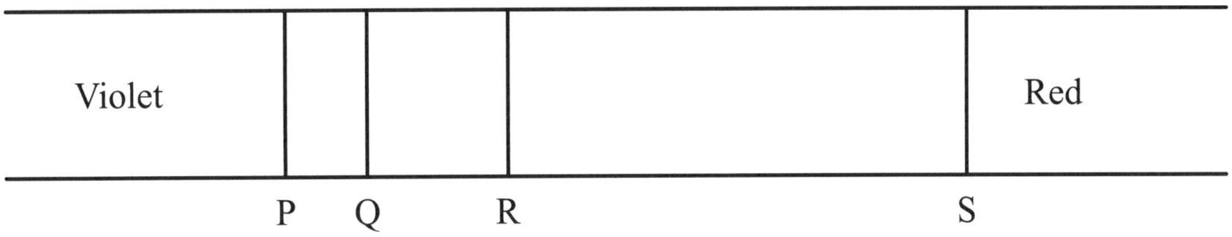

The wavelengths of the four emission lines are provided in the table:

Emission Line	**Wavelength (10^{-7} m)**
P	4,10
Q	4,34
R	4,86
S	6,58

Frequencies associated with these wavelengths are emitted when electrons move from a higher energy level to the –3,4 eV energy level.

33.2.1 Calculate the value of the energy of the light associated with the emission line S. (4)

33.2.2 Which emission line is produced by the transition from the highest energy level to the –3,4 eV energy level? Briefly explain your answer. (3)

33.2.3 State why knowledge of the emission line wavelengths is useful to scientists to identify substances. (2)

[17]

TOC 1 Data Sheet 2 Definitions 3 3 solutions 4 4 solutions 5 5 solutions 6 6 solutions 7 7 solutions 8 8 solutions 9 9 solutions 10 10 solutions

Question 34 (2019 IEB Supplementary Examination) (Solutions on page 490)
A Physics student measures the maximum kinetic energy of photoelectrons emitted from the surface of metal X, using different frequencies of the incident radiation. The student uses his data to plot the graph shown below.

Graph showing the relationship between the maximum kinetic energy of photoelectrons and the frequency of incident radiation for metal X.

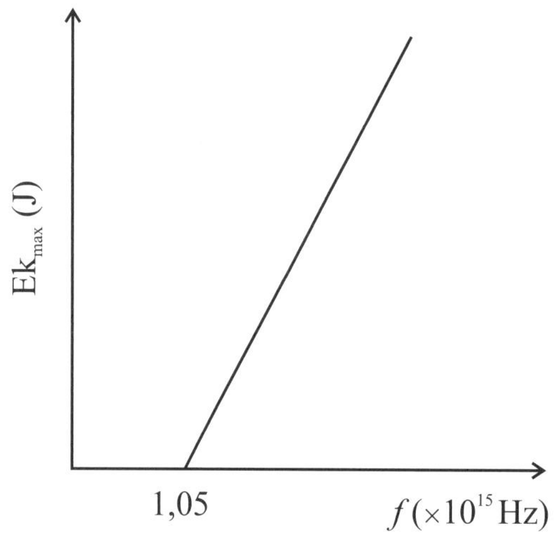

The following table shows the work function of a variety of metals:

Metal	Work Function (J)
Sodium	$3,82 \times 10^{-19}$
Zinc	$6,97 \times 10^{-19}$
Copper	$7,52 \times 10^{-19}$
Platinum	$1,02 \times 10^{-19}$
Calcium	$4,78 \times 10^{-19}$

34.1 Define *work function.* (2)

34.2 State the independent variable in this experiment. (2)

34.3 Show that the gradient of the graph has units N·m·s. (2)

34.4 Use information from the graph and the table above to determine the identity of metal X. (4)

34.5 The wavelength of blue light is given as 475 nm. When this blue light is shone onto a certain metal surface, the maximum velocity of emitted electrons is $2,77 \times 10^5$ m·s^{-1}. Determine which metal from the table above is being used. (6)

[16]

10. PHOTONS AND ELECTRONS (SOLUTIONS)

Question 1

1.1	A	(2)
1.2	B	(2)
1.3	C	(2)
1.4	D	(2)
1.5	D	(2)
1.6	C	(2)
1.7	D	(2)
1.8	B	(2)
1.9	B	(2)
1.10	C	(2)
1.11	B	(2)
1.12	C	(2)
1.13	C	(2)
1.14	D	(2)
1.15	B	(2)
1.16	A	(2)
1.17	B	(2)
1.18	B	(2)
1.19	A	(2)
1.20	C	(2)
1.21	C	(2)
1.22	D	(2)
1.23	B	(2)
1.24	D	(2)
1.25	B	(2)
1.26	C	(2)

[52]

Question 2

2.1 The minimum amount of energy needed to emit an electron from the surface of a metal. (2)

2.2 $E = \dfrac{hc}{\lambda}$

$= \dfrac{(6,6\times10^{-34})(3\times10^{8})}{350\times10^{-9}}$

$= 5,66\times10^{-19}$ J (4)

2.3 $E = W_o + E_{k_{max}}$

$E = W_o + \dfrac{1}{2}m_{e-}v^2$

$5,66\times10^{-19} = 3,36\times10^{-19} + \dfrac{1}{2}(9,1\times10^{-31})v^2$

$v = 710981,37\,\text{m.s}^{-1}$ (2)

2.4 $N_{photons} = \dfrac{E_{total}}{E_{per\ photon}}$

$= \dfrac{8,49\times10^{-9}}{5,66\times10^{-19}}$

$= 1,5\times10^{10}$ photons

$\therefore$ Number of electrons $= 1,5\times10^{10}$ (2)

2.5.1 Number of electrons emitted will increase. (1)

2.5.2 Number of electrons emitted will not change. (1)

[14]

Question 3

3.1 The minimum frequency of incident radiation at which electrons will be emitted from a particular metal (2)

3.2 $W_o = 4,28\left(1,6\times10^{-19}\right)$

$= 6,848\times10^{-19}$

$W_o = hf_o$

$6,848\times10^{-19} = \left(6,6\times10^{-34}\right)f_o$

$f_o = 1,04\times10^{15}$ Hz (3)

3.3 $E = W_o + E_{k\max}$

$hf = W_o + \frac{1}{2}m_{e-}v^2$

$6,6\times10^{-34}\left(2\times10^{15}\right) = 6,848\times10^{-19} + \frac{1}{2}\left(9,1\times10^{-31}\right)v^2$

$v = 1\ 181\ 543,04\,\text{m.s}^{-1}$ (5)

[10]

Question 4

4.1 $f = \frac{c}{\lambda}$

$= \frac{3\times10^8}{6,65\times10^{-7}}$

$= 4,51\times10^{14}$ Hz (2)

4.2 $E = \frac{3,04\times10^{-19}}{1,6\times10^{-19}}$

$= 1,9$ eV

Change in energy between n = 2 and n = 3:

$\Delta E = -1,5-(-3,4)$

$= 1,9$ eV

$\therefore$ It is a transition from the 3rd to the 2nd energy level. (2)

[4]

Question 5

5.1 The shortest wavelength corresponds to the highest energy. Therefore:
Transition C is in the UV spectrum.
Transition B is in the visible light spectrum.
Transition A is in the infrared light spectrum. (3)

5.2 $\Delta E = -1,5-(-13,6)$

$= 12,1$ eV

Energy in Joules:

$E = 12,1\left(1,6\times10^{-19}\right)$

$= 1,936\times10^{-18}$ J

$E = \frac{hc}{\lambda}$

$1,936\times10^{-18} = \frac{6,6\times10^{-34}\left(3\times10^8\right)}{\lambda}$

$\lambda = 102,27\times10^{-9}$ m

$= 102,27$ nm which is in the UV spectrum. (6)

5.3 Free electrons have an energy of zero. The negative implies that energy is released as electrons move to lower levels. (2)

5.4 Energy of transition C:
$\Delta E = -3,4-(-13,6)$
$= 10,2 \text{ eV}$

Energy of transition B:
$\Delta E = -1,5-(-3,4)$
$= 1,9 \text{ eV}$

Energy of transition C:
$\Delta E = -0,85-(-1,5)$
$= 0,65 \text{ eV}$

Work function of caesium:
$W_o = hf$
$= 6,6\times10^{-34}(5,1\times10^{14})$
$= 3,366\times10^{-19} \text{ J}$

In eV:
$W_o = \dfrac{3,366\times10^{-19}}{1,6\times10^{-19}} = 2,1\text{eV}$

$\therefore$ Only C will cause photoelectrons to be emitted. (4)

5.5 $E = W_o + E_{k_{max}}$

$E = hf_o + \frac{1}{2}m_{e^-}v^2 \rightarrow E$ was calculated in question 5.2

$1,936\times10^{-18} = 6,6\times10^{-34}(5,1\times10^{14}) + \frac{1}{2}(9,1\times10^{-31})v^2$

$v = 1874877,29\text{m.s}^{-1}$ (5)

5.6 6 (2)

5.7.1 $E = \dfrac{hc}{\lambda} = \dfrac{6,6\times10^{-34}(3\times10^8)}{485,29\times10^{-9}}$

$= 4,08\times10^{-19} \text{ J}$

$E = \dfrac{4,08\times10^{-19}}{1,6\times10^{-19}} = 2,55\text{eV}$ (4)

5.7.2 Change in energy between n = 4 and n = 2:

$\Delta E_k = -0,85-(-3,4) = 2,55\text{eV}$

$\therefore$ It is a transition from the 4th to the 2nd energy level. (2)

[28]

Question 6

6.1 The minimum amount of energy needed to emit an electron from the surface of a metal. (2)

6.2 Frequency of incident light (2)

6.3 $W_o = hf_0 = 6,6\times10^{-34}(1,6\times10^{15})$

$= 1,056\times10^{-18} \text{ J}$

$W_o = \dfrac{1,056\times10^{-18}}{1,6\times10^{-19}} = 6,6 \text{ eV}$

$\therefore$ The metal must be platinum. (4)

6.4 $E = W_o + E_{k_{max}}$

$\dfrac{hc}{\lambda} = W_o + \frac{1}{2}m_{e^-}v^2$

$\dfrac{(6,6\times10^{-34})(3\times10^8)}{400\times10^{-9}} = W_o + \frac{1}{2}(9,1\times10^{-31})(191000)^2$

$W_o = 4,78^{-19} \text{ J}$

$W_o = \dfrac{4,78^{-19}}{1,6\times10^{-19}}$

$= 2,99 \text{ eV}$

$\therefore$ The metal is calcium (7)

[15]

TOC
1 Data Sheet
2 Definitions
3
3 solutions
4
4 solutions
5
5 solutions
6
6 solutions
7
7 solutions
8
8 solutions
9
9 solutions
10
10 solutions

Question 7

7.1

Emission line	Wavelength ($\times 10^{-7}$ m)
S	6,58
R	4,86
Q	4,34
P	4,10

(4)

7.2 $E_R = \dfrac{hc}{\lambda}$

$= \dfrac{6,6\times10^{-34}\left(3\times10^{8}\right)}{4,86\times10^{-7}}$

$= 4,07\times10^{-19}$ J

(4)

7.3 $E_R = \dfrac{4,07\times10^{-19}}{1,6\times10^{-19}}$

$= 2,54$ eV $\rightarrow$ an unrounded answer from 7.1 would yield an answer of 2,55 eV

$\Delta E_k = E_x - (-3,4)$

$2,54 = E_x + 3,4$

$E_x = -0,86$ eV

(4)

7.4 $E_p = \dfrac{hc}{\lambda} \div 1,6\times10^{-19}$

$= \dfrac{6,6\times10^{-34}\left(3\times10^{8}\right)}{4,10\times10^{-7}} \div 1,6\times10^{-19}$

$= 3,02$ eV

$\therefore$ P is the highest energy emission and is below the work function of zinc.

$\therefore$ None of the emissions would cause photoelectrons to be emitted from zinc.

(4)

[16]

Question 8

8.1 The minimum frequency of incident radiation at which electrons will be emitted from a particular metal (2)

8.2

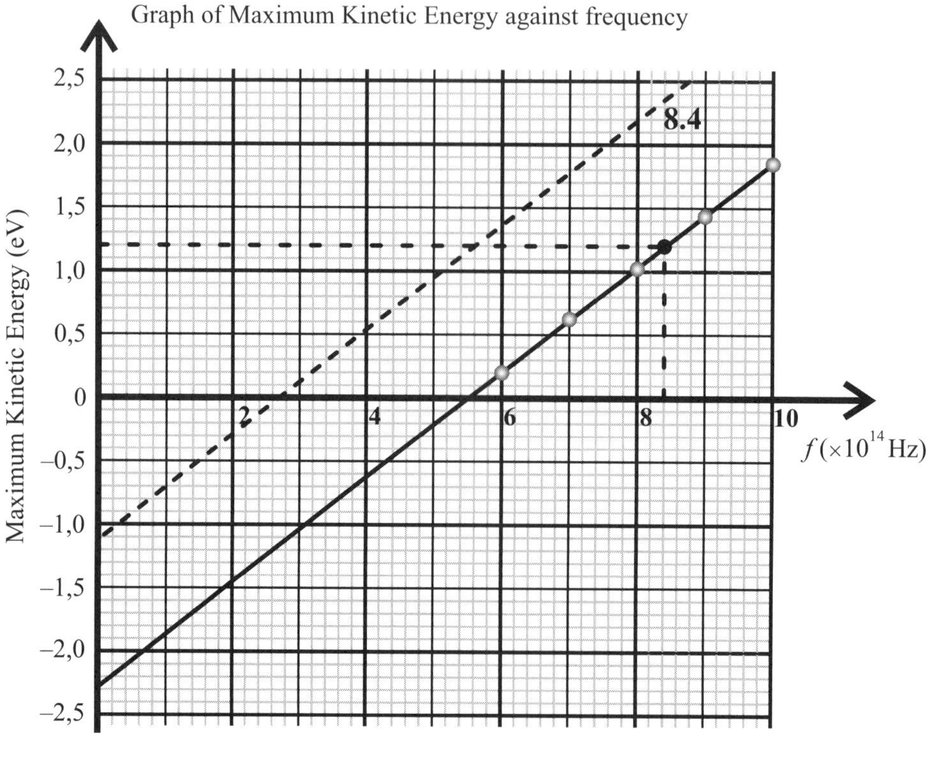

(6)

8.3.1 $5{,}49\times10^{14}$ Hz (read from the x-intercept of the graph) (2)

8.3.2 $W_o = 2{,}28\left(1{,}6\times10^{-19}\right)$

$= 3{,}65\times10^{-19}$ J (2)

8.4 Shown on the graph. (line must be parallel to the first and have an x-intercept half that of the graph for sodium) (3)

8.5 The learner is not correct.
The gradient of the graph would be equal to Planck's constant in J.s if the units on the y-axis were in joules. As the y-axis is in electron volts the gradient will be equal to Planck's constant in eV.s instead of J.s. (4)

8.6.1 $E_{k_{max}} = \dfrac{1{,}92\times10^{-19}}{1{,}6\times10^{-19}}$

$= 1{,}2$ eV

$\therefore f = 8{,}4\times10^{14}$ Hz (3)

8.6.2 $\lambda = \dfrac{c}{f}$

$= \dfrac{3\times10^{8}}{8{,}4\times10^{14}}$

$= 3{,}57\times10^{-7}$ m (3)

[25]

Question 9

9.1 The process that occurs when light shines on a metal and electrons are ejected. (2)

9.2 The minimum amount of energy needed to emit an electron from the surface of a metal. (2)

9.3 $W_o = \dfrac{hc}{\lambda}$

$= \dfrac{6{,}6\times10^{-34}\left(3\times10^{8}\right)}{600\times10^{-9}}$

$= 3{,}3\times10^{-19}$ J (4)

9.4 Yes. (1)

9.5 The threshold wavelength of the metal is 600 nm. As the new light is a shorter wavelength thAn 600 nm electrons will be emitted irrespective of the intensity of the light. (2)

[11]

Question 10

10.1 The photoelectric effect.
It establishes the quantum theory and it illustrates the particle nature of light (3)

10.2 The frequency of red light is below the threshold frequency of zinc while UV light's frequency is above it. (3)

10.3 $W_o = 4{,}33\left(1{,}6\times10^{-19}\right)$

$= 6{,}928\times10^{-19}$ J (1)

10.4 $E = W_o + E_{k_{max}}$

$$\frac{hc}{\lambda} = W_o + E_{k_{max}}$$

$$\frac{6,6\times10^{-34}\left(3\times10^{8}\right)}{100\times10^{-9}} = 6,928\times10^{-19} + E_{k_{max}}$$

$$E_{k_{max}} = 1,29\times10^{-18}\ \text{J}$$

(4)

10.5.1 Red light: No effect (the ammeter would still read zero).
UV light: The reading would increase. (2)

10.5.2 Red light does not have sufficient energy to eject an electron from the surface of zinc. Increasing the intensity of the light does not increase energy and therefore electrons will still not be ejected.
Increasing the intensity of the UV light will increase the number of photoelectrons emitted from the plate which will increase the current. (4)

10.6 Graph of Maximum Kinetic Energy against frequency

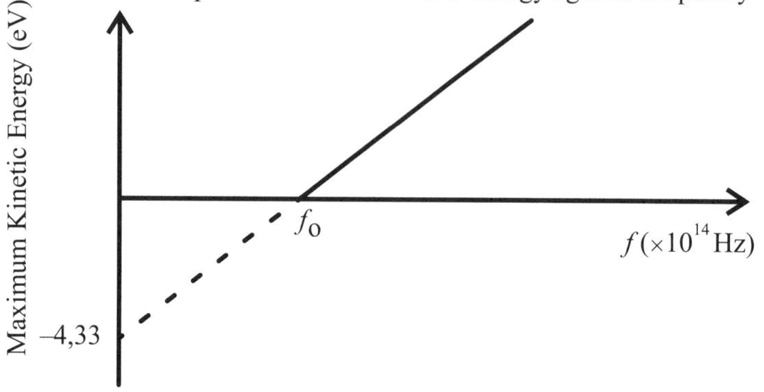

10.7 eV.s (2)

10.8

$$\text{Gradient} = \frac{h}{1,6\times10^{-19}}$$

$$= 4,125\times10^{-15}\ \text{eV.s}$$

(2)

[25]

Question 11

11.1 The photo electric effect. (1)

11.2
- When a customer walks through the door the beam of light from the emitter is broken.
- This will cause current from the receiver to stop flowing to the relay switch causing it to close.
- This completes the circuit for the doorbell causing it to ring. (3)

11.3

$$W_o = \frac{hc}{\lambda_o}$$

$$1,5\left(1,6\times10^{-19}\right) = \frac{6,6\times10^{-34}\left(3\times10^{8}\right)}{\lambda_o} \rightarrow \text{convert eV to J}$$

$$\lambda_o = 8,25\times10^{-7}\ \text{m}$$

(4)

11.4
- When the intensity is decreased the number of photons incident on the metal is decreased.
- This causes the number of electrons being emitted from the metal to decrease which will cause the current to decrease.
- If current is not strong enough to turn on the relay, the switch inside the relay will close causing the doorbell to ring without the beam being broken. (3)

11.5.1 $E = hf$

$= 6,6\times10^{-34}\left(9,5\times10^{14}\right)$

$= 6,27\times10^{-19}$ J (3)

11.5.2 $Q = It$

$= \left(928\times10^{-12}\right)(10)$

$= 9,28\times10^{-9}$ C

$N_{e-} = \frac{Q}{q_{e-}}$

$= \frac{9,28\times10^{-9}}{1,6\times10^{-19}}$

$= 5,8\times10^{10}$ electrons

$\therefore$ Number of photons $= 5,8\times10^{10}$

$E_{total} = E_{photon}N_{photons}$

$= \left(6,27\times10^{-19}\right)\left(5,8\times10^{10}\right)$

$= 3,64\times10^{-8}$ J (7)

[22]

Question 12

12.1.1 $E = hf$

$= \left(6,6\times10^{-34}\right)\left(15\times10^{15}\right)$

$= 9,9\times10^{-18}$ J (3)

12.1.2 $E = W_o + E_k$

$E = W_o + \frac{1}{2}m_{e-}v^2$

$9,9\times10^{-18} = W_o + \frac{1}{2}\left(9,1\times10^{-31}\right)\left(4,58\times10^{6}\right)^2$

$W_o = 3,56\times10^{-19}$ J (4)

12.1.3 $W_o = 2,1\left(1,6\times10^{-19}\right)$

$= 3,36\times10^{-19}$ J

The maximum speed of the electrons will be faster as the work function of cesium is lower than that of the original metal. (3)

12.1.4 (a) Increase. (1)

(b) No effect on the number of electrons. (1)

12.2.1 X. Spectral line A has the lowest wavelength which corresponds to the highest frequency and greatest energy. (4)

12.2.2 3×10^{8}. The speed of light is constant irrespective of the frequency. (2)

[18]

Question 13

13.1 The process that occurs when light shines on a metal and electrons are ejected. (2)

13.2 The threshold frequency. (1)

13.3 $W_o = 2,2\left(1,6\times10^{-19}\right)$

$= 3.52\times10^{-19}$ J (2)

13.4 $\text{gradient} = \dfrac{0,4125\left(1,6\times10^{-19}\right)}{1\times10^{14}}$

$= 6,6\times10^{-34}$ J.s (4)

13.5 $W_o = hf_o$

$3,52\times10^{-19} = 6,6\times10^{-34} f_o$

$f_o = 5,33\times10^{14}$ Hz

$\therefore x = 5,33$ (4)

13.6 $W_o = \dfrac{4\times10^{-19}}{1,6\times10^{-19}}$

$= 2,5$ eV

$W_o = hf_o$

$f_o = 6,06\times10^{14}$ Hz

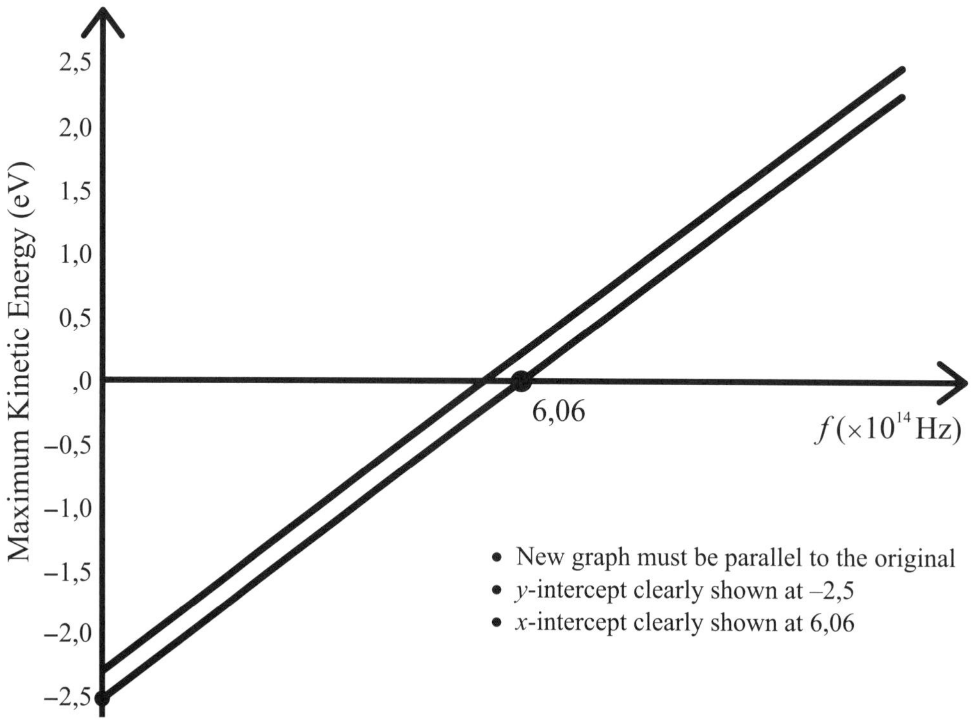

(5)

[18]

Question 14

$E = -0,8 - (-1,5)$

$= 0,7$ eV

$E = \dfrac{hc}{\lambda}$

$0,7\left(1,6\times10^{-19}\right) = \dfrac{\left(6,6\times10^{-34}\right)\left(3\times10^{8}\right)}{\lambda}$

$\lambda = 1,77\times10^{-6}$ m

[14]

Question 15

15.1 The process that occurs when light shines on a metal and electrons are ejected. (2)

15.2 When the beam is crossed, light to the photocell is blocked and current stops flowing. When current stops flowing the siren is triggered. (2)

15.3 15.3.1 The minimum amount of energy needed to emit an electron from the surface of a metal. (2)

15.3.2 Maximum energy of the white light:

$$E = \frac{hc}{\lambda}$$
$$= \frac{(6,6\times10^{-34})(3\times10^{8})}{400\times10^{-9}}$$
$$= 4,95\times10^{-19}\text{ J}$$
$$= 3,09\text{ eV}$$

The maximum energy of white light is lower than work function of the photocell. This means white light does not have enough energy to cause electrons to be emitted. (5)

15.3.3 Increasing the brightness (intensity) of the light does not increase the lights energy. If the light's energy is not greater than the work function, electrons will not be emitted, irrespective of brightness. Therefore, he will not be successful. (3)

[17]

Question 16

16.1
1. Atoms contain energy levels.
2. Electrons can only exist in these specific energy levels and not in between them.
3. The energy levels are unique for every element. (3)

16.2 E_3 to E_2. (the longest wavelength has the smallest energy) (2)

16.3
$$E = \frac{hc}{\lambda}$$
$$= \frac{(6,6\times10^{-34})(3\times10^{8})}{532\times10^{-9}}$$
$$= 3,72\times10^{-19}\text{ J}$$
(3)

[8]

Question 17

17.1.1 Energy radiated by the bulb per second:

$$E = 0,2(0,1\times10^{-3})$$
$$= 2\times10^{-5}\text{ J}$$

Energy per photon of the violet light:

$$E = \frac{hc}{\lambda}$$
$$= \frac{(6,6\times10^{-34})(3\times10^{8})}{450\times10^{-9}}$$
$$= 4,4\times10^{-19}\text{ J}$$

Total number of photons incident on metal plate per second:

$$N_{photons} = \frac{E_{total}}{E_{photon}}$$
$$= \frac{2\times10^{-5}}{4,4\times10^{-19}}$$
$$= 4,55\times10^{13}\text{ photons}$$
(5)

17.1.2 $4,55\times10^{13}$ electrons (assuming each photon ejects an electron) (3)

17.2.1
$$f_o = \frac{2\left(1,6\times10^{-19}\right)}{6,6\times10^{-34}}$$
$$= 4,85\times10^{14}\text{ Hz}$$
Therefore, current is 0 as the frequency is lower than the threshold frequency. (4)

17.2.2 30 (2)

17.2.3 45 (2)

17.2.4 7,5 (2)

17.2.5 200 (2)

[16]

Question 18 (2008 IEB Final Examination)

18.1.1 Electroscope. (1)

18.1.2 The photoelectric effect (1)

18.1.3 The minimum frequency of incident radiation at which electrons will be emitted from a particular metal. (2)

18.1.4 a, b and c. The gold leaf will fall. (4)

18.1.5 The frequency of the ultraviolet light is higher than the threshold frequency of aluminium and electrons will be emitted. (2)

18.1.6 The frequency of infra red light is lower than the threshold frequency of copper. Therefore, no electrons are emitted and there is no change to the position of the leaf. (1)

18.1.7 The leaf will fall back faster as more electrons will be emitted per second. (1)

18.1.8 There will be no change observed as the number of electrons emitted per second will remain the same. (1)

18.1.9
- If the frequency of the light is lower than the threshold frequency, nothing will happen to the gold leaf.
- If the frequency of the light is the same as the threshold frequency, the gold leaf will fall back slightly.
- If the frequency of the light is greater than the threshold frequency, the gold leaf will fall back slightly the same as in the previous experiment.
- If the intensity of the light in the previous two experiments is increased, the leaf will fall back faster. (4)

18.2.1 The frequency is inversely proportional to the wavelength. (2)

18.2.2
$$\lambda = \frac{c}{f}$$
$$= \frac{3\times10^{8}}{6,67\times10^{14}}$$
$$= 4,5\times10^{-7}\text{ m}$$
(2)

18.2.3 (a) To perform X-Rays (1)

(b) Radio, television transmission (1)

(c) Infra red heating lamps, night vision for cameras, heaters (1)

18.2.4 (a) $E = hf$ (1)

(b) The frequency of this radiation is very high. This means there is a large amount of energy associated with this frequency which damages living cells. (2)

(c) Gamma radiation. (1)

[28]

Question 19 (2009 IEB Final Examination)

19.1 A negatively charged plate was repelling particles. Therefore, the particles must be negatively charged. (Zinc plate must be losing electrons whereas the positive plate would attract electrons, so no such effect is noticed) (2)

19.2 19.2.1 Intensity of the light
Frequency (or wavelength) of the light (2)

19.2.2
$$E = \frac{hc}{\lambda}$$
$$= \frac{6,6\times10^{-34}\times3\times10^{8}}{440\times10^{-9}}$$
$$= 4,5\times10^{-19}\ \text{J}$$
$$= 2,81\,\text{eV}$$
(6)

19.2.3
- Intensity of red and blue light does not affect the kinetic energy of the photoelectrons.
- The maximum kinetic energy of the emitted electrons is only dependant on the frequency of light.
- The photon of light is absorbed by a (valence) electron in the metal. If the energy of this electron is greater than the work function of the metal, the electron will be emitted. It will have kinetic energy = energy of the photon less the work function of the metal.
- Because blue light has a higher frequency than red light, its photons have higher energy than those of red light. The electrons emitted when blue light is shone on the metal will therefore have greater kinetic energy. (6)

19.3 19.3.1 Caesium (1)

19.3.2 It has the smallest work function. Therefore, it would have the most electrons ejected per unit time. (2)

19.3.3
$$E = 2,75\left(1,6\times10^{-19}\right)$$
$$= 4,4\times10^{-19}\ \text{J}$$
$$E = hf_o$$
$$4,4\times10^{-19} = \left(6,6\times10^{-34}\right)f_o$$
$$f_o = 6,67\times10^{14}\ \text{Hz}$$
(5)

[24]

Question 20 (2010 IEB Supplementary Examination)

20.1 The minimum amount of energy needed to emit an electron from the surface of a metal. (3)

20.2 So that the metal attracts the electrons back to the surface, stopping them from reaching the collector (so that no current passes through the circuit). (2)

20.3 d, b, a, c, g, e, f **or** d, b, c, a, g, e, f **or** b, a, d, c, g, e, f **or** b, d, c, a, g, e, f (7)

20.4 20.4.1 She included the units for wavelength (nm) in the table instead of the in the heading. (1)

20.4.2 (a) $6{,}82\times10^{14}$

(b) 0,15

(c) $7{,}84\times10^{-20}$

20.4.3 Frequency (wavelength is also acceptable) (1)

20.4.4

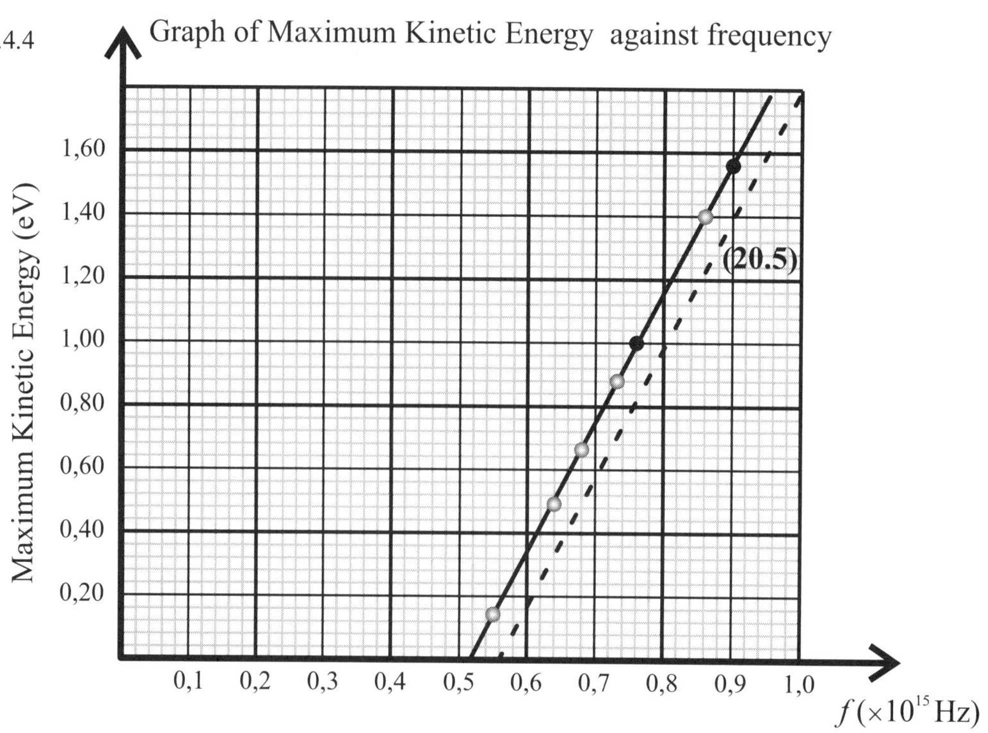

(1)

20.4.5 $m = \frac{\Delta E_k}{\Delta f}$

$= \frac{1,56 - 1}{0,9 \times 10^{15} - 0,76 \times 10^{15}}$

$= 4 \times 10^{-15}$ eV.s (4)

20.4.6 Planck's constant (in eV.s) (1)

20.4.7 $0,52 \times 10^{15}$ Hz $\rightarrow$ read from the x-intercept of the graph (1)

20.4.8 $W_o = hf_o$

$= \left(6,6 \times 10^{-34}\right)\left(0,52 \times 10^{15}\right)$

$= 3,43 \times 10^{-19}$ J (1)

20.4.9 No. The Experiment should have been repeated for each metal and the intensity of the light should have been kept constant for each experiment. (3)

20.5 $2,3\left(1,6 \times 10^{-19}\right) = \left(6,6 \times 10^{-34}\right)\left(f_o\right)$

$f_o = 0,56 \times 10^{15}$ Hz

Shown as a dotted line on the graph for 20.4.4. The threshold frequency must be at 0,56 and the line must be parallel to that drawn in 20.4.4. (3)

[41]

TOC
1 Data Sheet
2 Definitions
3
3 solutions
4
4 solutions
5
5 solutions
6
6 solutions
7
7 solutions
8
8 solutions
9
9 solutions
10
10 solutions

Question 21 (2012 IEB Final Examination)

21.1 Graph of Maximum Kinetic Energy against frequency

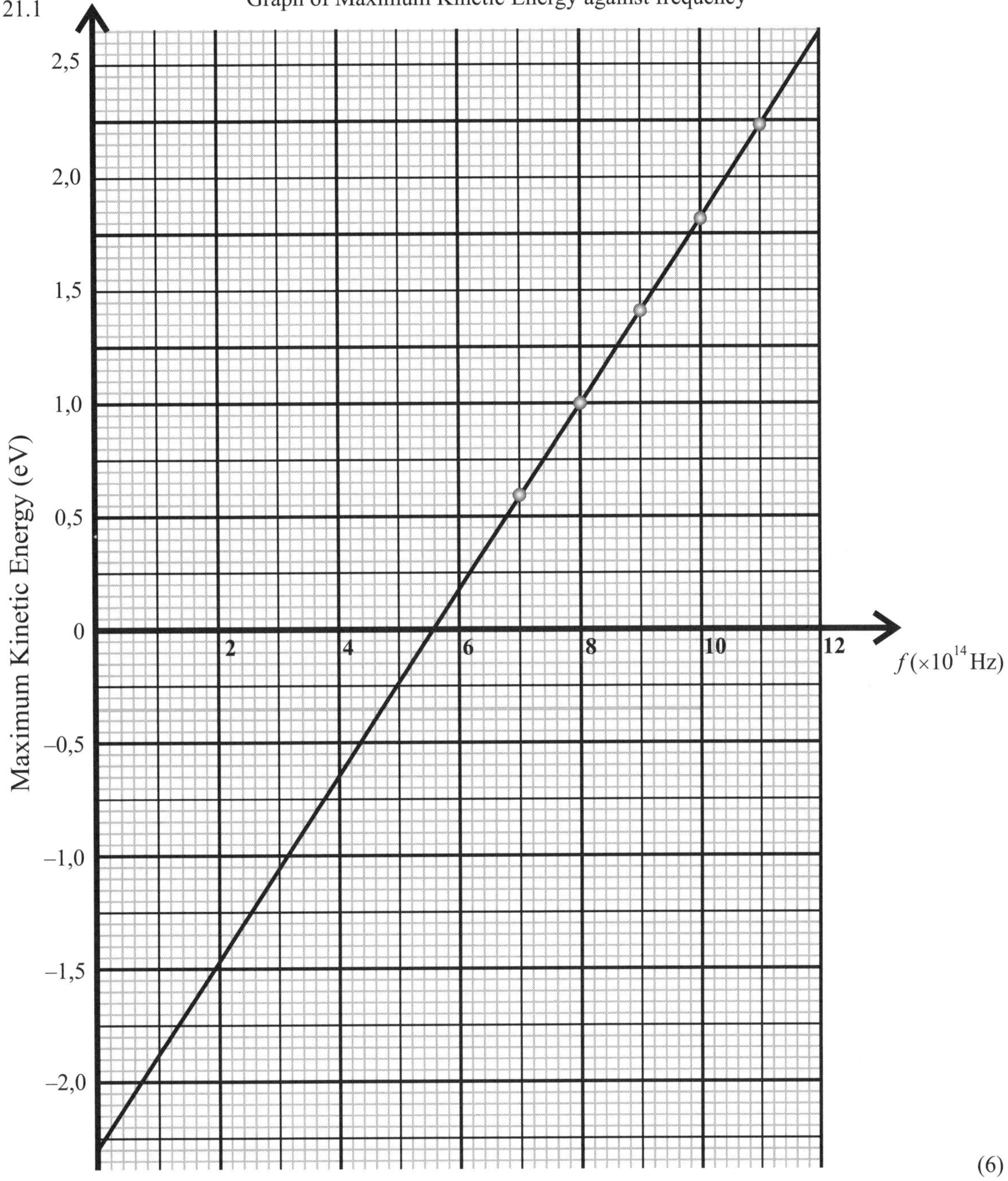

(6)

21.2 The minimum frequency of incident radiation at which electrons will be emitted from a particular metal. (2)

21.3 $5,6 \times 10^{14}$ Hz (2)

21.4 21.4.1 $10,4 \times 10^{14}$ Hz (1)

21.4.2 $\lambda = \frac{c}{f}$

$= \frac{3 \times 10^8}{10,4 \times 10^{14}}$

$= 2,88 \times 10^{-7}$ m (3)

21.4.3 $E = hf$

$= \left(6,6 \times 10^{-34}\right)\left(10,4 \times 10^{14}\right)$

$= 6,86 \times 10^{-19}$ J

21.5 There would be no change to the graph. Increasing the intensity would only increase the number of electrons emitted. (3)

21.6 21.6.1 2,25 eV (1)

21.6.2 $W_f = 2,25\left(1,6\times10^{-19}\right)$

$= 3,6\times10^{-19}$ J (1)

21.6.3 $E = W_f + \frac{1}{2}mv^2$

$hf = W_f + E_k \rightarrow E = hf$ and $E_k = \frac{1}{2}mv$

$E_k = hf - W_f \rightarrow y = mx + c$

Writing the equation in the this form it can be seen that the gradient of the graph represents Planck's constant and the y-intercept is the work function of the metal. (3)

[25]

Question 22 (2013 IEB Final Examination)

22.1 Photoelectric effect. (1)

22.2 22.2.1 No effect. (1)

22.2.2 Increase. (1)

22.2.3
- With bright light more photons strike the metal surface per second.
- One photon transfers its energy to one electron which is emitted.
- Therefore, there are more electrons emitted per second.
- This results in a greater current.
- The energy of each photon is the same, therefore the kinetic energy of the emitted electrons is constant. (4)

22.3 Increases. (1)

22.4 In the equation $hf = W_o + \frac{1}{2}mv^2$ the work function is constant. This means that as frequency increases so does the velocity of the electrons. (3)

22.5 22.5.1 $f = \frac{c}{\lambda}$

$= \frac{3\times10^8}{480\times10^{-9}}$

$= 6,25\times10^{14}$ Hz (4)

22.5.2 $E = W_o + E_{k_{max}}$

$hf = W_o + \frac{1}{2}m_{e^-}v^2$

$\left(6,6\times10^{-34}\right)\left(6,25\times10^{14}\right) = 3,8\times10^{-19} + \frac{1}{2}\left(9,1\times10^{-31}\right)v^2$

$v = 2,67\times10^5$ m.s^{-1}

22.5.3 The energy of the light is lower than the work function of the metal. (2)

[24]

Question 23 (2014 IEB Exemplar Examination)

23.1.1 The minimum amount of energy needed to emit an electron from the surface of a metal. (2)

23.1.2 $W_o = hf_o$

$4,08 \times 1,6 \times 10^{-19} = 6,6 \times 10^{-34} f_o$

$f_o = 9,9 \times 10^{14}$ Hz (4)

23.1.3 $\lambda_{max} = \dfrac{c}{f_o}$

$= \dfrac{3 \times 10^8}{9,9 \times 10^{14}}$

$= 3,03 \times 10^{-7}$ m

∴ Source B will release electrons as its wavelength is smaller than the threshold wavelength.

(4)

23.1.4 Increase intensity of light, more photons per second means more electrons per second. (2)

23.2.1

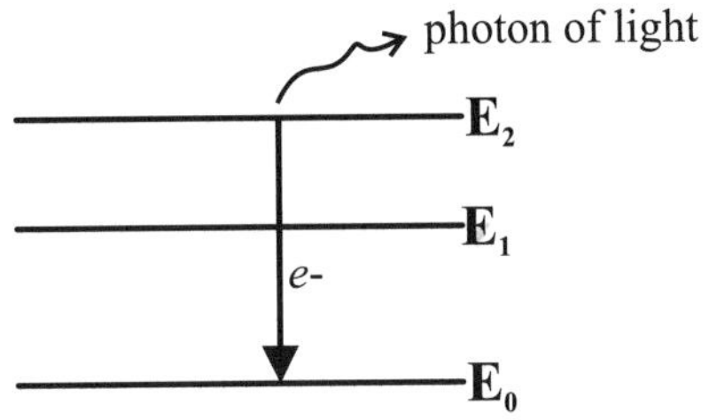

An electron in an excited state would rather occupy a lower energy level. Electrons must release energy in the form of a photon to occupy a lower energy level. (3)

23.2.2 Each atom has unique energy levels which electrons may occupy. Only transitions between energy levels are possible and so photons emitted have unique energies and hence unique frequencies. (2)

[17]

Question 24 (2014 IEB Final Examination)

24.1 $11,9 \times 10^{-19}$ J

24.2 As the wavelength of the incident radiation increases the maximum kinetic energy of the emitted electrons decreases.
You cannot say that maximum kinetic energy is inversely proportional to wavelength or vice versa.
You also cannot say that as the maximum kinetic energy of the emitted electrons decreases, the wavelength of the incident radiation increases (2)

24.3 The longer the wavelength of the incident radiation the lower the frequency and the lower the energy of the photons therefore the emitted electrons will have less kinetic energy as $E_k = E_{light} - W_o$ and W_o is constant. (3)

24.4 $f_o = \dfrac{c}{\lambda_o}$

$= \dfrac{3 \times 10^8}{4,9 \times 10^{-7}} \rightarrow \lambda_o$ was read from the x-intercept of the graph

$= 6,12 \times 10^{14}$ Hz (4)

24.5 $W_o = hf_o$

$= \left(6,6 \times 10^{-34}\right)\left(6,12 \times 10^{14}\right)$

$= 4,04 \times 10^{-19}$ J (3)

[13]

TOC | 1 Data Sheet | 2 Definitions | 3 | 3 solutions | 4 | 4 solutions | 5 | 5 solutions | 6 | 6 solutions | 7 | 7 solutions | 8 | 8 solutions | 9 | 9 solutions | 10 | 10 solutions

Question 25 (2015 IEB Final Examination)

25.1.1 Photoelectric effect (2)

25.1.2
- UV light has a larger frequency than visible light.
- The frequency of UV light is greater than the threshold frequency.
- Therefore, UV light can eject electrons. (3)

25.2.1 The minimum amount of energy needed to emit an electron from the surface of a metal. (2)

25.2.2 $W_o = hf_o$

$$3,36\times10^{-19} = \left(6,6\times10^{-34}\right)\left(f_o\right)$$

$$f_o = 5,09\times10^{14}\ \text{Hz}$$

(2)

25.2.3 $f = \dfrac{c}{\lambda} = \dfrac{3\times10^8}{400\times10^{-9}}$

$$= 7,5\times10^{14}\ \text{Hz}$$

$$hf = W_o + E_{k_{max}}$$

$$\left(6,6\times10^{-34}\right)\left(7,5\times10^{14}\right) = 3,36\times10^{-19} + E_{k_{max}}$$

$$E_{k_{max}} = 1,59\times10^{-19}\ \text{J}$$

(4)

[14]

Question 26 (2015 IEB Supplementary Examination)

26.1 $E = hf$

$$-2,4\times10^{-19} - \left(-5,4\times10^{-19}\right) = \left(6,6\times10^{-34}\right)\left(f\right)$$

$$f = 4,55\times10^{14}\ \text{Hz}$$

(4)

26.2 Wavelength A is greater than wavelength B. (1)

26.3 $E = \dfrac{hc}{\lambda}$. Wavelength is inversely proportional to energy. The lower the energy of the photon released in the transition, the longer the wavelength. (3)

26.4 If energy is inversely proportional to n^2, then $E.n^2 = \text{constant}$:

n	*E*	$E.n^2$
1	21,6	21,6
2	5,4	21,6
3	2,4	21,6

$\therefore E.n^2 = 21,6$

[21]

Question 27 (2016 IEB Final Examination)

27.1 The minimum amount of energy needed to emit an electron from the surface of a metal. (2)

27.2 $E = \dfrac{hc}{\lambda} = \dfrac{\left(6,6\times10^{-34}\right)\left(3\times10^8\right)}{296\times10^{-9}}$

$$= 6,69\times10^{-19}\ \text{J}$$

(3)

27.3 Sodium and aluminium. (2)

27.4 $hf = W_o + E_{k_{max}}$

$$6.69\times10^{-19} = 3,94\times10^{-19} + E_{k_{max}}$$

$$E_{k_{max}} = 2,75\times10^{-19}\ \text{J}$$

(3)

27.5 No, intensity increases the number of electrons, and the energy of the electrons is not affected by intensity of the light. (4)

[14]

Question 28 (2016 IEB Supplementary Examination)

28.1 A process that occurs when light of sufficient energy shines on a metal and electrons are ejected. (2)

28.2.1 3 (2)

28.2.2 E_3 to E_1 (2)

28.2.3

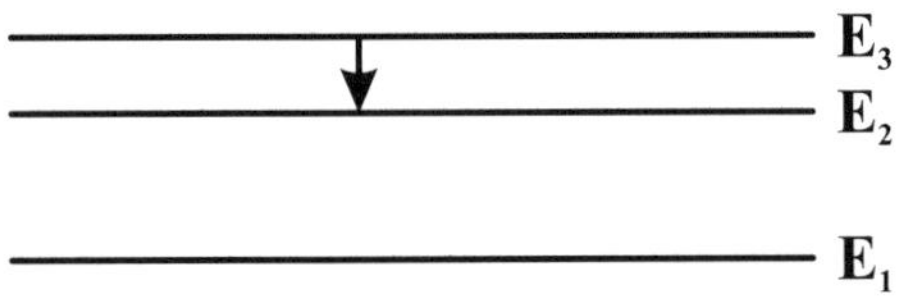

(2)

28.2.4 $E = \frac{hc}{\lambda} = \frac{(6,6\times10^{-34})(3\times10^{8})}{618\times10^{-9}}$

$= 3,2\times10^{-19}$ J (4)

28.2.5 electrons can't possess any more energy than allowed in an energy level. When they move to a lower energy level, the difference in energy between the levels has to be discarded. (2)

[14]

Question 29 (2017 IEB Final Examination)

29.1 3 (2)

29.2 $E = hf$

$[-3,4-(-13,6)](1,6\times10^{-19}) = (6,6\times10^{-34})(f)$

$f = 2,47\times10^{15}$ Hz (4)

29.3.1 $E = \frac{hc}{\lambda} = \frac{(6,6\times10^{-34})(3\times10^{8})}{655\times10^{-9}} = 3,02\times10^{-19}$ J

$E = \frac{3,02\times10^{-19}}{1,6\times10^{-19}} = 1,89$ eV (4)

29.3.2

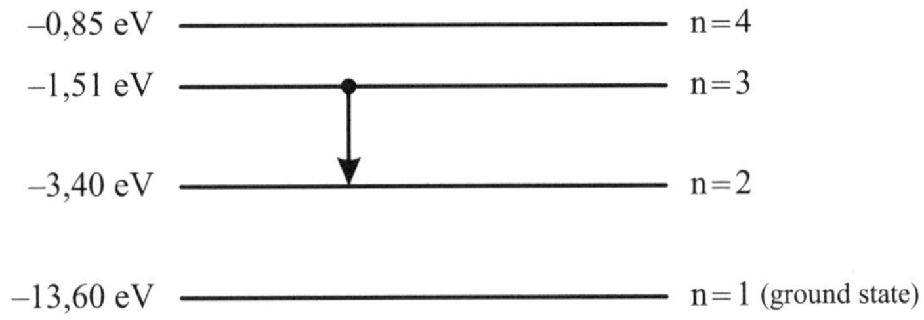

(2)

29.4 Free electrons have an energy of zero. The negative implies that energy is released as electrons move to lower levels. (2)

[14]

[18]

Question 30 (2018 IEB Supplementary Examination)

30.1.1 $E = hf = (6,6\times10^{-34})(9,1\times10^{14})$

$= 6,01\times10^{-19}$ J (3)

30.1.2 The minimum amount of energy needed to emit an electron from the surface of a metal. (2)

30.1.3 $E = W_o + E_{k_{max}}$

$E = W_o + \frac{1}{2}m_{e^-}v^2$

$6,01\times10^{-19} = 3,5\times10^{-19} + \frac{1}{2}(9,1\times10^{-31})v^2$

$v = 7,43\times10^{5}$ m.s^{-1} (4)

30.2.1 A photon is a particle of light. (2)

30.2.2 $E = \frac{hc}{\lambda} = \frac{(6,6\times10^{-34})(3\times10^{8})}{524\times10^{-9}}$

$= 3,78\times10^{-19}$ J (3)

30.2.3 $E = \frac{3,78\times10^{-19}}{1,6\times10^{-19}}$

$= 2,36$ eV

$E_5 - E_2 = 2,36$

$E_5 = 2,36 + E_2$

$E_5 = 2,36 + (-2,81)$

$E_5 = -0,45$ eV (3)

[17]

Question 31 (2017 IEB Supplementary Examination)

31.1 The minimum frequency of incident radiation at which electrons will be emitted from a particular metal. (2)

31.2 $E = hf = (6,6\times10^{-34})(4,4\times10^{14})$

$= 2,90\times10^{-19}$ J (3)

31.3 If the frequency of incident radation is greater than the threshold frequency, then the maximum kinetic energy increases as frequency increases.
If the frequency of incident radation is less than the threshold frequency, then the maximum kinetic energy is zero and no electrons are ejected. (3)

31.4 B. The threshold frequency is double as the work function is double. Therefore, the x-intercept will be a greater value. The slope of both graphs would be the same as the slope is equal to Planck's constant. (4)

31.5 $hf = W_o + E_{k_{max}}$

$(6,6\times10^{-34})(15\times10^{14}) = 2(2,90\times10^{-19}) + E_{k_{max}}$

$E_{k_{max}} = 4,1\times10^{-19}$ J (4)

[16]

Question 32 (2019 IEB Final Examination)

32.1 The minimum frequency of incident radiation at which electrons will be emitted from a particular metal. (2)

32.2 $f_o = \frac{c}{\lambda} = \frac{(3\times10^{8})}{583\times10^{-9}} = 5,15\times10^{14}$ Hz (3)

32.3 $W_o = hf_o$

$= (6,6\times10^{-34})(5,15\times10^{14}) = 3,40\times10^{-19}$ J (3)

32.4 $\frac{hc}{\lambda} = W_o + E_{k_{max}}$

$\frac{(6,6\times10^{-34})(3\times10^{8})}{450\times10^{-9}} = 3,40\times10^{-19} + E_{k_{max}}$

$E_{k_{max}} = 1\times10^{-19}$ J (4)

32.5.1 Higher intensity has no effect (2)

32.5.1 Higher intensity increases the number of ejected electrons. (2)

[16]

Question 33 (2018 IEB Final Examination)

33.1.1 The minimum amount of energy needed to emit an electron from the surface of a metal. (2)

33.1.2 $W_o = hf_o$

$= (6,6\times10^{-34})(6,90\times10^{14}) = 4,55\times10^{-19}$ J (4)

33.1.3

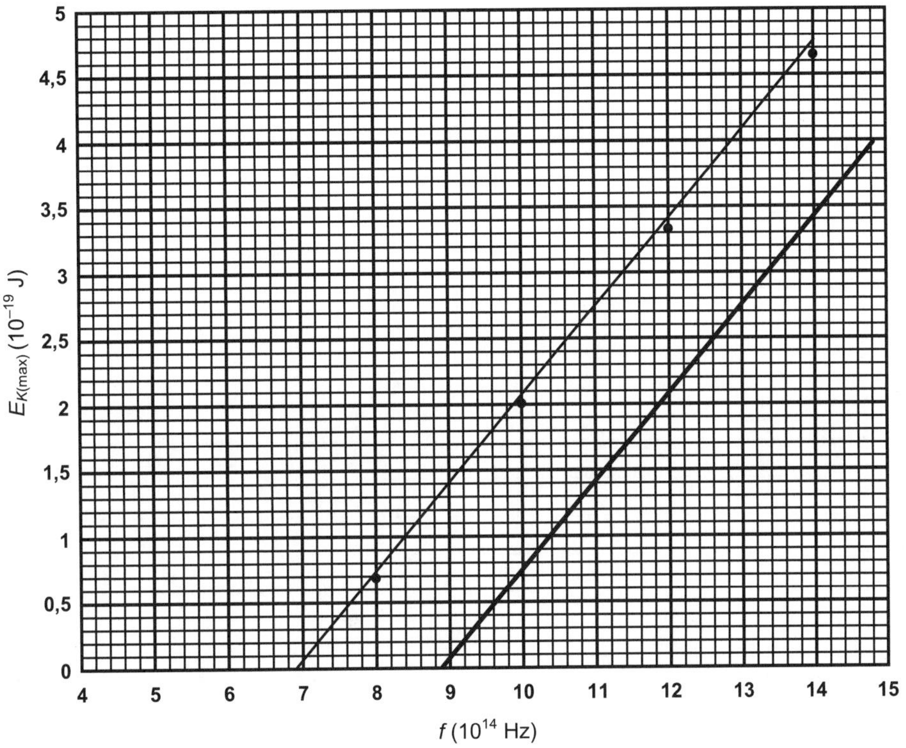

33.2.1 $E = \frac{hc}{\lambda} = \frac{(6,6\times10^{-34})(3\times10^{8})}{6,58\times10^{-7}} = 3,01\times10^{-19}$ J (4)

33.2.2 P. Wavelength is inversely proportional to energy. Therefore, the smallest wavelength will be associated with the highest differenc in energy. (3)

33.2.3 Emission lines are unique to each element. So they can be used to identify substances. (2)

[17]

Question 34 (2019 IEB Supplementary Examination)

34.1 The minimum amount of energy needed to emit an electron from the surface of a metal. (2)

34.2 frequency of incident radiation (2)

34.3 Gradient $= \frac{\Delta y}{\Delta x} = \frac{\text{J}}{\text{s}^{-1}}$ = J.s = N.m.s (2)

34.4 $W_o = hf_o$

$= (6,6\times10^{-34})(1,05\times10^{15}) = 6,93\times10^{-19}$ J

∴ The metal is Zinc (2)

34.5 $\frac{hc}{\lambda} = W_o + \frac{1}{2}m_{e\text{-}}v^2$

$\frac{(6,6\times10^{-34})(3\times10^{8})}{475\times10^{-9}} = W_o + \frac{1}{2}(9,1\times10^{-31})(2,77\times10^{5})^2$

$W_o = 3,82\times10^{-19}$ J

∴ The metal is sodium. (6)

[16]

Notes

Use these pages to make your own important notes

Notes

Use these pages to make your own important notes

Notes

Use these pages to make your own important notes

Notes

Use these pages to make your own important notes

Notes

Use these pages to make your own important notes